A DISCIPLE'S LIFE

A DISCIPLE'S LIFE

The Biography of
Neal A. Maxwell

BRUCE C. HAFEN

DESERET
BOOK

SALT LAKE CITY, UTAH

All photos are from the Maxwell family collection, except as noted. The following are used by permission and/or courtesy of Busath Photography, pages 21 (far right), 198; *Deseret News*, pages 243, 303, 405 (O. Wallace Kasteler), 409 (Howard Moore), 439, 443 (Tom Smart), 555 (Chuck Wing); Filmedia Studios, Inc., page 253; Hugh Hewitt, page 545; Intellectual Reserve, Inc., pages 451, 559; LDS Church Archives, pages 143, 382, 435, 475, 479; Mary Naegle, page 241; Newman Photography, Inc., page 77; Mark Philbrick, pages 421, 495; Ronald Reagan Library, page 493; *Salt Lake Tribune*, pages 5 (Al Hartmann), 197 (Russell B. Odell), 341; John Snyder, page 565; Anne G. Stewart, page 561; *This People*, page 387 (Bill Dean); University of Utah, page 159; Zeke Studios, page 563.

Library of Congress Cataloging-in-Publication Data

Hafen, Bruce C.
    A disciple's life : the biography of Neal A. Maxwell / Bruce C. Hafen.
        p.   cm.
Includes bibliographical references (p.) and index.
    ISBN 1-57008-833-0
    1. Maxwell, Neal A.   2. Church of Jesus Christ of Latter-day
Saints—Apostles—Biography   I. Title.
    BX8695.M335 H34   2002
    289.3'092—dc21   2002000998

Printed in the United States of America   72876-30021
Quebecor World Book Services, Fairfield, PA

10 9   8   7   6   5   4   3   2

For Colleen
The story is theirs

CONTENTS

PREFACE

THE STORY BEHIND THE WRITING OF THIS BOOK really began in 1976, when Elder Maxwell invited me to take a leave from Brigham Young University and work for two years under his daily direction in the new Correlation Department at Church headquarters. In later years, when I was an administrator and a teacher at Ricks College and then at BYU, I saw him often in Church Educational System meetings, where he was a key figure on the Church Board of Education.

In 1996 I was called to the Seventy and assigned to an Area Presidency in Australia, where I remained until returning to Utah in August of 2000. Like so many other Church members, my wife, Marie, and I were stunned by the news of Elder Maxwell's leukemia in late 1996, and we worried and prayed about his health. During October conference 1999, he invited me to come by his office. As we talked, he indicated he was not certain about his condition. He said he was receiving an experimental treatment but "one of these days" the leukemia just might fully return. That was the main reason, he said, why he'd finally yielded to prodding from others that he allow the writing of his biography. I thought a book on his life story would be wonderful—until he asked if I would write it.

As honored as I felt, I honestly thought my doing this was not a good idea. I believed that he, his family, and the Church deserved thorough research and writing, and the work needed to be done at once to maximize the possibility of being published during his lifetime. He shared those hopes. But given the frightening uncertainty about his health; given that acceptable biographies can take years to document and write; given that he hadn't kept a personal journal, which would necessitate additional months of original research; and given that I was half a world away on a Church assignment—I replied that someone who could give this project immediate and full-time attention was needed.

Nonetheless, after more visits with Elder Maxwell and with others, within a few days I had agreed to begin the project and to move as quickly as possible. In the weeks that followed, I worried about having committed myself to something as unreachable as this task seemed. As I would awaken to hear the colorful birds that rule those fresh Australian mornings, I would sometimes wonder if—indeed, I would hope that—I had agreed to write Elder Maxwell's biography only in a dream. Then the reality would hit me again. At times I would remember Nephi's words about the Lord preparing a way for people who have a work to do.

As time went on and as I found able people eager to help, my anxiety gradually subsided. I learned about peaceful intensity. Marie and I increasingly sensed that we had been given a rare privilege and that whatever came of this experience would bless us. As we worked we also prayed often, along with so many others, that the Lord would lengthen Elder Maxwell's life. After such prayers, I would sometimes recall a scriptural phrase I'd first heard him quote: "But if not . . ." (Daniel 3:18)—meaning, we must do everything we can to make this work, and then if it doesn't, "it matters not" (Mosiah 13:9).

Looking back now, especially after having talked at length with Dr. Clyde Ford, Elder Maxwell's oncologist, I know we are all witnesses to a genuine miracle. The preservation of Elder Maxwell's life was not, and couldn't have been, anticipated by medical science. Along with its far more substantial blessings, the miracle made it possible to have a biography that draws on lengthy interviews with him and reflects his having reviewed the entire text. We do not cease to pray that the miracle will continue.

As the project began, I thought perhaps the main theme of Elder Maxwell's life would be his rare contributions to the Church as a role model for educated Latter-day Saints. The evidence from researching his life story, however, revealed a different focus and, hence, the book's title. Discipleship is without question the central message of Neal Maxwell's life and of his teachings. His background and contributions as an educator still matter—in fact, they matter even more in light of the more fundamental discovery that his story is, as Sheri Dew said after reading the manuscript, a kind of manual on trying to become a follower of Christ.

At one point, I considered saying something in the book about the characteristics of a modern disciple's life that are common to disciples we meet in the scriptures—Peter, Nephi, Paul, Alma, and the others. Elder Maxwell's story is in many ways like theirs. These stories reveal some common elements, both for *Disciples* (Jesus' followers who are called and given authority, such as Apostles) and for *disciples* (people who choose to follow Him, regardless of their callings). I soon realized, however, that while it is appropriate for a biography to build on the framework of a core theme like discipleship, the theme could easily intrude enough to detract from the life story. I hope I have avoided that. In any case I can say that Neal Maxwell's quest to become a disciple emerged from the research on his life rather than being imposed on it.

His quest leads to a general observation on why we are drawn to life stories. Why do we read, let alone write, biographies? Since ancient days, we have been taught the gospel by stories. The accounts of the war in heaven, the Garden of Eden, and Cain and Abel are the first stories showing what happens when people try to live God's teachings—or don't live them. The New Testament is itself a story—about Jesus, who He was, what He taught, and what He did. Christ's life is the story of *giving* the Atonement. The story of Adam and Eve is the story of *receiving* the Atonement. As we experience mortality the way our first parents did, struggling with the opposition between good and evil, we can look at Eve or at Adam and say—that is the story of *my* life. Then when we tell our own stories to others, we realize that the cosmic quest to overcome evil and find God is our very personal quest.

Our own testimonies are true and often powerful stories that capture in vivid detail how the Lord blesses us, protects us, changes us, and helps us to overcome. Nothing brings the Spirit into a conversation or a classroom more than hearing people bear honest testimony, not so much by exhortation as by just telling the story of their personal experience.

The scriptures are primarily a collection of stories, given to us because God directed prophets to recount their experiences to His people. In His desire to give us guidance about life, God could have given us a large rulebook or a series of grand philosophical essays. But he didn't. He gave us stories—about people like ourselves. Again and again the Book of Mormon writers tell us about some person's experience and say, "And thus we see . . ."

What *do* we *see* from these stories? We can see, for example, that "by small means the Lord can bring about great things" (1 Nephi 16:29) and that if people keep God's commandments, "he doth nourish them, and strengthen them, and provide means" for them to keep going (1 Nephi 17:3). We can see that "the devil will not support his children at the last day" (Alma 30:60), that "the children of men [are quick to] forget the Lord. . . . And we also see the great wickedness one very wicked man can cause" (Alma 46:8–9).

J. R. R. Tolkien's understanding of the power of stories played an important part in the conversion of his friend C. S. Lewis to Christianity. Tolkien helped Lewis see that the *story* of Christ's life conveys a fuller meaning to our minds than abstract statements of doctrine and reason can convey. He explained that the abstract ideas of Christianity "are too large and too all-embracing for the finite mind to absorb them. That is why the divine providence revealed himself in a story." This insight helped Lewis realize why he had *felt* that certain classical stories were "profound and suggestive of meaning beyond [his] grasp even tho' [he] could not say in cold prose 'what it meant.'"

Like the stories of other disciples, this book is the story of one person's discoveries about applying the story of Jesus to his own life. Neal Maxwell's *story* offers more understanding than at least my "cold prose" could offer in an essay about discipleship and "what it means."

I now see why a biography cannot be better than its primary source material. The parts of this story that draw on such contemporaneous documents as letters and journals are richer than the other parts. Only limited documentation of this kind was available for several time periods. Finding Elder Maxwell's brief personal history and the early letters he wrote—from Okinawa, during his mission, and to his son, Cory, on his mission—were rare treasures. Churchill's biographer called such letters "history's gold." The issue here is the depth of real evidence. Memories recalled years after an event are helpful, but they make it harder to present uninterpreted evidence that allows readers to draw their own conclusions.

At the same time, Elder and Sister Maxwell's reading of the drafts of each chapter assured me as we went along that I would have the main facts straight, whatever happened with Elder Maxwell's health. I realized that the Maxwells might be uncomfortable with details that revealed less than flattering dimensions of their lives. Fortunately, both of them understood this concern and actively encouraged me to avoid hagiography (an "idealizing or idolizing biography"). Both prefer a candid account that includes a person's challenges and limitations. "It isn't that we're searching for weakness as much as we are for growth," Elder Maxwell said, having earlier written:

> We must be careful . . . not to canonize [our role] models as we have some pioneers and past Church leaders—not to dry all the human sweat off them, not to put ceaseless smiles on their faces, when they really struggled and experienced agony. Real people who believe and prevail are ultimately more faith-promoting and impressive than saccharine saints with tinsel traits.

There are pros and cons about whether my association with Elder Maxwell over the years has benefited his biography. My having spent so much time with him in the world of Church education and in life at Church headquarters makes it difficult for me to stand apart from that environment and describe those parts of his life with what might be a desirable objectivity. Moreover, I cannot conceal my affection and admiration for him and for Colleen, even if I wanted to. So this is not a dispassionate work, even though I've tried to present an honest story.

Yet there is also a place for biographers who are well acquainted with their subjects. James Boswell, who wrote the classic biography on Samuel Johnson, regarded their friendship as a strength. It allowed

Boswell to look beyond mere events to "interweav[e] what [Johnson] privately wrote, and said, and thought." Moreoever, friendship hardly constrained Boswell to tell only a positive tale. On the contrary, he wrote, Johnson's life, "great and good as he was, must not be supposed to be entirely perfect. To be as he was, is [praise] enough to any man." Indeed, Johnson himself said, "There are many who think it an act of piety to hide the faults or failings of their friends," which leads to biographies with "whole ranks of [indistinguishable] characters adorned with uniform [applause]."

Johnson underscored the advantage of personal knowledge over public records. Those records, he wrote, reveal so little of a person's nature and character that "more knowledge may be gained of a man's real character, by a short conversation with one of his servants, than from a formal and studied narrative, begun with his pedigree, and ended with his funeral." And, speaking of funerals, Johnson also gave this encouragement to a biography published while its subject is still on life's stage: "If a life be delayed till interest and envy are at an end, we may hope for impartiality, but must expect little intelligence; for the incidents which give excellence to biography are of a volatile and evanescent kind, such as soon escape the memory."

Neal and Colleen Maxwell have given me an intimate and prolonged entrance into their well-ordered and compassionate lives, thus enriching my own life. Their full story is a joint one, and although I have not really captured Colleen's part of the story here, I hope her graceful influence somehow distills upon these pages, as it does upon his days. I also understand now why a published biography can only hint at the real nature of lives well lived. Much of a true disciple's life is not susceptible to being documented, weighed, and written down. The real story is theirs.

ACKNOWLEDGMENTS

THIS BOOK WAS A MARATHON PROJECT that needed to be done at a sprint pace. That pace would have been impossible without the devotion and skill of many people. My primary collaborator was Gordon Irving of the Family and Church History Department, who is one of the Church's primary oral historians. During most of the research phase while I was in Australia, Gordon and I were in frequent communication by e-mail. Using agendas we outlined together, he conducted eighteen interviews with Elder Maxwell over a period of seven months. Gordon then edited these transcripts, which totaled 560 pages, as well as my own several interviews with Elder Maxwell. Gordon also recorded thoughtful interviews about Elder Maxwell with each member of the First Presidency, several members of the Quorum of the Twelve and the Quorums of the Seventy, and others named in the bibliography and notes.

Gordon, who was a student in Elder Maxwell's political science classes at the University of Utah in 1967 and 1970, was also a lively source for research questions, research sources, and stimulating conversations about history, biography, and most major topics in the book. Then he meticulously read an early draft of the manuscript, offering many helpful comments. He also outlined the bibliographic essay. Both as a professional historian and a companion in a shared cause, Gordon's well-schooled and faithful touch has made this a much better book.

Members of Elder Maxwell's family provided indispensable help. Cory, his son, was my other frequent e-mail companion during the research phase, and his diligence yielded many sources we otherwise might have missed. Assisted by Jan Jensen, he combed, inventoried, copied, and shipped as a weekly care package across the Pacific portions of large annual scrapbooks that Elder Maxwell's secretaries have compiled since the late 1960s. Cory also conducted interviews with Maxwell family members, helped unearth the buried treasures of personal and family letters, and gathered the photographs from which the final selections were made.

The family history work of Elder Maxwell's sister Ann M. Washburn was an invaluable source for the chapters on the ancestral stories and on their family. His other sisters—Lois Maxwell, Sue M. Skanky, Carol M. Wright, and Kathy M. Parker—gave candid and helpful background and comments on the early family chapters. Elder and Sister Maxwell's children and their spouses provided similarly valuable reviews of the chapters on their family.

I thank Eric d'Evegnee, a graduate student in English at Brigham Young University, who is married to our daughter Sarah. Eric read and analyzed all of Elder Maxwell's numerous books, speeches, and articles, identifying literary patterns and illustrations with both depth and detail. Even though I also read this material for myself, the chapters that discuss Elder Maxwell's writing reflect Eric's insight and diligence more than is apparent from either the text or the notes.

Several secretaries made helpful contributions. B. Jean Hyde and Cherie Best typed most of the oral history transcripts. Elder Maxwell's secretary, Susan Jackson, helped in numerous ways, providing details about the sequence of events during Elder Maxwell's illness and finding speeches, letters, and other materials that seemed always at her fingertips. My secretary in Sydney, Maureen Young, contributed both research skills and keen insight. My secretary in Salt Lake City, Barbara Madsen, has been a tireless research assistant who worked along many fronts.

The staff at the Church History Library and the libraries at BYU and the University of Utah were always responsive and generous in providing books, sources, and suggestions. I profited from counseling with many of the people whose interviews and letters are cited in the notes and with Kent Brown, Elder Spencer J. Condie, Sheri L. Dew, Ronald Esplin, Elder Kenneth Johnson, Leslie Norris, Lea Rosser, Ronald Walker, and others among Elder Maxwell's friends and associates. I also drew on the support of Elder L. Aldin Porter, Elder Earl C. Tingey, and other members of the Presidency of the Seventy.

I thank those who read early drafts of the manuscript and gave valuable suggestions—Sheri L. Dew, Eric d'Evegnee, Joy M. Hafen, Marie K. Hafen, Thomas K. Hafen, Gordon Irving, Martha Johnson, Colleen H. Maxwell, Cory H. Maxwell, Elder Neal A. Maxwell, Phillip C. Smith, and Richard E. Turley Jr. In addition, Deseret Book's Suzanne Brady, Richard Erickson, Tonya-Rae Facemyer, Amy Felix, Lisa Mangum, Michael Morris, Richard Peterson, Sheryl Roderick, and Anne Sheffield contributed high standards and much effort in preparing the manuscript for publication.

I am deeply grateful to my family, especially to Marie and our daughter Rachel, who supported and encouraged me when "the book" made me seem perpetually absent even when I was physically present. Marie's serene confidence that the Lord would sustain me let us discover afresh the spiritual gift of peace of mind.

PART I

THE FELLOWSHIP OF CHRIST'S SUFFERING

I SHOULD HAVE
SEEN IT COMING

Aᴌᴌ Aᴘᴏsᴛʟᴇs ᴀʀᴇ Dɪsᴄɪᴘʟᴇs ᴏғ Jᴇsᴜs, but not all of Jesus' disciples are Apostles. This is the story of one Apostle's personal journey of discipleship.

A few weeks before April conference in 1997, Elder Neal A. Maxwell was released from the hospital after forty-six days—and nights—of debilitating chemotherapy. Now he wanted to speak to the Church, if only to thank people for their prayers. The First Presidency left the choice to him. To avoid the risk of infection arising from crowd contact, they would make special arrangements for his entry and exit from the Tabernacle.

What about his hair, which the chemotherapy had uprooted? Someone got him a brown toupee, which he tried out on his family and a few friends. And there was a far more basic question—could he, in his weakened condition, even make it to the pulpit and back?

In the end, he kept it simple—no vanity, no hair, and a six-minute talk. He felt he "needed to make a statement, and my special audience within an audience were all the people who'd lost their hair because of chemos. I wanted them to see that shining pate and feel a sense of hope." His simple acceptance of his own appearance showed how far he had come since the now-forgotten years of his severe adolescent acne.

Midway through the Saturday morning conference session, Elder Maxwell approached the pulpit. For those who had not already heard the news of his deadly leukemia, the piercing frankness of the TV camera immediately told them that something unusual was going on. There he stood, this man known for the power of articulate speech and spiritual insight, now barely strong enough to hold on to the pulpit. His once full head of hair was replaced by stark baldness; his glasses seemed larger than usual. Some may even have wondered who was speaking. Yet the voice was warmly familiar. As he spoke, "his courage and countenance reduced the next speaker, Apostle Robert Hales, to tears."

Some have likened this moment to Elder Bruce R. McConkie's final general conference testimony on April 6, 1985, which one person said meant more to him than if he had read all of Elder McConkie's books. So it was with Elder Maxwell. One Church member said, "That is how I'll always remember Neal A. Maxwell—that honest, visual image of bravery and submission, rising from his sickbed to speak to the Church in utter humility. That captures everything he's written and said for years about being meek and lowly. That day his heart spoke fully to mine. I want to be that kind of disciple."

He began the talk with self-deprecating humor: "My thanks to the First Presidency for this opportunity, during which, as you can see, the lights combine with my cranium to bring some different 'illumination' to this pulpit." Next a modest medical report: "treatments to date have proved encouraging." Then his waiver of any claim to a miracle: "If I have any entitlement to the blessings of God, it has long since been settled in the court of small claims by His generous bestowals over a lifetime."

He thanked the many who had helped and prayed, and then he became distinctly but subtly autobiographical. He expressed special gratitude for the Holy Ghost, "for the recent ways in which He has been the precious Comforter, including in the midnight moments." That was an understatement, after his wrenching 1,100 hours of medical

Giving the thumbs-up sign during the April 1997 general conference, shortly after undergoing extensive chemotherapy

confinement. Typically for him, he offered lighthearted candor rather than a heroic flourish: "Those who emerge successfully from their varied and fiery furnaces have experienced the grace of the Lord, which He says is sufficient (see Ether 12:27). Even so . . . such emerging individuals do not rush to line up in front of another fiery furnace in order to get an extra turn!"

The allusion to grace introduced his central message—the enriched understanding of the Atonement that had come to him in his reflections on his trauma. "The more I learn and experience," he said, "the more unselfish, stunning, and encompassing His Atonement becomes! When we take Jesus' yoke upon us, this admits us eventually to what Paul called 'the fellowship of [Christ's] sufferings.'" Then, if we are meek enough, our suffering "will sink into the very marrow of the soul." The mention of "marrow" by a leukemia patient was not coincidental.

To provide context for this moment, let us go back about a year to 1996, when Elder Maxwell was enjoying easier days. That spring had seemed busier than usual. But he relished a full agenda and was enjoying this season of his maturity as a senior member of the Quorum of the Twelve Apostles.

It had been pleasant for him a short time before, as new chairman of the Church's Public Affairs Committee, to accompany President Gordon B. Hinckley on a trip to the White House, where they presented two volumes of personal family history to President Bill Clinton. Elder Maxwell never went to Washington these days without smiling inside as he remembered how intimidating the place had seemed to him when he and Colleen were first there in the early 1950s, unable to afford their own car. He had worked then on the staff of Wallace Bennett, United States senator from Utah, where he discovered that while Potomac fever might be contagious, it wasn't addictive.

As chairman of the Temple and Family History Executive Council, Elder Maxwell had closely followed the staff's preparation of the Clinton history. He had asked them to highlight what he called "by the ways" that added a personal touch to their visit—such as their discovery that Hillary Clinton's English ancestry tied into a family line of Vice President Al Gore. President Hinckley encouraged the Clintons to hold a family home evening to look through their new books. As they left, Elder Maxwell mentioned to President Clinton that the First Presidency and the Twelve had recently prayed for him and for the country in the Salt Lake Temple, following a longstanding custom regarding the occupants of the Oval Office.

In the weeks that followed, Elder Maxwell was involved as the Church Public Affairs staff supported President Hinckley's preparation for his now-celebrated interview with Mike Wallace on *60 Minutes.* Twenty-five years earlier, Neal had confided to a friend that if he could choose one person to represent the Church on national television, it would be Gordon B. Hinckley. The two had worked behind the scenes on Church public affairs issues since the early 1970s, when Brother Maxwell was a regional representative of the Twelve. The Church had come a good distance "out of obscurity" (D&C 1:30) since those days. Given his lifelong fascination with the media, politics, and the Church, nobody appreciated this development in media attitudes more than Neal Maxwell did.

By the time April conference ended, the issues were piling up, not only in Public Affairs and Family History but also in the Church

Historical Department and the Area Committee, in which Elder Maxwell now chaired key committees of the Twelve.

When not assigned to headquarters meetings or trips, the Maxwells would be home for "free weekends," as they were in mid-April. On Saturday the 13th, he spoke about King Benjamin's sermon during the annual FARMS Symposium at Brigham Young University. The next day he talked in three meetings—the missionary farewell for his grandson Peter Maxwell, a sacrament meeting in south Salt Lake Valley, and an evening missionary fireside at the University of Utah.

As the gray haze of Salt Lake's tedious winter air inversions gradually gave way to the warm, clearing breezes of late spring, some of Elder Maxwell's attention turned, with great zest, to tennis. Inside the honed discipline of this man's public demeanor lurks a competitive spirit that has regularly found a way to "let go" on the tennis court in a playful intensity that might surprise the average general conference goer. For nearly half a century, he has frequently played sandlot tennis (earlier it was basketball) with such partners as Oscar McConkie, a life-long friend.

When spring finally yielded to summer, Neal's other, less-concealed juices began their rhythmic flow. For him, when July approaches, it's time for some serious writing. Since coaxing him to write his first book, Colleen wondered if she should now try harder to slow down his intoxicating, almost annual exercise in self-expression. But she had seen the value of its fulfillment, for both reader and writer. Still, she was relieved that this summer he wasn't ready to tackle a whole book.

This year he actually seemed to relax into the more modest project of drafting a talk called "The Education of Our Desires," a favorite Maxwell idea, for Education Week at BYU–Hawaii. And rather than planning the usual big vacation trip for their entire family, it was enough for 1996 to celebrate his seventieth birthday on July 6 with a family ride on the Heber Creeper antique train, followed by dinner in nearby Midway.

In June, Elder and Sister Maxwell traveled to a conference in Sapporo, Japan, and then attended the dedication of the Hong Kong

Temple. Traveling to Japan was always emotional for him, because the trauma and the spiritual epiphany of his youth in a muddy battlefield on Okinawa were etched into every cell of his body. As for Hong Kong, having a temple in what would soon be part of the People's Republic of China fanned the embers of a spark he had felt as a personal quest since his first visit to China in 1982. He hungered to share the gospel with the mainland Chinese, but his political realism kept his inborn impatience under control.

Throughout these months, sandwiched between meetings, speeches, trips, and writing, Neal and Colleen would, as their highest priority, assemble their extended family in evenings with their children and spouses for a "Grandpa Neal's fireside" with the grandchildren. And somehow, in the invisible corners of such a schedule, he and Colleen were always showing up in hospitals or on telephone calls, in a private ministry to a throng of people whose physical and spiritual well-being had come to have a permanent claim on their attention. By now, the regular rhythm of these familiar patterns flowed freely from his heart's earth like a mountain spring.

Oddly, this summer, as the reduced writing output hinted, Elder Maxwell's flow of energy seemed to be diminishing. He had always been so fit, his circles of concern so large and so full, that he simply shook off a pesky sense of fatigue. One day he leaned slightly against the doorway to his office and asked his secretary, Susan Jackson, to "remind me to ask the doctor when I go in for my physical why I'm so tired. Maybe I'm just getting old."

In early September, he met his politically astute friend, Bud Scruggs, for lunch—the political version of his occasional escapes to tennis. Neal would drain Bud with as many questions as the time allowed, feeding his insatiable curiosity about every nuance in current events. Bud enjoyed the mentoring his friend gave him, a lens that enlarged his view of every subject. As they paused between topics, Bud asked routinely, "So how are you feeling these days?" Neal hesitated before replying. "I just had my annual physical, Bud. The doctor tells me I'm anemic."

"That's not a big deal," said Bud. "You just need some iron pills."

"No," said Neal, "for a man my age, anemia may be bad news." He didn't know yet how bad the news would become, but he didn't like what his instincts were sensing.

His internist, Dr. Larry Staker, didn't like what he was sensing, either. Neal's blood wasn't yet seriously anemic, but Dr. Staker wanted to measure further blood counts while sending him to specialists who checked for such possibilities as thyroid problems, bleeding ulcers, and vitamin deficiencies. During the next few weeks, his white blood count dropped steadily. Feeling more concern than he let on, Dr. Staker sent Neal to Dr. Clyde Ford, a Latter-day Saint oncologist at the Salt Lake Clinic, for cancer tests. This was his first referral to Dr. Ford in more than ten years of Salt Lake City practice, but Dr. Staker felt a prompting to call him.

After further investigating the abnormal blood tests with a bone marrow biopsy, Dr. Ford called his findings to Neal and Colleen on a speaker phone in Neal's office on Wednesday, September 11, 1996. They leaned forward and listened with careful attention to the doctor's restrained, matter-of-fact diagnosis. It looks like myelodysplastic syndrome, he said, an aggressive, deadly disease that is hard to treat, especially in older patients.

Technically, Dr. Ford explained, Neal's was still a "preleukemic condition," because the "blasts," or abnormal blood cells forming in the bone marrow, were still only 18 percent of the cells. "But if the blasts reach thirty percent, it will be, by definition, full-blown leukemia. And if you get leukemia at age seventy, you're too old for a bone marrow transplant—so you could be . . . not necessarily, but you could be . . . looking at a life expectancy of three to twelve months. We need to watch it carefully for a few weeks—and pray it doesn't develop as we fear it could."

Neal and Colleen hung up the phone and looked in silent shock at each other. Soon Colleen's gentle fingers were wiping away a tear that ran down Neal's cheek, her vision blurred by her own tears. She began to whisper that it would be all right, that they needed to wait and see, learn more about it. Modern medicine can do so much now. The Lord will not forsake us, not now.

Surrounding them there in the office, even enveloping them, were the familiar echoes of past years: the faded, autographed picture of Neal's mentor Harold B. Lee; the photo of Flat Top Hill in Okinawa; the small but elegant bronze statue of Joseph Smith; the group picture of the Twelve when Neal joined them in 1981; mementoes from friends in the Church Educational System, the Pacific Islands, Europe, Africa, Asia, the University of Utah, and elsewhere. On the credenza behind the tidy desk stood his ancient manual typewriter, flanked by the pictures of Becky and Mike, Cory and Karen, Nancy and Mark, Jane and Marc—and the loyal little band of grandchildren. And, where Neal could always see it from his swivel chair at the desk, a rendering of the outstretched arms and penetrating gaze of Bertel Thorvaldsen's *Christus*.

"You know, Neal," said Colleen, her voice still close to a whisper, "you've talked and written so much lately about trials and suffering. Maybe the Lord wants to let us see how we can deal with that ourselves."

"Maybe so," he returned. "Maybe so."

Moved by his instinct to share what people ought to know, he urged that, despite the uncertainties, they had to tell Becky, Cory, Jane, Nancy, and their spouses and families, tonight. Also, he had to tell the Twelve, who were having their regular temple meeting the next morning. He didn't want any of them hearing the news from someone else. And he wanted a blessing at their hands. Now he and Colleen, the comforters of so many for so long, stood in need of comfort. Who comforts the comforters? They knew the rational answer to that question. But they hungered for more than rationality.

Early Thursday morning, the Twelve filed into the historic upper room of the Salt Lake Temple, with its antique doors and the fixtures of Church history. After warm personal exchanges, they took their places in the semicircle of large chairs. The portraits of each President of the Church, beginning with Joseph Smith, stood on the wall behind them, seeming to join their little circle of disciples. In front of them, above the three chairs that awaited the First Presidency, restful paintings of the Savior graced the wall, completing the room's circle of discipleship. Fifteen years earlier, Neal Maxwell had been ordained an Apostle in this same room.

He had asked that a personal matter be added to the meeting agenda. When the time came, after the First Presidency had joined them, he told them the news—what he knew, what he didn't know, and how serious he thought it probably was. Elder Jeffrey R. Holland said of this dreadful surprise, "I will never forget the morning he announced [his illness] in the temple. I started to cry. I could not conceive of a Quorum of the Twelve in which Neal Maxwell wasn't present. I just thought, 'He is too good. He does too much.'"

After Elder Russell M. Nelson anointed him with consecrated oil, President Boyd K. Packer gave him a blessing as all of the First Presidency and the Twelve joined in placing their hands on his head. After the blessing, each one embraced him, sharing tears and private words of love, each in his own way conveying a spirit of peaceful confidence.

It had been more than fifty years since Neal had first discovered the security of an unseen peace that was stronger than very visible fears—on Okinawa, in miserable battlefield conditions, with shells raging and exploding all around him. That was the only experience in his life that could compare with what he felt now, and the comparison was eerily close. Already he found himself drawing again on what he had discovered so long ago about the Lord's awareness of him. The warm, steady hands of his brethren felt like a tangible symbol of that awareness.

In the astonished gratitude of his youth, shaking and crying in a foxhole full of mud and foul water, he had pledged his life in service to the Lord. He had no clue in those days what such a promise meant or where it would take him, but none of that mattered then. And it didn't matter now. The point was still the same. Whatever the details and the unanswered questions, Neal could say to himself with unqualified assurance: "I know that [God] loveth his children; nevertheless, I do not know the meaning of all things" (1 Nephi 11:17). He had read that passage often in recent years with people in trouble. Now it spoke to him with surprising freshness, like a letter from home, the kind his gentle father so often used to send him during the war.

It was not lost on him that he had spoken with increasing frequency, it seemed, about what he has called the postgraduate course in the curriculum of discipleship, teaching the Latter-day Saints that God sometimes gives tutorial afflictions to those who have tried hardest to follow Him. Neal titled the last book published before his illness *If Thou Endure It Well,* which, he said later, was almost an invitation to his own experience with adversity.

That theme had even earlier roots. Nearly twenty years before, his book *All These Things Shall Give Thee Experience* described three sources of suffering: Our own mistakes, life's adversities, and afflictions that "come to us because an omniscient Lord deliberately chooses to school us." Of the third category, he wrote:

> The very act of choosing to be a disciple . . . can bring to us a certain special suffering. . . . [Such] suffering and chastening . . . is the . . . dimension that comes with deep discipleship. . . .
>
> It appears to be important that *all who will can come to know "the fellowship of his sufferings."* (Philippians 3:10.) At times, we are taken to the very edge of our faith; we teeter at the edge of our trust . . . [in] a form of learning as it is administered at the hands of a loving Father. (Helaman 12:3.)

In 1991, Elder Maxwell had quoted this "wintry verse": "The Lord seeth fit to chasten his people; yea, he trieth their patience and their faith" (Mosiah 23:21), noting that this "divine purpose ought to keep us on spiritual alert as to life's purposeful adversities, especially as we seek to become more saintly." And in April conference 1990, he had said: "The enlarging of the soul requires not only some remodeling, but some excavating. . . . Even the best lectures about the theory of enduring are not enough. All the other cardinal virtues . . . require endurance for their full development. . . . He [Jesus] was determined that He 'not drink the bitter cup, and shrink' (D&C 19:18) or pull back."

As he now traveled the well-known path from the temple back to his office, Neal Maxwell, the ardent student of discipleship, sensed that his new course of study had just begun. Perhaps he should have seen it coming—but he hadn't, even though he knew that the very act of choosing to be a disciple can bring to us this special suffering.

TWO

WINTRY DOCTRINE

O VER THE NEXT FEW DAYS, Neal and Colleen forced themselves to maintain the appearance of a normal routine. But as the wheel of their consciousness made its rounds, like the fixed hour of a clock, the stark dread of the unknown rang its dark chimes. Then that, too, would pass while they attended to other things, until the wheel came round again.

The afternoon following the temple meeting, Neal went, like any good grandpa, to see his grandson Brian play football for the East High sophomores. A few days later, he played tennis with Oscar, Dick Boyle, and Bill Bailey. After the doubles match, Neal shared the news with them. He told others with whom he had frequent contact—members of the Seventy and other people at Church headquarters.

For example, he invited Bruce Olsen, managing director of Public Affairs, to his office. As Bruce sat in the outer office, he sensed that "something awful was going on." Neal invited him in with his distinctive cordiality and then, as they sat at the little table in his office, told Bruce "gently and simply" of his condition. He wondered aloud whether the Church should make some public statement, so that whatever the rumor mill said, the members of the Church could hear the news accurately from those who knew it best. Eventually, on October 26, the Church did issue a statement that he had a "pre-leukemic condition," was "receiving excellent medical help," and was "going about his duties."

Bruce couldn't deal with the Public Affairs dimensions just then. Unable to control his emotions, he groped for words, trying to focus his thoughts. Instinctively empathizing with Bruce's shock, Neal kept control of the conversation. He spoke warmly of his affection for Bruce and his wife, Chris, reflecting his habit of tracking the details of other people's lives so attentively that it often surprises them. Bruce embraced him with words of encouragement but felt he'd been "comforted by the afflicted." As he left the office, he tried to regain his composure, standing by a filing cabinet trying not to sob.

That weekend Elder Maxwell flew to Lethbridge, Alberta, for his assigned stake conference. On short notice, President Boyd K. Packer asked Neal's good friend and a Canadian, Alexander Morrison of the Seventy, to go along, just to be with him. At home in the familiar conference pace, Neal gave no hint to the congregation about his inner turmoil, even though he confided to Alex that he believed he would live only another few months.

Elder Morrison and others close to Elder Maxwell soon learned that he felt he had no claim to a special miracle. He would talk about such people as Richard L. Evans, Bruce R. McConkie, A. Theodore Tuttle, Marvin J. Ashton, and other General Authorities who had met death early. They were better men than I am, he would say. He didn't want to give anyone false hopes, and, as one friend put it, he didn't want "to promote a fan club to demand a miracle."

This attitude explains what looked like pessimism to some in his closest circle. He had worked so long on making himself "willing to submit" to the Lord (Mosiah 3:19, a verse he had quoted often), that some people thought he was actually too resigned, too ready to yield. He had a related tendency that prompted some to lecture him a little. Since boyhood, he was ever the anticipator—impatient, anxious to get on with whatever was to come next. His typical remark was, "Let's get this show on the road." And if it was time to face death, he had no need to argue or, for him, much worse, to shrink from drinking whatever bitter cup was his.

Colleen saw things differently, and she didn't hesitate to coach him with the loving directness she had long cultivated. She could see that in his desire to accept what had been allotted to him, he was reluctant to importune the Lord with much pleading. But she pointed out that Jesus' first cry in the Garden of Gethsemane was, "If it be possible, let this cup pass from me." Only after he had made this earnest plea did the Savior finally submit Himself with, "Nevertheless not as I will, but as thou wilt" (Matthew 26:39). With Jesus as our example in all things, she said, it must be permissible to plead. Then of course we submit, as He did. Neal saw her insight and agreed.

When they reviewed the statistical tables and other material Dr. Ford gave them, Neal was quick to point to graphs showing that at his age most people with leukemia just didn't make it. But Colleen, not usually a fan of statistics, noted the data showing that chemotherapy brought remission to 25 to 50 percent of older patients. If the "blasts" went up, of course he should try the chemotherapy, she said. Then she showed him her tough-love side: "And if you've only got a short time, we'll deal with it. What do you want most to try to do?"

In November, the Maxwells traveled to Europe for meetings with mission presidents and other leaders. President Packer phoned Elder Cecil Samuelson, who was Area President in England and a longtime friend of the Maxwells, urging him to make sure Neal took it easy in the unforgiving pace of normal meeting schedules. Cecil, a physician, already knew about the illness, having talked on the phone several times with Elder Maxwell about it. He arranged a visit to the Preston England Temple, then under construction, and also to Chester, a charming old English town he thought the Maxwells would enjoy. But after a few minutes there, Neal was ready to move to something he found more substantive.

By December, further blood tests and bone marrow biopsies showed that the blasts were now above 30 percent. This result upgraded his official condition to acute nonlymphocytic leukemia. Dr. Ford gave in to Neal's desire to make one more trip—an assignment in Hawaii, where he'd promised to take Jane and Marc with their baby. By the time they returned, his blood condition demanded immediate hospitalization. It was time for all-out chemotherapy.

On January 17, 1997, he entered the hospital isolation ward where bone marrow transplants are performed. There he would remain for forty-six days of intense immersion into a world of trauma unlike anything he'd ever known, even in the war. He was no stranger to hospitals, having supported an uncounted number of people in their agony there, often through afflictions that lasted for years. But he'd never gone down that fearful road himself.

A bright and seasoned oncologist, Dr. Ford has at close range watched many patients endure chemotherapy and cancer's other terrors. Asked what the treatment is like for the people involved, the doctor says quite honestly, "I have no concept. It really can't be described unless you've gone through it." And even those who've been there cannot really explain it.

As the wintry day descended toward its close, Neal and Colleen drove up the streets of Salt Lake City's Avenues district to LDS Hospital. They were anxious but not perplexed. Perhaps they were comforted by the sight of the grand old homes, the fresh snow on the stately trees, and the familiarity of so many past visits to patients in that hospital. Then too, LDS Hospital is close to the spot where, a century earlier, Neal's great-grandfather Thomas Ash owned a tiny cobbler's shop, where he taught his five sons the shoemaker's trade he'd learned as a young apprentice in England. Neal Ash Maxwell had always liked the theme of masters, apprentices, and tutorials. As they pulled into the parking lot, Neal breathed a deep sigh and looked at Colleen. He reached for her hand and said, once more, "I just don't want to *shrink.*"

Shortly before learning of his illness, Elder Maxwell had prepared an article for the April 1997 *Ensign* called "Enduring Well." There he wrote, "Certain forms of suffering, endured well, can actually be ennobling. . . . Part of enduring well consists of being meek enough, amid our suffering, to learn from our relevant experiences . . . in ways which sanctify us." There was no doubt in Colleen's mind that day that her companion of forty-seven years had become meek enough to learn from the tutorial that awaited them inside.

Almost immediately, Neal faced the full fury of chemotherapy's side effects. His blood pressure plunged, his temperature jumped with fever, and his body struggled to retain fluids. Some conditions soon improved, but other troubles followed. The first night, a doctor entered his room at midnight and plopped a huge sandbag on his chest to help stop bleeding caused by I.V. lines in his chest and by his lowered platelets. Later on, just when he was learning to live with other unpleasant side effects, he developed a painful sore in the roof of his mouth that made it feel impossible for days to eat, drink, or even swallow.

For a week, the flow of chemotherapy drugs, antibiotics, and transfusions was continual and then became intermittent as periodically the doctors called a halt to test whether the powerful drugs were killing the leukemic cells without killing too many good cells. The first tests were encouraging, but the chemicals continued to pound him, pushing his physical stamina to its limits.

Because few visitors except immediate family were allowed for the first month, Neal felt cut off from his loyal network of extended family, Church colleagues, and other friends. He was heartened when his dear friends Thomas S. Monson and James E. Faust came to give him a blessing. He had a constant yearning to thank the many others who, he knew, were fasting, praying, cheering. He seized any moment of temporary respite to dictate notes by phone, which his secretary prepared and mailed. To two grandchildren who were baptized during his confinement, Timothy and Katie, he wrote, "Please know that I will be thinking about you while you are at the Tabernacle, and probably shedding a few tears. . . . I am so grateful that we are a forever family, and this ordinance of baptism and receiving the Holy Ghost are two more steps in that marvelous process."

He became acquainted with two young fathers, Richard Nebeker and Gordon Hillier, who were being treated for leukemia in the same hospital ward. One night a nurse came into Neal's room and found him pleading in prayer for Richard's life. Unknown to the nurse, this moment echoed a night when young Neal had come home and overheard his parents in their bedroom, praying for him and his sisters. Richard and Gordon both died while Neal's chemotherapy continued. His dictated letters were read at both funerals. The Maxwell family knew he meant it when he said he really should have gone before Richard or Gordon did.

On February 26, Truman and Ann Madsen in Provo listened to his voice—tender but faint with fatigue—in a recorded message on their answering machine:

> Truman and Ann, this is Neal. You've been so kind to inquire and to write. I feel deprived of a chance to talk with you personally but wanted to tell you how much I love you. We're in this interesting *valley,* and hoping we can get extracted, with the key things that my body needs to produce, which can't come from the outside. . . . We're not releasing the hospital number, but I may try again to get to you. This is Wednesday afternoon about 3:25. I love you both so much. It's the kind of experience [pause] in which I need some tutoring; and yet, at the same time, [a tired chuckle], I won't mind when the course is over. We love you.

Late the next night, Dr. Larry Staker made one of his frequent visits to Neal's room. The two were longtime friends, but Larry's intimate involvement with Neal's illness brought them very close now, like buddies in combat. Larry entered the room, its dim hush punctuated only by the colored numbers that flashed like heartbeats on the monitors surrounding Neal's bed. Neal was awake and conscious but likely unaware of Larry's presence—or much else. Larry spoke his name. Neal tried to look up, but he was so utterly spent that he couldn't even raise his head. Larry ached at his friend's pitiful condition, "the weakest that a person can possibly be" and still be alive.

He thought Neal might respond to serious conversation. Good questions grabbed his attention when food or television never could. He pulled a chair up close. "This is Larry. I wonder if you know what day this is." Neal looked back at him, his eyes trying to focus. "It's forty days," Larry said. "Forty days you've been in this wilderness. You've endured it well." Larry paraphrased some Bible verses. Neal tracked him exactly. The conversation was launched.

As Neal found enough energy to talk, he shared what he'd been thinking during the unknown hours, not sure whether it was day or night. "I want to play in the game," he said, barely audible and only partly to Larry. "I want a jersey. On the team, on this side or that side. I don't want to sit on the sidelines." Larry recognized the prayer embedded in his plea. So typical of Neal Maxwell. He wanted to be where the action was. Better to be suited up and playing on the other side of death's veil than to be benched on this side. But Larry didn't know the connections between these earnest words and Neal's past.

One primary theme of Neal's life is that he has always been passionately engaged in causes that mattered to him. As a boy, he prepared himself for years with his backyard hoop and worn leather ball. He was determined that nothing would keep him from playing basketball on Cec Baker's celebrated teams at Granite High in Salt Lake City. His greatest boyhood disappointment came when he didn't make Baker's team. The pain of that loss has remained with him so long, one senses it's still there. "I want a jersey. Let me be on the team."

Then came his time in the infantry, then fighting in the Lord's army as a missionary, the intellectual engagements of university studies, the political skirmishes in government and education. And then, on an ever-broadening scale, the struggle between the sacred and the secular in American life, the tension between faith and reason in Church education, and finally, his greatest cause—his full-time spiritual ministry. With every breath, Neal had embraced the engaged life of which Oliver Wendell Holmes said, "It is required of a man that he share the action and the passion of his time at the peril of being judged not to have lived."

There was another echo in Neal's plea for the Coach to play him. He had ministered over a span of several years to a young father in Provo named Joe Clark, whose quadriplegic paralysis had been caused by a rare brain virus. Joe's wife, Janice, was the daughter of Doug and Corene Parker, friends of Neal and Colleen from college days.

When Neal gave Joe a blessing in the early stages of his illness, some within the family circle thought Elder Maxwell's apostolic power would surely liberate Joe from his awful bondage. But Neal told them it doesn't work that way. The righteous are not always spared. Once inside Joe's room, Neal focused intently on him. Verifying that Joe could hear and understand him, he pronounced a blessing that said nothing definite about his recovery but included this thought: God would not leave him abandoned between two worlds where he could participate in neither one. Rather, the Lord would walk with him now, through the dark valley. Joe would be consulted and his voice heard in spiritual decisions about his life and which world might be his.

Over the next five years, Joe gradually recovered modest powers of speech and a little upper body movement—just enough to maintain a "constant conversation of love" with his family. Then he passed quietly away. Doug Parker said at Joe's funeral that he "probably changed more lives" for good in those five bedridden years "than most people do who live to an advanced age." In his remarks, Elder Maxwell said: "Joe had a special consultative arrangement with the Lord on whether he would stay or go and when he would go. Not many people have that. I think it was . . . bequeathed to Joe because of his purity and goodness." Then he said:

> There are in the gospel warm and cuddly doctrines, and then there are some that are just outright *wintry* doctrines. [These doctrines are true, but] we avert our gaze [from them], because we don't wish to contemplate them. One of them, frankly, is that we cannot approach the consecration that Joe has achieved without passing through appropriate clinical experiences [because we don't achieve consecration] in the abstract.
>
> [Sometimes the Lord hastens His work in] our spiritual development [by] a compression of experiences. . . . Sometimes the best people . . . have the worst experiences . . . because they are the most ready to learn.

Perhaps when Neal asked the Coach to play him that night in the hospital, on one team or the other, he too was having a consultative conversation—the apprentice asking the Master to guide his faltering

Shortly after returning from   During his years in administra-   Soon after his call to the
his mission   tion at the University of Utah   Quorum of the Twelve

steps, like Peter on the sea, as he learned the wintry doctrine of consecration.

What is it about forty-six days of chemical bombardment that can
turn a hospital into a clinic for spiritual development? It can't be mere
physical pain, as much as that may test us. The larger context of life
creates the conditions of exquisite *mental* pain—feelings that your life
will never again be as it was and may well be nearly over, dashing all
hopes about tranquil twilight years or about continued senior service
among the Lord's anointed. For Neal, that included not only the fear
of a shortened mission but also an inner worry that he had somehow
not measured up. Doesn't the coach take you out of the game only when
you're not playing well?

Psychic pain runs bottomlessly deep. There you are, drugged up
and cooped up for a month and a half, confused whether it is day or
night, unable to rest or to turn off either the pain or your darkest
thoughts. The constant threat of death keeps crashing through
your barriers of mental resistance. Does such suffering somehow *teach*
everyone who tastes it? Anne Morrow Lindbergh didn't think so. She
wrote, in lines Elder Maxwell admires, "I do not believe that sheer
suffering teaches. If suffering alone taught, all the world would be wise,
since everyone suffers. To suffering must be added mourning, understanding, patience, love, openness, and the willingness to remain
vulnerable."

Because he knew all this, Neal's spiritual submission was not passive. He and Colleen worked to learn whatever the experience might teach them, an attitude that reflected decades of exertion to master the Lord's curriculum for the school of mortality. That commitment alone distinguished him from many cancer patients. Dr. Staker said that many "probably terminal" patients become consumed by their trauma and slip into inevitable self-absorption, unable to see, let alone attend to, needs beyond their own. Dr. Lyman Moody said that as soon as some patients hear "the awful C-word," they begin to die. But others begin to live, often more fully than ever before; for life has suddenly become more precious.

For Neal, the question was not just about a richer life but always about discipleship, trying to be like Jesus. As his treatment began, he wanted to learn more empathy and "to learn still more of Jesus by taking upon me a very small version of His yoke." During Neal's treatments, Dr. Staker watched him extend himself with concern for other patients or members of his family—a personal effort he seldom saw in such a disabled patient. "That's what Jesus did at the Last Supper," said the doctor. "He knew that tonight was Gethsemane and tomorrow was the cross." Yet in the hours just before, he gave his disciples his "most sublime, most powerful teachings." Neal would later marvel how Jesus, in his hours of greatest agony, attended to individuals—the guard who lost his ear, the thieves on the nearby crosses, and Mary, his mother.

Colleen chose to make their season of wintry doctrine a winter of her contentment. She believed she had a doctrinal mandate to *be* cheerful. The Savior, she would say, often "instructed his disciples to be of good cheer," even when there seemed "little to be cheerful about." But he had "overcome the world." So Colleen consciously chose to brighten Neal's room and cultivate her gratitude toward his nurses and doctors. She admitted she was a total "bluebird of happiness" during Neal's hospital stay, even though she knew "many people felt we were in a serious state of denial." But she knew that in dealing with cancer, "attitude is everything." She wanted to "speak of the joy to be found in all of life— whether amidst pain or [life's] pleasures. . . . And there is joy in both." She found, through experience, that "it is more difficult to maintain the spirit of gratitude and humility when times are easier than when times are difficult." She remained "realistic about what we were facing," but with her native "optimistic temperament," this "seemed [like] the time to summon all the . . . good cheer that was in me. After all, there is little to be lost and *much* to be gained."

Colleen's attitude drew on the inner wellsprings of her nature—lifting, encouraging, and choosing to view the bright side of people and events—but not because she didn't know better. She knew exactly what she was doing, and why, and for whom. To her, it is vital that women "convey hope to our families."

Shadowlands, a movie on the life of C. S. Lewis, one of Neal's favorite authors, imagines a conversation between Lewis and his wife, Joy, who has a terminal illness. As they talk about Lewis's fear of losing her, Joy tells him, "The pain then is part of the pleasure now. That's the deal." Neal and Colleen understood the same deal—our peripheral awareness of impending separation enriches our savoring of the love we may still have.

In early March, Neal left the hospital. The therapy had been successful—his leukemia was in remission. He was weak, he would need further treatment, his hair was gone . . . but, for now, the winter was past. His suppressed immune system left him vulnerable to infection until his red blood count could return to normal. Among his first outdoor ventures, he went with Dr. Staker to speak—at more than arm's length—to the doctor's daughter's early-morning seminary class at Skyline High. It felt sweet to be back in the classroom. Back in the ball game. He lifted the students, but they wouldn't understand how much they lifted him.

This experience whetted Neal's appetite to speak at April conference, and he wanted to share what he was learning about the Atonement. He was realizing that his ordeal could admit him into "the fellowship of [the Savior's] sufferings" (Philippians 3:10). He'd found that if a person's heart is receptive enough, those who taste this peculiar fellowship begin to appreciate not only Christ's suffering but also His "character"—which helps them not only adore but emulate Him. So, as he said at conference, "Jesus knows how to succor us in the midst of our griefs and sicknesses precisely because Jesus has already borne our griefs and sicknesses. He knows them firsthand; thus His empathy is earned." Then he cited but didn't read Alma 7:11–12:

> And he shall go forth, suffering pains and afflictions and temptations of every kind . . . that the word might be fulfilled which saith he will take upon him the pains and the sicknesses of his people.
>
> And he will take upon him death . . . ; and he will take upon him their infirmities, that his bowels may be filled with mercy, according to the flesh, that he may know according to the flesh how to succor his people according to their infirmities.

Neal was finding new meaning in Alma's idea, which he had talked about for years but which his firsthand experience was now changing from theory to practice. He was discovering that in his own suffering, in a small way, he could learn about emulating Christ—not by suffering alone but by letting his grief give him a "feel" for what other people taste in their sorrow. He could see more clearly that those who let themselves become "afflicted in [the] afflictions" of their loved ones (D&C 30:6) are doing something Christlike—really following Jesus (see D&C 133:53).

Trying to become a true follower of Christ—discipleship—is the central message both of Neal Maxwell's teachings and of his life story. The meaning of that message has developed for him through his personal experience. Having now seen glimpses of this process since 1996, let us go back and walk the winding path that led him there—and to what happened next with his illness. Then perhaps it will be more clear why he feels he should not have been surprised when leukemia arrived at his door.

PART II

THE ANCESTRAL STORIES

NEAL A. MAXWELL FAMILY

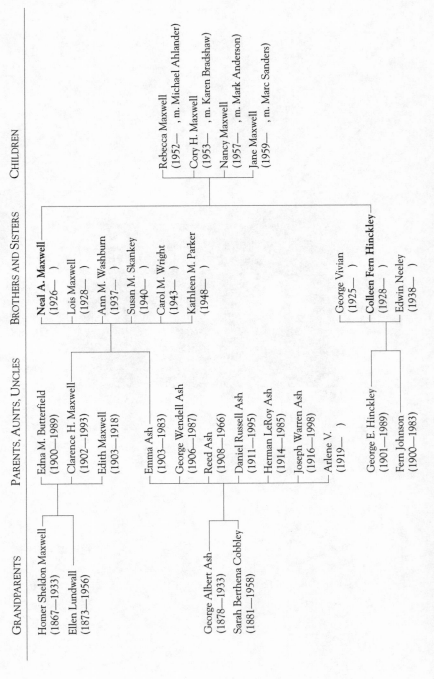

GRANDPARENTS | PARENTS, AUNTS, UNCLES | BROTHERS AND SISTERS | CHILDREN

Homer Sheldon Maxwell
(1867—1933)

Ellen Lundwall
(1873—1956)

Edna M. Butterfield
(1900—1989)

Clarence H. Maxwell
(1902—1993)

Edith Maxwell
(1903—1918)

Emma Ash
(1903—1983)

George Wendell Ash
(1906—1987)

George Albert Ash
(1878—1933)

Sarah Berthena Cobbley
(1881—1958)

Reed Ash
(1908—1966)

Daniel Russell Ash
(1911—1995)

Herman LeRoy Ash
(1914—1985)

Joseph Warren Ash
(1916—1998)

Arlene V.
(1919—   )

George E. Hinckley
(1901—1989)

Fern Johnson
(1900—1983)

Neal A. Maxwell
(1926—   )

Lois Maxwell
(1928—   )

Ann M. Washburn
(1937—   )

Susan M. Skankey
(1940—   )

Carol M. Wright
(1943—   )

Kathleen M. Parker
(1948—   )

George Vivian
(1925—   )

Colleen Fern Hinckley
(1928—   )

Edwin Neeley
(1938—   )

Rebecca Maxwell
(1952—   , m. Michael Ahlander)

Cory H. Maxwell
(1953—   , m. Karen Bradshaw)

Nancy Maxwell
(1957—   , m. Mark Anderson)

Jane Maxwell
(1959—   , m. Marc Sanders)

THREE

CONVERT ORIGINS

ONE VIVID METAPHOR FOR THE JOURNEY of discipleship is the idea of going to Zion. Neal Ash Maxwell's birth in 1926 united two primary paths that lead to Zion—the path of the convert (the ancestry of Clarence Maxwell, his father) and the path of the pioneer (the ancestry of Emma Ash, his mother). Along those paths, Neal's heritage would teach him about the links between faith and sacrifice, about the temptation to shrink from bitter cups, and about the fruits of going to Zion—or choosing not to go.

Clarence Maxwell came from convert stock. He was born in 1902 in Bozeman, Montana, a wildly beautiful place that still surged with the untamed flavor of the Western frontier: trout-filled rivers, stunning mountains, scary saloons, and small country church houses. Young Homer Maxwell (Clarence's father, 1867–1933) taught a Sunday School class in the Butte, Montana, Methodist church, where he met and then married Ellen Lundwall (1873–1956). Clarence, their son, would also come to know more about his own future wife (Neal's mother) by listening to her teach Sunday School in an LDS church.

Homer's parents, John and Minerva Maxwell, had reared their

five sons on a rocky farm in Vermont. In 1879, when John was sixty, the family moved to Kansas. Within a few years, four of the sons went to seek their fortune in the big sky country of Montana. Gold had been discovered there in 1862, not far from Butte, attracting Civil War deserters from both the Union and the Confederate armies.

By 1890, John and Minerva joined Homer and their other sons in Bozeman. Both parents were religious. Minerva had been "a Christian from early girlhood, being of staunch Puritan ancestry." The Methodist pastor who penned John Maxwell's obituary in 1896 described him as a "man of strong character" who battled "against the forces of evil . . . particularly . . . the saloon." John was known in Bozeman as 'Father' Maxwell, because the community knew him as the "father of the four Maxwell brothers of this city." The pastor interpreted the attendance records with optimism: John was "always seen in the house of God on the Sabbath, when able to get there."

Perhaps the most poignant story in Clarence Maxwell's heritage involves the family of his mother, Ellen Lundwall. Ellen's father, Martin Lundwall (1842–1912), along with his family, joined The Church of Jesus Christ of Latter-day Saints in Sweden at the age of fifteen. Even as a boy, Martin had a testimony of the Restoration that was clear and strong. He "was brought up poor" and "worked with my hands for my support." But he had also "studied the Mormon faith as the Lord knew that I wanted to serve him and do his will." Five years later, in 1862, Martin and his family decided he should remain in Sweden to serve a three-year Church mission while his family sailed for Zion.

The voyage turned out to be so traumatic that it shook the faith of this family of Swedish converts. Anders Lundwall, Martin's father, discovered after the *Humboldt* set sail that he should have brought more food to sustain his family during the forty-day trip. The crew was supposed to provide essential rations, but the ship's provisions "gave out before half the journey was over." The sea was rough, everyone became sick, and the Lundwalls had virtually nothing to eat for the last twenty days of the crossing. Reflecting his knowledge of the Book of Mormon as well as his humiliation as the failed provider for his family, Anders wrote, "It pained me to have my small children call on father for something good to eat and I couldn't get it for them before I reached land. . . . [By comparison, however,] I think that the Jaredites when they came over were denied even the privilege of going upon deck to get fresh air."

After at last arriving in New York, the Lundwalls made their way to Florence, Nebraska, the departure point for overland trips to the Salt Lake Valley. A late winter and unexpectedly high water along the intended route then delayed their departure. These factors, combined with the debilitated condition of his wife, Hanna, and two young sons, persuaded Anders to stay in Florence. Then in nearby Omaha, he found a four-acre farm he could work to save money and help his family recover their strength, both physical and financial.

Anders's letters to Martin in Sweden show that the idea of now taking another leap of faith across the vast American wilderness was just too much. What if they ran out of food, again, halfway across the plains? No one could guarantee their protection. Anders began to shrink at the prospect of one more bitter cup, at least right then. He wrote to his son that he had decided to stay in Omaha a while rather than head for Zion then, because if he "worked and saved $160" he could "buy oxen, a wagon and cow . . . and then when I get [to Zion] it will be mine." He realized that "some of my brethren . . . think I am a poor Latter Day Saint to stay here," but he wasn't ready to leave. Besides, his daughters could work for a dollar a week, and "we have good people here."

Martin, the clear-eyed missionary, wrote back with great concern. He thought his family should push on to Zion, where they could all be reunited after his mission. Anders replied that Martin's mother and small brothers had suffered from the ocean trip, yet "now thanks to the Lord, . . . we have our physical needs supplied and our spiritual condition has never been better. . . . I understand that you are somewhat concerned because we have stayed in Omaha, but . . . I thought it was my duty to take care of my children's health and life." He added, candidly, "I didn't have faith enough to travel over the burning desert in the condition their health was in. . . . I can't write the kind of a letter that I know you expect from me."

His father's hesitation about going to Zion alarmed Martin, so he decided to leave his mission early and go to Omaha. "It was mostly for the sake of my parents that I wanted to go to bring them back to the faith," he wrote. But when he couldn't raise funds for a ship ticket, he could only write his family "for their good that they might come back to the right way again."

Within a few months, Anders sent good news to Martin. The family was headed to Zion—almost. They kept encountering obstacles that seemed so reasonable. When Martin's sisters bade farewell to their employers, "they persuaded them to stay till next year." Moreover, Anders had been hearing rumors that "the reputation from there [Utah] isn't the best but I want to try for myself and if it is a good place I want to let you know as soon as I get there." He thought "we are just as good Mormons now as we were five years ago [but] I have believed the bad as well as the good things."

In an apt symbol of Anders's apparent state of mind, the family record then becomes cloudy. Martin's journal offers only this clue: "They had left Utah and were [again] living in Omaha, where they fared well in material things." Evidently Anders had spent some time in Utah, but it is unclear what he found there, how long he stayed, or why he returned to Omaha.

Martin finally finished his mission and joined the family in Nebraska in May 1865. We do not know whether he tried to persuade his family to try for Zion once more or why he decided to remain with them. Whatever the reason, he stayed in Omaha, married Hanna Larsson, who was not a Latter-day Saint, and worked as a bricklayer.

Anders died in Omaha in 1871 at age fifty-two. His widow, Hanna, soon took all of the family except Martin to Montana. Some time later, in a journey as filled with irony as with adventure, Martin also removed his family to Montana. In 1880, they traveled eight hundred miles by train from Nebraska to Corinne, Utah, not far from Promontory Summit, where Charles Cobbley, Neal's pioneer great-grandfather on his mother's side, had helped complete the first transcontinental railroad in 1869. There Martin and his family changed trains and took the northern rail line as far as it went—to Red Rock,

*Neal's paternal grandparents,
Homer and Ellen Lundwall
Maxwell, with their children
(clockwise from left): Clarence,
Edna, and Edith*

Montana. From there they found their way to Bozeman, where they
remained until Martin's death in 1912. They had traveled not to Zion
but through it.

Yet the hunger for Zion never fully left Martin Lundwall. Perhaps
because Bozeman had no branch of the LDS Church, Martin affiliated
with the local "Josephites"—the Reorganized Church of Jesus Christ
of Latter Day Saints. But he was not content with what he found there.
In 1906, he was rebaptized into the Church he had first embraced in
his native Sweden as a boy. Hanna, his wife, never did join the Church.
In 1908, at age seventy, four years before his death, Martin took the
train to Salt Lake City, where he was endowed in the Salt Lake Temple.
After a lifetime of longing, wondering, and wandering, Martin
Lundwall had come at last to Zion.

Martin and Hanna's daughter Ellen Lundwall enjoyed Homer
Maxwell's Methodist Sunday School class enough to marry him in

Butte in 1900. Two years later, Ellen bore a son, Clarence, the second of three children. Homer made his living by running a corner grocery store in Butte, where the family lived for a time in an upstairs apartment next to a saloon. Clarence remembered Butte as a noisy, crowded mining town with few lawns and trees. He could barely wait until summer each year, when the family returned to the Lundwall ranch near Bozeman. After his grandfather Martin Lundwall died in 1912, ten-year-old Clarence rejoiced at the news that his family would move to the ranch to be with his grandmother Lundwall.

The next seven years were the happiest of Clarence's boyhood. He reveled in caring for the farm animals in a bucolic atmosphere that later influenced Neal Maxwell's home environment—including Neal's 4-H pig-raising project. For all the rancher's joys of fresh air and open space, however, the Bozeman winters were often severe, with deep snowdrifts and icy wind blasts barring the way to school, neighbors, and town. Grandmother Lundwall died in 1915, leaving the ranch to Ellen and Homer. They kept the ranch but moved into Bozeman—just when the influenza epidemic of 1918 hit the town, closing its schools. The flu took the life of Clarence's younger sister, Edith, to whom he'd been very close. "Nothing seemed to be the same again with Edith missing," he wrote.

In 1920, Homer and Ellen sold the ranch and took Clarence, his older sister, Edna, and everything they owned on a train headed for Salt Lake City. It wasn't a happy move for Clarence, who yearned for the wide open spaces of ranch life. With a population of 100,000 people, several miles of paved roads, a trolley system, and even a new airport, Salt Lake was the Intermountain West's largest population center. To eighteen-year-old Clarence, though, those were all reasons to avoid the place.

As the train chugged and whistled its way southward from Montana's big, mountain-studded skies, Clarence would have been astonished to know what he would one day say about this move—why his parents moved to Utah, and why in their first year in Salt Lake City they moved to four different locations, until finally arriving in the Wandamere Ward. He would conclude, "[I] am sure my parents were guided when they purchased [our home] so that I might be exposed to the Gospel and become a member of the true Church, and to meet and marry the girl chosen for me in accordance with Neal's patriarchal blessing, which states, 'Your line of descent has been prepared before hand.'"

FOUR

PIONEER ORIGINS

<hr />

Neal's mother, Emma Ash, was from Mormon pioneer stock. Indeed, Emma was "four-square British"—three of her grandparents were born in Britain, and then they sailed, rode, and hiked to Zion; her other grandparent was born shortly after her English pioneer parents arrived in Utah.

This flow of believing blood in Emma's veins followed directly from the historic English missionary harvest of 1839–41. In fact, as the first of Emma's grandparents headed for Zion in the 1850s, more members of the Church lived in the United Kingdom and Ireland (35,000) than in Utah (12,000). This ratio gradually reversed itself as vast numbers of British and other European converts streamed across the ocean and the plains to Zion. Thus the stories from Emma Ash's ancestry reflect the very mainstream of Latter-day Saint pioneer history from 1850 to 1900—the gathering of Israel, especially from Europe, to the valleys of Utah.

Thomas Ash (1833–1907) was Emma's paternal grandfather. His family's story captures the grinding tension many English Saints felt between their poverty and their yearning for Zion—which sometimes went many years without fulfillment. Born in Cheshire, young Thomas began an apprenticeship with a shoemaker soon after his parents joined the Church. His master was so disagreeable that he ran away to Birmingham to find better tutoring. There he married Sarah Ann Hick (1838–1911), and they eventually had twelve children. A stalwart in the Birmingham branch, Thomas often tucked missionary tracts into his customers' shoes, he freely repaired missionaries' shoes, and he led the choir.

Thomas was a man of slight build, about five feet, four inches tall who, despite little formal education, had a "literary turn of mind and loved all kinds of books, especially histories. He would frequently sit up until daylight reading" books borrowed from neighbors. Sarah, by contrast, was never able to read or write. Thomas was "gentle and refined" by nature, not really "adapted for the life of misery and struggle which he was called to endure."

The Ash home was in a typical working-class neighborhood in sprawling Birmingham, that smoky urban symbol of the Industrial Revolution. Row upon row of housing clusters—high, soot-dusted brick houses—were joined together in quads of sixteen homes, like ancient condominiums, sharing a small common backyard. Alma Ash, Thomas's son, called this neighborhood "a nest of poverty and barbarism," with a "continuous fight against temptations to bad habits."

Despite Thomas's continued work as a cobbler, his family remained so poor that they often had to take clothes and even bedding to the local pawnshop to borrow money to pay their rent or buy food. Each week was a struggle to earn enough shillings to "fetch our clothes" by paying off the pawnbroker. Almost every Saturday night, one or more of the Ash children would be designated to stay home from church—and anywhere else—the next day, because the family couldn't pay enough to redeem all their clothes. Nothing was harder for Sarah Ash than sending her baby clothing to the pawnshop, for fear she wouldn't get it back.

As time went on, the Ashes watched a steady stream of fellow Latter-day Saints leave for Zion. For twenty years, the children often played a game they called "Going to the Valley" by lining up the kitchen chairs in a journey of fantasy. They gradually despaired of ever seeing Zion, yet they prayed continually, feeling it would take "a stupendous miracle" to deliver them from "Babylon." In 1880, the branch president visited the family with the news that, as the ones "most entitled to be emigrated that season," they would receive that year's allotment from the Church's Perpetual Emigrating Fund. The family was "overwhelmed with joy." Then the plans suddenly changed. Feeling that the allotment should be shared with other families, the mission president offered Thomas only enough money to take himself to Zion, where he could earn enough to send for his family after him.

Thomas and Sarah were despondent. Their children were old enough that if they didn't go now, some might marry outside the Church and stay behind forever. They had no assurance that Thomas could find work in Utah, had no idea how long it would take to save the cost of tickets for the whole family, and felt torn apart at the thought of indefinite separation.

In the end, Thomas went alone, embarking for Zion with the family cheering him on, reassuring him that he could soon bring them all along, too. He found work in Utah but soon learned from a mutual friend that he and Sarah were expecting another child. Meanwhile, Sarah and the children had written a letter advising of the pregnancy but begging Thomas to stay in Zion—a letter he never received. Torn by conflicting emotions, he was eventually overcome by his sense of duty to Sarah. Unable to borrow money for the family to emigrate, he decided to return to England on a cattle freight ship, which nearly sank in a vicious storm.

When Thomas reached Birmingham, he was greeted by cynics in his crowded neighborhood with, "Well, Sir Thomas, old chap, you didn't stay long in the Holy Land." More difficult was the response of Church members, some of whom "received [him] rather coldly," presumably judging him to lack sufficient faith. Some taunted him afterward about not having taken his family to Zion yet. With restraint, Thomas would say, "No, but I shall go someday." And some of them would reply, "You have been saying that for twenty years."

In 1885, Thomas's third child, Alma, sailed for America, determined to send for his family later. As his train puffed into the Utah landscape, Alma was shocked with disbelief. He had expected "Zion" to look far more inviting: "It seemed so rugged and barren and the whole country looked as if it had leprosy, being covered with white alkali and nothing visible but a few huts." He "longed to gaze on verdant and smiling [green] fields once more."

Alma was befriended by missionaries he had known in the old country, and soon he had his first look at the Salt Lake Temple, still under construction after more than thirty years of work. Before long, he landed a job interview at the ZCMI shoe factory, where he was asked to make two pairs of shoes. He found others' tools strange to use but met the test. Wrote Alma, "Oh, how the Lord works in his might and power. He aided me in the making of those two pairs of shoes, for on that one effort depended the emancipation of my father's family from England." After working a short while, he was able to borrow the money needed to bring his family to Zion.

Thanks to his enterprising son Alma, Thomas could now open his own tiny shop on Seventh Avenue in Salt Lake City, where he made boots and repaired shoes. His grandchildren saw him often there, noting his "genteel, kindly manners, his hair and skin so white and so frail looking."

Sarah, Thomas's wife, was memorable in her own right. She was five feet tall, had a reddish cast to her hair, and possessed great energy. She "believed in expressing her opinion," a trait she passed along to her granddaughter Emma. When she first tasted ice cream, she thought it was too cold—so she put it on the stove to warm. She was a delightful mimic and on demand would perform skits, playing all the parts and dropping all the h's. A favorite line was "By 'Arry, we shan't give up— if the rich lord on the 'ill would only pay us, which 'e never will."

In 1898, at age sixty-eight, Thomas was called on a mission back to England and assigned to his home city of Birmingham, where he served for two years. He died a few years after returning to Utah, the deepest desire of his heart fulfilled: Thomas Ash really had come with his family to Zion.

Thomas and Sarah's son George Albert Ash (1878–1933) was seven when the family came to Utah. He was excited at seeing his first Indians and buying American chewing gum. Assisted by his father, George perfected the cobbler's trade at the ZCMI shoe factory. He later owned the Monarch Shoe Shops, with stores in Salt Lake City, Ogden, Provo, and Eureka. At the height of his business success, George amassed a profit of two thousand dollars. He suggested to his wife, Sarah Cobbley Ash (1881–1958), that they use the money for a trip to California, which he had always wanted to see. But she hankered for an automobile—a rare treasure in those days. Not finding agreement a necessity, George went to California with his brother, and Sarah used her half of the money to buy a Model A. She learned to drive (which George never did), loved the car, and did her own automotive repairs. Sarah was always independent and resourceful. After the family had lived in a series of small apartments and homes in Salt Lake City, she surprised George by announcing that she had saved enough of "her money" that she'd just bought a building lot for the family at the end of the streetcar line at Twenty-Seventh South on State Street, where they later built a home. Soon, however, the Great Depression wiped out the Monarch Shoe Shops, along with all their other assets except their home. They never again knew financial security.

George had inherited his mother's wit and dramatic flair, which he sometimes put to practical uses. For instance, as a young man he sold homing pigeons, some of them over and over. After buying the same pigeon several times, one customer finally told him, "I don't want that pigeon no more!"

George's use of his imagination also anticipated what his grandson Neal would later do with his own children. George loved to make up stories for his children, such as "Goldilocks and the Three Ball Bearings." Neal's later version would be "Tweedledee and Tweedledum," which featured the "Friends of the Forest."

Whenever George read about anything educational, the children "had to discuss it and play act it or have fun that way. We were practically as well informed as the teachers on history and geography," his favorite subjects. When he wanted his children to experience the

Neal's maternal grandfather,
George Albert Ash

Neal's maternal grandmother,
Sarah Cobbley Ash

Amazon River, he turned their old kitchen table upside down, invited the family aboard, and pretended they were sailing in South America. He taught them the history of the American colonies and "the Spirit of '76" in the same way.

George Ash died at age fifty-five in 1933, when Neal was seven years old. George had had stomach pains for years—but never severe enough, in his view, to warrant a trip to the doctor's office. Not long afterward, at age fifty-two, Sarah had a stroke and later developed Parkinson's disease. She was an invalid for the next twenty-five years, with the family caring for her most of that time as she lived near the home of her son Herman ("Herks").

One day in 1958, Neal felt prompted to go see Sarah, his grand-mother, who by then had been in the hospital for several years. He had always felt an unusual closeness to her and to her father, Charles Cobbley. As he stood alone at her bedside that day, he felt impressed to give her a blessing, in which he asked the Lord to release her from her suspended state. She passed away a few weeks later at the age of seventy-seven.

George Ash had married Sarah Cobbley in 1902, and their daughter Emma, Neal's mother, was born the next year. Sarah's father, Charles Cobbley (1855–1937), became an important figure in the life of his great-grandson Neal Maxwell. When Neal touched his great-grandfather Cobbley's old hands, marked with the toil of carving a life for his family from the desert, he clasped his own tangible bond to the real pioneers. That linkage was represented by Charles's presence in the circle when Neal was blessed as a baby in Salt Lake's Wandamere Ward in 1926—and again when Charles laid his pioneer hands on Neal's head to confirm him a Church member and give him the gift of the Holy Ghost eight years later.

After sailing the Atlantic in 1855 with the "wind-rocked" ship *Thornton* as his "cradle," Charles spent his first five years in Pennsylvania, where his parents worked to save the money needed to travel onward to Zion. When the family finally set out from Florence, Nebraska, in 1861, they had just buried two of their seven children, and six-year-old Charles was near death. He soon recovered enough that his "small legs trudged almost the whole of the one thousand miles across the vast plains" to Utah. The Cobbleys settled in Pleasant Grove, south of Salt Lake City.

Charles grew up knowing "the privations . . . incident to pioneer life" and also the "simple . . . joys" of that life. His first home in Utah County had a dirt floor and a partly dirt roof. The family grew subsistence crops and took their wheat on an all-day wagon trip to Springville to be ground, a two- or three-day process. They brought in wood from the nearby mountains to cook food and heat their little home. Some winters were so cold their wood would run out, and then they had to walk to the foothills of Mount Timpanogos to gather sagebrush for their fires.

At age eleven, Charles witnessed the Black Hawk War of 1866, the largest conflict between the pioneers and the local native Americans. By age thirteen, he was carrying tools to the blacksmith shop for a Latter-day Saint crew working for the Union Pacific, because Brigham Young had arranged to build the "forty miles of the worst road" of the westbound railroad. Charles and his father soon helped finish the first transcontinental railroad near its famous joining place at Promontory Summit in northern Utah.

Charles marveled at the new day brought by the railroad to Utah's once-isolated valleys. Now the Saints had broader markets for their grain and other crops. Sawmills opened, so they could build homes of lumber, and trains could bring coal to heat their stoves. Mines were opened nearby, boasting fabulous discoveries of gold, silver, lead, and copper. Mining attracted new elements to pioneer Utah—new kinds of people and new forms of greed. Watching his world change, Charles was cautious: "I believe there was nothing any safer for a man than to stay with his farm. . . . I have seen lots of money lost in mining." Because mining requires so much capital and entails so much risk, he thought, it is "no place for a poor man."

On June 28, 1878, Charles married Emma Louise Davis, whose mother had helped Charles's parents care for him during their ocean voyage from Liverpool twenty-three years earlier. Emma was only sixteen when they married, but the young couple were well prepared to begin their life together: the enterprising young Charles took Emma to his thirty-acre farm, where he had already built a small house for their future family.

The Cobbleys eventually reared ten children in Pleasant Grove, where Charles worked as a blacksmith and a farmer. After the harvest each year, he would "fix up a freight team" and haul goods between Lehi, the end of the railroad line, and Pioche, Nevada, along with trips into Wyoming and California. At the Pony Express station in Pioche on one trip, Charles had the experience his posterity, including Neal, would always coax him to retell: "One of the drivers of the Wells Fargo Express threw off a box of money and it broke. [Gold coins] scattered all over. If I had wanted to be dishonest, I could have been a rich man . . . no one else was there, only me and [a drunk] fellow. But it didn't even tempt me. We gathered all of it up and put it back."

A hard test for Charles and Emma arrived in the mail three days after Christmas in 1892. The stately signature "Wilford Woodruff" rested at the bottom of a letter calling Charles to serve a two-year mission in the Southern States. With a houseful of young children, an unpaid debt from having just expanded their home, and no way for Emma herself to do the blacksmithing and freighting work that had kept food on their table, the couple were driven to their knees.

Charles could have felt himself shrinking a little at the thought of leaving his family right then. But Emma was an "intrepid soul, energetic and prudent," and she encouraged Charles to accept the call, knowing fully what the Brethren asked of her as well as of her husband. So, "being moved" by her support and his own "devotion to the gospel," he posted a letter to the First Presidency on a wintry January 7, 1893:

> I will merely state my circumstances and then leave the matter as to my going entirely with my Brethren over me.
>
> I have seven children under the age of thirteen, the oldest boy is six years old. I have a small farm. I also do some black smithing for my neighbors. During the last two years . . . with my work and farm and by using the strictest economy, I have been unable to make ends meet.
>
> During that time I have put a small addition to my house which I am still indebted for, not able to pay before the coming summer. These are the facts in regard to my condition and while not wishing to shirk any duty to which I may be called, . . . I will leave the matter entirely to your wisdom and judgment.

After the Brethren received this letter, a note was penned at the bottom, followed by the initials "JFS" (likely Joseph F. Smith of the First Presidency): "I would not ask him to go now, but leave him to decide whether he can go or not and when he concludes, let him report." Charles did accept the call, serving for two years "without a five-cent piece in my pocket." His "only means of transportation was my two legs." He never rode a train and once walked eighty miles to reach a new field of labor.

Emma and the children shouldered their own missionary burden, sustaining Charles's call both physically and spiritually. Emma, who "had little time for the tinsel and bubbles of social life, but [who] had a zest for genuine fun and the companionship of friends," simply went to work. For two years, she drove a team of horses between Pleasant Grove and Provo, selling butter and eggs from the Cobbleys' farm. She also found work cleaning houses, and the children helped out from jobs of their own. By the time Charles returned, the family had not only taken care of themselves but also paid off the ninety-dollar debt for their expanded home.

In 1902, Charles and Emma Cobbley's daughter Sarah married George Albert Ash and moved to Salt Lake City. A year later, Sarah and George Ash became the parents of Emma, named for Sarah's mother. During her childhood, Emma (who would become Neal Maxwell's mother) looked forward to occasional wagon trips from Salt Lake to Pleasant Grove to visit her Cobbley grandparents and enjoy the farm animals and other delights unknown to a city girl.

The Cobbleys lived in Salt Lake City's Wandamere Ward during the last few years of Charles's life—and the first few years of the life of his great-grandson Neal. Emma was glad to be closer to her Cobbley grandparents. She was always stirred by the "fervency" of her grandfather's ongoing "tribute to his wife as a help meet and homemaker." Emma also drew spiritual support from her grandmother Cobbley, who accompanied Emma to the Salt Lake Temple on the day she married Clarence Maxwell in 1923.

FIVE

CLARENCE AND EMMA

IT WAS STILL DARK OUTSIDE IN SALT LAKE CITY as nineteen-year-old Clarence Maxwell hurried along the snow-crusted walkway toward the trolley stop at Twenty-Seventh South. The new year, 1922, had just begun. The morning was chilly by Utah standards, but these winters were nothing compared to the freezing, massive drifts that buried the fence lines around Bozeman for weeks at a time.

As Clarence stood waiting in the cold for the streetcar, "an event took place which changed the course of [his] life and put purpose into it." A man just younger than Clarence arrived to wait for the same trolley. He said his name was Judd Flinders. Judd and Clarence climbed aboard, chatting over the noisy clatter of the metal streetcar wheels as they rode into town. Judd said his youth group was having a social that evening at the Wandamere Ward, not far from Clarence's home. "Mutual," Judd called it, inviting Clarence to come along.

Clarence wouldn't usually have been looking for anything new to fill his evenings, but just a few days before he had heard "by way of her mother" that the young lady he had been dating was no longer interested in him. So with "time hanging heavy on [his] hands," he told Judd yes, he'd be glad to go. This was a good night for that.

Before beginning the social part of the evening, the Wandamere M-Men class took a few minutes to choose new officers for the coming year. In 1921, a year earlier, the Church had adopted a program called M-Men and Gleaners for young people aged seventeen through twenty-one. Even though this was his first meeting, and even though he wasn't a Latter-day Saint and really knew nothing about the Church, the group invited Clarence to be the M-Men class secretary. They wanted him to feel welcome, and he did.

A few days later, Clarence attended a meeting of the class officers to plan a trip to Pine Crest Inn up Emigration Canyon. Emma Ash was there from the Gleaners with her friend, Gladys Rutter, whose English mother operated a little store next to the chapel. Emma and Gladys always made each other more "impish," and this night they directed their impishness at Clarence. They sat on either side of him on the couch, teasing him and sitting ever closer to him. "He sat very upright," said Emma, then "finally smiled and talked a little with us."

Clarence had seemed so shy that Emma was surprised when he asked to walk her home after the meeting. After they had talked playfully on her front porch for a few minutes, Emma related, "Surprise! He leaned over and kissed me! I wondered, 'Shy??' I couldn't wait to tell [Gladys]." Emma just stood there. "I didn't know what to do and I thought, 'Well, you can't tell a book by its cover.'" Later she learned that Clarence really was shy and quite proper. So proper, in fact, that he had just thought the kiss was expected of him.

The ward chapel was the social center of the neighborhood that surrounded the big Wandamere Resort on Twenty-Seventh South. The ward held a Valentine's Day dance on February 14, 1922. By then Clarence and Emma were seeing each other often. Clarence hadn't missed a Sunday in going to church. It helped that Emma taught the Sunday School class he attended.

Meanwhile, Clarence was also feeling drawn to the Church's teachings. He began attending the priests quorum meetings before Sunday School, and Bishop Arthur Shurtleff took a personal interest in him. His work with the M-Men officers put him in touch with MIA leader Jesse Fox, who enjoyed answering Clarence's frequent questions. Clarence found these two men "very considerate of me." They encouraged him to keep coming and "to become one of them."

Years later, Clarence's son, Neal, would say that when Clarence was introduced so naturally to the Church, "he had a friend and a job and was nurtured." No one gave Clarence any formal missionary lessons, but his feeling about the rightness of the Church's teachings just kept growing. Later that spring, he asked Bishop Shurtleff about becoming a member. He was baptized in the font at the Salt Lake Tabernacle on June 24.

At Judd Flinders's funeral more than seventy years later, Neal Maxwell would say, "When Judd Flinders reached out his hand in greeting . . . to my father, he [took] not only . . . the hand of Clarence Homer Maxwell, but . . . four subsequent generations"—by then nearly a hundred people. Clarence eventually shared with his own family what he had found, baptizing his parents in 1933, just before his father's death, and his sister Edna a little later. Once he knew the Martin Lundwall story, perhaps Clarence felt that these steps reconnected his mother's Lundwall ancestry to its original but interrupted yearnings for Zion.

By the time Clarence joined the Church, he and Emma were seeing each other almost every day. Emma worked in her father's shoe repair shop at Second South near Main Street, and Clarence worked at Booth Fisheries, just around the corner from First South and Main. She had no trouble convincing her father's errand boy to make detours from his trips about town to deliver her notes to Clarence and to bring back Clarence's replies.

As the courtship grew more serious, there were also occasional moments of misunderstanding. One night when Clarence was at Emma's house, their conversation turned into a disagreement. "Angrily I went out the back door," he said, "thinking this was the end." He walked off the doorstep into the mud and wet of a heavy rainstorm. Looking at his shoes, Clarence realized he'd left his rubber overshoes inside Emma's house. He was perturbed, but "because of my Scotch

Clarence and Emma Ash Maxwell
about the time they were married

descent and dislike for muddy shoes" he went back for them. Emma welcomed him, both apologized and began talking, and Clarence returned home, retiring "for the night at my usual late hour." Years later, he was amazed at what he had almost lost—and how his budding relationship with Emma was saved by a pair of shoes.

The Wandamere Ward could have thought that the wedding of Emma and Clarence was arranged by the ward activities committee. They met in the ward, they courted in the ward, and they shared their company with the ward. One night during their courtship, they together won first prize for best costume at a ward costume ball. They kept up their work on the M-Men and Gleaner committees. And the night before their wedding on February 28, 1923, they both acted in the ward play. Clarence, who played the role of an English butler, still had flour makeup from the play in his hair when they went to the temple the next day.

That next morning they rode the streetcar up Seventh East and along South Temple to the Salt Lake Temple, accompanied only by Emma's grandmother Emma Louise Cobbley and Clarence's friend Bill

Rutter. No one else in Clarence's family was a member of the Church, and Grandmother Cobbley was evidently the only one in Emma's family who could go. Joseph Fielding Smith of the Twelve, whom they had never met, was assigned to perform their sealing that day. Afterward, the newlyweds celebrated by going to a movie. Then they rode the streetcar to the home of Clarence's sister Edna, who lent them her place for their honeymoon. Ever conscientious, Clarence had asked for only two days off work from his job at Oxweld Acetylene. Then he was smart enough to suggest that Emma call his boss to ask for a third day—which she did, successfully.

In the Maxwell-Ash marriage, the pioneer stream and the convert stream converged in a river of harmony. Emma and Clarence were part of what their son Neal calls that "critical mass" of decent people who hold together families, neighborhoods, communities—and the Church. "He comes from a very humble beginning," said President Boyd K. Packer, "and it shows in his sensitivity to people." Within three years, on July 6, 1926, Neal would be born into this welcoming cradle of values and attitudes—a modest, sunny environment that built the earliest pathway for his spiritual journey on a foundation of peace and security.

PART III

CHILDHOOD STIRRINGS

SIX

BORN IN SALT LAKE CITY'S ROARING TWENTIES

T HE DECADE OF THE 1920s WAS A BRIEF, carefree, and sometimes heady window of time for most Americans. As frightening as World War I and the national influenza epidemic had just been, both the nation and the world now seemed safer and stronger. For the first time, there were more than 100 million Americans. Constitutional amendments had recently said yes to women's right to vote and no to the sale of intoxicating liquor. Babe Ruth was hitting more home runs than anyone had thought possible, the automobile worked so well that it promised to put the whole nation on wheels, the stock market just kept moving up, and people flocked to the movies— especially when the "talkies" replaced silent films in 1927.

Meanwhile, in an event whose future significance was not yet foreseeable, Lenin and the Bolsheviks had toppled the czar in Russia. Totalitarianism was barely beginning to cast dark shadows across the world, as the figures of Hitler, Stalin, Mussolini, Tojo, and Mao Zedong prepared their moves toward the center stage of world history. Some future historians would say that the U.S. withdrew in the 1920s from its responsibility to protect the world's peace. "Emerging from

World War I as the leading world power, the United States proceeded to dissipate that power," as it declined to help maintain security in the postwar world.

But at home, Jack Dempsey and Gene Tunney boxed with a muscle that reflected the nation's growing confidence, and the Four Horsemen played football at Notre Dame the same way. Clarence Darrow and William Jennings Bryan brought eloquence to both sides of the Scopes trial in Tennessee, Eugene O'Neill's plays brought a rich depth to Broadway, and F. Scott Fitzgerald's *The Great Gatsby* did the same for American literature. And thousands of flappers danced away their cares with the Charleston.

By the time Neal Ash Maxwell was born in 1926, Calvin ("Silent Cal") Coolidge was a "benign presence in the White House, content to let the bankers, industrialists, and speculators run the country as they saw fit." No one could have predicted the calamities that waited just around the corner of history—the Great Depression and yet another great war, either one of which would threaten the very survival of the American experiment in self-government more seriously than anything since the Civil War.

Heber J. Grant had been President of the Church since 1918, Church membership stood at just over 600,000, and about 2,500 full-time missionaries were serving. The Church was still largely agrarian and rural, with 75 percent of its population living in Utah and the Intermountain states. Yet the Church had its own reasons for renewed confidence in 1926, as important long-term developments were taking root.

Salt Lake City, for example, was becoming urbanized. The location of Clarence and Emma Maxwell's home on Twenty-Seventh South and Seventh East symbolized the change. Their house almost straddled the boundary between Salt Lake City and Salt Lake County—and the city part was expanding. That line also captured the point where city life and country life intersected. Each spring and fall, in their early years, the Maxwell children would watch as local stockmen drove sheep past their home, to and from the nearby mountain grazing land. Emma always worried about errant critters trampling on her tulip beds when the street was "covered from one side to the other with moving herds of sheep."

The Church itself was also in a transition time. The Saints' geographical and social isolation from United States society during the latter half of the nineteenth century had gradually come to an end. This process had been hastened by the completion of the transcontinental railroad in 1869, the general settlement of the West, Utah statehood in 1896, the development of local mining interests, and the emergence of Salt Lake City as a major economic center in the Western region.

Utah was among the world's largest producers of silver, lead, and copper by 1920—and only 40 percent of the population of Salt Lake County was Latter-day Saint. Also, just as more people of other faiths were making Utah their permanent home, the Church and its members were becoming more assimilated into the larger American society. In one symbol of these movements, Elder Reed Smoot of the Quorum of the Twelve Apostles had successfully represented Utah in the United States Senate since 1903 and would remain there until 1933.

In a field that would affect Neal Maxwell's future life as commissioner of education, Utah was developing a strong state educational system to meet needs once served almost exclusively by Church schools. So the Church scaled back its involvement in schools and began to emphasize religious education. The seminary program had begun as an experiment in 1912 at Granite High School, located within walking distance of Neal's home. This was the high school and seminary he would attend in the early 1940s.

David O. McKay became the first General Authority to serve as Church commissioner of education in 1919. During the 1920s, the Church expanded the seminary program throughout the Intermountain area and launched the first institute of religion at the University of Idaho in 1926, the year of Neal's birth. By the early 1930s, the Church had donated all of its colleges—except Brigham Young University, Ricks College, and LDS Business College—to the states where they were located. In Utah, these schools included Dixie, Snow, and Weber colleges.

The Church was also on the cusp of a major shift in the meaning of "gathering to Zion." Historically, Church members were concentrated in Utah and contiguous states because the Church had expected its converts to "gather" to the center stakes from all over the world. Now, however, those stakes had become mature enough that it was time to look toward establishing a permanent Church presence in other locations. These were the early stirrings of what would become a truly global Zion during Neal A. Maxwell's lifetime.

For example, the Hawaii Temple was dedicated in 1919, followed by temples in Cardston, Alberta, Canada, in 1923 and in Mesa, Arizona, in 1927. The Los Angeles California Stake was created in 1923. Church membership in North America increased by almost 25 percent during the decade of the 1920s. On May 6, 1922, President Grant delivered the first gospel message over the air waves by means of radio. People heard him for a thousand miles in every direction, speaking from atop the Deseret News Building. General conference was first broadcast by live radio in 1924, and the Tabernacle Choir began its still-running weekly radio broadcasts in 1929.

Church leaders in the 1920s were discouraging people from migrating to be with the main body of the Saints in the Intermountain region; however, European members suffering from the dislocations of World War I understandably continued to flow to the United States. The subsequent shocks of the Depression and World War II undermined the conditions needed to establish permanent communities of Saints in Europe and elsewhere. The Church had not grown much in Latin America by the 1920s, and the Japanese Mission was closed in 1924 after twenty-three years of very limited growth in Asia. Yet long-term centers of Church strength had already taken root in Polynesia—Hawaii, New Zealand, Tonga, Samoa, and Tahiti.

The Wandamere Ward, where Neal spent most of his growing-up years, reflected the early twentieth-century gathering. Latter-day Saint emigrants from the great cities of Europe gravitated to the edges of Salt Lake City, where they could be close enough to find work in the city but live far enough away to find affordable housing. Neal found his ward was "loaded with converts from Europe: Swiss converts to the south, Germans to the north, and Dutch just north of them."

The European converts retained their national character, which included a strong work ethic. For example, Rutters' store, located next to the Wandamere chapel, was operated by an English convert couple whose children were good friends with both Clarence and Emma. Neal and his friends would press their noses against the glass covers that arched over the Rutters' candy counters, able to buy several treats with one nickel. Sister Rutter would never go to the ward old folks' dinners, because she was too busy running the store even in her early eighties.

One of Neal's youth advisers was another British convert with thick glasses. He was a strict theologian who didn't relate well to young men—but no one doubted the depth of his faith. Having once trained for the ministry in England, he'd "preach to us the whole class period with his chin resting on his cane" and "give unrequested encores at testimony meetings."

Young Neal's ward teaching companion was a German convert who "talked too much when we visited the homes," gave "regular orations" in fast meetings, and "would have been genuinely puzzled by the concept of two-way communication." Yet the youth of the ward, including Neal, knew that he loved both them and the gospel.

New buildings rose on the Salt Lake skyline as the city grew from 100,000 to nearly half again that many people between 1920 and 1930, in part because Utah's birthrate led the nation. This growth came not with blight but with beauty, as a local "city beautiful" movement tried to make the city "second to none in the United States." The city boasted the "broadest and most beautifully laid out streets" anywhere and was said to be one of the country's "most scientifically arranged cities."

An example of the city's commitment to its quality of life was the Wandamere (meaning "beautiful lake") Resort, the central backdrop for the stage on which Neal Maxwell grew up. Located just down the street from his home, the resort opened in 1907 as a recreational center, with concession stands, "airplane" rides that swung out over the lake, a theater pavilion, a zoo, and a small train that circled the park. The city boundaries jogged south at Seventh East just enough to include the park within the city limits. Emma Ash Maxwell had girlhood memories of people coming from all over the valley to the dances, picnics, and summer theater productions. The city eventually sold Wandamere to Charles W. Nibley, Presiding Bishop of the Church, who later donated it back to the city in 1922, hoping that coming generations would find "healthful enjoyment and rare pleasure here in playing that splendid outdoor Scotch game known as golf."

Wandamere then became Nibley Park, a golf course, where young Neal Maxwell had his first personal—though brief—conversation with a General Authority, President Heber J. Grant, in his red golf sweater. Neal and his friends would wait at the ninth hole to shag any stray golf balls hit over the park fence. When President Grant played, he hit the ball with consistency, perhaps because he played only with his irons. Most golfers would pay the self-appointed crew of ball retrievers a nickel per ball, if anything. But if he hit a shot off course, President Grant "was good for about fifteen cents, and that was really good!"

It was at Nibley Park during this era when President Grant finally enticed the office-bound James E. Talmage out for his only try at golf. Elder Talmage went, on the condition that he could quit whenever he chose. President Grant, confident that Elder Talmage would fall in love with the sport, agreed not to bother him again about playing. After watching President Grant hit a couple of practice shots, Elder Talmage seized a club, hit his tee shot straight down the fairway, put his suit coat back on, bade his brethren adieu, and returned to the office.

The city's Main Street in those days was a "maze of urban technology, with trolley wires and rails lacing the centers of streets lined on both sides by parked automobiles." The Hotel Utah had been completed in 1911, and on October 2, 1917, the stately new Church Office Building was opened at 47 East South Temple Street. Paving gradually transformed city streets "from thoroughfares for pedestrians, trolleys, and horses into auto roads." Salt Lake City's prominence was suggested by its new airport, which brought both airmail and passenger service to town. The region composed of Utah, southern Idaho, eastern Nevada, and southwestern Wyoming had a population of 700,000.

Air pollution may seem like a modern Salt Lake City problem,

As a toddler

but concerns about that issue ran high in the 1920s. The leading local figure in addressing that and other public health issues was Amy Brown Lyman, first secretary and later general president of the Relief Society, a member of the Utah legislature, and the wife of Apostle Richard R. Lyman.

The city itself was expanding to the south and southeast of its original core toward Sugarhouse, Murray, and Midvale. Some "country living" estates began to emerge in the Holladay-Cottonwood area, interspersed with the farms that dominated the larger valley. Wandamere remained rural enough that, on a good day, Neal could still go catch a trout in a stream that ran fifty yards from his house.

Into this place of peace, in a season of both promise and risk, Neal Ash Maxwell was born early on the morning of Tuesday, July 6, 1926, the first of six children. A friend drove Emma and Clarence to the hospital. Having used up his allotted vacation days the previous week in premature anticipation of the baby's arrival, Clarence went back to his job after the delivery and "didn't lose any time from work." The delivery "cost—$50 for each the doctor and hospital" left them enough to buy "a nice wicker baby carriage brown in color" for baby Neal.

The same day, Neal's five Ash uncles all went out to their sand-lot basketball court behind the family home on Leland Avenue and gave a collective cheer. Because Emma had had a boy, they intended to make sure their first nephew became an all-state basketball player.

Neal was an ordinary boy, not born under any condition that would make him feel entitled to anything in particular. The main thing was that he was born of decent, good parents who tried to teach him all they knew. And, like Abraham of old, he soon concluded that "there was greater happiness and peace and rest" for him in seeking for "the blessings of the fathers" (Abraham 1:2). For Neal would grow up with an unspoken sense in some uncharted region of his heart that as much as he would come to love basketball and as much as he would come to hate war, he wanted more to become a disciple, "a follower of righteousness, desiring also to be . . . a greater follower of righteousness, and . . . desiring to receive instructions, and to keep the commandments of God."

SEVEN

CLARENCE MAXWELL
AND SON: MASTER
AND APPRENTICE

NEAL ENJOYED AN UNUSUALLY SECURE, open relationship with his parents, especially his father—though because that all seemed so natural, they hardly sensed its significance. So Neal's primary spiritual mentor was a self-effacing convert who never held a highly visible position, never knew material wealth, and had only a high school education. It probably never crossed Clarence's mind (or Neal's, for that matter) that he was the master for an energetic young apprentice who was unconsciously modeling every shade and hue of his father's discipleship—which is one reason Clarence fit the role so well. His unawareness of his own meekness was one hint that it was genuine.

Clarence was a shy and unassuming man of slight build, about five feet, eight inches tall, with light brown hair. Carol, Neal's sister, has a favorite, typical memory of their father sitting on the couch in their living room, his daughters laughing and repeatedly combing his sparse hair while he read the Sunday "funny papers" aloud to them, changing his voice for each comic strip character. "Dad didn't need many worldly things," said Neal's sister Sue. "In fact, he often didn't even seem aware of them. His eyes saw only the meaningful things in life, and almost all conversations were related to the gospel."

For Clarence, then, having a gospel conversation was no big deal—that was just what you talked about, because that was real life. He was also methodical, orderly, and frugal. He used his pencils down to practically nothing; he wanted all of his tools kept in place and not left outside; he wasn't judgmental; he didn't raise his voice or speak unkindly of other people. He ate his lunch at his desk while at work, and he read Church books as he ate there. He would wait on customers during his lunch hour and not count that as company time. He went on his lunch break to his daughter Sue's baptism and then returned to work while Sue and her mother went out for lunch to celebrate.

Looking back, Neal doesn't think his father enjoyed great job satisfaction, partly because in the days of the Depression, he was grateful to have a job at all. Clarence learned on the job to be a stenographer and a meticulous bookkeeper. For the first twelve years of Neal's life, Clarence worked for a subsidiary of Union Pacific railroad, taking that same Seventh East streetcar every day into town to work. Neal remembers going often to meet his father at the trolley stop after work to walk home with him, "which gave me real joy."

When Union Pacific moved its office to Omaha in 1936, they told Clarence he could move to Nebraska with them, or he could leave the company and receive fourteen hundred dollars—a year's salary—as severance pay. Clarence might have thought of his grandfather Martin Lundwall as he considered moving back to Omaha. He showed his ten-year-old son the check and "even let me hold it for a brief moment." Neal thought he'd never see a check for so much money again. Going with the railroad hadn't been a close question for Clarence, who stayed in Salt Lake City and found another job. He later worked many years in the office of Sterling Furniture Company.

With the Maxwells' modest financial station, aggravated by the depressed economic climate, the family had no car and few other material goods. Most others in their neighborhood were in the same fix— they were all poor but hardly knew it. Neal doesn't remember ever going out to dinner with his parents. They couldn't have afforded it, nor could most others then.

Yet Clarence maintained his sense of humor. One Sunday when Neal was a baby, Clarence and Grandfather Ash heard a crackling sound, smelled smoke, and discovered that a small fire had broken out in the attic of the Maxwell house. Clarence climbed upon a stool he'd placed on a chair so he could look through the ceiling trap door into the attic. When Clarence yelled "Fire!" Grandpa Ash ran for help. In his haste, he let go of the stool, which fell over, leaving Clarence dangling from the rafters. Clarence would laugh remembering that incident, telling Neal that "your part in the story" was "a rough ride in that new baby buggy down the six or seven front steps," after Clarence dropped to the floor. Another treasure he rushed to safety was the bureau drawer that contained the tithing and fast offering money, which Clarence, the ward clerk, had brought home from church that day. In the end, the fire didn't damage the house significantly.

Clarence enjoyed recalling that Emma's doctor had predicted Neal would be born on July 4 but, in fact, he arrived two days later. "It wasn't your fault," Clarence wrote, "that you were not a firecracker as Dr. Pinkerton predicted." He also smiled at the coincidence that Neal was a patient in Holy Cross Hospital only twice—once when he was born and once when he was called to become an apostle in 1981.

Despite the family's economic circumstances, Clarence was happy with everything that mattered to him—his family, his Church assignments, his farm animals, and his garden. His attitudes rubbed off onto his son. Neal's daughter-in-law, Karen B. Maxwell, thinks Neal learned "his gentleness with children" and his "lack of ego and self-importance" from Clarence, who worked hard behind the scenes for the railroad and the furniture company, innately meek and loyal about fulfilling his duties. Those attitudes were linked in Clarence's world to his "dedication to doing things right" and his "love for the doctrines of the gospel."

Clarence and Emma valued education, and both read often to Neal. With their parents' encouragement, nearly all of the Maxwell children would graduate from college. Scriptures, Church manuals, and other books were open and accessible around the house, like welcome friends. And whether his parents read to him from the Bible, *The Secret Garden*, or *Kidnapped*, the books conveyed to Neal a message much like the one he received in the family's continual, informal gospel conversations: learning and literature were worthwhile—and beyond that, or as part of it, "life seemed to have an overall, purposeful, and divine design. Some things were right and other things were wrong."

Clarence always read the daily newspaper, a lifelong habit Neal acquired early and ardently. His parents both prized their *Book of Knowledge* set and used the books often. The children found that Emma was much quicker to answer their questions, because Clarence always wanted to think about it, which gave him time to look in the scriptures or other books for the most reliable answer.

Neal was never very adept at mechanical things, so he's not had the skill he wishes he'd had in solving his own household problems. Colleen said, "Neal was not as methodical as his father and neither gifted nor interested in working with his hands, yet he "really wanted to please" his father. Pleasing Clarence was one reason Neal became interested in his purebred pig project. Whatever the job, he could see his father's approval, or lack of it, in one glance at his face.

In his early years, Neal sometimes thought his father was too fussy about his expectations for work quality, which may be one reason that mechanical things didn't seem to come easily. Neal would have been content to follow his mother's more relaxed style, which sometimes meant "just throwing things together and saying, 'Let's get this thing done!'" Emma thought it wasn't worth the trouble to build pigpens to Clarence's high standards, because "the pigs wouldn't care if things weren't exact."

But Neal's earliest work experiences were under Clarence's watchful eye, "loving but exacting." And though Neal "worked hard, my work was often not carefully done. I was a stranger to excellence." One thing he didn't like about farm work is that "you were never through with it." Irrigation turns always seemed to come in the middle of the night; and even if he had just fed the animals, it was always about time to feed them again. As one dairy farmer put it, the trouble with milking cows is that they don't stay milked. So, while young Neal didn't always put

Front row: Clarence Maxwell, Herks and Joe Ash; second row: Wen, Reed, and Russ Ash; back row: Arlene Turner (Emma's sister), Neal, Afton Ash (Emma's sister-in-law) with son Vic, and Emma Maxwell

his shoulder to the wheel with a "heart full of song," he did "learn about shoulders and wheels, which helped later in life, when the wheels [of work] grew larger."

One day, Neal gave his best to satisfying Clarence's high standards in putting in a row of fence posts on the little farm plot near their home. He worked all day to align the posts in a straight row, burying each one at exactly the same depth. When Clarence came home, Neal "watched anxiously as he carefully inspected the fence posts, even checking them with a level bar before pronouncing them to be fully satisfactory. Then came his praise," which Neal knew he never got unless he'd earned it. "My sweat of the brow had earned Dad's commendation which, in turn, melted my heart." When that happened, "the importance of pride in workmanship . . . finally reached me. . . . The posts were not the only thing that fit into place that summer."

Neal also felt over his shoulder the same look of Clarence's well-calibrated eye when he was keeping records on his 4-H purebred pig project. Neal's annual report to his 4-H leaders when he was sixteen states that he was "constantly faced by an experienced bookkeeper"— "my Dad," who records "the most minute details." He acknowledged

Clarence's help when he won two state championships in the record book contest for livestock production projects.

Later on, Elder Maxwell would often talk about work to Church members. He had first learned to value work because his father did, and then he discovered its value for himself. So, he would teach, work is a spiritual necessity, even if it weren't an economic necessity. He learned from his own sweat that "though joyful, missionary work is work. Though joyful, temple work is work." He urged Latter-day Saint parents to teach their children to work—by working. Don't insulate them, he said, "from the very things that helped make you what you are!" He wrote in the *Friend* that people who learn to work will be "better disciples of Jesus Christ, who Himself learned to work as a carpenter. . . . There won't be any lazy people in heaven. They would not be happy there anyway, because there will always be so much to do."

Many of Neal's early interests grew as if grafted onto his father's interests. Clarence later acknowledged as much, looking back with nostalgia to the pig project and the trumpet he had bought for his junior high–age son: "Your 4-H achievements [and] trumpet lessons" fulfilled "my ambitions [more] than yours," even though they also provided good training. When Neal's interest in the trumpet waned after about a year, Clarence taught himself to play it—eventually well enough to play his favorite song, "The Holy City." The song meant enough to Clarence that one of his grandsons, Andrew Skankey, played it—on the trumpet—at his graveside service.

His testimony of the gospel was the major premise for all of Clarence Maxwell's reasoning, not only about religious topics but everything else, like work, keeping records, and music. He had what Neal called a convert's zeal—a childlike freshness with which he applied the gospel to life, drank in spiritual learning, and approached his Church callings.

Clarence served in the bishopric while a young man and then was the ward clerk for many years. As the clerk, he felt responsible to guard every nickel of the members' tithing. Among Neal's earliest memories was the sight of Clarence carefully opening the ward's little bank bag and placing all of the tithing and fast offering money on their round dining room table to count it each fast Sunday after Church. Few people had checking accounts then, and much of the money was in coins. To wide-eyed young Neal, surrounded by the poverty of the Depression, that seemed like a great deal of money. It was not what Clarence said but the way he felt and acted about the tithing money that told Neal these were sacred funds. Through their advanced years, Clarence and Emma always contributed funds to missionaries leaving from their ward.

Neal also watched Clarence ask good gospel questions and find good answers as intuitively as he breathed. Clarence was always raising faithful questions, born of his thirst to understand and expand the doctrines that guided his life. The idea of asking skeptical questions or trick questions or even amusing questions would never have occurred to him.

Church members in those days felt free to write to General Authorities of the Church. Not many people wrote such letters, but Clarence Maxwell did. So when he couldn't find a good answer to his gospel questions any other way, he would carefully tap out a letter to one of the Brethren.

Looking at those letters now, it is difficult to tell whether they were typed on Clarence's typewriter or on the battered manual machine Neal still uses. Neal's typewritten notes, even today, look just like the ones Clarence typed more than half a century ago: the small, old Smith-Corona characters, single-spaced, occasional strikeovers, and using every inch of the paper.

In 1946, for example, Clarence wrote to Elder Joseph Fielding Smith of the Twelve, asking about repentance, forgiveness, and exaltation. Elder Smith wrote back a two-page response in which he wondered "why this question is so constantly rising." He quoted a scripture and then highlighted the quotation with an asterisk and a long, handwritten marginal note. Neal would remember this exchange when President Smith, as the President of the Church, asked him to serve as Church commissioner of education in 1970.

Such an exchange of correspondence between a Sunday School teacher and a General Authority wouldn't occur in today's much larger

Church, in which members are encouraged to go to local priesthood leaders with their questions. But in Neal Maxwell's formative years, this exchange of letters let him see the Brethren as accessible tutors—men who wrote personal letters and, two at a time, visited stake conferences four times a year.

As a stake missionary, Clarence wrote to Elder Smith, wondering if he'd given the right answer to an investigator about the Godhead. And as stake mission president, he wrote to Elder Bruce R. McConkie to clarify the possibly erroneous teaching of a stake missionary about the various appearances of the Lord. Later, in doing his own family history work, Clarence wrote to Elder Howard W. Hunter, asking about the sealing relationship of children born to temple-married parents who are later divorced and the sealing is canceled. The Brethren always replied specifically and courteously.

Because Clarence typically showed Neal both his questions and the replies he received, Neal took for granted that discussing faithful, constructive questions was part of the natural culture of the Church. He also couldn't help noticing that sometimes those with broader responsibilities in the Church took a more deeply informed view in the way they answered the questions. The seeds of these early assumptions, born of Clarence's combination of devotion and desire to learn, bore fruit in Neal's later attitudes.

Conversations about gospel and other topics were daily fare around the Maxwell dinner table or as they worked together in the yard. Generally Clarence wasn't as active as Emma in their wide-open family discussions, but "if you got him talking about the gospel, that was a different matter." He was a "real believer," sharing his blend of believing attitudes with his native curiosity.

So Neal's understanding of the gospel and the Church was gradually shaped by the way he and Clarence shared their thoughts, openly and easily. For Clarence, it was second nature to look for and find the answers to life's questions in gospel teachings. His attitude created a climate of spiritual confidence for Neal, partly because both of them found that the process worked. Their specific, friend-to-friend exchange shows in their written correspondence while Neal was in the war and then on his mission in Canada, as his father faithfully "kept [up] a steady stream of letters to any of his family who were away." Colleen remembers that Neal maintained a constant conversation with his parents, phoning them almost daily during his early married years.

Neal sometimes went with his father to the Tabernacle for general conference. Given his slight personal observations of President Grant at the Nibley Park golf course and his emerging interest in political affairs, which began long before he ever heard the term *political science,* he was fascinated with President Grant's comments at conference. President Grant once said he was exercised about the New Deal, adding that President J. Reuben Clark, counselor in the First Presidency, "tells me I'm not supposed to talk about this, but I'm going to talk about it anyway." "To a boy up in the gallery," said Neal, "that was interesting."

Neal later said that his testimony came in three ways. Early in his home life, he experienced the witness of the Spirit, followed afterward by intellectual and experiential conversions. He found that the witness of the Spirit is more sure but that the other witnesses would increasingly corroborate his spiritual impressions.

He vividly remembers returning home one night and inadvertently hearing his kneeling parents in a nearby room praying aloud for the welfare of their children. Neal was touched with their concern and how the concern fit within their faith. He also prayed as a child during the Depression that his father would be able to find employment, and he felt his prayer was heard.

His most stirring boyhood experience with the faith of his father occurred late one night in 1943, as sixteen-year-old Neal returned from his swing shift as a grease monkey at the local Greyhound bus terminal. As he walked in the darkness, he noticed an unexpected light burning inside the house.

Quietly opening the door, Neal heard voices from the kitchen. Several people were there. He tiptoed closer, wondering what was going on. He sensed serious, even somber tones in the hushed voices. Two family friends stood under the dining room light next to Clarence and

Emma. They were working, unsuccessfully, to revive Carol, Neal's six-week-old sister. None of them noticed Neal standing in the entry to the room. He saw the baby lying on her back on the round dining room table, the same table where Clarence counted the tithing. He'd heard his parents say earlier that Carol had whooping cough and they were worried about her. Now she had turned blue and, so far as Neal could tell, had stopped breathing and was about to die.

He watched as his father and the other men placed their hands on the baby's head. Speaking in quiet but direct tones, Clarence blessed Carol to live, adding other words Neal no longer remembers. When the blessing ended, Neal could see Carol begin to breathe. Emma bundled up the baby, and the adults whisked her to the hospital. After they left, Neal crept to his bedroom. Moved by what he'd felt as he saw Carol breathe again, he knelt to thank God for his parents and their convictions. He prayed for little Carol, asking that his father's blessing might be accepted. Carol survived the illness and grew up to became the mother of six children.

In 1995, Neal told PBS interviewer Hugh Hewitt in *Searching for God in America,* a television series of probing conversations about spiritual life with American religious leaders, that this experience gave a strong spiritual witness to his boyhood testimony: "I watched my father, after the manner of the New Testament, bless her with the power of the priesthood, and saw her begin to breathe again."

A crowning tribute that showed Neal's attitude toward his father's gentle tutoring came when Neal learned about the concept of fathers blessings. Because Clarence had not grown up in a Latter-day Saint home and because he hadn't learned the concept elsewhere, he was unfamiliar with Church policy authorizing fathers' blessings, as distinguished from patriarchal blessings and general priesthood blessings for health or comfort.

When Neal was in the bishopric of a student ward at the University of Utah in 1957–59, he heard Bishop Oscar W. McConkie, a brother to Elder Bruce R. McConkie, teach ward members about the nature, the procedure, and the importance of fathers' blessings, which may be recorded verbatim in family records, even though they are not retained in official Church records. Neal found this such a rich doctrine that he thereafter gave his own children blessings and would often teach of such blessings in his ministry among Church members.

He also went to Clarence, even though Neal was by then married and a father himself, to tell his father about the doctrine and to ask for a blessing at Clarence's hands. Clarence was reluctant. He said he just didn't see how he could do that for an adult son to whom he now looked for spiritual leadership himself.

Like young Nephi, who restored his father's confidence by asking him, "Whither shall I go to obtain food?" (1 Nephi 16:23), Neal patiently coaxed Clarence for more than ten years. Finally he "sand-bagged him" into giving the blessing. Knowing of Clarence's love for family history, Neal, by then a General Authority, invited his father to visit the Church Office Building to do some genealogical work. Once Clarence was in Neal's office, he said, "Now, Dad, I want a father's blessing. And then we'll go do the family history work."

So Clarence placed his hands on his son's head on January 17, 1976, and pronounced a blessing. He prayed that the Lord would direct what he should say to "one of His faithful servants." Then Clarence blessed Neal with "strength to bear the burdens which may come upon you in physical ways . . . that you may bear [them] as [Paul] did, without complaint." Neal would remember this part of the blessing when he entered the valley of his illness twenty years later. In other parts of Clarence's blessing lie echoes of the tutorial in discipleship with which his father had guided Neal through his boyhood years. Clarence blessed him

> that you may be humble . . . and seek not in any way to glorify yourself but that you may do all for the glory of our Father. . . . That your testimony may be a power to those who hear you, that even if they may not themselves know, as you know, that they may, through your words, come to know that Jesus is the Christ. . . . [That you may] devote your time and your attention to the work of the Lord, not neglecting your family in any way . . . that

you may . . . feel at rest in these things . . . that He may come to you in great strength. . . . Keep the commandments, study the scriptures, . . . learn the ways and the will of the Father and of the Son . . . [and] you will have joy in heaven throughout eternity . . . with your posterity.

EIGHT

EMMA, LOIS,
AND LIFE AT HOME

CLARENCE AND EMMA'S MARRIAGE exemplified har-
mony amidst diversity. They had just the right blend to be model team
teachers for the ward M-Men and Gleaners, a class they taught for
several years. The two enjoyed a marriage of warm, spirited friendship
that was big enough for two very different personalities. Clarence
believed—and practiced—the idea that marriage is an "equal partnership," where "neither partner is a servant to the other." He believed the
"husband [should] wash dishes or clothes, [and] change diapers," with
"both father and mother" sharing "equally the privilege of teaching and
training and enjoying the children."

Where Clarence was of slight build, shy, methodical, and
restrained, Emma was quite the opposite. She had dark brown hair and
stood five feet, two inches tall but was fairly rotund most of her life.
Emma was also gregarious, impatient, and opinionated. At her funeral,
Neal said she had never been confused about what was right, and she
loved people enough to reprove them. On the whole, he would "give
her an A for correctness but a B for diplomacy." After the funeral, one

relative whom Emma had often tried to motivate toward greater Church activity told Neal, "Let's make that a C plus for diplomacy."

Her instructions about her own funeral illustrate her style. When her life was ebbing, she told Neal she didn't want her family to have a big dinner after the funeral—she wanted them to give the food to shut-ins or sick members of the ward. She also wanted the funeral to be both "brief" and "accurate," with "no big buildup." And "if it's a good day," she wanted everybody to go home from the funeral and plant some flowers. Emma loved flowers, especially roses. Lois, Neal's sister, once said, "If plants know when they are loved, it is no wonder that her roses did so well." Because it was "a good day," Elder Maxwell passed along Emma's request to those at the funeral, noting, "We know that one day we will face her equivalent of a personal priesthood interview" with her.

At the same time, the consensus among Emma's children is that obedience was her defining quality. Her children were always impressed that, once she knew how her Church leaders felt on an issue, "she lined up." Characteristically she would say, "He's the bishop, you know. So we should do what he says." And she always would.

Emma was a stalwart, matriarchal figure who led out assertively on religious issues. To Neal, her greatest lesson was that her life reflected clear priorities—the family and the Church come first. She especially liked children, having taught and led them for thirty-two years in the Primary organization. Children liked her, and they liked her directness. When Neal was little, he sometimes bit the piano bench when he got upset, leaving teeth marks. Once when he bit a young friend in some childish frustration, Emma told the small boy, "Bite him back!" The friend did, helping to cure Neal of his problem.

She was also blessed with creativity and intensity of focus that found their way into Neal's personality. She had a way with words, once earning the then-sizable sum of ninety-eight dollars from the Paris Company in Salt Lake in a public contest to find a new marketing slogan. Emma's winning idea was "Dependable Merchandise." In 1952, when she and Clarence bought their first television set, she burned the family's dinner on two occasions after getting engrossed in western movies. Emma also liked to organize things, planning activities with enough detail to anticipate Neal's penchant for organizing family trips and structuring group conversations.

Emma shared the action in her ward. As stake Primary president, she helped pilot Cub Scouting as a test stake for the Church. She enriched her Primary lessons with frequent references to good litera-ture, which she loved and often shared at home. She made the costumes for the stake Primary program when little Neal was in the cast and members of the Church's Primary General Board attended as special guests. Emma loved a good time, hamming up her role as the fortune teller at the ward carnival. She also made the gravy for ward dinners until she was in her seventies.

Emma reflected a contagious interest in other people. Her daugh-ters remember their teenage friends often coming over "for talks with Mom." Within and beyond the ward, Emma nurtured and volunteered, in both conventional and unconventional ways. She believed in citi-zenship enough to serve as a voting district election judge for many years. She also gave older neighbors the shots they needed for diabetes and other ailments, which Neal doubts "the local medical association" would have appreciated. Emma "really cared about those often over-looked in life," which included many friends and women in the neigh-borhood who often "came to her for counsel."

Even though Clarence was perhaps more of a mentor for his son, Neal's relationship with Emma was so secure and so fruitful that she strongly affected the way he developed. Her confidence in him, in her-self, and in the Lord were powerful offsetting forces when Neal struggled with self-esteem during his adolescence, when he was dis-covering his own identity during the war, and at other times of stress. No other force quite equals a mother's touch of love when it is given as fully and freely as Emma gave it, conveying to her child the inner strength and resolve to cope with life's buffeting.

When he was in kindergarten, Emma helped him draw and cut out some paper pumpkins, which he took to school on a day when Emma would be away from home until late afternoon. An older boy tore up the pumpkins just before school started. Neal was stunned and hurt. He had never been bullied like that before. He still remembers "crying and coming home alone, realizing with a special kind of terror that my mother was gone and that no one would be home" when he arrived. The five-block walk from school to home felt like five miles that day. He instinctively needed Emma, the champion of the underdog, as he struggled to cope with his hurt feelings.

Neal's most pronounced childhood memory about Nibley Park is also associated with his mother's protection. The two of them had been at the park's theater and were running home in the midst of a thunderstorm. Suddenly lightning hit a tree very close to them, and Neal huddled close to the safety of Emma's strong presence as they ran for shelter.

When Neal was around twelve, his family was renting a home in rural East Millcreek that belonged to a couple serving a mission. He loved the larger house and spacious grounds, where he was introduced to serious livestock production. One season they had a pony at their place, which Neal was free to ride—if he could. Emma watched one day through a window as Neal tried and tried to stay on the frisky little horse. After being thrown several times, Neal finally gave up—only to see a younger boy come along later and tame the pony enough to ride him.

Neal was dejected, his self-confidence more bruised than was his rumpled body. He was sure he'd never be much of a horseman—or much else. But Emma saw it otherwise: "I remember looking out of the window and seeing you bucked off. You were angry, but you gave him a hard look and took the bridle and led him back to the barn. You were always kind to the animals." She helped Neal see that, in the long run, it said more about his character to be kind to animals (especially one that had just dumped him like that!) than to ride them the very first try.

As the first Ash grandchild, Neal received unusual attention from Emma's five brothers, who took seriously their self-appointed role of indoctrinating him in the best family traditions of basketball, fishing, hunting, and devotion to Granite High School. Both the Ash backyard and his uncles seemed huge to little Neal. They would pound the dirt near their basketball hoop, wet it, and pound it some more, until it felt like clay. Then, as Emma put it, they would "play like mad." Neal loved watching their frequent scrimmages, following "the cloud of dust, which marked the progress of the ball going to and fro, up and down that court."

Lois was born in 1928, when Neal was two. From the beginning, Neal and Lois were warmly encircled in the arms of extended family. They lived within walking distance of both the Maxwell and the Ash grandparents and their families. On pleasant weekends, Clarence, Emma, Neal, and Lois would often walk the eleven-block round-trip along unpaved sidewalks to see both sets of grandparents, perhaps pushing Lois in the brown wicker buggy.

At home, the Maxwell family enjoyed serial radio programs, listening together to *Little Orphan Annie, Jack Armstrong,* or *One Man's Family.* Emma was "a stringer of some kind for one program's sponsor," having signed up to test their recipes. On a warm Sunday evening, the Maxwells would all four sit on the front porch and munch homemade sandwiches and drink milk or Emma's fresh lemonade as they chatted and watched over the neighborhood.

In 1933, when Neal was seven, Franklin D. Roosevelt began serving as president of the United States. That year both of Neal's grandfathers passed away. His parents took him and five-year-old Lois to one of the funerals, but the experience unsettled the children enough that they didn't attend the second one. That was a hard year for the family in other ways, because Clarence was sick at home with pneumonia and therefore out of work for some time.

Lois and Neal became what he calls a "duet brother and sister" during their childhood together. The two would race from their front porch to the big tree near the street. In the backyard, they dug a hole big enough for four children to stand in. One winter, Clarence helped them build an igloo large enough to turn around in. Neal also taught Lois most all she would ever know about sports. They reenacted many events from the 1936 Olympics in their yard, using orange crates for hurdles and bamboo poles for the high jump.

Lois had been born with limited eyesight, which became an important influence in opening Neal's own eyes, and his heart, to the needs of people from varying and sometimes sensitive circumstances. He developed great admiration for Lois's courage and good cheer as he watched her travel alone each week on the Bamberger train to and from Ogden, where she attended the Utah School for the Blind from the third grade onward. She later completed her college degree, taking notes in Braille and relying on friends who read to her. She went on to enjoy a productive teaching career in the public schools, specializing in helping children with learning disabilities.

Like her parents, Lois is down-to-earth. During one time of family reminiscing, Neal thanked Lois for setting a high standard, because "she has never been given to any self-pity." Lois responded with Emma-like candor, "How do you know?" And everybody laughed.

Neal's other sisters, Ann, Susan, Carol, and Kathy, were all born after he was eleven, and in a few years he was off to war and the mission field. So they have known him mostly as a grown-up big brother, who was their close and willing mentor in all things athletic, political, romantic, and religious. Neal has stayed close to his sisters, visiting often and having lunch with them every time there's a birthday.

Clarence and Emma filled their later grandparent years with "unhurried, unlimited attention" to their grandchildren, some of whom were in their home almost daily, enjoying Emma's cooking, games, and sleepovers. Emma "especially gave encouragement to those grandchildren with challenges and reminded [their] parents to be patient and trust in the Lord." Emma struggled during her final years with health problems that required her to carry an oxygen tank, but that didn't keep her from attending Church and family events.

As she was near death in 1983, Emma spoke in subdued tones. Clarence, who had developed a hearing problem, couldn't hear her. He leaned over her bed, thinking she was saying something tender. She was actually telling him he had his elbow on her hair and it was hurting her. In another near-end conversation, Clarence, always on task and always a believer, was concerned that they didn't have much time left to talk. He told her he was having trouble locating people in a certain ancestral line in their family history research—and, "when you get there, Emma, I need to have you get me some help." After her passing,

With his sisters (clockwise from left): Susan, Kathy, Lois, Ann, and Carol

someone from the family asked Clarence if he wanted anyone to stay with him at home that night. "No," he said matter-of-factly, "I have a testimony of the gospel." From then on, in the room with twin beds which they had shared, he slept in Emma's bed.

Some time after Emma's death, Clarence was thinking of marrying Helen Larsen Nielsen, who had lost her husband. When he asked his daughter Kathy how she felt about that idea, she replied, "I guess it's going to take me a little time to get used to it, Daddy." Clarence patted her on the knee and said, "How long do you think it will take? I don't have much time." Clarence married Helen in 1987 and died in 1993. Helen passed away in 2000 amid warm feelings of mutual appreciation between the Maxwell and Nielsen families. Because Helen had been on Emma's board when she was stake Primary president, the Maxwells felt that in a sense Emma, once more in character, "picked her successor."

NINE

A TRUE STORY?
OR WERE YOU JUST
PREACHING?

As THE RANGE OF NEAL'S EXPERIENCE BROADENED, he encountered some contradictions between the honest love of the gospel he felt at home and the institutional ineffectiveness he sometimes found in the church meetings he attended. The deeply settled state of his parents' faith helped their son gradually construct a bridge between the spiritual security of his family life and the comparative insecurities he felt, early on, at church.

During Neal's childhood, Clarence spent hours at the ward meetinghouse as a bishopric member; however, Neal had not yet made the connections among church, home, and his real but unarticulated trust in the Lord. One Sunday Emma and Neal made the familiar walk from home to the meetinghouse. Clarence, as usual, had gone ahead much earlier for his bishopric meetings. As they walked, Neal said to her, "Church, church. When I get big, I'm not going to church."

This was one of several hints during Neal's childhood that he was finding his experience at church less than fulfilling. His first attempt at public speaking hardly heralded the verbal fluency he would one day develop. The Maxwells were in the East Millcreek Ward, and Neal was about thirteen. He had been asked to talk about tithing and had worked hard to prepare and then memorize what he would say. When he stood at the pulpit, he began, "Tithing. The law of tithing." Then his mind went blank. Embarrassed, he groped for words and pled with himself, but the screen of his memory remained empty. Finally, he snapped his fingers in frustration and said, "Nuts!" The congregation laughed, and Neal stumbled on with a few words he no longer recalls. He regarded this first church talk as a complete failure.

Neal felt that the teachers and speakers in church often didn't connect all that well with him or with his friends. When he was eleven, he wore a Roman guard costume in a Primary festival in the Grant Stake. His picture ended up in the *Children's Friend,* the Primary's magazine for the entire Church. Looking at himself in that strange outfit as a snapshot of his moods, Neal said years later, "I look so bored, and I probably was."

He revealed his thoughts about one or two leaders with whom he associated at Wandamere in his memories about teachers who gave "unrequested encores" in testimony meeting. He thought that the high councilors who came to their ward were sometimes "too stern and too preachy," even though they were "good men." As for his ward teaching, he wasn't "thrilled over it, but I did it." He also remembers, with chagrin, the day the bishop's wife taught their Sunday School class. His class gave her such a hard time that she went home in tears. The bishop later asked the class to stand before the entire ward, while he scolded them for the way they had behaved. Neal knew they deserved this, even if the bishop didn't handle it with "a great deal of finesse."

He found the Church activity program no more appealing. He "did not connect with Scouting." He "never could tie a square knot. I always tied grannies." So he "rose to the dizzy heights of Tenderfoot and then quit," because he was more interested in hanging around with the much older M-Men during their basketball games and practices.

Some of his difficulty was, in retrospect, that the Church in the 1920s and 30s was "much less effective institutionally" than it would become in later years. His ward, typical for its day, was huge, but only about fifteen percent were active members, and it seemed that an even tinier fraction of the more affluent members were consistently involved. Neal recalls, for example, that it was unheard of in that era for a medical doctor to be a bishop or stake president. A ward in that same neighborhood today would probably be three times that active, with higher levels of commitment, peer support, and supporting resources. This development reflects in some ways how the Church itself has matured.

Wandamere was something of a homespun community, but that was not atypical of the times, an interior-decorating era some have affectionately called "early Depression style." The chapel had no carpet, just wooden floors and "wooden benches that squeaked every time you moved them around" or moved on them. The ward house was multifunctional. The same room served alternately as chapel, drama stage, activity center, and, on Friday nights, a movie theater for those who had paid their ward budget assessment. Rolling his eyes a little, Neal remembers the good times at the ward movies: "The films always broke, and the audience would finally stamp their feet, hoping the man in the booth would get the film spliced" so the show could go on.

With its down-home flavor, Wandamere was a nurturing place for Neal—especially because of the constructive attitude his parents had about life in the ward. He had his frustrations, but he never had serious doubts about the values his parents both taught and modeled. Much later, after seeing intellectual arrogance, the vanity of wealth, and other forms of pride, Neal would say, "I give my parents a lot of credit for those homely, unfashionable virtues of family prayer and tithing, which were so pronounced for me."

His parents patiently and lovingly negotiated their son's transition from home and private religious feelings to the more public, behavioral reflections of his private values. He always knew they had "a set of givens, that you try to help people and you try to be patient." But "they didn't harp on it," and he didn't ever feel "pounded upon." He was sometimes irritated and, later on, "a little feisty and independent." But, "while my parents winced, they respected my agency. I knew somewhat how they felt, but they backed off a little bit in this almost sacred zone where our agency touches parental counsel." After they would say, "You know how we feel," he found himself "loving and respecting them all the more!"

Like other strong-willed children, Neal experienced occasional contradictions between the love and the discipline his parents gave him. By working through these tensions in an atmosphere of high mutual trust, he gradually internalized a conscience and faith of his own. He "felt a sense of belonging, that God cared about me, that my parents loved me, and that they would help me," when he wasn't so sure others would help. The Wandamere Ward, despite its limitations, was also "a warm and nutritive environment that was free of so many troubles that confront [numerous] neighborhoods today."

As time went on, the seeds of testimony in Neal's infant discipleship began to sprout, even if almost imperceptibly. He found that teachers and leaders in the East Millcreek Ward, where he lived from age ten to age thirteen, seemed to connect with him a little more. He also enjoyed singing in an Aaronic Priesthood chorus at the priesthood session of general conference when he was about fourteen. In his early teens, Neal first began to notice some distance emerging between his religious feelings and those of some of his friends. He was gravitating closer to the Church, even as some of them were moving more away from it.

One of Neal's sisters remembers when he was out with some friends who wanted to buy some beer. Neal asked them to take him home. Hearing that recollection, Neal said, "That makes me sound judgmental of my friends." Replied Colleen, "Not really. You went home and cried." And when he remembered the incident, Neal agreed, "I did."

Neal took enough seminary classes to graduate, though he recalls, wistfully, "If I could listen with one ear and get away with it, I didn't listen with two ears the way I should have." He had not read the Book of Mormon by the time he entered the military at age eighteen. But he did listen enough in class—even with only one ear—that forty years later he could tell the Church's seminary teachers, "I still remember the voice of my seminary teacher, James Moss, reading the scriptures."

During this season, Neal encountered an Aaronic Priesthood

adviser named Steve Monson, whom he dearly loved. This affection led to a deep sting of sadness when, not long after he had been Neal's teacher, Steve was shot down in the air war over Europe in World War II. He was one of the first people Neal knew who went away to fight in the war. Losing Steve suddenly gave the war a very personal dimension for Neal, perhaps contributing to his desire to fight there himself.

The difficulties Neal encountered during his boyhood church experience arose not because he didn't value the gospel's teachings but because he valued them so much. His most serious connection to spiritual things had taken hold in what he learned with his father and mother and in his private reflections about those experiences. His religious feelings were real, embedded in an unusually sensitive young heart. He instinctively knew the difference between responses to those feelings that were superficial and responses that were genuine—even though he couldn't have explained why the responses felt different to him.

Neal's dilemma calls to mind the story of a little boy who heard his grandfather speak in church. The boy asked, "Was that a true story, Grandpa, or were you just preaching?" Young Neal Maxwell had heard, seen, and felt true religious stories for years—at home, from parents in whom there was no guile. Because his soul had resonated to those true stories, he sometimes felt a little dissonance when his early church experience felt more like "just preaching."

As the years went by, Neal would reflect often on both the true stories and the preaching he had known. These memories would become an intense motivating force, prompting him to help other people have a church life that encouraged authentic spiritual realities. This same hunger would later lead Neal to try so hard to improve church shortcomings that he sometimes felt guilty for "steadying the ark" too much. However it expressed itself, his desire for quality in the church environment had much of its origin in the sweet satisfactions he had tasted in the gift of a childhood home full of genuine spirituality.

TEN

HOOPS AND HOGS

THROUGHOUT HIS EARLY YEARS, Neal felt driven by an intense commitment to excellence, which expressed itself especially in his zeal for basketball and in a 4-H project with purebred pigs. During the three years when the family rented a home in East Millcreek, he loved the rural "Tom Sawyer solitude" of this two-and-a-half acre place surrounded by orchards and fields. Here he looked after the animals and crops his family relied on for sustenance—cows, pigs, chickens, ducks, and enough vegetable crops and fruit trees that, for a season each year, he and Lois would try to sell their Bing cherries.

Neal almost always had a part-time job after that, and he often gave his mother some of his earnings to help with household expenses. He worked at Interstate Brick for twenty-five cents an hour, making and hauling bricks three nights a week after school, walking to and from work an hour each way. Then it was the grease-monkey job at the Greyhound bus depot and water boy for a construction crew, as well as bottle boy for Denhalter Bottling Company. These jobs cut into both his social life and his study time, but they reflected the necessities of his life. They also exposed him to people whose values and vocabularies were different from what he knew at home, but all of that inoculated him against what he would soon find in the U.S. Army.

Not yet a terribly serious student at school, Neal still became a voracious reader—of what he liked to read. He would spread out the daily newspaper on the floor and devour it with an appetite that indirectly trained his ear and instincts toward journalistic language. He also loved reading newsmagazines and whatever adventure books or fiction he could find lying around the house and on Clarence's bookshelves. His Aunt Arlene, Emma's sister, said that her most typical memory of young Neal is that of a teenage boy reading stacks of books with piles of sandwiches at his elbow. His penchant for both news commentary and good books would develop over the years into something near addiction.

But among all of his early interests, Neal found two primary outlets for his inborn passion for quality—hoops and hogs. The love of basketball was virtually unavoidable, because his five Ash uncles had programmed that into his being like computer software on a hard drive. His natural gifts matched the environmental pressure: He was quick on his feet, and his left-handed shots were finely honed and hard to block.

Perhaps his best childhood Christmas came during the East Millcreek years, after his father had prepared Neal for the reality that they simply couldn't afford to buy a basketball. But on Christmas morning, there was a new ball, somehow, along with a secondhand hoop Clarence had painted to look as good as new. Neal put up the hoop on the front of their garage and played hour after hour, dreaming of the day when he fully expected to be on Cec Baker's winning team at Granite High.

The family moved back to Wandamere after three years. They left the spacious Millcreek farm and moved in with Neal's grandmother Ellen Lundwall Maxwell in her four-room, frame house on Adams Street (Twenty-Ninth South and 450 East). Now, instead of having a roomy home, they lived in a tiny, crowded place where, for a little while, the only toilet was outside.

Living conditions were cramped, but the family relationships were

The Wandamere Ward basketball team with Neal on the back row, far left

strong enough to handle the natural stress. Neal's greater trouble came at school, where, though blessed with many friends, his living circumstances made him feel not quite good enough for the "in crowd." He may have thought he needed to compensate for this perceived limitation by excelling at basketball. Until leaving East Millcreek, he had played the game as well as anybody in the larger neighborhood. But when he moved into the smaller house, his basketball fortunes seemed to shrink as well. He didn't even make the sophomore team at Granite High.

Part of the problem was that Neal had stopped growing, a process that didn't resume until after he graduated from high school. Whatever the causes, "It was a bitter pill for me. I had always wanted to be all-state for Granite." It was his "first real disappointment in life," "a very difficult time." Neal still winces when recalling that a friend whom he had earlier helped teach to play basketball did make the team and enjoyed great success. In junior high, he had also told his friend Lynn Cahoon that Lynn would surely be an all-stater in football some day, a goal he did reach.

Meanwhile, however, Neal found another source of unique and real achievement—although eventually, and ironically, even this area of his success would become a source of social stigma. But while it lasted, he had some happy days with his purebred Duroc pigs.

The hog project began in rural East Millcreek in 1937, when Neal was eleven. LeRoy W. Hillam, who later became Neal's Granite High agriculture teacher and "one of the finest friends of my life," invited him into a 4-H project that started with a purebred gilt named Lady Era, 1st. Five years later, in a formal report called "My 4H Club Experiences and My 4H Project Achievements," Neal wrote that until meeting Mr. Hillam, he was kind of "a 'city slicker' . . . unappreciative of what farmers and other men like them do for us each year. . . . In fact I now wish to be a veterinarian." He thought he might someday attend vet school at Colorado State, although Lois later said Neal would have been "outstanding in education, politics, almost any field but veterinary medicine."

In his first pig shows, Neal showed mostly his inexperience. Lady Era didn't do well at the county fair competition, and he soon saw that "there is pigs and there is PIGS." So "back home she went and I fed her better." Then, under Mr. Hillam's seasoned tutelage, Neal gradually mastered the process of breeding, judging the quality of his own stock, and keeping the "best animals for herd improvement."

He also learned to be resourceful about finding low-cost pig feed. He would buy dozens of three-day-old loaves of bread from bakeries for a penny a loaf. And, if he came by at the right moments, a local dairy would often give him seventy gallons of waste skim milk at no cost. The general public had not yet discovered the dietary place of nonfat milk. Having that favorite pioneer dish of bread and milk put his pigs at troughs of luxury.

Within a year, Neal won first prize awards in the county fair. Then he bred his only sow to a sire that "netted thirteen dandies" in a litter. This breeding was so successful that he tried the same match again, producing "one of the greatest sows I have ever owned, Red Riding Hood," eventually a fine producer herself and a great show animal. "Mr. Evans of the Duroc Association says she is a marvel."

The rest of Neal's pig project report reads like something from the sports pages, describing the thrill of finally meeting some of "the 'big boys' of the show ring" in the Utah State Fair. By 1940, when he was thirteen, he slept near his beloved Red the night before some shows. Then, with Red in contention for state champion, the chief

Watching over pigs after they were judged at a fair

judge saw her "with an experienced eye," asking how many pigs she had produced and raised. Since female pigs were judged for both their appearance and their litter production, Neal knew the implications of his answer. At that early stage in Red's career, he could only breathe deeply and reply, "None, sir."

Speaking in "his true English accent," the judge said, "Well, laddie, your being honest has cost you the Grand Championship, but nevertheless she's a beautiful animal." He did win first prize for showmanship that year, gaining "prestige enough . . . to be asked by the large outsiders to show their pigs for them." From this he learned that "it pays to tell the truth even though it hurts."

Among his other 4-H adventures, Neal once hauled some pigs to the Ogden livestock show in a friend's station wagon. He also became a stock judge himself. County Agent Marden Broadbent wrote that he was "one of the competent stock judges from his study and interest." Moreover, Neal "kept the other boys encouraged and even sold them [some of his own pigs] at a losing price to keep them coming along." In recommending Neal for a scholarship, Mr. Broadbent said, "You may depend upon him for anything he commits himself to accomplish. . . . He will uphold the standards of the trust vested in him."

The next year, 1941, was "the best year in my 4-H history," despite the "major setback" of losing Lady Era by accidental poisoning. He took eight blue ribbons that year, along with five red ones and "a lonely white ribbon." His total prize money for the year was $116, and, he wrote, "that 'ain't hay.'" By 1942, pork prices rose because "more pork went into Johnny Doughboy's stomach," and Neal won a war bond "for contributing the 'most' for victory in the animal line." He also gave two radio talks "to encourage 4-H boys to do more for American victory" in the war. Finally, he was selected as Utah's most outstanding 4-H club member in livestock, which won him a trip to Chicago in 1942—by then his most distant trip away from home.

ELEVEN

ADOLESCENT
DISAPPOINTMENTS
AND DIRECTIONS

NEAL WAS NOW SIXTEEN, and he was beginning to encounter the social downside of being an expert on pigs. Always in the background was the wound he would long feel about not making that high school basketball team. He felt as if he'd been cut off from an anticipated inheritance of sporting success, like some kind of athletic prodigal son. And "being at home feeding the pigs was not like working out with the varsity." Then came the day of infamy for his perceived social status. Emma called Granite Junior High, trying to find him because some of his animals had escaped their pens. The principal came to his class to announce that Neal Maxwell was urgently needed to rush home and round up his straying pigs.

Not long afterward, Neal attended a party at a classmate's home. When the refreshments were served, someone asked him with a laugh, "Why don't you eat your ice cream the way your pigs do?" Neal felt a sting from that thoughtless remark. The world of middle adolescence is difficult enough for anyone trying to live through it. As humorist Richard Armour is reported to have said, "Adolescence is a disease." A young person's hunger for peer approval and social acceptance often balloons out of all proportion to reality. And Neal's self-perception created a world of hurt—pig ridicule and basketball failure.

As if that weren't enough, his skin also broke out in a severe and unsightly case of acne. In the early 1940's, medical science hadn't yet discovered the wonders that would later be wrought by antibiotics and other treatments for one's complexion. Some teenagers during that era, if they could afford it, would go to a dermatologist to have their faces scraped with a scalpel and other instruments. This could sometimes relieve the infections and reduce the danger of permanent scars associated with a very visible disorder that sometimes fully covered both cheeks and much of the neck. Neal felt some emotional rejection during this time, and his pock-marked scars are still visible, permanent reminders of a condition that evoked a variety of reactions in a high school crowd, most of them unspoken and almost all of them negative.

It would have been natural for him to compensate by trying hard to establish his worth in other ways, seeking acceptance in the fickle world of adolescent popularity and peer acceptance. Whatever else it did, the acne probably reduced the inclinations he might have had toward pride and vanity. Sometimes the school of discipleship requires a high tuition, including the way teenagers measure emotional costs.

Very gradually, Neal's innate reserves of self-worth, instilled from the peaceful and spiritual security he had known as a child at home, gave him the perspective to sense that he would survive this temporary trauma. Beyond that, he would later realize that his experience gave him empathy for all those who feel excluded, rejected, put down, misunderstood, and left out—whatever the reason. And he would find that nearly everyone has had some reason to know something of those feelings. For instance, Neal once urged a group of Church leaders to avoid harsh attitudes toward returning prodigals who have strayed and returned. He encouraged them not to worry about the fragrance some prodigals carry as they return from eating with the swine.

Years later, after he had come to know Neal by conducting two long TV interviews with him, Hugh Hewitt said that when he learned about these hard days in Neal's adolescence, when "he wasn't gifted with a great head start," then he understood the source of Neal's "enormous sensitivity to people," which included the PBS camera crew.

Introducing him once at BYU, Elder Jeffrey R. Holland said that in the compassion he found in Elder Maxwell's speaking and writing, "I seem to hear the echoed accents of a boy who has known the anxiety of a severe case of acne; what scarred the skin seems to have softened the heart. I hear as well empathy, born of ridicule cast at a late-developing boy living on the wrong side of town—a keeper of pigs, prize-winning 4-H pigs though they were." Against this background of his youth, "The discipline of his prose recalls to me the even more remarkable discipline of his character."

Perhaps connected in some way to this season of character growth, the discipline of Neal's prose actually found some unexpected roots during these same years. Preoccupied with his disappointments, Neal was coasting through his classes, earning only average grades. He never felt confident in math and science. He enjoyed history, and English was always easy for him, because he felt at home with the written word. Then one day his English teacher, Mary Mason, gave him some shock therapy that would change the course of his life.

Neal had just handed in an essay in Miss Mason's class. He was well read for his age and natively verbal enough that he could dash off an easy writing assignment and do well enough. But Mary Mason had other ideas. She could have given him a B or C and let it go at that. Yet she saw a real talent going to waste and wanted to motivate him. So Mary gave Neal his grade—a D. He was shocked and hurt, protesting that he didn't deserve a grade like that. Looking at him intently from her dark brown eyes, Miss Mason said, "Neal, you're capable of doing A work."

Once his irritation subsided, Neal decided to respond to his teacher's intervention, feeling a duty to do more with whatever capacity he might have. He took greater interest in his writing assignments, even coming alive to the exercise of diagramming sentences and understanding grammar. Soon he took a job as coeditor of the school paper, although he remarked that his fellow student "Carolyn Fagg did most of the work." Neal stayed close enough to Mary Mason to give her a blessing years later when she was dying of cancer, and then he spoke at her funeral.

Before long, Neal had begun an adventure with the world of words that would ultimately last a lifetime. He also found increased acceptance among his friends as he became the leader of his speech class in addition to leading the agriculture club. He even found a direct link between his 4-H interests and the world of politics and words, when the West Jordan Farm Bureau group invited him to give a speech. Representing other 4-H students, Neal gave "quite a speech on the political potential of the Farm Bureau" to the largely adult audience. He was afterward amazed at his temerity but realized he was becoming fascinated by his first glimpse at using the spoken word to help "connect groups with political power."

Neal eventually came to see, in retrospect, that the path of his discipleship had been taking a needed, if uncomfortable, turn. "The Lord was nudging me away from basketball—maybe the acne gave me greater empathy for people. . . . He was doing things with me that I wasn't conscious of."

Part IV

World War II

TWELVE

VOLUNTEERING FOR IMMEDIATE INDUCTION

N EAL MAXWELL'S EXPERIENCES IN World War II were, in two important ways, defining moments in his early life. One way was how the war shaped his attitudes about politics, power, leadership, and involvement in public causes. The other was a purely spiritual sense. In the war, he came to know divine reality in a way that permanently changed his orientation.

Until the bombing of Pearl Harbor on December 7, 1941, most Americans thought that Hitler's bold aggression was Europe's problem. Isolationist attitudes had persisted in the United States since the end of World War I. But the Japanese bombs that shattered American ships and lives on that sleepy Sunday morning in Hawaii roused the nation to its feet, angry and ready to fight back.

The next day, some students at Granite High hurled verbal abuse at the few Japanese-American students attending there. Further away, from his English country estate, Winston Churchill telephoned Franklin D. Roosevelt and asked, "'Mr. President, what's this about Japan?' Roosevelt replied, 'It's quite true. They have attacked us at Pearl Harbor. We're all in the same boat now.' Churchill couldn't have been happier." The United States of America was now fully committed to the worldwide war.

From then on, throughout the early 1940s, the war dominated American life. As the national draft and a surge of volunteering took hold, many of Neal's older friends went off to war, and some of them never returned. Thousands of U.S. servicemen were stationed in the Salt Lake Valley for training and military support work at Fort Douglas and the Kearns Army Air Base. Overnight, Utah became a regional center for defense-related industrial production. For instance, Colleen's father, George Hinckley, a chemist at Utah Oil Refinery, was instantly immersed in rearranging his company's facilities to produce aviation fuel.

Every school and 4-H club in the country took up the charge. As part of his club duties in 1942, Neal's personal commitment to "4-H Victory Achievement" produced 180 pounds of scrap metal, thirty-five pounds of rubber, the purchase of war bonds, summer work at a defense plant, and raising more pigs for meat and fewer for breeding in order to supply troops and meet national food priorities. "This coming war year I will increase my efforts to help until victory is achieved," Neal pledged in his "Victory Achievements" report submitted to the state 4-H office.

When Neal graduated from Granite High School in May of 1944, the week's newspaper headlines were all about the war: "Two German Strongholds Fall: Nazis Quit Cassion, Formia," "Allies Make Burma Gains," and "Bad Weather Retards European Air War." It was therefore neither surprising nor unusually heroic for the times when Neal told his parents he wanted to volunteer for service immediately. He was not yet eighteen, but he was "anxious to be involved." "I wanted to go," he said. "I felt it was my duty." Neal's feelings were like those of many others his age, who "had a fairly well developed sense of duty and no sense of entitlement."

Neal marched to the local U. S. Army selective service office and volunteered to go as soon as possible after he turned eighteen in July. He could have waited for the normal draft process to find him, or he could have enlisted for some specialized training program, but he wanted immediate induction. "I didn't want to wait around," he said, reflecting the "let's get on with it" attitude that would repeat itself often through his life. Clarence and Emma, especially Emma, struggled to understand and support him. Emma later said that when Neal told them he felt he had to volunteer, his parents' "hearts were full, but we knew you would not feel right unless you did your part."

It didn't ease Emma's anxiety to discover the service branch to which her son had been assigned—the infantry. He would be on battle-fields, live in foxholes, and even engage in man-to-man combat. Emma was very troubled. But the infantry suited Neal just fine. He liked direct engagement. There was a world war on, and he wanted to help win it.

Neal completed basic training at Camp Roberts, California. Having been outside Utah only three times before, he now felt home-sick and insecure. He was also shocked by the attitudes of some of the men in his outfit, many of whom had little use for the Latter-day Saint lifestyle standards he had largely taken for granted. He also didn't think he cut much of a swath as a swaggering military hero. He was so young that he "didn't even need to shave in between inspections." And when he first wore his military leggings (which preceded combat boots), he put them on wrong, so that "the buckles were on the inside of the leg and therefore would catch on each other when I would walk." He thought he was "a stupid and yet laughable" sight.

No wonder he wrote his parents from Camp Roberts in September that he thought by the time he finished basic training he'd "be a real man." After all, "I've been shooting the M-1 rifle, The World's Best, all week." But he was also seeing his family's values in a new light: "Our home was heaven," he wrote, "and now I realize how swell and grand you and Dad have been. That's sincere." Then, "I owe $5.50 tithing," which he would send for them to take to the bishop.

In January of 1945, Neal was given a seven-day "delay en route," which meant home leave in Salt Lake City before shipping out for the Pacific. This phrase was typical of the army style that would come to irk Neal. The army wouldn't acknowledge to the public that it gave soldiers a real leave or furlough, because the war had made everything appear so urgent. The trip home was labeled a delay, as if somehow unavoidable. From this context, Neal took the phrase he would later use to describe his remission from leukemia as a "delay en route."

He would again feel irked a short time later, when his group stopped in Hawaii for jungle training. The army had a rigid policy against sunburns, because sunburned men couldn't carry field packs. After Neal unwittingly overstayed a visit to Waikiki Beach, he couldn't acknowledge his nasty sunburn to his superiors without facing a court martial. So he carried a full combat pack on a back covered with ugly blisters. It was the army way.

His short stay at home reinforced Emma's fears that her only son was walking into the jaws of hell. When he reached his Pacific departure point near Seattle, she called him to say she knew a colonel there who might have a way for him to fulfill his military duty without having to "go overseas." Neal repeated: "Mom, I *want* to go overseas." He wondered why she was so upset that he actually wanted to go. He didn't think she understood why he "needed to go." He felt that "we were in a righteous war [and] we needed to win." Perhaps Neal wouldn't understand what Emma was feeling until he had children of his own.

The infantry. A foot soldier, in the most ferocious war in world history. By some accounts, you can't get much lower on the pecking order of humanity. So why would he do that, if Emma really did know a colonel who might have found an honorable alternative? Part of the answer was in Neal Maxwell's fundamental character. His decision to volunteer for immediate induction and stay in the infantry was perhaps the boldest—but it wouldn't be the last—example of how simply being engaged was and is, for Neal, essential to being alive.

As time went on, he would be the same way as a missionary about engaging both opposition to the Church and inadequate missionary teaching resources. He would be that way about college students engaging secular arguments over religious questions. About universities being engaged in their local communities. About parents engaging the real needs of their children, and leaders engaging the real needs of their people. About Latter-day Saint scholars drawing on gospel principles to engage the secular dilemmas of their day. About the true Church realistically engaging the problems faced in establishing Zion in all the world. About engaging adversity in the lives of afflicted people. And about meekly engaging every duty and hazard that may be required to experience the complete process of becoming a disciple of Jesus.

Some people, with good reasons of their own, prefer isolationist, or at least arm's length, stances on some of these issues. But starting with the war, Neal demonstrated a personal makeup that wanted to be *engaged*, with a real intent to serve the common good, in every form of "combat." One of his favorite quotations, shared often in talks during his ministry, is from the Duke of Wellington, who, "falling exhausted after the crucial victory at Waterloo, permitted himself a brief moment of immodesty, saying, 'I . . . don't think it would have done if I had not been there.'" And for Neal, having "been there" does not mean in the luxury suite. Whether in wartime or otherwise, the infantry—or its equivalent in other realms—is just fine. Maybe better.

In addition to this personal inclination, some of Neal's motivation for wanting to serve on the front lines was that he was part of a time, a place, and an entire generation of people who were ready to do what the nation—and the world—needed in World War II. In a popular 1998 book, Tom Brokaw called this age group "The Greatest Generation"—those who "came of age during the Great Depression and the Second World War. . . . This generation was united not only by a common purpose, but also by common values—duty, honor, economy, courage, service, love of family and country, and above all, responsibility for oneself." They "went on to create . . . useful lives and the America we have today."

Like Neal, most of them "didn't think what they were doing was that special, [because] everyone else was doing it too." Brokaw's book captivated Neal when he read it, because it "seemed familiar [to] him . . . his generation, their sacrifice, and the great war that conditioned" them, even though he always felt like the least of them, since he was only at the tail end of those who saw action. America's World War II generation possessed extraordinary character, both during and after the war. Much of Brokaw's language about the group in general describes Neal in particular:

> They answered the call to help save the world from the two

most powerful and ruthless military machines ever assembled.
. . . [After the war,] disciplined by their military training and
sacrifices . . . they stayed true to their values of personal responsibility, duty, honor, and faith.

[Through the GI Bill] they became part of the greatest
investment in higher education that any society ever made. . . .
[They brought] to industry, science, art, and public policy . . .
the same passions and discipline that had served them so well
during the war. . . .

Although they were transformed by their experiences and
quietly proud of what they had done, their stories did not come
easily. . . .

World War II . . . was the common denominator and the
defining experience in the lives of millions of young Americans.

One of them was John F. Kennedy, who "gave voice to his generation" about "the importance of entering the arena beyond the battlefield. In the postwar years, politics was a noble calling and a natural
extension of the lives of [those] who had made so many sacrifices and
learned so many lessons during the war." Neal came to share that general view of politics.

Another was George Bush (senior), who was shot down during a
bombing run against the Japanese. Like so many other veterans, Bush
didn't like to talk about the war, but in a candid moment he invoked
the key lesson: honor. "His service in the war was 'a duty, yes, but truly
an honor.' He also feels strongly it was an obligation of citizenship that
requires no additional reward. . . . As he says, 'Serving in World War
II, I was a tiny part of something noble."

That too was Neal's attitude. For that reason, he would struggle
during the 1960s to understand the cynicism provoked by the Vietnam
War, when some disillusioned young people had trouble seeing how
war could ever be justified. Being cynical about patriotism would
remain unthinkable to Neal, as it did to most others who fought in
World War II—against a more clearly defined enemy in a more obviously moral struggle than has been the case in some other wars. Neal
would later quote John Stuart Mill to a group about the United States
Constitution, articulating the personal belief that took root in his

personal war experience: "A people may prefer free government; but if
. . . they will not fight for it when it is directly attacked . . . they are . . .
unfit for liberty."

Commenting on how the war shaped Neal's world view, his friend
Bud Scruggs believes that people of more recent generations "have a
hard time understanding the notion of good versus evil" and "the
importance of actually fighting for what you believe." Totalitarian enemies, such as Hitler, helped "define our virtues." The war was "a remarkable time, when people understood that evil needed to be faced
down." The terrorist attacks in New York, Washington, D.C., and
Pennsylvania on September 11, 2001, were reminiscent enough of Pearl
Harbor to let people gain something of that realization for themselves.
In one horrifying morning, the current generation could suddenly
understand, and perhaps draw strength from, the instinctive willingness of "the greatest generation" to sacrifice everything to preserve a
free society.

Elizabeth Haglund, who worked closely with Neal at the
University of Utah and for years afterward, also noticed how the war
had affected him, including in the strictly private realm. "He had a
severe experience in the war," she said, "and he came back with an
intense sense of purpose." She believed "something deeply spiritual
happened there, though he didn't talk enough about it for her to know
what had actually occurred."

THIRTEEN

OKINAWA

AFTER LEAVING HAWAII, NEAL'S huge military ship steamed and tossed through endless miles of dark blue waves past the Marshall Islands and into the Mariana Islands. He was gulping at the vastness of both the Pacific Ocean and the implications of going to war. He wrote to his mother from Saipan: "Have [now] seen dead [people] and wrecked equipment. There are still [enemy troops] in the hills, but don't worry. . . . I know your prayers are with me."

From then on, military policy wouldn't let him share any details about his troop movements. But he could, and did, say: "I wish I'd done so many more things for you folks [in appreciation] for the wonderful life you and Dad have given me. . . . I've only accomplished one thing . . . well, and that was the fence. Maybe [even] that's fallen down [by now]. . . . Ten sons couldn't love you parents more than I do." He needed the reassurance of that love now as never before. The next stop was Okinawa.

It was May of 1945, and the tectonic plates that had grounded Neal Maxwell's world were beginning to shift drastically. He learned upon arriving in Okinawa that President Franklin D. Roosevelt had just died. He soon learned also of President Heber J. Grant's death. Those two men had been tall trees in the foreground that had framed his view through most of his life. But new views were appearing all around him. As the troop ship pulled into Okinawa harbor, Neal could see "the artillery blazing on the island." A "dull sickening sensation" began to fill him as reality struck. "This was real war and it was far less glamorous up close." Until now, "it had been kind of a game."

What Neal didn't know—fortunately, for the sake of his peace of mind—was that the Japanese had developed a grisly strategy for the Battle of Okinawa. Their backs were against the wall, and Okinawa had become their last hope. If the Yanks prevailed here, nothing would stop them from attacking the Japanese homeland—something the Japanese military had vowed could not, must not, ever happen.

Consider briefly the larger military context. The Japanese had bombed Pearl Harbor to establish their command of the South Pacific. Both the United States and Britain immediately declared war against Japan, but the Japanese knew the Allies would be preoccupied—and they were—with the war in Europe. By early 1942, the Japanese had moved almost at will through Thailand, Burma, and the British Malay Peninsula. Soon they took the Philippines, a territory of the United States. The Allies, strung out across the entire globe, tried to respond, but, embarrassingly, they failed to hold onto even their most secure positions in Hong Kong and Singapore.

In a crucial turning point, the Allies finally stopped the Japanese eastward expansion in the Battle of the Coral Sea off the Australian coast in 1942. Then they stopped the Japanese westward expansion in Sri Lanka and began the arduous work of retaking everything the Japanese had seized. By 1944, Japan was gradually losing its control of the sea, which threatened its key geographic advantage—that Japan itself was out of range from Allied air bases in the Pacific.

When General Douglas MacArthur won back control of the Philippines in October 1944, Japan was suddenly on the defensive. Germany was losing momentum in Europe, which allowed the Allies to shift more resources to the Pacific. The Allies undertook an

island-hopping strategy, launching air and naval attacks on islands
throughout the trackless Pacific, wherever the Japanese had established
control. Island hopping was ugly in its human and other costs, but it
was effective. United States warships would pound an island with
artillery shells, and then troops would wade ashore under the cover of
continued artillery barrages. Once ashore, these soldiers would take on
the waiting Japanese with more artillery, mortar fire, machine guns, and
finally the hand-to-hand combat that made the work of the infantry
even worse than Emma Maxwell feared it would be.

Using this technique, the Americans kept on the move, eventually winning control of the Marianas with the fall of Saipan. This news
stunned the Japanese people, who had believed the propaganda that
their troops were winning the war. General Hideki Tojo and his cabinet resigned. Their successors saw clearly that unless they could hold
off the advancing Yanks on Iwo Jima and Okinawa, Japan itself would
be next. For the Americans, taking those two islands would provide
staging areas from which they could cut off crucial Japanese fuel supply routes—and put Japan within reach of B-29 bombers.

When Iwo Jima fell, some Japanese leaders argued that it was
time to negotiate a peace settlement. But another view prevailed—
throw everything they had at the Americans in one last, lunging effort
to shift the momentum. Okinawa thus became a deadly "Tennozan"—
"a site where a sixteenth century Japanese ruler staked his entire fate on
a single battle." Defending this island was now "the key to whether
Japan would survive as an independent nation."

So it was that General Ushijima planned a "monster ambush" on
Okinawa, allowing "the Americans to come ashore unopposed so that
they would stroll unwarily into the trap" of an island "filled with riflemen . . . artillery, batteries of mortars, and light tanks." Then Ushijima
would unleash a barrage of kamikaze suicide bombers on U.S. ships and
troops, smashing them "so shatteringly" that the Japanese could then
"take the offensive and destroy them." Ironically, as it turned out, the
fierceness of Japan's defense of Okinawa became a major factor in
President Harry Truman's decision to use nuclear weapons on Japanese
cities to end the war.

By the time Neal joined the Seventy-Seventh Division, the Battle of Okinawa was underway. He was one of the replacements sent to maintain United States momentum. On his first night there, a big kamikaze battle lit up the entire harbor. Amid those fireworks, Neal received the somber news that his group would be going up to the "line" the next morning. Within a few days, he would receive news that produced a very different emotion—Germany had surrendered, ending the European conflict.

He found that the next day was "a poignant morning as the eight or so of us who had come all that way together were finally broken up into different units, realizing we might never see each other again." In a fateful choice, as Neal waited for instructions, a soldier named Sisk asked him and his friend Paul "Joe" Montrone, a Catholic from Salt Lake City (who has since died of leukemia), if they wanted to be in a mortar squad. They didn't understand what they were deciding but said yes. Later they learned that, in their case, firing mortar was safer than being regular riflemen. Their buddies whose last names began with "M" went into a platoon that attacked Hill 140 (Flat Top). Few survived.

Neal's overall odds were hardly reassuring. To begin with, of the eleven million uniformed Americans in 1945 (some 7 percent of the U.S. population), only about 5 percent served in the infantry, and of those, 60 percent would actually fight on the front lines. That computes to roughly a 3 percent chance that anyone who had enlisted or was drafted would actually go into battle as an infantryman—those placed in "mortal contact with the enemy."

On May 13, Neal wrote his family:

> I've been assigned to the famed 77th Division. . . . They're killers, out of necessity, but fine fellows. I'm proud to be one of them. . . . Seen a lot of terrible things lately, but the worst is ahead. Met some fine LDS fellows on the last boat, had planned services, but were rudely interrupted by an air raid. . . . I'm all alone as far as spiritual companions are concerned, except for One. I know he is always with me. I feel your prayers for me in my heart. . . . I'm so glad [the war is] over in Europe, we need help here . . . It's rough here, but not too much for us to bear.

As he waded into this, his first experience in combat, Neal from his vantage point couldn't have realized the "vicious sprawling struggle" that raged around him. "Never before . . . had so much American blood been shed in so short a time in so small an area. . . . Okinawa was the largest combined operation [ever] fought on, under and over the sea and land." As horrible as were the later nuclear attacks on Hiroshima and Nagasaki, when "measured by sheer suffering . . . the battle of Okinawa was a greater tragedy."

About four hundred miles from Japan, Okinawa is a small island—sixty miles long and eighteen miles across at its widest point—with a normal population of 500,000. But for this battle, more than one million people were locked together there in a death struggle, and about a fourth of them would die—Okinawan, Japanese, and American.

At Neal Maxwell's spot in the center of the island, his division had been assigned to take out the entrenched Japanese positions on a complex of hills—Chocolate Drop, Wart Hill, and Flat Top. This forbidding area "bristled with mortars and interlocking machine-guns and 47mm antitank guns. . . . Casualties were frightful." Only about 800 of 2,400 men from the 306th Regiment—one-third—who had begun the battle in this location were left to be formed into a single battalion. A similar fate awaited the 307th Regiment—Neal's unit—as they faced these hills.

Neal felt like one of the youngest, greenest soldiers there. He wrote home that the soldiers "could barely put our feet together and do what we were supposed to be doing." He already knew the names of some casualties. He heard soon after they arrived that Ernie Pyle, World War II's most celebrated American correspondent and a hero to U.S. troops, had just been killed on a nearby island by a hidden machine gun. But the casualty stories and statistics didn't wait for the young, new soldiers to mature before becoming abruptly personal.

The first American Neal saw killed was a big man from his company named Partridge. As their group walked single file toward Flat Top, a shell exploded nearby. They hit the dirt. When they got up, someone said to Partridge, "Come on, get up, let's get going." But

Flat Top Hill, Okinawa, in 1973

Partridge had caught a big piece of shrapnel, and he was dead. Neal was so shocked that "for five or six hours I was in a daze. I was only 18 and very frightened. Then as we saw more and more [of the] battle, the worse it got." Later, as they approached Flat Top, Neal saw Japanese corpses all around him. Then he looked up to see a buddy named Claude Phillips squirting a flamethrower. Suddenly Phillips took a fatal shot himself and rolled down the hill.

May 19 marked two commemorations: the worst night in combat, and the one-year anniversary of Neal's graduation from high school. By then, the savage battle had already "rendered the entire landscape bare of almost any vegetation." Then, beginning on May 21, heavy rains "turned the battlefield into a quagmire. Even tanks and amphibious tractors could not move to support the infantry. . . . Disease swept through the [U.S.] ranks. . . . The American drive literally bogged down in the center. . . . All the troops were exhausted."

The living conditions were deplorable. The mud was so bad that "sometimes you slept standing up in it." Even "tanks disappeared in lakes of ooze." The soldiers "struggled with the weight" of heavy packs and ammunition. Dysentery "plagued nearly everyone to some degree." Sleeping was a "near impossibility." Their foxholes were "filled with mud and water." They "ate wretchedly. . . . All had almost constant thirst, and worried about supplies of water only less than of ammunition. Brought up in five-gallon tanks, the water always tasted of oil." When the men "were lucky enough to be pulled off the front line for rest . . . hot coffee often waited." One soldier "craved coffee . . . despite his dead appetite," because of the unrelenting thirst—and because the coffee, having been boiled, was at least edible. It was "an existence not conveyable by words or film." To be surrounded by the trauma of combat amidst such field conditions left some who survived it unable to talk about it for forty years.

This scene gives a poignant, sacrificial quality to Neal's modest comment in a letter to his parents during this time about his mood and about trying to keep the Word of Wisdom:

> Had a dream the other night. You folks were holding Carol up to a window and I was saying Boo to her, and she laughed just as she does. Boy, if that didn't make me blue. . . . It's rough here. . . . It will be wonderful to bathe again. Still not smoking, drinking tea or coffee, nothing great but the coffee is tempting some times.

To a boy struggling through an exhausting battle with constant thirst and only foul water to drink, boiled coffee offered more than its usual temptation. Drinkable water was so scarce that Neal had to use rainwater and a biscuit from his can of rations for the sacrament he prepared and blessed in his foxhole each Sunday. Sometimes he obtained water by making good trades. More than thirty years after the war, he received a letter from a Latter-day Saint woman whose husband, Chris Seil, not a Latter-day Saint, had been on Okinawa with Neal. After hearing about this boy for decades, Sister Seil finally learned that his name was Maxwell, so she wrote to Neal. Her husband clearly remembered a "Mormon boy who really lived his religion." He "gave Chris all of his beer, coffee and cigarette rations in exchange for [his] water."

Neal never would drink the coffee. He sensed that a core principle was at stake, not merely the color of what he drank. On June 8, when he had been pulled back from the front lines for a brief respite, he wrote home, "Still haven't drunk any coffee, more proud now 'cause it meant considerable suffering, but always something comes along and I'd have a substitute. I have a little testimony right there. . . . I pray God will continue His wonderful help in these small but important things."

Years later, Neal would say that his wartime experience tested and transformed him in many ways. Especially important was how the war helped the seeds of testimony that had been sown in his youth begin to sprout, sending up recognizable little green shoots from the soil of his heart. He would quote C. S. Lewis to explain why:

> You never know how much you really believe anything until its truth . . . becomes a matter of life and death to you. It is easy to say you believe a rope to be strong and sound as long as you are merely using it to cord a box. But suppose you had to hang by that rope over a precipice. Wouldn't you then first discover how much you really trusted it?

The battle also damaged Neal's hearing. His father, Clarence, had trouble with his hearing for years, and Neal may have inherited some of that. But being too close to U.S. Marine artillery one night on Okinawa probably caused further damage to his hearing in at least one ear, which became more noticeable as the years went by.

During the middle of the battle for Okinawa, Neal had the most transforming experience of all. He was part of a mortar squad that fired at Japanese positions hidden in the hills. His own mortar position created an obvious invitation for the enemy to locate and eliminate his firing capacity—and him. They needed only to direct their own artillery and mortar fire at the place where Neal's squad sent up its shells. By identifying his position and comparing where their shells hit, they could direct their fire closer and closer until they had done their deadly job.

One night in late May, the shrieking noise of artillery fire caught Neal's attention with a frightening realization. Three shells in a row had exploded in a sequence that sent a dreadful message—the enemy had completely triangulated his mortar position, and the next series of shots would hit home. Suddenly a shell exploded no more than five feet away from him. Terribly shaken, Neal jumped from his foxhole and moved down a little knoll seeking protection, and then, uncertain what to do, he crawled back to the foxhole. There he knelt, trembling, and spoke the deepest prayer he had ever uttered, pleading for protection and dedicating the rest of his life to the Lord's service.

Neal later called this "one of those selfish, honest prayers" that many people offer in times of great stress. He didn't feel entitled to anything in particular, and he knew many of his combat buddies prayed that night as fervently as he did. Yet he did have very personal reasons for looking to heaven for protection. He was carrying in his pocket a smudged carbon copy of the patriarchal blessing he had received before leaving home. He had read the blessing frequently enough to know this part especially well:

> I bless you that as the agencies of destruction are manifest . . . you may be preserved in body and in mind and your intellect be quickened by the spirit of truth . . . that you may rejoice in the power, the love and the mercies of the Redeemer. I seal you up against the power of the destroyer that your life may not be shortened and that you may not be deprived of fulfilling every assignment that was given unto you in the pre-existent state.

After the prayer, Neal turned his attention again to watching the night sky, which was earlier ablaze with flashing, fiery noises. His body spontaneously tensed up as he waited, searching the darkness for sounds and clues. But no more shells came near him.

Later he wrote:

> After that triangulation occurred, the shelling stopped at the very time they were [about] to finish what they had been trying to do for days. I am sure the Lord answered my prayers. . . . The following night they began to pour [more] shells in [on our position], but almost all of them were duds—either the ammunition had gotten wet or they were not exploding in the very thick, oozing mud. . . . I felt preserved, and unworthily so, but have tried to be somewhat faithful to that promise that was given at the time.

Neal (second row, far left) and some buddies shortly after returning from the front lines; in the center is Paul Montrone, Neal's foxhole buddy from Salt Lake City

He would occasionally talk about those two nights in the years that followed, never offering more details about the experience but usually adding something like, "I foolishly thought at the time that I could pay the Lord back, and now, of course, I'm in greater debt to Him than ever."

Over the next few weeks, Neal wrote several short letters home, some of them scrawled on postcard size military "V-mail" notes designed for the haste of combat conditions. He was not ready at first to share what had happened. Perhaps he didn't want to worry his family, and army policy limited what he could say. Beyond that, the experience had been almost too personal to describe in writing. Its meaning went far beyond what mere words could explain.

At the same time, Neal had discovered a sublime kind of spiritual knowledge and without self-consciousness showed in his letters how the influence of that knowledge was already distilling quietly on his soul. Without much explanation, he began sending some of each military salary check with his letters to be saved for his mission. He also offered a few restrained hints about the barely tolerable conditions that surrounded him. Both the frequency and the content of the letters illustrate how close Neal felt to his family:

> May [no date]: My thoughts are constantly of home. I think today is Mother's Day. Many happy wishes, Mom. . . . I'm writing on a can of mortar ammo, it's kinda bumpy. . . . Please don't worry. I'll be OK. I'm in good Hands.

> May 24: I had a ration biscuit and rainwater for my sacrament. That proves it's not the ingredients, but the Spirit. It was wonderful. Mud is terrible here, . . . my mind is home always. Many things have so strengthened my faith that I can hardly wait to go on a mission.

> May 28: I have a beard ½ to ¾" long, unusual for me. . . . I get lonely for an LDS [friend]. Perhaps after the campaign I can get together. I pray constantly . . . to be worthy of my parents, [the] church, and the wonderful chances [I've had]. . . . I know I shall return.

> May 30: Dearest Mom and Dad, Oh my loved ones, I'm so lonely for you, sometimes I feel like crying. . . . All I have to do is be worthy of my patriarchal blessing, your prayers, and my religion. But time and so much action hang heavy on a man's soul. Today is Sunday. I have to make it a point to know [the day] so I can bless my sacrament. Otherwise it's just another day. . . . When I get home I'll probably cry the first week, but never fear, there is no diversion strong enough to draw me from my home.

> June 1: [After being on the front lines] I'm terribly tired. . . . We've seen some tough action but . . . will have to wait [to explain]. I can say only God prevented my death at times. My prayers are just as ardent as they were up at the lines. I have a testimony no one can crumble.

> June 4: We're having rain, rain, and now typhoons. . . . We're supposed [to see the movie] "Gone With the Wind" tonite and [we] may be [gone with the wind], too, as we're expecting a

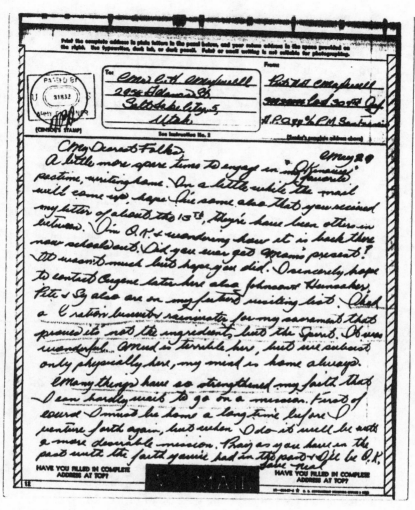

A V-mail Neal wrote from the front lines (actual size)

typhoon. . . . Reading my Book of Mormon and . . . praying in secret [daily].

June 8: [Since a recent promotion, I earn] $74.80 a month now and you are to get all but $10 so I should have a little nest anyway. Use it if you need it, money is less significant to me than it ever was. . . . The testimony I have concerning my Patriarchal Blessing concerning wars pass[ing] over me is very strong.

June 10: Momentary relief [the break from the front lines] is usually the first opportunity . . . to forget God, but this is one little boy that will never forget what He did for me while in action. . . . Combat has stamped itself indelibly on my mind, but I'm not one of those psychos yet. . . . I laughed for the first time for a long time yesterday. I've smiled before then but never laughed. Relaxation does strange things after long tension.

June 12: After seeing some of the deeds my buddies performed in making the Supreme Sacrifice, I have a strong desire to destroy this thing [war] that causes such grief. I can't say I hate any race because they are God's children. I can plainly see the only way to avoid future wars is by missionary work and that's an opportunity I want more than ever. . . . I [have] placed myself completely in [God's] trust many times, and cryed I felt so good, no tears but it's so easy to cry inside, especially with joy.

After another several weeks, when he was in the Philippines, Neal could write more freely, because he was outside the sensitive combat zone:

August 5: I miss our L.D.S. They are my people. I pray to God I can someday labor in return for all [the] prayers I've had answered. Where would you like me to go on a mission? I've had two great prayers answered in my life. One at Carol's stricken time, and another one night on Okinawa. . . . I shall never forget God's aid in those cases.

September 5: We caught hell on Flat Top. [After one] week, [from a total of 157 men] there were 58 of us left. Many times I'd write a v-mail letter and hafta stop cause the artillery would pin us down. . . . What a horrible feeling, when you're under sniper fire. I could hear them crack over my head but You Know Who was always with me. I owe Him so much. All the maggot eaten [bodies] within a few yards of my hole. . . . What a mess.

Finally, almost a year after the Okinawa ordeal, he gave his family the most explicit description:

May 2, 1946: About eleven months and twenty days ago I knelt in a foxhole and asked for the seemingly impossible, that

Pointing to the approximate location of his foxhole on his return to Okinawa in 1973

the shelling that had just [driven] me from my foxhole would cease. The last round was zeroed in. There was no reason in the world for them to stop now, but they did. No one can tell me it was a coincidence.

Decades after the war, Neal learned from his aunt Arlene what Emma had told her during May of 1945. Emma said that one evening (we don't know the exact date), she and Clarence had knelt by their bed to pray, as they did together each night, for Neal and his sisters. As they got into bed, Emma said, "Clarence, we must get up and pray again. Neal is in grave danger." They knelt and prayed once more, believing the Lord would extend special protection. When he first heard this story in 1996, Neal simply said he did not doubt his mother knew it.

In 1973, he returned to the spot where his foxhole had been located, "which, for me, is a sacred spot. Sugar cane has since covered the little plateau, but not my poignant memories." As a reminder, he still keeps in his office a framed photograph of Flat Top Hill, with a piece of sugar cane attached. Only a few ridges away stands a relatively new LDS chapel. He taught the gospel at the Okinawa stake conference on a subsequent visit.

He would always feel that he is "still trying to keep that commitment to serve Him all of my days." That night Neal had clearly "sensed that the Lord had some things for me to do." He couldn't have begun to say what that meant, for his heart was telling him things his mind did not yet know. "With this blessing and pledge, I was nudged toward discipleship without realizing what service would be required. I had been blessed, and I knew that God knew that I knew." This event thus set in motion the steps leading toward his mission, his temple marriage, and all that would yet follow.

One of the survivors of the Martin and Willie handcart tragedy once said something hard to grasp, unless one has stood in shoes like his: "We became acquainted with [God] in our extremities, . . . [and] the price we paid to [know Him] was a privilege to pay." That was Neal Maxwell's feeling about what happened on Okinawa and what has happened through his experience with leukemia. He has described both traumas as "a great spiritual adventure, one I would not want to have missed"—because here, at the peril of his life, he came to know God.

If he had waited to be drafted, he might "never have seen any action" in the war. He might have escaped being stretched to his extremities—but he would also have missed the heights that a disciple can discover in his depths.

FOURTEEN

LEARNING AND
LEADERSHIP
IN WARTIME

LEARNING IN WARTIME IS the subject of an essay by C. S. Lewis about British education during the war. The phrase also describes the remainder of Neal's military experience. He was on a steep learning curve not only about spiritual discoveries, patriotism, and the horrors of war but also about a new world of experience through his relationships with his fellow soldiers. He had sailed into the Pacific as a green, frightened teenager who didn't know how to buckle his leggings, and he returned two years later having discovered a major new theme that would fascinate and engage him from then on—leadership.

Soon after his first days in battle, Neal's writing skills—"primitive though they may have been"—took him into military administration. When his commanding officers discovered his natural talent, one request multiplied into several. Soon Neal was spending much of his time with two main writing tasks—letters of comfort and honor to the families of men who lost their lives in the war, and stories for hometown newspapers about their local soldiers.

In late June 1945, Neal wrote his family that "the memory of black days [on Okinawa] sorta hung over a guy, especially when you

write letters of condolence to the bereaved ones of your buddies. . . .
While it's an honor it's a task a man doesn't relish." Yet "drafting those
letters furnished lessons in compassion for the young soldier." Mary
Mason, Neal's high school English teacher, would have been pleased
to see him at work—partly because he could see that writing skill had
real value and partly because he now realized he needed more education to develop and inform his talent.

Once Okinawa was declared secure by the Allies, his division
headed for the Philippines, preparing to invade Japan. Then Neal, and
the world, learned on August 6 about the fateful events in Hiroshima
and Nagasaki, which brought a swift end to the war on August 14.
Neal's innocent reaction showed his limited perspective on the significance of the atomic bomb. Just before the bombing, he had written his
family, "Hear much about this new bomb? It may do the trick."

Neal considers his first reaction to the bomb a self-centered one—
joy that the war might be over, that they wouldn't need to invade Japan,
and he would soon be going home. There was no philosophical debate
among his fellow soldiers about the merit of dropping the bomb—they
simply lacked perspective about the implications of its awesome power.

Neal also remembers being puzzled by the prediction of a fellow
soldier from New York who warned that Russia would now become
America's primary enemy, not the Japanese. He couldn't see the other
soldier's point, because Russia and the United States had been allies in
the war. Then he began to see the difference between particular wars
and longer-term political developments.

After Japan's surrender, Neal's outfit was shipped to Japan as part
of the army of occupation. He spent a year there—in Sapporo,
Hokkaido, and then in northern Honshu. Neal expected they would be
welcomed in Japan as conquering heroes, but he soon found the realities of occupation not all that glorious. He felt intuitive empathy for
the Japanese people. He still remembers a painful and all too typical
moment in Hokkaido, watching Japanese children and a few adults
crowd around U.S. Army garbage cans to scoop out whatever they could
find. That scene, and many others like it, wrenched him with the reality
of how little the Japanese had and what the war had cost them in

personal ways. He knew that, heavy as the American casualties had been on Okinawa, the Japanese had lost far more. Years later, Elder Monte Brough would hear Neal speak to the Japanese Latter-day Saints there, asking the Lord to bless the descendants of those who lost their lives in that awful battle.

It was thus especially tender for Elder Maxwell in the 1980s to meet a stake president named Kensei Nagamine in Okinawa. President Nagamine had been an eight-year-old boy during the battle. His mother had rushed him to safety during the American strafing. He had not heard of the Church then, but he would later be president of the Tokyo Temple. When Neal first met President Nagamine, he hugged him good-bye at the airport but longed to stay closer to him. On a later visit, Neal called on him in a church meeting to express his feelings about the war, which fully matched Neal's own. By then many of President Nagamine's family had served LDS missions.

After arriving in Japan, Neal was moved up the ranks of enlisted men until he was appointed first sergeant in a large company. When the company commander was looking for a new leader, he wondered aloud to Neal's boss about possible people. With Neal working within earshot on clerical duties, the commander said, "How about Maxwell? He could do it." The first sergeant replied, "Maxwell? He's only nineteen." That didn't stop a later commander, who saw enough of Neal's capacity to make the promotion—to the young soldier's complete surprise. His demonstrated skill with paper and administrative work had now placed Neal in a leadership role, but he felt utterly unprepared for it.

Even in the early stages of his leadership experience, he worked with a friendly, unified group whose support helped compensate for his trying sense of inadequacy: "I sure have some nice fellows working for me in the Intelligence Section," he wrote home, "all of them fathers and older men who really treat me swell. Seems funny to be Sarge to older men. . . . [But] the experience is invaluable."

He was gaining in both experience and confidence, which he would need in his next assignment more than he could yet foresee. As he wrote his family in two letters:

I get a little thrill out of setting goals in the Army and making them despite many hard obstacles, hope I can be as successful in civilian life. Course we know the reason—I've had some very important gifts or at least guidance in many matters.

I suppose you know the legend on how tough we 1st Sgt. are supposed to be. Well, I have quite a theory on the treatment of G.I.'s to get results. I'll expound it one of these days. Believe me it gets results, and operates on the theory that each man can be made to do his best with the use of a little practical psychology. . . . I'm bragging too much today.

Before long, Neal became first sergeant in a big ordnance company of three hundred men, people drawn together from several different units. That diversity of background and the company's swollen size created a situation that was not easy to manage. So Neal, still a teenager, was thrust into the role of primary disciplinarian for an unwieldy group of sometimes grumpy men, most of whom were older than he was and all of whom just wanted to go home. Most of the company's officers were happy to let him worry about discipline among the troops, because they had other interests.

Neal recalls that this situation became "one of the significant tests of my life to win respect and impose discipline on the company where the officers were reluctant" to do much themselves. "I'm in an awkward position," he wrote home. "Here I am issuing orders to sergeants, buddies, etc. It's rather hard . . . for a 19 year old to tell men 32 etc. what to do, and bawl 'em out when they're wrong."

In retrospect, Neal could see that "armies of occupation are not usually happy armies," partly because "soldiers are not apt to appreciate the strategic considerations" at work in postwar circumstances. In addition, it was not his nature to be a stern disciplinarian. But it was clear that he couldn't always wait around for his men to solve their own problems. One soldier got drunk and broke a number of windows, so Neal ordered him to dig a six-by-six foot hole in the ground one day and fill it in the next day—all in full view of the other troops.

As Neal stretched and groped for guidance, he found two sources of help that compensated for his total inexperience with leadership.

One was that he had been in combat himself, while many in his new company had not. Something about his own experiential battle scars, young as he was, qualified him to be taken seriously by older men who hadn't been there themselves. His other source of comfort was a spiritual one. He frequently found himself seeking a private place to pray for help, both about his general concerns and about specific cases. He wrote his parents, "I still wander out alone often and pray under the star-studded sky. It gives me a feeling that praying amid other atmospheres just can't do."

At times the responsibility seemed too much. In one letter he wrote his family, "Time is heavy here now, nearly fifteen months . . . too long. . . . I can't take this too much longer. . . . I do many things here that require such mature judgment I shiver when I think of the responsibility. Way down underneath I'm just a kid, so homesick and young that he doesn't know what to do."

But with experience, he found not only that his men would accept him but also that if he listened to them carefully, his own ideas about how to solve seemingly impossible problems actually yielded solutions. As he saw this, the field of leadership opened up as an exhilarating opportunity for serving people, helping organizations, and learning about human nature. Here, perhaps, were the beginnings of Neal's future work and thoughts on leadership of all kinds.

His leadership perspective increased his interest in how the army did things—even though he was seldom in a position to do much about policies or decisions he didn't like. From those days onward, Neal would worry about institutions that, in effect, shoot themselves unnecessarily in the foot. He was terribly dismayed, for example, by "friendly fire," which he had seen on Okinawa, when a communications mix-up led to an incident of American guns firing on American troops. He was similarly disturbed by U.S. military orders to dump excess jeeps into the ocean when the Japanese people had such a desperate need for vehicles.

Such thoughts provoked his emerging larger interest in military tactics, strategy, and history. Grounded in the sometimes messy realities of his own field experience, he developed a fascination for military history and leadership. In later years, he would often instinctively speak about "tactical concerns" and "strategic implications," as if everyone in his audiences shared his second-nature feel for the difference between the military concepts of strategy and tactics.

As he added his college training and his political experience in Washington, D.C., Neal would begin to devour biographies and other books on Churchill, Truman, MacArthur, Roosevelt, and many other leaders who struggled with the inherent conflicts between military and political interests. This context enriched his own views of history and leadership across the entire spectrum of applications.

Neal's feeling of responsibility for so many men also developed his appreciation for the contributions that some made to the group's well-being. Despite some of his early adjustments to people who had different lifestyle perspectives from his own, Neal couldn't hold back his feelings of gratitude for "the good guys" after serving in combat with them. When he said good-bye to some old timers from his outfit, he wrote home that "it was a privilege to have fought with such fine men. . . . There [are] men ripe for the Gospel who are just as Christian as ourselves but have a great need of the Gospel to guide them."

He later praised the courage of "a rugged sergeant under fire on Okinawa" who "had difficulty complying with formal military requirements." The man was "a steadying influence" for "those like me— frightened and wide-eyed with wonder." He learned that "non-conforming individuals can contribute to common causes," if good leaders will help them do that.

The sense of appreciation ran both ways. In April 2000, more than fifty years after his military experience, Neal received a note from Kenneth Buesing in Wisconsin, to whom he'd sent occasional notes over many years. Buesing was a lieutenant in the same company in which Neal was first sergeant. He said he'd been reflecting on his life, now that he had Parkinson's disease, and felt he hadn't thanked Neal enough for his influence in Japan. "You were a good one," he wrote. "You could not only take orders, but you could translate and give orders. You had a good understanding of your subordinates' problems and needs."

And in the 1970s, a former soldier named Harry White was in an

Arizona hospital for surgery. He had been in Neal's outfit in Japan. His wife and children were Latter-day Saints by then, but he wasn't. Harry's hospital roommate was a Latter-day Saint named Ivan Bates, who read his Book of Mormon regularly. Noticing the book, Harry told Ivan he had known an LDS man in the war named Neal Maxwell—he remembered him as "old Mac"—who "was never brash with the men. He always spoke quietly, but with great authority." Ivan Bates passed this comment on to Elder Maxwell, who called Harry White on the phone. Next time he was in Arizona, Neal contacted Harry, stayed in his home, and performed his baptism.

Not all of Neal's experiences with his fellow soldiers left him with happy memories. Watching some of them behave unwisely and sometimes recklessly verified his own moral convictions. It also prompted later teachings about irresponsible pleasure seeking. He remained disappointed, for example, with those who would spend their nights in drunken escapades of unfaithfulness to their companions at home. He could never erase from his memory "the boasting words of army buddies following their night of adultery, which I heard while trying to go back to sleep on an army cot," Neal once told a BYU group. "I saw the shame of . . . those same men in the days and weeks that followed. It seemed to me . . . that the raucousness and the shouting of sin, the Cain-like glorying in it, is also the sound of pain trying to erase itself."

Neal also reflected these feelings when he wrote a story called "The Dilemma of Madame Butterfly and Mary Jones" for a literary magazine during his university student days. He described two American soldiers in Japan, "knights of MacArthur's round table," who objected to the demeaning way Japanese men treated women and then, hypocritically, went off to their own "comfort girls," who were "convenient . . . submissive and unquestioning."

After one episode of hearing his buddies boast of such so-called conquests, Neal wrote home about the links he was seeing between this American behavior and the issue of moral leadership. Clarence had just sent Neal a copy of the *Church News*, which "had quite an effect on me." Neal compared that vision of "our people . . . in Zion" with the people he'd just seen "swaggering in drunken victory." He continued: "The dire need of humanity is leaders," but "I fear greatly for the United States," unless the nation has morally reliable leaders. "Despite all the planning to insure peace I see it fleeing from the world." He worried about developments in China and Russia and then repeated his concern about Americans who are "still unheeding of God. . . . How many faithful wives will accept untrue husbands after years of separation overseas? . . . I have seen all I need ever see of the world to know my place is in the Priesthood with our people."

At the same time, Neal did like how General Douglas MacArthur performed as leader of the U.S. occupation forces in Japan. The long-term strategic implications of postwar policies intrigued him, but he didn't pretend to understand them yet. He once had his photo taken when he was standing by MacArthur's five-star limousine in Tokyo. Later he would say he thought postwar Japan was probably MacArthur's finest hour.

Another group of soldiers with whom Neal felt an increasing bond of identification were the LDS servicemen. His letters reflect real growth in that bond during his two years away from home. Since arriving in Okinawa he had sorely missed the friends who had accompanied him until they went on to other assignments, and he later formed life-long friendships with such LDS soldiers as LeRoy Nydegger and Eugene K. England. After seeing the distasteful conduct of some other men, Neal felt special appreciation for the returned missionaries, who were his own "visual aid" to demonstrate "the need to persist in discipleship" amid the widespread temptations of worldliness. His sense of belonging to "[his] people" in the Church was clearly beginning to blossom.

The most memorable sacrament meeting he had yet experienced took place on Okinawa, just after he and others from his division returned from the front lines. When Neal learned that a meeting for all Latter-day Saint servicemen had been called by a chaplain from Idaho named Lyman Berrett, he was genuinely excited about seeing his friends again—then he realized that some of them might not have survived the battle. He and the others thus gathered, knowing that the ones who didn't make it to the meeting probably hadn't made it through the battle.

One who didn't make it was Dean Nielson from Delta, Utah, whom Neal had admired for the way he "strove to put on the whole armor of God." "One of the rendezvous to which I look forward," Neal would say later, "is to see my friend again and to thank him" for his example and his friendship. Another person who attended a Latter-day Saint servicemen's meeting that Neal later attended in Japan was a young bomber pilot from Brigham City named Boyd K. Packer. Boyd's group had borrowed a jeep and driven sixty miles to the meeting. Neal and Boyd didn't know each other in those days, but they would one day attend more than a few meetings together.

World War II had changed both the world and Neal Maxwell forever. At the level of political ideals and democratic society, Neal would always retain a passion for the values of freedom, personal responsibility, and civic duty, which he came to cherish by defending them with his life. He would develop his own deep convictions about, and his own ways of teaching people about, the way these values make a free society possible.

Neal was also changed spiritually. For his development as a disciple, the war had been his first rite of passage. Far from parents and Church leaders, he faced both physical and spiritual ordeals. He discovered that his internal strength could be a resource to his country and a force against its enemies. He also felt the brotherhood of his fellow soldiers, which reinforced his understanding that he was defending interests larger than his own.

Beyond this, he found God's reality for himself. Alone in a foxhole, unable to rely on familiar sources of authority and protection, he turned to the Lord. Then he found that he was not just his father's son, or a faithful son of the fathers of his Latter-day Saint community, or a servant to the leaders who represented his country. In an echo of what Nephi, Paul, and other early disciples discovered for themselves, Neal now also knew that he was a son of God, able to access directly a divine perspective on his life.

PART V

MISSIONARY DAYS IN CANADA

FIFTEEN

TEACHING
THE GOSPEL

L̲ONG BEFORE RETURNING FROM the Pacific, Neal had decided to serve a mission—he just wasn't sure when. He wanted to fulfill the serious commitment he'd made on Okinawa. Yet he'd ached with homesickness during the long wait in Japan, and the idea of just being home for a while had great appeal. He was also eager to begin his college education, but even with the GI Bill, that was expensive. He had sent home enough money that a savings account of twenty-four hundred dollars was waiting for him. But that felt to him like mission money.

Soon after arriving home, he kept feeling he "had promises to keep"—and that meant a mission, now. He thought his bishop might approach him with a call, but all young men weren't expected to serve missions in those days, and few had been called from the Wandamere Ward since the war ended. His mind made up, Neal grew tired of waiting for the bishop. In an early example of what he would call his "ark-steadying tendencies," he went to the bishop's home. He said he had the money, was worthy to go, and wanted to "get this show on the road." The bishop hesitated and then said he'd been meaning to ask Neal about going.

Years later, Neal would learn from that bishop's ward clerk that the bishop had felt Neal needed more time with his family after having been so far away for a tenth of his life. That's why he hadn't yet asked him about a mission. Hearing this, Neal chastised himself for having been too judgmental and impatient. But by then, his mission was long since completed.

Young Elder Maxwell was called to serve in the Canadian Mission, headquartered in Toronto. As he prepared to leave, he had two important experiences with General Authorities. First, as was customary with many full-time missionaries then, he was ordained a seventy in December 1946 by Elder S. Dilworth Young of the First Council of Seventy. Before ordaining him, Elder Young asked with his endearing, pioneerlike bluntness if Neal was willing to be a missionary all his life.

Thirty years later, when the new First Quorum of the Seventy was reconstituted, Neal was sustained as a member of both the Quorum and its Presidency. The First Council of Seventy had consisted only of seven full-time General Authorities, who had responsibility, among other duties, for the work of the part-time seventies who were scattered throughout the stakes of the Church. One of these seven in 1976 was Elder S. Dilworth Young.

In that historic conference, Neal said he hoped his "little footnote on a page of the [Seventies'] Quorum history" would "read clearly" that he had "[worn] out [his] life in helping to spread Jesus' gospel." Then he affectionately remembered 1946:

> Thirty years ago President S. Dilworth Young ordained me a Seventy, but only after extracting a promise that I would preach the gospel the rest of my life. His stern demeanor was such that I felt I'd been asked to jump off a tall building. I went over the side saluting. Now I salute that same selfless, sweet seventy . . . once again.

Neal's second encounter with a General Authority before his mission occurred when Elder Matthew Cowley of the Quorum of the Twelve Apostles was assigned to set him apart as a full-time missionary. The two had not met before, and they did not discuss Neal's interests before the setting apart. In the blessing, Elder Cowley counseled him quite directly to "avoid political discussions," because he was "going to preach the gospel." This statement struck Neal as pure inspiration, because he had become so interested in political matters during the war that he felt sure he would not have thought of Elder Cowley's well-principled advice had he not heard it so clearly.

As it turned out, he remained fascinated with the 1948 United States presidential election between Harry Truman and Thomas E. Dewey. He occasionally kept up on campaign news during his mission, at times discussing the issues with a companion. After the Republican nominating convention, Neal wrote to Clarence, "I say Dewey on 3rd ballot or Vandenberg on 7th ballot. Either man is OK." But he otherwise tried hard to focus on missionary work—not an easy assignment for one with emerging political instincts so strong that they would capture his interest for decades afterward.

Neal arrived in Toronto on February 1, 1947. His mission president was Octave W. Ursenbach from Alberta, who was replaced by Floyed G. Eyre of Ogden in September 1947. Neal joined 143 other full-time missionaries working primarily in Ontario and Quebec. The mission had 1,388 Church members in early 1947 and 1,652 two years later.

Eastern Canada, especially Ontario, had a rich missionary heritage. There Parley P. Pratt had baptized John Taylor, who became the third President of the Church. Parley found Joseph Fielding there as well, along with his two sisters, one of whom, Mary, became the wife of Hyrum Smith and the mother of Joseph F. Smith, sixth President of the Church. Ontario was also the birthplace of Ira Nathaniel Hinckley, grandfather to President Gordon B. Hinckley—and great-grandfather to Neal Maxwell's future wife, Colleen Hinckley.

The Canadian Mission had a distinctive postwar flavor. On the positive side, most of young Elder Maxwell's fellow missionaries were war veterans, which created a splendid resource of spiritual maturity: "We were there because we wanted to be, not because we had been pressured into it." This was true of most missionaries the Church sent out in those years—the Latter-day Saint version of "the greatest generation." One Australian Church member said they were

> veterans with a maturity not simply the result of their extra years but born of their experiences in battle on sea, air and land. Unlike many of their predecessors, their testimonies [were] strong before they [ever began] their missionary service. . . . We who knew them think there has never been another generation of missionaries like them.

The war had strained leadership resources in many smaller Church units, which had unavoidably gone untended by the Church's depleted missionary force. For example, in the city of Orillia, Ontario, Neal's first field of labor, he found "things were in some disarray" among the branch membership. He and his companion could locate only two or three people who would still attend church. Several others not only declined to attend but had taken actions that required the missionaries, in their role in the branch presidency, to terminate their membership.

This less than auspicious beginning provided the basis for Neal's sobering missionary reality check. In later years, his children would occasionally remind him that on his mission he baptized two people and excommunicated four—a net loss of two. This comment was included in an article about Elder Maxwell written for publication at the time of his call to the Twelve in 1981. He had thought the comment an appropriate way to reassure current missionaries who struggle, as he had, when they don't fulfill their expectations about convert baptisms. When someone in a prepublication review wondered about including this sentence, the inquiry went back to Elder Maxwell, who smiled and said gently that the reviewer must not have much of a sense of humor. The sentence remained in the text.

When it came to proselyting, Neal plunged in all the way—then promptly encountered a number of well-known obstacles to missionary work. Yet his responses both showed and shaped his character, as he took on each barrier as it came—bad weather, his own limited gospel knowledge, the resistance of local ministers, and the absence of meaningful teaching resources.

For missionaries working outdoors virtually all the time, Ontario in February could feel a little chilly. In one of his first letters home, Neal wrote: "It gets about 20 below and pull-lenty of snow. . . . I got a frost-bitten left ear in Toronto. . . . I bought some ear muffs and fur gloves ($.50 more than the ones I had, but real gloves, nuts to ZCMI)." Years later, he would write to his son, Cory, trying to cheer him up about wintertime tracting in Germany:

> My first three weeks in the mission field found us knocking on hundreds of doors without a single invitation to come in. It was in the middle of a Canadian winter and the snow was four feet high. I am not trying to impress you with my nobility, but simply empathizing with you. Frankly, I was glad that it started off rather rough, since everything after that initiation seemed to be an improvement.

Neal's frequent letters to Cory (about 150 during Cory's two-year mission) echoed, in one more way, the influence of his father, Clarence, who maintained a similar stream of correspondence to Neal during both the war and his mission.

Neal's missionary letters to his family continued to reflect his wonder about surviving the harsh winter—quite a contrast to the mud and heat of Okinawa. Compared to his letters from the Pacific, he now wrote in clipped phrases and capitalized words that reflected the missionary's ever-hustling pace but kept alive the close, constant conversation with his parents. For instance, he wrote on February 19 with the return address "No'th o' th' Boda'" about other physical plagues besides the snow which he hadn't encountered in the islands:

> Everyone from States is plagued with Dandruff to such an extent many Elders are losing hair. I have more than ever before (dandruff). Is there anything I can eat to Bolster My Hair or Remove this dandruff? Shampooing helps for a couple of days. You might ask around if you get a chance. What was the dosage of those calcium pills? I don't think I need them but as a rule the Peoples teeth are Bad here so I'll take them.

Neal's limited gospel knowledge was another barrier to his

effective proselyting, but he had more control over this problem than
he did the cold winter. Orillia was located in something of a Canadian
Bible Belt, which meant that Neal, the war veteran, was about to discover a new version of artillery—a frequent barrage of theological
riddles and biblical arguments against the Church. From the moment
he encountered such questions, instead of being dismayed by his relative ignorance of the scriptures, he was off and running for answers.
Like Clarence, Neal instinctively began his searches with the premise
that every question had a good answer in the doctrines of the
Restoration—he just needed to find it.

He began to devour the scriptures like a man just escaped from a
starvation cell. His second companion, Stephen Call, remembers that
Neal's "reading ability . . . was remarkable—fast and with understanding," even though he also talked "so fast it was difficult for some of us
to understand him." Neal wrote a steady stream of questions to
Clarence, asking along the way for one church book after another.
Those books had been there all the time before his mission, but he
hadn't been ready for them. Now his need and his love for discovery
together created an omnivorous hunger for the intellectual framework
of the gospel, which he would erect on the deep footings and foundation of his already secure spiritual knowledge:

> Am through with all tracts and Pearl of Great Price, start-
> ing Doctrine & Covenants. Lots and lots to learn. . . .
> Finished B. H. Roberts, *Falling Away*. Very good. I can't
> read enough of this now. I love it. Too cold to tract now. Mostly
> study classes. . . . It is a great and marvelous work we are doing.
> Our only fears should be can we do it well enough. . . .
> Sorry if I disturbed you about my question on New
> Jerusalem. I later ran across explanation, so I should be more
> patient. Your Outline was very good, Dad. Where will the Ten
> Tribes (lost portion) stay? In Zion or with Judah? I've read both.
> . . . I too wish you Parents could be with me as we go forth daily,
> the three of us—[my companion], myself, and God.
> I could use some [more Church] books, *Priesthood and
> Church Government, Gospel Interpretations* [both] by Widtsoe,

Restoration of All Things [by] J. Fielding Smith, and *Presidents of the Church,* dunno who it's by.

Over the ensuing months, Neal embarked on his first attempt at "binge reading"—reading several books at a time—a pattern his reading still follows. He read whatever he could find from B. H. Roberts, Joseph Fielding Smith, John A. Widtsoe, James E. Talmage, and other Latter-day Saint authors. His interest was in doctrinal literature, not motivational works. He could hardly have been more motivated. As he remembered it later, he was hungry to catch up on things he felt he should have known sooner. Now his reasoned understanding of the gospel was emerging as "a response to real life," and he felt his confidence growing as he filled in doctrinal gaps. This process added to his earlier spiritual witnesses, creating a testimony that came "cumulatively, . . . experientially, . . . rather than in one blinding flash."

Clarence, Neal's librarian for much of this research, was a ready and able tutor. One of Neal's missionary associates, Web Adams, said that Neal told him during their mission that Clarence really was "a student" of the gospel, and he could sense that Neal had "great respect for his father." Web also noticed that Neal was "engaged to the nth degree" in his gospel study—and in following the issues of the day not only about religion but trends in society.

Part of what ignited Neal's gospel scholarship was the resistance, and sometimes the hostility, he and his companions encountered from ministers of other churches, who warned their flocks to watch out for the Mormon missionaries. On one occasion, Neal and his companion were invited to a confrontational meeting with a number of ministers who challenged them with numerous scriptural questions. At first Neal could offer little response, but he relished the process of preparing himself to deal responsibly with such issues. The opposition provoked him to action, spurring his own learning.

These theological encounters also awakened Neal's not-always-suppressed competitive streak, which was emboldened by his high confidence in the spiritual roots of his testimony. He felt compelled to respond, to take a stand. As he wrote his family, "Local minister slammed us over radio Sunday with bitter untruths. But he's a rabble-rouser anyway. I love competition. Called on him to 'call him on the carpet' for some of his lies, but he wouldn't see [us]. . . . More about him later. That is why I like it here."

The minister was a Baptist named Guthrie, whose Sunday radio broadcasts had a large audience in and around Orillia. The citizenry took the minister at his word, and the missionaries encountered stiff resistance everywhere—for weeks. Many years later, Hugh Hewitt asked Neal what kept him going during this time, which was so frosty in every sense. Neal replied it was because he was "there on the Lord's errand. If I'd been selling widgets, I'd have bagged it after the first day." But soon he caught "the sense of adventure [and] challenge" of trying to respond in a mature way. The combination of his feelings of inadequacy and the strength of the opposition was good for him, "because it helped me to balance advocacy . . . with humility, which I needed to learn. If one has an unbroken string of successes, he misses the chance to learn from . . . disappointment." The indifference of the people also taught him how unusual the message of the Restoration really is. So he worked at not judging people for responding as they did, when they didn't really understand the message.

The other proselyting obstacle Neal faced was a lack of good teaching resources. In the postwar period, the missionaries were left to their own devices, teaching investigators however they thought best for their circumstances. This approach had its merits, as Neal's case attests—it developed the missionaries' gospel scholarship and their spiritual self-reliance. The downside was a lack of systematic training, teaching, and criteria to prepare investigators for baptism.

This laissez-faire environment troubled Neal when he noticed that the missionaries "were all fumbling around out there. Everybody must have felt as I did, that there's got to be a better way." One of his companions liked to visit investigators and read a chapter from the Book of Mormon each week—to which Neal later responded, "I don't know how many chapters there are in the Book of Mormon, but it would take you forever to join the Church that way." His reactions weren't harsh—he just believed they could find more effective missionary methods. It was the same reaction he'd had when he saw

While on his mission

so-called friendly fire in the military or he wished for better teaching of the youth in the Wandamere Ward: we can do better than this.

For example, after one of his first attempts at a missionary street meeting, he was convinced this was "the least efficient means of proselyting ever invented." People would make fun of the missionaries as they sang "on a street corner, attracting the town drunk." Then when they would walk by a factory, people standing at upper-story windows would throw things at them. As "rites of intensification" for new missionaries, he thought all of this perhaps served a purpose, but he felt there had to be more effective tools for seriously teaching the gospel.

As time went on, his tolerance for street meetings increased. By July, he wrote the family, "I never thot I'd like Street Meetings, but it is [an] invigorating and edifying experience. We have lots of competition here." And he still remembers when Floyed Eyre, his new mission president, took his own turn preaching at a street meeting. A very unkempt man shouted at President Eyre, "You are a liar!" The president calmly replied, "And you, sir, are a gentleman. However, I think we're both wrong." The unkempt man harrumphed and turned away without catching the point, but the missionaries loved it.

Nudged by his desire to improve things and emboldened by his crash course in the scriptures of the Restoration, Neal responded with alacrity when President Eyre asked him if he'd like to prepare a written plan for teaching the gospel to investigators. He had been on his mission just under a year. In its final form, the plan was called "The Sword of Truth." It contained thirteen lessons—the Godhead, the Plan of Salvation, the Church in the Meridian of Time, the Apostasy, the Restoration (five lessons), the Word of Wisdom, the Book of Mormon, the Second Coming, and a wrap-up lesson on spiritual gifts, tithing, and the sacrament.

Each lesson included a central objective, suggested visual aids, and usually two single-spaced pages of typewritten text, with scriptural references sprinkled like salt throughout the text. These mimeographed lessons resemble a cross between something Clarence Maxwell would have written on his old Smith-Corona and a Neal A. Maxwell general conference talk, with parenthetical references to scriptures after every few sentences.

The foreword to the lesson plan contains the author's message to "Fellowservants of the Messiah." He explains the need for a "systematic and effective technique to build testimony and desires for membership." After a few suggested instructions, the concluding lines, full of metaphors and stirring figures of speech, sound like a young Elder Maxwell:

> Do not feel it necessary to extract all of their old stumps of doctrine in one evening. After [teaching them fully], the uprooting will be simpler. . . .
>
> The majority reject this work as being of God. But men who sail in ships of reason, who have set their sails to catch the winds of truth, will eventually . . . land upon the shores of salvation. . . .

The 'Sword of Truth' is yours then. Wield it well, for the time is short.

President Eyre liked Neal's work enough that he adopted the plan throughout the mission. A few missionaries in other missions began to use it as well, as they randomly happened upon it through friends from Canada. A missionary in the Northwestern States Mission named Richard L. Anderson (who later taught religion at BYU) wrote the "Anderson Plan" during this same era to serve the same purpose. Neal always felt that Elder Anderson's plan was "better by far," but at least he had made an effort, and it spurred in him an increased desire to develop his writing skills.

SIXTEEN

ESTABLISHING
THE CHURCH

Missionary work involved Elder Maxwell and his fellow missionaries not only in proselyting but also in building up the organized Church. In the postwar years in Canada, as in most other far-flung places in the mission field, missionaries were the primary support for Church members as well as investigators. So a young missionary like Neal might be home teacher, branch mission leader, youth advisor, missionary zone leader, spiritual counselor, and priesthood leader—all rolled into one. Among the members, his primary purpose was to teach and lift them until they could assume leadership duties for themselves.

As had happened in the military, the needs of the day pushed young Neal once more into very adult roles for which he felt unprepared. This time, the nature of Church leadership added a spiritual dimension he hadn't seen in the army. For the maturing Neal Maxwell, being asked to ride these next, higher waves of compassionate leadership came at a good time to advance his discipleship.

Barely nine months into his mission, Neal was called as district president in Toronto, responsible to oversee the missionary work and the spiritual welfare of 540 Church members—331 of them in the Toronto Branch and the remainder scattered through the expanse of Ontario. Because Elder Ezra Taft Benson of the Twelve was touring the mission that month, he was involved in Neal's call and then set him apart. Neal wrote in his journal about his brief interview with Elder Benson and added, "As they sustained new officers, I was stunned by the reading of my name. . . . Spoke words of appreciation and testimony, near weeping. Set apart under the voice and hands of President Eyre and Apostle Benson. . . . Resolved firmly to try and uphold this confidence God has given me even though I feel undeserving."

It was unusual for a member of the Quorum of the Twelve Apostles to set apart a district president, but this brief contact began an association that would endure. Neal served later in the Washington, D.C., stake mission presidency as a counselor to Elder Benson's son Reed and then in a university ward bishopric with Elder Benson's son Mark. A few years later, Elder Benson was among those who set Neal apart as an Assistant to the Twelve and then, not many years afterward, as a member of the Twelve.

Two days after Neal was set apart as district president, he wrote home about the missionary testimony meeting that followed the district conference: "My testimony is the most precious thing I have. . . . This burning testimony has been mine for months now and I owe so much of it to you. May God strengthen me."

Tutored by President Eyre, Neal began to learn about Church leadership. On one occasion, the president set a deadline for remodeling a chapel, but the missionaries, who were in Neal's district, thought the deadline was unrealistic. Neal felt caught between the president and the missionaries. President Eyre taught him, "Elder, because we all believe in the Church and care deeply about what happens, there are times when we will disagree because we care so much. Isn't it wonderful that those elders are that committed to do their task well?" The president had taken the missionaries' feelings into account, but he left the problem's resolution in Neal's hands. Neal appreciated this approach enough that he would later cite the case to illustrate to leaders the importance of listening to people and not oversupervising them.

Neal also remembered his mission president's teachings. Nearly fifty years later, he told an Aaronic Priesthood fireside, "My mission president used to say we may not always be able to keep an evil thought from entering our minds, but we don't have to offer it a chair and invite it to sit down." And he has always remembered how moved he was in a Toronto district conference when President Eyre bore witness of the First Vision and then told the congregation they were accountable for having heard his witness. Neal would one day conclude one of his first general conference talks with his testimony, adding, "I know I will be held accountable for this testimony; but, as hearers or readers, you are [also] now accountable for my witness."

By the time of his first Christmas in Canada, Neal's growth was in full stride. Laura Merrill, a senior missionary in Neal's district, wrote in a Christmas card to Clarence and Emma:

> Your son is a scholar, keen as can be, a great memory, a high sense of what is expected of him, and never an idle minute. He is an ideal leader and his help to all the missionaries is bound- less.

She wrote them further:

> I am old enough to be his grandmother, so you know I speak from mature judgment.

The next July, Neal's assignment was changed. He became dis- trict president in Montreal, with 225 members, 188 of them in the Montreal Branch. President Eyre felt a particular need for Neal to con- centrate on lifting the district's missionaries spiritually. By then Neal was developing a sense of his own spiritual independence, "because you really do have to make decisions," especially when feeling responsible to help others. The mission leadership pattern in those days nurtured his spiritual self-reliance. As district president, he usually traveled alone when working with missionaries and members, even though he might

Neal (second from left, front row) at Toronto district conference; second row, fourth from left, are President and Sister Octave Ursenbach, President and Sister Floyed Eyre, Sister Flora Benson, and Elder Ezra Taft Benson

be the companion to another missionary leader with whom he'd stay when he wasn't traveling the district.

The missionaries enjoyed Neal's playful and competitive streak. When visiting them, he would often broker "a really good round of ping pong" or they'd play a little basketball. But the elders and sisters "knew he was a leader, all business, and he got the job done." They felt that he liked them, he loved life, and loved missionary work. He tried hard to teach them, sometimes drawing on the ideas in his "Sword of Truth." After one visit, he wrote his family that he had explained "how to answer the 'I am Saved' group, for which I received an undeserved lauding, but I know the Lord guided me in my preparation."

In September 1948, Elder Marion G. Romney, then an Assistant to the Twelve, toured the mission. During this trip, Neal saw some early hints of Marion Romney's gifts as a personal mentor, a relationship that would return more than twenty years later when Elder Romney, then of the Twelve, gave Neal considerable coaching as the new Church commissioner of education. Neal wrote his family that his informal time with Elder Romney had given him a

> better than average chance to draw upon his Wisdom and Personality. He's certainly humble and unpretentious. Gave a lot of good counsel to us. . . . Regarding money, my mission has cost much more than I anticipated. Being a D.P. twice is a major factor [he needed to pay some travel costs himself]. I'll be Bone Dry upon arrival Home, maybe have to borrow from you, but I'll pay you back soon as I can. . . . Elder and Sister Romney have in times past had a rough go financially, but they merely Smile about it and say, "it was good for us," so we shouldn't (speaking to myself) ever get too dollar minded.

Neal afterward felt a little sheepish about having offered his assessment of Elder Romney's own potential Church influence. He remembers "imprudently" and "foolishly but nevertheless accurately" introducing Elder Romney to the missionaries as "a man whose spiritual star had just begun to rise."

As the months progressed, Neal's Church leadership role also introduced him to many new and faithful questions to ask his father, Clarence, in their ongoing and now intensifying gospel conversation. In addition to the echoes of the sorts of questions Neal had seen Clarence ask in his own letters to General Authorities, Neal's letters also reveal the introspective self-discipline that would mark the learning style he applied to his budding discipleship:

> Can one holder of the Priesthood anoint and seal in case of emergency in administering to the sick?
> What do you know about the propriety of taking consecrated oil internally, [or] rubbing it on parts of the body? I have been under the impression that it wasn't called for, but . . . would like something authoritative on it. . . .
> I felt the presence of the Lord in the [district] meeting telling me who to call on for testimonies even tho I had other [names] written down. . . . Now I have found the greatest thrill one can have, serving his God, a joy that if you had not at times applied counsel and brakes to me I might never have received.

I'm so simple. Sometimes (1) Still a bit impulsive, (2) self aggrandizing, (3) not completely mentally righteous thinking, (4) Talk too much. But I shan't despair, as I think I've developed some and matured a little.

He also described blessing a Church member, when he felt

> God's strengthening help [enabled me] to . . . rebuke the power of the Adversary. It will always be a testimony. She was relieved of great emotional distress, bringing her sleep and calm . . . according to my blessing. I had to retire in prayer to ask for faith to support my actions in company with the Elder who assisted. Surely my God . . . must be grieved that despite such great blessings, [my] spirituality . . . is not cultivated more. I thank him for the principle of Repentance. My testimony grows daily and I rejoice at its succor to me.

Neal's association with, and growing sense of responsibility for, the members of the Church came to mean as much as his relationships with the missionaries. One of the stalwart Church members he came to appreciate and to strengthen was Mary Linklater, who lived too far from Orillia to attend Sunday meetings. Mary's husband strongly opposed her Church activity. Her only contact with the Church was when the missionaries made a monthly visit. After a few visits, Neal wrote his family about this "isolated Saint" who "treated us grand. She has a marvelous testimony. Her husband has persecuted her relentlessly, burning her books, . . . publicly humiliating her, etc. But as age is upon him, his fury is spent." Some years later, Neal and Colleen visited his mission field and went to see Mary again. In a tender reunion, she introduced Neal to her frail and ailing husband as "the one you liked."

The relationships Neal developed with converts and other members in the branches of Ontario and Montreal bore sweet and long-term fruit. During his assignments in Montreal, for instance, he and a companion met and taught a woman who was later baptized by other missionaries. Years later this woman's daughter, Olive Tooth Arbuckle, wrote:

More than 30 years ago Elder Neal A. Maxwell knocked on my mother's door. . . . She had been looking for many years for something but didn't know what. . . .

I remember that day. . . . I'd just come home from school and there was my mother with all her books around her and these two young men. I was so mad that I just went straight into the kitchen and slammed the door. . . . About fifteen minutes later my mother came into the kitchen waving her arms and dancing around saying, "I've found it, I've found it! I've found what I've been looking for and they're coming back to teach your father tonight."

Although I was rebellious at that time . . . and was determined not to join, I'm so grateful I promised my mother I would. She lived only ten months after she was baptized.

Neal's growing sense of kinship with the members in Canada also nourished his feelings of belonging with his ward back home. As he wrote with appreciation to the Wandamere Ward during his early missionary months, he perhaps unconsciously reflected the influence of his intense scripture study in his choice of words—and some hints of a unique style of gospel prose that was barely beginning to develop:

May I take this opportunity to thank all of you for the splendid treatment you accorded me in divers manners before my leaving for Work in a part of God's vineyard. . . . I have grown to love this work. . . . I have but sipped the cup of joy. . . . But to compete against the Satanic opposition [has made it] necessary to "Put On the Whole Armor of God." . . .

May we realize that to appreciate the Eternal Life that is ahead of Us it was necessary that We come here and Partake of the Bread of Adversity so readily proffered one in Mortal Existence.

Another sample of Neal's early efforts to find the distinctive voice of his gospel language occurred in an earnest letter he wrote to Clarence and Emma when he learned that his mother was expecting a baby (Kathy) at a relatively late age:

It gave me a great thrill to know that you are allowing

another of God's spirit children a privileged spot on this earth, an earth peopled for the most part by unrighteous and decaying people, leaving Father Elohim little opportunity for placement of his chosen spirits. . . . Many in Zion will say "all is well" and complacency shall reign over many, thus your willingness and self sacrifice, tho perhaps it leaves the confines of conventionalism, is pioneering in 1947, your labors with past spirits has been recognized by the Most High. . . . I have long prayed that you both might be permitted to tarry on this side of the veil til your task . . . was done and all the children firmly grounded in the gospel.

As Neal's associations with the Canadian members multiplied over time, he felt great empathy for their circumstances. Once he returned to Utah, the modest Maxwell home became a refuge for anyone from his mission who came to Salt Lake City. In 1949, Neal helped organize "Samaras," a lively group of returned Canadian missionaries that would endure more than fifty years. Samaras sponsored missionary reunions and other events, and it helped fund missionaries' travel to and from their mission. Its first major project was what Colleen called a "big production" to help Church members travel from Ontario and Quebec to Salt Lake City to visit the temple, because no other temple was any more accessible to them.

Neal not only arranged buses and raised funds for this trip but was so anxious to have the Eastern Canadian Saints feel close to the Church's leaders that he invited President J. Reuben Clark of the First Presidency to speak to them at a small fireside. President Clark met with Neal long enough to reprove him gently. He worried about the risk and expense of such long-distance temple trips, and he didn't want to encourage more trips by speaking to the group.

Undaunted, Neal approached Elder John A. Widtsoe, whose books he had so thoroughly devoured during his mission. Elder Widtsoe accepted. When Neal drove by to pick him up for the fireside, the Apostle was sitting in a swing on his front porch, waiting. "I was not late; he was early. As I helped him into the car, he gave me a brown sack which included a warm, fresh loaf of brown bread his wife, Leah, had just baked. He wanted me to have it, though we had never met before." And as they drove, Neal enjoyed asking him doctrinal questions.

This small act of kindness touched Neal, who recounted the experience at the inauguration of the John A. Widtsoe Chair in Chemistry at the University of Utah in 1995. He had already admired how Elder Widtsoe's writings "let his ideas have a life of their own." Then this glimpse of Elder Widtsoe's personality drew Neal to him. He was a role model in more than his gospel scholarship. "The more I see of life," Neal said, "the more I admire individuals in whom there is a combination of brightness and sweetness and of goodness and gentleness. Such were delightfully combined in John Andreas Widtsoe."

Neal Maxwell's mission accelerated his discipleship in a natural sequence. He had felt some deep but unnamed spiritual stirrings during his childhood and on Okinawa. Yet he was still so young, lacking real understanding of the gospel and the Church's place in the world. His mission opened the eyes of his understanding, explaining and confirming his earlier spiritual impressions with the added witnesses of reason and experience.

When Neal finished his mission, President Floyed Eyre wrote Neal's bishop on January 22, 1949: "He has with rare ability put forth unstinted effort to spread the great message of truth that has been vouchsafed to him." Then he added a handwritten postscript, which the bishop showed to Neal. Neal would later cite—without quoting it—this expression of confidence as a good example of how leaders who give specific, sincere praise can provide needed motivation and affirmation. "It took President Eyre thirty seconds to write this," Neal would say, "but it gave me encouragement for fifty years: 'Dear Bishop, Elder Maxwell is in my humble knowledge the top missionary I have yet had. Congratulations to your ward and his home.'"

Part VI

University Student

SEVENTEEN

A POSTWAR
STUDENT'S LIFE

B Y 1949, NEAL WAS LIKE A SPIRITED RACEHORSE, pawing the earth, raring a little, feeling overdue to get on with the race. The war was over, his mission was behind him, and at age twenty-three he had finally enrolled at the University of Utah. But now, ready to run, with a full life ahead of him, much of his agenda was a blank slate. He had taken no college classes, he had no clear ideas about a major or a career, and he had left no sweetheart waiting back home. Though mature for a college freshman, in some ways he remained impressionable and unformed.

Neal's uncertainty about a career choice didn't slow his intense college pace—he rushed through a four-year program of eleven straight quarters in three calendar years with no summer breaks. Having long since abandoned his boyhood notion of becoming a veterinarian, he at first leaned toward education. Then his interest in government pulled him to a political science major with a Russian minor. With the Soviet Union emerging as a threat to democracy, his instincts were drawing him toward some new kind of front lines.

Neal Maxwell's attitude and his pace weren't that unusual among the millions of veterans who flooded the nation's campuses after the war. Those of the "greatest generation" were motivated by a no-nonsense hunger for higher education. They were ready to move on, wanting better lives than the ones they remembered from their childhood years during the Depression.

Fortunately, a grateful nation matched their commitment with one of its own—an unprecedented educational investment called the Servicemen's Readjustment Act of 1944—the GI Bill of Rights. The GI Bill provided a veteran like Neal with full tuition plus seventy-five dollars a month expense money, so long as the student stayed enrolled in higher education. With this support, the number of enrollments in colleges and universities in the United States jumped from 1.7 million in 1945 to 2.4 million in 1948. Nearly 8 million veterans would use the Bill to enroll in some kind of educational program.

The GI Bill transformed American society by making higher education the key to upward mobility for average citizens rather than a prize for the elite few. Previously, it was common for a family to share one bathroom, heat their home with coal, wash their clothes on scrub boards, and use iceboxes as refrigerators. Most people rarely ate in restaurants, dances were the entertainment of choice, and ice cream was the favorite treat. In wartime even that was rationed.

After 1945, however, the nation shifted its vast war production energy to the private sector. This move was accompanied by "a spirit of confidence never experienced before. Americans felt they could literally do anything." Most people wanted their own car, their own home, and a higher standard of living. The ticket to all of this was a college education, and the GI Bill put that ticket within popular reach, making "trained minds, rather than land or minerals, America's most important resource." Thus began "the shift to the knowledge society" of today, launching the entire modern "postcapitalist society." This was such a major shift that management expert Peter Drucker believes "future historians may consider it the most important event of the 20th century"—an economic and social transformation so large it is still in process.

This context shows not only how and why Neal and his fellow

veterans went to college but also introduces the Church's own postwar educational and cultural transformation. Reflecting the same economic and social patterns that would sweep the country, the creation of a knowledge-based society would produce a more educated Church, as new thousands of Latter-day Saints in the United States went to college during the middle and later decades of the 1900s.

When Neal became Church commissioner of education in 1970, he illustrated, and in some ways personified, this generation of Church members. Like so many others, he came from modest origins, gaining far more education than his parents had enjoyed. His parents valued education, but college just hadn't been possible for them. As a student Neal also worked his own way through the conflicts that education can create between the sacred and the secular.

Symbolizing the postwar era, Neal took many of his classes in military barracks, which the government had simply given to the University of Utah. He "sat in old, wooden army chairs—carefully stenciled with obsolete unit numbers—for most of [his] political science classes. In one room, they turned on the light bulbs by hanging pieces of string." Fifty years later, he would contrast these chairs with an expensive endowed "chair" the university named in his honor.

He didn't consider himself much of a student, even though he graduated with honors. Typically, he didn't study beyond the essentials needed to prepare for tests. He enjoyed reading books but mostly when the book caught his high interest in politics and public affairs. In that field, he invested himself enough that Professor G. Homer Durham, his political science mentor, who went on to an impressive career in higher education, could tell a national scholarship committee that of the "thousands of undergraduate students" he had known, he placed Neal "No. 1 for a National Convention Fellowship."

Neal also dabbled in a variety of extracurricular interests, most of them drawing on his growing skill as a writer and a commentator on public issues. In a creative-writing class in English, Professor Clarice Short gave him a left-handed compliment by asking if he had plagiarized a short story he wrote for her. When she realized that the story was his own work, she encouraged him to write for the school's literary magazine. He made a few efforts, curious to continue his exploration with writing, but he was "in too big a hurry to do much."

His published stories drew on his wartime experience, using familiar images from his Okinawa experience—like wounded soldiers falling down and not getting up. He also experimented with the rhetorical devices that would mark his later writing. One story began, "A sooty, sweaty hand clawed into the dirt. Its turgid tendons surfaced in response to the throaty cry, 'Hang On!' . . . The body lurched backwards in silent agony and then bounced down the precipitous hill. Behind rolled a clattering steel helmet like a dog looking for its master." The story probes how little the average person understands what war is really like.

Homer Durham found Neal a job moderating a weekly program on public issues aired by the university's educational radio station, KUER. Neal welcomed the income of twelve dollars and fifty cents a week, and he felt challenged by the spontaneity of live interviews with such public figures as Utah governor J. Bracken Lee, Senator Wallace F. Bennett of Utah, and Senator Paul Douglas of Illinois. He began his broadcasts with a recorded "ominous voice" that stated, "It is out of the collision of opinions that the whole truth can be found." This was the forerunner to Neal's later interview show *Tell Me* on KUED, the university's television station.

His relish for creative writing and current issues also drew him into writing and producing skits for Delta Phi, the fraternity for returned missionaries, which he preferred over the traditional campus fraternities. Along with Oscar McConkie, this crowd included Web Adams, a friend from the Canadian Mission; Douglas Parker, later a law professor at the University of Colorado and then at Brigham Young University; and Truman Madsen, later a teacher of religion and philosophy at BYU.

Neal and Web became known on campus for their satirical political skits, presented at student assemblies for homecoming and other events. One skit, performed in Kingsbury Hall, portrayed a tight-fisted Utah governor J. Bracken Lee sliding by the university on roller skates, tossing out a few paltry coins for the school's budget. A lighthearted performance at BYU parodying the extremes of missionary life brought down the house with laughter at a gathering of returned missionaries. Neal was very "fun loving" then, but his friends also noticed his impatience. Awaiting their turn to perform, Neal would be "agitated [and] looking at his watch. He wasn't a slow-moving, patient guy."

Corene Cowan, who later married Doug Parker, dated Neal a few times. She found him uninterested in typical dates such as movies and dancing. He preferred walks and study groups, where they could talk about ideas. Not always so serious, their "most outrageous and memorable" time was with Web Adams and his date. The four went to a dance at BYU, where the girls were surprised to see Web and Neal suddenly appear in one of their comic skits as the official floor show.

As his membership in Delta Phi suggests, Neal preferred to avoid the "higher spheres" of campus social status, as viewed by those in the fraternities and sororities. Oscar, who came from Salt Lake's urbane East High, thought Neal "unnecessarily insecure" about his Granite High and agriculture background. But Neal enjoyed his mildly iconoclastic role, which let him poke occasional holes in the pretense he sensed among some campus socialites. He managed Rick Clayton's successful campaign for student body president, after the "East High crowd" had dominated student government for years. Neal wasn't really interested in student government, being motivated more by "audacity and vanity." Mostly, he was intrigued "just to see if [we] could beat the Greek crowd."

Neal had the reputation among his campus friends of having been a good missionary in Canada. He organized a study group, in which he would often end up leading gospel discussions. "An incredible conversationalist," he "kind of took control" of discussions in an inoffensive way, just by being informed as well as having a clever way of expressing ideas.

He was only one of an interesting group of young believers in the gospel who enjoyed growing together on the campus. Doug Parker didn't see him then as one necessarily marked for some unusual future contribution. Rather, Neal's life shows "how it takes thirty years of slow, incremental spiritual and character growth—to become what you are" later. "You're not that way, full blown," when you're young. Neal, like others, went from experience to experience and "took with him those qualities he possessed, and as he did, [those qualities] blossomed and flowered."

EIGHTEEN

INTELLECTUAL AWAKENING AND MENTORING

A SIDE FROM MARRYING COLLEEN HINCKLEY, the most important development in Neal's university life was the igniting and shaping of his intellectual interests and attitudes through his political science classes and his association with Homer Durham.

Neal found most of his university classes not all that exciting. His teachers ran the complete spectrum from brilliant agnostics to sedate religious believers. He was eventually drawn most to professors Francis Wormuth and Homer Durham, the founding fathers of the U's political science department, which was once in the history department. As department chairman, Durham had hired Wormuth, a gifted teacher whose views generally opposed Durham's. That opposition both fascinated and benefited Neal. Wormuth was a skeptic about both religion and politics, but he was well-read and incisive. He once reportedly said, "There are only two geniuses amongst us [Utah thinkers]—myself and Hugh Nibley." Neal at times found himself dazzled by Wormuth's intelligence, especially when Wormuth's views challenged Neal's own intuitions and beliefs.

President J. Reuben Clark startled Neal in 1952 by agreeing with

Wormuth on the important postwar issue of U.S. isolationism. The occasion was a campus lecture sponsored by the political science department, with Neal as a member of the student planning committee. President Clark gave a thoughtful address, later published, in which he described himself as a "thoroughgoing isolationist." He had previously enjoyed a distinguished career in the State Department, including service as ambassador to Mexico. Other than their coincidental agreement that the United States should avoid foreign entanglements, President Clark and Professor Wormuth had little in common.

Neal was unsettled. He disagreed with both of them, and that pushed him to clarify his own thinking. He had returned from the war convinced that the United States had made a major contribution in helping to win the war, preserving democracy, and establishing itself as the leader of the free world. His penchant for engagement, which his commitment to the infantry had illustrated, probably influenced him as well. If he saw a political problem looming over some distant horizon, his visceral urge was to go deal with it. As the years have gone by, Neal has sensed that on many issues he was moving more and more toward President Clark's viewpoints. But he wasn't there in 1952. It comforted him then to know that when President Clark had taken the same isolationist position against the League of Nations in 1919, Church President Heber J. Grant, speaking "as an individual," had said he favored the League.

Neal also felt discomfort in April 1951, when he confronted the opposing views involved in President Harry S Truman's decision to fire one of the nation's most admired World War II heroes, General Douglas MacArthur, who was commander of United States and United Nations forces during the Korean War. Truman was a Democrat, and Neal's leanings, like those of his parents, had been toward the Republicans on most issues. He still remembers being one of only a few children in his public school to declare themselves in a straw poll for Republican Alf Landon for president of the United States in 1936, when Democrat Franklin D. Roosevelt was the overwhelming choice of almost everyone else—in the nation as well as in Neal's classroom.

In addition, most Americans saw MacArthur as a soldier's soldier

G. Homer Durham, a political science professor and mentor to Neal, with colleagues in the political science department; back row: Neal (far right) and good friend Ralph Mecham (far left)

and a hero's hero. One historian thought this general "may have been the most brilliant commander in the country's history." Neal hadn't forgotten the thrill he felt when he learned that MacArthur had kept his promise ("I shall return") in retaking the Philippines. He also remembered the patriotic pride he felt the day a friend took his picture next to MacArthur's limousine in Japan.

President Truman had been trying to negotiate a settlement with the Chinese to end the Korean conflict, even as MacArthur was urging the strategic bombing of China. After an intense struggle over their differences, MacArthur publicly threatened to attack China, directly disobeying Truman's orders that MacArthur remain silent. That did it for Truman. Despite MacArthur's 69 percent popularity ratings, the president fired him to preserve civilian control.

Neal and a few other students huddled with Homer Durham in his tiny office in the old Fort Douglas Surplus Building, listening by radio to MacArthur's farewell speech to Congress. Thirty million other Americans listened as well. Neal felt the emotion as MacArthur closed, "his voice dropping as he began the famous last lines . . . 'Old soldiers never die. They just fade away.' And like the old soldier of the ballad,

I now close my military career and just fade away—an old soldier who tried to do his duty."

Fifty years later, Neal recalled that some Congressmen were so stirred by MacArthur's speech that one Democratic senator said, "If he'd spoken another twenty minutes, I'd have marched on the White House myself!" But Neal also admired how Georgia Democratic senator Richard Russell thoughtfully directed the ensuing Congressional hearings, diverting the emotion and restoring confidence in the constitutional principle of civilian control of the military.

When the emotion subsided, Neal decided that Truman was right, as a matter of constitutional doctrine. He admired Truman's courage and integrity, and he was disappointed in MacArthur, feeling that while his "place in history will be rightfully generous . . . his bravery was, on occasion, matched by his vanity."

The events with President Clark and President Truman were part of a process that helped Neal think through his own philosophy. He found that his views depended more on particular issues than on party affiliation. This approach was also shaped by the close relationship he developed with Homer Durham, whose student Douglas Alder said, "I couldn't figure out if he was a Republican or a Democrat." Alder had never heard anyone deal with Franklin D. Roosevelt in such an "objective manner" as Durham did. That stunned him, because in his world, nobody had much "good to say about FDR." Durham's approach intentionally pushed his students to form their own views in responsible ways.

Homer Durham often invited students to his home for evenings of serious conversation. Sometimes a little austere, he had the reputation of not suffering fools gladly, not seeming very tolerant of those who didn't think as fast as he did. He was also not one for small talk. Neal picked up some of these attitudes himself in his early years, perhaps because he found it stimulating to try and think as fast as Durham did, and he enjoyed Durham's substantive discussion of ideas. He also found that his mentor would "go to the wall" to help his students find good professional positions—an attitude that benefited Neal on several future occasions.

Neal would later acknowledge with gratitude that he was "one of Homer's boys." In addition to admiring Durham's quest for intellectual rigor, Neal came to appreciate his attitude toward public service as an ethical dimension in political science. And he was especially blessed to discover that, along with everything else, his mentor's life reflected a sometimes understated but deeply real commitment to the gospel of Jesus Christ.

In 1987, Brigham Young University created a G. Homer Durham Lectureship, encouraged by two more of "Homer's boys," L. Ralph Mecham and Martin B. Hickman, who was then a dean in the social sciences at BYU. On that occasion, Neal would comment on Durham as a role "model for professional public servants," because he was "wise, good, and honest" (see D&C 98:10), in contrast with many modern civil servants "who are barely civil." He recalled how Durham quietly blended his religious faith with his commitment to public service, serving "family, friends, neighbors and others" in ways that would prepare them for eternity, "along with serving them here and now." "For all the diplomas Durham signed," Neal was especially glad that Homer's mentoring marked Neal with his "spiritual signature."

Neal's tutorial relationship with Homer Durham illustrates some key mentoring relationships among Latter-day Saint educational leaders in the twentieth century. In these relationships, each master modeled for his apprentice how to reconcile the competing demands between the spirit and the intellect, teaching by example how to contribute to the world without becoming worldly. That modeling was part of the genius and purpose of the Church schools, not just for the leaders but for all students and all teachers.

To begin with, Karl G. Maeser was the "founding father" of Church education, having tutored Brigham Young's children before being sent to start BYU in 1876. Karl Maeser later oversaw all Church schools, assisted by an examining board that included James E. Talmage and Joseph Tanner, whom Maeser had mentored at BYU. When Talmage was later president of the University of Utah in the early 1900s, his research assistant was J. Reuben Clark, who went on to Columbia Law School and then worked in the U.S. State Department.

Then James E. Talmage was called to the Quorum of the Twelve Apostles. Meanwhile, Joseph Tanner went to Utah State University, where he found a promising young scholar named John A. Widtsoe, whom he encouraged to attend Harvard to study chemistry and then return to Utah.

Over the next generation, J. Reuben Clark became a member of the First Presidency and mentored a young stake president named Harold B. Lee in developing the Church Welfare Plan. During that same era, John A. Widtsoe became president of Utah State University and then the University of Utah, before being called to the Twelve. Elder Widtsoe knew and influenced young Homer Durham, who later became Neal Maxwell's mentor. In addition, Harold B. Lee later tutored Neal Maxwell before recommending him as commissioner of education in 1970. Neal would in turn mentor future Apostles Dallin H. Oaks, Jeffrey R. Holland, and Henry B. Eyring as key leaders in the Church Educational System.

These close teacher-student relationships illustrate the natural process by which several generations of Church leaders have passed along to leaders they helped select for the next generation a shared vision about educating both the mind and the heart. Many other teachers and leaders in Church education during these years similarly found their own mentors and role models—discovering, as Neal did from Homer Durham, that for all students, example is the best teacher. Having been well mentored as a student, Neal Maxwell would thus know why and how to mentor others when his turn came.

NINETEEN

CONNECTING THE SECULAR AND THE SACRED

Neal's college years gave him experience with a new and significant converging of secular and sacred ideas. Until this time, the "Church track" and the "educational track" in his life had run parallel to each other. Now the two tracks began coming together. As he delved into political theory, for instance, he just couldn't see that field in a complete way without including the gospel's teachings about man's nature and about government. Before long, Neal "didn't see how one could go on in secular education and not pay attention to what the gospel teaches" about every relevant topic and issue.

He welcomed this time of engagement between the secular and the religious, even though he knew that some people feared it. For him, it was simply natural to look for ways "to connect gospel principles with my secular learning." It helped that his most basic spiritual questions had been settled by his experience from childhood through his years as a soldier and as a missionary.

As he faced the philosophical puzzles of university life, then, he felt "a special zest of trying to connect secular learning with gospel learning." Based on his prior experience, he now "assumed a connection" with the gospel "could be made." It no longer seemed to him a serious alternative that the gospel "wouldn't connect, or that if it didn't, there would [not] be a preeminence for spiritual things." As his college experience reaffirmed this basic attitude, instead of threatening his faith, Neal's education gave him "more confidence in the capacity of the gospel to respond to the human condition."

All of the people described in Neal's heritage of mentors shared a primary commitment to the religious life. Still, in practice, not all of them would have approached the issues of the day in the same way Neal eventually did. Some, like Homer Durham, spent their professional lives in state schools, where church-state separation constrained them from developing many written or publicly spoken attempts at treating secular problems in the light of gospel teachings—or vice versa. In that sense, Neal would later feel much greater academic freedom as the Church's commissioner of education than he ever felt at the University of Utah, because he was more free to articulate the active integration he felt personally between the sacred and the secular.

Others, such as J. Reuben Clark, simply had a different attitude about actively integrating secular and religious issues. President Clark was personally more comfortable maintaining something of a separation between his professional and religious worlds, even though he used his ample scholarly tools in both places and his profound religious depth prevailed in all he did. Perhaps President Clark's views about isolationism between the interests of the United States and international needs also reflected his instinctive preference for maintaining an internal boundary between faith and reason—while Neal's irrepressible urge to engage possible conflicts made him less concerned about boundaries.

Neal would later find affirmation for his proactive integration in the approach of his closest spiritual mentor, Harold B. Lee. Indeed, that might have been part of what drew Elder Lee to Neal when they first became acquainted. From the time of his call as an Apostle in 1941, Elder Lee had sought to achieve "the learning of all wisdom and intelligence from the scriptures, and the learning of all secular knowledge. . . . [Said Neal about Elder Lee:] 'Being secure spiritually and intellectually he could be eclectic in gathering [secular] ideas, concepts, and truths which would be helpful to the work of the kingdom.'" Elder Lee and Neal Maxwell had both established their spiritual moorings before reaching out, as they did, for secular perspectives. And both tended to evaluate secular matters in the light of the gospel, rather than vice versa.

Other University of Utah friends reinforced Neal's outlook. One of these was Henry Eyring (the father of Apostle Henry B. Eyring), whom Neal regarded as "the most distinguished Mormon scientist of this dispensation." Dr. Eyring shared Neal's basic stance: "Since he felt that all truth comes from God, and since he knew that God refused to require him to believe anything that was not true, Henry had a very large view of truth, sparing him the unnecessary conflicts and contortions which some have." Another friend was Russell Nelson, a renowned cardiac surgeon at the U of U Medical School who would later join Neal in the Twelve. Russell said, "Many years ago a medical colleague chastised me for failing to separate my professional knowledge from my religious convictions. That startled me because I did not feel that truth should be fractionalized. Truth is indivisible."

Neal never worried that the findings of science or other disciplines would challenge the gospel, because he always believed, and then his experience consistently confirmed, that "the lessons from secular history buttress gospel principles" more than they challenge them. Thus, for him, every dimension of "the gospel is relevant to every social problem."

So Neal felt sorry for those who were too suspicious of, or too trusting in, reason and intellect. He saw some people have real crises in their faith when they were unable to understand some difficult human experience. They may have found that it eroded their faith to try to reason their way through what is essentially an unreasonable experience, yet the greatest religious tests often require sacrifices that go well beyond reason. Some of them would then decide not to use reason at all in considering religious experience, in order to avoid the risk of floundering over the limits to reason's powers. Ironically, the fears that fuel this position may arise not from placing too little trust in reason but too much. Neal had a more tolerant approach:

> In my own education . . . I found that the basic gospel truths . . .
> could be harmonized with the great secular truths. [And] those
> gospel truths which, for the moment, could not be harmonized
> could . . . be regarded expectantly, for, ultimately, all truths
> belong to the gospel. Not all theories . . . but all truths. To so
> realize was an emancipating feeling then, and is now, for the
> feeling has never diminished, only increased.

As he told one group of students, "The Lord sees no conflict
between faith and learning in a broad curriculum. [See D&C 88:78–79,
118.] . . . The scriptures see faith and learning as mutually facilitating,
not separate processes. Robert Frost's line, 'Something there is that
doesn't love a wall,' is applicable regarding a wall between mind and
spirit."

Neal's view on this subject, from its beginnings in his student days
to its maturity later on, was never a generic attitude of simply balancing faith and reason. Nor did he think it sufficient simply to integrate
the two realms indiscriminately, as if they were of equal importance.
Further, he always sensed the risks of unwise integration that allowed
an academic discipline to judge the gospel or the Church, knowing that,
as one student said, "there is a danger that use of scholarly tools—which
requires the privileging of those tools—will breed habits of mind that
reflexively privilege secular scholarship over the gospel."

From the first time he heard them teach in some of his university
classes, Neal was always dismayed by Latter-day Saint professionals
who let their disciplines take priority over their understanding of the
gospel. He would later express concern about teachers who "fondle their
doubts" or "conceal their doubt of doubt" in the presence of Latter-day
Saint students who were looking for spiritual mentoring. Neal was also
disappointed in Latter-day Saints who remained "anti-intellectual
about the gospel." He thought it ironic when someone couldn't see "the
intellectual depth of the gospel," let alone its full spiritual dimensions,
because they measured everything with the limited tools of their academic disciplines.

Neal's approach to integration, then, looked at all knowledge
through the gospel's lens. He found that he could integrate a secular

map of reality into the broader religious map, but the smaller secular map, with its more limited tools and framework, often wasn't large enough to include religious insights. Thus the gospel's larger perspective influenced his view of the academic disciplines more than the disciplines influenced his view of the gospel.

Elder Cecil Samuelson has noticed, for example, that "early on [Neal] developed a notion that the gospel encompasses all truth." So "he will pick up a Steven Hawking article about theoretical physics and think about ties to the book of Abraham. Or he will think about Churchill's role in preserving the freedom of the world" so the Church could continue teaching the Restoration. He believes that "faith and learning are symbiotic [and that] any apparent inconsistencies between gospel verities and scientific truth are the result of incomplete or inappropriately interpreted data. When a matter remains unresolved, he shows the same restraint employed by Alma: 'Now these mysteries are not yet fully made known unto me; therefore I shall forbear' (Alma 37:11)."

Neal also came to wish that those of other religious faiths could know more about the Book of Mormon—not just to prove the book is true but to see the Restoration's witness of Christ, so that "a confused mankind can have certitude about the . . . reality of the resurrection." For him, the insights of the Restoration not only held up under scrutiny but they increasingly hold up a Christianity threatened by higher criticism of the Bible and endless other attacks.

As a college student, Neal also enjoyed discovering that George Washington and James Madison both called the drafting of the Constitution "a miracle." For Neal, only divine intervention would explain why there would have been "so many bright minds together in a small country at the same time." Arthur M. Schlesinger thought the Founding Fathers were "the most remarkable generation of public men in the history of the United States or perhaps of any other nation." Historian Barbara Tuchman wondered aloud, "It would be invaluable if we could know what produced this burst of talent from a base of only two and a half million inhabitants." When he read that, Neal wanted Tuchman to know that God had "established the Constitution of this land, by the hands of wise men whom [he] raised up unto this very purpose" (D&C 101:80).

Similarly, Neal's understanding of early Christian apostasy illuminated his university courses on the Greek philosophers—and vice versa. He drew on this background when he gave a conference talk on the Apostasy, explaining how obvious it is that Greek philosophy distorted early Christian teachings rather than "some misguided monk in a monastery making things up."

Neal's early interest in sacred-secular convergence also prepared him to welcome the writings of C. S. Lewis, a gifted British champion of Christianity who wrote during Neal's early years, critiquing modern secularism with unusual skill. Neal first read *The Screwtape Letters* in the 1950s, soon followed by other Lewis works. He admired and would later emulate the way Lewis's writing style reached the common reader with uncommon religious insight.

In 1960, he sent Lewis a letter of gratitude—accompanied by a copy of the Book of Mormon: "May I express my deep appreciation for your contribution to literature and Christianity through your excellent writings." Your work has "held special pleasure for me. Perhaps you do not realize that you have acquired quite a following in this area of America" in recent years. He explained the Book of Mormon only briefly, adding that his gratitude for Lewis's work "is not conditioned upon your appreciation of this Book." Rather, "my sending it to you represents an effort to share with you some of the things that have brought me satisfaction as a token of the appreciation I feel for your writings."

Along with Neal's discoveries about secular and religious learning, his attitudes toward institutions—including the Church—also developed during his student years. His tendency toward what he called his "institutional chafing" had earlier made him impatient about the quality of classes and meetings in his home ward, about the United States military bureaucracy, about waiting for his bishop to approach him with a mission call, or about missionary teaching resources. Part of Neal's chafing came from his inborn impatience. "I thought, All right, Heavenly Father, if I've got to be more patient, let's get it over with right now."

One example of this attitude was that he thought it wasn't worth the time to attend the university commencement where he would have been awarded his diploma, so he just skipped it and waited for the diploma to be mailed. Colleen has since joked that it was poetic justice when he later had to attend many commencement ceremonies as a university administrator in both the state and Church educational systems. He felt the same way about such formal affairs as wedding receptions, though he was a good sport about his and Colleen's own wedding reception. He felt more justified in his attitude when he found that C. S. Lewis thought that attending receptions is like reading the first page of a hundred different books. He has told his family that someone should create a conveyor belt that keeps reception lines moving, giving each person only 3.7 seconds to speak with the bride and groom.

Young Neal also needed to work on his attitude toward sacrament meetings. He had come alive with his excitement for fresh gospel teachings, both as a missionary and from his discovery as a student that the gospel could illuminate so many other issues. With his engine running in such high gear, he sometimes found it frustrating, or perhaps a little boring, to sit through classes and meetings that fell short of what he thought the gospel really had to say. As a result, when a sacrament meeting seemed to drag a little, Neal, sitting in the congregation, would quietly pull out his scriptures and start reading about some topic that held his interest more.

Once more, Matthew Cowley rescued him. Earlier, without knowing any of Neal's tendencies, Elder Cowley had cautioned him in a blessing to avoid political discussions during his mission. When Elder Cowley later performed Neal and Colleen's marriage, still without any reason to know Neal's attitudes and habits, Elder Cowley counseled the young couple to pay attention in their sacrament and other meetings "whether you like the quality of the speakers or not." Neal felt appropriately chastised: "When you get that kind of laser-like precision, you know you're dealing with somebody with apostolic powers."

He didn't forget this mild but inspired rebuke. It was still with him when he was asked to write an article for the *Ensign* about President Spencer W. Kimball after President Kimball's death in 1985. Among all the things he might have chosen to quote from President Kimball's writings, Neal felt to include this: "We do not go to Sabbath meetings to be entertained or even solely to be instructed. We go to worship the Lord. If the service is a failure to you, you have failed. No one can worship for you; you must do your own waiting upon the Lord."

Another provocative student-era example of Neal's institutional chafing was the visit he and a friend requested with Elder Harold B. Lee of the Twelve. This was the first time he and Elder Lee ever met, and neither could have imagined how closely they would one day work together. The two university students just wanted Elder Lee to know how disappointed they were with the quality of instructional manuals the students were finding in their Sunday School and other classes. Neal was audacious but earnestly sincere. Later on he could hardly believe he had been so bold. Elder Lee "was very nice to listen to this young punk who was telling him what ought to be done."

This small incident was important to Neal, though in retrospect he thought the nature of his concern hardly justified taking Elder Lee's time. It was natural to him to make such an approach, partly because the Church was much smaller then and partly because he'd seen his father approach the Brethren with those early letters. Besides, his concerns were honest, faithful ones. He really felt that the gospel was much richer than what he saw many Church teachers presenting. Elder Lee's attitude signaled to Neal that Church leaders will listen, and should listen, to faithful questions. That attitude not only helped Neal develop a desire to work within the system but would also later make him want to listen closely to others who had concerns like his.

Toward the end of Neal's student time at the university, he experienced another incident that made him chafe a little. He and Colleen, just married, were struggling for every dollar. They had no car and not much else. Their bishop, in a typical request for the times, assigned them to contribute funds to help buy a stake welfare farm south of Salt Lake City. They swallowed hard and paid their share, but privately Neal was murmuring. He thought the farm was "a perfectly abysmal place, where you couldn't grow anything." He couldn't understand why busy Latter-day Saints should go "hoe rocks and sagebrush," unless as a general "test of obedience" rather than to "feed the poor." He later felt the same way when their stake in Washington, D.C., bought a dairy farm outside the city. The farm later became part of Dulles Airport, so at least, Neal thought, the Church got a good return on its investment.

He recalled these incidents later as a member of a General Welfare Committee subgroup, chaired by then-Elder Thomas S. Monson. The subgroup recommended that the Church sell many of its stake welfare farms, because it was more efficient to feed the poor in other ways. Their group asked the general committee if the members' working on those farms was really central to the welfare program or if welfare was concerned primarily with efficiently feeding the poor, urging members to avoid debt, and encouraging adequate protection against possible calamities. When the general committee agreed with them, Neal felt vindicated.

His early tendency toward institutional chafing reveals a part of his personality that he has continued to work on. Even though Elder Maxwell has learned to discipline his impatience, Elder Jeffrey R. Holland thinks it hasn't always been easy for him to work within the sometimes laborious institutional process of central Church administration. "He's so bright and able, a kind of free spirit—in the sense that he knows where he wants to go and how to get things done." So to work proposals through "a big group" in "a process that has review after review has probably been a little nerve-wracking to Neal over the years. . . . But he's handled it well." Experience taught Neal the value of holding his tongue until the right time and place, rather than just complaining and running for cover.

PART VII

COLLEEN

TWENTY

EARLY LIFE

CLARENCE, NEAL'S FATHER, was probably the most formative religious influence in his early years. Later on Neal would be guided by the wise and attentive mentoring of Harold B. Lee, N. Eldon Tanner, Marion G. Romney, and Spencer W. Kimball. But in the shaping of his spiritual life's most personal and subtle dimensions, no human hand has left a more enduring touch than Colleen's.

In this day of "tell it all" investigative reporting, a person like Colleen poses a problem for a biographer who wants at least to present her as she really is, with no sugar coating. But Corene Parker, a fair-minded observer who has known Neal and Colleen since their college days, says Colleen has simply always been "the same considerate, other-regarding person that she is now—wholesome and delightful." Corene knows that such assessments are "always questioned in public life," but that's just how Colleen was—and is. And this understanding of her nature is necessary to understand Neal's own growth.

Though Neal didn't know Gordon B. Hinckley until many years after he had married Colleen, President Hinckley is a first cousin to Colleen's father, George Hinckley. President Hinckley describes

Colleen as "a very able woman. She's done wonders for Neal, and he'd be the first to give her credit." President James E. Faust sees in Colleen "a certain resilience and strength beyond that softness and kindness which she has. She is sometimes a restraining influence" for Neal. "She's perfect for him."

Elder Dallin H. Oaks, who has been unusually close to the Maxwells for thirty years, believes that Colleen's "influence on him is profound." She is "a very gentle person on the exterior," but "he values [her influence] very highly and speaks of it with reverence and appreciation." Reflecting her own lifelong instincts to reach for those whose lives ache for encouragement, she has almost unintentionally nurtured the development of Neal's personal ministry to individuals. Elder Oaks found that this kind of compassion was more inborn with her than it was with him. "I didn't see that in him much when he was Commissioner [of Church Education in the early 1970s], but now it's pervasive."

Adds Elder Jeffrey R. Holland, Colleen is "a strong woman— quiet, gentle, but strong. I think Neal has loved that. They're very much alike. I don't know who's fed whom, or whether two kindred spirits found each other already this way, but with courtesy and sensitivity," both "still have a pretty good steel rod running down their backbones." But "whatever you'd say about Neal" regarding meekness and peace-making, "you could say it in spades about Colleen. She's a wonderful mix of velvet and steel." When introducing Colleen at Brigham Young University, then-President Holland said, "I cannot help but feel that much of what your husband now is, is due in part to what you always were."

These observations from intimate friends are important to an understanding of Neal Maxwell's life story. "I don't think you could really know him without knowing her," says Elder Marlin K. Jensen. She is "responsible for much of his refinement and growth; she's given him honest feedback; shaped the kindness, the meekness, the service ethic." Colleen Hinckley was born on April 8, 1928, Easter Sunday, in Salt Lake City, the only daughter of George Hinckley (1901–1989) and

Fern Johnson (1900–1983). She has two brothers, George V. and Ed. Her lineage on both sides draws on a strong pioneer heritage.

Colleen's paternal grandfather, Lucian N. Hinckley (1862–1950), was a half-brother to Bryant Hinckley, father of President Gordon B. Hinckley. Their father was Ira N. Hinckley (1828–1904), who was born in Ontario, Canada, the province where Neal served much of his mission. Ira first heard of the Church as a child and then lost both of his parents to early deaths. At the age of fourteen, he found his way to Nauvoo, Illinois, where "he frequently heard the Prophet Joseph Smith and his brother Hyrum preach in the grove west of the site where the temple was under construction." Soon he was baptized and lived with the Saints until they left Nauvoo.

In 1850, Ira and his young wife, Eliza, left the Midwest with their baby girl to join the Saints in Zion. Only partway along the trail, Eliza died from cholera. Ira buried both Eliza and his half-brother Joel on the same day. When Colleen's father told this story, he would conclude, "And after the burial, the wagon rolled on." Rolling on in the face of adversity became a theme in Ira Hinckley's life.

After arriving in Salt Lake City, Ira married Adelaide Noble. Soon he took her sister, Angeline, as his plural wife. When he was thirty-eight, Ira accepted Brigham Young's call to move his families to what became known as Cove Fort in Millard County. There Ira took charge of constructing and then maintaining the fort, a midway stopping point on the key north-south route between Salt Lake City and St. George. In 1877, President Wilford Woodruff called Ira to preside over the Millard Stake, the newest of twenty-five stakes in the Church. He served a quarter century as stake president for a large portion of central Utah. Ira's vision and sacrifices as a pioneer leader set an enduring example for his posterity. His son Frank said of him, "I think I have never seen as good a man as he was. He preached the loudest by practice and the least by noise or talk of any man I ever knew."

Colleen, who has always felt both linked to and moved by her ancestors' pioneer spirit, kept a copy of two letters Ira sent from Fillmore to one of his sons in the mission field in the spring of 1883. Among other things, Ira wrote:

We have had a very cold winter here but most of the folks have got hay enough to feed their stock. . . . Every time it snowed it only made me happier, looking to the future for more water to grow more grass and grain. On the whole, I feel first rate. Getting so that I would not miss having some ups and downs in life to gain the experience to prepare us for the future. It is a good world we live in. . . .

My son, . . . be prayerful and watchful that the destroyer may not have power over you, for he will do his best to lead the servants of the Lord astray.

Although you have to fare hard, stand it like a man and never . . . look toward home until the servants of the Lord say it is enough.

Ira Hinckley, the farsighted optimist, saw future irrigation water in the same snow that made some others complain of the cold. Yet he was also bluntly realistic about the threats of opposition and the power of obedience. Colleen would innately reflect that same tough cheer.

Colleen's father remembered that his grandfather Ira had a passion for education, even though "in those pioneering days, some folks frowned on much learning as unnecessary and affectatious." Ira had learned from experience about "the need for manual labor," but "in his position of leadership" he could also "clearly see the great need for education." He hungered to learn more himself, to become "equal to the honors [of leadership] and their attendant responsibilities."

George had also been encouraged by the educational attitudes of his father, Lucian, and his mother, Ada. Though she had little formal schooling, Ada loved reading, read often to her children, and had books and magazines freely available around her home. She gave Colleen's parents a book of Bible stories and then wrote to them, "Do you have time to tell the children stories from the bible book? If you could tell them one every evening before they go to bed, they would always remember it, and it is sowing seeds in their minds and hearts."

The attitude that education is a valuable investment, not a wasteful expense, motivated George to earn a master's degree in chemistry at the University of Utah, even against the odds of the Great

*Colleen's parents,
George Edwin Hinckley
and Fern Johnson Hinckley*

Depression of the 1930s. As a child of the Depression, he would later always park his car a few blocks from his city destinations to save the cost of parking meters.

George worked for Utah (later American) Oil Company in a Salt Lake refinery, playing an integral role during World War II in converting the refinery to the production of fuel for airplane engines. He was later industrial relations manager for the oil company, which gave him an office in the city rather than at the refinery.

George Hinckley applied his love of learning to the gospel. He taught his ward's Gospel Doctrine class for years and, like Clarence Maxwell, loved to discuss doctrinal topics. He memorized many scriptures and a good deal of poetry. He liked gospel discussions enough that he hated to end them. Neal would say at his funeral, "When it seemed as though he had finished, he would sometimes then say, 'Actually . . .' and continue an elaboration of the point at hand." He was also steady, well-read, and gentle. He loved flowers, the earth, and the temple.

When Cory Maxwell was serving his mission in Germany, he sent home a little German doll with bushy eyebrows—which the family soon designated "Hinckley eyebrows." George and several of his male relatives were noted for "those really distinguished eyebrows."

From her earliest days, Colleen felt the embrace of the Hinckley family heritage. As a child, she accompanied her parents to Hinckley family reunions, where President Gordon B. Hinckley's father, Bryant, a well-known Latter-day Saint figure in his own right, often acted as an informal kind of patriarch for the group. Bryant would tell family stories that taught the clan what a blessing the Hinckley name was, encouraging the children to "never do anything to bring disrespect or dishonor" to the family. The sense of family belonging stirred Colleen, who felt Bryant to be a great man.

Colleen's mother, Fern Johnson Hinckley, was petite—at five-foot-three, much shorter than George at five-foot-ten. She was attractive and caring. When Fern's grandchildren thought of going to see her, the picture that came first to mind was of Grandma Hinckley putting her small hands on their upturned cheeks, kissing them, and telling them how very glad she was to see them.

Fern's paternal grandfather, William H. Johnson (1839–1911) crossed the plains with other pioneers in 1856. He and his wife, Eliza, settled in Fountain Green, near Manti. After losing a son and two grandchildren to diphtheria and finding the doctors "didn't know what to do for it," William "prayed for enlightenment." In 1884, at age forty-five, he began to study medicine. Soon he was known throughout the Sevier River valley for his success in treating both diphtheria and typhoid. He "always had a cheerful word" and "served faithfully in any case of sickness" without regard to remuneration. When he and Eliza died, the local newspaper said the "venerable pair" had been "separated by death only three weeks."

Eliza Snyder (1839–1911), who became William's wife, had been born in Canada. Her family joined the Church there and then moved to Nauvoo during her early childhood. Colleen loved hearing Fern recall her grandmother Eliza's memory of the time Joseph Smith held her on his knee and talked to her. Eliza went to live near Provo in 1851 and grew up during the time of the Walker War with the local Native American tribe. During the war, she had fearful memories of riding with her father as he often had to drive their team and wagon between the pioneer settlement and their farm. The Indians later told him they could have ambushed him and his "papoose" many times, but "he had always been kind to them and given them food, so they would not harm them."

Fern cultivated the habits and traits of her pioneer grandparents. Always knitting and sewing for her family, she made many sweaters for her grandbabies long before they arrived—in some cases even before a marriage had occurred. A favorite phrase from Fern, whenever family members ate at her home, was, "I am so glad to have my family around me." Later in life, she could rarely speak those words without tears coming to her eyes.

After Fern met Neal Maxwell the first time he arrived at the Hinckley home to pick up Colleen, her reaction was, "Well, he's a nice-looking young man. What's wrong with him?" She thought Colleen had been single long enough. As time went on, Fern and Neal developed an unusually close in-law relationship. Neal found her to be "one of the most appreciative people I have ever met. She responded so generously to the smallest act of kindness." And Fern never hesitated to tell Neal to sit down again when, in the early years of the marriage, he would habitually stand up and say they needed to be going within a few minutes of arriving for a family visit.

Just before Colleen was born, George and Fern moved from Provo to Salt Lake City, where he pursued his studies and then worked for the oil company. During most of Colleen's growing-up years, they lived on Logan Avenue near Fifteenth East. At age two, Colleen nearly died from pneumonia. She always felt that her father's priesthood blessing helped protect her life. When she was older, George gave her a father's blessing in which he blessed her to be an "advertisement for the Church in far lands," promising her that the spirit of her father and mother "shall ever attend thee."

Colleen's was an idyllic childhood. She thought the song "Over the River and through the Woods" had been made up just for her family, to accompany their frequent trips to the Chester Johnson home in Provo and the Lucian Hinckley farm home near Delta, Utah. Her grandmother Hinckley would often be waiting for them on the back step, wearing her little white night cap.

The family home in Salt Lake City was similarly warm and welcoming. George often built a fire in the fireplace, and the family would gather to enjoy homemade root beer and read scriptures or recite poetry. Even though family home evening wasn't as well established in the Church then as it became later, Colleen's warm feelings about the pattern ran deep enough that she and Neal consciously chose to cultivate a similar home atmosphere.

December 7, 1941—the day Pearl Harbor was bombed—was a traumatic day for Colleen. She has never forgotten her feelings of dread about bombs and war, which always seemed a terrible nightmare. Her family felt the effect of the war directly, because the oil company called George to stay in Chicago or New York for weeks at a time, helping to coordinate the refinery's production with the military's need for aviation fuel. The war also imposed rationing on sugar, gasoline, and even nylon stockings. Not having free access to nylons wasn't so bad for teenage Colleen, because "many of the young men of dating age were away" anyway.

Young Colleen loved life—her home, her school, the Church, and her friends. Especially her friends. Her brief personal history, written later in life, recounts that "while in Garfield [Elementary] School some of my closest friends were . . ." She then lists nine names. And a few pages later, her "good friends" at East High include a list of sixteen names, followed by "and a number of others."

Because of labor shortages brought on by the war, Colleen worked full time each summer from age fifteen onward. She spent one summer at a power sewing machine on an assembly line. Factory work opened her eyes. "It was kind of dark and dismal and you never saw the finished product—just the part you were working on." This experience prompted her to desire a college education, both for "a more stimulating vocation" and for preparation to be "a more capable wife and mother."

Colleen with her older brother, George

During one period in her late teens, Colleen became so involved in school and work activities that she stopped attending that era's equivalent of the Young Women program meetings on weekday evenings. A sensitive class adviser reached for her attention, inviting her to become more involved with the seventeen-year-old Gleaner girls. She was soon president of the class, helping to plan activities in the large Edgehill Ward building, which became a focal point for youth and ward and stake projects in the eastern part of Salt Lake Valley. She maintained those interests long enough to earn a Golden Gleaner award.

Her earning that award deserves mention mostly because of the contrast between it and Neal's Master M-Man award. Neal, whose teenage heart had rarely connected with Scouting and other Church youth activities (except basketball), was called to the Young Men's MIA General Board in 1964. At one meeting, the leaders announced that they wanted all board members to understand and exemplify the Church's youth achievement program, so they gave honorary Master M-Man awards to every board member who hadn't earned one earlier. Colleen was a little nonplussed when Neal returned home and kidded her that, after all the effort she had devoted to earning her Golden Gleaner award, they just "passed out our awards with the sack lunches."

Colleen enrolled at the University of Utah in 1945, where she enjoyed four full years—academically, socially, and spiritually. She loved learning so much that she couldn't get quite enough of most subjects. She had been drawn to homemaking as her core subject, but she followed her intellectual curiosity and energy to many other places. Neal later said she "racked up" more than fifty credit hours beyond the graduation requirements, with courses that included "everything from spring flowers of the Wasatch to Obert Tanner's philosophy class."

All that variety left Colleen well educated but without the credentials for a specific job, so she extended her coursework long enough to add a public school-teaching certification in home economics education, with an emphasis on foods and nutrition. This qualified her, as 1950 began, to accept a job teaching home economics at a high school in Thatcher, Arizona, replacing a teacher who had left at mid-year.

University social life had also appealed to Colleen's natural inclination toward friends and activities. She joined the Chi Omega sorority but eventually lost interest in the fraternity-sorority culture. Though she formed several close friendships there, the sorority life "seemed a bit superficial." And the selective nature of group membership also ran against her feeling that everyone "should be appreciated and acceptable." She felt more at home in Lambda Delta Sigma, the social group at the Latter-day Saint Institute, which had an open membership.

Colleen also took religion classes at the institute, feeling especially drawn to T. Edgar Lyon and Lowell Bennion, the humane and thoughtful institute director, who nurtured a grateful generation of students at the university. The institute gave her refuge from the socially "competitive spirit of the campus." It also exposed her to Lowell Bennion's deeply ingrained compassion, which inspired in Colleen a service ethic that would flourish in her own life from then on.

Colleen met Neal in Lowell's class in 1949. She was a senior, preparing to leave the campus and teach in a public school. He was just back from his four years in the military and his mission. Colleen noticed that Neal was a pal to Web Adams and that the two of them

Colleen in her late teens

wrote and produced funny skits for Delta Phi, the fraternity sponsored by the institute for returned missionaries. She first saw him socially at a gathering attended mostly by institute students at Steve Smoot's home. As the evening unfolded, Colleen noticed how much the other students turned to Neal with their questions about the gospel, politics, or other topics. She noticed even then his skill at drawing quiet people into the discussion and thought to herself, "Who is this guy?"

Meanwhile, Colleen was torn about a personal relationship she had been developing with another young man since junior high. They had exchanged letters during his mission, but after he returned, Colleen didn't feel quite ready to take the relationship to a more serious level. She went off to Arizona to think about it while she tried her hand as a schoolteacher.

Their correspondence continued during her months in Arizona. Interestingly, her friend kept writing "nice things" about Neal Maxwell. She had heard similar comments from others by then. So when she returned home for the summer, it was not an unpleasant surprise the day Neal called her to ask for a date. The only problem was that "he talked so fast." His approach on the phone somehow "made her feel she was number fifteen on a list of girls he'd been calling." In her version, she turned him down "just for spunk." Looking back, Colleen and Neal have somewhat different perspectives on this event. She remembers she "was impressed that he seemed to have so much charisma. People were looking to him for answers and just had a great regard for him." Then Neal adds, "So much charisma [that] she turned me down when I first asked her for a date." Fortunately for both, he called again, and this time she said yes.

It didn't take them long to overcome slight differences in their backgrounds. Neal recalls that he "was this kid from Granite High who, I'm sure, didn't dress that well and was a little disdainful of the Greek [sorority and fraternity] system. She was much more prominent socially, and her friends became my friends." For those who believed in a "class system" at the university, she "was of a different order of magnitude" than he was.

Even so, Colleen found herself increasingly drawn to him. She found him "really cute and interesting," even if he did lack just a little social polish. He didn't care for dancing and didn't like small talk, both of which were more important to other people than they were to her. He "was so knowledgeable and such a good speaker, even though he did talk fast. But if you could listen fast you could learn a lot." As Neal came to know her better, he was impressed with her maturity, her sensitivity to other people, and the depth of her spiritual convictions. He began feeling a "spiritual impetus that this was a young woman out of the ordinary."

After a few dates, Neal's irrepressible "let's get on with it" attitude began to express itself, and Colleen found herself feeling a little rushed. The first time Neal proposed marriage to her, she thought he "used so many big words . . . that [she] said yes before [she] knew what [she] was getting into." His memory is that they just walked around the block near her home, had an especially good conversation, and the shared feelings that followed led to a joint decision to marry.

Neal and Colleen at their wedding reception

Somewhere during this relatively brief courtship, Colleen decided she needed to take things into her own hands. She found herself thinking "I don't know him that well. I wonder if this is really the right thing to do." She knew that each of them had earlier felt relatively close to marriage with someone else, and those experiences probably helped them both by offering a comparative experience. So she prayed earnestly, alone, on two different occasions. Both times, "the Spirit came really strongly. . . . I think that is the most powerful witness I had. It was a confirming spirit that it was the right thing to do."

They had begun dating in July, were engaged by September, and planned to marry in December. Colleen's parents went on a couple of trips after the wedding date was first set and found each time when they returned that the wedding date had been moved up. So they decided not to take any more trips. Meanwhile, at the Maxwell house, Emma remembered, "Our first introduction to Colleen was when you came home one night and said, 'I've got to see more of that girl. She has some thinking under her hood.' It was your habit to sit on the side of our bed when you came home from a date and tell us about it. There was never anyone who compared to Colleen."

Colleen and Neal were married in the Salt Lake Temple on November 22, 1950. They weren't exactly rich in this world's goods—he was still in college, they had no car, Colleen got a teaching job at Jackson Junior High, and Neal found part-time work. They couldn't afford their own car until a few years and two children later, after they had lived in Washington, D.C., for a while. They borrowed the Hinckley family car for their honeymoon, and their first home was a basement apartment in a home near the university, the home where, coincidentally, Colleen had received her patriarchal blessing at age twelve.

TWENTY-ONE

SPEAKING THE
TRUTH IN LOVE

IT DIDN'T TAKE NEAL LONG TO REALIZE, as he put it, that he had "married up" spiritually in ways that would lift and bless him. No wonder his patriarchal blessing had told him, regarding his marriage, "your love may be without end."

Neal had his first in-depth look at Colleen's character very early. From the accumulation of such experiences at their real-life level, he would later say, "There is romantic love, and then there's the affection that's born of admiration. I have that for her too." Within the first year after the wedding, their first pregnancy ended in a miscarriage. A few months later, Colleen was expecting Becky. By the seventh month of this pregnancy, Colleen began having terrible headaches and nausea. When she lost five pounds in the last month before Becky's birth, her doctors were mystified. They gave her phenobarbital, took out her wisdom teeth, and sent her to specialists. One neurosurgeon suspected a brain tumor. In the meantime, however, they had to bring the baby to a safe landing.

Becky was born safely in February 1952. During a noon recess at the April 1952 general conference, Elder Mark E. Petersen, who was an acquaintance of Colleen's parents, joined Neal to give Colleen a blessing. In May she returned to the hospital for tests. Before the ordeal ended, Colleen had been subjected to months of spinal taps and electroencephalograms. When the indications of a brain tumor didn't materialize, the doctors finally settled on a diagnosis of viral meningitis that would eventually run itself out, which is essentially what happened.

During this drawn-out mixture of trauma and uncertainty, there were moments when Neal honestly feared he would lose Colleen. He began to feel again the way he had felt when he first arrived at Okinawa. "Suddenly you realize that, with the guns blazing, this is for real." Her graceful handling of the pain and pressures, both physical and otherwise, made a deep impression on him. Neal couldn't help noticing that Colleen "didn't think of herself at all. There was no self-pity, no sense of martyrdom."

Watching her bravery in the midst of a fiery trial was moving to Neal. Then he saw Colleen's attitude as she recovered—not only did she feel no resentment but having pulled through the illness made her feel this was an ideal time for them to "recommit themselves to be more worthy of their blessings." As they did that, they learned together about the connections between opposition and drawing closer to God.

Another almost-incident soon gave Colleen a close look at Neal's character. Near the end of the Korean War in the early 1950s, the national draft had reduced the Church's number of full-time missionaries. The Church sent out a letter to bishops, inviting them to recommend seventies who could serve missions away from home. When Neal heard of this need, he went to his bishop, noted that he was an ordained seventy, and offered to serve again, if needed.

Colleen gasped as she realized the depth of Neal's commitment to the Church. Then her thoughts reverted to her pioneer heritage. She thought again about those women "who stayed home" in the Church's early days "when their men went off for years" as missionaries. Her commitment was equal to theirs—and to Neal's. But still she was relieved when their bishop explained that the request was for men who had not yet served missions.

Neal also came soon to see how right he was about that thinking going on beneath Colleen's "hood." "I knew I was not dealing with an eighteen-year-old co-ed who was so anxious to please me that I'd have my way when I shouldn't," he said. "We hadn't been married long before I knew I had a kind of Gibraltar—someone who would be tough and strong in the storms of life." For example, despite his Republican leanings, Neal was quite taken by Adlai Stevenson's intelligent grasp of the issues in the 1956 presidential election. Colleen simply responded that Eisenhower is "smarter than you think he is." Neal later saw that Eisenhower's biographers had found that his down-home approach was "a deliberate ploy on his part with the press" and that he was "much more cagey and savvy than some people thought."

Neal also found that Colleen had reading interests different from his own. His preferences were strong enough that he wasn't sure why anyone would read Anne Morrow Lindbergh or Mother Teresa if one could read military history or political biography. Then, taking Colleen's subtle hints, he began to read some of what she enjoyed. Soon Neal discovered a whole new genre of valuable literature, such as Lindbergh's *Gift from the Sea*, which became the source of a quotation he liked so much he later had it framed and placed on the wall of his busy office: "My life cannot implement in action the demands of all the people to whom my heart responds." That insight later became a poignant and practical reminder to Neal that the extent of his actual influence would never quite reach the broader extent of his idealistic hopes.

He also found that, in his writing and speaking, Colleen could be a gentle but very constructive critic. Once in his early years as commissioner of education, he was trying hard to use a series of rhetorical devices to develop the theme of a written speech. He asked a colleague at work to read through the draft and offer suggestions. The friend thought his stylistic tools were calling too much attention to themselves. As the friend groped for a polite way to say what he was thinking, Neal sensed the concern and said, "It's too cute, isn't it? That's what Colleen thinks." The friend sighed and said, "She's right." Neal completely reworked the draft.

Over the years, Neal's respect for Colleen has just kept growing, along every front. He found in her some qualities he often described as the rare but ideal combination—meekness combined with brightness. Hers is a kind of natural intelligence, which unites with her spiritual gifts and character traits to form a personality uniquely suited to a full partnership with him.

One pervasive influence on him has been Colleen's tasteful manner of doing whatever she does. Neal feels she is "a more complete Christian" than he is, with a high desire to serve and a low need for recognition. Partly through the example of her own parents and partly as an innate attribute, there is an unusual kindness and refinement about her. As one neighbor wrote, Colleen is "love personified and gives to others as naturally as she breathes." Or, as Elder Henry B. Eyring wrote, thanking her for a service she had rendered, "You've always had the gift to make me feel that when you were kind to me I had somehow done you a favor."

Seeing these qualities helped Neal develop more tenderness and patience. If he murmurs or gets overly irritated, for example, "she just has to say my first name in her own special way . . . and that's the end of the streetcar line." This was a nice antidote to help young Neal tame his early temptation at times to be a little too critical in his observations. Elizabeth Haglund, a close friend of many years, commented that Colleen doesn't like any degree of sarcasm, and she has helped raise the bar of Neal's tolerance levels. "Colleen is superb at deflating Neal when occasion warrants." Her "surgically precise prick bursts his bubble and, without wounding him, brings about needed change."

An illustration of their interaction occurred in late 1989 and early 1990 when Colleen developed a staph infection in her knee after a fall. She eventually underwent minor surgery when the knee kept filling with fluid. Later she required knee replacement surgery. During the time of the staph infection, she required injections of antibiotics every few hours, night and day. Unable to give them to herself, Colleen relied on Neal.

One very late night, he couldn't get the needle into the injection cap. After several tries, he pricked his finger with the needle. Then he had to change the needle on the syringe. By then he was murmuring. With that "Colleen way" of hers, she "just patted my hand from the bed

Colleen about age forty-five

and said, 'It will go in next time,' and it did. So she's met my impatience with her patience."

Not long afterward, Colleen wrote Neal a love letter that began Dearest Husband,

> After having seen myself as a care-giver . . . I found I was the one needing care. . . . I soon discovered that one scarcely knows anything about love until love is tested. It's a tender and humbling experience to find that your life is literally dependent upon someone else. . . . That knowledge becomes especially heart-warming when one knows that this person is not inclined to tedious, regular, exacting things. And then to see that such is done without complaint or murmuring begins to tell you just a little of love. . . . To know of your genuine love and self-sacrificing spirit has truly touched my heart. . . . How could I be so blessed? Please know of my humble and heartfelt gratitude.
>
> All my love,
> Colleen

Another dimension she helped add to Neal's experience was the place of physical affection. Colleen's mother had a spontaneous, genuine way of greeting her family members with welcoming hugs and kisses. Over time, Colleen has gently and successfully encouraged Neal to be more demonstrative with his children and grandchildren, something that was more typical of her family background than his.

Her innate serenity has also blessed the atmosphere of the Maxwell home. Neal was characteristically fast-paced and impatient, and she has been a great "calming influence" for him. He told a student research assistant in the late 1960s that he lived in a hectic world full of pressure and commitments but that when he came home, he found a "stress-free environment," because Colleen "always calmed him."

Mike Ahlander, Becky's husband, recalls a family Thanksgiving dinner when Colleen's gift of calm was in effect. Neal, who, Mike said, "is in high speed all the time," had just carved the turkey and put it on a large platter. As he carefully carried the overflowing plate into the dining room, his foot accidentally caught something and the plate fell to the floor. With the hungry family looking on, Neal was upset with himself. But Colleen immediately and calmly rescued the situation. With a voice so serene she didn't even sound surprised, let alone concerned, she stepped right in with an immediate alternative for the main dish. "We'll be okay," she said. "We'll pick it up, and do this, and be just fine."

In no other realm has Colleen's serenity been more important than in her own spiritual attitudes. Neal looks to her for spiritual companionship, as she does to him. He loves to hear her pray. She is "very prayerful," naturally expressing an "ardent kind of prayer that's wonderful." Yet "she's so calm and serene" that someone who doesn't know the range of her heart might not realize the intensity of her pleadings.

Neal has also learned to listen to Colleen's promptings as what he calls his "auxiliary conscience." She is restrained about when and how she shares, because she knows he listens to her. Since the early days of their marriage, when Neal worked in sensitive government offices or when he served as bishop, she has also found it easy to respect the need for confidentiality—which means she doesn't intrude or volunteer opinions in such areas; rather, he usually has to ask for her views on some topic of appropriate discussion. He thus regards her as "an additional prompter, along with the Holy Ghost. . . . She's not always convenient. I don't want to hear what she tells me sometimes, but I've learned long since to pay attention."

That was not his natural instinct when they were first married. After Neal finished his undergraduate degree in 1952, for example, he spent the next four years working in federal government offices in Washington, D.C. When they felt it was time to relocate, they had a number of options. One choice that struck Neal as an unlikely one was a public relations job at the University of Utah. Colleen felt strongly impressed that he should take this job, because she thought being on the campus would give him an opportunity to "have an influence on young people, the way Lowell Bennion did." That's where she thought his greatest strengths lay.

Although Neal kept pointing out that the job involved little more than writing press releases, Colleen's feeling persisted, until they both prayerfully concluded that the move was a good one. It turned out to be exactly that, including the reality of influencing students. But they couldn't have foreseen that outcome at the level of pure reason.

Colleen has learned to coach her husband in ways that have let his confidence in her accept her confidence in him. She recognized his talents very early, seeing also some of the undeveloped edges as those talents emerged. She would find pleasant and honest ways to encourage him to take his Church callings seriously, telling him, "You have some talents. You'd better use them. You can do this." In such an attitude, she recognized his gift to communicate in speech and writing, gradually persuading him that he had ideas worth sharing, all the while seeing whatever he did as service rather than as self-serving.

It has helped in all dimensions of their relationship that they can communicate freely. Neal has found that Colleen is so strong that he's never had to "hold back and try to calculate, now how can I talk with her about this." So they've learned they can be "fairly direct" in their conversation, though both have learned to temper that directness with the breath of kindness. Neal once offered his experience with Colleen to illustrate the meaning of Paul's phrase "Speaking the truth in love" (Ephesians 4:15). "What she says may not always be convenient, but I don't have to decode her motive or her meaning. She does everything in a spirit of love."

Neal once wrote his daughter Nancy about the great

> source of strength and comfort . . . that your mother was not only at my side but was often ahead of me spiritually. Her righteousness seems to be so reflexive when at times mine is more labored. I . . . trust her completely. . . . This level of security is an exceedingly important blessing. Such relationships might be enormous exceptions today, but they are attainable, and you deserve and need such a marriage.

Among Colleen's most significant sources of influence has been her gift of personal empathy, combined with her commitment to humanitarian service. The personal part was there for a long time, but she learned the service dimension as a college student from Lowell Bennion. With such instincts, Colleen has long been alert to the circumstances of people in her ward, her neighborhood, her extended family, and anyone else within her natural spheres of movement. She is an excellent cook—a skill she learned both from her mother and from her college major in food and nutrition. She willingly offered that skill during Neal's days as a student ward bishop, when the Maxwells would invite a table full of guests for Sunday dinner virtually every week for months at a time.

But Neal and Colleen's family also came to know that the fragrance of fresh bread in her kitchen or even the scent of some delicious dinner, was often from baking that was intended for someone outside their home. On other occasions, the cooking would be for everyone in the family except Colleen, who, without comment, was fasting for someone who was on her mind. Her daughter-in-law, Karen, has found that Colleen's home management reflects her background and her sense of taste. For instance, she uses "leftovers wisely and effectively," but when something has been left over "a couple of times, then it's out of there."

Colleen's skill in the kitchen is matched by her capacity to take a

A scene typical of the table set by Colleen during the period when many guests, including college students and neighbors, dined at the Maxwell home

sincere interest in people in all roles and stations. As she and Neal have circulated in some distinguished circles, she has not given preference to those circles over other relationships. She has respected the station of educational, political, and Church leaders but has never been "overly bowled over" by the appearance of prestige as such. In their Church ministry, Neal has found—and has been helped by—how naturally Colleen fits into any social situation from a state dinner in Washington, D.C., to a modest table in the primitive dwelling of Church members in Third World countries.

On any given day, she typically would have done a half dozen things for people—taking food, making visits, or lending a hand in some other way. "That's just going on all the time and has for years, says Neal." Her actions have always flowed so naturally that people sense it isn't forced, just instinctive—which gives it even more meaning. After her children married, Colleen had more freedom to direct her energies into what Neal calls a "crescendo in the circles of her

Neal and Colleen Maxwell in the mid-1990s

Christian service." In recent years, her service has included tutoring first-grade children in reading at Salt Lake's Guadalupe Center and assisting nurses to care for children and families in the spina bifida clinic at Primary Children's Medical Center.

Colleen has managed to keep a kind of quiet independence about her outreach. She's always been available for church callings or activities that supported Neal's various roles, but she has also avoided what he calls "role suction," the tendency to get pulled exclusively into roles that others have expected her to play—whether mother, grandmother, Relief Society president, or General Authority's wife. She accepts her various roles, but she has always been her own person, with her own quiet circles of influence quite unrelated to her husband's callings.

Colleen's intuitive Christian service has clearly rubbed off on Neal. Some of that was fairly direct, as she would tell him about someone's need and then ask if he could deliver a potted plant or a custard for her. Then she might suggest that they go together to see someone who was sick, or she'd make him aware of someone he could help with a phone call. He soon learned that if she felt someone needed them, "she was probably right." He found that her "spiritual antenna on Christian service" was always "more highly attuned than mine. So I learned to pay attention over the years when she had those impressions and feelings."

Two other influences would later augment Colleen's, helping Neal learn how becoming a follower of Jesus often involves some kind of private ministry. One was the example of President Spencer W. Kimball, whom the Maxwells first came to know well as a neighbor in the 1960s. The other, much later, was Neal's own illness in 1996. In the meantime, it is clear enough that Colleen was her husband's first and best teacher about the spirit and art of personal ministering.

No wonder Neal has often told Latter-day Saint congregations that for too long, the women of the Church have been the Christians while the men have been the theologians. Stirred by Colleen's example, he has encouraged a sharing and balancing of those functions, so that all Latter-day Saint men and women might seek to be both Christians and theologians. Her public profile may be less visible than his, but Colleen's inconspicuous influence has gradually become more pervasive in Neal's understanding and practice of his own unfolding discipleship. The story from this point forward is theirs.

PART VIII

STARTING OUT TOGETHER

TWENTY-TWO

WASHINGTON, D.C.

B Y 1952, NEAL MAXWELL felt drawn to Washington, D.C., a bit like a heat-seeking missile, but the force that drew him was a general, undefined one. As Colleen put it, he just "loved that political thing." Though he had graduated from college with a political science major, he didn't really have in mind a career in politics or government service, nor did he plan to use his Washington experience as a springboard to something else. He was fascinated by national politics, and he wanted to find out for himself what it was like to be at the very center of political process, policy, and power. As with so many other steps in his life, he actually seemed to enjoy proceeding quickly but fearlessly in the mode of "Lead, Kindly Light": "I do not ask to see / The distant scene—one step enough for me."

During the next four years, Neal gained a significant real-world education that informed and shaped him. He learned about the process of building consensus and cooperation among competing groups—and about the limited effectiveness of dogmatic extremists on both ends of the political spectrum. About the place of a commitment to the common good among statesmen who contribute to real problem solving—

and about the limited contributions of ambitious, egocentric show horses. About the inner workings and the genuine value of the American political system—and about the limitations of bureaucracies.

Grasping such lessons gave Neal an important level of insight into his own approach to leadership, both organizationally and in the formation of public policy. When he left Washington in 1956, he returned to Utah not because he couldn't handle the world of big-time political forces but because he could. He handled it well enough that he preferred to draw on that foundation in a sphere more suited to his real interest—higher education. But no matter what else he would do later, he would think, teach, interact, and lead with a honed set of "political" skills, in the best and largest sense of the term.

George Hinckley offered to help pay Neal's way through law school, in Washington or elsewhere. He could see his son-in-law's interest in what looked like a law-related world, he knew that Neal and Colleen didn't have the money to pay for tuition or much else, and he thought more education and a specific career track might give Neal a desirable focus. But Neal was tired of school after his intense sprint through the U, and he couldn't see himself as a lawyer anyway.

For a young and wide-eyed Utah Republican who was a World War II veteran, the early fifties were a good time to be in Washington. Dwight D. Eisenhower, a celebrated World War II general, had just been elected President of the United States—the first Republican elected to the White House since Herbert Hoover in 1928. The Republicans were energized, the postwar economy was beginning to move, and the Korean War was about to end. On the other hand, the Cold War was intensifying. The Soviet Union had now become a sufficient threat to the United States that much of the country "was almost in a state of paranoia about international communism." In the face of that threat, Eisenhower's view that the United States should be engaged in global political developments affirmed Neal's views against isolationism.

As an added incentive for a politically oriented Latter-day Saint, President Eisenhower had appointed Ezra Taft Benson, a member of the Quorum of the Twelve, as Secretary of Agriculture. Elder Benson enjoyed an unusual degree of influence, because Eisenhower looked to his Cabinet for overall policy advice more than most presidents had done. In addition, wrote historian William Manchester, every Cabinet meeting "opened with a silent prayer or a few prayerful words from Benson. . . . If Eisenhower forgot it, [Secretary of State John Foster] Dulles would clear his throat and murmur a reminder, and Ike would blurt out, 'Oh my gosh! And I really need all the help we can get up there this morning. Ezra, please . . . '"

Among local Church members, J. Willard Marriott, his food service and hotel empire just emerging, was president of the Washington Stake, which stretched from Baltimore, Maryland, to Richmond, Virginia. Neal's and Colleen's involvement in this stake would expand their vision and attitudes about life among a community of Saints.

Neal's first job in Washington was as a staff economic analyst with a government intelligence department, but his assignments were well removed from exotic Soviet intrigue. He found the preparation of routine economic analyses a bland enough intellectual diet that he was ready to leave the organization after little more than a year. The most interesting thing about his work was that it gave him the opportunity for an insider's view of international relations. He gained much of this perspective in weekly briefing sessions, such as the time he heard former president Harry Truman give his perspective on several current international issues to a small group of staffers. Neal was impressed with Truman's candor and his grasp of detail.

During this impressionable stage of Neal's exposure to a large bureaucracy, he was alert to lessons about leadership. He was quite taken by the style of a particular branch chief, who was responsive and encouraging to Neal's staff team when they performed well even on small tasks. As an indication of her confidence, she gave the team increased responsibility. Because she was personally secure, Neal found "she was unthreatened by the progress of her followers, realizing that as they grew and improved she was succeeding as a leader." Thus she took "delight in [the] development" of her subordinates. This approach appealed to Neal enough that he sought to incorporate it into his own approach to leadership.

By contrast, he later became disillusioned with the department's overall approach to its internal management priorities. As he would later tell an audience at Brigham Young University,

> in one federal department . . . the methodology of filing came out by directive and assumed a preeminence over our primary task. This trend was symbolically accompanied by the domesticating appearance of sweet potato foliage on the desk (which was accompanied by my disappearance from that department in search of better tasks).

When they learned Neal was leaving, his superiors offered to help finance his education for a Ph.D. in international relations at Harvard. This would have qualified him for further responsibility with the department, because the upper-level staff people all had doctoral degrees. But he had already decided he preferred to work in the legislative branch of government. Nonetheless, Neal always retained certain work habits he developed by following the organization's standard protocol. For instance, he would never have any trouble keeping information confidential, because confidentiality had been so valued and so pervasive in his work environment. He learned instinctively to tear up or shred unneeded documents—a practice he frequently employed in later work assignments.

Neal's good friend from his college days, Ralph Mecham, was working as a staff assistant to Utah Senator Wallace F. Bennett. Senator Bennett had been elected in 1950, the first time he had run for public office. He was from a pioneer Latter-day Saint family, his father having crossed the plains in 1868. His wife, Frances, was a daughter of Church President Heber J. Grant. A prominent Utah businessman, Senator Bennett had become the first representative of small business to be elected president of the National Association of Manufacturers in 1949. This was a background Neal could, and did, appreciate. In addition, Wallace Bennett possessed some statesmanlike qualities that appealed to Neal's instincts about the political process.

When Ralph learned that Neal was looking for another position, he recommended him to the Senator and to Lyle Ward, Bennett's administrative assistant. Based largely on Ralph's influence, Neal soon joined the staff, which then totaled five people. Logistical support for

Senate staffers was limited enough that Neal's addition to the crew bumped both him and Ralph into an underground basement office in the Senate Office Building, rather than in Senator Bennett's fourth floor office, where Ralph had been.

In an extracurricular project that reflected the "brashness" Neal remembers about himself during this stage, he and Ralph worked during lunch hours in their shared basement office to invent a board game they called "Uranium Millionaire." Uranium was booming in those days, particularly in southeastern Utah. They submitted their game to Parker Brothers, whose rejection letter said they'd received "many games . . . with a 'uranium background.'"

The Senate soon became Neal's kind of place. He was immediately attracted by his opportunity to work on national issues related to Senator Bennett's committee assignments with Finance, Banking, and Housing and Urban Affairs. He became a devoted reader of the *Congressional Record,* a habit he maintained for years after leaving the senator's staff. He was frequently assigned to listen to floor debates and committee hearings, which gave him numerous opportunities to observe famous people and time-honored processes at close range.

He immediately noticed the wide variety of styles and commitments to the legislative process among various senators. He discovered that members of the Senate could hardly be experts on the details of every bill; consequently, they had to rely on committees and staff support. Such discoveries helped Neal understand the sage observation that people who love law or sausage should avoid seeing either one being made. As he once put it, "I got to see politics in the raw in the United States Senate. It was a great education."

For instance, Neal was standing in a Senate corridor one day when the bell for a vote rang all the senators to the main floor. Senator John F. Kennedy of Massachusetts rushed past Neal in the hallway. Looking around, Senator Kennedy turned to Neal and asked, "Which way am I supposed to vote?" Neal calmly replied that he thought the Democrats were voting 'aye' on this one, so the senator went to the floor and voted 'aye' on the proposition.

Neal's real-world education was underway.

TWENTY-THREE

THE SPIRIT OF
PUBLIC SERVICE

———————

NEAL SOON NOTICED A DIFFERENCE between show horses and work horses. That insight launched the development of his entire understanding of—and attitudes toward—public service, a set of perspectives that permanently influenced his personal desires and philosophy.

Once he stood in a Senate anteroom next to Senator Lyndon Johnson of Texas, who was then the Senate majority leader. Both were reading the ticker-tape news reports on an important bill coming out of a Senate committee after months of intense effort. One member of the committee who had not attended the sessions to hear the tedious testimony had managed to show up on the day the bill was reported so he could "take his bows before waiting TV cameras. He was one of those senators who would show up for the opening of an envelope," Neal observed. "The man at my side, later to become President, profaned in his disgust for the show horse senator, declaring that [he was] a lazy liberal who let other liberals do the work while he took the bows." He learned from such experiences how "the many depend upon the few to lead, . . . to show the way."

One of Neal's most memorable experiences with "show horses" led to his cameo appearance in the events leading to the Senate's censure of Senator Joseph R. McCarthy of Wisconsin. This was a strange tale that captured the nation's attention and ended with a sadly permanent legacy—"McCarthyism" now holds a place in standard dictionaries, a pejorative term referring to unfair and aggressive personal attacks.

In 1951, Senator McCarthy was "the most famous figure in the [Republican] party." As the flamboyant chairman of a Senate committee, he conducted extensive hearings on the influence of Communists in the federal government and elsewhere. The public initially took McCarthy at his word. But when a McCarthy aide sought preferential treatment from the U.S. Army, the army accused McCarthy of improper conduct. McCarthy retorted that the army had trumped up this claim to make him call off his investigation of Communists in the armed forces.

After dramatic public hearings, the Senate was so embarrassed by McCarthy's conduct that it appointed a select committee chaired by Utah Sentor Arthur V. Watkins, Senator Bennett's close friend, to investigate McCarthy. Acting firmly, Senator Watkins banned television from his committee's hearings. When McCarthy complained, Watkins declared him out of order. McCarthy then "bolted into [a nearby] corridor, where television crews were waiting, and spluttered into a microphone, 'I think this is the most unheard of thing I ever heard of.'"

When McCarthy attacked the committee as "handmaidens of the Communist Party," Senator Watkins wept on the Senate floor, saying he had "taken this thankless job" at the request of his colleagues and "now they were standing by watching while McCarthy vilified him." This scene so moved Senator Bennett that he asked Lyle Ward, with Neal's assistance, to draft a resolution condemning McCarthy for attacking the committee. The Senate's adoption of the resolution on December 2, 1954, paved the way for McCarthy's formal censure by the Senate.

On the day the Senate passed the censure motion, Senator

McCarthy rushed into a side room where people from the media were waiting. Standing nearby, Neal entered the room with the others. There he saw that the media representatives "knew [McCarthy] was through, he knew they'd given him a good ride, and they knew he'd been good copy." Neal would later say of this scene, "In their final exchanges in that room I saw how symbiotic sensationalism can be. . . . Crucial causes often fall into the hands of those least able to champion them effectively . . . and . . . the media use people—sometimes cruelly."

Neal thought McCarthy an "inept and phony" leader who undermined the cause of anti-Communism. He believed there were indeed some Communist influences in high places, but he found that McCarthy's arrogance impaired his judgment about the complexities of dealing with those influences.

Watching this case at close range helped teach Neal to be skeptical about celebrity status as a basis for public trust—since, as someone has joked, a celebrity is just a person who is well known for being well known. He would always remain cautious when he saw public figures driven to the spotlight of notoriety. Years later he would say of people with McCarthy's weakness, "craving power and the spotlight sucks out the spiritual oxygen, leaving some 'past feeling.' Strangely, though desensitized, some are still able to hear the beckoning click of a TV camera at a hundred yards."

While the McCarthy incident was the most extreme example, Neal also observed other Congressional disappointments. One was the confession of Utah Congressman Douglas R. Stringfellow just before the 1954 election that certain stories he'd told about his World War II experiences had been fabricated. Elected in 1952, Stringfellow had publicly claimed that he lost both of his legs while on a secret wartime mission behind enemy lines in Europe. In fact, his injuries did occur during the war but not in battle.

As a fellow war veteran, Neal felt real sadness over Stringfellow's embarrassing revelations and his withdrawal from Congress. Neal said he was, after all, "a legitimate veteran," so he didn't really need to make up the stories. He had also been a very promising Congressman. Neal had seen him "spellbind the House Interior Committee" regarding the need for the Upper Colorado River Project. The Republicans in Utah hastily persuaded Henry Aldous Dixon, president of Utah State University, to run for Stringfellow's seat. After Dixon was elected, Neal provided him with some staff assistance when he first arrived in Washington.

In general, Neal found that the show horse mentality among United States Congressmen was widespread. He eventually concluded that many of them were, "by and large, driven by [a desire for] power and perpetuation in office" more than by a genuine commitment to the public interest. "Power is so attractive [that] only a few people can handle it. . . . Meekness is not a common virtue." He often noted that his impression bore out Joseph Smith's words: "We have learned by sad experience that it is the nature and disposition of almost all men, as soon as they get a little authority," to "exercise unrighteous dominion" (D&C 121:39).

Neal was troubled enough by his discovery of this general tendency—which some people call "Potomac fever"—that "it shaped [his] views for the rest of [his] life," moving him to examine his own motives. He probably sensed within himself the same desire for recognition at times, and his honest effort to tame that urge became part of his commitment to discipleship.

Years later, he would often refer to his Washington experience or to similar examples in political and military biographies. He would talk about the "incessant strivings for glory . . . among the talented" and the "addicting nectar of recognition." At times he'd quote Abraham Lincoln about the way "towering genius . . . thirsts and burns for distinction." Frequently he would cite the Doctrine and Covenants: "Wherefore, *honest* men and *wise* men should be sought for diligently, and *good* men . . . ye should observe to uphold" (D&C 98:10; italics added). And then he would return to one of his signature themes—the quest for meekness.

These experiences tempered Neal's idealism about the American political system with a sober dose of realism, but he never became cynical about the system itself. One reason he retained his optimistic view about public service is that he also saw a few impressive examples of authentic statesmanship. In fact, he came to realize that the leader-statesman could make an indispensable contribution to the success of democratic institutions.

For example, he came to admire Senator Richard Russell of Georgia, a Democrat who was chairman of the Armed Services Committee. Russell had an engaging personal modesty that Neal found to be an essential part of his statesmanship. Neal liked this quality, sensing that Russell's self-effacing personality did not displace his natural talents; rather, the modesty channeled his skill and strength to serve the public interest without his even seeming conscious of self-interest. As he saw Senator Russell in action, he could see and appreciate more fully the role Russell had played a few years earlier in averting a constitutional crisis by the way he managed the dispute between President Truman and General MacArthur.

He saw a similar quality in Senator Bennett, and he noticed that these two senators from opposing political parties often worked together, usually behind the scenes, to build the consensus needed for wise action. Neal saw the value of Bennett's collegial style and gentle demeanor. And, although Neal sometimes wished Bennett would be more assertive in pursuing legislative initiatives, in general the senator was a fine mentor for him.

He noticed that Bennett often took work home so he could master intricate problems. This impressed Neal, who saw that a good leader must "rise above his staff" and "know the data better than anyone else." The senator also helped Neal develop his own skills of political advocacy. In a draft of proposed remarks for the senator's use in encouraging a certain piece of legislation, Neal wrote that "the situation was underlined with unparalleled urgency." Senator Bennett just said, "Neal, that's too much alliteration, and it's too graphic."

On another occasion, the senator taught Neal to tame his task-oriented tendency to push impatiently through the agenda of pressing issues. Neal was driving Senator Bennett someplace when the senator said he needed to change his schedule to attend the funeral of a good friend. Neal blurted out something about, "Oh, Senator, you don't need to be at the funeral. We've got to have you" at the planned political appointment. Bennett calmly replied, "Neal, I should be there. He's my friend." Neal immediately saw that as the "brash young staffer," he wasn't making allowance for the personal dimension. He would remember this incident, and his own priorities would gradually assign ever greater importance to personal and human needs.

With increased experience and with Senator Bennett's tutoring, Neal developed greater appreciation for the process of building personal relationships with trusted friends, across the political aisle and across the country. He also came to see the place of these relationships in doing the business of the Senate. The senator taught him that legislation is possible only at the highest level where real consensus exists and that this level is adequate, even when it falls short of what a dogmatic partisan might have wished—or demanded.

For instance, Neal watched Senator Bennett work closely with Democratic senators from the South on cane sugar issues that concerned Utah sugar beet farmers. He saw the importance of regional cooperation among senators from the West, in both parties, as the group mobilized support for the Upper Colorado River Storage Project. The passage of that legislation in 1956 would rank among Senator Bennett's most significant accomplishments. Issues relating to regional cooperation also formed the basis for some of Neal's later publications as a fledgling political scientist.

When Senator Bennett assigned him to work on an industrial dispersion bill, Neal tried his hand at managing a piece of legislation through its entire process. President Truman had first proposed this project as a passive defense method—dispersing key industrial facilities to various locations, both as a defense against enemy attacks and to meet possible demands for military mobilization. With Bennett's watchful coaching, Neal looked to the Western regional base for initial help and built the necessary coalitions to gain support for the bill. As support grew, Neal worked with the White House staff in arranging for President Eisenhower to comment favorably on the bill at a press conference. The law was eventually passed; however, it was never implemented as planned because of social and political obstacles that turned out to be more powerful than the policy behind the legislation. Some of those obstacles arose within the executive branch bureaucracy that had responsibility for the law's implementation.

Neal was thus able to say of the industrial dispersion bill that he saw it all the way through, from conception to nonimplementation. He later realized that many aspects of the concept were probably not realistic, especially when the enemy could multiply missiles faster than the government could move factories.

He later described this project in his master's degree thesis, because it illustrated both the coalition-building process and the challenge of blending the wills of the legislative and executive branches of government in implementing policy. This was only one of many ways his years in the Senate prepared him to specialize in "the American Congress as my little slice of political science" in the university classroom. He would also find that his frequent proximity to national leaders and national issues had given him an informed kind of confidence when he later dealt with Utah legislators or interviewed other public figures on KUED television.

Although he stood outside the political context, J. Willard Marriott was another person whose example Neal found heartening during this time of his intensive learning about public service. Already emerging as a national business leader, Marriott was the Maxwells' stake president. Neal had heard of the Marriott business acumen but was stirred even more by Bill's soft-spoken humility. Because that commodity was generally in such short supply in Washington, Neal noticed the contrast. He saw in Bill a certain "self-confidence enclosed in meekness that was a good thing for me to see, because he was [also] such a high achiever."

In his younger days, Neal hadn't really been conscious of his own father's innate meekness. And the military leaders he knew were not much into being meek and lowly. But during his missionary service, he had begun to sense that meekness mattered. Then, his general disillusionment with most political leaders only enhanced his appreciation for the few other-centered leaders he did encounter in Washington. When he saw their modesty, he recognized it and liked it. One Sunday he saw President Marriott quietly giving a branch president a substantial financial contribution for the branch building fund—something other stake members never knew. Their not knowing gave special meaning to Neal's view of the donation.

Out of all of these experiences, his understanding of the political process and public service came into balance. He retained his disappointment in political figures whose self-interest interfered with their commitments to the public interest. He also realized that political extremists at both ends of the spectrum suffered from "the same kind of myopia," as they played to their galleries and engaged more in sloganeering than in actual problem solving. Thus he saw for himself that "things get done in the center," that portion of the political spectrum where the interests of competing political parties overlap. If you're off too far to one side, you can maybe "make good copy in a newspaper," or "have a moment in the sun" with a speech but will otherwise be ineffective. At the same time, he came to appreciate "the dilemma of the centrist"—who may not be appreciated by those on either end of the spectrum.

When the centrists helped the political system work—and Neal saw that the system often did work, "even with all the mischief"—he found that "our whole American system depended on having strong political parties and that politics would be an honorable profession." For him, then, the "highest expression of politics was in our governmental/constitutional system." The key to that system was the honest commitment of even a few able leaders who together built the relationships and shaped the consensus that nourished effective public policy.

In that "world of public service," Neal concluded, the "shaping of choices in the political process" can have "greater impact and influence" than what happens in the voting booth. While "the voting booth is very democratic," the "shaping of the [policy] alternatives is aristocratic; it is work that is done by a few." And the people blessed with the capacity and the self-discipline to do that work well would not—if they were statesmen enough to deserve the duty—be "first in line as eager volunteers" to serve their country, because they would often need to sacrifice their own interests for the sake of the larger public good.

These insights would influence Neal's future approach to the resolution of problems among individuals and groups in any environment.
Whether he found them in biographies, history books, or real-life experience, he was often moved by the examples of people who, when called
upon, laid both their gifts and their egos upon the altar of public service. He wanted to be like that. Because of these deep feelings, one of
Neal's favorite moments in American history was an incident when
George Washington blended power with meekness in a way that confirmed his role as a father of freedom. This was a story Neal has often
recounted to illustrate the attitudes he came to prize.

Near the end of the Revolutionary War, despite the American
military victories, the colonies were disorganized, squabbling, and still
unwilling to finance a national government capable of paying its
debts—including what the country owed its soldiers for several years
of valiant service. In their frustration with the untidiness of democratic self-government, some of Washington's men tried to persuade him
to become king of America.

The general rejected a monarchy as contrary to all they'd fought
for. Then some soldiers plotted to overthrow the government and
establish a military dictatorship, with Washington or without him.
Washington called his men together in a meeting some consider "probably the most important single gathering ever held in the United
States." Washington was unable to dissuade them, until he tried to read
them a letter. Unable to read, he pulled some spectacles from his
pocket. "'Gentlemen, you must pardon me,' he said in apology. 'It
appears that I have grown gray in your service and now find myself also
growing blind.'" As the men realized Washington's attitude of sacrifice,
"They wept, many of these warriors. And the . . . plot was dissolved."

Neal loved biographer James Flexner's lines: "This homely act and
simple statement did what all Washington's arguments had failed to
do." Surely "in all history few men who possessed unassailable power
have used that power so gently and self-effacingly for what their best
instincts told them was the welfare of their neighbors and all mankind."

Earlier Flexner had written about Washington's conscious habit
of trying to learn from his experience, always assuming that he had

more to learn than he had to give. In these words is a distant mirror of Neal's own growing desire for self-discipline: "As [Washington's] character and his world view expanded, more meanings became clear to him. He accurately defined his failures and worked out the reasons why he had failed. The results of this protracted self-education were to prove of the greatest importance." Drawing on his impressionable years in Washington, D.C., Neal Maxwell's own expanding world view and "protracted self-education" about the link between meekness and public service would prove important to his ministry.

TWENTY-FOUR

FAMILY BEGINNINGS

Leo Tolstoy began the classic *Anna Karenina* with, "Happy families are all alike; every unhappy family is unhappy in its own way." Tolstoy knew that there are a thousand ways family life can go wrong, but, despite variety in personalities, backgrounds, and circumstances, there is only one way family life can go right—a disciplined adherence to certain root principles of commitment and affection. Without that discipline, there will be unhappy families, each one unhappy in its own undisciplined way.

Neal Maxwell and Colleen Hinckley both grew up in such stable families that some people in today's culture of fractured families might say life was never like that. But in the Maxwell and the Hinckley homes, life really was like that. Despite obvious differences in the personalities and environments of those two homes, there were fundamental similarities in matters of principle. Central to their common pattern was the gospel and parents who affectionately tried to impart its teachings to their children. Having tasted the sweet fruit of this pattern so personally and so long, Neal and Colleen both wanted their children to experience what they had known.

As their children were growing up, Neal became unusually structured in his efforts to "do it right" with his family. Some people might find his approach too structured, too planned. But for him and Colleen, the structure worked—partly because structured approaches and working always on his "protracted self-education" were so natural to his personality.

Beyond matters of personality, Neal came to believe passionately that family life really is at the center of society, the Church, and the gospel. Looking back on his life, he has said that as pleasant as was life in the Wandamere Ward, one can't be sealed to a ward—or a high school or a group of missionaries. What happened in the homes of society took on increasing importance in his ministry. He once told the lawyers of the Utah State Bar Association, "Winning points at the office roundtable is not as vital as that which happens at your supper table." He told the teachers of the Church Educational System, "We will be no more effective in the classroom than we are effective in the laboratory of life at home." And he wrote in the *Ensign* that "life's most demanding tests as well as life's most significant opportunities for growth in life usually occur within marriage and the family."

Those closest to Neal knew these were not just pleasant, pro-family cliches. Said President James E. Faust, "He's a great soul in so many areas, but none greater than in his role as a family patriarch. He [and] Colleen . . . have a great family. He is a noble father and grandfather to that family."

As time went on, Neal came increasingly to think about ways to strengthen not only his own family but also other families, especially those of Church members. During his years with the Correlation Department in the mid-1970s and then during his membership in the Twelve, Neal found himself following family issues and needs with great interest and concern. As he learned from Church research that children with temple-married parents were far more likely themselves to become, and remain, active Church members, Neal would think with gratitude about his own extended family. He had seen, over three generations, the fruits of the simple, faithful way Clarence and Emma had kept their covenants and taught their children. For him, that kind of family life in successive generations is how Zion will be built.

Elder Maxwell has taken unusual interest in learning what proportion of Latter-day Saint children in various countries are growing up in the homes of temple-married parents. He often reflects on how the Latter-day Saints can best pursue the vision of building a second- and third-generation Church throughout the world. His passion about family life always reaches broadly enough to include single parents and other single adults. Sometimes he mentions his admiration for his single sister, Lois, emphasizing that Church doctrine assures her of an eternal marriage and family life.

Neal and Colleen's efforts with their family reveal glimpses of their own laboratory of life at home. It helps to know in advance the high priority they have attached to this part of their lives. Yet the Maxwells are also quick to agree with Mary Hales, wife of Elder Robert D. Hales of the Twelve, that if you think you've seen a perfect family, you just don't know them well enough yet. They found that the surprises and adventures of rearing children inevitably make family life a perpetual exercise in managing the difference between the real and the ideal.

Bearing children was itself a challenge for Colleen and Neal. Over the years, she experienced three miscarriages, in addition to giving birth to their four children. To their real disappointment, surgery required after Jane's birth finally eliminated the possibility of having more children.

Becky, their firstborn, arrived in the midst of Colleen's health trauma in 1952. Neal's parental inexperience showed up early, in what has become a favorite family tale. They brought Becky home to a basement apartment near the home of Colleen's parents, anxious to follow their doctor's instructions not to let her be around other children. With Colleen preoccupied by her illness, Neal conscientiously felt that Becky should sleep in their bed. Then the concerned young father "slept with his head about six inches off the pillow." When he awoke one morning and couldn't see Becky where he had placed her, he was frantic for a few minutes, half awake, searching for her—until he found her safely asleep in a corner of the bed covers.

Neal (holding Cory) and Becky during Grandfather Hinckley's visit to Washington, D.C.

Becky was naturally the child on whom her parents first practiced their parental communication skills. One Sunday when the family was in church, Colleen asked Becky, then about nine, to go home and put some potatoes in the oven to bake for dinner. To prevent the potatoes from bursting, she told Becky, "Before you turn on the heat, poke a fork into each potato so the air will come out." When she arrived home and opened the oven, Colleen found a fork stuck into each baking potato— just as she had asked.

Cory was born in Washington, D.C., in 1953, when Neal and Colleen still couldn't afford a car. When Colleen's labor began, she called their friend Ralph Mecham, who drove her from their suburban home to a hospital in the city. Neal rushed to the hospital from his Senate office, arriving barely in time for the birth.

Nancy was born in 1957, the only one born on time—a "hard

charger, like her dad," Colleen said. Then Jane came along two years later, during a busy summer in her father's job at the University of Utah. As soon as Jane had safely arrived, Neal had to hurry back to the campus. When the nurses took Colleen from the delivery room to her regular room, they wondered where her husband was. About that time, Colleen's father, George, entered a hospital elevator to be with Fern, her mother, who was there for some tests. When the nurses saw George, they asked Colleen, "Oh, is this your husband?"

TWENTY-FIVE

THE MAXWELL FAMILY

ELDER MAXWELL PERHAPS UNCONSCIOUSLY summarized many of his own approaches to parenting in remarks he shared in some Saturday evening sessions of stake conferences in the early 1980s. He talked about building a happy "storehouse of memories" from a list of desirable family practices he had compiled. They included structuring family activities to create pleasant memories, fathers giving blessings to their children, husbands giving blessings to their wives, giving prime time to prime relationships, providing pleasant little surprises for family members, parents writing letters to their children, parents bearing testimony privately to their children, reading scriptures aloud together, having frequent gospel conversations, parents willingly learning from their children, helping family members deal with opposition, holding back clever but possibly cutting comments, and ensuring that the parents are both Christians and theologians.

The memories of the Maxwell children from their own home life track this list with unerring consistency. For example, it became clear to all of them early on that, with clocklike regularity, their task-oriented father would set aside his normal preoccupations so that he could just enjoy a good time with them. Son-in-law Marc Sanders has always been "impressed that someone in his position is home at five o'clock. He gets a lot done, but he doesn't let work dominate him." That has been a constant pattern. As a deliberate choice, Nancy said, Neal put both his time and "his money into the memories" he would build with his children.

Cory's earliest memory of his father is of the two of them and Becky raking leaves in their yard—and then, laughing together, diving into the pile of leaves. In the family's early years, Saturday mornings were always work time, with the schedule "pretty programmed" for everyone to pitch in to do household chores. Neal would rouse the slumbering masses with the University of Utah fight song, reminding them that they could play as soon as the work was done. Sundays were always a family day, with regular visits after church to both sets of grandparents, when other duties allowed.

One family excursion into Neal's creative imagination became so entrenched that he has carried it on, by popular demand, with his grandchildren. Somehow he got started making up "Friends of the Forest" stories, starring "Tweedle-Dee and Tweedle-Dum." He told these creative tales to Becky, Cory, Nancy, and Jane when they were very young—and the adventures still continue with his grandchildren; he recently recorded some favorites for the younger ones. What Neal liked best was that this spontaneous story time let him "put my arms around them and lie down on the carpet and just tell them stories."

The children loved how the animals who were the friends of the forest had names just like theirs—such as Cory Cucumber and Jane Jeppson—and each chapter would always have a subtle moral. In one typical tale, the friends of the forest had to find a way to negotiate with the snakes on Snake Mountain to rid the forest of people who wanted the animals to be at war with each other rather than at peace.

Neal's own love of basketball and tennis made it natural for him to engage his children in his playful side. He understood Elder Marvin J. Ashton's comment that a twelve-year-old boy doesn't so much want you to say you love him as he wants you to play ball with him. When Cory got interested in baseball and boxing, Neal practiced

The Maxwell children about 1959 (clockwise from left): Becky, Cory, Nancy, and Jane

baseball with him and then helped teach him to box—even though, Cory later realized, "baseball is a little too slow for Dad."

As the family grew older, they added other activities to their repertoire. Some were informal activities or competitions Neal would make up as the family drove on trips. He often led the family in flying kites, hiding Easter eggs, seeing movies, and making up races—some in which he would race the little ones while he was running backward and they ran forward. Their board games included *Boggle, Scrabble, Monopoly,* and one called *Landslide,* in which Neal's will to win simply couldn't be repressed. Somehow Colleen could never quite muster the competitiveness required of serious *Monopoly* players, because she would always make secret but forbidden side deals with losing players, giving them money under the table or giving away her choice properties, such as "Boardwalk," for a song.

In the pleasant images these events conjure up, one can hear the distant echoes of Neal and Lois racing, as children, from the porch to the trees in the front yard, or building snow forts with Clarence in the backyard, or Clarence's daughters perpetually combing his hair while he read the Sunday comics aloud, imitating each character's voice.

Once the Maxwell children began marrying, the in-laws were always included in ever more challenging competitions—such as some very serious tennis. The family outings have often made room for mixed doubles and other inclusive varieties, but the most intense tennis is reserved for the family singles championship. For years, Neal issued a standing challenge to Cory, Mike, Mark, and Marc that they had to beat him in singles before he turned sixty in 1986—or any victories after that date wouldn't count. Giving no quarter, Neal has always been a tough competitor in these matches. "He'll force you to play your best," says Cory, whose last victory over his father goes back to 1972, before his mission.

On Neal's sixtieth birthday, he sent a can of white Wimbledon tennis balls to each of his four partners in the family men's singles group, with this letter:

> Let the record show that so far as the singles matches between aging Neal Ash Maxwell and [these] aspirants are concerned, only two aberrations appeared: Briefly and fleetingly—before any challenge had been issued—in 1972 with Cory (was Calvin Coolidge President then?), and with Mike in a Henefer hiatus involving a borrowed racquet.

Neal's letter extended appreciation for "encouraging a senior citizen in his performance" and ended with "a plea for mercy" regarding future matches.

At the other end of the spectrum of family experience, the Maxwell parenting style called for quite a different set of skills and responses when a child needed discipline. Again reflecting the way they had been reared, both Colleen and Neal tended to govern their children as Joseph Smith governed his people—by teaching correct principles and leaving room for self-governance. Their children were not in doubt about how they were expected to behave, which allowed most of their parents' counseling to be suggestive and nondirective.

In general, the Maxwells were realistic and flexible. Both of them preferred a "suggestion-box climate" in their home, as opposed to "parental rigidity." The children got the message early that Neal saw himself as a father or grandfather first and a university officer or General Authority second, and his willingness to share time with the family affirmed the message. The good-natured spirit of their family activities also created an open, trusting climate.

When their children needed to learn a behavioral lesson, the parents usually tried to step back and let the children learn for themselves. They felt from the earliest stages that if they "butted heads" too often, they might do a child more harm than good. They also respected their children's agency and worked at helping all of them make their own good decisions.

Sometimes, however, directness was called for. In his teens, Cory habitually teased his sisters, especially Nancy. On one occasion, while driving in the car, Neal spoke directly: "Cory, you need to back off and be kinder to Nancy, because she's suffering under the teasing." Another time, Cory was playing typically loud teenage music on the home stereo system. When Neal heard a song that contained profanity, he "did not stroll, he marched in and said he would not have that music played in their house." After that, Cory was more careful to screen his own music, in or out of the home. They later worked out an accommodation by putting a small stereo player near Cory's bedroom—partly to appease him and partly to contain the sound.

When the Maxwell girls dated young men their parents weren't enthusiastic about, Neal and Colleen generally were patient. Neal did "roll his eyes a few times" about some boys the girls dated on the grounds that they didn't want to seem exclusive. It was also clear to all of the children that they were expected to be home by a reasonable hour—and that their parents would either be waiting up or be expecting them to check in at the master bedroom when they returned home.

Despite her gentle exterior, Colleen had no trouble showing tough love. Once when Neal was out of town, she became upset because the children had become so quarrelsome she couldn't get their attention. So she simply announced she was leaving—"Okay, I'm going out the door." And she did. The children looked at themselves and said, "Good night! Mom's leaving. What have we done?" Colleen was similarly direct on a later family vacation when a group of grandchildren were getting out of control in a swimming pool. She marched them "back to the motel room and read them the riot act" for the purpose of maintaining family peace—an environmental quality she values very highly.

Some other sensitive occasions called for unusually creative remedies. Once one of the children became very frustrated by a seminary class, feeling perhaps some of the disappointment Neal had known himself at times in his youth classes. The outcome of the class was in jeopardy because of repeated absences. Knowing of Neal's visible Church role and knowing how he felt about studying the scriptures, this youngster hardly dared raise the problem, but the absences were piling up. A candid conversation followed. Because all avenues for reconciling with the teacher seemed closed, Neal had an idea: "All right, you read your assigned material with great care, and we'll discuss your reading at length one evening each week." A period of home study followed, which proved satisfying for both student and teacher.

The children sometimes sensed clear inspiration in their parents' interventions. When one of them was working in a faraway city one summer, "out of the blue" Neal called the child and "asked if anything was wrong." The child was struggling a little and felt that the call was truly inspired. Child and father had another of those candid conversations, eventually agreeing on how to have the summer end better than it had started.

Every child's adolescence can sometimes be a little turbulent. During such a season, one of the children fell into some behavior that was wrong and potentially embarrassing. When Colleen learned of one such incident, she just said with a disappointed tone that she expected better. When Neal came home a few days later, this youngster had already gone to bed. Neal went into the room, sat on the end of the bed, and said, "I love you, and you've got more potential than this." The child felt more parental concern than real chastisement. Neal and Colleen weren't happy with what had taken place, but their focus was more on the child than on how the behavior might reflect on them.

One of Colleen's unique contributions to the Maxwells' parenting was her desire to teach her family the "service perspective" that motivated her so much. She taught this orientation almost constantly by example, as she visited people in need and invited to dinner a steady stream of members of the student ward, widows and widowers, or others she felt needed a little friendship. While they didn't dare say so at the time, some of her children recall that they sometimes would have preferred to have their parents to themselves for Sunday dinner. With the passage of time, they have come to appreciate more the compassion that was so naturally their mother's way.

Sometimes Colleen would more directly teach about service. Once when Cory was in junior high school, and without consulting him, his mother made a deal with a widow in the neighborhood that Cory would take her trash to the curb on the weekly garbage day. When he protested a little at being conscripted for such service, Colleen explained that this was his chance to help someone who really needed it—and besides, it would be good for him. So he did it—a little grudgingly at first, but he did do it.

Colleen taught about service not just to be nice but because she had learned from experience how serving others matures the giver. She never forgot having read about a sample of young people who were acutely withdrawn, backward, and unhappy. The study reported that "in every case," the youth "were withdrawn because of over-concern with self," which revealed a lack of concern for others. She was also influenced by her mother, who was always kind to strangers. During the Depression, Fern Hinckley was ever ready to welcome people who were "down on their luck" who were willing to work in exchange for a hot meal.

A favorite family story that captures Colleen's service instincts occurred during a vacation trip to California. Neal had run into a grocery store for some provisions while the family waited in the car. Looking out the car window, Colleen spotted a large number of shopping carts strewn all over the parking lot. She instinctively jumped from the car, rounded up the stray carts and, by the time Neal returned, had them herded all together at a pickup point near the store entrance. The rest of the family just watched her in amazement—which some of them have since realized was their much-too-common response to her energetic example.

Neal has often led his family into communications and activities in a relatively structured way. The modern Latter-day Saint family home evening program began in 1964. The Maxwells found that the regular pattern of meeting every Monday night was frequently interrupted by Neal's duties at a state university that couldn't realistically accommodate their desire to preserve Monday evenings for family time. But, as needed, they found other ways and times to fulfill the purpose of those evenings. They would occasionally share a church video or read scriptures together. The family was not rigid about their reading pattern, but Neal would frequently engage them during dinner or elsewhere in "gospel conversations" about a scriptural question or religious topic. He always looked for natural ways to draw his children into thought-provoking conversation.

One such moment was the day when he asked nine-year-old Cory for some feedback about his parenting. Standing in the kitchen, Neal pointed to the two ends of the oven door handle and said, "Tell me how I'm doing as a father. If this on the left-hand side is too strict and the right-hand side is too lenient, where would you say I am?" Cory wasn't prepared for such a question but felt complimented that his father "would care what I thought." He believed his dad was about in the middle, maybe slightly on the strict side. Later on, Neal and Colleen would hold a relaxed "exit interview" with their children at the time of their marriages, asking what they could have done better as parents. Becky, for instance, recalled in that visit how much it had meant to her that they trusted her in a certain situation that was more delicate for her than they had realized.

Sometimes at dinner, Neal would ask each one present to offer some specific and deserved word of praise for another family member. At other times, he would begin a family conversation with something like, "Let me tell you some good things I have observed about each of you." He had a kind of "amazing knack" for when and how to express

Neal and Colleen with their children in the late 1960s

himself at such moments. Becky remembers they were "not the least bit phony but very sincere" comments.

The expanded version of this practice came in the form of personal letters Neal would now and then write to his children, beginning when the older children entered adolescence. He wrote the first series during Thanksgiving 1970. The letters are similar in their general approach but carefully tailored to the individual child. Each begins with measured expressions of praise, followed by the gentlest of suggestions.

After describing some personal qualities he admired and liked, he told one child:

> If I were to make any suggestions to you in the spirit of love, they would not be many. One is that you have unused intellect that would give you much satisfaction and excitement if you could bring it to bear more frequently. You do have a tendency to "get by," and because you are quite bright you seldom press yourself to your limits. Since I was somewhat similarly inclined during my youth, I can only say to you that I had much more fun later when I . . . was more demanding of myself.

To another child he wrote:

> You are quite open and candid about your feelings. . . .
> While this trait is a strength, you will need to make allowance
> for the fact that when someone is candid, she or he needs to
> make an extra effort to show concern to compensate for the can-
> dor.

And to another:

> I trust you and respect you and simply want you to know of
> my love. You are wise beyond your years. Forgive me and your
> mother if in our high expectations of you we anticipate things
> prematurely [or] expect more from someone who is already
> doing so very much.

Because of his illegible handwriting ("unreformed Egyptian,"
President Harold B. Lee called it), Neal's letters were always more useful when his secretary typed them. He once left a handwritten note for
Cory as he was hurrying out of town. When Cory picked up the note,
he "stood at the kitchen sink and pondered it for the longest time and
then said, 'Mom, I just can't read this.'" When he handed Colleen the
note, they discovered Cory had been trying to read it upside down.
Either direction, it all looked the same to him. And Colleen was "not
sure I was able to help him a whole lot when we turned it right side
up."

The children recall having their own family testimony meeting a
time or two each year. And on one occasion in the late 1960s, Neal
invited each child to sit down with him alone so he could bear his testimony in private. He told Cory then that he had recently learned
Harold B. Lee had made a practice of bearing his testimony privately
to each of his children, and he liked the idea. He wanted Cory to know
that what he felt and said in private was the same as what he might
hear him say over the pulpit.

Jane remembered that his sharing of his private spiritual feelings
had a "real impact" on her. It showed her how much the gospel meant
to her father. She could see that he "really wanted to live the gospel
completely. He was serious about progressing." She then felt more

motivation for her own life. We have already seen how stirred Neal was when he learned about fathers' blessings from Oscar McConkie—he immediately wanted a blessing from his own father, which he finally received after a few years of gentle coaxing. Meanwhile, he adopted the practice of giving each of his children a father's blessing, recorded word by word for family records. He usually gave these blessings the night before each child's wedding.

In more recent years, Neal has been careful to coordinate his schedule with the family's, making sure he and Colleen spend regular time with family members. They have met monthly with their married children, attending the temple one month and planning something recreational the next month. When the adults are together, Neal will frequently "engineer gospel discussions." Sometimes those discussions have been about Neal's drafts of his books or conference talks, because he has found his own family members to be among his most trusted sounding boards. He has also maintained a regular association with his sisters, as he previously did with his parents and with Colleen's.

Neal's penchant for planning to ensure the success of major family events is illustrated by excerpts from two letters he wrote to his married children and their spouses in 1988, just before the group was leaving to join him and Colleen for some vacation time together in Hawaii:

> Do all you can to prepare your family for unity, stressing that this is a "once in a lifetime" trip, observing that we will need to be loving and patient with each other. . . . Each couple . . . [is] to bring a game or an inexpensive treat to be used at crucial moments. . . .
>
> Everybody should pack LIGHTLY. We will have laundry facilities [but] don't forget swimming suits.
>
> You probably ought to have a departure drill a couple of times before you go. . . . Remember our tickets are nonrefundable. . . . If we miss the flights, that is the ball game!
>
> It will be wonderful to be with you.
>
> Remember to allow enough time for both parking and checking in [at the airport]. . . . Somewhere along the way, if we

could have 15 or 20 minutes with just the [grandchildren],
Colleen and I would like to visit with them. . . .

Begin to think now of the things that you are apt to remember too late. . . .

We will pray for your safety and health, and for a rich stockpiling of memories.

His style as the conscientious tour guide was evidently influenced by past experience, because he had already established a reputation among the family for his dedication to keeping the flock moving along. The family has not let him forget about the time his anxiousness about staying on schedule deprived them of seeing some picturesque castles on the green hillsides of the Rhine River in Germany.

The story is that Neal cut off the sightseeing early and urged the family from the top deck of their vessel down into the hold, so they could get off quickly when the ship docked. They ended up waiting, with no room for a view, for more than half an hour in the heat of a stifling crowd before the tour concluded. Not long thereafter, Neal hustled the family off one side of a very long train as it stopped. Then they discovered, too late, that they were on the wrong side of the train, bags and all, unable to get to the correct side of the tracks. The waiting express train they were to catch pulled away without them. The family has since teased that, as Nancy said, they "missed a fair amount of Europe just sitting inside [boats and] train stations."

Such moments from the Europe trip, with Neal pacing to hurry up the family, led to the inside joke that has affectionately become known as his "Europe face"—a "help-me-endure look" of "exasperation and frustration that still appears occasionally. Instead of yelling or getting frustrated, that was kind of . . . how he let off steam. Mainly it just made us all laugh." But the family understands the look, and they try to take signals from it.

Another feature of the family trips was that Neal and Colleen were determined to make each experience educational. Without that dimension, Neal might well have lost interest in family travels, because, as some of his General Authority associates have noticed, he is "probably the world's worst tourist," getting easily bored with typical tourist

"Grandpa Neal" telling stories to grandchildren while on a family vacation

stops—cathedrals and art museums. When the Maxwells were with Russell and Dantzel Nelson in Bangkok, for instance, between Church meetings someone offered them a boat trip along the klongs, the picturesque local canals. When Neal "politely declined, . . . Sister Nelson, Sister Maxwell, and Brother Nelson" made the trip.

At the same time, Neal has an unusually high interest in places and artifacts that reflect his interest in politics, history, and capable leaders. Colleen has usually taken charge of assigning family members to do research on each area they might visit and then report to the family when they reached that spot. As Cory and Nancy recalled, with Neal and Colleen "you never just sort of go someplace; it's an educational experience—a working vacation."

They followed this same approach with their grandchildren when taking the extended family on a two-week bus tour across the country to visit Church history sites in 1994. Some family members were a little apprehensive about the trip's extensive structure and homework. Sons-in-law Marc Sanders and Mark Anderson "thought it would be a bust, but it was fabulous."

A family videotape during one moment of this trip captured Neal saying a few words to the family group at a spot near the Peter Whitmer home in New York:

> We're probably within 100 yards of where the witnesses saw the golden plates. So it's very special. . . .
>
> Thank you for being patient with me. . . . One of the things that happen when we love each other, is that we . . . see each other's little imperfections. . . . Those are things we have to work on. We're bound to notice them in each other, and I'm sure you notice them in me. To know that we're given time by Heavenly Father to work on those faults and overcome them is a remarkable and generous thing.
>
> [Lorenzo Snow said he] saw the minor imperfections in the Prophet Joseph Smith. But instead of being offended by them, they made him grateful, feeling that if the Lord could use [Joseph], with his imperfections, maybe there was some hope for him.

As the Church history trip illustrates, Neal and Colleen have worked consistently to include their grandchildren in regular family activities that usually have some spiritual or educational purpose at their core, visible or not. Colleen also tries to take each grandchild to a special lunch on his or her birthday—where just being together is purpose enough.

With experience, Neal has learned to create conversations and interactions that include those of all ages. Said Karen, "He does it even with the smallest grandchildren," always drawing them into a conversation. "He's very attentive, listens very carefully, and you know by what he says back . . . that's he's processed what you've said and gone a step beyond . . . and you have to think more."

One favorite tradition already established among the grandchildren is "Grandpa Neal's firesides," which they are invited to attend every few months at the Maxwell home—as soon as they're ten. (The informal "Grandpa Neal" grew out of a time when both Neal and Colleen's parents were still alive, and their first grandchildren were confused by the sheer number of relatives who were all named Grandpa

The extended Maxwell family at Winter Quarters in 1994

and Grandma.) Colleen has made little briefcases marked with the name of each grandchild, so they can collect handouts and other materials that launch them with their own filing system for gospel topics. She has also created a successful "peacemaker" project—each grandchild whose parents judge him or her to have been a good peacemaker during a given period is invited to the Maxwells' home for a family sleepover.

The view of the grandchildren about all of this was captured when Neal dropped by Mike and Becky's home one day. Becky called upstairs to three-year-old Robbie, asking if he'd like to come down and see Grandpa Neal. "Should I bring my scriptures?" Robbie called back. Well, not really. As one observer described it, Neal "can play in the leaves, move in for the kill at tennis, read stories or make jokes [with his grandchildren] . . . He is often jovial and—most emphatically—does not require family members to carry around Bibles all the time. Still, he returns again and again to the scriptures . . . drawing refreshment like water on parched lips" in his frequent "gospel conversations" with any group, including his grandchildren.

The grandchildren have echoed back the same combination of loving commitment and deliberateness that they have felt from Neal and Colleen. On the Maxwells' fortieth wedding anniversary, the sixteen grandchildren old enough to write their names signed the following "family pledge" and presented it to their grandparents:

> In honor of our grandparents' . . . anniversary and because we love them so much, we sign this pledge to live worthy to marry in the temple of the Lord, and to fulfill honorable missions as we are called. We will do our best to insure there will be no empty chairs when we meet in the life beyond. Signed with love and admiration.

The spouses of the Maxwell children have been able to watch the family's style with the objectivity made possible by comparisons with their own families. Cory's wife, Karen, also came from a large and close Latter-day Saint family, but she found the Maxwell family style rather different from what she'd known—especially in its degree of organization. Her parents had always "just trusted that things would happen" all right, and they usually did. By comparison, the Maxwell "vacations were so civilized, compared to what I was used to." As a child, she had "hardly ever stayed in a hotel or motel," because her family just camped. But the Maxwells "always had to have a tennis court." And "agendas for a vacation? . . . That would not happen in my family."

But Karen has come to see that being so structured and getting on to the next thing on the agenda is simply "interesting" to Neal. From the time he helped arrange things in 1975 so that Cory could surprise Karen with a marriage proposal on the scenic lookout atop the Church Office Building, she has seen his unique creativity at work. The careful planning also shows how the Maxwells give. They will "feel the spiritual needs" of family members or other people, and "come up with a practical way to meet" the need, "polishing the idea until everything is packed as full of goodness and meaning as one of Neal's talks. Getting an idea and finding a way to embody it in either words or deed, or both, is their specialty."

Mark Anderson, Nancy's husband, brought the family a fresh perspective. He said, "I never would have guessed in a million years that

I was going to marry a General Authority's daughter." On his first trip to the house, he spotted Neal through a window, wearing a white shirt. "Great," he thought. "What am I going to do, and how am I going to act?" As he walked in, Neal began offering him waffles, pancakes, and juice—"he was firing food at me."

Then began what the family calls The Conversation. Neal asked Mark if he had a "wanderlust." Mark "wasn't quite sure what *wanderlust* meant." They skipped that, and Neal went on to the topic of literature. He asked, "Who is your favorite author?" Mark said he had only a "dimly lit perspective" about "books—who writes them and who's good." Then he remembered "some things I was forced to read in freshman English" and offered the only book he "thought was the slightest bit literary—*Catcher in the Rye*." Whereupon, Neal "looked like he'd swallowed a lemon."

Moving on, Neal asked if a certain course Mark mentioned was a "garden variety" class. Mark "didn't know if he was talking about snakes or flowers or soil—I had no idea." To Mark's relief, they finally discovered a mutual interest in tennis, at which point Neal "seemed quite perky and offered to play me." When their match began a few weeks later, in the fall of 1975, Neal started playing with his left-handed and "completely unorthodox form." Mark, who had played some pretty demanding tennis in his day, thought "this is going to be a long afternoon." Then, "pretty soon, he was hacking me to shreds." Mark beat him only twice after that, years later, after "many, many matches. For a hacker, he's remarkable."

By the time Mark was ready for induction into the Maxwell clan, he was prepared to appreciate the formal welcome given him at the wedding breakfast by Becky's husband, Mike Ahlander. Mike warned him about family tennis and other games: "Neal doesn't like to lose. Of course, you'll soon be grateful" for Colleen's generosity, because "if you're losing she's always willing to . . . give you money in a grueling game of *Monopoly*."

"You'll come to know Neal's 'Europe face,'" when people aren't there an hour early for a train, or when one of his daughters is still using the electric curlers with two other daughters waiting to use them—and the family is "supposed to be at the Tabernacle in three minutes." You'll "soon learn that if Colleen isn't fasting for the garbage man, she's straightening the grocery carts" at the supermarket. You'll help Neal's limited mechanical aptitude if "you can just label what few tools he does have, so he'll know what each is for." Then Mike recalled going to California with the Maxwells before he and Becky were engaged. "Neal kept calling me [Becky's former boyfriend's name]. Colleen was working on our engagement sampler, and my name was already stitched in."

Time has drawn the family closer, where all have seen in Neal a gradual "warming and mellowing" and an increase in patience. Some of that has come from stretching together in their shared experiences. For instance, the first grandchild, Mike and Becky's Rachel, was stillborn after a full-term pregnancy. As painfully sad as it was for the parents, Colleen also found it the hardest trial of her life to that time. Even after they had shared many feelings about the incident with Mike and Becky, Neal wrote a note to them that would foreshadow some ideas to which they would all return at the time of his own leukemia:

> Peter tells us that when we suffer [while] keeping the commandments, this redounds to our eternal good. . . .
>
> This experience will increase your abilities to help others who suffer, and it will give you a deeper . . . perspective of the gospel and of life. Sometimes . . . we can learn . . . only . . . with experience.
>
> I love you . . . and appreciate the strength you have been to us all, for . . . we have wept . . . twice, once for you and once for ourselves.

Another unexpected sorrow came later, the day Karen and Cory learned from an ultrasound examination that their newly expected baby girl would be born without a left hand and might have other difficulties. When they shared the news with Neal and Colleen, Neal's response was, "We really have a special spirit coming."

Karen reflected on Neal's attitude not long afterward while she attended the dedication service for the Bountiful Temple. As the choir and congregation sang "The Spirit of God," Karen found new meaning in the song's phrase "angels are coming to visit the earth." She wrote to Neal and Colleen, "I knew that our personal family angel is coming,

Elder and Sister Maxwell with their children, their spouses, and all the grandchildren in 1997

and that her visit will be a precious revelation if we will be righteous and ready. . . . Your efforts are never unnoticed—only too seldom acknowledged."

By the time Anna Josephine was nearly five, she was already teaching her family, including her grandparents. As Neal recounted in a general conference talk, Anna Jo's cousin, Talmage, age three, had tried to reassure her:

> "Anna Jo, when you grow up you will have five fingers."
> Anna Jo said, "No, Talmage, when I grow up I won't have five fingers, but when I get to heaven I will have a hand."

Neal added:

> If Anna Jo, who has difficult days ahead, stays steady within what has been allotted to her, she will continue to be a great blessing to many people! . . .
> I pray for this in the name of Him who counts all sparrows and all fingers.

So Anna Jo, Neal told Hugh Hewitt, "is already lighting up the landscape." Not only she but her family and others "are getting an experience in love" from her presence—such as the time when Anna Jo was still four and her father, Cory, offered the family prayer. After he finished, Anna Jo said, "Good! You did it all by yourself." Mr. Hewitt later said that the knowing tenderness in the way Neal talked about Anna Jo during their TV interview reflected clearly to him Neal's "conviction of God's involvement with her."

After half a century of parenting and grandparenting, Elder Maxwell has never been more sure that family life is the central place where children—and parents—learn to live the gospel. As a Church leader, then, "you'd have a pretty hollow victory if you failed as a father, even though you might be a terrific visitor at stake conference." He counts it among his greatest gifts that he and Colleen have been "equally yoked" in their own marriage, that they grew up in homes with attentive parents, and that they have been showered with the riches of a faithful posterity. There is no group with whom Neal would rather share, and learn about, the gospel than his own family. And in his mature years, he's "never been more engaged in or excited about the gospel than right now," and "sharing with each other and with family is the centerpiece of our spiritual nourishment."

That feeling of being so much "at home" with the gospel now seems to represent the full flowering of the seeds that were planted in the warm spiritual soil of Neal's own childhood—at home, with his parents. And what he feels now is simply the mature version of what he felt then, with each life stage giving meaning to the other. Perhaps, in the most essential ways, happy families really are very much alike.

PART IX

A UTAH MAN AM I
1956–70

TWENTY-SIX

SINGULARITY IN DIVERSITY

WHEN NEAL MAXWELL BEGAN WORKING at age
thirty as assistant director of public relations at the University of Utah
in 1956, he couldn't have imagined what awaited him over the next
fourteen years. He had no academic training beyond a bachelor's
degree, he had no experience in higher education administration, and
he had no career path in mind.

Nonetheless, his experience during those years provided a nearly
ideal preparation for two different roles to which the First Presidency
would eventually assign him. He would be called in 1967 to a leadership committee that would help prepare the Church organization for
its expansion across the world. And in 1970, he would become commissioner of education at a time when the Church would need to
respond to a far more educated and more global membership.

Because Neal didn't know he would be given responsibilities of
such breadth and complexity, he didn't know that he needed to gain
experience in as many fields as he did—and that he needed to hurry.
But with wind-ripping speed, the experiences came—not because he
was always qualified for them, nor because he sought them, nor because

he knew where all of this was going. On the contrary, he almost unintentionally pursued an unusual, multitrack career path that, in some ways, makes sense best when it is understood as Nephi understood his path of discipleship: "I was led by the Spirit, not knowing beforehand the things which I should do" (1 Nephi 4:6).

In fourteen years at the university, Neal was given roughly fourteen different jobs, often overlapping with each other, almost any one of which required particular training and each of which could have been the basis for an entire specialized career. His assortment of tasks (some part-time and some full-time) included public relations officer, journalist, recruiter of scholarship students, executive staff assistant, TV talk show host, university administrator, political lobbyist, fund-raiser, teacher, scholar, public commentator, leadership consultant, citizen leader, student life expert, educational consultant, political consultant, and bridge builder between the Latter-day Saint and the non-Latter-day Saint communities in the Mormon heartland.

Many of those who knew Neal in a single role considered him a budding specialist in that field. But in fact, his U of U career is best understood as a *composite* of many specialties. His uniqueness was in his versatility. He was a generalist who had a knack for picking up on-the-job training, even when he wasn't formally qualified. Much of that training was like his tennis game or his speaking style—self-taught and distinctive. Each new experience made him more valuable for the next job, as each field improved his perspective on other fields.

Because he lacked some traditional qualifications and specific aspirations, his selection for each job was often "on the merits" by leaders who were drawn more to his innate capacity than to his resume. In fact, for some of these jobs—if he had applied in writing—his paper credentials might not have been competitive enough even to earn a finalist's interview.

Neal began looking for a job in Utah after he and Colleen decided it was time to return home from Washington, even though they had several options for continued employment in the nation's capital. A Washington-based insurance company had offered him an attractive position. And, more of a temptation, Senator Bennett encouraged him to stay on the staff to begin the Senator's second term in 1956. But Neal felt he had learned the essentials he had gone there to learn. And though politics would always fascinate him, he'd become disenchanted with what government programs could do. Although "the governmental approach to human problems is helpful," he increasingly believed, it "doesn't really do the job. The gospel does."

By this time, Neal was feeling, if only in a vague way, that he could address the individual needs of other people more effectively by working in higher education—and at the center of the Church population. In some way that wasn't connected to his employment interests, he also felt a desire to take the freshness and vitality he had felt in Washington's Latter-day Saint community back to Utah. He told Doug and Corene Parker in 1956 that he and Colleen had found refreshing spiritual strength among the D.C. Church members of the "mission field," and they wanted to take that attitude of deeper commitment back home, somehow to help make a difference. Ralph Mecham sensed that Neal was preprogrammed to return to Utah for an unclear purpose that Ralph felt had spiritual overtones.

The Church had provided an exhilarating dimension for their Washington experience. With Colleen serving as ward Primary president and Neal in the stake Young Men's presidency and then in the stake mission presidency, church life in the D.C. stake had been "totally consuming" for them. Their church commitments "took over our life. And we liked it."

The Maxwells were part of a stimulating study group among young LDS couples then living in Washington, including Russell and Dantzel Nelson, who had known Colleen during her college days. Russell Nelson said they "hadn't dealt with anybody who was interested in conversation and . . . idea development" about religion and politics quite the way Neal was—and they found it "refreshing and invigorating." Brother Nelson assumed at that stage that Neal "would go into politics" as a potential senator or congressman.

Neal served in 1955–56 as a counselor to the stake mission president, Reed Benson. Through this association, Reed's father, Elder Ezra Taft Benson, then Secretary of Agriculture, came to know Neal well enough that he offered him a position in that department. Neal was grateful for this interest, but he had already decided against working in a federal agency long term. Elder Benson wrote him that his decision to return to Utah was "understandable" but "somewhat disappointing to me."

In early 1956, the *Deseret News* published an opinion piece Neal had written about Democratic Minnesota senator Hubert Humphrey and agricultural price supports, which reflected Neal's interest in journalism as well as politics. He even toyed with the idea of becoming a writer for a Salt Lake newspaper but found no openings. Elder Benson wrote Neal, "You will be interested to know that the President [Eisenhower] read the editorial to a group of us yesterday. We all got a good laugh. Keep writing."

Neal traveled throughout Utah during 1956 helping with Senator Bennett's reelection campaign. He met a variety of community leaders, relationships that would later aid his work for the University of Utah. He also learned that Parry Sorensen, director of public relations at the university, was looking for an assistant director. He met with Parry, who offered him the job. Uncertain whether to take it, Neal talked with his and Colleen's friend, Lowell Bennion, at the Salt Lake Institute of Religion. Lowell encouraged Neal to stay in Washington to capitalize on what he had already invested there. In the end, it was Colleen's intuition about taking this job that made the difference.

In the fall of 1956, Neal moved into a shared office in the university's administrative center, the Park Building, absorbing a hefty salary cut and occupying a "splintered oak desk and a chair that broke every once in a while." He found that "disengagement from the Potomac was not easy" and that writing press material in fact yielded little contact with students. Still, writing about university news introduced him to many faculty and administrators.

His talents were soon put to work in other ways; Homer Durham saw to that. Durham, Neal's student mentor, was now academic vice president to A. Ray Olpin, president of the university from 1946 until 1964. Durham arranged a welcoming party at his home, introducing a number of administrators and faculty leaders, including President

Olpin, to his "protégé newly returned" from Washington. Neal reported about life in Washington, especially the Senate, telling stories and commenting on current affairs. Lowell Durham, Homer's brother and a faculty leader, enjoyed Neal's "beautifully-paced report," which disposed of "the layman's cloak-and-dagger concept" of international intrigue in the nation's capital.

President Olpin confided to his journal that Neal Maxwell was "very frank and used fine English, made a good presentation and caused me to think he would be a good field man or off-campus representative of the university." Within a year, Olpin asked him to become coordinator of scholarships, in addition to his public relations duties.

Neal worked with scholarships during 1957–58. Utah law allowed the university to waive tuition for a small proportion of Utah students. Rather than leaving these as randomly assigned waivers, Neal began traveling the state to recruit promising high school graduates to attend the university by offering the tuition waivers as scholarships. President Olpin thought his approach too generous, but Neal stood his ground, urging that the university needed to recruit aggressively the state's brightest students, using the scholarships as an incentive.

To Neal's surprise, Ray Olpin must have been persuaded not only about the scholarship policy but also about Neal's ability to articulate a position. Perhaps nudged by Homer Durham, in 1958 Olpin invited Neal to become full-time assistant to the president, which would become a tutorial in university administration. Now Neal found himself drafting presidential speeches, memos, and overseeing calendaring as well as acting as the executive secretary for the university's management team—President Olpin, academic vice president Homer Durham, and business vice president Paul Hodson.

Meanwhile, Neal simultaneously pursued other interests. He decided to capture some of his Senate experience on paper while his impressions were still fresh, publishing an article entitled "The Conference of Western Senators" in 1957 in a U of U departmental political science journal. By 1958, he hungered to teach on the campus

and saw he'd need an advanced degree to do that. Reassured by his publication that his Senate experience was a good source for political science research, he set up a graduate program with the political science
faculty, who had earlier been his professors. He had to schedule his
classes and research around his full-time job demands, but he was energetic enough and the department flexible enough to make it work. He
completed the M.A. degree in 1961. "Regionalism in the United States
Senate: The West" was his thesis, in which he showed how senators
crossed party lines to cooperate on such shared regional interests as
developing water resources in the arid western states.

In 1958, Neal wrote a graduate student paper on the United
States Senate's role in foreign policy. To his amazement, a national
magazine, *The Nation,* printed it, with the daring title "Congress
Abdicates on Foreign Policy." His issue was whether there is any real
role in foreign policy for the Senate Foreign Relations Committee or
Congress, or is the constitutional power of congress to declare war a
mere anachronism? He was a little uncomfortable about appearing in
a fairly liberal publication, but the article enhanced his hopes for some
kind of career in political science. It would remain his most nationally
visible publication.

The diversity in Neal's university interests was beginning to multiply by 1958. That year the university launched KUED, its new public television station. In what would become a kind of marquee offering
for KUED, station manager Keith Engar invited Neal to become the
moderator of a weekly interview series called *Tell Me.* Neal had no specific training for such a job. His only comparable experience had been
his student radio interview show several years earlier. But he had developed enough poise during his Washington years to feel comfortable
interviewing public figures on a live TV show—so he took on the project, continuing it for ten years, despite the increasing demands of his
other assignments.

As the moderator for *Tell Me,* Neal became known as a "sort of
Larry King Live for the university"—although that comparison is too
dramatic. Television was still in its infancy, the country was not yet
dominated by TV celebrities, and the program's technical quality was

On the set of the weekly KUED television program Tell Me, *which aired for ten years*

"fairly amateurish," compared to the talk shows of today. It was transmitted in black and white, and its style was that of a pleasant conversation rather than a probing, confrontational drama. This was long before the era of investigative ambush reporting.

In a relaxed atmosphere, Neal asked questions of general interest and then listened respectfully as the guest often rambled about his views and experience. Audiences enjoyed the novelty of television enough that they weren't "as sensitive then to background noise," nor did they mind the simple camera angles, the talking heads, and the interviewer's only occasional interruptions to paragraphs of narrative. Most shows went smoothly, although one guest "froze up" ten minutes into what was to have been a thirty-minute interview. Neal rescued the show by asking many extra questions to compensate for the guest's "Gary Cooper style" one-word answers.

Happily for Neal in several of his duties, 1958 was also the year Elizabeth Haglund arrived at the university, filling the vacancy in public relations created by Neal's appointment as assistant to President Olpin. Liz became a loyal and able ally behind many of the scenes where Neal was increasingly onstage. She didn't know what to make of Neal when she first arrived, fresh from a long career of working for NBC in network broadcasting in New York City. When she moved into Neal's former office, she found no "evidence of Neal's work," because the office files were mostly empty. That was her first glimpse of his clean desk mentality.

Soon, however, Liz and Neal became trusted professional colleagues. She was a bright New Yorker with years of professional experience and a deep commitment to the Church. As she got to know him, Liz could see that "he had great physical energy, drive, and focus. If you got into a conversation with him, you talked about what he had asked you, and then he was through." Yet she "realized the breadth of his intellect and the practicality of his understanding" and saw that "he was not fooling around." Noting that Neal "caught on so fast to that interviewing stuff," Liz decided to support the *Tell Me* show. Her NBC experience gave Liz both good contacts and "enough chutzpah to go after good people for him to interview."

Liz soon brought her friend Arlene Francis from New York for Neal to interview. Francis was in those days a nationally known and "witty 1950s television personality" on, among other things, the classic game show *What's My Line?* After the *Tell Me* interview, Francis told Liz that Neal "is network material!" She found him skillful and incisive as an interviewer. To prove her point, she returned for another interview a few years later.

During the *Tell Me* years, Neal interviewed United States Supreme Court Justice William O. Douglas, Senator (later Vice President) Hubert Humphrey, Averell Harriman, Utah governors, senators, business leaders, and various Latter-day Saint Church leaders. The experience steadily increased his "grasp of public affairs" and his appreciation for good and influential leaders. He enjoyed what he called "the small talk of great men and women." When he interviewed Elder Joseph Fielding Smith of the Quorum of the Twelve Apostles, he said, "Your father [Joseph F. Smith, sixth President of the Church] was gone

In Chicago covering the 1968 presidential election for National Educational TV

a lot during your childhood. Did you resent that?" Neal expected him to say no, that his father was doing the Lord's work. Instead Elder Smith said, "Yes, it was very hard. But I would go see my aunt after school, and she would talk to me about the Prophet Joseph."

Neal remembers asking Elder Richard L. Evans, also a member of the Twelve, what it was like in his childhood to be poor and to have no father. Elder Evans said his mother made his shirts from used sugar sacks, adding how glad he was when the sugar company began putting floral patterns on their sacks rather than just the company's initials.

Local newspapers praised the TV series as "one of the most stimulating programs seen hereabouts" and "Channel Seven's big show of the evening, the season premiere of *Tell Me*." With this experience, Neal later became a part-time regional editor for the educational network that preceded the Public Broadcasting System, helping to produce TV specials on pressing public issues. In 1968, the network took him to Chicago to provide live commentary on the presidential election. The teleprompter jammed just as he began reporting on election returns from the Western states. He had no choice but to recall voting numbers and states from memory—hoping he would be accurate.

To Elizabeth Haglund, the Neal Maxwell who came into view on the U of U campus in 1958 was barely becoming aware of his gifts, and he felt certain inadequacies in himself and in his background. His "intellect was so alive," he had "an inner light" that reflected itself in a curious combination of meekness and confidence, yet he "worried about not being humble enough." At the same time, as he was trying to make sense of all this, "there was a competent graciousness about him" that was unusual. Eventually Liz saw Neal develop and mature until he had "reached into the mind of the Lord," where he would "know what's there." He would one day become, in her eyes, an Apostle "for all times . . . particularly to the unbelieving, the non-believing, and the once-believing. That makes him enormously valuable . . . because he is so singular a spirit."

TWENTY-SEVEN

PRESIDENT OLPIN AND POLITICAL SCIENCE

WHEN A. RAY OLPIN BECAME PRESIDENT of the University of Utah in 1946, a liberal arts college embarked on a massive transformation to become a full-fledged university. G. Homer Durham said at Olpin's funeral that "more than any single individual" he had "made the University of Utah what it has become and may yet become."

Nationally, the GI Bill and other postwar trends opened American college campuses to a flood of increased enrollments. Conditions in Utah accelerated these trends. With a historic commitment to education and a high birthrate, Utah's high school graduates attended college at twice the national rate. From the time Neal Maxwell went to the university in 1956 until he left in 1970, enrollment doubled, from 10,000 to 20,000 students.

Knowing this flood was headed his way, Ray Olpin searched for growing room. He discovered that in 1850 Brigham Young and the other founders of the university (then called the University of Deseret) originally planned for a campus more than six hundred acres in size. Later the federal government used much of that land to create the military's Fort Douglas. With World War II now over, the fort became a tempting target—its land adjoined the campus to the east. When General Dwight Eisenhower visited Utah in 1948, Olpin had the pluck to hold an impromptu huddle with him.

When Ike saw the original campus maps and heard Olpin's plea for space to educate "the boys that went overseas," the general "scribbled out an order" that eventually transferred 300 acres of Fort Douglas to the university. As Paul Hodson later wrote, "No one ever did a better half hour's work for the state of Utah" than President Olpin did that day. The university soon moved half of its departments into what had been military buildings.

This incident illustrates the creative energy Ray Olpin employed to create a fine university under the sturdy gaze of that white block "U" on the northeastern hills overlooking Salt Lake City. He helped build a major graduate institution that eventually attracted many new students, research funding, a medical center and other major buildings, several superstar faculty, and a reputation as one of the best state universities between the Midwest and California.

President Olpin was from Pleasant Grove, Utah. He had served a Latter-day Saint mission in Japan before doing graduate work in physics at Columbia University. He worked at Bell Labs and then at Ohio State University before his appointment as university president at Utah. In addition to expanding the U of U campus, Olpin relentlessly scoured the nation to recruit faculty members. He believed passionately that "it was preferable to bring a great scholar to many students in Utah than to send a few Utah students east or west in search of graduate and professional training." Many of the people he hired went on to distinguished careers elsewhere—Meredith Wilson became president of the University of Oregon, G. Homer Durham became president of Arizona State, and Sterling McMurrin became U.S. Commissioner of Education. Olpin also made the university into a cultural center, with a summer theater program and arts festival, and he encouraged the creation of KUED, the educational television station.

Those who knew President Olpin well praised his capacity and contributions even as they acknowledged that his aggressive style ruffled a few feathers. Elizabeth Haglund said that although he "did remarkable things for the university, he wasn't a smooth man." He had "unostentatious courage" but needed the diplomatic skills Neal Maxwell brought to his office. He was nonetheless effective in his own way. Once Utah governor J. Bracken Lee sent some regents to "rein in" Olpin's expansionist tendencies, and Olpin ended up persuading them to support his aspirations.

Neal said at his funeral that Olpin's "deep caring for the university was encased in an exterior which covered that caring to the casual viewer. He may have done this to protect the institution at a critical time when it was . . . becoming a genuine university." Working at his side, Neal found him "stern, but strong and courageous," a man who often "took criticism that should have gone to others."

Neal performed a variety of tasks for Olpin—background staff work, agendas, and follow-up for meetings ranging from the three-person university management committee to the board of regents. When Olpin needed help on a speech, he might tell Neal his general themes and then invite him to draft language for Olpin's review—which usually took several revisions. The caption under Neal's smiling, youthful picture in the 1961 U of U yearbook said, "Hard work and quick efficiency help Mr. Maxwell keep abreast of his unending duties."

The board of regents appointed Neal as their secretary in 1961, a job he held for two years. Although ostensibly a clerical task, it put him in contact with board chairman Royden Derrick, president of Western Steel Company, and the other regents. As Neal's stature gradually increased with that group and across the campus, the regents apparently looked to him for more than a clerical role—which may have made President Olpin a bit uncomfortable. Olpin wrote in his journal on July 2, 1962: having "my executive assistant as secretary to the Board" is a "most unusual organization." The secretary "does not manage the university—all he does is make records of the activities of the Board . . . and follow their instructions."

Neal also represented the university in other functions beyond the role of a typical staff assistant—more evidence of his growing influence. In 1960, he was the university Founder's Day speaker, citing founder Orson Spencer's desire for the university to produce "a hun-dredfold and be pleasing unto the Lord." He also represented President Olpin with remarks at a university banquet. Afterward, Elder Marion D. Hanks of the First Council of Seventy wrote Olpin, "While I have known Neal for many years and have always [respected] his abilities and character, I was never more sure that we have in this man great and powerful capacities." The next year Neal gave the baccalaureate address at Carbon College in Price, Utah.

In the meantime, with Homer Durham's help and the credential of Neal's new master's degree, he began in the fall of 1961 to teach a political science class. He held class in the Biology Building, conve-niently located near his office in the Park Building.

His class was titled "American Political Thought," a year-long course divided into three quarters, treating the history of American political ideas since the nation's founding. He gave his students a demanding reading list, sparked discussion with provocative questions, and sprinkled his lectures with anecdotes from his Washington experience. At first he assigned his students a research paper but found he didn't have time to read the papers carefully. For nine years, Neal's classes became a stimulating, well-directed group conversation about history, politics, and the ideals of the Founding Fathers. He loved the teaching, and his students responded in kind.

Jim Jardine, one of those students, would later graduate from Harvard Law School, serve as a trustee at the University of Utah, and head up the project to create an endowed chair in Neal's honor in the political science department in 1999. Jim considers Neal his most influ-ential teacher. To describe Neal's effect on him, Jim quotes Oliver Wendell Holmes that a mind expanded by an idea can never return to its original dimensions. Neal sparked just such ideas in Jim's mind. "His classes were full of the electricity, the crackle of ideas." He was moved by Neal's "joy in learning and exploring new ideas." He also shared wonderful reading lists that passed on to his students his infectious pas-sion for "the best books."

In addition to the intellectual stimulation of Neal's classes, he was a natural role model for such promising students as Jardine. Liz

At a University of Utah function with (from left) Reed Brinton, President A. Ray Olpin, Parry Sorensen, and J. Willard Marriott

Haglund has seen former students from "all over the country who feel that Neal is their mentor. Hundreds of them are different today because he helped them see what they could do." In 1966, the Delta Gamma sorority gave him their "Favorite Professor Award."

Neal's influence had particular meaning for Latter-day Saint students. Though he was circumspect about the limits on religious teaching at a state institution, students "saw his commitment to the gospel, that it was rational, spiritual, wholehearted. He really was a shining young man," without being "self-conscious or goody-goody" about his religious beliefs. His example encouraged them to take on "some of his attributes and [they] found it working for them."

Opinions about Professor Maxwell on the campus were generally favorable, but they weren't unanimous. One student thought that while he was an able teacher, he occasionally came across in class as "a bit officious, even arrogant." That same student has "seen the metamorphosis" since those early years, as he watched Neal, over time, become more "humble and spiritual-minded."

Differences about his performance also cropped up in the political science department. Most of the faculty recognized his strengths as a teacher, a writer, and a practicing political scientist. Because he taught only part-time and never earned a Ph.D., however, some of them muttered about his academic title. Neal was given the title of "instructor" when he began teaching in 1961 and was promoted to assistant professor in 1964. In 1961, he published an article that drew on his master's degree research, "The West on Capitol Hill," in a book called *Western Politics*. He later updated his research on this topic, his writing full of characteristic Maxwell prose about "political patriarchs" and "regional redwood." He concluded, "What we see, therefore, is clearly neither a requiem for a region nor a resurgent regionalism, but change."

During the 1960s, when Neal's students and his political science colleagues viewed him mostly as a member of the faculty, he was actually a full-time administrator, along with forays into public television, public service, and many other projects. Neal wasn't even aware during those years that on two occasions some of the department faculty recommended that his academic title be changed from assistant professor to lecturer. Both times, the proposal failed to carry the needed votes because of his strong record in teaching, writing, and public service. Indeed, in 1970 the university promoted him from assistant to associate professor—an unusual step for a part-time professor with no doctoral degree. His department chairman wrote that "all members" of the relevant committee "wished that Professor Maxwell had been able to finish his Ph.D." before being consumed in university administration. But "after considerable discussion," it was their "almost unanimous consensus" that Neal's "long involvement and manifest contributions in government, politics, and civic and public affairs, both in Washington and in Utah, had compensated for the lack of the Ph.D."

The record showed that Professor Maxwell was "a truly excellent classroom teacher" and his scholarly publications were "first-rate work reflecting careful scholarship and felicitous craftsmanship." Professor J. D. Williams wrote that "Neal is worth his weight in gold to our students" by showing that political science "has something to contribute to the public good." This comment referred to Neal's service as chairman of Utah's Constitutional Revision Commission, which began in 1966.

When he learned about these academic disputes, Neal thought the committee had raised legitimate questions about his title, but he knew that under the circumstances he couldn't have been a full-time, Ph.D.-holding faculty member. He wasn't that concerned about his academic rank, so long as he "could teach students." Colleen had been right, then. By accepting that first public relations job, he did end up influencing students—in a way he couldn't have predicted. And more student contact was just around the corner.

TWENTY-EIGHT

DEAN OF STUDENTS

BACK IN THE PRESIDENT'S OFFICE, Ray Olpin was about to give Neal his first opportunity to serve as a line administrator, introducing him to concepts of leadership that would claim his serious attention from then on. His first Church book, in 1967, would be subtitled *Essays in Leadership for Latter-day Saints*. One of that book's central themes, "participative" leadership, drew directly on Neal's experience in the field of student life—a world that was being turned upside down during the turbulent 1960s.

It was summertime in 1962, and the dean of students had just left, giving President Olpin little time to find a replacement before school began in the fall. Perhaps knowing this need was on Olpin's mind, Lowell L. Bennion, who had been director of the LDS institute of religion near the campus and Neal's former teacher, went to see Olpin. According to the president's journal, Dr. Bennion explained that he "wouldn't be kept at the institute next year" and did "not want to teach at BYU," as he had been invited to do by Latter-day Saint education leaders.

So Lowell Bennion was looking for a job at the university, and President Olpin was looking for a new dean of students. Dr. Bennion said he wasn't interested in doing detailed administrative work, but he would enjoy working in the dean's office, especially if the university could hire Tom Broadbent, a Latter-day Saint who was then dean of students at the University of California at Riverside. He recommended that Olpin try to recruit Broadbent. Olpin then learned that the current associate deans had said they wouldn't stay in the dean's office "if someone untrained" in their field of student personnel were made dean. He knew they had reservations about this gap in Dr. Bennion's background, even though they also "respect[ed] him highly." So Olpin called Tom Broadbent, who visited the campus, considered the job, but concluded, after making it "a matter of prayer," that he wasn't ready to leave Riverside.

With his time and his options running out, President Olpin conferred with Daniel Dykstra, the academic vice president since Homer Durham had gone to Arizona State as president. They talked about people already on the campus. Finally Olpin suggested Neal Maxwell's name, and Dykstra said, "Tremendous. He would command the respect of the students, the faculty, and everyone who works with him." When Olpin raised Neal's name with faculty council leaders, someone there asked the same question the associate deans in student life had raised about Bennion—did Neal have the requisite training? Not easily outfoxed, Olpin simply replied that "we didn't know what kind of training was best for a dean of students."

President Olpin next approached Neal about the new job, mentioning Lowell Bennion's possible role as associate dean. Neal's own account was that the president "came to work one day and said he'd had some inspiration while he was shaving." Neal was totally surprised. He did lack the typical training to be dean of students, and he was concerned about the reaction of non-Latter-day Saint personnel if both he and Lowell Bennion moved into the dean's office at the same time. Nonetheless, he admired Lowell as his mentor and friend, he knew the dean's staff would soon see Lowell's gifts, and he felt President Olpin had been so good to him that he should accept the request.

Neal thus became dean of students, and he always felt that his associate deans—Lowell Bennion and Virginia Frobes—were better at student life tasks than he was. Still, a *Salt Lake Tribune* editorial welcomed the appointment: "Dean Maxwell, well known as a speaker and writer as well as an administrator, has a special interest in and talent with young people and their problems."

Neal soon saw Lowell's skillful touch at work when a group of student athletes were accused of misbehavior. He defused the emotion and counseled constructively with each student, "as only Lowell could," drawing on his rich background from the institute years.

The new job altered and expanded Neal's role on the campus. One change came when President Olpin advised him that as one of the university's senior administrators, he should no longer serve as the bishop of a student ward, which he had been doing since 1959. Olpin wanted to avoid the appearance of any church-state conflict of interest. Student wards were a new enough phenomenon that Olpin mentioned his concern to Church President David O. McKay, who concurred with him.

Olpin also released Neal as his assistant, but the two retained an advisory relationship, with Neal becoming a member of the university deans' council and a member of Olpin's extended management team, which had always included the dean of students. Neal also found that as dean he had contact with the legislature, especially when the university sought state approval to add a small building fee to student tuition and fees, letting students help fund construction of the new Special Events Center and other buildings.

Neal's relationship with Olpin was not limited to student life issues. Since his days in the public relations office, Neal had found a serious "gap locally between higher education . . . and the business community." Borrowing from an idea he saw working at another state university in 1963, he proposed a program of conferences between faculty and community leaders. For too long, Neal felt, Salt Lake City business leaders had seen the university as a "hilltop hideaway," and local media people had found it difficult to "get any information out of the university." Neal continued raising this issue until the campus opened up more fully.

The public speeches he gave during this period reflected both his attitudes and his expanding circle of contacts. When invited to speak at a devotional for the Latter-day Saint institute of religion near the university just before the 1964 national election, he discussed what some would have considered a relatively secular topic—Utah voter attitudes. But Neal, a political scientist who looked at his discipline through a gospel lens, wanted to discuss the practical implications of some doctrinal overtones. He said he thought local voters were sometimes overly influenced by a candidate's ideology or personality; sometimes unwilling to become seriously involved in the political process, despite feeling they had a "rendezvous with destiny"; sometimes tended to overly moralize such temporal political issues as water resources; and sometimes didn't seem aware of the Church's support for a two-party political system.

In June 1964, Neal was asked on short notice to fill in for an unwell Hugh B. Brown of the First Presidency as the speaker at the university's baccalaureate service. By this time, Neal's secretary, Edith Bronson, was learning to make "nine copies on onion skin" carbon paper (photocopying was still in its infancy) because increasingly people asked for copies of his speeches. Delivered with authority and awareness at a time when student unrest in the United States was just beginning, his theme was "Speaking the truth in love," from Ephesians 4:15.

His message included an appeal to both Latter-day Saint and non-Latter-day Saint members of the university community. Neal was becoming an interpreteter between both groups: "The man of religion and the humanist . . . have far more in common than they realize. . . . It is this duo to whom we look for shared concern in behalf of the individual. . . . It is they to whom we look to effect needed change, whether it is the result of empiricism or in response to the broad doctrine of repentance."

After President Brown read Neal's talk, he sent a letter of apology for his illness, adding that his "inability to be present was . . . a blessing to all concerned." President Brown's gentle praise for this talk suggests what others may have felt—that people in the community were coming to appreciate Neal Maxwell's inclusive approach. A few years later, Neal would be asked to dedicate President Brown's grave.

Being dean of students taught Neal about human interaction, group process, and leadership. He received an intensive on-the-job education that continued later when he supervised the dean's office as vice president. He came quite unprepared to the field of student life, but he was dean of students through a difficult and historic era, when the protests of the 1960s raged across American campuses. Virginia Frobes and Martin Erickson, her assistant, were his best teachers about the issues and the research on students, including counseling and psychology as well as leadership methods. He also dived into the professional literature, went with student leaders to training seminars, and learned by daily experience.

One typical example of his practical education in conflict resolution occurred in January 1964, when a student and faculty art exhibit displayed a few nude statues in a prominent spot on the campus. When members of the public and the board of regents called the university to complain, Neal was caught between the clashing views of those who complained and those who claimed that freedom of expression must protect the exhibit. He hadn't helped sponsor the exhibit, but he was the administrator who, along with President Olpin, "took the heat" about it, from both sides. The next week he wrote to a friend that this "flap over an art exhibit" had made him "the man in the middle" and left him feeling "very weary."

But this was tame compared to what happened later when the tremors of national student unrest occasionally shook the Utah campus. The university remained relatively calm, compared to what happened elsewhere, but it was still a perplexing time. Once Neal was responsible to oversee the arrest of some students who made an obscene demonstration, and then he had to give a deposition in a court proceeding. And he was the vice president responsible for student life when the campus was engulfed in turmoil in the sad spring of 1970. At Ohio's Kent State University, National Guardsmen tragically shot four students during a student revolt over the Vietnam War. In reaction,

Utah students burned the Intercultural Center, an unoccupied frame building that had once been used as a university bookstore.

Many of the student disturbances during this time lacked a clear focus, both at the University of Utah and across the country. Edith Bronson said of one student sit-in at the Park Building that she "didn't know exactly what they're objecting to," but with students all over the second floor of the building, she "had to step over bodies" to leave her office. Her uncertainty about the students' real purpose captured a central feature of the entire national movement—its goals were, unfortunately, very unclear. It was especially unclear what the protesters had in mind to replace the system they set out to disrupt.

Although Neal's colleague Martin Erickson had been predicting some kind of student protest movement for some time, the "revolution" actually began at the University of California at Berkeley in 1964, when a few students challenged that university's right to limit student protests. The events at Berkeley quickly blended with two other forces—first, the civil rights movement, which had drawn many college students to the South, and second, anger over the government's conduct of the war in Vietnam. National feelings were also tragically aggravated by the assassinations of President John F. Kennedy in 1963 and then both Robert F. Kennedy and Martin Luther King Jr. in 1968.

In its extremes, the student movement challenged universities as surrogates for a corrupt, white, and corporation-dominated society. The self-appointed national leaders in this often bewildering drama traveled from one campus to another, urging students to find any handy target for their rebellion. They sometimes said, "The issue is not the issue," urging students to protest against any campus policy, because civil disobedience was an end in itself, designed to revolutionize the entire culture. They chose universities as their target not because the schools were repressive but, ironically, because they were open institutions and centers of influence. The "counterculture" thus lashed out at "any institution attempting to assert authority over young adults."

The visible turmoil of the 1960s gradually faded during the 1970s, but in some deep and disturbing ways, the student movement—in all

its turbulent interaction with other forms and groups of social protest—
sowed seeds that changed not only universities but American culture
forever. And Neal Maxwell, like others who cut the teeth of their social
understanding on this battlefield, would also never be quite the same.
It always amazed him that something so big could happen so fast. He
had once wondered how the society described in the Book of Mormon
could change as rapidly as it did ("thus had they become weak, because
of their transgression, in the space of not many years"; Helaman 4:26),
but now he understood: "Anybody who watched the sixties understands
how our society changed quickly."

In a general sense, the "movement" had a way of shifting the burden of proof about the place of many traditional values. In the past,
society had accepted long-standing cultural mores as legitimate, until
someone proved conclusively otherwise. The civil rights movement did
prove otherwise regarding historical American patterns of race discrimination. Some protesters felt they had similarly proven otherwise
about extending trust to governmental institutions that declare war.

Certain assumptions about right and wrong began to shift in the
public mind. In a confusing, erratic way, secular values increasingly
seemed to transcend religious ones; civil disobedience at times seemed
to transcend patriotism in the hierarchy of citizenship values; and
Americans began feeling freer to walk away from such institutional
bonds as marriage. Instead of assuming that sexual permissiveness was
wrong, more of the younger generation began to talk and behave as if
the defenders of traditional moral values had to prove *their* case. Movies
and television began to change, allowing a sexual explicitness that no
one would have imagined only a few years earlier. The nation's basic
sense about the nature of acceptable public expression yielded to an
increasingly standardless culture.

This was a very different world from the one Neal Maxwell had
known as an idealistic young soldier defending freedom on Okinawa
or as a patriotic young Senate staffer who believed deeply in the nation's
political system. This strange new world left a permanent mark on him,
because his daily occupation required him to think through his
responses to the conflicts on his own campus. As a result, he became a

sensitive and unusually articulate defender of well-established values, forging his views in settings that ranged from personal conversations with students and faculty to the larger audiences who heard his speeches and read his writings.

In this context, Neal soon saw that "power sharing" was a big issue in the student protests. Fortunately, his predecessor dean, Bill Blaesser, had anticipated this concern well enough in advance to place many students on university committees. But Neal kept learning about the need for, and the value of, participative leadership. He would have more to say about that in the future, in many settings.

He also saw that the concept of *in loco parentis* (the idea that a university stands in the place of parents regarding its students) was fading fast at state universities, in marked contrast to its mainstay role at such religious schools as Brigham Young University. As that concept frayed, like a thread in an unraveling social fabric, many universities relaxed their control of such customary functions as dormitory rules and behavioral and dress codes. This development saddened Neal, who always remembered a plaintive and telling line from a Berkeley student: "If the university isn't going to worry about me, who *is*?"

Neal's attitude toward dissenters was to listen to them, care about them, try to understand them—and still try to help them see the big picture that he thought many of them missed. He wrote to students in the campus newspaper in 1963, for example, respectfully urging them to develop "the capacity to express rational dissent" and "achieve identity within a community." It is ironic, he wrote, that while many Americans "enshrine rugged individualism," history shows that "cooperation" is the nation's real genius.

Neal also became interested in the concept of self-esteem, an idea he found in the work of student personnel specialists who were helping students and authority figures to communicate with one another. When the national College and University Personnel Association met on the Utah campus in 1966, Neal talked to them about self-esteem as "a major personnel problem." He urged university leaders to help employees and students understand the need to help one another bring their personal self-concepts into line with reality, so that their self-esteem was deserved and they could help one another grow. With more honest feedback and better listening, leaders could give specific, deserved appreciation and guidance that honestly lifted those "whose self-concepts are too demeaning, too unflattering." In this way, people could assist one another with "individual redemption." He also talked about self-esteem in some of his Church speaking during this time, and he wrote about it for a national 4-H publication, recognizing how the discipline of 4-H had earlier helped him develop "self-esteem through achievement."

Such ideas as leaders asking for honest feedback and giving deserved, specific praise became staples in the insights Neal developed during these years—and those ideas grew from what he was learning about helping people build genuine self-esteem. In his personal leadership style, in his parenting, and in his teaching of leadership principles, he would return often to these concepts in future years, even as they merged with his expanding view of the gospel.

While Neal was learning how to work with students under the demanding conditions of the times, he was called to serve as a member of the Young Men's MIA General Board of the Church—first assigned to the board's speech committee and then to its leadership committee. At the same time, Elizabeth Haglund, his university colleague, was called to the Young Women's MIA General Board. In 1965, the two MIA general presidencies appointed Neal and Elizabeth to write the 1966 MIA leadership manual. Many of the ideas in this manual later found their way into Neal's first book, *A More Excellent Way*. In the book's preface, Neal thanked Martin Erickson from the office of the university dean of students for many of his ideas and illustrations.

Neal's approach to Church leadership was clearly influenced by his university experience, although he was conscious of, and grateful for, the difference between Church and university environments. He felt much more freedom in the Church setting, where he could explore his growing understanding about leadership in the light of scriptural patterns. One significant difference he found was that in the Church, authority flowed from God to divinely appointed leaders, while in a democracy the people themselves retained ultimate authority.

Joe J. Christensen, who worked closely with Neal in the Church Educational System after 1970, found that Neal often employed leadership terms or methods he had first seen in the student life context, but Joe found that Neal was "always fitting those ideas into the gospel" rather than vice versa. Perhaps for such reasons, the minutes of the meeting of the MIA General Boards for October 20, 1965, state that after Neal and Elizabeth presented some leadership material to the boards, someone noted that the material they presented "was not a University of Utah program but had been prepared" as requested by the MIA executives.

Having learned about leadership by practical experience among soldiers, missionaries, senators, and now students, Neal was learning how to teach leadership to others.

TWENTY-NINE

UTAH STATESMAN
AND UNIVERSITY
VICE PRESIDENT

D URING THE UNIVERSITY'S SEARCH for a president to replace Ray Olpin in 1964, some thought the regents should consider Neal Maxwell. He himself regarded his candidacy as "a Harold Stassen sort of thing" (Stassen was a frequent candidate for the presidency of the United States in the 1950s and 60s but was never among the front-runners). Neal thought his candidacy improbable, mostly because he didn't have a doctorate and partly because of his visible association with the Church on the MIA General Board.

Nonetheless, a few regents, graduate school dean Henry Eyring, and others urged both Neal and the search committee to take his candidacy seriously. Neal's friend from college Douglas Parker, by then a faculty leader at the University of Colorado, wrote an unsolicited letter to the search committee. He said Neal's "credentials and capacity for true greatness as a University president are stamped within the man himself." Others might have stronger qualifications on paper, but "Neal possesses the needed empathy for people, the fairness, the youthful vision and energy to be one of the country's great university presidents.

*Making a presentation
at a University of Utah
board of regents meeting*

. . . I do not believe you could find a person with more potential for inspired leadership."

Most of the regents felt that James C. Fletcher, a research scientist who held a Ph.D. in physics from the California Institute of Technology and had taught at Princeton, would maintain the U's momentum toward becoming a major research university. The son of Harvey L. Fletcher, a world-renowned scientist who had earlier been a dean at Brigham Young University, Dr. Fletcher, at age forty-five, became president on September 9, 1964. The University of Utah regents had persuaded him—even though he had declined their first two offers—to leave his position as vice president of Aerojet General Corporation, the nation's third largest aerospace company. After serving seven years at the U, he would be appointed director of the National Aeronautics and Space Administration (NASA).

Jim Fletcher was brilliant, but he was shy by nature. He once told a colleague that he'd never fit in at BYU because he was "absolutely incapable of saying hello to everybody he passed on the sidewalk." Paul Hodson, one of his vice presidents, reported that although some in the community found Fletcher exciting and dynamic, others thought him aloof and, at times, a little abrasive. When Hodson once told Fletcher that a few people might interpret a certain proposal as "intellectually arrogant," the president replied, only half jokingly, "Let's face it, Paul, we *are* intellectually arrogant."

Because Fletcher was used to running a large organization based on sophisticated data, he installed management information systems that were new to the campus. He had a knack for identifying talented people and "interacting with them in ways that increased their confidence and presence in the [campus] organization." Neal learned from Jim that spotting and using bright, dedicated people was an important skill. When Neal needed to entrust someone with a highly responsible task, he increasingly looked for one who was both bright and meek.

From their first meeting, Neal and Jim Fletcher hit it off. Soon after Fletcher had been appointed, he returned home from an intense visit to the campus. He told his wife, Fay, "I struck gold. . . . Neal Maxwell is there. . . . Nobody in this world can use the English language as well as [he] does, and nobody in this world has a better [sense] about how people feel and what they might be able to do. He is just a genius."

Fletcher was used to working with a larger team, so he increased the number of vice presidents from two to six. At the same time, he was impressed enough with Neal's gifts that he increased his responsibilities, partly to give him an incentive to stay around. Neal's new title was vice president for planning and public affairs—which included overseeing student life, public relations, fund-raising, alumni, and long-range planning. The yearbook summarized his duties as "interpreting the university to the community." In 1967, Fletcher changed Neal's title to executive vice president, making him responsible for all of the U's nonacademic functions.

Of the 1964 appointment, the *Deseret News* editorialized, "Though still a young man [age thirty-eight], Mr. Maxwell has won great stature in the community and among his colleagues." He also

President James C. Fletcher (left) awarding Neal an honorary degree

received a letter about his new duties from Elder Harold B. Lee of the Twelve, with whom he had attended his first stake conference as an MIA General Board member earlier that year. Elder Lee wrote:

> I have long admired you as one of our solid educators. . . . Many will hope that under this new administration you will be instrumental [in helping avoid a letdown] on standards of dress or conduct on the campus. . . . Your new president needs one like you.

Perhaps this letter made Neal long for some way to retrieve the waning concept of *in loco parentis* or at least for a way to explain to Church members why state universities were losing some of their traditional authority to supervise students' behavior.

During their six years together, Jim and Neal learned to move around the campus and the community like experienced tennis doubles partners. Neal had energy, personal contacts, and an inclusive style that opened doors with many university constituent groups, doorways that President Fletcher would enter and exit with focused emphasis on his own role and strengths.

As time passed, Jim Fletcher saw Neal's abilities grow. Looking back in 1981, President Fletcher said that Neal was "one of the most competent administrators I've ever come across. I can think of only one other, at NASA, who compares; and I've been in some large organizations." He had an "unusual sense of people and how they'll react." At the university, Neal's "Church loyalties always came first, but that didn't affect his effectiveness. Given the natural conflicts about Church attitudes" at the university, it was "amazing that he could handle it so well. His honesty and trust had a lot to do with it."

Neal became a two-way interpreter between the university and the community. In an alumni magazine article published just after Fletcher's arrival, Neal made the case he would make with state legislators, prospective donors, prospective faculty, and local business and community leaders—namely, that the university gave more to the community than it took. The U, he wrote, "is not Utah's fancy, expensive trotter but the state's 'workhorse' in higher education," carrying more than 54 percent of the state's college enrollments between 1947 and 1962, awarding more than 61 percent of its four-year degrees, and building 60 percent of the U's new buildings from sources other than state funds.

Fletcher and Maxwell took their energetic appeal for support to alumni and friends all over the country, organizing the university's first National Advisory Council. Assisting from her public relations office, Elizabeth Haglund joined them in a meeting to launch the NAC in New York City. She saw a young and anxious Neal Maxwell pacing the lobby of the Waldorf Astoria "nervous and impatient" one morning when the president wasn't ready to go, ahead of schedule. "I don't think he knew he was in such a hurry during that era. It was intrinsic with him." Neal called the Fletchers' room; they said they'd be there at the planned time, and they were.

With this urbane group of Utah alumni, Elizabeth said Neal's portrayal of the university was "so gilt-edged that they would have bought anything from him. He was marvelous," displaying a social ease that belied the innate shyness and mild sense of inadequacy that Elizabeth knew still lurked a little in Neal's interior. For him, it helped that he was telling a story in which he had complete confidence: Jim

Fletcher wants to move the U up a notch in national influence and quality, and he is gratefully standing on Ray Olpin's shoulders to do it.

Neal was even more at home when his duties took him to the Utah legislature, where he represented not only the University of Utah but also, in some ways, the larger face of Utah higher education. By the mid-1960s he had come to know many of the state's civic and business leaders, and they knew him—from his ties with Senator Bennett, his TV show, the numerous hats he wore at the U, and his own commitment to local civic projects.

Utah's "movers and shakers" found Neal easy to like—partly because he got so involved in their world. In 1963, for instance, he chaired Salt Lake's United Fund Drive with a gusto that led some to call him the campaign's "million dollar angel." He helped the fund achieve its first million-dollar goal in an annual drive, partly because he liked the fund's public service dimension. He confided to a friend that he had tripled his own monthly payroll contribution to the United Fund when he saw where the money was going. He also believed that the university was "tied to the state socially and politically. Each will rise or fall with the condition of the other."

During this season, Neal also became a director of Mountain Fuel Supply Company (later Questar), a governor of the Salt Lake Area Chamber of Commerce, and president of the Milton Bennion Foundation—a project that fulfilled his earlier plea to Ray Olpin for dialogue between educational and business leaders. James E. Faust, a state legislator and president of the Utah State Bar during some of these years, came to know Neal the way others did. To him, Neal was a bridge-builder: "He'll cross the river in a relationship and build a bridge. He's the first one to put the girders out."

Neal was both direct and practical in reassuring legislators and other leaders that the university wasn't growing too large and that it was an economic asset to the state. One of his favorite projects was to invite influential people to the campus and let them observe the U's top-flight researchers at work. He would ask the professors to open up their offices and labs and then bring visitors to hear them explain how their work helped the state. He might take them to the greenhouse

Celebrating achievement of United Way fund-raising goal in 1963

where Professor John Spikes was doing creative work with biology and atomic energy. Or, a favorite moment for Neal, they'd go see Henry Eyring demonstrate his "drunken molecule" routine, in which Henry showed how molecular actions worked while he stood in front of an office chalkboard full of complex equations.

Neal wanted Utah's legislators to see for themselves the interactive relationships between vocational education and the university's research role. "One man with an idea from a university background will found a business in which students from trade techs will be employed." Therefore, "it was so clear . . . that the people of the state were getting a bargain" in their support for the university. Neal felt this was a more practical, and therefore more persuasive, argument for supporting the U as a major university, than trying to promote the value of pure research as a desirable but academic abstraction.

One of the university's most difficult, but finally most successful, legislative challenges was how to fund the construction of some urgently needed, expensive new buildings—including a major medical center. Enrollments had expanded until the place was bulging at its seams, and army barracks were hardly adequate for either the size or the quality of university the U was becoming. But most Utah legislators came from the old school about debt—they didn't believe in it. So it took herculean efforts between 1963 and 1965 for Neal and many others to persuade the legislature (and the public) that it was a wise investment, not merely an expense, to adopt "the biggest bonding effort for education that this state has ever had." The bonds were financed by a one-half percent state sales tax increase.

An obstacle to the bonding-for-buildings problem was that each of the state's nine colleges and universities had its own direct line to the legislature, which created both confusion and competition. Neal next became involved, then, in finding a way to coordinate all nine institutions while still honoring a needed degree of autonomy at each school. Neal's own university was the biggest player on this field—with, therefore, the most to lose in any compromise of its direct relationship with the legislature. But the bruises the players had collected during the building fund crisis showed a clear need for a stronger state system of higher education.

President Olpin had initially opposed the creation of a state higher education coordinating council in the late 1950s because he couldn't yield one whit of the University of Utah's preeminence. He was finally persuaded by the promise that the new council would prevent the creation of additional state colleges and would assure increased funding for the university. But he still resisted the council's having any more than "coordinating" authority. A coordinating council thus created in 1959 at least put yellow "caution" signs at the intersection where the college presidents all came to meet the legislators. But some collisions were inevitable, because the council needed but lacked the authority of a traffic cop. The council had no authority to create or manage a state master plan for funding or anything else.

By the time Calvin Rampton became governor in 1965, Utah's higher education was in trouble. Student enrollments had increased 31 percent in one year (1964–65), BYU was limiting its enrollment, and the *Salt Lake Tribune* editorialized that a "'tidal wave' of post-war babies" threatened to overwhelm the state's higher education capacity. Determined to solve the problem, Rampton appointed a committee chaired by Peter Billings and including Neal Maxwell, charging them to recommend a permanent state system of higher education. After a complicated struggle, the legislature in 1969 fashioned the plan that led to today's Utah system of higher education, which is governed by a single board of regents and assisted by institutional advisory councils at each school. The first commissioner for the new system was Neal's mentor G. Homer Durham, fresh from his term as president at Arizona State University.

A recent study of the origins of this new system identified the University of Utah as a key historical obstacle to a unified system—and Neal Maxwell's attitudes as a key source of resolution. President Fletcher fatalistically saw more centralization as inevitable. He was also persuaded by Neal's being "philosophically more comfortable with . . . centralization . . . as a means of improving Utah higher education." In the end, Fletcher and Maxwell "jointly brought [their] somewhat unwilling institution along during the master planning process." Along the way, "Maxwell was an eloquent advocate for centralization who could both 'deliver' the University of Utah and also flesh out in persuasive prose the principles" he believed in.

Working with state senator Dixie Leavitt on the system's final recommendations, Neal drew on his United States Senate experience to shape public policy in the area of overlap between competing interests and principles. His approach tried to balance the need for institutional freedom with the need for statewide planning, limiting the authority of the system's commissioner to that of "executive secretary to the board" of regents, leaving line authority running directly between the board and each campus president. These experiences developed Neal's later attitudes about the role of the Commissioner in the Church Educational System, teaching him why system leaders need to help their boards find strong presidents and then avoid micromanaging them.

By the later 1960s, the state asked Neal to help solve another problem—reorganizing the state's own governmental branches.

Governer Rampton was committed to strengthening both the executive and the legislative branches of state government, reflecting a national movement to upgrade the power of state-level governments. "At no time in the nation's history [had] the states' basic law been under such widespread scrutiny." After hearing a Rampton-appointed Little Hoover Commission on the executive branch, the legislature concluded that it first needed to revise the state constitution's legislative article. The power the typical nineteenth-century state constitution gave to state legislatures was, as one expert said, "the most serious failure in American political development."

This weakness in state legislative power had two causes. First, corruption in nineteenth-century state legislatures had prompted severe constitutional limits on their power, a model on which Utah's 1896 constitution was based. Second, the federal government's power had gradually increased until it now dwarfed state power, endangering the very concept of federalism (shared power between state and federal governments) that was at the heart of America's complete constitutional system. With U.S. cities bypassing their state governments and turning to the federal government to solve urban problems, it was time to revitalize state constitutions.

The legislative study committee (LSC) launched in early 1966 was overseen by House Speaker Kay Allen and Senate President Oscar W. McConkie. To Oscar, Neal's longtime friend, Neal Maxwell was "the ideal guy" to chair such a project. He had a political science background, knew the legislators, had a good rapport with the Church, and brought the perspective of his staff years in the federal Congress. The LSC initially included N. Eldon Tanner of the First Presidency, who had served in the Alberta legislature in Canada, and James E. Faust, a Salt Lake City attorney who had served in the Utah legislature and as president of the Utah State Bar Association.

Cautious about change, Utah voters rejected the committee's first recommendations in 1966, including a proposal for a constitutional convention to deal with all needed revisions. Neal thought the proposals failed because the Salt Lake Chamber of Commerce opposed them. The public was also spooked by the open-ended implications of a constitutional convention. Learning from this defeat, the legislature reconstituted the committee as a longer-term constitutional revision commission (CRC), leaving Neal as chairman. The new group proposed a "Gateway Amendment," which allowed the public to consider clusters of constitutional amendments without reviewing the entire document. The CRC adopted a media campaign and obtained public endorsements from groups that included the Salt Lake Chamber of Commerce. In 1970, the electorate adopted the Gateway Amendment.

Roger Porter, who later served as an economic policy adviser in the White House and on the faculty at Harvard University, was a BYU student during the CRC years, working as Neal's student assistant during two summers. Watching Neal manage this process, Roger said he'd "rarely . . . seen anyone move so surely or adeptly in bridging the differences between Republicans and Democrats, LDS and non-LDS, power brokers in one sector of the economy and leaders in other sectors."

For example, Neal had turned to his friend John W. (Jack) Gallivan, publisher of the *Salt Lake Tribune,* for advice. Jack, who wasn't a member of the LDS Church, was one of Utah's leading community statesmen. He and Neal had together attended a national conference on strengthening state legislatures. Jack helped persuade the influential Salt Lake Chamber of Commerce to back the CRC proposals. To address local leaders, Neal also imported Michigan governor George Romney, who had previously helped revise his state's constitution. Roger found that Neal had an "astonishing lack of interest in who received credit" for the work and that he'd help create "an environment in which people could reach agreement without feeling like some won and others lost."

Authorized by the Gateway Amendment, the CRC developed several proposals for the 1972 ballot—annual legislative sessions (rather than every two years), increased legislators' compensation, and new positions of legislative auditor and legislative legal counsel. The *Salt Lake Tribune* published Neal's article that urged passage of the amendments as a way to revitalize federalism, increasing the state's power compared to that of the federal government. When the amendments

With the Utah Legislative Study Committee, forerunner of the Constitutional Revision Commission; back row: mentor N. Eldon Tanner (second from right) and long-time friend James E. Faust (fourth from right)

passed, Neal wrote to Cory, "All the amendments passed . . . by wide margins, so I feel good. Later today our Constitutional Revision Commission will meet" to begin consideration of similar changes for the executive branch.

The CRC eventually recommended creating the office of lieutenant governor as "second in command" to the governor; abolishing the office of secretary of state, and changing the membership of the state board of examiners—all of which the public approved in 1974. When Neal was released as CRC chairman, a *Salt Lake Tribune* editorial noted his commitment to public service, his balance between detail and vision, his "knack of identifying the most likely approach to a successful public presentation," the "versatile nature of his leadership," and his "genuine selfless way [which avoided] the turmoil and disharmony" that could have occurred. These attitudes reflected not only the political scientist rendering public service but Neal's peacemaker skills. One friend said Neal has an unusually "irenic" quality—peaceful in purpose and able to promote unity. This gift had drawn him from university life into civic service, where he helped people of differing views resolve complex public policy issues to serve the common good.

Elder Alexander Morrison thought Neal's years at the U of U enhanced his education about people, history, and institutions—a process that motivated him to learn from experience as well as books. The university years added a diverse and valuable set of tools to his understanding of the American political system, leadership, managing people with varying views, public policy, and his sense of history. All of this laid foundations on which he would soon need to build.

THIRTY

THE MAXWELL STYLE

B Y THE MID-1960S, NEAL'S DISTINCTIVE personality had settled into a number of telling habits and attitudes. Some of them were well known around the campus, including a playful streak that would become a little more (but not completely) sedate once he began his full-time association with the Church. The playful streak included a mixture of Neal's quick sense of humor and his innate competitiveness. One time the secretaries to Neal and to Parry Sorensen discovered that both men typed hunt-and-peck style, with one finger of each hand. They proposed a race with two manual typewriters side by side, testing which of the two could type the same pages first. Neal won, but he never would have raced someone who typed with all ten fingers.

Another time, while Henry Eyring was dean of the graduate school, Edith Bronson proposed that they do something for their faithful campus postman to honor his retirement. Henry and Neal put together a "nice certificate," recognizing the mailman with an honorary "doctor of letters" degree.

Nothing was more competitively playful than the Coronary Club, the twice weekly (Mondays and Fridays at 4:00 P.M.) pickup basketball

*Playing basketball with
the Coronary Club at
the university*

games with friends from the faculty and administration. Here Neal's intense "drive to win," which he usually kept under tight control, would cut loose with an unsuppressed energy that must have taken vengeance on the demons that had haunted him since he failed to make his high school basketball team. If it didn't do that, at least it gave him a place to let off the steam generated by the increasing pressure of his daily duties.

One faculty partner said Neal rarely missed a game in fourteen years. Edith would just write "seminar" on his schedule, and he'd be there. Jim Jardine remembers being in Neal's office as he dashed out the door for a 4:00 P.M. game. Edith signaled to him that the governor was phoning, but Neal waved and shook his head, so Edith told the governor's secretary that Neal had a pressing appointment and would need to return the call later. Some of Neal's teammates played basketball "as if it were a contact sport" but Neal played with a more "finesse," relishing his "very accurate left hand set shots from the sidelines." Neal's typical shot was "novel," like his slightly quirky but well-polished tennis shots. He sparked fast-paced team action with his hustle and tough defense. His quick hands would "swipe the ball away" without mercy, but he wouldn't ever lose his temper.

By 1970, the campus newspaper did a story on the club. When Neal left the U that year, the other players gave him a certificate recalling his "solicitous concern for injured teammates, whether or not the injury was inflicted by him." They noted too his "consistent confounding of the laws of physics," making his shots "despite all manner of impossible trajectories."

Neal's passion for action also surfaced when he played tennis, which eventually replaced basketball as his physical and emotional outlet. His regular tennis matches began in the 1960s and stopped only for his chemotherapy in 1997—and then began again, and still continue. Neal's tennis partners found what his "hoop" friends did—that he was very competitive and played with a unique style. In general, said Jim Jardine, "he'll dive for every ball but give you every line call." And "he's developed all these crazy strokes"—drop shots, spin shots, unorthodox serves, and disguised volleys——"and this isn't just for fun. These are tools" to win.

His tennis style reflects his offstage personality, as well as his desire to stay fit: "A one-minute warmup is plenty for him. Let the games begin." If the game drags a little, "out come Neal's spin shots— 'junk tennis' they call it. His doubles partners never know where the shots are going to or coming from." And if there's "even a brief lull," Neal wants to hear the latest political news: "How are things going for the president? What have you heard about the governor?" And when he gets unhappy with his own shots, he will "scold himself: 'Oh, Neal! Oh, Neal!'"—a lament "somewhere between an exclamation and a grunt." Faculty colleague J. D. Williams found a similarity between Neal's tennis game and his office style. Neal was "a clean desk man, and

With his doubles group that has played together for more than twenty-five years: Oscar McConkie Jr., Bill Bailey, and Richard Boyle

I've never been able to abide them." In "tennis you never knew where the ball was coming from. And in his office you never knew where he hid the papers."

Friends who have been in touch with Neal through the years have noticed that when he's in town, he just might call to arrange a quick game. When he visited Oscar McConkie while Oscar was presiding over a mission in Arizona, Neal set up a basketball game in the mission office parking lot. And Beverly Campbell, who worked with Neal on Church international affairs in Washington, D.C., said that on his visits he loved it when the Campbells could find him some tennis clothes and tennis partners. Then he'd rise early, play a hard game, and arrive at his meetings with ambassadors from other countries, refreshed and on time.

Elizabeth Haglund believes that his passion for sport is not an isolated aberration but a window to a soul full of strong, deeply rooted emotions. She knew all about the playful streak, from stories that filtered back from the gym and the tennis court; but she thought Neal consciously "bridled his passions" with a self-discipline that arose from his "sense of mission."

One day Liz also happened to glimpse the deeper springs of Neal's passions. She dropped by his home to deliver something and, before he knew she was there, she saw him in a rocking chair "on the front porch of his house [holding] one of his new grandbabies. It was the most emotionally moving vignette. He was totally fulfilled in the presence of this child." It was as if the baby were "telling him about the next world by osmosis."

The idea of bridled passions introduces Neal's demanding self-discipline. Since his mission, Neal had worked consciously to develop desirable character traits. His interest in such themes as meekness and discipleship in the later books and talks of his ministry reflects his discovery in earlier years that he needed, and therefore wanted, to work on developing those qualities within himself.

For example, Neal surprised one of his faculty basketball friends at the U in the 1960s by confiding that he had to make himself work hard to do a better job in teaching, speaking, and leadership. He was the same way about his parenting. Other close friends saw that he "has tried very, very hard over the years to make himself a better person. For most people, New Year's resolutions don't last. But his do." His later call as a General Authority enhanced this tendency, but he's long had "a determination, the perseverance, to do it and do it and do it again." All of that has produced gradual changes as he has matured. Said one friend, "No one I know requires such extreme effort of himself." Another said Neal is a Type A personality "with a capital A, yet he has learned such exquisite skills that he does not really appear hurried when he's hurrying, and he doesn't appear to be dismissive when he's dismissing."

There was almost a Ben Franklin quality about Neal's quest for self-mastery. In his 1771 *Autobiography,* Franklin recorded his disillusionment with the churches of his day for paying insufficient attention to morality and citizenship. So he decided to write his own "lesson plan"—as Neal has done when not satisfied with existing missionary approaches and Church leadership texts. Neal never went to the

Franklin-like extreme of keeping a scorecard on his own performance with each of thirteen ideal virtues, but some of Franklin's language sounds very Maxwellian: "Avoid trifling conversation. . . . Resolve to perform what you ought. . . . Lose no time. . . . Avoid extremes. . . . Imitate Jesus and Socrates."

For Neal, self-mastery was simply part of the gospel. To him, mortality is designed to help us learn and grow. We can't take material things with us, but character and understanding are portable. "We talk glibly about eternal progression," he told some students at Brigham Young University, "yet that idea really must be broken down into day by day improvement." In addition, much of his on-the-job training to fulfill unexpected occupational assignments was self-taught—just like his basketball and tennis shots and his typing, speaking, writing, and leadership styles.

He has worked on himself in small ways and large ones. Edith noticed that when Neal ran across a new word in his reading, he would deliberately use that word several times the next day in speaking or writing—and then he'd have it in his vocabulary. He once wrote to Cory and Karen, "Deliberately cultivate what your mother has done better than I—a certain resilient and glad spirit, so that even when you are in the midst of a pressure situation you can smile and have an upbeat manner." The key words here are "deliberately cultivate."

Another example of the self-mastery quest was Neal's preoccupation with patience. Cory has said his father is not a "naturally patient" person, but he has worked on that quality over the years, including giving a devotional talk on the subject at BYU after he had just returned from a difficult trip that tried his patience. Even now, his family and friends can tell when he's "biting his tongue" or may "start to say something"—and then check himself.

Neal also decided he wanted to understand and practice empathy. Drawing on the way he learned to listen to students who were trying to understand their own rebellion, he wanted to become more fully aware of other people's feelings. He told one interviewer during those years, "I don't know that empathy is natural to us. . . . I have to work at it. I have to make sure that, in my task orientation to get things done, I do not forget the feelings of people."

When he first began working at the university, he was so focused on his own tasks that he sometimes didn't listen fully to the answers other people gave to his own questions. Oscar McConkie found that as time went on, Neal was much "more likely to *listen* to your response and not be thinking about what he's going to say next." Part of this skill came as Neal learned to believe, "more than he used to, that the other guy may have something worth listening to."

In earlier days, Oscar had noticed that Neal "didn't suffer fools gladly." In fact, before he began consciously to develop empathy, he had "the capacity for a very acerbic wit." Neal acknowledged as much, once telling a BYU audience that in the early years of his marriage, he once privately spoke "less than worthy words" of criticism about someone just before being called to work with that person in a church assignment. "In such circumstances one winces for his words, and pride goes first" as one learns "experientially." As time went on, however, Neal "just buried it," simply choosing to avoid clever sarcasm or criticism by suppressing it.

So Neal's "talents in ministering with sympathy and empathy to people is a learned [skill]. The more he did it, the better he got at it." He learned empathy from Wallace Bennett, who wanted to attend a funeral when Neal thought they should stay on the regular schedule. He learned of it from noticing that Ray Olpin was sometimes too task oriented—and in Olpin he saw much of himself. Neal once wanted to tell Olpin, "Look, somebody is going to come and give you a million dollars. Make them feel good on their way out, rather than arguing with them over something," as was his tendency.

Neal also began learning about empathy from being asked to talk at funerals. In the early 1960s, a woman called him to say her husband had passed away and she wanted him to speak at the funeral. Neal was so saddened by the news that he sat alone, crying, after hanging up the phone. When Cory saw his father, he thought he must have done something to make Neal feel bad—the empathetic son was watching his father learn empathy from experience. Gradually, Neal's empathy increased, as did the requests for his presence at funerals.

After Neal had gained some experience at Church headquarters, he began to see the traditional rivalry between BYU and the University of Utah more empathetically. In the past, he'd seen BYU through Utah's eyes; now he could also see Utah through BYU's eyes. Then he realized the folly of being so competitive as to "stereotype each other in a way that is not only inaccurate but unfortunate." As this insight came, it reminded him of the unfortunate polarization he'd seen between political extremists in the U.S. Senate, who likewise suffered from the myopia of stereotyping.

Neal's growing empathy responded when the president of a student stake at the University of Utah invited him to speak. The stake was made up mostly of married students but included a number of LDS single parents. The stake president told Neal, among other things, that the single parents needed encouragement. As Neal spoke, he said he'd been watching the diving competition in a televised Olympic event. In that sport, he said, the score given to a diver is the multiplied sum of the degree of difficulty of the dive times the quality of executing the dive. People may watch others do their dives, but one can never know the difficulty of another person's dive. Only God knows our degree of difficulty. That's especially true for single parents. From his having seen and said this, the meaning of Neal's expression of admiration and encouragement to the single parents was itself multiplied.

Neal's empathy began to express itself in his approach to leadership. Through their years of interaction in leadership settings, President James E. Faust would find that "even when he's presiding he's very, very sensitive in reaching out to get the opinions of everybody and not imposing his own thoughts and ideas on other people. . . . He can almost read your thoughts."

For example, he enjoyed drawing other people into interaction, whether in leadership training, a classroom, a social setting, or private conversation. He might ask people to write down their goals for their life, their goals for the next year, and their goals if they had only six months to live—then to list their main activities for the past week, to see if they were spending time on their most important values. He might also ask people to identify a skill or quality they need to develop and then write down one thing they would stop doing and one thing they would start doing in order to improve. Once he asked members of a study group to say what they would do if they had unlimited financial resources.

Some of this was "a tool for inclusion," to be sure people weren't being left out of group conversations. Colleen had noticed this tendency in Neal when she first met him. In teaching and training, he also found that "there is generally more learning when members of an audience have some involvement."

In one of his first Church Educational System staff meetings, Neal asked each participant to take three minutes and write what they'd like to be remembered for after leaving their current position. Then-BYU President Dallin Oaks preserved and often referred to what he wrote down that day, having found it a "very significant question." Neal would do the same thing in informal conversations, asking such questions as "How do you study the scriptures?" Then he'd listen to the merits of various study habits. He took a similar approach in asking his children questions designed to produce thoughtful discussions around the dinner table.

Not all of the Maxwells' friends were unqualified fans of his penchant for so much structure, even when it did produce involvement. When one group was having dinner together, he asked each person to take turns responding to a certain question. Elizabeth Haglund became exasperated. She had participated in such exercises so often with Neal that she wondered why they couldn't just enjoy "wonderful, warm, meaningful"—and spontaneous—conversation.

Related to his interest in empathy was Neal's conscious choice to take a positive view of human nature in dealing with other people. He had learned, both with students and with those he supervised, that people do better when they're valued than when they're scolded. "I have found," he told a BYU audience, "that it is better to trust and sometimes be disappointed than to be forever mistrusting and be right occasionally. This is to endorse empathy, not naivete."

Those who worked for him found that if he wasn't happy with their performance, he would just not increase their responsibility. "If you didn't do the job, you never got asked a second time." Those with ears to hear would sense his gentle style of correction, and he preferred working with people whose ears were finely tuned enough to hear his understated direction.

Elizabeth Haglund found that he worked best with self-starters who could keep up with him without much direction. His best allies were "whole-souled" people who had their "own sense of direction that dovetailed with his." Not everybody who thought they'd like to work with Neal "wanted to work as hard as Neal works you. He just squeezes the last drop . . . out of you without always realizing he's doing it." Further, "if you had to have someone explain the whole thing to you, if you couldn't see the vision from the words he used," the collaboration probably wouldn't work.

Typically, then, Neal's corrections would come in a "feedback sandwich," with the correction surrounded by positive comments. For instance, one scholar missed two deadlines on a project that Neal's office had helped to fund. When the person requested another extension, Neal wrote that he could "understand in part . . . the many burdens that have fallen upon you." And "I surely want it to be done well . . . which is, of course, your style." But "we will probably have to hold" to any new date "to bring this matter to closure. I am looking forward [to seeing] what you will have done." Probable interpretation: Don't ask again to extend the deadline.

Others found that Neal's sensitivity about people's feelings made him reluctant to give direct criticism—he'd find another way to send a needed message. When Russell Nelson, then a regional representative, assisted Neal in a stake reorganization, Elder Nelson forgot to include the normal reference to the stake high priests quorum presidency when setting apart a new stake president's counselor. Rather than whispering in Brother Nelson's ear or asking him to repeat the blessing, Neal just explained to the group afterward that the counselor's office in the stake presidency included his presiding role in the high priests quorum.

Another part of the Maxwell style was his innate commitment to efficiency. While in his office, Neal focused on the task or person before him, and people typically left his office feeling he had nothing else on his mind but whatever they had discussed together. If he had papers or projects on his desk, he would do whatever was needed to work through them and move on. By about 5 P.M., he would be ready to go home, and that was usually without "anything left over." Edith also said he cleaned out his correspondence files once a year and "just threw everything away." That habit has continued through the years, making his biographer's task at once easier and harder.

In conversations with work colleagues, his quickness and his focus always shortened conversations. Often when he saw where someone's point was going, he would ask questions about bottom-line implications, perhaps before the other person was prepared to be there. Some colleagues found, as Dallin Oaks once said, "That confounded Neal Maxwell sometimes finishes my sentences!" One friend noticed that "in their young married lives it was not uncommon for Neal to finish Colleen's sentences." Some of this was because Neal anticipated so intuitively that he would detect where a thought was going as soon as it began to unfold.

Neal's interest in efficiency was intentional. He practiced habits he learned from others, such as President N. Eldon Tanner. Neal knew that when business pressures began to affect President Tanner's health as a young man, he "had a talk with himself" and decided "he would give the problem before him, whatever it was, his full and best attention. Once he had disposed of it, having done his best, he would forget it and move on to the next one" rather than recycling his problems.

The passion for efficient focus sometimes made it hard for Neal to relax and slow down. His family knew if they went on a family vacation, he'd often take work along; or if they went out to dinner, he'd want to structure a "gospel conversation." At times this part of his personality made him seem always in a hurry—early for appointments, airplanes, and trains and impatient with having to wait in lines, get through traffic, or attend receptions.

His haste even showed up in his typing, where his friend with a printer's eye, President Thomas S. Monson, could always tell when Neal had typed something himself, "because he's too [impatient] to wait for the capital key to go down. So . . . the capital letters are all . . . a sixteenth of an inch higher on the line than all the rest of the letters." He still often types little notes on his manual machine in half-space lines, rather than regular spaced lines, perhaps because he doesn't want to take time to click the carriage return twice.

Edith saw his hastiness when she typed his dictated speeches. Often Neal would be so anxious to keep moving that he would take a sheet half-full of typing from her machine so he could begin revising it. She was a fast typist but couldn't keep up when he was "so anxious to get into it, make the corrections, get it done, and get started on something else."

At times during the early university years, his fast pace put work needs ahead of human ones. But he gradually became more "humanized," adjusting his gait to that of other people. "There's something to be said about not getting too far ahead of other people," said one friend. Even later, President Boyd K. Packer said Neal "likes to get something done right now. . . . You have to slow him down once in a while." Adds President Monson, "When it's time for the meeting to end, he doesn't look at his watch. He's not rude. But you can just tell, because there's a little shoulder movement that says, 'I ought to be moving on to something else.'"

Neal's inborn mental quickness was related to what would become his distinctive verbal style—laced with one-liners, alliteration, and word pictures in speaking, writing, and informal conversation. During his university years, he increasingly looked for ways to turn a phrase or create a fresh metaphor that would compress and capture meaning and insight—a stylistic urge that has heavily marked his work ever since. The exercise of crafting memorable phrases and images required real exertion, especially because his natural creativity was always bubbling up an array of word choices. In that sense, the Maxwell style of expression hardly saved his time because it added to his preparation effort. But the process yielded fruit that packed entire sentences of meaning into brief phrases, thus economizing his listener's time.

Edith noticed he was always moving paragraphs, cutting, compressing, and looking for vivid images and symbols. She also thought that some of "his talks are so hard for an ordinary person to keep up with, because he doesn't have any extra stuff in them. It's all meat, and the little things that give you time to catch up with what he's saying have disappeared." As one later associate put it, "You take that raw ore, sprinkled with gold, compress it, and extract the gold and you have his books." Edith thought this style more fitting for the university audience where it was first forged than it was for the younger kids. "He was a little above them."

During the late 1960s and early 1970s, when Neal was still developing his speaking style, he sometimes experimented with language that became saturated with rhetorical devices. One 1973 talk at BYU, for instance, included these phrases:

> A distinctive, differential valuation of truth could be a more profound protrusion. . . .
>
> We live in an age that is flooded with facts . . . a process which [reflects] futility as much as humility. Much of the factual flood flowing from research is very valuable, but from some undiscriminating research comes a deluge of data and a blizzard of conceptual confetti. . . .
>
> Without the divine disclosures God has given to us, we face all the usual dangers of incomplete information, but these are compounded by cosmic consequences. . . .
>
> Without divine guidance, cerebral calisthenics . . . can provide us with . . . but empty exercise. . . . Freedom is the catalyst in the chemistry of choice. . . .
>
> Distinctive education must therefore pay more than a curricular curtsy to those kingly truths about family and freedom. . . . After all, rhetoric is an easy religion, and conversational Christianity makes few demands of us. . . .
>
> Distinctive education . . . is a temporizing tutor. . . .
>
> In moral education, a chameleon curriculum is not usually conducive to . . . selflessness.

The Maxwell language style did not go unnoticed on the BYU campus, which led to some good-humored and constructive feedback to which Neal, over time, would respond. Indeed, many years later, when asked about his diminished fascination with alliteration, Neal would smile and say, "I'm now down to two packs a day." In 1976 Donald T. Nelson, the director of fund-raising for CES, introduced Neal to his staff with language that caused then-BYU President Dallin Oaks to "laugh himself almost under the table":

> Neal A. Maxwell is a connoisseur of communicative cadences and one for whom we have ample affection and affinity. As such we believe he will recognize in the introduction that is to follow the compliment of imitation which has been to exaggerate not castigate. . . .
>
> Brother Maxwell, an accumulator of accolades, is an admirable administrator who has been our boon and booster for the last five years. He can bolster and bless, becalm and bedazzle, befriend and beseech, but he balks at balderdash and begrudges ballyhoo.
>
> He is a baron of brevity, the best of the breed, who has helped us as a broadminded brother to banish barnacles of brainless and bankrupt behavior.
>
> He has counted the cadence for us, calm and candid. His cardinal care was to act as a captivating catalyst . . . in the awful arithmetic of the year-end fund results. . . .
>
> Now, Brother Maxwell, if you are not too taxed to testify, nor too anguished to appreciate, we will await your tender tutoring.

One further dimension of Neal's style was that he learned to create bridges between the Latter-day Saint and the non-Latter-day Saint communities, both on the campus and in Salt Lake City. His deepest loyalties were to the Church, but he respected the U as a state institution, and his peaceful nature helped him foster good relationships between Latter-day Saints and members of other faiths—especially those for whom the Church presence in Utah was a difficult issue.

Neal's religious attitudes were no secret. People knew he had a "complete spiritual commitment," but he "always enfolded [it] in respect, generosity, and openness toward those who didn't accept or understand him fully." As dean of students, he knew of the discomfort some in that office felt about his and Lowell Bennion's closeness to the Church. Nevertheless, "instead of allowing them to be enemies, [Neal] made them his colleagues, and that wholly changed the complexion of things." In his approach to the religious issue, "he never confronted it, never made speeches about it," and "was very successful in conveying to other people that it really didn't matter." He "earned his spurs" by simply creating authentic professional ties.

Bill Loos was a student body officer who worked closely with Neal when he was dean of students. After Bill later joined the Church, he recalled:

> [Neal's] warmth did much to "thaw" the cold feelings of some students toward the Church. . . .
>
> We never discussed the Church, yet years later when I took the missionary discussions, it was Neal's example . . . that propelled me into continuing with my investigation into the Church. . . . [His] unspoken influence seemed to always give me confidence in the Church. . . .
>
> I felt his love and respect just as much before joining the Church as after. It was not conditional on my believing, or living or acting like he did.

Neal took a proactive approach that reflected his empathy for faculty members who were not Latter-day Saints. He helped prepare a paper the university gave to non-LDS faculty prospects and their families, conveying an attitude of welcome and acceptance and offering well-informed suggestions about their natural questions. He often reassured his non-LDS friends about what "the local culture" contributed to the university. Sometimes he would say, for instance, that the Church should send the university a bill for a million dollars for attracting such people as Henry Eyring, who never would have come to Utah but for the attraction he felt toward the Church.

Russell Nelson, who was a faculty member at the medical school when Neal first returned to the university, saw two reasons why Neal had earned so much respect from his non-LDS friends. One was that he "was so unarguably good," professionally, doing his work so well that he "was immune from attack" on other grounds. Besides, people simply liked him as a person, and "you can't quarrel with a man you love."

On the other side of this judicious balance, Neal constantly looked for ways to reassure Latter-day Saints in the legislature, the Church leadership, or elsewhere about the university's environment and direction. He was well aware, as Oscar McConkie put it when he was Utah senate president, that it was "hugely important that the state university have some sympathetic understanding of 70 percent of the Utah population" who were members of the Church.

This wasn't always easy, or completely possible, given the constraints inherent in a state institution. Neal once heard from a friend that two General Authorities were concerned about some issues on the campus and wondered why Neal hadn't done more about those concerns. He immediately asked to see the two leaders, telling them he'd heard of their questions and wanted to discuss them openly, in the spirit of Matthew 18:15—a favorite Maxwell scripture, and by then a hallmark Maxwell process: "If thy brother shall trespass against thee, go and tell him his fault between thee and him alone: If he shall hear thee, thou hast gained thy brother."

As an interpreter between the two communities, at least in Utah higher education, Neal tried to interact honestly with both groups. Looking back, he felt it was good for his own growth to "learn to defend my principles in a setting where you didn't get a free pass. I had to be sure of what those principles were, and the strength of that position became more apparent to me." His approach was "a great source of strength and courage for [other] faithful" Latter-day Saints at the university who looked to Neal as a role model.

During his university years, he developed many close friendships with people from all across the spectrum of belief and attitude toward the Church. He kept many of those relationships alive for years after leaving the campus. As just one example, in 1996 he baptized Willam Christensen, the university's distinguished ballet director, when Christensen was past ninety years of age. During his years of observing the U community, Jim Jardine believed that "non-Mormons and less-active or disaffected Mormons" in "the university community related to him, respected him, [and] connected with him" to "a degree that was probably true of no other Latter-day Saint" of that era. This was because Neal was "always so centered on the gospel" and was also so genuine and thoughtful that "people who might feel a distance from . . . the Church . . . felt like they had a relationship with him."

In 1969, the board of regents surprised Neal with a gesture that showed how leaders from diverse perspectives felt about him. They awarded him an honorary doctor of law degree at the June commencement. Major universities seldom give honorary doctorates to their own faculty, let alone to one of their own administrative personnel. The regents, chaired then by Edward Clyde, appreciated Neal not only because of his long university service but also because of the statesmanship in his approach to shaping a Utah system of higher education and revising the legislative and executive articles of the Utah state constitution.

PART X

"GOING TO THE CHURCH"

THIRTY-ONE

STUDENT WARD
BISHOPRIC

Neal's secretary at the university, Edith Bronson, typically described his 1970 appointment as commissioner of Church education as "going to the Church." To her, that's how it felt. She continued working for Neal as they moved from the University of Utah to the Kennecott Building in downtown Salt Lake City, where the Church Educational System was housed until the new high-rise Church office building was completed two years later.

With Neal switching from blue shirts and sports jackets to white shirts and dark suits, with office meetings now opening with prayer, and with a calendar of frequent appointments with General Authorities, it might have felt to Edith like stake conference every day. It was clearly a watershed time for Neal, but he'd actually been gravitating toward ever more involvement with the Church and its leaders for several years.

When the Maxwells moved back from Washington, D.C., in 1956, they bought a small home on Evergreen Avenue in the East Millcreek stake, not far from where Neal had grown up. Their stake president the first two years was Gordon B. Hinckley, though they had little personal contact with him. Neal served briefly in ward callings, including helping other members construct a chapel across the street from their home—a task he felt ill-equipped to do: "A few of the bent nails still in that roof are mine. I wasn't much help."

The Church also expected the ward to help pay for its new chapel. Neal and Colleen responded, gladly, if gulping slightly, when their bishop asked if they could contribute, in addition to their tithing, an amount equal to 10 percent of their annual income. When the Church later began to construct chapels entirely from churchwide tithing donations, Neal applauded, though he also wondered if "we could have lost something in the process" of reducing the sacrifice expected of faithful members.

In 1957, Oscar McConkie was made bishop of one of the first two student wards at the University of Utah, and he called Neal to be his counselor. Student wards had just been introduced at Brigham Young University, where Ernest Wilkinson would later say this concept was the most important innovation to occur during his BYU presidency. Oscar McConkie and Wilford W. Kirton Jr., who were partners in the law firm that did most of the Church's legal work, had served in a stake presidency together near the University of Utah campus. When they heard about the BYU student wards, they went to see Elder Henry D. Moyle of the Twelve, assuring him that there were "fit candidates for salvation at the University of Utah." Elder Moyle encouraged them to create a student ward in their stake, adapting normal programming to the needs of university students. They hadn't the slightest idea how to approach the task but thought they had a relatively blank check to find the best format.

Looking back, Neal felt the idea of student wards was inspired. He thought that if all those Latter-day Saint college students after World War II "could have been somebody's counselor in a Church calling when they were students," the Church might have avoided the "needless hemorrhage" of many promising young people during that era. In student wards, they would see their inquisitive but believing friends develop their religious faith honestly, fearlessly, and successfully under the tutelage of experienced bishopric and Relief Society leaders.

Elder Moyle and Elder Richard L. Evans, also of the Twelve and a member of the board of regents at the university, took a special interest in the U of U wards. Elder Evans set Neal apart as a member of the bishopric and occasionally spoke at ward functions. Once President Hugh B. Brown, then of the First Presidency, was scheduled to speak to the students. When he was delayed, Elder Evans "warmed up the crowd" until President Brown arrived.

Neal had first met Elder Evans just after his mission, when Neal occasionally assisted Elder Evans and Elder Marion D. Hanks in their assignment to oversee the program for visitors to Temple Square. As a regent at the university, Elder Evans also saw Neal in his various university roles. Elder Evans had been unusually close to his own mentor, Elder John A. Widtsoe, whose approach to the relationship between higher education and the Church had long been a role model that shaped Neal's views. Neal's friendship with Elder Evans and his admiration for Elder Evans's eloquent style of speaking and writing kept that same model alive.

Bishop Oscar McConkie's innovative approach to student wards sometimes surprised certain general Church officers. When the Presiding Bishopric called in the McConkie bishopric and some BYU bishoprics to ask how the regular Church youth manuals were working in the student wards, Oscar said they'd found the manuals less than relevant, so they had designed their own curriculum. As others in the group looked on in mild shock, a member of the Presiding Bishopric said, "Well, I'm glad there's somebody here who agrees with me." President N. Eldon Tanner offered similar support for program flexibility in student wards, calming the anxieties of some general auxiliary leaders.

Oscar found that thirty-year-old Neal, with all his talent, was still in the early stages of his development. He was sometimes "not sympathetic to those who didn't catch on quickly," but over time he learned from experience. His conscious effort to "cultivate Christian works" prompted him to develop more kindness and empathy. For example, if Neal stated "some political maxim in a bishopric meeting and I didn't get" it immediately, "he'd look at me like I wasn't bright enough to understand . . . and he was probably right." Another time, Oscar visited a graduate student who was estranged from the Church. When he told the bishopric about the visit, Neal, perhaps wanting to empathize with the student's perceptions, said, "So when he decided that Jesus didn't want him for a sunbeam, he quit." Oscar found this an early reflection of Neal's impatience with people who criticized the Church without understanding it.

A key experience that expanded Neal's compassion was his call as bishop of a student ward from 1959 to 1962. In that capacity, he learned to delegate administrative functions to his counselors so he could spend the hours needed to counsel young ward members who were dealing with behavioral or intellectual challenges. Often, though not always, he found that an intellectual issue masked a behavioral one. When he didn't know the answer to some intellectual puzzle, he would say something like, "I don't know. But what do you think about the Book of Mormon?" Or, "Is this something you're going to let keep you from being touched by the rest of the gospel?" His ward members learned and grew from his counseling, and so did he. Neal would later say that being bishop was his most satisfying local Church experience, because he could "touch people's lives directly" and was "present at the moment of truth in an individual's life."

President Olpin, to whom Neal was executive assistant at the U when he was called as a bishop, was bothered about the call, feeling that it risked church-state conflicts between Neal's university and ecclesiastical roles. Neal told the president he saw no conflict and thought his church life was strictly a personal issue. Olpin accepted that response but only until Neal was named dean of students in 1962.

Neal's call as bishop took him away from his home ward, but Colleen compensated for that when she took their children to add a little life and youth—and family role modeling—to student ward sacrament meetings. Colleen also insisted on inviting all two hundred ward members, a few at a time over many months, to the Maxwell home for Sunday dinner.

Bishop Maxwell was a proactive shepherd for his flock of single and married students. When he might have been sitting on the stand

Bishop Maxwell greeting University Sixth Ward members outside meetinghouse

in the minutes before ward meetings started, he was probably still standing in front of the chapel, hoping to catch someone walking by from one of the nearby sorority or fraternity houses. He collected information from Church headquarters showing him the names and addresses of Latter-day Saint students who lived within the ward's large boundaries, and then he and other ward leaders would call on them to invite them to come join with the ward. One of the people he touched in such a visit was Michele Monay, who would become the wife of Larry Staker, the physician who, years later, was so close to Neal when he first learned he had leukemia.

Neal learned for himself about the workings of inspiration while watching his congregation, from the stand or in hallway conversations. Then he'd follow up on these impressions, sometimes telling a student, "I don't know why, but I have a feeling you and I need to talk." And he would learn in the quiet privacy of those talks about walking the road to repentance or about clearing up some doctrinal misconception.

Sometimes these ward members wrote back, years later, thanking him for interventions that turned out to be life-altering.

From these experiences, he discovered he needed a slower, more flexible interview schedule, because these were human issues, not just tasks on a list. He also found that he needed to wait, listen, and interact, resisting his urge to give quick, direct answers. Yet whatever he learned about ministering more effectively, he also saw that he couldn't hold every marriage together or ignite every wavering testimony. But he did learn to take every personal problem seriously, and that alone expanded both his vision and that of the people he counseled.

Bishop Maxwell found that the gospel, applied person by person, was the heart of his work, not the activities that sometimes appeared to be the ward's main function. A young woman once told him, "Bishop Maxwell, we don't need more activities. We need the gospel." He also found that questions from busy graduate students about accepting a Church calling were more about faith than about time schedules, even though he followed President Moyle's counsel about helping Latter-day Saint students take school seriously. As the proportion who accepted ward callings gradually increased, he saw how student wards helped to increase faithfulness among educated members throughout the Church.

While Neal was bishop, Elder Harold B. Lee of the Twelve visited their stake on an assignment. During that visit, Oscar remembers, Elder Lee placed a hand on Neal's shoulder and whispered to President McConkie, "The Lord has great things in store for this young man."

THIRTY-TWO

YMMIA GENERAL BOARD AND *A MORE EXCELLENT WAY*

NEAL WAS RELEASED AS BISHOP when he was made dean of students at the University of Utah in 1962. Then in 1964, he was called to the Young Men's Mutual Improvement Association (MIA) General Board.

Marvin J. Ashton, a loyal U of U alumnus who would later serve in the Twelve, was Assistant Superintendent of the YMMIA. He introduced Neal to the board on November 18, 1964. Elder Thomas S. Monson, a new member of the Twelve and adviser to the MIA, set Neal apart. Elder Monson was also on the university's alumni board. There he had found that "Neal Maxwell's reputation was legendary already," partly because he had "those jobs no one else wanted," like "having to fire the coaches." But he could do even that with a personal touch that left a fired coach feeling "it was the right thing."

The MIA general boards were large in those days, with more than fifty people on each one, many of them specialists from BYU and the U of U, who served on such committees as drama, sports, music, Scouting, and leadership. This was before the correlation era, so each auxiliary general board wrote, implemented, evaluated, and oversaw its own entire program. As a member of the MIA speech committee then, Neal trained stake and ward speech directors, helping them to coach youth when they gave talks in their Church meetings. He also helped organize the annual Churchwide June conference for all MIA leaders, and he attended stake conferences with members of other auxiliary boards and a presiding General Authority.

Shortly after his first board meeting, Neal was assigned to a conference in Ogden's Ben Lomond South Stake, accompanied by two other general auxiliary leaders and Elder Harold B. Lee. The auxiliary leaders met with their stake and ward counterparts for afternoon training, and then all the leaders met together on Saturday evening. Elder Lee asked Neal to talk for ten minutes. When he took only seven, Elder Lee said he should have spoken longer. Neal later commented that he thought it audacious for board members to hold "forth as if we really had something to say."

The stake clerk recorded that Neal spoke in the Saturday night meeting about the need for youth to have good role models. In an early use of what would become the central concept of his future Church teaching, Neal told the leaders that "a *disciple* should follow the good life so he may feel and see the works of the Spirit. To some it is given to know the truth, but some must rely on others for their faith." In the Sunday afternoon general session (stake conference had both morning and afternoon sessions then), he said that each young person needs to love and be loved, have a sense of belonging, feel recognition, and submit to authority. Those themes echoed some of what he'd been learning as dean of students.

Neal had six or seven stake conference assignments each year in his MIA calling. He attended the Boston Stake in early 1966, at which, coincidentally, three other future Apostles were also involved. Boyd K. Packer, then an Assistant to the Twelve, was serving there as president of the New England Mission; L. Tom Perry had just moved into the stake and would soon be called into the stake presidency; and Robert D. Hales was released from the stake presidency at this conference to take a new job in England. The clerk recorded an attendance of 677, which was 25 percent of the membership—a good turnout, considering the snowy weather. Elder Packer later recalled having heard Neal speak at this conference. He never forgot his early "impression of the man—and it's never changed. I was impressed with his ability . . . with words. He's the master of the one-liner," with meanings "crystalized into one phrase or one sentence."

After Neal had served on the MIA board less than a year, he and Elizabeth Haglund, by then on the YWMIA board, were assigned to the leadership improvement committee. One of their tasks was to show board members how to teach the entire MIA program in their stake conference visits, rather than speaking only about their specialities. In this capacity, Neal trained the trainers—in ways that in hindsight he would consider rather brash, partly because he still felt a little guilty about not having been a very "gung ho" MIA participant in his own youth.

At one board meeting, for example, Neal assigned impromptu speech topics and then evaluated each member's talk. Another time, he talked to board members about "not being our own worst enemies," which included not "overdoing their protestations of humility." He often talked about participative leadership, urging board members to be less formal, involving their audiences when training them—which was quite a departure from their traditional style of simply giving talks.

Elizabeth and Neal were also assigned to prepare the 1966 MIA leadership training manual and introduce it at June conference. That annual event had become a huge project by the mid-sixties, with thousands of MIA leaders traveling to Salt Lake City for training in every activity department. The general boards also staged a giant youth festival of music, dance, or drama that demonstrated a pattern the stakes would follow in their own local activities. As a separate assignment that year, Neal and Chieko Okazaki also co-chaired the theme presentation committee—a major production in itself. The MIA had a new scriptural theme each year, which the youth recited as they began each ward's midweek MIA evening program.

As the MIA approach suggested, each Church auxiliary organization in those years had its own organizational and training line to the stakes and wards. The Church also had a more developed auxiliary activity program than would be possible when it had spread further across the globe. Looking back, Neal would feel that "the change to a less-structured local program is lamentable, but in other ways it was inevitable." When the Churchwide MIA June conference was discontinued in 1974, President Spencer W. Kimball announced that the Church would fulfill the conference purpose in a more decentralized way—a still unfolding pattern, as suggested by the revised youth program the Church introduced in January 2002.

The 1966 leadership manual formed the basis for Neal's first book, published in 1967, *A More Excellent Way: Essays on Leadership for Latter-day Saints.* Neal's experience as dean of students had introduced him to several concepts he included in this material, adapting it to the Latter-day Saint environment. The book illustrated the tendency he had developed in his college days to integrate secular and scriptural learning; however, it also illustrated how his approach to integration consciously placed secular ideas within the gospel's primary context.

A More Excellent Way was more about leadership approaches than about Church doctrine, and it relied less on scriptural sources than would his later books, yet it was based on such gospel principles as love and personal spiritual growth. Neal wrote with a serenity that reflected his authentic commitment to the Church, deeply rooted in the religious experience of his home, the war, and his mission. Those experiences had reassured him that his instincts about helping to improve Church leadership would be welcome, just as his writing an original lesson plan for missionaries had been welcomed. This implicit tone of unqualified gospel acceptance let Neal write about Church leadership with a freshness and candor that a less spiritually secure person might not have attempted.

The book's introduction, for instance, addressed the challenge of being an authoritarian church in a day (the 1960s) of increasing secularism, international Church growth, and the unpopularity of authoritarian organizations—all topics that reflected Neal's experience as bishop and dean of students. He acknowledged the clear significance of authority in the Church but wrote candidly that leaders should help members develop trust in that authority. The book was concerned not just with leadership mechanics but with "developing a climate of trust" to help leaders accept members as individuals, inviting their participation, not simply directing them. Leaders, he wrote, need to blend directive and participative styles:

> Many of us . . . in an authoritarian Church [have excused] ourselves from the need to act participatively in our leadership and followership roles. We have relied on the weight and prestige of the Church to support us in styles of leadership . . . which were heedless of the feelings of others. . . . It is the worth of souls that is great—not statistics.

And because the gospel net "gathereth of every kind" in this age of skepticism about institutions and authority, he continued, leaders must allow for individual differences and let people know that their ideas matter. Moreover, the "only moral authority to which people respond is example." So leaders must develop Christlike attributes if they would lead well in His Church. In that sense, "our ability to individualize is . . . a test of our capacity to love." And leaders who "overreact to dissent or to doubt" are not helpful to members who have honest questions. Authority is still essential to carry out the Lord's purposes, so leaders must not defer to people so much that they "minimize the gravity of sin or give gushy, casual reassurances too quickly." But, on balance, "there is in the admittedly authoritarian structure of the Church much more opportunity to use participative approaches than is realized."

With this blend of participation and direction as a framework, the book offered ideas and practical tips to leaders about getting adequate information, being open and candid, how to give "specific" and "deserved" commendation and reproof, and working in small groups—including the family. Several short training exercises were sprinkled through the book. Those who worked closely with Neal recognized here many of the leadership habits he has cultivated for years.

This book revealed much about Neal's development by the late 1960s. Fundamentally, he thought, students and other followers want their leaders to *empathize* with them and *level* with them—trademark Maxwell terms. To do this in the Church, leaders must love, be candid, include others, and be sensitive. Moreover, these are "acquired and cultivated traits," not "natural gifts." In that sense, *A More Excellent Way* was Neal's first effort at leaving written notes tacked onto the trees along the pathway of his discipleship, left for those who'd be coming behind. This process would continue with each book he wrote. He was sharing what he'd been learning, and he learned from deliberately practicing what he discovered from his life experience.

In early 1967, the YMMIA leaders assigned Neal to make an extensive trip through Latin America with two other board members—seven countries in three weeks. They'd see only two stakes; all the other units were mission districts. He'd never been in that part of the world but really didn't want to go. He was pressed for time at the university, he didn't feel competent to teach all facets of the MIA's complex program, and the whole idea of transporting an American activity program to the international Church unsettled him. "I am supposed to go to Brazil and teach *them* to dance the rumba?" he said to Colleen with a perplexed "Europe face" look.

By then the Maxwells had moved to a home on Herbert Avenue, closer to the university. They discovered after the move that three members of the Quorum of the Twelve lived in their ward—Elders Spencer W. Kimball, Delbert L. Stapley, and Marion G. Romney. Once when Neal was asked to teach a ward Gospel Doctrine class on the duties of the Apostles, he found Elders Kimball, Stapley, and Romney all sitting in the classroom. On another occasion, the three elderly Apostles sang a trio at a ward party, "I'll Serve the Lord While I Am Young."

Soon after he'd been asked to travel to Latin America, Neal passed Elder Kimball in a hallway one Sunday. Knowing nothing of his private reservations about the trip, Elder Kimball said, "Neal, I wish you would take that trip to South America." That comment settled anything he was unsettled about. He made the trip.

Neal returned home with a stirring sense of the Church's coming growth there—and that discovery convinced him that the Church needed a simpler organization internationally, one that could adapt to every part of the world while emphasizing the gospel's fundamental elements. He could also see how impractical it would become to follow the traditional pattern of sending people from Utah-based general boards and priesthood committees, along with General Authorities, to teach a detailed Church program all across the globe. Little did he know that within a few months, he would need to draw directly on those impressions in helping to devise, teach, and implement a new approach to Church leadership—the correlation program and regional representatives of the Twelve.

THIRTY-THREE

CORRELATION AND THE CHURCH LEADERSHIP COMMITTEE

B Y 1 9 6 7, THE CORRELATION PROGRAM of the Church was developing well under the piercingly watchful eye of Elder Harold B. Lee, who was then second in seniority in the Quorum of the Twelve Apostles after President Joseph Fielding Smith. During the next few years, Elder Lee would become Neal's most significant mentor.

Few superlatives could overstate the historical importance of correlation, both as a doctrinal concept and as an organizational movement. Those writing the history of the Church later identified correlation as "one of the principal themes of the Church's history" from 1960 until well into the 1970s. And Harold B. Lee's biographer wrote that "some historians may well argue" that correlation, developed pursuant to an assignment from President David O. McKay, was Elder Lee's "most significant lifetime work for the Church," including his service as President of the Church for about eighteen months in the early 1970s.

Elder Lee's vision of correlation had its roots in his conversations as a young Apostle in the early 1940s with President J. Reuben Clark and Elder Marion G. Romney. One issue they discussed was the relationship between the priesthood and the auxiliary organizations, which was intertwined with questions about the respective roles of the First Presidency, the Twelve, and the Presiding Bishopric. Another was the question of multiple organizational lines between headquarters and local Church units—as demonstrated by the MIA's line from general to stake and ward leaders, which Neal saw in his general board experience. By 1960, these issues were still there but were both augmented and eclipsed by two other massive developments that Elder Lee's prophetic instincts foresaw: the deterioration of the family in Western society and the internationalization of the Church.

In 1961, the First Presidency launched correlation by announcing the creation of general committees for children, youth, and adults. Each committee was chaired by a member of the Twelve and was charged to review Church curriculum planning by age group rather than by organization. In 1963 came the first general priesthood committees on welfare, genealogy, missionary work, and home teaching. Members of these committees traveled with general board members and General Authorities to stake conferences from 1963 to 1967, a season that prepared both the Brethren and the Church for the calling of regional representatives in 1967.

Other elements of correlation announced in the early 1960s included the change from ward teaching to home teaching, the creation of stake and ward priesthood executive committees and councils, family home evening, and the new positions of ward and stake executive secretary. In 1971, the Church correlated its magazines to reflect the primacy of age-group perspectives over those of auxiliary (such as Relief Society and Sunday School) or quorum organizations.

Organizationally, correlation was a simplified and "integrated Church program led by the priesthood." This meant that the main organizational line should be the natural ecclesiastical channel from the First Presidency through the Twelve to stake presidents, bishops, and families. All quorum and auxiliary programs would then be "correlated" by the presiding priesthood officers within that line at each geographic level, including Church headquarters. The distinction between the "ecclesiastical" line (the Twelve) and the "temporal" line (the Presiding Bishopric) had its seeds in this era but was not fully clarified until the mid-1970s.

Conceptually, correlation emphasized the family as the heart of the Church. Each priesthood officer's highest mandate was to apply the entire set of new concepts—the correlated curriculum, ward councils, and everything else—to the strengthening of every home, making the family the center of gospel instruction and living. The First Presidency's direction on that subject was conveyed in a letter to Elder Lee and his associates in terms that have been quoted frequently and reverently by subsequent First Presidencies: "The home [is] the basis of a righteous life and . . . no other instrumentality can take its place or fulfill its essential functions, and . . . the utmost the auxiliaries can do is to aid the home in its problems."

By the spring of 1967, Elder Lee was brooding prayerfully over a major unresolved question in the full implementation of correlation—how to fill the space in the priesthood line between the General Authorities and the stake presidents, which would only grow greater as the Church grew larger. This situation was both an organizational issue and a serious training problem. Elder Lee and his associates could see clearly what Neal had just seen in South America: It was unrealistic to keep enlarging general boards and general committees and expect them to train the entire Church leadership from Salt Lake City in all of the Church's programs.

In June, Elder Lee took the concept of regional representatives to the First Presidency and the Twelve, where it was approved and set for implementation at the 1967 October general conference. He was mindful throughout this time of the "inherent hazard of introducing an entirely new level of leaders" between stake presidents and General Authorities.

Against this weighty historical background, with which Neal had had virtually no contact, he was released from the YMMIA Board in June of 1967 and called to a new Church Leadership Committee. This new committee, chaired by Elder Thomas S. Monson and reporting to

Elder Lee, was initially a subset of the Adult Correlation Committee, but it soon became independent of the age-group committees.

When Elder Lee assigned Elder Monson to chair the new Leadership Committee, he said, "You may have any two men you choose in the Church . . . stake presidents, mission presidents, anybody." Their first task was to flesh out and implement the concept of regional representatives. In addition, they were to design training programs for these new officers and other leaders, including a bishops' training manual and, later on, plan the annual seminar for regional representatives and the training portions of stake conferences.

Elder Monson searched prayerfully and came back with the names of Wendell Ashton and Neal Maxwell. A year later, with their tasks growing rapidly, they were joined by two other men selected the same way—James E. Faust and Hugh W. Pinnock. The executive secretaries to the committee were Henry D. Taylor, an Assistant to the Twelve, and later David B. Haight, another Assistant to the Twelve.

From the moment he first saw Thomas Monson in action at such close range, Neal would always think of him "like Larry Csonka, the fullback. President Lee would give him the ball and open a hole in the line, and Tom would be good for seven yards. It was just a great team."

The feeling was mutual. Elder Monson saw that Neal was "young, vigorous, and was not steeped in anybody else's traditional philosophy." Moreover, "the leadership of the Church at that time wanted a new look at things." In the years that followed, Elder Monson and Neal often served on the same committees. During one of their early assignments together, Neal passed Elder Monson a note of gratitude and affection. Now in the First Presidency, President Monson still carries "that same little shriveled note" in the pocket of his scripture covers as a token of their friendship.

Early in his assignment on the Leadership Committee, Neal arranged to have Osmond Harline, director of the Bureau of Economic and Business Research at the U, prepare careful projections of Church growth over the next quarter century, country by country. It was probably the most sophisticated demographic study done for the Church to that date. As soon as Elder Lee saw Neal's presentation of these findings, he concluded that all of the General Authorities needed to see it, because the size and momentum of the coming trend made obvious the need for some office such as regional representative—which validated and illustrated all that Elder Lee had been feeling.

In a special meeting called for that purpose, Elder Lee gave a brief welcome to the General Authorities and then astonished Neal by saying, "Now Neal Maxwell will present this material to you." As Neal stood up, he "felt about as smooth as a sack full of old door knobs." But the point of his presentation was clear to all: The future would soon bring not just more members but more stakes, more inexperienced local leaders, the need for more training, and a new set of issues about managing a multinational church. The Church was on the cusp of such expansion that the current leadership approach couldn't possibly manage what was coming. It was a prototypical moment, capturing Neal Maxwell as the Brethren would see him from that day forward— presenting extensive data, looking ahead for trends, sensing implications for leadership and training, and articulating his thoughts in memorable phrases.

From 1967 on, Elder Lee became Neal's seasoned master, bringing along and relying upon a promising young apprentice, with both of them always tilted toward their ultimate discipleship of the Savior, whom Elder Lee loved to call "the Master." The Leadership Committee worked hard to assist Elders Lee and Monson prepare to unveil the plan for the regional representatives to the Church's stake presidents, who'd all been invited to general conference. The presentations included not only projections of Church population growth but the reasons for, the nature of, and the future training pattern proposed for the new officers.

To Neal's surprise, his name was included in the list of sixty-nine regional representatives announced at conference. He had seen himself strictly as a young staff support person who'd never served as a stake or mission president, but he concluded that Elder Lee must want him to gain enough experience "in the field" to help their committee do its work. That made sense, because they still had to work through the job description, let alone develop all of the support material for the new officers who would be training the stake presidents in the total program of the Church.

The very concept of regional representative was a change of breathtaking proportions to the presidencies and boards of the general auxiliary organizations and priesthood committees and to others who had seen these traditional offices as essential to operating the Church. The general priesthood committees were dissolved, with many but not all of the former committee members now called as regional representatives of the Twelve. Auxiliary board members would no longer attend stake conferences but would give training only at the regional, or multistake, level. Within a few more years, the boards would shrink to a dozen people each. And every Church headquarters department—for both men's and women's organizations—would be subject to the single priesthood line to the field, a line that now involved the regional representatives as primary trainers for a geographic region of several stakes.

The specific nature of the regional representative's role took a few years to develop. Some things were clear from the beginning, such as the general point that these men were to watch over the entire program of the Church within their regions, not just selected priesthood or quorum programs. Each was also to "act as an advisor to the stakes and as a liaison officer between stake presidents and the Council of the Twelve," representing the Twelve to the stake presidents rather than vice versa. This meant that stake presidents first discussed their questions about many Church policy issues with their regional representative—which, for the first time, gave each stake president an assigned person to whom he could turn for counsel. The new leaders would also hold training meetings with stake presidents, conduct regional meetings in which general board members would train auxiliary leaders from several stakes at a time, review proposed stake boundary changes, and occasionally be assigned as a stake conference visitor to a given stake in their assigned region.

Although the Brethren recognized the need for some kind of officer to help with such functions, they were not ready to give the regional representative full "line authority" over stake presidents. This reluctance stemmed partly from the sheer newness of having a priest-hood leader between stake presidents and General Authorities, and the Twelve didn't want them to "come on like gangbusters," giving authoritative direction. Rather, they were to serve as teachers and coaches, not as "super stake presidents." When assigned as a stake conference visitor, for instance, the regional representative was to defer to the stake president as the presiding authority.

This left some people, including many regional representatives, unclear about the boundaries of their ambiguous job description. One of these men said in a seminar a few months after the new office was instituted, "You've told us so many things we can't do. When are you going to tell us what we can do?" And "sure enough," Neal soon found, one regional representative called together the stake presidents in his region to tell them the details of how he wanted them to do their home teaching. When this report came back to the Twelve, the regional representatives were told at the next seminar even more things they couldn't do.

At the same time, the Brethren recognized the new office as an inspired step in the direction of working out an appropriate organization for the expanding global church. More than twenty years later, regional representatives would be superseded by Area Authority Seventies, functioning under the direction of Area Presidencies composed primarily of General Authorities. But in all of these steps, there was never any question about the fundamental principles of correlation that guided the unfolding process.

As Neal watched all of this, he thought it illustrated how revelation guides the Church. "Revelation works in a natural way. There is an unmet need [such as Church growth]. As we ponder over it, the mind and experience can put forward an adequate alternative [for the season, and] the confirmation is the inspiration." Neal didn't think "the Lord should have to do our research for us," nor "should [we] have a feeling that revelation is a push-button kind of thing." Rather, as the Twelve worked out the best organizational pattern, "their experience and their logic will take them well down the trail towards a solution, and often all the way."

Drawing on the entire cluster of correlation concepts, then, the new office of regional representative would seek to implement much that Elder Lee had been teaching for years. The "prime objective," he said, was to place

> the Priesthood as the Lord intended, as the center core of the Kingdom of God, and the auxiliaries as related thereto; including a greater emphasis on the Fathers in the home as Priesthood bearers in strengthening the family unit. . . .
>
> And all of this under the direction of the Twelve . . . acting under . . . the First Presidency; and you [regional representatives of the Twelve] are to carry this to the ends of the earth.

From a sociological perspective, Jan Shipps, a non-Latter-day Saint observer of the Church's history, thought that correlation was made necessary by the success of the Church's missionary emphasis after 1950, which sparked a rapid growth spurt that moved the Church beyond its Intermountain cultural base. This created such a need for buildings, training, and other forms of support that without it the Church risked "devolving into 'little more than an institutional umbrella' over a family of diverse congregations." To prevent this "disintegration . . . into a diversity," she thought, correlation created a "more centralized system" that was more efficient and coordinated, producing a "'standardized and simplified brand of Mormonism' that emphasizes families, temple work, and the preeminence of the Book of Mormon." Thus, "correlation is the key to how Mormonism became a movement that did not fracture and fragment."

Of more fundamental importance, Neal increasingly felt that the Lord had prepared Harold B. Lee for "such a time as this" (Esther 4:14), because these developments were all part of the Lord's plan to "hasten [His] work in its time" (D&C 88:73), establishing the Church among all nations. For Neal to be so close to this major transition would bless him through the rest of his ministry, because Elder Lee's mentoring transmitted to Neal a prophetic vision of the future of the Church.

Elder Lee continually expanded Neal's understanding, even if the process occasionally had its stresses. For example, the seminar for regional representatives soon became established as a significant time every year for the Brethren to assess candidly the state of the Church. Because of the small audience of key leaders and the absence of public media, the sermons given by Church leaders at these meetings "emerged as being among the most significant addresses to the priest-hood leaders attending general conferences since 1967." The Church Leadership Committee was responsible, in a staff role, to help plan what would happen at these meetings. In 1969, Elder Lee was unable to attend the annual seminar due to minor surgery, so he asked Neal to read his talk to the group. Neal was very uncomfortable, feeling the situation "put him on the spot" in front of the General Authorities, but he learned a "different form of obedience" from doing as Elder Lee requested, in spite of his personal discomfort.

As this incident suggests, it took Neal a little time to feel his way into his relationship with Harold B. Lee, who had a reputation among his brethren for being both intimidating and demanding. In the days before a regional representative seminar in the late 1960s, Neal saw Elder Marion G. Romney working in his yard, which was not far from Neal's home. Feeling a little uneasy about whether he was communicating adequately with Elder Lee, he stopped to ask Brother Romney what he thought about Neal's asking Brother Lee if he felt all right about what Neal was doing.

Elder Romney, long a close friend of Elder Lee and now a friend and neighbor of Neal's, was characteristically blunt: "Listen, if he wants to tell you something, he'll tell you. He'll take the hide off you if it isn't going well. You don't need to go ask him" anything. A few years later, when Neal was working closely with Elder Romney on Church education issues while President Lee was in the First Presidency, he got another dose of Romney-style straight talk when he wondered if he had been too candid. "Neal, you're no . . . good if you won't tell us the truth." Thus did Elder Romney mentor Neal into his mentoring with Elder Lee.

Actually, Harold B. Lee's intimidating nature may well have been one reason he welcomed Neal's assistance on such sensitive projects as establishing the concept of regional representatives. Elder Jeffrey R.

Holland, who was watching the unfolding of correlation in the late 1960s as the director of an institute of religion, thought Elder Lee's use of Neal's "immense personal skills, superb negotiating and navigating and sensitivity" on delicate matters of organizational change inherent in correlation "was quite probably intentional"—because Neal's deft touch could sometimes put velvet gloves on the Lee hands of steel.

As a regional representative himself from 1967 until 1974, Neal at times accompanied General Authorities on special assignments in addition to working with the stake presidents in his assigned regions, first in Tremonton, Utah; then Ogden, Utah; and later Reno, Nevada. Some of his work was designed to field-test certain Leadership Committee initiatives about training church leaders, but some of it was to carry out ecclesiastical duties that General Authorities had previously performed.

In one early stake conference, Neal was assigned to accompany Elder Lee in choosing a new stake president. There he "saw the Lord reveal his will rather dramatically." After the two visitors had interviewed about two-thirds of the priesthood leaders, the next man on the list entered their office. Neal said that Elder Lee "just looked at me and nodded before the man had ever taken a seat. . . . He had his man and he knew it, and I did too." Also at this conference, they were to select a new stake patriarch. Having met more than twenty leaders during their interviews, Elder Lee asked that a certain man come in with his wife. When he said, "The Lord wants you to be a patriarch in this stake," the burly farmer began to weep. At his wife's urging, he explained that "two weeks ago the Lord told me this was going to happen." Elder Lee turned to Neal and taught him, "You see, Neal, why we have to operate by the Spirit?"

The relationship between Harold B. Lee and Neal Maxwell was not limited to leadership issues. In October 1969, the First Presidency assigned Elder Lee to recommend a statement the Church could release to the public on the subject of civil rights. This need arose from protests during that volatile era, especially against athletic teams at Brigham Young University, which grew out of the Church's policy of not ordaining blacks to the priesthood. Elder Lee asked G. Homer

Durham and Neal each to draft a statement the Church might use for public comment and then gave their drafts to Elder Gordon B. Hinckley, who prepared a further draft for review by Elder Lee and the First Presidency. The First Presidency released their statement on December 15, 1969.

Another incident illustrates the relationship that had developed between Neal and Harold B. Lee. With the help of the Leadership Committee, the First Presidency and the Twelve focused on how the Church might do a better job of reclaiming men, especially fathers, who weren't active in the Church. Strengthening the role of priesthood-holding fathers in Latter-day Saint homes was at the very center of correlation's objectives. In 1971, the Church adopted the term "prospective elders" to replace "Senior Aaronic Priesthood," a change that "shows some faith in the future, more optimistic than" the former title, which focused "on past failures."

When President Lee introduced this change at the seminar for regional representatives, he asked Neal to explain some data on sacrament meeting attendance, temple marriage, and the growth in the number of less-active men. The two discussed the information in a team-teaching mode. Summarizing, Neal said, "We are losing ground [at the rate] of about 6,500 men a year, most of whom are fathers." President Lee added, "We are losing more men than we are rescuing." Asking Neal to read a list of ways to engage prospective elders in the Church, President Lee said, "This is . . . [the] kind of thing that can stir people's imagination." The list included inviting prospective elders to serve on phone calling committees, as greeters, ushers, and ward choir members, and by helping "widows and the home-bound." President Lee finished the thought: "And so on and on we could go if we have the talent and imagination."

At other times, however, President Lee might not rely on Neal's help. He was very much his own man, and he did his own homework. During one regional representatives' seminar, for example, Brother Lee asked Neal what information he had on a certain topic. Neal gave him some papers, which Brother Lee scanned quickly and then ignored when he spoke.

Through organizational developments that have flowed naturally from the principles clarified in President Lee's day, the roles of other Church leaders are now more clear than they were then. The functions Neal performed on the Leadership Committee are typically carried out in today's Church organization by General Authorities among the Quorums of the Seventy and the seven-member Presidency of the Seventy. This realization throws into sharp relief the significance of the organizational transition in which he so actively participated in the late 1960s and early 1970s. It also explains the discomfort Neal always felt when asked to perform tasks that his instincts told him belonged more appropriately to people with more authority than he had.

His staff role let Neal serve as a constructive interpreter among the General Authorities, regional representatives, and other general Church officers. Thus he listened to some of his former colleagues on the general boards who worried that the regional representatives were overemphasizing such "priesthood" programs as home teaching and missionary work, with which they were personally most familiar, rather than teaching all of the programs, including those of the "auxiliaries." Neal tried to help those with such questions see that the point was to strengthen all families and all individuals, not to shift from auxiliary "programs" to priesthood "programs." In retrospect, he has wished that this clarification could have been made both earlier and more clearly.

Former auxiliary board members from the 1960s continued to meet annually to reminisce about "the good old days" of their role in a much smaller, mostly western American, Church. In 1995, on the evening the group formally dissolved, Neal told the "EXBOS" (EX-BOard memberS), "We were all privileged to have been a part of something when it was in its crescendo—not in its decline." Theirs had been an era of "essentially a North American Church," for which the former approach was "cherished and effective." By 1995, the Area Authority Seventies had replaced the function of regional representatives, and Area Presidencies were well established. "Even so," he concluded, "our nostalgia is understandable." Fortunately, "families and wards will remain human sized," no matter how large the Church grows.

THIRTY-FOUR

COMMISSIONER
OF EDUCATION

IN JANUARY 1970, PRESIDENT DAVID O. MCKAY
passed away, ending his abundant twenty years as President of the
Church. During that time, the Church's membership had nearly
tripled, from about one million to three million members, with much
of the growth coming outside the United States. Indeed, growth and
internationalization had emerged as the Church's primary challenges,
inviting, even demanding, a fresh look at everything the Church was
doing.

Joseph Fielding Smith became President of the Church with
Harold B. Lee as his first counselor. With the momentum of correlation well underway and with President Smith's complete confidence,
President Lee was the leading figure in what became a complete
reexamination of the Church's structure and programs—a natural
extension of the correlation process. The Church's educational system
soon came within President Lee's searching scrutiny.

It was a natural time to reexamine the future of Church education. Brigham Young University had reached its enrollment ceiling of

25,000 students, which signaled an end to a period of rapid expansion. Ernest L. Wilkinson, who was serving as both president of BYU and chancellor of the Unified Church School System, was seventy-one years old. Other leaders in Church education were also at or near retirement age. The seminaries and institutes were growing fast but had yet to develop a strategic response to the pressing needs for education among Latter-day Saints outside the United States.

The larger American environment also invited a reassessment of the assumptions on which all education, especially higher education, had proceeded for generations. The student revolts of the 1960s had questioned every basic assumption of traditional educational methods, especially the authoritarian attitudes reflected in the personalities of university presidents like Ray Olpin at the University of Utah and Ernest Wilkinson at BYU. So the early 1970s were a time when governing boards throughout higher education in the United States were looking for leaders of a different kind—people who were "open, candid, 'men of low profile,' characterized by 'an ability to mediate rather than to polarize.'" They needed leaders who had "a compassionate spirit," who believed that "youth is neither a disease nor a crime." For Latter-day Saint education, that sounded a lot like Neal A. Maxwell.

Since the end of World War II, gaining a college degree had shifted from being an American luxury toward being an American necessity. The GI Bill and the economic and technological expansion of the postwar period had truly democratized higher education not only by making a college education financially available but also by stimulating the entire culture toward education as the basis of "the good life." College was no longer just for the elite and wealthy few—it was for everybody who had the will and the wits to give it a try.

As if these forces weren't enough to create a demanding environment, the Church was facing important challenges of its own in the field of higher education. Latter-day Saint youth throughout North America felt the same economic, social, and demographic forces that were motivating almost everybody else to head for college campuses. In addition, the Church, as powerfully exemplified by the life and teachings of President McKay, had given its young people clear religious reasons to seek higher education.

The Church's theology was full of such motivation: "Teach ye diligently, and my grace shall attend you," the Lord had said, not only about religious doctrine but "of things both in heaven and in the earth, . . . the wars and the perplexities of the nations" (D&C 88:78–79). "Seek ye out of the best books words of wisdom; seek learning, even by study and also by faith" (D&C 88:118). And "I, the Lord, am well pleased that there should be a school in Zion" (D&C 97:3).

President McKay had taught and encouraged that vision from one end of the Church to the other throughout his long and influential life. He had been a teacher of English literature and an administrator at the Church's Weber Stake Academy in Ogden when he was called to the Quorum of the Twelve in 1906. Later, as commissioner of education for the Church in the 1920s, he was a persuasive advocate for education among Latter-day Saints of all ages. Then, during his presidency of the Church, he established his optimistic vision of education by leading the expansion of BYU, Ricks College, the Church College of Hawaii, and elementary and secondary Church schools in the South Pacific and Latin America. His decades of teaching were full of exhortation to the Saints about education as a quest for knowledge, wisdom, and character.

In an important sense, then, the far-flung educational system of the Church by 1970 clearly reflected the educational philosophy of David O. McKay—a philosophy long shared, though with variations in emphasis, by his predecessors and colleagues in Church leadership. Yet the rising demand for education among young Latter-day Saints was on a collision course with the internationalism and growth of the Church. Just as with its general boards and committees, the Church simply could not continue to fund colleges and schools to match expected growth. What had been possible for a small church in western America was not economically or logistically feasible for a large, international church. Further, in the eyes of some observers, the Church's deep commitment to the value of education in an increasingly secularized society ran some serious risks.

Thomas O'Dea, a Catholic sociologist who taught for a time at the University of Utah, published a book entitled *The Mormons* in 1957. He described the Church in sympathetic, fairly objective terms. In his conclusion, O'Dea summarized the major "sources of strain and conflict" he believed the Church would face in the near future. Heading his list was the conflict he saw coming between the Church's emphasis on education and its authoritarian theology: "Perhaps Mormonism's greatest and most significant problem is its encounter with modern secular thought." He continued:

> From their earliest beginnings, the Latter-day Saints have placed great emphasis upon education. . . . [Yet] little did they realize that in placing their hopes in education they were at the same time creating the "transmission belt" that would bring into Zion all the doubts and uncertainties that, in another century, were to beset the gentile world. . . .
>
> . . . The Mormon appreciation of education emphasized higher education and thereby encouraged contact between Mormon youth and those very elements in modern thought that are bound to act as a solvent on certain aspects of Mormon beliefs. The Mormon youth, who usually comes from a background of rural and quite literal Mormonism, finds that his entrance into the university is an introduction to the doubt and confusion that his first real encounter with secular culture entails. He has been taught by the Mormon faith to seek knowledge and to value it; yet it is precisely this course, so acceptable to and so honored by his religion, that is bound to bring religious crisis to him and profound danger to his religious belief. . . .
>
> Clearly, the dilemma of education versus apostasy is one to which Mormonism has as yet found no genuine solution. . . .
>
> The encounter of Mormonism and modern secular learning is still taking place. It is a spectacle of the present, of which no history can as yet be written. Upon its outcome will depend in a deeper sense the future of Mormonism.

In 1970, Neal Maxwell entered this scene of contradictory currents as the Church's commissioner of education, with a new First

Presidency and a new mandate. His response to these issues would make a fresh and lasting contribution to the Church, and to educated members of the Church, that would be among his most substantial legacies. Only his apostolic ministry, with its example of Christian discipleship, is more significant. Working closely with President Lee and his associates, Neal would help devise long-range policies that clarified the place of education in a global church. As for Thomas O'Dea's provocative questions, Neal himself represented the dilemma of which O'Dea wrote—and Neal's own example, as much as his speeches and writing, would speak for itself as a productive response to the O'Dea paradox.

Neal came "from a background of rural and quite literal Mormonism." He had encountered with zest the confusion and doubts of the modern secular world at sophisticated levels and had emerged with a spiritual maturity that was enriched rather than undermined by his educational and professional experiences. Then, as a role model, he taught what he had learned to other educated Latter-day Saints, and he brought into key positions in the Church Educational System several people whose encounters with O'Dea's concerns had been as valuable and as positive as was his own. To the extent that the future of Mormonism really was affected by the outcome of the conflict O'Dea described, Neal Maxwell's example suggested a promising future.

In this lofty historical context, Neal's entrance onto the public stage of Latter-day Saint history in 1970 came from a life story that wasn't calculated to leave big footprints on that, or any other, stage. He had the innate ability to play an influential role, but he hadn't designed a career path that was likely to leave very visible marks.

About 1969, Neal was feeling closer to discouragement than he had ever felt before—or since. By objective measures, he was not very discouraged; that would have been foreign to his "can-do" nature. But he felt unsettled, as if it were time to "break camp and move down the trail," and he wasn't sure what to do. He felt he was "topping out" at the university, regarding both what he could give and the satisfaction he found, even though his experiences on the U campus and in Utah public service vastly exceeded any expectations he'd had in 1956.

In more recent years, he'd been approached about a possible college presidency, running for Congress, working for a national organization dealing with state legislatures, or heading up the Utah Coordinating Council for Higher Education. Yet none of that had seemed to fit. But fit what? Just as he'd felt when leaving Washington, D.C., to return to Utah, he really lacked a long-term sense of personal direction.

One day he and Jim Fletcher were driving somewhere together, and Neal confided to Fletcher his feelings of uncertainty. Jim responded quickly, telling Neal he was capable of doing anything he wanted to do—so he should just pick a path and take it at any level. Neal was honestly surprised at Jim's high assessment of his capacity, and Jim was surprised at Neal's surprise. But Neal "had never thought of myself quite that way. Part of me was still the youngster" not quite good enough for the "in crowd" at Granite High. "I didn't have any game plan. I didn't know what was coming. There was no sense of the commissioner thing, because that didn't exist."

So Neal didn't have calculated ambitions, and he wasn't the elitist that his sometimes highbrow manner of speaking and writing might have suggested to people who didn't know him. He saw himself as something of an underdog, trying hard to do his best to help society, happy to work wherever needed until something or someone drew him elsewhere. "I believe we are supposed to make the world as good as we can make it," he would say. "We should not be like Jonah and sit on the mountain top waiting for Nineveh to go up in flames."

Yet there was in his background an enigmatic lack of conscious preparation. After graduating from college, he worked for a few years as a Senate staffer but chose to forgo further educational or career options that might reasonably have prepared him to wield real influence. When he took the public relations job at the U, he was following a spiritual urge that he didn't fully understand. If he had been serious about a political career, arguably he should have stayed on Senator Bennett's staff. Or, after returning to Utah, he should have become more involved with the Republican party—doing what people do who later plan to seek political office, such as supporting candidates and taking on political tasks that pay one's dues with the party.

And if he had been serious about a college teaching career, or even an administrative career in higher education, arguably he should have obtained more educational credentials. If he had wanted to qualify for a college or university presidency, or work in academic administration, those jobs called for a Ph.D. or some equivalent level of advanced study. As Elder Dallin H. Oaks has said, however, Neal Maxwell is "the only master's degree person I know of who leads and supervises Ph.D.s who hasn't apologized for not having a Ph.D. He's not the least bit apologetic because he saw himself as a *practitioner.*" Paradoxically, "this man, more than any Ph.D. I've ever met, is incredibly visionary. He's a theoretician. And he's so good at the theoretical that he doesn't need to have a Ph.D. It's as if Abraham Lincoln had to explain why he didn't have a political science degree. The man had it in his bones to do what had to be done." Or, as American philosopher William James is reported to have said, "Native distinction needs no official stamp."

Something about Neal's "native distinction" evokes a memory of his choosing to hasten his service in the infantry. He never felt sorry for himself about that, never felt he was somehow above that humblest of military choices. On the contrary, he would say with the Duke of Wellington that it would not have done for him not to be there. Still, it seems inexplicable that he would have pursued the infantryman's version of a career in higher education or politics, especially to those who came to appreciate him for the richness of his intellect and his natural gifts of statesmanship. As *Deseret News* staffer Jerry Johnston wrote in 1981, Neal "has a reputation for having one of the brightest intellects in the Church." Yet in earlier years, perhaps Neal didn't know how full of promise he really was. Perhaps, despite his outward appearance of competence and assurance, he was more inherently meek, like his father, than he was even aware.

As it turned out, this combination of personal willingness and lack of career planning actually let Neal accumulate the experience, the practical skill, and the insight that President Harold B. Lee was looking for and that the Church now needed—but without the personal agenda or

With President Harold B. Lee in the spring of 1972 at a Boston young adult conference

self-absorption that had troubled President Lee about some self-conscious intellectuals. President Lee was known for his distrust of so-called Church liberals, but he had said a liberal is a person "who does not have a testimony," someone who reads "by the lamp of [his] own conceit." Intelligence, as such, is different—disciplined by faith, it is always a blessing, whereas what Neal has called "unanchored brilliance" is a threat. Thus President Lee had respected and embraced such bright "schoolmen of spiritual stature" as West Belnap, Reed Bradford, Daniel Ludlow, and Antone Romney—BYU professors he had mentored among the executive secretaries to the first Church correlation committees.

Harold B. Lee's confidence in Neal didn't arise in a vacuum. For one thing, several of President Lee's most trusted confidants had already come to know Neal's nature and his heart—Presidents N. Eldon Tanner, Marion G. Romney, and Spencer W. Kimball. And President Lee's own experiences over several years let him see Neal in an unvarnished way for who he really was, including his paradoxically loyal tendency to consider steadying the ark.

There was, for instance, Neal's visit during his college days to

Elder Lee's office, muttering in good faith about the quality of Church manuals. Neal's role with Oscar McConkie in shaping student wards at a state university in ways that didn't match existing Church programs. Neal as a young YMMIA General Board member traveling with Elder Lee on his first stake conference assignment. The Leadership Committee, in which Elder Lee saw Neal at his unique best—analyzing the issues, casting up fresh alternatives, and blazing new trails in a context where he "felt free to make suggestions, to think about the unthinkable." The times called for fresh and energetic thought, which could emerge only in a climate of total two-way trust. The relationship between Harold B. Lee and Neal Maxwell enjoyed just such a rich blessing.

On a sunny June day in 1970, then, President Lee called Neal's office at the university, asking if he could drive right down to a meeting with the First Presidency—Presidents Smith, Lee, and Tanner. Neal was halfway there before he realized he was wearing an informal sport jacket. But there wasn't time to change to a suit. Besides, the members of the First Presidency knew him.

President Lee spoke for the Presidency, informing Neal that they had decided to re-create the office of commissioner of education, and they wanted him to accept that assignment. They wanted the entire system of Church schools and religious education evaluated and reorganized as needed; they wanted the president of BYU to report to the commissioner—no longer directly to the First Presidency; and Neal had their total confidence.

Neal asked only three questions in the fifteen-minute interview. Would he move to BYU, where Ernest Wilkinson and the seminary and institute leaders all had their offices? The answer was no—they wanted the commissioner to be "near the Brethren," in more ways than one. Did all of the First Presidency and Twelve support Neal's appointment? Yes, without question. Was there any job description? Not in detail—they'd work that out.

A few days later, Neal wrote a short letter, to which President Lee replied, reflecting

> upon the delightful relationship I have had with you over the
> last few years when I have had the privilege of sounding the

depths of your soul—intellectually and spiritually, and have never found you wanting. . . . My associates . . . have entertained similar feelings, but likewise I am profoundly impressed that the Lord has had you in mind as one of His choice ones to meet the challenge of the great need of our youth, particularly in the educational field today. I have, since the first of my acquaintance with you, felt assured that the day would come when you would have a prominent place in our educational structure. We . . . are thankful that the Lord has brought forward one like you to fill that need.

. . . President Tanner . . . remarked to me how delighted he was to see the manifestation of your grasp of the situation and your attitude of loyalty and faith and earnest desire and selfless qualities seldom to be found among us today.

Be assured of my full confidence and my prayers. As you now set up your organization, my door, my heart, and my time will always be open to you.

Later on, Neal would feel that perhaps some inspiration had prevented him "from going off and doing some of these other career things," like the options he raised with Jim Fletcher in the car that day. Had he been more logically ambitious about planning his life, the path of his discipleship probably would not have developed as it did. Ralph Mecham, who was especially close to Neal since their college days, wasn't surprised. He had a "feeling back in the early 50s" that Neal "sensed early on that he had a mission to perform" for the Church, somehow, someday. Neal's relationship with President Lee had become the catalyst for that mission to begin to unfold.

Part XI

The Church
Educational System
1970–76

THIRTY-FIVE

CREATING THE CHURCH EDUCATIONAL SYSTEM

O N   J U L Y   1 9 ,   1 9 7 0 ,   G .   H O M E R   D U R H A M —who had a sense of history about such things—wrote in his journal that his former student and close friend, Neal Maxwell, was the new commissioner of education for the Church. The Brethren, he wrote, are "reviving the old office held by JAW [Elder John A. Widtsoe, a member of the Twelve and Durham's father-in-law, commissioner from 1921 to 1924 and 1934 to 1936], JFM [Elder Joseph F. Merrill, also of the Twelve and commissioner from 1928 to 1933], and F. L. West [Franklin L. West, commissioner from 1936 to 1953]." Homer called Neal's appointment "a fine choice," though it "leaves a gap in the U of U leadership of a strong, visible churchman who is also respected, and has commerce with the sensitive Utah non-Mormons."

In August, the university held a farewell dinner for Neal, at which President Fletcher quipped, "I don't really feel we've lost an executive vice president, but we've gained a church." He added that in his "short career," Neal had found "the realization of the American dream: successful and happy." When the lights on the block U on the hill above campus blinked their farewell that night, Neal was emotional. After three years as a U student and fourteen years in its administration, he felt a tender nostalgia. He told the dinner guests that he was "a better Mormon because of my non-Mormon friends at the university. In a gentle way, they have reminded me of what I should be."

A *Deseret News* editorial noted the problems Neal faced now—growing enrollments, a complex educational system, Brigham Young University at its enrollment ceiling, and LDS youth "exceptionally beset by unsettling tests of faith in an era of uncertainty and instability." But his appointment "brings together a man who's used to meeting challenges [with] a program that faces them."

Meanwhile, Edith Bronson, still Neal's secretary, found that not everybody was all that impressed as she and her boss began their new jobs. On the day she arrived at the Kennecott Building, where they would office for two years, she could find neither a typewriter nor a desk. So she called the Church purchasing staff and said, "This is Neal Maxwell's office. We're trying to furnish an office." After a pause, the purchasing secretary replied, "Who's Neal Maxwell?"

This was but one of several hints that "going to the Church" would create a few adjustments. Soon after they received their furniture, President Lee called and asked if Neal would come to his office. Caught off guard, Neal had to run next door to ZCMI to buy a white shirt he could hurriedly don before crossing the street to attend the meeting. Further, Neal had been known to let a mild cuss word slip out occasionally when he was trying to do something mechanical that wouldn't work. But not any more. The same with his driving. His congenital impatience had made him a Type A driver, wearing out brakes "more rapidly than a lot of people would." Now he was taming his road style as well.

Edith already knew that "above all, Neal was religious. That was his main thing." But she was still unprepared for the day she walked into the commissioner's office to give him something and "he was praying at his desk." She apologized for interrupting, but Neal said calmly, "It's okay. I'm through. I just had a question I needed an answer to."

These little examples are but subtle hints of what those closest to

Neal began to see on a larger scale—he took the new job seriously, he liked it, and it let him be himself. The Church and the gospel had long been his highest priority, and now he could breathe and drink what he called "the inexhaustible gospel" all day, every day. His family noticed that he was more fulfilled and happy, even though he had thoroughly enjoyed his university years.

Joe J. Christensen, who had known Neal at the U and would now work with him in CES, watched the new commissioner teach a religion class at the U institute. Joe said Neal seemed liberated, "much more free to talk about what he wanted to than he'd ever felt" in a political science class. Now he could "overtly express his testimony" to students, no longer constrained by the realities of a state university. It was "a flight to freedom," where he welcomed "the values of the gospel [in his professional work] with the joy of the returning pilgrim." As Edith said, "I think he loved it. . . . I think he finally felt like he was home."

But now came the huge project of turning the Church's loose-knit confederacy of educational entities into a real system built to serve whatever long-term purposes would contribute most to the Church's future. Neal quickly found that although some elements of a system existed, there was little overall strategy. He would have felt "blessed if I could have been given a couple of pages that say this is the policy . . . , this is who we are going to educate, this is what we can afford, but there was none of that."

A big issue was whether higher education—especially BYU—should claim the lion's share of both budget and attention. Should BYU be expanded? Reduced? Should the Church build other college campuses? Should the Church try to build new elementary and secondary schools in other countries where it was expanding internationally, as it had already done in a few locations? Where did religious education fit—seminaries and institutes—when compared in priority to schools and colleges? How important were educational needs compared to other growing claims on the Church's budgeted funds?

To begin with, it helped that President Lee could personally tutor Neal in a vision of Church education that, as noted earlier, had a short but potent chain of title over the generations. Karl G. Maeser had been the tutor to Brigham Young's children. Then in 1876 Brigham Young sent him to Provo to start BYU (originally Brigham Young Academy). There he let the best of his German intellectual discipline serve the broader vision of his unqualified commitment to Brigham Young's primary request—not to teach even the alphabet or the multiplication tables without the Spirit of God. As the first general superintendent of Church schools from 1888 to 1901, Karl Maeser passed the torch of this vision to an entire generation of LDS teachers, including young James E. Talmage, who mentored young J. Reuben Clark, who mentored young Harold B. Lee, who mentored young Neal A. Maxwell.

With natural variations on the theme of this basic vision, Church education had gone through several adjustments as the Church adapted to its own growth and a changing Utah environment. During Karl G. Maeser's day, the Church established "academies" (high schools, some of which later became junior colleges) throughout the intermountain Church, because there was no adequate state school system. As early as the 1890s, the First Presidency had also dreamed of having a genuine university to lead this armada of schools. They even designated James Talmage as the first president of such a campus, to be located in Salt Lake City. But the economic depression of 1893 made that project impossible. Then, gradually, Brigham Young University assumed the flagship role.

By the late 1920s, state high schools in the West were becoming stronger, and the First Presidency could see that it wasn't feasible or necessary to duplicate them with expensive Church schools. The concept of providing religious education through seminary classes for LDS students attending state high schools had worked well since its introduction at Salt Lake's Granite High in 1912. So the Brethren decided to encourage support for the public schools and to expand religious education. In 1926, they established the first institute of religion for college students at the University of Idaho in Moscow, and other institutes soon followed.

In the early 1930s, the Church donated nearly all of its post-secondary academies to the states where they were located. In Utah, these academies included Dixie College, Snow College, and Weber

College. The Church also offered Ricks College to Idaho at no cost, but the state found even that price too high. Idaho was unwilling to assume the annual operating costs, so the Church kept Ricks. This context established fairly early the principle that, if it had to choose, the Church would give higher priority to religious education than it gave to Church schools, because that would offer a spiritual perspective on education to the most students at the least cost.

Then, as the Church began to expand internationally during President David O. McKay's tenure, a renewed interest in Church schools arose. With some LDS schools already operating in the Pacific, the Church established a college in Hawaii, a high school in New Zealand, and a few primary and secondary schools in Latin America. In the mid-1960s, the First Presidency approved, then later withdrew, the idea of creating several junior colleges as a feeder system for BYU.

From Karl Maeser's day forward, the Church's commissioner of education theoretically oversaw all LDS schools, seminaries, and institutes of religion. By the time Commissioner Frank West retired in 1953, however, each Church school was really operating independently from the others and from the seminaries and institutes. William E. Berrett, who supervised the seminaries and institutes during much of the 1950s and 60s, described this situation with polite understatement: "This independence of the various educational units was prompted by personality differences among those heading the various units." To Neal, that history had a familiar sound—it was much like Utah's colleges before the state adopted the centralized system he had helped design in 1969.

This situation meant that each school had its own governing board, sometimes duplicating the Church Board of Education or the Pacific Board of Education for the schools operated by missionaries in the South Pacific. The Brethren tried to achieve some unity by appointing Ernest Wilkinson as "chancellor" of a "Unified School System" during the early part of Ernest's service as president at BYU (1951–70). Although that helped, Ernest was often preoccupied with the growth of BYU and issues related to a possible system of junior colleges.

In 1965, Harvey L. Taylor, a vice president at BYU, was appointed as administrator for all Church schools other than BYU, and William E. Berrett continued to lead the seminaries and institutes under Taylor's direction. Just as his old friend Ray Olpin at the U of U had felt about his relationship to the Utah legislature, Wilkinson didn't want to give up his direct reporting line to the First Presidency. So BYU stayed outside the Church school system.

By the time of Neal's appointment, however, Wilkinson, Taylor, and Berrett had all reached retirement age, as had John L. Clarke, the president of Ricks College. With these personnel openings, with numerous big and unresolved issues, and also with a new First Presidency in place, Neal felt the urgency of establishing both unity and a clear strategy for all of Church education. That feeling matched the attitude of the First Presidency. Elder Thomas Monson said the new First Presidency definitely "had an idea of where they wanted the program to go," beginning with an "amalgamation" of the various educational entities.

Perhaps the most important factor in developing the needed unity and strategy was the two-way relationship of confidence and trust that developed between the First Presidency and Neal. Like ripples from a pebble thrown into a pond, the strength of that relationship soon reached in all directions to create a mutual sense of harmony that included, on one hand, many other General Authorities and, on the other hand, many faculty, administrators, and students in the Church's classrooms everywhere.

Joe Christensen, who became Neal's associate commissioner, looked back on those years as a Camelot-like "era of intense creativity and a feeling that you could plumb the depths of your imagination" and "your ideas would at least have a hearing." In trying to help the Brethren create a real "system" of education, Neal's staff kept sensing they had "pretty well a blank page," and the Brethren were "so supportive and accepting of [their] ideas" that they felt great responsibility to do their homework prayerfully, because the "chances were they'd approve" what Neal's people would submit.

From the perspective of BYU, Neal's six years as commissioner rallied most of the faculty troops there with fresh vision. By 1976, one senior faculty member would say, "I don't suppose the Church has ever had a commissioner so incomparably fluent in both the language of faith and the language of scholarship . . . [and] so admired by the rank and file of the LDS academic community, particularly the faculty and students at BYU."

Dallin Oaks also saw how Neal brought the BYU faculty into a relationship of mutual trust with the Brethren. "More than anyone I've known," he said, Neal "was able to do that. He was very, very good at it." From the standpoint of seminary and institute faculty, Joe Christensen saw the same thing, that Neal was "as significant as any individual in the Church in raising the confidence level" of senior Church leaders in their religious educators.

Neal became a genuine two-way interpreter between LDS faculty members and the Brethren. And the way people in those two groups felt about Neal clearly affected the degree of confidence they felt in each other. That mutual confidence was the important point. This wasn't a popularity contest about Neal; it was a conscious exercise in directive-participative leadership. Neal believed in what he was doing, as he candidly and honestly looked for ways to help those in both groups understand, appreciate, and trust one another.

He nourished this harmony as he interacted with them both. His talks and writing showed the faculty that he understood and participated in their world, yet he always looked at their academic disciplines through the lens of the gospel. He also built their confidence informally, occasionally inviting promising new faculty members to his home for dinner, or participating actively in faculty conferences. Much of what Neal did in these settings was more a reflection of his personality than any particular techniques. As historian Richard Bushman put it, Neal's "genius [is the way he appealed to] people with quite different temperaments. . . . Something in his personality . . . won the confidence of academics and people with little sympathy for [academic matters]. It was something about his openness, the sense you got that he understood and liked scholarship." His "irenic touch" also generated feelings of peace and cooperation between people with differing bases of experience and attitude.

Truman Madsen added to this perspective that, during Neal's years as commissioner and later as a General Authority, he developed a remarkably broad set of relationships. His interest and his support have not been reserved for people in the areas of his personal interest; rather, he has nurtured and encouraged LDS scholars all across the spectrum of the professions and academic disciplines, from psychology, literature, and history to law, business, and the sciences. Madsen reached this conclusion after making a list of all the people he could think of who felt that Elder Maxwell had taken a special interest in their work.

With the Church leaders, Dallin Oaks said Neal took a "much more subtle" approach than "lecturing the Brethren in a trustees' meeting," which is how some people would have tried to help—and which is "totally counterproductive." Neal's style was to provide "informal explanations" about educational issues or personalities to General Authorities, in conversations of all kinds. At the same time, he helped faculty members at BYU and elsewhere in Church education understand the unique perspectives and concerns of the Church leaders. Said Elder Oaks, then president of BYU, "Neal helped me . . . to understand the Brethren. He'd give me little tutorials about, 'Well, bear in mind that this is [what] they're worried about, and you'd do well not to use that argument. It's a good argument, but it will be misunderstood, or it's counterproductive.'"

Some of Neal's service was that of a translator, building communications bridges between people within and outside the academic world. This function was not new to him—at the University of Utah, he'd been interpreting the university community to the local community, and vice versa, for years. On a later occasion, for example, BYU presented to its board of trustees a sensitive document that had been labored over for months by a faculty committee. A senior board member entered the meeting room a little early, having just read the long memo. He held it up and asked with a wink, "Why does this thing have to sound like it was written by a bunch of professors?" The first to respond, Neal said good-naturedly, "Well, the Doctrine and Covenants says everybody's entitled to hear the gospel in his own tongue."

In this climate of growing harmony, the Commissioner's office engaged head-on the diverse interests, policies, and reporting lines of its far-flung educational network. Their task was to bring unity and coherence out of great diversity. Elder Boyd K. Packer watched Neal bring it "together in a way that somebody from BYU might not have been able to do. . . . This is a big Church and BYU may be the flagship, but it isn't the only ship in the armada. He could see the other ships, even the rowboats."

Soon the commissioner's office recommended, and the board approved, a new organization called the Church Educational System (CES), with its own sense of identity, visibility, and brotherhood. For Neal, the task was analogous to creating the American Constitution to replace the old Articles of Confederation. Jeffrey Holland, who would replace Neal as commissioner in 1976, agreed. "Neal created this new world and new logo, new offices, and new appointments. He legitimized [CES] in a new way, and it's been that way ever since."

This development didn't occur in an exclusive, private corner. Neal, the student of participative leadership, wanted the plans to reflect the collective desires of the Church leadership, so that it would be both right and lasting. His access to President Lee let Neal sense almost continually the First Presidency's concerns and priorities. President Lee had many long-held views about most of the general issues they faced, but he respected Neal's own vision and skill enough that he wanted the commissioner to scrutinize all assumptions and options to verify "our scope" and "our limitations" before making key decisions.

Neal also obtained permission to take several new, inclusive steps to broaden the base of participation in that entire process. One such step was the appointment of a personnel search committee from among members of the Church Board of Education. Elder Marion G. Romney chaired the committee, joined by Elder Boyd K. Packer of the Twelve, Elder Marion D. Hanks, an Assistant to the Twelve, and Neal. Because principal leaders in Church education would soon retire and new positions needed to be filled in the commissioner's office, there would be a clean sweep of leadership posts. Neal worked closely with the search committee for most of two years as they actively helped select his three associate commissioners (Joe J. Christensen for religious education, Kenneth H. Beesley for schools and colleges, and Dee F. Andersen for finance), new presidents for Ricks College (Henry B. Eyring), BYU (Dallin H. Oaks), Church College of Hawaii (Steven Brower), and the first dean of the BYU Law School (Rex E. Lee).

At Neal's urging, all of the institutional governing boards began meeting in one combined meeting, even though separate minutes were kept to meet the legal requirements for each entity. At that time the board included the First Presidency, all of the Twelve, one or two other General Authorities, the Presiding Bishop, and the general president of the Relief Society. Next, Neal requested that each of his associate commissioners attend each board meeting, along with the president of BYU. The First Presidency initially wondered why all of these people were needed in the meetings, but Neal felt, and experience confirmed, that their participation would enhance both the board members' understanding of the issues and the CES leaders' understanding of the board's attitudes.

Then, in order to make the meetings both meaningful and efficient, the board agreed to several guiding principles Neal proposed. One of these was that, helped by the commissioner's staff, the board would develop a series of general policies and then delegate to the staff and the CES institutions the authority to make certain decisions that were "within policy." The development of basic policies in Neal's early months as commissioner thus took on considerable long-term significance.

Neal also built a style of candid teamwork among his associates and the school presidents. In a departure from some past practice, he assured board members that they'd all receive full disclosure about any important issues—good news or bad—and that nothing would come to them outside regular channels or without having been carefully reviewed at his level. He also wanted his team members to hear and respond to one another well before they took proposals to board meetings. These approaches helped build a unified system, and they ensured valuable peer review through internal critiques as proposals were developed.

In the early months of CES, after two decades of feeling free to take BYU needs directly to the First Presidency, Ernest Wilkinson was less than keen about attending weekly commissioner's staff meetings. Neal valued his relationship with Ernest, but his instructions were clear: BYU now reported through the commissioner. In one early board meeting, Wilkinson asked if he might raise a certain BYU matter, although he hadn't yet discussed the topic with Neal. Neal spoke up, explaining that until the two of them had considered the issue, it wasn't ready for board discussion. The board supported Neal's response, and everybody learned together about creating a real system of education.

Neal's own role in shaping the new system was significant, but much of what he did was simply catalytic. For one thing, he believed that the board's agenda was the CES agenda, even though someone in his role was needed to ask hard questions and do thorough homework. He also believed deeply in participative governance, knowing that a true sense of ownership among the participants was essential to developing a lasting CES strategy. Sometimes he referred to "those future First Presidencies" that would emerge from the members of the Twelve seated around the table, and that gave his search for consensus a long-term character. At the same time, as Dallin Oaks could see, "They respected him greatly, and he had a great vision of what ought to be done." Besides, Neal's vision was "in accord with the direction they wanted to go. So I think the new CES policy formulation process was 60 percent Neal and 40 percent" the board.

THIRTY-SIX

NEW LEADERS

As soon as Neal saw the scope of his task and the approaching retirement of so many key individuals, he began praying to find the best possible people. There really would be a clean sweep of Church Educational System leadership. It was a bold stroke, but it appealed to him. As Jeffrey Holland said, "Neal likes a new broom." Neal also must have believed in the maxim that the most important factor in solving human problems is the competence and the character of the people trying to solve them—and he was willing to search hard for both qualities. He had long believed that "80 percent of leadership is to get the right people." Choosing these people would be as significant as anything he would do as commissioner, and some of the choices would affect the future leadership of the Church.

Working closely with Elder Marion G. Romney and the search committee, Neal first found his associate commissioners. He had come to know Joe J. Christensen at the University of Utah, where Joe had replaced Lowell Bennion as director of the institute of religion. When Neal discovered in August 1970 that Joe had just left Utah to preside over a mission in Mexico, he could have assumed Joe was unavailable. The willingness of the Brethren to interrupt Joe's mission before it was really underway showed the level of their support for Neal's recommendation that Joe become associate commissioner for religious education. Other committee members also knew him. Elder Romney later said of Joe, "He's about as conservative as you can be in the gospel, but still have new ideas." Joe would later serve as president of Ricks College and then in the Presidency of the Seventy.

Neal had exchanged letters with Kenneth H. Beesley, a Salt Lake native who had been on the faculty at Columbia Teachers' College in New York before becoming executive dean at Fresno State University in California. Neal liked Ken's background, and he liked the idea of including the perspective of LDS educators from outside Utah. One of his hopes as commissioner was to create a feeling of community among all Latter-day Saint scholars, wherever they taught. Ken was appointed associate commissioner for colleges and schools, with supervisory responsibility for Ricks College, the Church College of Hawaii (CCH), LDS Business College (LDSBC) in Salt Lake City, and all elementary and secondary schools. He would later serve as president of LDS Business College and then play a leading role in opening far-off Mongolia to missionary work.

Dee F. Andersen rounded out the commissioner's office with his assignment for finance and budgeting. Dee was another U of U administrator with a strong background in accounting and campus financial planning. Neal knew and respected Dee from their U days. He would later serve as Church budget officer, administrative vice president at Brigham Young University, and then as a mission president and temple president.

So far this made it four for four—nobody on the commissioner's staff was from BYU. Jeffrey Holland thought that bringing in all young outsiders perhaps unsettled a few "old timers" in Church education who were used to seeing people within the system work their way up into leadership positions. And Neal wasn't through yet.

Hal Eyring, the thirty-eight-year-old son of Neal's longtime U of U colleague Henry Eyring, taught at the Stanford Business School, having earned his doctorate in business at Harvard. He also served as bishop of the Stanford student ward. One Saturday night a few months after Neal's appointment had been announced, Hal's wife, Kathy, awoke and asked, "Hal, are you sure you're doing the right thing with your life?" They discussed her question. Then she asked, "Are you sure you shouldn't be doing studies for Neal Maxwell?" Neither of them knew Neal or his work well enough to know what that could mean. Hal was having trouble seeing Kathy's point. "Would you pray about it?" she asked. So he did pray, right then, and felt no answer.

The next morning during his bishopric meeting, Hal had a strong impression that he shouldn't do again what he had done the night before. Then the previous night's puzzled feeling returned. He had recently received some calls about intriguing job options that would take him away from Stanford and away from education, and Kathy knew his heart was in education. So he concluded that he had erred, not having prayed about those inquiries, and he promised himself he would pray about any other job offer that might come along.

Meanwhile, Neal and the search committee were looking for a replacement for John L. Clarke, the retiring president of Ricks College. The committee was at an impasse when Neal "went back to my office and one of those strong impressions came through to me . . . about Hal Eyring." So he immediately called President Romney and asked if the committee could reassemble, which it promptly did. Neal presented Hal's name, and "it was warmly received."

Within a week of the midnight conversation with Kathy, Hal received a call from Neal Maxwell, asking him to go to Salt Lake the next day. They met at Hal's parents' home. Getting right to the point, Neal said, "Hal, I'd like to ask you to be president of Ricks College." Stunned but remembering his experience of the previous week, Hal said he'd need to pray about it. Neal said that was fine, but they'd be seeing the First Presidency the next morning. Hal, who knew absolutely nothing about Ricks, prayed hard that night.

The next day, after a brief visit with Neal and the First Presidency, Neal told Hal that the position was his if he wanted it. Within a few days, he accepted. Later on, after his own call to the Twelve, Elder

Commissioner Maxwell at a meeting of CES leaders in Hawaii with Kenneth Beesley, associate commissioner for Church Education (fourth from left); Dallin H. Oaks, president of BYU (third from right); and Henry B. Eyring, president of Ricks College (far right)

Eyring said his experience "gives you a feeling for Neal's style as commissioner. I would say the main characteristic of it is that the Lord went before him."

Replacing Ernest Wilkinson at BYU was the next big step. Wilkinson had written a letter of resignation to the First Presidency just before Neal's appointment as commissioner. But the board delayed announcing his release as long as possible, not wanting to make him a lame duck president. Neal pushed for an early announcement and a wide-open search, feeling that the Romney search committee and the natural leaders of the BYU faculty really needed an extended two-way conversation about BYU's future. He knew that some BYU faculty members were restless, feeling that the Wilkinson years, despite remarkable growth at that university, had lacked some of the participation and political tolerance Neal had already written about.

On March 9, 1971, President Lee and Neal announced Wilkinson's release at a BYU devotional. They paid tribute to Ernest, whose energy and vision had created a university of great size and substance. They also announced that he would help to establish the J. Reuben Clark Law School at BYU. Then Neal said the search committee would proceed openly but quietly to find "whom the Lord would have preside over this institution," adding that there were no "prior commitments" to anyone, "in spite of some of the speculation that you have heard." The committee immediately began soliciting names and interviewing people about BYU's needs.

The committee was looking for a leader who had spiritual and academic depth but who also would accept Neal's role, ensuring that BYU not dominate the newly minted CES. Still, Neal believed deeply that BYU must have a strong president. He had learned from his years in the Utah system that the board should pick a president in whom they had confidence and then support him, rather than expect the commissioner to micromanage him. When the search began, neither Neal nor anyone else on the committee knew Dallin Oaks personally.

In his early searching for possible candidates, Neal heard high praise for Oaks from very divergent sources—and that fact alone got his attention. One source was his friend Jerry Andersen, University of Utah academic vice president, an able, tough-minded, and politically liberal non-LDS law professor who had tried to recruit Dallin for the U law school faculty. The other was the politically conservative Ernest Wilkinson, who had known Dallin as a BYU student, had encouraged him to attend the University of Chicago Law School, and had referred Dallin to Carl Hawkins at the Wilkinson law firm in Washington, D.C., who helped him obtain a Supreme Court clerkship. In 1971, Dallin was a thirty-eight-year-old University of Chicago law professor who had served as acting dean of the law school there and was executive director of the American Bar Association's professional research organization. He was also in a stake presidency.

Dallin and June Oaks were driving late one night to Williamsburg, Virginia, for some professional meetings. June was asleep. Dallin heard on the radio about Wilkinson's resignation and about the new law school at BYU. When June awoke, he told her the news and said he had the feeling that this announcement would affect their lives in some way and that they'd probably receive a phone call about it in Williamsburg. The next day Neal called Dallin to invite him to meet with the search committee. Because Dallin's schedule didn't allow a trip to Utah for another two weeks, he met with the committee after Neal had gone to Europe for a prior educational commitment. Before leaving Utah, Neal briefed the committee about Dallin and then talked often with President Romney by phone during the search process.

When Dallin went to the Chicago airport, he found a problem with his flight to Salt Lake City, so he switched his ticket to a different airline. As he boarded, he saw Harold B. Lee on the flight, next to a vacant seat. Dallin introduced himself, and President Lee invited him to visit for fifteen minutes until the plane took off. President Lee and President Tanner also met with Dallin after he saw the committee. Weeks later, when the search committee had decided to recommend Dallin, President Lee said, "'We all know who the next president is going to be.' Apparently [he] knew before the ... committee [made its decision], although the impromptu interview aboard the plane in Chicago had never been mentioned to anyone."

Soon President Lee called to invite Dallin to be the president of BYU. He called back in a few days to say the Brethren wanted Neal and Dallin to meet before making a public announcement. So Neal flew from England and spent a day at the Oaks home in Chicago. Elder Romney thought this step would "impress upon BYU's new president that he would be reporting to the commissioner" and would be part of CES.

Dallin believed "the Brethren probably wanted Neal to meet my wife and feel the spirit of my home before they really went ahead with this. I was unknown to any of the authorities of the Church when they interviewed me. . . . If the purpose of his visit was to test the chemistry of the Oaks-Maxwell relationship, that was resolved very quickly." The two men found almost "instant agreement" on their most essential goals and approach—and the rapport between them simply kept growing. One day Elder Maxwell would say he'd gladly give Elder Oaks authority to act as his proxy well in advance of any decision, and Elder Oaks would say he'd never known a person with whom he had "more harmony in thinking and decision-making." And the more important the issue, the more likely it was that they would agree—whether in CES or later on, when both were members of the Twelve.

Neal's involvement with Jeffrey Holland's appointment as dean of religious education at BYU was more indirect but it illustrates how certain seeds of future Church leadership were being sown during Neal's years as commissioner. Jeff, a career teacher in the institutes of religion, knew Neal just well enough to call him for advice about his job options when he finished his doctorate in American Studies at Yale. Neal remembered the call nearly a decade later as he spoke at Jeff's inauguration as the BYU president who replaced Dallin Oaks. Jeff remembered it years after that, when he wrote to Neal, "I wouldn't even have been in CES if it hadn't been for your natural willingness to shepherd young unknowns."

With Neal's encouragement, Jeff taught briefly at the University of Utah Institute before taking a staff position in a new program at Church headquarters for single adults. There the two of them interacted frequently enough that Neal could respond warmly when the BYU administration recommended Jeff as the new dean of religious education at BYU in 1973, when he was thirty-two years old.

In the search for their new dean, a number of religion faculty members at BYU had expressed a preference not to have someone who was either young or an outsider. Because he was both, Dean Holland's appointment was one more reflection of the fresh breezes blowing in CES. Within only three more years, he would replace Neal as commissioner of education and would always think of him as "my mentor and tutor on Church education."

THIRTY-SEVEN

RELIGIOUS EDUCATION AND CHURCH SCHOOLS

As the commissioner's team gradually came together, so did a set of long-term strategic policies for the Church Educational System. Since his military days, Neal had been conscious of the distinction between strategy and tactics. He often used such adjectives as *strategic* and *tactical*, but by now he had discovered that not everyone recognized the difference between the two. Nor did others always assume, as he did, that institutional boards and top executive officers should focus more on strategy than on tactics. So, as he saw an endless array of tactical issues looking for some path into CES staff and board discussions, he looked for ways to draw the Church Board of Education into a process of developing a broad CES strategy.

It didn't seem to him a good use of the board's time, for example, to spend twenty minutes deciding whether to build new animal pens at the Church school in Tonga. Nor did it seem sensible to talk about approval for a new school in a South American country until the board had clarified its criteria and goals about Church schools in general. Historical precedent was an insufficient guide because the Church's present, let alone its future, was starting to look very different from its past.

Neal's first step was to allocate time in board meetings for broad discussions of what he called "reaction papers." He would ask his associates to help sketch the background, alternatives, costs, and benefits regarding approaches to a given issue even though no immediate proposal was before the board for decision. For instance, he urged the board to develop guidelines for the number of students required to justify building a new seminary building or adding a full-time teacher. Then, when a policy was in place, CES staff members were less likely to pursue something the board really didn't need to see, unless an exception to policy was clearly justified. This also allowed a more efficient approval process when specific projects were "within policy." The approach was new and refreshing for many on the board, and it seemed to work.

Neal brought what turned out to be his most important reaction papers to the board as early as the fall of 1970. He prepared himself by testing his questions on President Lee and the CES staff and then took early drafts of the papers to the board's four-member executive committee, which functioned as a filter for action and discussion by the full board. One of the papers asked whether CES should move faster to develop seminary and institute programs in international areas. It included data on membership growth and college-level enrollments in various countries. The second paper weighed the pros and cons of establishing more two-year business colleges, like LDS Business College in Salt Lake City, listing advantages and disadvantages. The third paper outlined a summary of general aims and future directions for CES. The executive committee was not interested in the second paper, and it saw the first one as related to the third. Thus began the process of CES strategic planning.

As revised for full board discussion, the general reaction paper asked what consensus existed about certain assumptions that would shape other policy principles. The first assumptions addressed the value of education and the connection between religious and educational goals: The Church has "an excellent history of membership growth in which we did not simply 'enroll' new members, baptizing and forgetting them; rather, we have helped them to prepare to cope with the practical problems of life." Education could thus help with personal development, economic self-reliance, building the Church's local leadership base, and contributing to the local culture. Another basic premise was that religious education, designed to build faith and testimony, should have top priority.

The ensuing discussions led to a formal report in 1971 from the commissioner of education entitled "Seek Learning Even by Study and by Faith." It presented three guiding policies for CES—(1) literacy and basic education are gospel needs, (2) the Church will not duplicate available state-sponsored education, and (3) all Latter-day Saint high school and college students should have access to weekday religious education. Within these policies were several general goals CES would seek to develop—youth with firm testimonies of the Restoration, stronger local Church leadership, parental effectiveness, community leadership, job skills, self-esteem, problem-solving ability, and preparing youth for missions and temple marriages.

The report discussed specific implications that flowed from the goals. For example, religious education should be expanded to follow the Church's growth, no new campuses for higher education should be added, and additional Church schools should be considered only when state systems aren't available. Data on all CES operations followed.

With three decades of hindsight, combined with his own experience from 1976 to 1980 as commissioner, Elder Holland regards this report—and, more importantly, the process that created and implemented it—as "the best illustration I know" of Neal Maxwell's strategic thinking.

> It was new. It was the kind of thing that was expected of him. . . . But he had to wrestle with where Church education was going. Would there be feeder schools for BYU? Would we set up more elementary schools? What came out of this was remarkable, calling the future about as accurately and persuasively as anyone has done forecasting around here. . . .
>
> And the freight train, the lifeblood vehicle, would be seminaries and institutes. In the last few years, the Twelve have

revisited where Church education should be going, and almost
to the bullet, it was the Neal Maxwell call of 1970.

Consider now the way Neal and his associates applied these criteria over the next five years—in religious education, LDS primary and
secondary schools, and higher education.

It was clear to Neal that President Lee wanted to give religious
education a higher priority than Church schools or Church higher education. This was the Church's unique and most essential educational
contribution, it was the least expensive, and it was the most adaptable
to the enormous variety of circumstances to be found in an international church.

So Neal looked to Joe Christensen to recommend ways to expand
seminaries and institutes—even internationally, if possible. The Utah
style of released-time programs (classes during regular school hours) in
Church-owned seminary buildings wasn't realistic. And the prospects
for replicating weekday religion classes across the globe in multiple languages, complete with manuals and faithful teachers, were truly daunting. Since its beginning, seminary had been confined to the Church's
areas of high population in the western United States. But Harvey
Taylor and William E. Berrett had already sensed the international
need enough to do some pioneering. In the late 1960s, they had introduced a few seminary and institute classes into selected other countries,
even though by 1970 no regular course materials had been translated
into any non-English language. Their experiments laid the foundation
for the most significant expansion of Church education during Neal's
tenure—taking religious education wherever the Church went, as missionary work took hold around the globe.

The hunger for religious education had clearly been growing in
the international Church. In Mexico, for instance, seminaries were
established in several locations in the 1960s. This was done, in part,
because Mexican law forbade religious instruction in the Church's
numerous elementary schools in that country, so the students took religion classes in nearby LDS chapels. The first early-morning and home-
study seminaries in South America were introduced in early 1970, after
an "eloquent appeal" to the First Presidency from Buenos Aires Stake

president Angel Abrea, along with repeated requests from other priesthood leaders. CES personnel who had earlier served missions in those countries went back to launch classes on a trial basis. Europe, Australia, and New Zealand took similar first steps during the late 1960s, mostly on a home-study basis in pilot stakes.

But the priorities of the new CES strategy gave these experiments an unprecedented momentum. Joe prepared a complete proposal for expanding the seminaries and institutes "wherever the Church went." Neal defended the proposal in the next budget review so strongly that he said he would take the needed funds from other CES operations, if new money was not available.

Joe constantly felt the pressure of Neal's desire to move "very, very rapidly," even though Neal tried to be empathetic about the complexities of language, distance, and quality in maintaining CES standards. Soon, aided by skilled and creative zone administrators, Neal and Joe sent out American CES people with a mission to return home as soon as they could accomplish three "scaffolding" mandates in each country: (1) start the program among the youth, (2) develop and maintain good relationships with local priesthood leaders, and (3) train local people to take over all administration and teaching within three years. In other words, they were to set up the scaffolding with teachers from the United States, build the building, and then remove the scaffolding.

They began in Latin America and Germany, enrolling in the first year about 700 students in Guatemala, in Argentina, and in Uruguay, with more than 900 in Brazil. Soon they expanded to Japan, Korea, Taiwan, and the Philippines. Joe Christensen would later say, "I know of no other Church program that moved toward globalization and nationalization so quickly."

Traditionally, seminary and institute teachers were full-time personnel, but it was impossible to sustain the international expansion on that basis. CES leaders hired some full-time supervisors, but eventually nearly all international teaching was done part-time by the most faithful local teachers they could identify, hire, and train with consultation and support from local priesthood leaders. They also learned from experience that, surprisingly, both enrollment and completion ratios were higher with early-morning seminary than with home study classes.

And they didn't wait until the Church was already established. Joe and Neal traveled to Madrid, Spain, when missionary work was just beginning in that country. They worked out with the mission president, Raymond Barnes, how they could start seminaries and institutes at "virtually the same time the Church's missionary efforts were starting."

By 1976, Neal could report to the board that CES had expanded its standard materials from one to sixteen languages, moving from seventeen to fifty-one countries, using classroom-based programs in such flexible locations as chapels and homes. Moreover, all teaching and local supervision was in the hands of local personnel. As Elder Jeffrey Holland saw it,

> This whole dream that religious education would be the wave of the future, the idea that we would take it everywhere, was all under Neal's direction. . . . It was part of this larger vision . . . those sparks flying off the flint and steel, as his unique creative energy latched on to the strategic vision CES had developed with the Brethren.
>
> Pretty soon people started to recognize that if youth went to seminary, they usually went on a mission. Then that returned missionary would be a good branch president someday, and next thing you knew, he would be stake president. The connection of what seminary was doing to build first a missionary force and then a kind of priesthood/family base in the Church was almost instant. . . .
>
> Over time it really has had an impact. That's where much of the future strength of the Church is.

By 2001, the total seminary and institute enrollment outside North America was about 340,000 students, almost half of the CES worldwide enrollment.

Interestingly, as Elder Henry B. Eyring noted, this high-energy effort got underway just ahead of President Kimball's stirring call in 1974, which took the Church's international missionary efforts to a new and higher level. President Kimball challenged each country to prepare itself to supply its own missionaries, who would sorely need exactly the preparation that seminary offered them.

It was with gratitude for President Lee's prophetic instincts, then, that Neal told the seminary and institute teachers in 1983 that the eventual "history of the Church . . . will show . . . a strong, even profound, correlation between the growth and quality of our seminary and institute program . . . and the growth of the Church's full-time missions. It is not accidental that the seminary and institute program spread coincidentally with the spread of the missionary work around this globe."

Developing a consistent policy for Church-operated schools—as distinguished from religion classes only—in international areas became Neal's most vexing problem. The arguments for Church schools were strong ones, even with a general CES policy against establishing more Church schools in countries with acceptable public systems. Many countries had only marginal schools, the educational immersion of students in an LDS atmosphere with LDS faculty would better fulfill the complete purpose of Church education, and a number of Church schools were already operating successfully in the island countries of the Pacific and in Latin America.

Nevertheless, schools were very expensive to build and maintain, experienced and faithful LDS teachers were hard to find in many countries, and financial factors made President Lee very reluctant to give the impression that the Church would provide schools whenever local Church members desired them. Additionally, the desire of Church members for LDS schools was not just an international issue. A number of American Latter-day Saints had requested Church schools for their children because they were disenchanted with the quality of U.S. public schools, especially with the increasing influence of secular values in those schools.

The closer they looked at public school systems, however, the more Neal and the board became convinced that the Church should do all it could to support public schools, in every country, as a matter of basic citizenship. Nonetheless, as he noted in his final board meeting before leaving the commissioner's post, this commitment to public education was contingent upon the schools' maintaining an acceptable moral and educational climate, a concern that would grow in his mind as he experienced the increasing influence of secularism.

Always desiring good homework before making policy, Neal requested a "study of educational needs" in the international Church. One of the first studies called for a review of Church schools in Mexico. Many of these schools had originally been established not because public schools were unavailable but because of a desire to nurture students' religious faith more fully. This study became the basis for a board policy that no new schools would be created unless there were 150 LDS students in a given location who had no access to public schools. This policy later led the Church to close most of its schools in Mexico.

In Asia a team of researchers from BYU, assisted by Neal's CES staff, assessed educational patterns and opportunities among Church members. They found that a higher proportion of Korean Latter-day Saints had college degrees than Church members anywhere, with other positive reports from Japan, Hong Kong, Taiwan, and the Philippines. Because they found that local school systems were adequate, the study team only recommended expanding seminaries and institutes into these countries. Then, to minimize costs and to build the Church locally, they suggested a Church-sponsored international student loan fund to encourage LDS students to seek education in their home countries.

The international loan fund did get a very modest start during this era, but, more importantly, it planted the seeds for the more comprehensive Perpetual Education Fund that President Gordon B. Hinckley would announce nearly thirty years later as a major effort to support local education for qualified students.

Neal also worked hard to understand local school conditions for himself. One of his first and most extensive data-gathering trips as commissioner took him in October 1970 through the Church's school system in Hawaii, Samoa, Tonga, Fiji, New Zealand, and elsewhere in the South Pacific. He knew the stories of David O. McKay's first trip through that region in the 1920s, which had ignited Elder McKay's affection for the Polynesian Saints and his desire to support their access

Receiving ceremonial whale's tooth from Fijian tribal chief during a visit to Church schools in the South Pacific

to education. He knew of President McKay's commitment to the Church College of Hawaii (CCH), established near the Hawaii Temple in 1954 on the wings of prophetic promises about the school's future.

Neal soon developed his own deep admiration for the Polynesian Saints. As just one example of this feeling, he spoke to a BYU group in 1975 about President Kimball's call for each country to supply its own full-time missionaries, so American missionaries could go elsewhere. "The first country to comply," he said, "wasn't western Canada or some other place where the Church has been for a long time, but the little kingdom of Tonga in the Pacific, where there are 156 full-time missionaries, of whom 150 are Tongans."

Still, his early probing failed to uncover a clear set of goals for CCH, or a clear enough connection between that college and the Church's schools for younger students in other Pacific islands. He had assumed that CCH would be concerned primarily with "returnability"—returning to their island countries the students it had educated. But he found no real data on that issue. He was also concerned whether the CCH curriculum had enough of a vocational orientation to make returnability feasible. In other locations, he was troubled to find a few cases where junior high school students were living away from home to attend Church boarding schools. Neal found himself feeling that these schools needed more local teachers and leaders, rather than being "colonial" places staffed mainly by American expatriates. Only in this way would the schools fulfill the long-term spiritual goal of building local Church leadership.

Neal encouraged Alton Wade, later the president of CCH (by then BYU–Hawaii) to study the actual "return home" patterns of CCH graduates as part of his doctoral dissertation. Wade's findings showed no clear pattern in the rate of student returns, and in time, the entire subject became more complex than Neal had originally thought.

Then he remembered a presentation he'd once made to Native American students from many tribes at the University of Utah. He had told them, "You've got to decide whether you want to live on the reservation or be part of American society. Until you make that decision, all these other decisions [about education and career] can't be made." The reaction of his audience had told Neal he touched a nerve with that question—their fundamental concern was that they were uncertain about their own identity. Finding out who they were and where they fit in a shrinking, global, multicultural society was very difficult for them to do, except as each individual gradually found his or her own answer.

During his six years as commissioner, Neal helped the board work to clarify its policy on Church schools. The first case of closing a school arose in 1974, when the government in American Samoa asked to buy the Church school there. The board agreed, concluding that the local public schools were adequate. This case later became a precedent for the painful process of closing Church schools in Mexico, Chile, and elsewhere, because administrators courageously applied the board's clarified policy—if local systems are adequate, no Church schools are needed. In three other cases, after Spencer W. Kimball became President of the Church at the end of 1973, exceptional local conditions prompted the board to open new schools in Fiji, Tonga, and Kiribati (the Gilbert Islands). Over time, however, the overall number of Church schools shrank dramatically.

In that same time span, the schools also progressed toward Neal's strongly held goal of having local administrators and teachers. He knew this policy wouldn't be easy to implement, because the local people needed to measure up professionally, and it would take time to locate and develop the needed talent. Competent expatriate Americans, who often served as educational missionaries, were far more experienced and more plentiful. But, in the long run, Neal wanted to build up the Church locally, not simply have a few good classes taught by missionaries.

In February 1974, he wrote from Australia to Cory, who was serving on his mission: "We are in the most delicate stages now of the policy [we] started three years ago of passing the baton of leadership to non-Americans in the Pacific portion of the CES. If we move too fast or too slow we will hurt the work. Each country is a separate challenge. Generally, the 'passing of the baton' is going well."

Ironically, the board's policy of entrusting CES supervisory duties to strong, local LDS educators occasionally bumped up against an unexpected concern. Because they were moving so quickly toward local governance, CES at times identified, hired, and trained able local leaders, and then, because of their spiritual maturity, those leaders were more rapidly prepared to serve—and were at times so called—as stake and mission presidents. Some people worried that these decisions might create the appearance of a paid ministry, which obviously ran counter to Church doctrine on lay leadership.

Neal responded by identifying and encouraging strong personal role models among those who first faced this challenge. He began by saying, "Well, [the man involved] wasn't stake president when we hired him." He also liked to quote Alma 29:8, because this point was for him a doctrinal key to establishing the international Church: "The Lord doth grant unto all nations, of their own nation and tongue, to teach his word, yea, in wisdom, all that he seeth fit that they should have." It really didn't surprise Neal that the same people might be the most qualified for both ecclesiastical roles and for Church employment, especially in the early stages of establishing the Church. Over time, the risk would gradually take care of itself because those faithful enough to be asked to serve in both positions were usually mature enough to keep their roles separated, setting an example for others as the Church grew in their country.

THIRTY-EIGHT

HIGHER EDUCATION AND BRIGHAM YOUNG UNIVERSITY

Among the most clear-cut of the new priorities of the Church Educational System was the ceiling on both enrollments and new institutions in higher education. By 1970, Latter-day Saint colleges enrolled 32,900 students, while 200,000 LDS students were enrolled in other institutions, with 50,000 of them also enrolled in institutes of religion.

During the mid-1960s, Ernest Wilkinson had proposed the creation of a complete system of Church junior colleges in the western United States as "feeder schools" to Brigham Young University. President David O. McKay was especially sympathetic to the plan for junior colleges, but he and others, including Harold B. Lee, worried about its financial costs. The board at first approved the concept but then dropped it after a thorough feasibility study. Yet the hunger among Church members for more access to Church-sponsored higher education increased, as the population of college-bound LDS students continued to grow after the board capped BYU's enrollment at 25,000.

Neal's appointment was barely announced when a group of Church leaders from California asked to see him. They asked if the Church might buy a college campus that was available in their area. Because Neal wasn't involved in earlier discussions on the junior college system, he went to the First Presidency, to whom he expressed his own concerns about funding, faculty availability, and the effect of such a precedent on future expectations. The Brethren were unequivocal, reiterating the factors that led them not to pursue the earlier junior college plan.

This showed Neal that the strategy for higher education in the CES policy document needed to state clearly that BYU's enrollment would remain capped and that no new institutions would be considered. Nonetheless, Neal "didn't want to lock the Brethren in forever," so the statement consciously said that no other institutions were "presently" planned. Then, over the next few years, he and other CES leaders "kept saying that, and people finally realized we meant it," despite repeated requests for other campuses, including some from Europe.

Within the boundaries of existing campuses, however, Neal urged the leaders at BYU, the Church College of Hawaii, and Ricks to look for every possible way to accommodate more students. The first significant innovation occurred when BYU adopted a new academic calendar. After considering numerous options with his staff for several weeks, President Oaks one day took his notes and disappeared for an afternoon into Provo Canyon. There he prayerfully considered the complex variables and came back with a unique calendar proposal, which he called "4–4–2–2." Fall semester would begin early enough to end before Christmas and then, after a regular winter semester, would come two half semesters—spring and summer terms. It was a creative and demanding idea, but it worked, adding thousands of student credit hours to BYU's annual educational output.

Neal believed the inspired spirit of cooperation at BYU would help the new calendar succeed, even though other universities had been unsuccessful with trimester-style formats. When the new system was clearly working by 1974, he thanked the BYU students, faculty, and staff for their "unique and deeply felt commitment to 'making things work out.'" It also helped that enrollments at Ricks College had not been capped, so the Ricks student body gradually increased, easing somewhat the pressure on BYU.

Another step that increased overall enrollments was the 1974 decision to change the name of CCH to BYU–Hawaii (BYU–H) and then have BYU-H report to BYU rather than to the commissioner's office. CCH was already a four-year school, but its educational mission needed clarification, and it needed logistical and academic support that BYU–Provo was better equipped to give than was the commissioner's office. The change instantly enhanced the school's academic credibility, and its enrollment moved from around 1,000 toward a ceiling of 2,000. It also resolved what Neal considered one of his "most complicated" challenges, by clearly establishing BYU–H as a university campus.

The presidents of Ricks, CCH, and LDSBC did not attend the regular CES meetings in Salt Lake City in the early 1970s, because they reported through Associate Commissioner Kenneth Beesley. Those presidents therefore interacted less frequently with Neal than did BYU president Dallin H. Oaks. Still, reflecting his interest in Ricks president Henry B. Eyring and in system-wide long-range planning, in 1971 Neal asked President Eyring to chair a select committee on higher education. He charged the eighteen-member committee, with its representatives from all of CES higher education, to "make fresh exploration of the possible need for change or refinement in present academic patterns or policies in the [CES] colleges and university." The committee's 1972 report explored a wide range of long-term issues, recommending that CES (1) focus on academic areas where Church doctrine made the most difference, (2) organize experiences that produce leaders of families, and (3) produce ideas that serve the Church while blessing the world. Interestingly, many concepts in this report prophetically sowed seeds that would sprout more than twenty years later when Elder Eyring served as commissioner of education in the 1990s and beyond.

Even if BYU couldn't grow much numerically, one of Neal's hopes as commissioner was to nourish BYU's growth spiritually and academically. The university was clearly sailing in the CES armada now, not off on voyages of its own. And it was still the flagship, so the way BYU flew the Church flag sent important messages to the community of LDS scholars, teachers, students, and other Church members. As the system's major university, BYU played an especially important role in demonstrating how "Mormonism's . . . encounter with modern secular thought" could truly bless the Church's future.

Just as Neal's relationship with the First Presidency was the most critical factor in his overall contribution to CES, his relationship with Dallin Oaks became the most critical factor in his contribution to BYU. Their friendship, forged in the trenches of trying together to mold a good Church university into an excellent one, would last to become a productive partnership for the contemporary Church.

It took a few experiences to launch the Maxwell-Oaks relationship. At first, Dallin was so overwhelmed with the combination of BYU's size and his newness that he was less than thrilled about driving to Salt Lake City for a weekly commissioner's half-day staff meeting— in addition to two monthly meetings with the board and with its executive committee. A colleague in their first few staff meetings watched Dallin quietly reading his huge stack of daily mail during an extended discussion of some CES issue in which BYU's interest was obviously remote, but Neal wasn't troubled, because he "knew what [Dallin] was trying to do."

By contrast, in another early staff meeting, an issue arose in which Dallin saw serious trouble for BYU's interests, so he took ten minutes to articulate a strong argument against the proposal. He concluded by telling Neal firmly, "If you decide to go ahead on this, I will oppose it and insist" on discussion before the full board of education.

After the meeting, Neal drew Dallin aside and said, "You don't need to do that. Let's just work it out between us. Give me a phone call." Suddenly Dallin realized that someone other than Neal had wanted the issue raised, and Neal didn't think it wise for staff relationships for Dallin to use such "overkill" in their meeting. Dallin should have answered in thirty seconds, not ten minutes. This incident taught him that Neal's mind is so quick that "often he'll make up his mind before you've spoken one and a half sentences." He is also so skillful at reading other people and solving problems outside formal settings—and knowing the best way to handle formal settings—that it's best just to tip him off and follow his instincts. That day was the only time Neal ever gave Dallin any direct advice, and for Dallin, "it was a formative event in our relationship."

On another occasion, Dallin had taken great pains to prepare a lengthy memo on an issue important to BYU. He showed it to Neal, who read it in a flash and began tearing it up. "I thought at first that he was rejecting it," said Dallin, but "soon learned that meant he was persuaded and was glad to have me handle it." Joe Christensen had a similar experience. Both came to know soon enough that Neal read fast, approved what he liked, didn't want extra paper, and would rely on a memo's author to keep his own file copy.

After a few such get-acquainted sessions, the Maxwell-Oaks partnership moved into high gear, where it has remained ever since. As their mutual trust grew, so did their ability to anticipate each other, like two musicians in a very harmonious jazz group, and each learned when to let the other improvise. They had two very different, highly complementary, working styles. Neal's style was that of the visionary chief of staff who works on strategic plans at army headquarters; Dallin's style was that of a field commander—a nice balance for running BYU within the broad goals of CES. Neal became Dallin's foremost mentor about higher education, teaching him at the level of concepts and principles and never looking over his shoulder or saying "here's how we did it at the U."

As time went on, other synergistic contrasts emerged. Dallin found that Neal "is a speed reader," while Dallin's reading is "painfully slow." "He reads a book a week. I read a book every fifteen or twenty weeks. But I will find things in the book he has not seen." His visionary approach gives Neal "an incredible perspective," while Dallin inclines toward "a thoroughness and noting of detail. He keeps a clean desk; I keep a cluttered one." Dallin once told some BYU leaders in Neal's presence that one reason Neal's desk is cleaner is that he "can sweep everything off his desk and onto mine," because "I'm the one who works on the detail to bring the vision to fruition."

Elder Oaks added that Neal's talks are "filled with poetic imagery; mine are dominated by explanations and declarative sentences. He is something of a pessimistic worrier; I am an incorrigible optimist." Comparing their speaking styles, Dallin once said he uses words the way he'd use work horses—to pull a load. He wouldn't dare try to use words as show horses, for fear he couldn't control them as Neal does, and then the show-horse words would "jump a nearby fence and run around in the field with their tails in the air."

Their work on BYU matters grew in future years into collaboration, often by assignment, on many other Church projects. Through it all, Dallin found that Neal's "major contribution" is his "remarkable vision," from which "over the years, thousands have benefited." Neal will "raise strategic problems, present and prospective, that I have never seen. But when I study the things he has raised, I see ramifications in detail that he has not seen." Elder Oaks also offered this comparison between Neal and another visionary colleague, President Boyd K. Packer:

> President Packer's vision . . . is what I would call a "seeric" vision, in the sense that he sees far ahead on the basis of spiritual impression, not necessarily by an analysis of the facts. Neal Maxwell's vision . . . is an analytic vision, or a vision of wisdom. He takes facts available to everyone (which he absorbs at an incredible rate) and then with unique spiritual gifts finds meaning in those facts that is not evident to the rest of us.

As their relationship has ripened with time, including more than sixteen years together in the Quorum of the Twelve, Dallin would feel "like I've always known him and always worked with him." And Neal would sometimes feel that his long and intimate friendship with Dallin Oaks gave him the brother he never had in his own family.

With this unusual degree of mutuality paving the way, Neal and Dallin in 1971 joined in a quest to increase the spiritual and the academic capacity of BYU. Their first priority was to lift both the religious faithfulness and the professional quality of the faculty. The faculty retirements they were most glad to see, said President Oaks, were not the academically unqualified people but those "who weren't totally loyal to the Church. . . . We were trying to raise the *spiritual* quality . . . at the same time we were raising the *academic* quality. . . . We worked very hard at both" goals.

A prerequisite to pursuing this two-pronged strategy was to invite the academic departments, the faculty, and the board into a participative process, decentralizing many university functions in ways that both depended on and increased the level of two-way trust. Each of the groups was in the mood for such a change, and Neal and Dallin possessed the attitudes and skill that made the changes possible in ways the Brethren warmly supported.

Ernest Wilkinson had been at BYU for two decades, and he had assembled a capable team of administrators, had recruited many able faculty, expanded the enrollment fivefold, and built an impressive campus. Dallin kept Ernest's two key vice presidents, Robert K. Thomas and Ben E. Lewis, as his own closest associates. But the Wilkinson presidency had been an intensely personal one, and some faculty members had resented his aggressive, controlling style, even though that style had in many ways helped BYU become as large and strong as it was. By 1971, the BYU community was anxious to enjoy greater communication and participation at every level.

An early, major theme of the Oaks administration, then, aided both by Neal's philosophy and his role with the board, was decentralization of tasks, authority, and responsibility. This changed the campus atmosphere, relaxing a climate that had at times been contentious. Both Neal and Dallin emphasized spiritual, not political, priorities as the guideposts to understanding the major premise of BYU's educational mission. They also made clear that BYU would remain an undergraduate university where the main purpose of research was to strengthen teaching quality. BYU would remain a culturally conservative place by national standards, but Dallin told the faculty very early that he thought the words *conservative* and *liberal* usually were not helpful labels. His view affirmed Neal's long-held conviction about the ineffectiveness of dogmatic approaches at either end of the political spectrum.

The board thus authorized the delegation of a new level of university governance to deans and department chairs, involving them much more in faculty hiring and promotions, salaries, budgeting, and other decisions. This shift in overall philosophy brought with it an increase in candor, efficiency, and flexibility across the campus, helped by the board's responsiveness to Dallin's recommendations, which had in turn been encouraged by the high level of confidence the board felt in Neal, who fully shared Dallin's views and attitudes.

Neal and Dallin were wholehearted in their harmony with the board. They shared President Marion G. Romney's understanding that BYU was "a Church institution . . . administered the same way the Church is administered—that is, by the priesthood. . . . We are aware that there are universities in which the administration [or] faculties [or] students" play the primary role in policy formation. "Whatever justification there is in such universities for this type of government does not exist here." The Brethren always had ultimate responsibility for policy. At the same time, the board remained "deeply interested . . . that scholastically BYU be unexcelled," so long as the quest for that excellence and the "urge to compete with other universities in academic honors" were always subordinate to "the . . . saving of souls."

As he encouraged decentralization and participation across the campus, Neal continually reiterated that BYU's greatest strength was in its unique relationship to the Church, in which hierarchical authority was an honored, even divinely revealed, pattern. Within that pattern, BYU would always be part of CES and subject to board direction, but the university community would be included in a fruitful blend of participation with authority—a Church leadership philosophy Neal had articulated well before becoming commissioner.

Neal found his own ways to send this message to BYU faculty. He would tell them that they must always keep their citizenship in Jerusalem and use their passports to go to Athens. Or he would say, "LDS scholars can and should speak in the tongue of scholarship, but without . . . losing the mother tongue of faith." Another time he put it this way:

For a disciple of Jesus Christ, academic scholarship is a form of worship . . . another dimension of consecration. Hence one who seeks to be a disciple-scholar will take both scholarship and discipleship seriously. . . .

No wonder a true community of scholars would qualify to be part of a larger community of saints. . . .

Consecrated scholarship thus converges both the life of the mind and of the spirit! . . .

Genius without meekness is not enough to qualify for discipleship [because] meekness facilitates working on what is lacking. . . .

Though I have spoken of the disciple-scholar, in the end all the hyphenated words come off. We are finally disciples—men and women of Christ. . . .

The greater the submission, the greater the expansion!

Neal always taught the BYU faculty and other LDS scholars in a way that lifted their scholarly and teaching aspirations, even when he was making it clear that one's religious citizenship, mother tongue, and discipleship were really the highest priorities. Once he told the BYU faculty, for example, "We cannot let the world condemn our value system by calling attention to our professional mediocrity." On another occasion, he told BYU students and faculty they must be like Joseph in Egypt. In times of great famine, Joseph drew on divine power to be part of the solution—not just another hungry mouth to feed—but he leaned "into the fray" and was "involved with mankind."

Neal taught this perspective in an informal retreat for university leaders in August 1974 at Timp Lodge in Provo Canyon. After updating the group on recent CES developments, thereby reinforcing BYU's identity with the larger armada, he concluded with a metaphor about BYU that reflected his own lifelong attitude about the value of being engaged in helping the surrounding society, rather than trying, Jonah-like, to escape it.

Taking his cue from the remark of a recent convert to the Church, Neal compared BYU with the Abbey of Cluny, founded in 910 A.D. in France. Most monastic orders in that era were concerned only with their own salvation. Having "turned inward," they didn't feel a duty to the surrounding culture. But "the Abbey of Cluny under some special leadership was like a pebble thrown into a pond [whose] ripples reached the most distant shore of the then Christian world." The abbey rallied people against the forces of immorality and materialism, creating a "cultural counterpoint," concerned with both spiritual reform and "social responsibility." "The monks left their cloister" and provided "leaven for a much wider world of which they were a part."

Neal urged that Latter-day Saints should do the same thing in their own times and places. Despite the deterioration of medieval society, this tiny group of monks blessed their church spiritually while preserving the best of human knowledge from barbarians. And the value of their work later rippled its blessings across the waters of history. That's what BYU must do, he said, because there is so little hope for secular reform. The Abbey of Cluny "didn't remain monastic, an island of excellence." Rather, the people at Cluny influenced others, long term. For BYU to do this in its time, its scholars must be "unarguably on a par with" the professional excellence of their peers, so that they will be "listened to and be influential."

These were fresh and encouraging insights from a commissioner of education who increasingly exemplified the common ground on which the Church Board of Education and LDS faculty and students everywhere could meet—not only to gather but to mutually reinforce one another, joined by their shared vision of having a university in Zion.

Standing on that common ground, Neal and Dallin gained approval from the board for several specific developments that illustrate their shared vision about BYU and its place in CES. For one thing, they clearly established a pattern for future BYU presidents and CES commissioners, showing that BYU could successfully report through, and be part of, CES. Neal's "ecumenical" style about CES institutions also brokered an attitude of sharing and cooperation, such as when he asked BYU to assume responsibility for the Hawaii campus. When he encouraged a blending of BYU's continuing education programs with those of CES. When he encouraged BYU and CES personnel to work together to develop the first CES literacy projects in Bolivia. When he urged the consolidation of several CES fund-raising organizations into the LDS Foundation. Or when he asked that BYU's

President Marion G. Romney at the dedication of the J. Reuben Clark Law School at BYU; front row: Elder Neal A. Maxwell; Lewis F. Powell, justice of the United States Supreme Court; Chief Justice Warren E. Burger; and BYU President Dallin H. Oaks

physical facilities staff assist all CES higher education institutions in planning buildings, thus avoiding the need to have a second facilities staff working directly for CES.

One of BYU's challenges when Dallin Oaks arrived was that the campus clearly needed additional physical facilities, although the board had already stated its intent not to authorize more BYU buildings as one way of controlling the enrollment ceiling. Neal had learned at the University of Utah that the best way to help legislators evaluate major building requests was to show them the problems and let them decide for themselves. So Neal and Dallin eventually took the board to Provo to show them the campus needs. These trips resulted in such decisions as closing the "lower campus," a set of venerable buildings some distance from the main campus, building a new library that doubled the previous space, and eventually constructing the Kimball and Tanner buildings.

With Neal's encouragement, Dallin also conducted a major review of religious education at BYU, which resulted in several changes that reflected what Neal had long sought in his own approach—closer integration of the religious and the secular. These changes signaled that, as

Elder Packer put it, "religious education [should] be an influence contributing to, and drawing from, every segment of the university." They invited more BYU faculty from regular academic departments to teach religion classes, and they invited others to do research related to religion. This included the creation of an Institute of Ancient Studies, headed by Hugh Nibley. Neal took a special interest in this field, anticipating his later support for the Foundation for Ancient Research and Mormon Studies (FARMS), the Joseph Fielding Smith Institute for Church History, the *Encyclopedia of Mormonism*, and the Center for Religious Studies.

The J. Reuben Clark Law School, which had been announced at the time of Ernest Wilkinson's retirement, opened its doors in 1973. Adding a major new professional program was truly an exception to the board's pattern of limiting rather than expanding BYU's offerings, but Presidents Lee and Romney had taken particular interest in the law school project, originally proposed by Ernest Wilkinson. Their interest was strong enough that they chose to go ahead with it even after Dallin Oaks, who had a rich background in legal education, told them during his BYU presidential search interview that he saw no need for the new school. Then they deferred continually to Dallin's judgments about the nature and approach of the school, which favored a school of national academic and professional influence rather than a narrower, practitioner-based approach.

The Romney search committee, which had chosen Neal's original CES leaders, added Elder Howard W. Hunter and then chose the law school dean—one more young person who would have future influence. Dean Rex E. Lee, then a thirty-six-year-old lawyer in Arizona, later served as Solicitor General of the United States and eventually as president of BYU from 1989 to 1995.

President Romney, who took a strong interest in the law school, also reflected the religious, nonpolitical nature of the First Presidency's attitudes toward education, a model both Neal and Dallin gladly followed. He once said his committee had selected Dallin Oaks, Hal Eyring, and the others in the only way he knew how to choose a leader—by following the same spiritual process he had come to know in choosing new stake presidents: searching interviews, much prayer, and an openness to inspiration.

As for depoliticizing attitudes, one of President Romney's assignments was to interview all prospective faculty for the new law school. He said to one candidate, "Now let's talk about your politics. Are you either a John Bircher or a Socialist?" Startled, the candidate replied that some people think those are the only two choices. President Romney said, "I know. That's why I asked. So are you in one of those groups or the other?" When the candidate said no, President Romney said, "Well then, you're all right."

Another major development that Neal felt reflected the high level of trust between the First Presidency and BYU was the decision in 1974 to build the Church's new Missionary Training Center near the BYU campus. Neal told BYU leaders that this expensive, complicated task "could not have been ventured at all" without that level of trust. "That building will probably have more influence on this planet than anything else I can think of [except a temple]." And it's at BYU. "That ought to tell you something."

THIRTY-NINE

BECOMING A
SPIRITUAL AND
EDUCATIONAL LEADER

C OMMISSIONER MAXWELL'S TALKS IN 1970 showed
the growing variety and reach of his voice. In his first talk to the
Brigham Young University faculty and staff, he shared his strategic
vision for the Church Educational System and BYU's place in it. BYU,
he said, should be "the nerve center of Latter-day Saint scholarship"
but must "play its role as part of the total system, rather than standing
apart from that system. You have much to offer to your institutional
partners, and something to learn from them."

A few weeks later, the First Presidency asked the new commissioner to speak in the priesthood session of October 1970 general conference. He addressed directly the enrollment ceiling at BYU, stressing
the Brethren's encouragement that LDS college-age students should
attend school near their homes and enroll in institute classes. Then he
told priesthood leaders how to help with the education of their young
people, showing how comprehensively he saw CES. Leaders, he said,
should help youth identify with seminary and institute, direct them
toward vocational counseling, assure them they can pursue learning

without fear, teach by the eloquence of example, and strengthen the families of the Church.

Neal's writing and speaking were becoming more visible to LDS and other public audiences. In the September 1970 *Improvement Era*, he called the Church "an ecclesiastical Everest," rising "above the Himalayas of secular philosophy." That year he gave a "Last Lecture" talk to BYU students, reflecting on the connections he'd discovered between political science and the gospel. He also published an essay entitled "Democracy and Dissent" in the December 1970 issue of *Perspectives on Utah Education.* Here he wrote with an experienced voice to the general public about dealing with the disturbing legacy of student revolt in the 1960s: "With so much change under way . . . dissent may be our constant companion."

In December, Neal spoke to the Maryland state legislature, drawing on his experience with legislative reform in Utah. He was also introduced as a Church representative at a time of some public criticism against the Church's then-current policy of not conferring the priesthood on African-American men. His audience included numerous African-American legislators. He prayed for, and felt he received, spiritual help; he also received a standing ovation.

Perhaps Neal's most influential message to educators outside Utah was his speech in 1972 to the Association of College Unions meeting in St. Louis. This was a national audience of student life personnel. His identification with the Church this time drew vocal opposition from a dissident delegate, who tried from the floor just before Neal's talk to urge the group to pass a resolution censuring BYU for the Church's policy on eligibility for the priesthood. Although the motion failed, the atmosphere remained a little tense.

Neal spoke about "the now and future student." He began by describing two LDS schools he'd recently seen in Bolivia and Samoa, observing that students are "impatient with marshmallow men and institutions, for [they] seek a hard core of meaning." He said higher education was caught between higher student demands and lower public support, partly because colleges and universities had let themselves "be seen almost as a substitute religion." Then college students

*With son, Cory, for an
article in THIS PEOPLE
about fathers and sons*

discovered "that the cathedral of learning was . . . manned by mere mortals, some of whom dispensed—to a society hungry for hope—doctrines of existential despair." He concluded that democracy itself depends on what higher education does now, and colleges must focus on students. By the time he'd finished speaking, the audience had become increasingly attentive.

During his early years as commissioner, Neal's letters to Cory in the mission field (he served in Duesseldorf, Germany, from 1972 to 1974) offer some rare glimpses of his private reflections amid his busy public life. These excerpts suggest how his letters echoed Clarence Maxwell's faithful and detailed messages written to Neal years before in Japan and then in Canada. Because of what those letters meant to him, Neal knew what his would mean to Cory:

> You are my only son, but what a fine son—and your future is bright with promise. . . . I . . . am so happy that our separation is for such a sweet and significant purpose.
>
> We savored your letter written Tuesday with great relish.
>
> I am . . . pleased with your indication that these communications did not make you homesick. You . . . have crossed an important psychological phase line.
>
> We fasted for you this Sunday.

There's mundaneness in proselyting, but duty and routine serve us well. Sometimes duty simply carries one over the discouragement—we are past the low points almost before we notice them. . . .

Keep your fine sense of humor, because missionary work has, like all of life, its own incongruities and implausibilities.

Often, when I wake up in strange hotel rooms with my hectic schedule of travel, I might wonder 'what am I doing here?' except that I feel encapsulated in our Father in Heaven's love and have that sense of purpose which makes the little inconveniences bearable.

I had a busy trip—can you imagine 38 takeoffs, or landings, in the space of 12 days? I did not sleep in the same bed twice, but we got everything done . . . and were blessed with health and safety.

[Written during the midst of the Watergate affair in Washington, D.C.] You work for the only 'Outfit' that is going anywhere in the world, Cory. It has divine leadership [and] direction.

On November 15, 1972, Neal received an unexpected visitor in his office, who came with a proposal that would cause him no little anguish over the next several weeks. Senator Wallace F. Bennett closed the door and told Neal, confidentially, that he had decided to retire from the United States Senate after serving more than twenty years. After much thought, he wanted Neal to run for his seat in the 1974 election. Bennett was prepared to give Neal's candidacy his full support, including the use of all his contacts, access to fund-raising, influence with the Republican Party, and anything else he might need. The senator said he was confident that Neal would win, for Neal had ripened and prepared himself in a way that would attract wide support, and his candidacy would please Senator Bennett greatly.

Neal looked at Senator Bennett in astonished wonder. He had first been encouraged to consider running for Congress in 1962 by Utah Congressman Sherman Lloyd. His name was mentioned as a possible congressional candidate in the Salt Lake press in 1965. That same year, the *Utah Alumnus* magazine teasingly said in the introduction to

The Maxwells on a trip to the Middle East with Elder and Sister Howard W. Hunter in December 1972

an article Neal had written, "It's an open secret that Neal likes the heady taste of Potomac water." But he'd never been seriously interested in the House—too many Congressmen in one body and having to run for reelection every two years, and neither he nor Colleen wanted to live in Washington, anyway.

But the Senate? It was the one political office that had long appealed to him. As Abraham Lincoln's biographer wrote of Lincoln's failed campaign for the Senate, "All of Lincoln's talents seemed to point him to the Senate—his literary gifts, his love of rational debate, of delivering logical and eloquent speeches from a prepared script." Yes, Neal was "somewhat tempted" to reach for "the laurel wreath in politics." Not that he was a shoo-in to be elected, even with Bennett's support. Yet he did learn later that both Jake Garn and Wayne Owens, who ended up running against each other for Bennett's seat, would have chosen to step aside had Neal been a candidate.

Bud Scruggs, who managed senatorial campaigns for both Garn and Orrin Hatch, knows Neal and politics unusually well. Upon hearing the story of Senator Bennett's 1972 inquiry, Scruggs thought Neal would have been a fantastic senator, because he is such a student of history and . . . policy, and his eloquence would have made him a national figure. He is so intensely interested in policy and its mechanics, and he understands human ambition. . . . He could . . . build consensus. . . .

He would have been not just a good senator, but a great one. Though perhaps not as great a candidate, because he doesn't like to talk about himself, doesn't believe there's anything qualifying in his background. And his interest in attributes like meekness and submissiveness, even in 1974, wouldn't have been particularly well suited to a Senate race.

The next day, Neal wrote to Cory, "I am not presently inclined to do this, but I will think about it and pray about it." For reasons he had a hard time expressing, he wasn't feeling the same "fire in his belly" about political office—even this one—that he might have felt even two or three years earlier. Still, the offer of Senator Bennett's total support blew a little oxygen on whatever sparks remained of that fire. So he went to see President Lee, who "was gentle and nondirective in his counsel, leaving the decision to me," though Neal sensed that he "wasn't that excited about my running." Then an experienced campaign manager called Neal to say he knew of Bennett's idea, and he wanted to help. He assured Neal that fund-raising would be no problem, and he thought he could win.

Meanwhile, the Senator went to see President Lee himself. By mid-December, Neal hadn't heard what came of that meeting, and he "wasn't too keen about asking" about it. Because being commissioner was a professional appointment, not a Church calling, he knew President Lee wasn't likely to tell him what to do. He wrote Cory that his prayer was, "I'll go where You want me to go." In a few days, he flew to Israel on a BYU tour, having promised Senator Bennett an answer soon. While traveling, he found a time to offer a special prayer for guidance, in which he said his own judgment was not to run, but he was willing if he should. He soon felt, definitely, that he shouldn't pursue it—and that was that, even though Senator Bennett went to see President Lee again in March of 1973 "to make one last effort to see if

I can be 'encouraged' to run for the Senate, [but] I am still content with my decision."

Some of Neal's closest friends thought this might have been a kind of Abrahamic test for him. Others were more matter-of-fact about it. Liz Haglund said, "If the Lord has your heart, you know what to do." And that's how it was for Neal. Her comment suggests an apt line from Neal's general conference talk in October 2000: "Discipleship may keep the honors of the world from us. As Balak told Balaam, 'I thought to promote thee unto great honour; but, lo, the Lord hath kept thee back from honor' (Num. 24:11–12)."

Within less than a year, Neal would be tested again, in an even more poignant way. Harold B. Lee, now President of the Church, told Neal in the fall of 1973 that he had "made up his mind to call [him] as an Assistant to the Twelve." At the time, that office was a lifetime calling as a General Authority of the Church. Neal was "surprised but said nothing to anyone, including Colleen." He thought a formal call might be extended at October conference, but no call came. President Lee repeated his intention after conference, and Neal didn't know what to say in response, so he said nothing.

Then on December 26, 1973, after serving as President of the Church for only eighteen months, President Lee died of a sudden illness at age seventy-four. The entire Church was stunned, having expected he would serve many years as the Lord's prophet. Most people felt as did President Spencer W. Kimball, who said at President Lee's funeral, "A giant redwood has fallen." "I never thought it could happen." On December 27, Neal wrote to Cory:

> It is my sad duty to inform you . . . of the death of President Lee. . . .
>
> I feel a special sense of bereavement because of the special relationship which it has been my privilege to have with this great and marvelous man. In many ways, he was like a second father to me. . . . [The last time I saw him alive,] his parting words to me were to tell that lovely queen, Colleen, of his love for her. . . .
>
> As a family, as soon as we heard the news we knelt in

[a] prayer [of] gratitude for [his] memory and powerful example. . . .

Yet I know that no man comes to the presidency of the Quorum of the Twelve who has not been foreordained to that task, and so President Kimball will bring his own specially impressed stamp to [the Church].

The last line in this letter restates the conviction Neal had shared with President Lee a short while earlier when Joseph Fielding Smith passed away and the prophetic mantle fell upon Harold B. Lee. On July 5, 1972, Neal had written him, "No man can come to the task you will assume who is not so foreordained, and in the soberness of these special hours you are entitled to that reminder." Reflecting the closeness of their relationship, President Lee mentioned this note, but not the name of its author, when speaking at President Smith's funeral: "I had a comfort from one who wrote [about the foreordination of those called to lead the Church]. If I didn't believe that, I wouldn't dare stand . . . where I am today."

President Lee's death brought Neal to his knees with sorrow. He really had lost a kind of father figure, and it had happened with awful suddenness. By now they had worked so intimately together on CES and regional representative matters that, for a time, Neal must have felt he'd lost not only his personal tutor but also his liahona of direction for the Church's future. It had motivated Neal to his soul's depth that this man for whom he had such respect had "trusted me so much," and that trust had moved Neal to "work so hard for him."

After the shock wore off a little, Neal couldn't keep himself from wondering what it meant, that President Lee had said he planned to call him as a General Authority. He was grateful he'd not mentioned it to anyone. He assumed that the likelihood of such a call had perished with President Lee. In January, as he was seeking some spiritual confirmation about that conclusion, Neal was in far-off New Zealand on CES business, having spent the day at the Church college near Hamilton. He was "weary and tired and missed Colleen and the family." Late that evening, "the sweetest spirit of reassurance and serenity came over me, [that] the Lord appreciated my labors . . . and was mindful of my concerns." He was at peace.

Within a few weeks, Neal and Colleen drove with President and Sister Romney to BYU to attend a meeting announcing that the expanded library would carry President Lee's name. With no forewarning, President Romney asked Neal if he had told President Kimball what President Lee had said about his call as a General Authority. Neal, very startled, said he hadn't mentioned it to anyone. Have you told President Tanner? No. President Romney seemed surprised. President Lee had obviously told him, as his counselor in the First Presidency, what he had said to Neal.

Soon President Kimball invited Neal to his office. He asked him to be frank and relate what President Lee had said to him. Neal answered his questions, making it clear he did not regard the conversations as a call. Then one evening just before conference, April 4, 1974, President Kimball, unannounced, visited the Maxwell home. He said he had parked down the street so no one would know he was there. Neal, who seemed to have a hard time being dressed with the formality appropriate for such occasions, was in a sport shirt and slacks with bare feet. (In 1981, President Kimball would call him to the Twelve while Neal was in a hospital bed.)

Neal hurriedly put on his slippers, and President Kimball extended an official call for him to serve as an Assistant to the Twelve. He was to remain as commissioner of education but would now also begin a regular routine of stake conferences and other purely ecclesiastical assignments. President Romney liked to remind Neal that the call was originally issued by Harold B. Lee. However the call was issued, President N. Eldon Tanner wrote to Neal, "There is no doubt that the Lord called you to this position."

When Neal was sustained as a General Authority, he had been commissioner nearly four years. His call seemed to give the First Presidency's stamp of approval to what he'd been saying and doing in the Church Educational System. It also assured those who had come to appreciate his attitudes and gifts that his influence in Church leadership would extend well beyond his interests in education.

Commissioner Maxwell had come to the stage of Church history at a time of unprecedented growth in the proportion of Church members who were college graduates. His visibility and example, along with that of the other CES leaders he brought to the attention of Church leaders, thus came at a time of increasing need among younger Latter-day Saints for role models whose lives would illustrate how to combine the worlds of the spirit and the intellect within the framework of a faithful gospel perspective.

Neal himself lived through, and so his own story illustrates, the transformation of American culture into an information-based society in the last half of the twentieth century. This vast change, enhanced and often fueled by increased educational opportunity, was accompanied by a postwar "baby boom" that magnified the social and economic effects of all the other changes. The birth rate in the United States nearly doubled between 1936 and 1957, from 2,315 babies per 10,000 population to 4,308. This demographic bulge has since moved through history like a python trying to consume a pig, fueling demands for education and many other needs and forces in the consumer society as never before. And the children of the baby boomers spiked the demand for college enrollments all through the decades of the seventies, eighties, and nineties, which included much of the enrollment pressures at BYU. Historian William Manchester wrote of this education-driven epoch:

> The sociological implications of this can hardly be exaggerated. In 1900 only 4 percent of Americans of college age were enrolled in a college or university. In 1957, the figure was 32 percent; when Kennedy . . . died [in 1963] it was 50 percent. . . . Between 60 and 70 percent of all Americans belonged to the middle class [which was] swiftly becoming the only class, the values of which were those which had once belonged to a small, highly educated upper middle class.

These cultural forces thrived on, even depended on, the increased availability of higher education. More recent data show that college enrollments in the United States tripled from 1947 to 1967 and then doubled again between 1967 and 1997. Some 2.3 million students were enrolled in 1947, and within fifty years, that number rose to 14 million.

The emphasis on education among Latter-day Saints visibly hastened these strong national trends in the Church. The number of eighteen-year-old Latter-day Saints in the United States and Canada nearly doubled from 56,000 in 1978 to 91,000 in 1998. Of this number, more than half attended college.

Among the general population, the nation's greater participation in higher education has tended to reduce religious belief because of the pronounced secularization of American society. This was a trend Neal Maxwell worried about and discussed often during his years at the University of Utah, in CES, and thereafter. As co-ed dormitories came to replace the old in loco parentis philosophy on American campuses, it was clear to all that the country's mores were changing. Secularization also meant that, as more people accepted higher education's nonreligious explanations of history and science, traditional religious ideas and standards simply enjoyed less social acceptance.

No wonder, then, that Thomas O'Dea would in 1957 wonder if "by encouraging [higher] education and giving it a more central place in both its own activities and its world view, Mormonism exposed itself more vulnerably to the danger" of a general intellectual apostasy. In this atmosphere, he speculated, educated LDS youth might be less willing to accept Church authority and less likely to believe literal interpretations of scripture. O'Dea had historical support for his concern, because highly educated people have "frequently been in the vanguard of . . . the 'secularization of culture,'" challenging religion's "fundamental viewpoints." And by the late twentieth century, the majority of Americans embraced these secular values, which "had once belonged [only] to a small, highly educated middle class."

What O'Dea might not have anticipated was that many of those young Latter-day Saints, who typically came from a background of "rural and quite literal Mormonism" to the nation's campuses, would emerge having mastered the intellectual world but with their literalistic religious commitments actually strengthened rather than weakened by their educational experience. Indeed, reliable research now shows that the greater the educational attainment of a member of The Church of Jesus Christ of Latter-day Saints, the higher will be the level of that member's church activity—a phenomenon that runs counter to the experience of other religious groups, for whom higher levels of education usually mean a lower level of religious commitment.

Neal Maxwell was only one of this number, but he was a very visible one, drawing on his rural pioneer heritage to give not only intellectual but also spiritual leadership to a community of believing teachers and students who turned a potential source of conflict into a source of strength. Neal and the others did this not by finding some clever way to outwit or avoid the authority and scriptural literalism of Church doctrine. Quite the contrary. Neal's unqualified acceptance of that authority and literalism let him put his own intellectual experience into a larger, spiritually based perspective. Then he found not only that education isn't a barrier to the religious life but that faithful Church members really can use education to enhance their spiritual contributions.

The apparent conflict between submissiveness to religious authority and the independence fostered by a liberal education creates a paradox that can seem difficult to resolve—until one sees the paradox resolved positively in the lives of real people, whose actual experience demonstrates both a stronger spiritual life and a more disciplined intellectual life. O'Dea himself saw that point, in the epilogue he wrote after he had first described the risks of more education to the Latter-day Saints. He put his questions to a small group of LDS graduate students at Harvard and "asked them what they really thought." Their informal, personal responses were "more persuasive than any analysis could possibly be." The students showed "thoughtfulness" and "awareness" in demonstrating creative "vitality." "Mormonism was meaningful to them," wrote O'Dea. "Their testimony must be admitted as eloquent."

Because personal resolutions are "more persuasive" than "analytical" ones, the best way for LDS students to grow through the natural paradox of freedom versus authority is to have a good teacher—a mentor, whose modeling they can watch and follow. Usually such mentoring occurs in a personal, student-teacher relationship of the kind Neal had with G. Homer Durham or Harold B. Lee. Former BYU social science dean Martin Hickman once said that he and Neal had both been among "Homer's boys" as students in the U political science department. Those young apprentices, said Martin, didn't all want to be political scientists like Homer, but they all did want to emulate his "striving for excellence," which for Homer embodied both spiritual and intellectual values.

Martin compared Homer's influence on his "boys" to Neal's influence on Latter-day Saint college students generally, both as commissioner of education and in his Church assignments. Martin could see how in the modern age, in which books and television provide broad access to the thought and influence of individual leaders and thousands of Latter-day Saint college students need mentoring, Neal has become

> a legend in the Church for the depth of his thought, his knowledge of the scriptures, the elegance of his language . . . , and for his compassion for those in and out of the Church who need comfort. . . . What G. Homer Durham did in the way of counsel and guidance for students [at the U] Neal Maxwell now provides for a generation of young Latter-day Saints, who come not only from the valleys of the Wasatch front but from the continents and isles of the sea.

Elder Alexander Morrison, an emeritus General Authority, described how Elder Maxwell has had that kind of influence on his life. Elder Morrison was once assistant deputy minister in Canada's federal health department. He first knew Neal in the same long-distance way that most Church members know him, but then they came into a few years of closer association. For him, Neal's "ability to have a foot in the camp of the intellect and a foot in the camp of faith" is a "great example of how" educated and professional "people can make sense of the secular world." Neal's whole approach shows that faith and intellect "are totally compatible and acceptable," especially when combined with his "personal example of humility and love and kindness." He has discovered that Neal

> has a respect for the intellectual life [but] he's not intimidated by scholars. They see him as one of their own . . . but he doesn't fawn all over them either. He sees the inability of the human

mind to explain everything in rational terms. So, for him, the intellect builds on a foundation of faith rather than replacing faith. . . .

His faith sustains him, but his intellect gives him . . . immense joy. Highly educated Church members have had his example before them, and they see a kind of spiritual kinship with him.

Elder Marlin K. Jensen of the Seventy has felt similar impressions about Elder Maxwell. For Elder Jensen, when someone so gifted has "ranged widely over the field of human knowledge" and believes so deeply in the Lord and the scriptures, "it is a great boost to my own faith when he . . . teaches and bears testimony." Because Neal is so cosmopolitan and can "respond to . . . the tough questions" while being "so secure in his own faith," he offers a "personal example of intellectual curiosity through a lifetime," enfolded in "a wholeness of Christian living."

Neal's mentoring of this kind is not limited to those who know him personally. Just one example is Craig Raeside, a young stake president in Australia who is a practicing psychiatrist. He once said it had been difficult for him to find mentors in the Church in Australia who could help him see how to put the gospel and his family first while also serving effectively in a demanding professional field. Then he said he did have one mentor—Neal Maxwell—and that mentoring has all come through talks and books: "I began to realise that I was being taught the scriptures, one on one, by an Apostle of the Lord, through the Spirit."

Craig has met Neal only twice. When Craig was twenty-four, he saw Elder Maxwell briefly at a stake conference priesthood leadership meeting. There, "with the impertinence of youth," Craig asked Neal why the plot in one of his books "seemed to get a bit lost in the middle." The second time was a quick handshake at a general conference just before Craig was called to be stake president. Then, as he read more deeply in the scriptures and in Neal's writings, he "started to see things in similar ways. I developed a great love for the scriptures and for the Savior . . . and a great love for the Brethren."

Over time, he has noticed that Neal has "tended to focus ever more on . . . truly Christ-like [personal] qualities." Finally, encouraged by a mutual friend, Craig wrote Neal the only letter he's written him, which ended, "You truly have been and are a close personal mentor for me. . . . Your instruction, your example, your testimony are precious to me. I hope to be able to do justice to the things you have given me."

These observations from such individuals as Martin Hickman, Elder Morrison, Elder Jensen, and President Raeside are not so much tributes as illustrations of the way Elder Maxwell has contributed to the lives of Latter-day Saints near and far, not only reassuring Church leaders about the value of education but reassuring educated Church members about the value of the spiritual life. Elder Dallin Oaks was once asked how he thought Neal has most helped educated Church members become followers of the Savior. Is it the way he writes or speaks, or is it more the content of what he says? Said Elder Oaks,

> Probably it is his personal example, more than any other thing. Anyone who knows him knows that he is an intellectual in the best sense of that word—always pushing to learn, always reading, always thinking, always using his critical faculties. And yet he has become a remarkably humble man, remarkably meek, a prototypical disciple of Christ.

With or without an extensive educational background, the best way to teach discipleship is to live it.

PART XII

EARLY YEARS AS A GENERAL AUTHORITY 1974–81

FORTY

CALLED TO HIS
MINISTRY

T HE DAY OF ELDER MAXWELL'S CALL as an Assistant
to the Twelve—April 4, 1974—was one of those hinge days on which
the doors of history turn; not because Neal was called then, but because
of two other events that same day which expressed, both literally and
symbolically, the dawning of a new era. One could almost hear the surrounding rocks tumbling as "the stone which is cut out of the mountain without hands" suddenly began rolling faster. With a burst of new
momentum, one sensed the stone would now surely "roll forth, until it
has filled the whole earth" (D&C 65:2).

The literal part that day was Spencer W. Kimball's first talk as
President of the Church to the regional representatives. It would
become known as The Talk about missionary work. No one who heard
it would ever forget having been there. Ezra Taft Benson, President of
the Twelve, said of it, "No greater address has been given before any
seminar. . . . There is in very deed a prophet in Israel." A few days later,
Neal wrote to Cory that this was "the greatest speech on the Church's
responsibility to missionary work . . . that I have ever heard! He is truly

going to insist that the Church preach the Gospel to all nations of the world. It was a dramatic and historical moment."

The themes that flowed from this talk, that day and in the months afterward, soon became household phrases throughout the Church: Every worthy young man should serve a mission. Every country should supply its own missionaries. Pray for the Lord to open the doors of the nations. As soon as the Church is ready, the Lord will open the doors. The Saints must prepare. Is anything too hard for the Lord? Do it.

The symbolic part was that, with no planning, during the same hour when President Kimball was delivering this message, Grant Romney Clawson was painting a huge new mural on the wall just outside the meeting room where the prophet spoke. Protected by a massive plywood barrier typical of construction projects, Clawson was painting a scene twelve feet high and seventy-five feet long, depicting the Savior commanding His disciples just before His Ascension, "Go ye therefore, and teach all nations" (Matthew 28:19). The painting was an enlargement of an original work by Harry Anderson. It would permanently adorn the east wall of the main lobby in the twenty-six-floor Church Office Building.

That mural would become nearly as well known throughout the Church as President Kimball's teachings on missionary work, and nothing could more aptly capture the central message of his presidency. This scene formed the backdrop for the globalization of the Church, which President Kimball's teachings so dramatically accelerated. Following in the wake of this primary thrust came several major changes attendant to his central message, including the organization of the First Quorum of the Seventy, the clarification of ecclesiastical and temporal lines of authority, the three-hour block of Sunday meetings, and the revelation that the priesthood is available to every worthy male.

On such a day and in such an historical context, the Lord's servants called Neal Maxwell to His full-time ministry. It was a fitting context not only because Neal had been present at the time of other recent changes but also because the vision of his own journey of discipleship would now begin to expand, reaching for the contours that would guide the increasingly global Church.

Elder James E. Faust embracing Elder Maxwell at the conference session in which he was sustained as an Assistant to the Twelve

In setting Neal apart on April 7, President Kimball blessed him that "you may use your unusual talents to build up the kingdom; that you may even have increased powers . . . to help spread the work about the world." He should "continue your closeness to your Heavenly Father, to bear witness." He was no longer the staffer or the educator but a full-time, set-apart servant of the Lord. That would expand him spiritually, but it would also require more discipline, as his general discipleship took on the more focused character of "called" discipleship: "Behold, I am a disciple of Jesus Christ. . . . I have been called of him to declare his word among his people, that they might have everlasting life" (3 Nephi 5:13).

The call introduced Neal to a new relationship with the members of the Church. He remained commissioner of education for two more years, but he began seeing the Church with fresh eyes. One colleague in Church Education said Neal didn't change his style of leadership, but "you could see the mantle of his call in his more overt spirituality." Now when he went to stake conferences, he felt an added degree of responsibility that he hadn't felt as a regional representative. When he was assigned to interview prospective missionaries whose worthiness was questionable, for example, he had to make the final decision about whether they would serve. He "felt the weight of that" duty "about as much as anything."

Along with his assignments in CES, his days now included telephone calls from stake and mission presidents about Church policy issues and personal worthiness issues involving members or missionaries. Often these were calls about matters not already clear in Church handbooks; otherwise, the call wouldn't have been necessary. As time went on, Neal was grateful for so much variety in his counseling diet, from very hard problems to spiritually poignant moments. His duties did not require that he deal only with difficult cases all day; if they had, he might have experienced burnout, which he once said is "caused by staring too long into the abyss of abnormality."

Among his more spiritually demanding experiences was the preparation of his general conference talks. When he was first called as an Assistant to the Twelve, all General Authorities spoke in each conference. His speaking style was so distinctive that some of his early talks left conference audiences a little breathless. They weren't accustomed to such phrases as "Included in the awful arithmetic of the Atonement are my sins." Or "The living of one protective principle of the gospel is better than a thousand compensatory government programs—which are, so often, like 'straightening deck chairs on the Titanic.'" Or, "Hearts 'set so much upon the things of this world' are hearts so set they must first be broken."

Neal's conference talks reached out to all Latter-day Saints more broadly than when he had spoken as commissioner. One memorable early example was "Why Not Now?" in October 1974. He spoke to those "who fully intend, someday, to begin to believe or to be active in the Church. But not yet! . . . They will not come inside the chapel, but neither do they leave its porch." In his tender yet piercing invitation, he said, "If, however, you really do not wish to commit now," then let me warn you:

> Do not look too deeply into the eyes of the pleasure-seekers about you, for if you do, you will see a certain sadness in sensuality, and you will hear artificiality in the laughter of licentiousness. Do not look too deeply . . . into the motives of those who

deny God, for you may notice their doubts of doubt. . . . Do not think too much about what you are teaching your family, for what in you is merely casualness about Christianity may, in your children, become hostility. . . . Do not think, either, about the doctrine that you are a child of God, for if you do, it will be the beginning of belonging. . . . Joshua didn't say choose you next year whom you will serve . . . 'Not yet' usually means 'never.'"

As a stake conference visitor, Neal's approach was informal, especially in the Saturday training meetings for leaders. Someone who was in a meeting during one of Neal's conference visits to Canada in the late 1970s said that Elder Maxwell encouraged "a great deal of group participation." He would move "into the audience and roam around with a traveling microphone" that involved people as he taught them. He was also "very receptive to whatever people had to say," and he conveyed "spiritual receptivity and humility" in moving the discussion toward the point of his intended message.

He would work at getting to know the stake presidents he visited, often teaching them about family priorities and leadership in ways they didn't quite expect. One Utah stake president said that as he and Elder Maxwell began a conference weekend with some time scheduled just for the two of them, Neal asked, "What would you be doing if I weren't here today?" The stake president said he would be "over in the school gym, watching my son play basketball." Neal's quick response was, "Let's go." So they went to the gym and sat "with the rest of the overzealous parents" and watched till the game ended. Then Neal met the young men and their coach. And the stake president learned "a lesson for a lifetime" about being a father.

In the stake presidency meeting, Neal put the brethren through an exercise that drew on his leadership training background. He showed them a diagram with a shield called "My Personal Crest," which was divided into four quadrants. Using that model, he had each man sketch a representation of what he would do if he had unlimited resources, a significant accomplishment in his life, and a truth he held dear. In the fourth quadrant, each was to describe himself in three words. As one by one the members of the stake presidency explained their answers, the stake president said, "We became more introspective, shared more, and became more intimate as a stake presidency" than they had in years.

In his later ministry, Neal was less likely to do this kind of exercise, because, over time, he found himself gravitating more exclusively toward scriptures, doctrine, and core spiritual insights about family life and the Savior. But he still maintained his instinct to mentor stake presidents quietly and personally, as the need arose. Once after he became a member of the Twelve, for example, he sensed that a stake president was worried that Neal had come as the conference visitor to release him because of difficulties associated with his daughter's troubled marriage. Neal soon realized that his main mission that weekend was not "to increase the home teaching by two percent" but to reassure the stake president "that the Lord loved him and needed him." So, among other gentle things, he played basketball with the stake president's son.

One of Neal's early assignments as a General Authority was to serve on the Church's Special Affairs Committee, which dealt with public communications issues. This combined his new Church perspective with his personal background. Elders Hinckley and Faust had led this committee until Elder Faust was sent to Brazil in 1975. Then Neal began working with Elder Hinckley. It was a natural spot for Neal, because he had previously accumulated much experience about civic matters and the people involved in them.

He continued to address civic groups, even though he now spoke as a general officer of the Church. In the late 1970s, for example, he addressed the Utah Conference on U.S. Social Security, the Utah Association of Counties, a governor's conference on Energy and Economic Development in Mississippi, and various Utah education groups. In these venues, Neal would quote some of his favorite lines about how to maintain limited government, such as, "If we are to restrain governments, we must first restrain ourselves." Or he would quote Will Rogers, who said he was thankful we don't get all of the government we pay for. Or Thomas Jefferson, who warned that government shouldn't attempt to do more good than the public can bear.

He often linked governmental themes with his concern about

Elder Maxwell and Elder Gordon B. Hinckley worked closely together on the Church Special Affairs Committee

secularism: "Secularists so often define 'good' as being more . . . creature comforts. [And yet] the governmental scratching goes on even after the [social] itching has stopped." With American society becoming more secular, he saw that when religious values wane, somehow government surges. "A religion of ten thousand regulations has emerged in place of the Ten Commandments." Thus, "it is increasingly difficult to render unto Caesar that which is Caesar's and also to render unto God that which is God's—because Caesar is asking too much."

Neal took opportunities to encourage Church members to be involved in civic affairs, rather than simply trembling on the sidelines, "filled with Martha-like anxiety about America." He commended the two-party system, urging Latter-day Saints to get involved, not waiting for others to create the political options and choices among candidates. "Going the second citizen mile includes not only Church service, but community service as well." These themes and attitudes had taken shape in Neal's mind years earlier.

His insight on public affairs issues helped the Brethren in what proved to be an unusually busy season. Traditionally, the First Presidency has been very reluctant to issue statements on public issues, preferring generally to encourage members to participate as individual citizens and to support the principle of separation between church and state. Between 1977 and 1981, however, a few exceptional cases arose, involving moral issues important enough to warrant official Church comment. These included statements opposing gambling, the Equal Rights Amendment to the Constitution of the United States, and deployment of the MX missile in Utah and Nevada.

Members of the Church arguably played enough of a role to affect in some degree the outcome of the national debate over the Equal Rights Amendment. Congress had approved the proposed constitutional amendment in 1972 and submitted it to the states. By 1980, thirty-five states had ratified it (though five of these later withdrew their ratification), leaving only three (or perhaps eight) more state ratifications needed to achieve the constitutionally required three-fourths majority. This circumstance created considerable pressure on the state legislatures in the remaining states, where Church members and leaders joined in the public discussion without apology. The First Presidency issued statements opposing the ERA in 1976, 1978, and 1980, urging Latter-day Saints to join the public process in their own states. As it turned out, the proposal fell short of obtaining ratification in the necessary thirty-eight states.

As an example of Neal's involvement, he spoke to an anti-ERA rally sponsored by a citizens' coalition in Florida on March 23, 1977. He expressed deep doubts about both the need for and the "safety" of the amendment. He said the action wasn't necessary, given the Constitution's equal protection clause in the Fourteenth Amendment and given the passage of many recent laws against gender discrimination. Of greatest concern, he said, the ERA would deprive lawmakers of their ability to "honor vital differences in the roles of men and women," especially in the family. That could produce "undesired, uncertain, unintended, unforeseen and unwanted consequences" for both family life and society.

Neal had watched the Brethren at close range for years, so he was fairly realistic about his new role. He'd seen their relentless travel schedules enough that, in his first general conference talk, he quoted Elder Richard L. Evans a little wistfully, "Have you ever gotten homesick on the way to the airport?" And he understood that he was, in some ways, less free now to dart across organizational lines or propose special projects. "There is such an important sense of seniority and protocol within the ranks of the General Authorities," said Elder Holland, "that you really defer to quorum relationships." When "Neal was a staffer, so to speak," he could more easily be called on and used by other leaders for a variety of "freelance work."

Once Neal helped prepare an agenda of challenging issues for discussion by a committee that included several senior General Authorities. When the meeting concluded after a lively discussion, staff members were gathering up a few papers left on the table. At the spot where Neal had been sitting, someone found a paper clip that was bent beyond recognition. "What on earth happened to this paper clip?" he asked. Still in the room, Neal looked at it and said with a little smile, "That's what you do when you're junior [in seniority]."

In another reflection of his realism, Neal attended a meeting in which several of the senior Brethren had been talking about issues related to President Kimball's stirring vision of taking the gospel to countries where the Church was not yet established. After the meeting, someone said, "Is President Tanner all right? He didn't say much, and he seemed a little pensive." Neal noted that President Tanner was responsible to oversee financial support for whatever the Church did. Then he said, "He's okay. He's just thinking about what it will mean to take the Church welfare program to India."

One demanding but elevating dimension of his new call was his growing need, and desire, to find spiritual guidance. He drew assurance from his patriarchal blessing, which told him that "the spirit of testimony may accompany all your acts," and that he would have "the spirit and power of inspiration . . . while representing the Lord in [laboring] for the salvation of mankind," for "there is an invisible power operating between you and the Master."

More experienced Brethren had taught him how to recognize the promptings needed for such lasting decisions as choosing new stake presidents. He wrote Cory, "I know personally that President Lee gets direct guidance from God, because I've been witness to several situations where the outcome made the reality of revelation apparent." As time went on, he was present several times when he knew revelation came to the First Presidency and the Twelve. After sometimes lengthy discussions, perhaps with periods of waiting for weeks or months, "then comes the prophetic intervention. There is a calmness and a serenity . . . even though a few moments before we might have felt differently about a matter."

Sometimes these impressions would come about individuals. "It doesn't have to be spectacular," he said. "It's the personalness of revelation that matters the most." For instance, once he thought he should pray for a woman he knew had cancer but almost instantly felt an inner sense that his prayer wasn't necessary. An hour later, he received a call informing him that she had passed away.

Another time he received a pleading letter from a missionary at the Missionary Training Center, asking if he could write to persuade the missionary's companion not to go home. He placed the letter in his stack of correspondence, planning to respond in due course. Then a feeling came over him that he should write immediately. He called in his secretary, dictated a letter, and arranged for the letter to go to the MTC that day. A few days later, the missionary wrote again. He said his companion had packed his bags and was waiting for a bus, unwilling to talk further with anyone at the MTC. He "went to the mailbox in desperation and there" found Elder Maxwell's letter. He dropped the letter in his companion's lap and left him alone in an office. "He completely broke down. . . . I don't know what went on in there, but ten minutes later he came out," unpacked, and stayed. "I refuse to believe that this is coincidence."

Individual premonitions had played a role when Neal and the CES search committee were looking for new leaders. That process continued in his new assignments. When he was made managing director of the Correlation Department in 1976, for instance, he needed someone to direct the department's new Evaluation Division. As he issued the invitation to assume that role, the man he selected confided that there had been a period a few months earlier when Elder Maxwell kept showing up in his dreams.

Neal also at times felt direction from what he called "the voice in the mind" in preparing his talks or writing, occasionally offering something as specific as a needed phrase or image. Colleen has often been aware of those moments, including experiences when she's been with him at Church gatherings. After hearing him as often as she has, she has sometimes been amazed at a new thought that will come to him to fit the local circumstance. In Neal's words,

> Unlike the roar and crash of artillery followed by a delivering silence, these smaller moments involve the Lord's periodic whisperings to my mind. Over the years, these whisperings have guided me and reassured me. They give me . . . sudden strokes of ideas and occasionally the pure flow of intelligence. These moments are as real for me as what happened on Okinawa. These are inward things, often taking the form of a directing phrase. I have found that the Lord gives more instructions than explanations.

At the same time, many spiritual experiences are "not shareable." Neal remembers President Romney's comment that we probably would have more spiritual experiences if we didn't talk so much about them. Sometimes that is because the Lord will "brace or reprove you in a highly personal process not understood or appreciated by those outside the context."

With all of this potential for both service and spiritual growth in Elder Maxwell's new duties, one can easily imagine that Clarence Maxwell might have wanted to write his son as did Mormon to Moroni: "My beloved son . . . , I rejoice exceedingly that your Lord Jesus Christ hath been mindful of you, and hath called you to his ministry, and to his holy work" (Moroni 8:2).

FORTY-ONE

LENGTHENING
THE CHURCH'S
STRIDE

I N THE LATER 1 9 7 0 s , Elder Maxwell told an interviewer
that "the volume of 'operational revelation'" in the Church "is at the
highest level it's ever been." Much of this was simply the Lord's tim-
ing but Neal also felt that some of it was the unique combination of
President Kimball's energetic vision, President Tanner's organizational
skill, and President Romney's closeness to the Spirit. Whatever the reasons, he felt that the Church had gone for years without seeing decisions of the magnitude it was then encountering on a regular basis.
From the recent foundation of President Lee's leadership, which had
clarified the principles of correlation, President Kimball launched the
international Church so fully that Neal said this "had never happened
before on this planet." It was the day of which all the prophets had
dreamed, when, for the first time, "the church of the Lamb, who were
the Saints of God" were truly "scattered upon all the face of the earth"
(1 Nephi 14:12–14).

In the judgment of Elder Bruce R. McConkie, whose service
as a General Authority spanned several decades, the three Church

developments in his lifetime that would do the most for the Lord's work all occurred within the five years from 1975 to 1980. They were the organization of the First Quorum of Seventy in 1975, the extension of the priesthood to all worthy males in 1978, and the publication of the Latter-day Saint edition of the scriptures beginning in 1979. Elder Maxwell shared particularly in the first two of these events.

The organization of the Seventy was significant because they would eventually become the leaders responsible for operating the daily affairs of the worldwide Church. This step would merge in a new light and a new unity what had earlier been the work of the First Council of Seventy, the Assistants to the Twelve, and the regional representatives. The Seventy, in several quorums, would become the only organizational layer between the stakes and the Quorum of the Twelve. The Area Presidency for each geographic area of the Church would be composed of three Seventies. Members of the First and Second Quorums of Seventy would be full-time General Authorities, and the members of the other quorums would be part-time (like bishops and stake presidents) Area Authority Seventies.

The process of reaching these conclusions, which now seem so natural, actually came one step at a time. President Kimball first announced the creation of the First Quorum in October conference 1975. A year later he expanded the Quorum by releasing the seven-member First Council of Seventy and the twenty-one Assistants to the Twelve, placing all of them in the First Quorum of Seventy. Seven members of the reconstituted First Quorum were then sustained as the Quorum Presidency. One of these was Elder Maxwell. All General Authorities were then members of the First Presidency, the Twelve, the Seventy, or the Presiding Bishopric. Within a decade, stake seventies quorums would be discontinued.

The idea of organizing the First Quorum of Seventy had been under discussion for many years at Church headquarters. The scriptures already authorized such a quorum to "preach the gospel, and to be especial witnesses unto the Gentiles and in all the world" (D&C 107:25), acting under the direction of the Twelve "in building up the church and regulating all the affairs of the same in all nations" (D&C

107:34). Seventies had been called and ordained at various times since the Church's early days, often to serve as missionaries. As part of his call to serve a mission, Neal himself had been ordained a seventy in 1946 by Elder S. Dilworth Young, who in 1976 was still serving in the First Council of Seventy.

The Brethren's questions in more recent times had sought to clarify the scriptural role of the Seventy and their relationship to other general and local officers—issues that the Church's international growth had now made urgent. Regarding the Seventy, the Lord had revealed to President John Taylor in 1882 that "everything that shall be necessary for the future development" of His kingdom would be given through appointed channels "from time to time." The First Presidency had asked Elder B. H. Roberts of the First Council of Seventy for a memo on the subject in the 1930s. In 1952, Elder John A. Widtsoe wrote about the increasing workload of the Twelve and their Assistants, adding, "The First Quorum of Seventy will no doubt be called into being to help meet the situation." In 1968, the entire First Council of Seventy proposed reconstituting the First Quorum, and they later offered to be released from their callings in the First Council if that would facilitate the Quorum's creation.

In the mid-1970s, the First Presidency asked Elder Boyd K. Packer for a complete review of the subject. Consistent with the Lord's words to President Taylor, during Elder Packer's prayerful homework in the scriptures, he discovered that "the call of a Seventy was not a local priesthood call; rather, it was henceforth to be as the Lord had said; the Seventy 'form a quorum, equal in authority to that of the Twelve special witnesses or Apostles'" (D&C 107:26).

During the summer of 1976, the First Presidency also asked Neal, as managing director of the Correlation Department, for a memo sharing his ideas about the new Quorum. He warmly endorsed the concept, as did others who saw it taking shape. Then, as a member of the Quorum's Presidency, he lived through the first few years of its implementation. As with correlation, the regional representatives, and the Church Educational System, Neal was again present at the creation of some historic steps—in Elder Holland's words, he was "clearly involved with the architectural work behind the Quorums of the Seventy concept and what that has become."

The next revealed step was the extension of the priesthood to all worthy males. On Friday, June 9, 1978, the First Presidency and the Twelve called the Seventy and the Presiding Bishopric into a special meeting in the Salt Lake Temple. Here President Kimball announced the culmination of his long pleading to the Lord for guidance about making the priesthood available to every worthy male. As the First Presidency's 1970 statement on civil rights had made clear, this subject had weighed heavily on the minds of previous prophets. But the revelation of which President Kimball spoke in the temple was about more than civil rights. It was the revelatory extension of the spiritual prodding he had felt with great intensity since that monumental 1974 talk to the regional representatives about fully establishing the Church in every nation. In process and direction, the announcement on the priesthood could only be compared with—in fact, its effect was a natural step in—the revelation Peter received to take the gospel to the gentile world: "Of a truth I perceive that God is no respecter of persons: but in every nation he that feareth him, and worketh righteousness, is accepted with him" (Acts 10:34–35).

Neal was profoundly moved as the group unanimously approved the statement proposed by the First Presidency and the Twelve. As President Kimball invited responses from all who cared to speak, each man responded. As they did, Neal felt a spiritual witness that this step was "revelation, not accommodation. The waves of the Spirit washed over us like surf, and I shed many tears." He gave the tear-soaked handkerchief he used in that meeting to Colleen for safekeeping, without its being washed, as a permanent keepsake from the experience. He later recalled this event as he carried another white handkerchief when he was assigned to create the first stake consisting entirely of black Latter-day Saints.

In his role with the Special Affairs Committee, Neal was assigned to call several people to notify them of the revelation before it was announced publicly. In every case, he couldn't read the statement without weeping again. Then, shortly after the public announcement, Neal received a call about it from the White House. The call came from his friend and former student, Jim Jardine, who was working as a special assistant to Attorney General Griffin Bell in the administration of President Jimmy Carter.

Jim told Neal that President Carter had heard the news and wanted to express his support to the Church. President Carter had met President Kimball on several occasions and developed a friendship with him. Because President Carter didn't understand the entire context of the announcement, he wanted to state his feelings appropriately. His press secretary asked Jim to draft a telegram that President Carter could send to President Kimball. Jim Jardine was calling to read Elder Maxwell his draft and ask for suggestions. After a brief review, "that was the telegram President Carter sent to President Kimball."

Two years later, Neal was asked to put this event into historical—and future—perspective. He said that the universal extension of priesthood blessings was the step that would move the Church toward true internationalization, making the Restoration's blessings available to everyone. The implications were dramatic. "Major quantitative growth is probably the greatest challenge the Church will face," Neal envisioned. Then would come a hastening of temple building and temple work. He quoted Brigham Young, who said that "there will be hundreds of [temples] built and dedicated to the Lord." Associated with the temple work, Neal expected that the Church would see "Elijah-inspired family research in ways not possible in the painstaking past." Spoken nearly two decades before the Church adopted FamilySearch™ on the Internet and before its current temple-building era, these were prophetic words.

The Brethren authorized two other changes during this time that visibly influenced the traditional patterns of local congregations. Both changes reflected their concern about the difficulties of carrying the practices of a western U.S. church to the distant parts of the globe. Neal was involved in the deliberations leading to these adjustments.

One change was the shift in 1980 to a three-hour meeting block on Sundays. Before this time, the typical schedule called for priesthood meeting and Sunday School during the morning hours and then sacrament meeting in the afternoon. Relief Society, Young Women, and Primary meetings were usually held on weekdays. That approach was far easier for Church members who lived close to their ward chapels in Utah or Idaho than it was in Asia, Latin America, or elsewhere, where each family's trip to the chapel could place heavy demands on their time and money. This was a time of increased energy costs and gasoline shortages but mostly, as Neal put it, "we're in a global Church. If a Filipino family can [barely afford to] make it to church on Sunday, do you want them to . . . go home and try to come back again for sacrament meeting?"

The other change dealt with the financial demands the Church made of its members. In 1980 Neal was assigned to the Member Finance Committee, which looked at ways of reducing the costs of Church membership. This committee, along with other groups among the Twelve, made recommendations leading to policies that emphasized tithing as the Lord's way of financing His work. This renewed focus on tithing allowed for the elimination of supplemental methods of financing Church costs, such as local building funds, ward budget requests, and welfare assessments.

Elder Mark E. Petersen, whose personal meekness Neal especially admired, chaired the Member Finance committee. "When any credit or praise was passed out, he would, as it were, sit in the corner hoping to be unobserved."

As President Kimball was lengthening the Church's stride, he was also conducting a tutorial in human kindness for Neal Maxwell. Because they had lived in the same ward for a few years, the Maxwells and the Kimballs were well acquainted. But after Spencer Kimball became President of the Church, Neal began to work closely with him on CES matters and then other Church assignments, until their acquaintance bloomed into a personal mentoring relationship. Neal came to see in President Kimball a rare blend of spiritual vision, tireless labor, and an unself-conscious tenderness toward other people.

Perhaps because Neal himself shared an instinct for visionary leadership and the energy for constant labor, which helped him develop additional appreciation for the tenderness, his admiration gradually moved toward emulation.

Long before he became President of the Church, the depth of Spencer W. Kimball's work ethic and religious commitments was already legendary. As one child said of him, "When I get big, I want to be like Spencer Double Dependable." But his tender, personal side became more visible to Neal as the two of them drew closer. By 1976, Neal said President Kimball had helped him see that

> you just keep going even when you're too tired to keep going. And he has a sweetness in the midst of great firmness. . . . He's taught me the importance of maintenance of relationships in sweetness, as seen in his visiting the sick and afflicted. He's just tireless . . . And there's a kind of innocence about him in that he doesn't realize how special he is. . . . That's a great lesson for me to see. I need to do more of that in my own life.

Seeing and responding to President Kimball's personal example brought Neal into a new apprenticeship—a renewed study in self-sacrifice, empathy, meekness, and ministering with compassion to those in affliction. Neal was already seeking these attributes of discipleship, and now he'd found just the right role model for some accelerated course work.

Shortly after President Kimball was sustained in 1974, he attended fast and testimony meeting in his home ward—where the Maxwells also attended that day. After enduring a meeting full of tributes to himself, President Kimball stood and expressed his love for the ward members but then he said, as Neal wrote in a letter to Cory, that "as long as he had studied the scriptures, he had never read of any special heaven for General Authorities. He then went on to give a splendid sermonette on the Democracy of the plan of salvation."

Soon the paths of the two men began crossing frequently. Sometimes, as was his self-effacing style, President Kimball would "just show up" at Neal's office and ask, "Is Brother Neal in?" At the end of a letter he wrote Neal about some Church business, he added, "I am

With President Spencer W. Kimball at the inauguration of Jeffrey R. Holland as president of Brigham Young University

mighty glad we have you where you are, with your humility and strength, with your clear thinking and your perfect organization." Another time, he sent Neal a draft of a talk he'd been working on and asked for his comments:

> I am wondering if I would dare to ask you to glance it over and see, first, does it have merit, second, have I made any statements that are improper, third, is it too long? . . . I realize . . . you are already so extremely busy, but I have such great confidence in your . . . judgment that it gives me a sense of security to know that you have approved it.

President Kimball sometimes met Neal's early attempts to be similarly self-effacing with his gentle humor. Once when the First Presidency had given a difficult assignment to Neal and Elder James E. Faust, President Tanner said, "President Kimball, I don't think we could find two better men for this task than Brother Faust and Brother Maxwell." Neal responded, "Surely, you can find better men than the two of us." With a smile, President Kimball replied, "Well, while we're looking for two better men, would you two mind going ahead with the job?"

As he watched President Kimball's quiet ministry to sick and other troubled individuals, Neal followed a similar pattern with increasing frequency. He enjoyed recalling a time when President Kimball was in the hospital as a patient himself and his nurses kept having to look for him in other rooms—where he had instinctively gone to "visit the sick." Often when Neal whispered to President Kimball that someone they both knew was in the hospital, President Kimball would say, "Yes, I know. I have already been there."

In 1979, while attending his home ward, Neal was seated next to President Kimball on the stand. Just before the meeting started, President Kimball took Neal by the hand and whispered to him, "Do you know that I love you with all of my heart?" The next week, the President asked him, "Do you remember what I said to you last week?"

On a warm spring day in 1982, Cory's wife, Karen, noticed President Kimball sitting in a lounge chair in the yard of his home. She and her children Peter and Emily went over to say hello to him. He took Peter by the hand and kissed it, saying, "I love all my boys. Elder Maxwell is one of the great men of this time." Neal confided these experiences to his personal notes, adding, "He is so marvelous to encourage us all. We feel his love, and we sense that he has no favorites."

When President Kimball passed away in 1985, the *Ensign* invited Neal to summarize his life and teachings. His article described President Kimball's prophetic vision, the courageous opening of the entire globe to missionaries, his multiple battles against illness and adversity, the revelation on the priesthood. But with all these strengths, it was President Kimball's gentle charity that most captured Neal's heart. He entitled his essay "Spencer, the Beloved: Leader-Servant," noting there "how uniquely beloved" this Church President was, creating a "discernible dimension of affection" for him:

> There was a pervasive warmth in [his] ministry . . . the loving but penetrating look of his eyes, his embrace, his holy kiss, his tenderness—felt by so many—all created a deserved aura about this man, not of unapproachability, but of special warmth. His love was inclusive; no one ever felt left out. [He] epitomized the central virtue in the first two great commandments—love of God and of his fellowmen.

Later, when Neal spoke at Camilla Kimball's funeral, he remembered "the authority of [her] example." He said, "President Kimball articulated and demonstrated 'lengthen your stride,' but there were actually two pairs of legs striding." The Kimball marriage, like the Maxwell marriage, was an equal partnership. And Camilla's attributes, many of them like her husband's, were, for Neal and Colleen, worth emulating: "In her meekness she did not fully realize how extensively she had developed Christlike traits."

Disciples learn much from knowing and following other disciples.

FORTY-TWO

THE CORRELATION
DEPARTMENT

As 1976 BEGAN, THE FIRST PRESIDENCY GAVE
Neal a new assignment, in addition to his duties in the Presidency of
the Seventy, which soon proved so demanding that it required his
release that same year as commissioner of education. He became managing director of the Correlation Department, a new department that
had resulted from the First Presidency's continued efforts to stream-
line the Church headquarters organizations in accordance with the
now-familiar principles of correlation. Neal was once again present at
the creation of a cutting-edge project, as the Brethren positioned themselves in one more way to understand and to lead a global Church.

The child, youth, and adult correlation committees originally created in the early 1960s focused on age-based curriculum reviews, while
other organizational steps—such as the regional representatives
concept—gradually trimmed the size and function of many general
boards and committees. The age-based committees were dissolved in
1972 with the creation of the Internal Communications Department,
which now directed the preparation of curricular materials for all

quorum and auxiliary organizations, using a combination of professional educators and Church-service committees.

These steps were consistent with the correlation principles of both harmonizing and simplifying all Church programs. Prior to this time, the general boards of the priesthood and auxiliary organizations, such as Relief Society or Sunday School, had each written their own lesson manuals, trained local leaders in their programs, and then evaluated "in the field" how the programs were being implemented and how they could be improved. Now, however, these general auxiliary presidencies and boards played a more limited role, giving general input and review to lesson materials prepared by a centralized curriculum department and providing only selective regional training and evaluation.

With this change in place, correlation could take on an additional role first envisioned by Harold B. Lee—the "correlation review" of all teaching and training materials to create a "single voice" and "final filter" in communications from Church headquarters to Church members. In 1973, President Lee had called this a plan to "'audit' the teaching materials of the Church" to ensure spiritual security and consistency. His biographer wrote that "this early insight was the forerunner of the . . . Correlation Department," which Neal would now manage. Even in 1973, President Lee already "had in mind the one man who had the vision and the ability to do what was needed in this [correlation review] venture, Elder Neal A. Maxwell."

By 1975 Presidents Kimball, Tanner, and Romney were ready to take this next step. And, as part of a new, centralized process that President Tanner especially had encouraged, they assigned to the Correlation Department two other functions not seen before at Church headquarters: evaluation and long-range planning. The new department with its three divisions reported to the Correlation Executive Committee, then chaired by Elder Mark E. Petersen and including five members of the Twelve plus the Presiding Bishop.

The first division, Correlation Review, was responsible to "audit" for doctrinal and policy consistency all lesson manuals, program changes, handbooks, Church magazines, and any other communications to local Church units from all organizations at Church headquarters.

Correlation Review was also charged to find ways to reduce the complexity and volume of Church programs, which meant Neal now found himself having to resist politely the advocacy of some of his General Authority colleagues who were advisers to Church programs or departments. As the years went by, this function became known at Church headquarters simply as "correlation," because every lesson, manual, or magazine article had to "go through correlation" before it was cleared for distribution to the Church.

Some of this function had occurred within Internal Communications since 1972, but by 1975 the Brethren desired a more arm's-length process, separate from the auxiliaries and other "originating organizations." When Neal began managing the department, he kept Daniel H. Ludlow as the director of Correlation Review, a function Dan had already been performing in Internal Communications, aided by Church-service committees. Brother Ludlow, the former dean of Religious Instruction at Brigham Young University, was a walking encyclopedia of Church doctrine and policy, which made him invaluable to oversee such a "final filter" review process.

In his role as managing director, Neal soon developed a few disarming one-liners and stories to help people see the need for this sometimes intimidating review function. He would say that every organization needs a chief skeptic who can ask dumb questions. Or he'd use a military analogy to comment wryly that we need to keep our friendly fire from having a bigger caliber than the fire of our enemies. Sometimes when new programs were proposed, Neal would try to help everyone see that those giving overall direction to Church programs need to be "in on the takeoffs as well as the crash landings." Another favorite was his tongue-in-cheek "apocryphal" account about "how correlation got started in the Church":

> A federal army [Johnston's army, in 1857] was sent out here to harass the Saints. The Brethren had decided on a policy of irritation without violence. In keeping with that policy, Porter Rockwell and Lot Smith were dispatched to a distant army camp where Lot . . . was to . . . remove the pins from the army's wagon wheels while Porter . . . was to drive off all of the army's horses.

In the dark of night, Lot was busily taking out wagon wheel pins, and Porter war-whooped into the camp and drove off all the horses, including Lot Smith's. Lot later walked wearily many miles back to Church headquarters and reportedly said, "Brethren, we've just got to get correlated."

The other two divisions—Planning and Evaluation—were brand new, and Neal needed to create them from the ground up. As it turned out, the long-range Planning Division never really got beyond a box on an organizational chart. Neal made some modest efforts to encourage a little long-range curriculum planning, but he sensed early on that the First Presidency and the Twelve were, by their natural, scriptural function, the true organizational planners whose seeric vision would always guide the long-term working of the Church. The idea of having staff people assist with this process in a centralized or "correlated" way had enough merit to be considered, but Neal and the Correlation Executive Committee never felt quite ready to propose a general planning staff.

The Evaluation Division, however, did come into being, and it has remained. Now called the Research Information Division, it employs about thirty full-time professional staff. The initial charge to the Evaluation Division was simple—to "evaluate the effectiveness of various Church programs," because the Church was now so large and so diverse that the General Authorities could no longer rely on their own firsthand impressions to know "what is going on in the field." As Neal liked to say about the limits of informal data-gathering processes, let's avoid being "victimized by our own personal impressions and anecdotes." He enjoyed quoting someone who said, "All Indians walk single file; at least, the one I saw did."

So here Neal was again, involved in an interesting new start-up organization that, like some of his innovations in the Church Educational System, would eventually become a routine part of the Church's headquarters work. But when it first began, the Evaluation Division, like some of what he did in CES, required incubation time before it was widely understood and accepted. Neal had always liked having reliable "data" as the "homework" for a large institution, including the Church, to understand what is really happening before making

major policy decisions. That was the impulse that had prompted him
to ask for demographic projections on Church growth, which helped
President Lee to explain the need for the regional representatives. A
similar urge had prompted Neal as commissioner to request a study of
the educational needs of international Church members, which helped
clarify the policy of giving high and rapid priority to religious education rather than simply building more Church schools. This approach
was Neal's "analytical vision" at its best.

At the same time, the Church had never used professional
researchers in any large-scale, systematic way before. Some senior leaders and department heads were initially quite cautious about the use of
social science or organizational behavior methods to study the Church,
its programs, and its people. There were good reasons to hesitate. For
one thing, the Brethren would need to have complete trust and confidence in the research staff before giving them access to the Church's
internal processes. Both institutional and personal privacy issues were
at stake in allowing research teams to study Church statistics or interview Church members and leaders with enough depth to yield reliable
findings. And a few Latter-day Saint researchers, like some LDS professionals in other fields, had sometimes let their secular training and
attitudes take priority over their Church commitments.

For Neal, these issues were similar to what he'd encountered in
trying to strengthen the BYU faculty in both teaching and research.
He believed that professional research tools in the hands of people who
clearly placed the Lord's work first in their lives could be a blessing to
the Church. Professionalism, like education, didn't need to be a master that subordinated Church loyalty; rather, Church loyalty was the
master and professional tools were the servant. It was second nature to
him that research yields only "data about the reality of things out there";
it won't ever "take the place of inspiration or scriptural direction."

Neal was also a realist about the limitations of statistical or other
social science research. While he always said he didn't understand
math enough to help his children with that part of their homework, he
had used research studies enough to know how to spot their implications. He knew the difference, for example, between causation and

correlation—a crucial factor in knowing what conclusions to draw from research.

Suppose, for example, that statistics show that BYU students are more likely to serve missions than LDS students at other colleges or universities. Neal could explain why that fact alone doesn't necessarily show "causation"—that is, it doesn't prove that attending BYU "causes" increased missionary service. It's quite possible that the same spiritual motivation that moves a student to attend BYU may also move him or her to serve a mission. Showing a cause-and-effect relationship would require more careful research that "controls for" the motivation variable, such as comparing the future missionary service of students who want to attend BYU but *are not* admitted with that of students who want to attend BYU and *are* admitted. Thus Neal "realizes that data [by] itself is not self-interpreting. It has to be put into a context and utilized."

In the end, it was not Neal's expertise so much as his personal credibility that let him become a two-way bridge of communication between Church leaders and the researchers in the Correlation Evaluation Division. His work as commissioner had earned the trust of both the Brethren and the LDS academic-professional community, and once more, Neal could help each group learn how to work with the other. He understood their worlds, and they understood him. Their confidence in that understanding built their confidence in each other.

To launch the Evaluation Division, Neal asked Bruce C. Hafen to take a two-year leave from his position as a law professor at BYU to help him figure out how the division should function, what kinds of research tools and professional staff to use, and how to approach the evaluation process. Neal got Bruce's name from Dallin Oaks at BYU, where he had worked the previous few years as President Oaks's assistant on special projects that included the staff work to help plan for the new law school. Dan Ludlow and Bruce became the Correlation Department staff, meeting almost daily with Neal and weekly with the Correlation Executive Committee. They were succeeded after about two years by Roy W. Doxey, former dean of Religious Education at

BYU, and Stan E. Weed, who had initiated evaluation research for the Presiding Bishopric.

As he'd done with CES and the Church Board of Education, Neal worked hard to build the trust of the Correlation Executive Committee in the evaluation process. He was careful to check basic signals frequently by taking general "reaction papers" to the committee, and he was very selective about both the research projects and the research personnel he recommended. That selectivity was aided by a Church-service Evaluation Correlation Committee composed of both professional researchers and lay Church members who helped ensure consistent quality control.

One of the first studies involved an evaluation of the effectiveness of regional meetings, in which general board members and regional representatives trained stake priesthood and auxiliary leaders. Partly because of these findings, the regional meetings were soon discontinued.

Another early project evaluated the effect of a TV special produced by the Church Public Communications Department. That study found, among other things, that being personally acquainted with a Latter-day Saint creates a more positive impression about the Church on the attitudes of individuals of other faiths than does a TV production.

Still another project examined which items on statistical reports were the most likely to predict overall stake activity or performance levels. The study found, for instance, that the proportion of adult males who hold the Melchizedek Priesthood is the single strongest predictor of a stake's other activity levels, such as attendance at sacrament meeting and youth activities. This work helped facilitate a simplification of the Church reporting system.

A later important study examined the influences that affect the decisions of young men to serve missions. That study, a summary of which was later published in the *Ensign,* found that children whose parents are married in the temple are five times more likely to serve missions and three times more likely to be married in the temple themselves than are children whose parents have not been married in the temple. It also found that "private religious behavior," such as personal prayer and scripture reading, was a much more reliable predictor of a young man's future missionary service than such "public religious behavior" as attendance at Church meetings.

In addition to undertaking its own evaluation studies, the new division also coordinated the work of other Church departments that were pioneering the use of research techniques to evaluate the effectiveness of training and programs. The Presiding Bishopric's office had already examined the effectiveness of the Church's bishopric training program, and the Missionary Department was using evaluation tools to improve missionary work.

Eventually the Evaluation Division also launched some large-scale, multiyear projects that drew on a series of studies and teams of researchers. A study of the conversion process, for example, looked at differences in the results of proselyting among various missions and countries and under different mission presidents. This project also examined, through personal interviews and other methods, why people moved toward conversion or away from it. The resulting data helped Church leaders consider where to deploy missionaries, how to improve the training of mission presidents and missionaries, and how to revise the missionary discussions.

Although these studies were for the Church's internal use, a few people who are familiar with such organizational research have seen some glimpses of the Church studies. Rodney Stark, a well-known sociologist of religion, wrote in a professional journal that

> the research efforts of other denominations shrink to insignificance when compared with the quality, scope, and sophistication of the work of the Mormon social research department. Much of this work is not yet readily available outside the Church. . . . Even if we must wait awhile, what is really important is that the right data are being collected in the right way. . . . Suppose that the Apostle Paul had not only sent out letters, but questionnaires?

As General Authorities and other leaders began to make use of these findings in their own teaching and program assessment, their confidence in the research process also grew until the Research Information Division became a tool of regular use. In retrospect, Elder Oaks believes the Church can thank Elder Maxwell for the utilization of this work, because it is unlikely to have won acceptance without him. As Elder Holland said, "All Neal Maxwell ever wanted to do was work good enough that it spoke for itself." "That's also part of the Maxwell legacy—that we're open" to using professional research staff who keep their work in channels and in perspective.

In February 1977 the First Presidency announced a clarification between the "ecclesiastical" role of the Twelve and the "temporal" role of the Presiding Bishopric, which for a short time involved Neal in a delicate task that grew out of his assignment with the Correlation Department. Although his role was temporary, the larger distinction between the ecclesiastical and the temporal arms of the Church has proven significant in supporting its international operations.

The First Presidency made clear that the Twelve were responsible for all spiritual or ecclesiastical affairs, including the work of the Seventy, the stakes, and the missions. They also stated that the Presiding Bishopric were responsible for all temporal or logistical support functions, such as physical facilities, finances, records, and translation and distribution of Church materials. Eventually this distinction led to a pattern in which each Area Presidency had the dotted-line support of a local director of temporal affairs who received training and line supervision from the Presiding Bishopric. Thus, the ecclesiastical and temporal functions came together at two points: once in the field at the area level, and once at Church headquarters in the relationship between the Twelve and the Presiding Bishopric.

Elder Maxwell became involved in the headquarters connection when the First Presidency created a Church Planning and Coordinating Council (CPCC). This was to be what Neal called the "junction box," where the ecclesiastical (Quorum of the Twelve) and temporal (Presiding Bishopric) organizational lines came together under the First Presidency's direction. As initially announced in 1977, Neal was the executive secretary to the CPCC, and the Correlation Department was to function as staff to this coordinating group.

This approach was intended to "take correlation to its highest level," arranging a setting in which every Church organization—ecclesiastical or temporal—would be represented in a planning body. Neal's role reflected the First Presidency's confidence in him, but he soon felt uncomfortable in it. "It was an awkward position to be in," he noted, because the relationship between the First Presidency and the Twelve needed to be direct. Neal finally went to President Tanner to discuss the "administrative awkwardness," which in part arose because he was a General Authority rather than a staff person. Within a few months, Francis M. Gibbons, secretary to the First Presidency, replaced Neal as executive secretary to the CPCC as a natural extension of his duties with the First Presidency.

Over the next few years, the Brethren moved away from the CPCC as they probed various ways to establish the optimal planning and coordinating relationship among the Twelve, the Presiding Bishopric, and—in their newly emerging role—the Presidency of the Seventy. Eventually the Brethren settled on a "council system." In 1982, the First Presidency created three executive councils that mirrored the three-fold mission of the Church that they and the Twelve had just adopted—a Missionary Executive Council (proclaiming the gospel), a Priesthood Executive Council (perfecting the Saints), and a Temple and Genealogy Executive Council (redeeming the dead). This approach brought together the governing quorums, offices, and Church departments in appropriate functional bodies, all under the direction of the First Presidency. The councils found a balance that has functioned well ever since. Each council includes members of the Twelve, the Presidency of the Seventy, and the Presiding Bishopric.

Neal thought the executive councils provided just the kind of headquarters correlation that President Tanner had been looking for when the CPCC was first proposed. Each council brings "together the three entities [the Twelve, the Presidency of the Seventy, and the Presiding Bishopric (PBO)] who, under the direction of the First Presidency, are responsible" for each phase of the Church's interests. As Elder Maxwell chaired the Temple and Family History Executive Council in the 1990s, for example, he saw how representatives from each of these groups contributed uniquely to the process of planning and building temples—staff from "temporal" PBO departments concerned with building construction issues, a member of the Presidency of the Seventy from the Temple Department concerned with operating the temples, and members of the Twelve concerned with bringing the spiritual blessings of temple work through the ecclesiastical line to Church members.

PART XIII

THE APOSTOLIC YEARS
1981–

FORTY-THREE

THE HOLY
APOSTLESHIP

By 1981 PRESIDENTS SPENCER W. KIMBALL, N. Eldon Tanner, and Marion G. Romney were in their eighth year as the First Presidency. The channels of continuing revelation had been filled with light during those years, as the Lord seemed to "hasten [His] work in its time" (D&C 88:73), creating the structure and momentum to establish an international Zion. In April conference 1981, the First Presidency announced a new "three-fold mission of the Church," providing a strategic vision that unified their previous statements about worldwide missionary work, the First Quorum of Seventy, universal access to the priesthood, and other globalizing steps.

> The mission of the Church is threefold:
> To *proclaim the gospel* of the Lord Jesus Christ to every nation, kindred, tongue, and people;
> To *perfect the Saints* by preparing them to receive the ordinances of the gospel and by instruction and discipline to gain exaltation;
> To *redeem the dead* by performing vicarious ordinances of the gospel for those who have lived on the earth. All three are

part of one work—to assist our Father in Heaven and His Son, Jesus Christ, in Their grand and glorious mission, "to bring to pass the immortality and eternal life of man." (Moses 1:39).

After this latest action in their full, even sometimes dramatic, years together, this First Presidency began slowing down. President Kimball had battled against one major health problem after another, and the health of Presidents Tanner and Romney was now seriously declining as well. By July, President Kimball had recovered just enough from recent surgery that he was feeling a restless urge to breathe needed vitality into the First Presidency.

He made up his mind to take the unusual step of calling a fourth member of the First Presidency, Gordon B. Hinckley. And, because of the Church President's key responsibility in choosing a new member of the Quorum of the Twelve, President Kimball decided to act while he could. Rather than wait until October conference, he would call Elder Neal A. Maxwell now to fill Elder Hinckley's place in the Twelve. President Kimball's secretary, Arthur Haycock, wrote of the two calls:

> For some time prior to [these] calls, . . . the President had not been at all well. . . . He was very noticeably suffering the effects of . . . his last . . . operation. It seemed difficult for him to concentrate and make decisions. . . . Nevertheless, when he called me into his office to advise that he was naming Elder Hinckley as a member of the First Presidency and Elder Maxwell to the Twelve, his mind was clear and his actions as definite and controlled as [they] had been 30 or 40 years ago. Immediately following [these calls], President Kimball seemed to revert at once to his former condition of . . . general ill health. . . .
>
> In my 46 years of close association with the last six presidents of the Church, . . . this is the greatest testimony of direct revelation I have ever witnessed. . . . There is no doubt in my mind that the Lord strengthened President Kimball in mind and body and . . . inspired him to call [President Hinckley and Elder Maxwell] to their high offices so that His work could continue on.

At the press conference announcing Elder Gordon B. Hinckley's call as a counselor in the First Presidency and Elder Maxwell's call to the Twelve

President Kimball extended the call to Elder Hinckley on Wednesday, July 15. Then he asked his counselors and the Twelve, who were away from their offices for the traditional July recess, to assemble for a special meeting in the Salt Lake Temple on Thursday, July 23.

On July 21, Neal Maxwell was in Salt Lake's Holy Cross Hospital, recovering from minor septal surgery on his nose. This was only the second time Neal had been a patient in Holy Cross Hospital; the first time was the day he was born there, almost exactly fifty-five years earlier. Arthur Haycock called the Maxwell home and then the hospital, where Neal was just out of surgery. After he asked Colleen how Neal was doing, President Kimball came on the line and said he was coming to the hospital. Moved by what she thought was his interest in Neal's health, Colleen thanked him but gently tried to dissuade him from making the effort. "It's not his heart, is it?" President Kimball asked, a little urgently. Colleen assured him it was nothing serious and suggested again that he need not feel he should come. But he was on his way.

Soon Arthur and President Kimball entered Neal's room with an unusual air of urgency, as hospital visits go. Neal, still a little groggy, tried gamely to be cheerful as he fought off the effects of the anesthetic. Brother Kimball bent over to kiss him on the cheek and inadvertently bumped his nose, "which was pretty hard not to do, because it was so swathed in bandages."

After they had exchanged a few kindly words about Neal's condition, President Kimball came quickly to the point. He explained what was happening with Elder Hinckley—news that Neal welcomed with great enthusiasm. Then, with loving soberness, he called Elder Maxwell to become a member of the Quorum of the Twelve. Neal would need to obtain an early release from the hospital to attend the temple meeting two days later, without being able to tell his doctor why he must go.

That night, after Neal had phoned the news to his children, Cory visited the hospital. When he entered the room, Neal was asleep. Cory later wrote to him: "I stood there just looking at you for a minute. . . . It just dawned on me what a great man you are and how much I love you. Tears started welling up in my eyes as I looked at you and thought about all you mean to so many people (and to our Heavenly Father). Just then you stirred and opened your eyes."

When Neal arrived at the temple on Thursday morning, he was ushered into the historic fourth-floor meeting room, where the new, four-member First Presidency and eleven other Apostles awaited him. It wasn't until after he'd taken a seat that he realized he was, inadvertently, still wearing his plastic hospital wristband—a little symbol of his dazed astonishment. President Kimball explained that President Hinckley had just been set apart and that Neal would fill the vacancy thus created. All of his Brethren then placed their hands on his head and, with President Tanner as voice, they ordained him an Apostle and set him apart as a member of the Twelve.

Fifteen years later, in this same room, the First Presidency and the Twelve would, again, all lay their hands on Elder Maxwell's head, this time to pronounce a blessing of health. His colleague from their remarkable 1981 experience, Gordon B. Hinckley, would again be there, this time as President of the Church.

Neal had promised his doctor that he'd go straight home from the temple meeting; however, he had to attend a press conference, where the new calls were announced. He was still running a fever, unsure how much of his anxious feelings were from the surgery and how much were from the events of the day. It helped him that the media's primary focus was on the health of the members of the First Presidency and on President Hinckley's new call. Within a week, President Kimball suffered another subdural hematoma, and Neal realized what a narrow window had opened, allowing the Lord's prophet to act with such confidence to strengthen the First Presidency.

In the days that followed, Neal and Colleen felt wave after wave of both human and heavenly interest. Friends called, and people wrote letters. Neal's granddaughter Emily wrote, "I'm glad you're my grampa. I'm glad that you're out of the hospital." The wife of one General Authority said she had recently had a dream that Neal would be called as an Apostle. Neal's colleagues from the Twelve reassured and bolstered him, telling him that the meaning of the call wouldn't sink in all at once and not to worry about taking time to "get himself together." He would be all right; he'd absorb it gradually, they said, repeating their love for him, affirming their confidence in him, and urging him to speak up in their meetings.

As for Neal, he felt a profound sense of inadequacy, worried that he wasn't ready to contribute what would be expected of him. "Even though I'd been around here in one role or another for a long time," he said, this was "just a different thing, totally different. . . . And it's not something that's over with in a day." He sensed that he now needed to be even more careful about everything he said. He was also deeply sobered by the "array of scriptures" he read about the importance of apostolic certitude as a witness of Christ and about the unique calling of the Twelve, who were the "repository of keys that lie nowhere else."

Then his thoughts turned to Harold B. Lee. How he hoped Brother Lee would approve of what had happened. That idea prompted a memory of Elder Lee's having told him of a spiritual experience he'd had as a young Apostle, when he learned that it was his *duty* to learn to love every person. He had found the message overwhelming— the Lord now *expected* him to "press forward . . . having a perfect brightness of hope, and *a love of God and of all men*" (2 Nephi 31:20; italics added).

Neal, having long since undertaken his personal journey of discipleship, had now entered the realm of all-consuming Discipleship. And there was a difference, although not so much in the basic process or the place to which the path leads, for both are very similar for disciples and Disciples. In fact, the LDS Bible Dictionary defines *disciple* as "a pupil or learner; a name used to denote (1) the twelve, also called apostles, (2) all followers of Jesus Christ." In moving from the second category to the first, however, Neal found a difference in the depth of his witness, the degree of his responsibility, and the urgency of the expectations now placed upon him. It was one thing to try in his own private, sometimes halting, way to pattern his life after the Savior's. But now he had been "called" to the Twelve as a lifelong, special witness of Christ, acting under the same authority and with the same unconditional commitment that Peter knew, and Paul, and Joseph, Brigham, Harold, Spencer, and the others.

Behind Elder Lee's words about loving everyone was a broad hint that Neal must now lay a more sure claim to the gift of charity, the pure love that Christ has for every human being. That was His message to the original Twelve Disciples: "By this shall all men know that ye are my disciples, if ye have love one to another" (John 13:35). Years earlier, Neal had perhaps unknowingly planted in his own mind the seeds of such a realization—such a duty and such a blessing—when he quoted Harold B. Lee at the very end of his first book, *A More Excellent Way:*

> I came to a night, some years ago, when, on my bed, I realized that before I could be worthy of the high place to which I had been called, I must love and forgive every soul that walked the earth, and in that time I came to know . . . a peace and a direction, and a comfort . . . I knew were from a divine source.

In the midst of such reflections, Neal wrote to President Kimball on July 29, apologizing for his condition at the time of his call: "My fumbling response in the temple . . . was heartfelt if not articulate." Then he added the key insight he'd been feeling, the one that had been

A favorite form of relaxation— playing with grandchildren

weighing on him with its deep blend of burden and privilege: "I realize, of course, that my real response [to the call] will come through the life that I live. That life . . . will be better not only because of the calling . . . but because of the [example] of your own life." A few months later, he would tell his Brethren of the Twelve, "My solemn obligation is to become more like Him step by step." And the core of becoming more "like Him" was to feel the same love He feels for others.

For Neal Maxwell, the injunction to seek charity resonated to the core of his soul. He had long nourished an inborn sense of empathy and compassion but now found this instinct everlastingly expanded by the call to the holy apostleship. He knew he was not called to this sacred service because of his intellectual or administrative gifts. Those things are helpful, but when the time comes to fill a vacancy among the Twelve, the inquiry is of a spiritual order—to find the one who should be "ordained to be a witness with us of his resurrection. . . . And they prayed, and said, Thou, Lord, which knowest the hearts of all men, shew whether of these . . . thou hast chosen, that he may take part of this ministry and apostleship" (Acts 1:22, 24–25).

There had been impressive flashes along the path of Neal's life. But more important was the fundamental direction the path had taken—in the quiet shadows, turns, and forks in the road; in sunshine and in shade; with footsteps quick and slow. He was now prepared to offer God his heart and his life, that he might more fully "receive true charity," "this love, *which he hath bestowed upon all who are true follow-ers* of his Son, Jesus Christ" (Moroni 7:48; italics added). In the years to come, the spiritual gift of charity would nourish the compassion Neal had already been learning, until President James E. Faust, without knowing how much Neal had tried to take Harold B. Lee's experience to heart, could one day say that Neal's most unique contribution to the Church was "his ability to love everyone. Whatever their circumstances, whatever their situation, their condition, he . . . carries with him the essence of the true love of the Savior."

Within a month, Neal and Colleen took their first international trip since the new call. They held meetings in Hawaii, Tokyo, Singapore, and Perth, Australia. In Perth, Neal was assigned to choose a new stake president for the Dianella stake, close to where the Perth Australia Temple now stands. They also met with the missionaries of the Perth mission, whose president was Daniel Ludlow, Neal's old friend from the Correlation Department days. Bruce Mitchell, an Australian regional representative who had assisted in the stake reor-ganization, said he was eager to hear what deep doctrine these two tow-ering intellects, Neal Maxwell and Dan Ludlow, would preach to the missionaries, especially given Elder Maxwell's new role. To Brother Mitchell's delighted surprise, Neal and Dan introduced their doctrinal instruction with personal stories about how they learned to set goals and work hard when both had raised purebred pigs as young men—a joint interest the two had rekindled that morning on their way to the meeting.

On the long airplane ride home from Australia, Neal began think-ing and praying about October conference. This would be his first talk as a member of the Twelve. So much about the call was barely settling in. He honestly felt that in that circle, he would "be the least, long after being the last so ordained." Still, although many other things might take him years to master, he was very clear about one thing—he felt an intimate, inexpressible gratitude for the Savior.

Not knowing quite where his feelings were leading, he pulled out a yellow legal pad and began to write down the ideas that flooded into his mind. As he wrote, high above the Pacific, he lost track of time and space. Soon tears were unself-consciously running down his cheeks. He brushed them away and kept writing. A flight attendant noticed him and asked if he was all right, if she could do anything. He assured her he was fine and kept on writing. Those notes became the basis for his talk.

Twenty years later, when asked which of his numerous publications had mattered the most to him, Neal said it would be this October 1981 general conference talk because his "life had been changed [so much] since the previous conference." He also received a greater outpouring of response from Church members to this talk than any he'd known, before or since. Arthur Henry King, a literature teacher at Brigham Young University whom Neal admired, once explained how the pinnacle of an author's creative form reveals what content matters most to that author—he will exert his highest skill to express the ideas that mean the most to him. That natural confluence of form and substance seems to have occurred in this talk, which Neal titled "O, Divine Redeemer":

> Can we, even in the depths of disease, tell Him anything at all about suffering? In ways we cannot comprehend, our sicknesses and infirmities were borne by Him even before these were borne by us. . . .
>
> Can those who yearn for hearth or home instruct Him as to what it is like to be homeless or on the move? . . . And when we feel so alone, can we presume to teach Him who trod "the wine-press alone" anything at all about feeling forsaken? . . .
>
> Can we teach Him about enduring irony? His remaining possession, a cloak, was gambled for even as He died. . . . Yet the very earth was His footstool! Jesus gave mankind living water so that we shall never thirst again, yet on the cross He was given vinegar! . . .
>
> Or can we inform the Atoner about feeling the sting of ingratitude when one's service goes unappreciated or unnoticed? . . .
>
> Should we seek to counsel Him in courage? Should we rush forth eagerly to show Him our mortal medals—our scratches and bruises—He who bears His five special wounds? . . .
>
> Indeed, we cannot teach Him anything! But we can listen to Him. We can love Him, we can honor Him, we can worship

Him. We can keep His commandments, and we can feast upon His scriptures! . . .

How dare some treat His ministry as if it were all beatitudes and no declaratives! How myopic it is to view His ministry as all crucifixion and no resurrection! How provincial to perceive it as all Calvary and no Palmyra! . . .

Soon, however, all flesh shall see Him together. All knees shall bow in His presence, and all tongues confess His name. . . . Tongues which have never before spoken His name except in gross profanity will do so then—and worshipfully. . . .

All will then . . . see how human indifference to God—not God's indifference to humanity—accounts for so much suffering. Then we will see the true story of mankind—. . . the mortal accounts of the human experience will be but graffiti on the walls of time. . . . Yes, Armageddon lies ahead. But so does Adam-ondi-Ahman! . . .

So as the shutters of human history begin to close as if before a gathering storm, and as events scurry across the human scene like so many leaves before a wild wind—those who stand before the warm glow of the gospel fire can be permitted a shiver of the soul. Yet in our circle of certitude we know . . . that there will be no final frustration of God's purposes. . . .

Humbly, therefore, I promise to go whithersoever I am sent, . . . acknowledging in the tremblings of my soul that I cannot fully be His Special Witness unless my life is fully special. I close with pleadings from the hymn, "O, Divine Redeemer!" which . . . are my pleadings:

> Ah! Turn me not away,
> Receive me, tho' unworthy, . . .
> Hear thou my cry . . .
> Shield me in danger . . .
> Grant me pardon, and remember not,
> Remember not, O Lord, my sins! . . .
> Help me, my Savior!

Neal was sensing by now what would become increasingly clear as each year passed—everything else about his life except his family would be subsidiary in significance to his apostolic call. "This is the Lord's work," he would feel and he would say. "There is nothing else that even approaches it in significance." His calling was not more significant than that of any other Apostle; indeed, it is the calling that makes each Apostle significant. Over time, Neal would give all of himself to the call, letting it shape and mold him, until President Boyd K. Packer would say:

> Neal is an Apostle, and it shows. It shows as much in our meetings, maybe more than it does outside our meetings. . . . The ordination and the office [are] the standard by which he makes his measurements. He's in the world but not of the world. . . . His call as "prophet, seer, and revelator" . . . isn't an idle designation or just a title. . . . The testimony of Christ is the spirit of prophecy. And he has that testimony and witness. [Against that standard,] you won't find him wanting. All these other things . . . personality, experience, capacity, efficiency [must] be measured against the more significant deeper things. If you're going to find Neal, you'll have to find him there.

The First Presidency and the Twelve have the unique right to bestow, when so prompted, an apostolic blessing not only upon individuals but also upon entire congregations. Elder Maxwell has experienced some sacred moments at the time he has given such blessings. They are not usually recorded in writing, but people have occasionally sent him letters that reflect what happened. Just a few examples will illustrate how Church members have responded to his influence.

Neal pronounced one of his early blessings on September 18, 1982, under unusual circumstances in the Chicago Heights stake. Just before the Saturday night session of a stake conference, a massive electrical power outage occurred in the area around the chapel. The meeting proceeded anyway, lit by a few lanterns and aided by a portable sound system. At the meeting's close, Neal pronounced an apostolic blessing on the group. Robert C. Nichols Jr., the former stake president, described in a letter what happened. As the blessing began, electric power was restored to the chapel, as "the bank of lights in the ceiling . . . stirred into an uncertain, brownish glow." The light increased as the blessing continued. When Neal concluded with his testimony of the Savior, "all the lights in the chapel . . . intensified to white, and bathed the awed assembly."

Stake president Robert Garff wrote Elder Maxwell after a stake conference in Bountiful, Utah, on May 18, 1987, that

> the highlight [of the conference] was the Apostolic blessing. . . . many people have said to me that it was a spiritual feast. Some . . . said they noticed a change in your countenance and a unique tone in your voice. . . . The journals of our stake [members] are full of reflections from that weekend.

This observation echoed something Neal mentioned in his personal notes during the early 1980s. He said that in recent years, on perhaps a half dozen occasions, he had the experience of sensing that "the Spirit of our Heavenly Father was especially present" in a conference or other meeting where he had spoken. In each case, one or two people had "come up after the meeting and reported that there was an aura or glow about [him as he] spoke." He believed that what they saw indicated to them, probably more than to him, "that the Lord was with us and approved" what was happening "at least at that moment."

Later in 1987, Neal left a blessing with the Orem Utah South Stake at the conclusion of a stake reorganization. President Leland Howell, who had just been released, wrote that the blessing was "an incredibly touching experience. The Spirit was so very evident and the content was personal to the needs of our people. . . . We were deeply touched by the Christlike way you related with us. That aspect of your visit was the most 'special witness' you could have borne." Another person in that congregation was Carl S. Hawkins, former dean of the BYU Law School, a thoughtful man for whom writing this letter to Neal was an unusual step:

> Your inspired and informative testimony of the Savior and your Apostolic blessing . . . added immeasurably. I observed and felt many members of the congregation moved as [my wife] and I were by the intimately personal import of the blessing, in ways that could only be explained as the influence of the Holy Spirit. I believe you know me well enough to know that I write this not to flatter you, but because I want to add my witness to the power of the Spirit that was operating through your holy Apostleship.

FORTY-FOUR

THE TWELVE
AS A COUNCIL

SITTING AMONG THE TWELVE for two decades, Neal gradually saw his Quorum begin to function more as a body of generalists
and less as a collection of specialists. More and more, they became the
Council of the Twelve, a brotherhood in which his inclusive, empathetic
personality came to feel very much at home. During these years, Neal
and his Brethren also became ever more aligned with their central role
as "special witnesses of the name of Christ in all the world" (D&C
107:23). One factor that contributed to this process was a Churchwide
pattern of increased delegation of authority. Another was the way
responsibilities were assigned for both the Church's programs and the
Church's geographical areas. And another, at least in Neal's case, was
attitudinal.

As the Church grew internationally, the First Presidency delegated an increasing load to the Twelve, and the Twelve delegated an
increasing load to the Seventy and to stake presidents. When Neal
was first called as an Assistant to the Twelve, for example, General
Authorities ordained every bishop and one of the Apostles ordained
every stake patriarch. Stake presidents now perform those ordinations.

A similar pattern prevails among the Church's governing quorums. President Kimball, for instance, had organized numerous area conferences, beginning in major international centers, and then, increasingly, in key cities of the United States. This was the First Presidency's way of bringing the feel of general conference to those who lived too far away ever to attend conference in Salt Lake City. Area conferences also let assigned members of the First Presidency, the Twelve, and the Seventy attend in small teams to draw closer to the Saints in a personalized setting, which was always presided over by a member of the First Presidency.

Then on October 16, 1983, Elders Boyd K. Packer and Neal A. Maxwell of the Twelve presided at the Church's first regional conference for four stakes in London and the surrounding area. Perhaps reflecting the unprecedented nature of the event, the Saturday afternoon priesthood leadership session in the Hyde Park chapel attracted nearly 100 percent of the leaders. Elders Packer and Maxwell both sensed the meeting's significance, knowing that the growth of the Church would make it ever more necessary for the Twelve to represent the First Presidency at such gatherings around the world—gatherings in which each congregation was large enough to fill the Salt Lake Tabernacle.

In a signal that both visitors recognized the prophetic calling of each member of the First Presidency and the Twelve, Neal stood to conduct the meeting and began, "Brethren, we've come to you today in our true identity as apostles of the Lord Jesus Christ." Within a few years, each multistake region would periodically experience a regional conference with one member of the Twelve assigned to preside, thus building an increased personal rapport between the members of the Church and those they sustain as prophets.

At Church headquarters, the First Presidency delegated a key form of authority when they assigned one of the Twelve to preside over each of the three Executive Councils that had mirrored the three-fold mission of the Church since 1982—the councils for missionary work, priesthood and auxiliary organizations, and temples and family history. This decision was significant because it authorized members of the

The Quorum of the Twelve shortly after Elder Maxwell's call

Twelve to preside in the key correlating bodies of the Church, which included members of both the ecclesiastical arm (the Twelve and the Seventy) and the temporal arm (the Presiding Bishopric). Neal presided over the Temple and Family History Executive Council from 1994 to 2000.

The increasing level of delegation from the Twelve to the Seventy may be seen in comparing some of the "firsts" that Neal experienced in his early service as an Apostle with the pattern that would prevail later. In the early 1980s, for instance, Neal felt it was "a big deal" to see the creation of a new stake or the selection of a new stake president. Since the Church's early days, new stake presidents had often been selected by two members of the Twelve, which was perhaps one reason why some stake presidents wondered if they were to be released when they learned that an Apostle was assigned to their stake conference.

At the time of Neal's call to the Twelve, it was typical for one Apostle to preside at stake reorganizations, assisted by a Seventy or a regional representative. In May 1982, for instance, Neal called a man in Idaho to be the new president of his stake. He was an older man who wore hearing aids in both ears. After Neal issued the call, the man said he had been awakened at 2:00 that morning by a prompting that he would be called to preside over the stake. Later that day, Neal called a new high councilor, who also said that he had been awakened the night before. He woke his wife and told her he'd had an impression about who the new stake president would be, that he himself would be called to the high council, and that he would decide to shave off his beard—all of which occurred in that order.

By the early 1990s, however, it was not uncommon for the Twelve to approve several new stakes in a given week, and full-time General Authorities from the Seventy presided at most stake reorganizations. A few years later, part-time Area Authority Seventies were authorized to reorganize stakes when so assigned. These changes reflected the reality that in Neal's lifetime the number of Apostles hadn't increased but the number of Latter-day Saints had increased nearly twenty fold. So the number of Church members for each of the fifteen Apostles grew from about 40,000 to about 800,000.

Neal also found notable during his first year in the Twelve the calls he issued to several new regional representatives, something only the Twelve did then. Within two decades, however, members of the Seventy were typically authorized to extend similar calls on behalf of the First Presidency to new Area Authority Seventies. Neal also heard his first report from a returning mission president in 1982—again, something only the Twelve did then. In earlier years, the First Presidency had always received those reports. A decade later, returning mission presidents had their exit interviews with Seventies in the Area Presidency who supervised their respective missions.

Another set of events in the late 1990s brought the First Presidency and the Twelve increasingly together in their roles as the Church's prophets, seers, and revelators. These fifteen Apostles issued three significant prophetic statements to the Church and to the world. One of these was in 1995, *The Family: A Proclamation to the World.* Another was *The Living Christ,* a solemn declaration of apostolic witness to the divinity of Christ, signed by each member of the First Presidency and the Twelve in January 2000 in celebration of the new millennium. The third step was a widely broadcast video presentation called *Witnesses of Christ,* fifteen apostolic testimonies of Christ, shown first at the time of April 2000 general conference. Neal welcomed these events because "the members of the Church deserve to hear our witness and to experience us in a way that belongs to the whole congregation," not just the local leaders. "We're getting better at that."

These examples suggest a general pattern in the 1980s and 90s that increasingly identified the Twelve with the First Presidency's spiritual ministry to the Church as a whole while gradually shifting the "operations" of the Church to Seventies and to stake presidents.

Another factor that enhanced the role of the Twelve as a council was a gradual shift in the nature of assignments to oversee Church departments and geographic areas. By the year 2000, Elder Maxwell would say, "We're Apostles first and then we may have assignments, rather than having the assignments seem to dictate our role to us." He thought this let the Twelve be more strategic and less tactical in their orientation. When he first joined the quorum, however, his brethren had sometimes seemed identified primarily as specialists in missionary work, or family history, or some other programmatic or administrative role. A similar kind of specialization, which sometimes led to advocacy, could occur in geographic assignments. Sensing that members of the Twelve shouldn't become overly identified with one part of the world, Elder Bruce R. McConkie used to say that he wasn't "the Archbishop of South America"—even when he was assigned to oversee the Church's affairs there.

The delegation of operational authority in the field took place primarily by increasing the responsibility of Area Presidencies, who were all Seventies. Delegation at Church headquarters occurred when members of the Presidency of the Seventy became the executive directors of most of the principal Church departments, aided by others from among the Seventy. These teams became the primary General Authority advisers to the departments, which in turn were made accountable to an executive council in which a member of the Twelve presided.

The movement of the Twelve toward being a council of generalists was further accelerated by a globalization process across many cultures that required more emphasis on the Church's general core values rather than on particular programs. Another factor was a conscious shift of attitude, as illustrated by the way Neal's own views became more general.

Before his call to the Twelve, Neal had been given a series of assignments to direct such specific operations as the Church Educational System or the Correlation Department. After his call to the Twelve in 1981, however, he began losing interest in being identified with any particular program or specialty, including education. He found himself wanting to focus on the "basics of the gospel," such as the scriptures, doctrine, temples, and families. He had always believed the Church's programs were to serve its people, rather than letting program needs dictate personal priorities. But more and more now, Neal would wonder which of the Church programs were really essential, especially in an international Church.

As part of this attitudinal change, Neal consciously worked on himself to repress his former instincts to advocate particular interests or solutions, not wanting his hobbies or passions to seek undue attention in quorum discussions. He came to prize the collegial relationship of the Twelve, in which "one gets a chance to see if his ideas will have a life of their own." And if those ideas don't fly with the group, then "maybe you'd better let them go." After all, "if my views are sound, why is it that my Brethren don't see it that way?"

At an earlier time in his life, he might have ground his teeth with impatience over a sometimes slow-moving group process that seeks unanimity before taking action. But now he not only could tolerate such a process but could increasingly see its wisdom. Drawing on his political science background, he saw in the deliberative process of the Twelve an analogy to James Reston's comment about the necessary role of both the "sail" and the "anchor" in comparing the executive to the legislative branches of government. The Twelve may seem "notoriously slow" at times, he said, but he could see that their need for unanimity ("And every decision made by [this quorum] must be by the unanimous voice of the same"; D&C 107:27) was not just a "procedural nicety." To have real agreement by "the next presidents of the Church sitting there in the Twelve" ensures "continuity of policy." So unanimity means not

*Greeting Elders
Bruce R. McConkie
and Boyd K. Packer
at general
conference*

mere assent but a willingness to support. And if it takes time for that willingness to develop, someone may have to "wait a little longer."

As one who had a tendency toward impatience and "steadying the ark" in his younger days, Neal was speaking with introspective modesty when he told the General Authorities in their June 2001 temple meeting that when he senses an obstacle in their decision-making processes, he now tries to ask himself, "Lord, is it I?" There had been a few times during his service in the Twelve when, he now realized, he'd been "trying too hard to fix things," putting his "shoulder to the wheel," only to discover that he was pushing not a wheel but "a stationary hitching post." In a similar meeting a few years earlier, he had said "how delightful it is to hear the small talk of great men, such as the First Presidency, and how each of us . . . [depends] on each other to take the wheat in our respective lives and with the breath of kindness blow the chaff away."

Elder Maxwell's effort to improve his own commitment to the nature of the apostolic call and the spirit of congenial brotherhood in the quorum has helped some younger members of the group. Elder Holland, for instance, says that Neal has

> grown into the office the way I want to grow into it. He thinks about the spiritual role of an Apostle, and [that role] has become

infinitely more important to him than any managerial or administrative role.

In his younger days, he liked to be in the thick of things,
and he always was. The senior Brethren drew him into it, often
whether he wanted it or not. He was in on 'the action.' I don't
think 'the action' intrigues him much now. . . .

Now he'd just like to be an Apostle, bear his testimony and
quote from the Book of Mormon.

He has grown and blossomed into a larger apostolic ministry, mindful of what it means to be a disciple of the Lord. . . .
He wants to be a disciple and he works at it.

Elder Holland finds that in Neal's relationships with other quorum members, this attitude has combined with his natural tendency to
facilitate group interaction and "bring people together," making him a
catalyst to help sustain the spirit of sweet counsel among his Brethren.
He encourages harmony in discussions where opinions on important
issues may differ. Always respectful of others' views, "regardless of how
strongly he feels," Neal will "find a way to offer the conciliatory comment." He's always been a good moderator, but "this is more. He has
grown." No matter what the issue, "he doesn't lose the spirit of his calling over it." And that lets him contribute to the *spirit* of the Quorum.

Of this same quality, Elder Eyring said that Elder Maxwell looks
ahead enough to "bring forward aggressive ideas," telling his Brethren,
"we really need to deal with this." Yet, at the same time, he "lifts the
level of the conversation." He is able to "offer an alternative without
inflaming anybody and yet getting it seriously considered. He's really
good at that."

Neal has had his own mentors about brotherhood among the
Twelve. In his early years in the group, he was on a trip to the Middle
East with Elder Howard W. Hunter. One day in Egypt, Neal said,
"When I awakened after a weary and dusty day together with him . . .
[Elder Hunter] was quietly shining my shoes, a task he had hoped to
complete unseen." Once President James E. Faust said his feeling for
Neal is "akin to that that I have for my own blood brothers. We seem
to be symbiotic, in terms of our approach to problems. . . . You're just

at peace with him." A few years earlier while in Brazil, Elder Faust had written to Neal, "Conferences come and go and we have too little time [together]. I feel an emptiness and a loss in not having been able to spend at least a relaxed . . . half an hour with you."

When Elder Russell M. Nelson was called to the Twelve, he sent Neal a note expressing gratitude for "the privilege of sitting beside you, that your effective teaching and tutoring may continue infinitely." After they'd been assigned to a regional conference together, Elder Nelson thanked Neal for his efforts to keep growing, having noticed "how much you have learned and are thereby able to teach since our last assignment together. This . . . stimulates me to try to do better."

Elder David B. Haight, who has enjoyed savoring Neal's "fertile mind" since their days on the Leadership Committee in the 1960s, has empathized with Elder Maxwell's "gallant struggle with leukemia." As his "heaven-sent remission" has continued, Elder Haight now rejoices "as I'm able to squeeze his hand and look into his face and witness the improvement in his health."

Another of Neal's early role models and confidantes in the circle of the First Presidency and the Twelve was President N. Eldon Tanner, who served as a counselor to Presidents McKay, Smith, Lee, and Kimball. From their first association on the Utah Legislative Study Committee, Neal admired President Tanner's quiet competence. As they worked together through the CES and Correlation Department years, he discovered President Tanner's "remarkable ability" in organizational, financial, and spiritual matters. "Take him a seven-page document, and he'll find the one thing in it" that has some "softness or fuzziness," not only with numbers but ideas. Neal noticed that "President Tanner had the meekness which permitted him to advance an idea and then let it have a life of its own rather than oversponsor it with his immense personal prestige in order to give it some advantage in the arena of decision making." In his general assessment, Neal felt that President Tanner was one of the greatest counselors in the First Presidency "in this dispensation." And "when the history of the Church is written, it will be very kind to President Tanner."

So there was tender personal meaning for Neal in their occasional exchanges, like the little homemade birthday poem President Tanner sent him once, writing a phrase next to each letter of the name "Neal A. Maxwell," including "Needless to say, it is/ Easy to express our sincere appreciation/ And love to you . . ." When President Tanner passed away in November 1982, Neal was asked to dedicate his grave.

One way Neal nurtured this spirit of brotherhood was by trying to discipline himself about preserving confidences, following channels, and avoiding critical comments about other people—even though he is sometimes passionate about his own views and is always communicating with other people, in and out of group settings. Most people who have worked closely with him during his years in the Twelve single out, with various adjectives, his peacemaker quality, which they say makes Neal a consummate team player, especially for a group desiring to function as a "council."

Elder Cecil Samuelson, for example, has noticed that no one at Church headquarters is more respectful of appropriate roles and relationships among the Brethren. Elder Monte Brough worked with Neal from 1993 to 1998, when Monte was executive director of the Family History Department and Neal was chairman of his governing council. He said nobody is more loyal than is Elder Maxwell to the people both above him and below him on the organizational chart, which gives him "enormous credibility" with his associates. Bud Scruggs said that for a person who is as open as Neal is, he is amazingly "circumspect about not criticizing the other Brethren," even if he may disagree, and he keeps confidences, even among friends and even on unimportant issues.

In the spirit of this commitment to one another, each member of the *Council* of the Twelve shares fully the scriptural mandate to "build up the church, and regulate *all* the affairs of the same in *all* nations" (D&C 107:33; italics added). Regardless of the rotating individual assignments in a given year, each Apostle in the worldwide Church has increasingly come to feel a worldwide ministry, embracing not only all Church programs but also all continents and all people. Consider, as an illustration, Elder Maxwell's official list of conference and special meeting assignments for 1993:

Date	Location	Assignment
January 30	Manti, Utah	Stake Conference
February 13	Provo, Utah	Regional Conference (BYU married stakes)
February 20	Salt Lake City	Dedication of Cathedral of the Madeleine
February 27	El Paso, Texas	Stake Conference
March 6	Hermosillo, Mexico	Regional Conference
March 13	Toronto, Canada	Stake Conference
April 9–19	Mongolia and Beijing, China	Dedicate Mongolia, visit Chinese officials
April 25–26	San Diego, California	San Diego Temple Dedication
May 1	Ogden, Utah	Regional Conference
May 22	Paris, France	Stake Conference
June 12	Twin Falls, Idaho	Regional Conference
June 19	Springville, Utah	Stake Reorganization
July 4	Provo, Utah	Freedom Festival
August 22	Salt Lake City	Training new Utah North Area stake presidents
August 28	Nyssa, Oregon	Stake Conference
September 11	Montreal, Canada	Regional Conference
October 16	Raleigh, North Carolina	Regional Conference
October 23	Hattiesburg, Mississippi	Regional Conference
November 6	Tokyo, Japan	Mission Presidents' Seminar, Area training
November 13	Seoul, Korea	Area training
November 17	Hong Kong	Area training
November 20	Manila, Philippines	Mission Presidents' Seminar, Area training
December 4	Chicago, Illinois	Chicago Temple workers' meeting

This was quite an array of major assignments, all over the world in one year—including mainland China and Mongolia. Yet it was typical of the pattern followed by all of the Twelve as the twentieth century came to a close. Within the span of Neal's own Church service years at the general level, he had personally witnessed the fulfillment of the Lord's words: the Quorum of the Twelve would not just hold meetings together in Salt Lake City. Rather, "The Twelve are a *Traveling Presiding High Council,* to officiate in the name of the Lord . . . in all nations" (D&C 107:33; italics added), traveling not just in the Western United States with a few international ties but everywhere. Indeed, as Neal was allowed to experience firsthand, the "Twelve hold the keys to open up the authority of my kingdom upon the four corners of the earth, and after that to send my word to every creature" (D&C 124:128).

At the same time, Elder Maxwell felt that the needs that inexorably sent the Twelve throughout the world must be balanced against the continuing need for them to counsel together as much as possible. Thus in a General Authority training meeting in October 2001, he quoted Joseph Smith's counsel to nourish the brotherhood and unity of the Twelve: "Let the Twelve Apostles keep together. You will do more good to keep together, not travel together all the time, but meet in conference from place to place, and associate together, and not be found long apart from each other."

FORTY-FIVE

OPENING THE DOORS OF THE NATIONS

No THEME IN MODERN CHURCH HISTORY is more dramatic than this one—opening the doors of the nations. By 1974, the Church had become secure enough organizationally, financially, and, most of all, spiritually that President Kimball was prompted to ask the Saints to pray that the Lord would open the doors of all nations to the preaching of the restored gospel. The Saints prayed. In 1978, he received the revelation allowing universal access to the priesthood for every worthy male. The Saints wept.

In 1989, four years after President Kimball's death, the Berlin Wall fell, symbolizing with resounding clarity the collapse of communism in Eastern Europe and the Soviet Union. As the Iron Curtain came down, the curtain in the next act of the Restoration's drama went up, as nation after nation opened doors long since closed to religion. To the people who lived through them, these events were so stunning that no ordinary Church member would have dared to predict what actually happened, even days before it occurred.

Yet the Lord had already announced as the Restoration began: "The voice of warning shall be unto all people, by the mouths of my disciples, whom I have chosen in these last days. And they shall go forth and none shall stay them, for I the Lord have commanded them" (D&C 1:4–5). Moreover, He had made it clear that the Twelve Apostles have a special charge to "build up the church . . . *in all nations.*" Thus they are "sent out, holding the keys, to *open the door* by the proclamation of the gospel of Jesus Christ" (D&C 107:33, 35; italics added).

Neal Maxwell, long curious about large-scale historical and political events, has felt deep personal gratitude at being given firsthand experience with this stirring apostolic charge:

> Since President Kimball, this sunburst of opening up the nations of the world has come and, for those of us who got to see that firsthand, it's just been a great privilege. You know, who would have guessed a stake in West Africa? . . .
>
> To have been in this niche of history has been a great blessing. . . . But it's happened so fast, when you think about it historically. . . .
>
> When I first went to Germany . . . I used to say to priesthood leaders, "How long before that Berlin Wall will come down?". . . "Oh, Bruder Maxvell," they'd say, "seventy years." And they meant it. It looked that way to me too.

President Hinckley has described Neal's keen interest in the globalization of the Church as "characteristic . . . of the Twelve generally. Neal has an understanding of the apostolic calling to open the doors of all nations. That calling is well defined by the Lord, and Neal is trying to carry out that mandate."

For Neal, the issues surrounding the Church's rapid internationalization are, from one perspective, very complex and daunting. He has taken a lifelong interest in the world's history, its peoples, and its cultures. He is well-traveled and well-read, experienced in analyzing the financial and demographic detail of both the costs and the benefits of expanding the worldwide Church Educational System. His personal heritage in the Church carries both the convert's perspective of his father and the pioneer heritage of his mother. He has noticed how the strength of his parents' temple marriage and deep gospel roots has blessed their posterity across four very faithful generations. Then he has faced the apostolic charge to help open the doors of the nations in the days of the Church's most historic global moment. He has wanted not to "shrink in the face of such a charge but to be realistic about the effort, the risks, and the patience needed to establish the Church" for the long haul.

Elder Alexander Morrison, who is himself well informed and reflective about the broad topic of international development, believes Neal has a remarkable capacity "to look at the Church worldwide . . . to look for trends, to look for things happening outside of Utah." His background and his sense of history help him "understand that what we do today influences where we will be ten years from now."

In addition, Neal is able to "separate culture from doctrine" in trying to understand the Church in various cultures. As he looks at a multicultural Church, he will often understand when difficulties faced by Church members in a given country stem from "a behavioral problem, a cultural problem, not a doctrinal issue." Having worked closely with Neal on such matters, Brother Morrison thinks Neal clearly wants to help all of us have "a better understanding of our world position," to grasp the implications of being "a church for the whole world. That's been the big issue of his apostleship."

For such reasons Neal understood, in ways few people would, why President Tanner was looking so pensive that day in the mid-1970s, after President Kimball announced his prophetic call to take the gospel throughout the world. With his stewardship for Church finances, President Tanner felt obliged to wear the hat of practicality and honestly wondered what it would mean to establish the Church welfare program in India—or Africa.

It was also President Tanner who first aroused Neal's curiosity about what today's Church calls the retention issue—how well the Church is retaining its new converts and building its base of experienced lay leadership, especially in countries where the Church is relatively new. Within Neal's first year as a General Authority, he was assigned to visit an international area of the Church that was experiencing very rapid growth. While there, he remembered having heard President Tanner wonder aloud whether this growth was coming too fast. Was the Church running faster than it had strength? (see Mosiah 4:27). So he listened carefully, dismayed at the report of a stake president who said of many new converts, "Our bishops have never known them." Soon after he returned home, President Tanner asked him, referring to convert retention, "I'm right, am I not?" And with what Neal had found, he had to say yes.

Another Apostle who has also long emphasized the need for better convert retention, beginning when "he was the entire staff for the Missionary Department," is President Gordon B. Hinckley, who has made improved retention one of the signature themes of his presidency of the Church. From the early years of his ministry in the Twelve, then, Neal was one among others of his brethren who spoke up persistently about retention—which he called "real growth." That is, when missionaries moved into new areas, when convert baptisms increased rapidly in certain missions, he would always ask whether the number of people attending sacrament meeting and paying tithing was growing at the same rate as the number of recorded baptisms. If only the baptismal numbers grew, there was little real growth.

Similarly, as the number of temples has multiplied in recent years, Neal has applied his concept of real growth to temple work, gently urging his fellow General Authorities to remember that "it will be easier to build these temples than to fill them" with temple patrons and ordinance workers. Elder Oaks says Elder Maxwell's concern and approach to real growth has been "a major contribution." He has kept "raising it and raising it" as a major issue in discussions about the stewardship of the Twelve "to build up the church and regulate all the affairs of the same" (D&C 107:33).

When he was first contact (the member of the Quorum of the Twelve assigned to oversee an area of the world in its relationship with Church headquarters) for the United Kingdom and Africa from 1987 to 1990, Neal asked Jeffrey R. Holland, then the Area President, to make a special examination of the U.K. files containing Church membership records with unknown addresses. Once enough records were identified, Neal urged a "lost sheep" project to locate and, where possible, reactivate those with whom the Church had lost contact. The project brought many back to the fold.

During his years as first contact for Asia, from 1990 to 1995, Neal had similar concerns about Church growth in Japan, where the number of less-active members had been growing at a faster rate than the number of active members. The Fukuoka Mission President was Cyril Figuerres, a former researcher for the Correlation Department, which Neal had helped create in 1976. With the combination of Cyril's background and his own interest in drawing on empirical data, Neal urged Cyril to identify and address the root problems in the mission's membership growth.

The result of these efforts was the "Ammon" pilot project, which drew on Elder Maxwell's long-term, multigenerational perspective to make significant adaptations in both member and missionary programs "without tampering with 'non-negotiables' such as doctrines and ordinances." The project recognized the unique needs of the Japanese people, who have stronger ties to group associations than is typical of Western culture, and only 2 percent of whom have a Christian background. Under Elder Maxwell's direction, with concurrence from the Area Presidency, President Figuerres designed the project to improve real growth on the individual level, the family level, and the "community of Saints" level.

Drawing on the research findings, the project implemented several interventions suited for Latter-day Saints in the Japanese culture. For example, the mission provided extended "greenhouse" nurturing for investigators and new converts, holding missionaries accountable for strengthening new converts every week for an entire year. The project also worked to "create a community of Saints where individuals and families could experience righteousness, joy, and social integration in a spiritually enriched, nurturing environment." Over time the number of convert baptisms nearly doubled, the proportion of converts who remained active increased significantly, and the number of newly reactivated members more than tripled.

For Cyril, working on the Ammon project with Elder Maxwell was "like a spiritual odyssey" that gave him "a glimpse of . . . the global leadership needed to develop a truly global Church." Elder Maxwell, he said, "never loses sight of the big picture and the grand 'why.' He is visionary, forward-looking, with an eye fixed just beyond the horizon." His "humble but serious involvement with the Japanese members" showed them "how much members of the Twelve care about their unique challenges and spiritual lives."

Elder Maxwell also invited Elder Alexander Morrison to help him study "real growth" issues during Neal's term as chairman of the Church's Boundary and Leadership Change Committee from 1982 to 1993. Their efforts to understand what happened to Latter-day Saint families in Britain over several generations led to the insight that "very clearly" the "key to having a multigenerational church" is to have "LDS marriages at the beginning." Converts who don't marry Latter-day Saints are far more likely to "drop off the radar scope" of Church activity. And when the marriage is in the temple, the likelihood of ensuring the continued Church activity of an entire family over the generations is extremely high. From an update of an earlier Correlation Department study on LDS youth, Neal learned that LDS children in international areas whose parents are married in the temple are nine times more likely to serve missions and marry in the temple than are LDS children whose parents were not married in the temple. In the United States and Canada, the rate is now four times higher when parents marry in the temple.

Neal drew on this background when he participated in a training session for General and Area Authorities in April 2001 on the need to strengthen families as the long-range key to establishing the Church. Elder Maxwell took his theme from Isaiah 58:12: "Raise up the foundations of many generations." He said, "We seek successive generations of grandparents, parents, and children who are 'grounded, rooted, settled,' (Eph. 3:17; Col. 1:23) and sealed in the holy temple."

Because the process of building successive generations in the Church takes so much time, and because that process can be threatened by so many obstacles in countries where all Church members are first-generation converts, it would have been both natural, even predictable, for Neal to drag his feet a little and ask for more data, playing the part of the anchor rather than the sail in opening the doors of the nations. Yet as realistic as he was, and as deep as were his concerns about "real growth," when Neal found himself face-to-face with the apostolic charge to take the gospel to every nation, his reverence for his calling and his charge would not let him shrink. In a striking example of the sheer faith he drew from the nature of his office, he refused to take counsel from his fears. Once more, Spencer W. Kimball was his role model.

During his own long years in the Twelve, President Kimball's reputation as a very thorough stake conference visitor was legendary among stake presidents. He would plow deep furrows of analysis, examining statistics and trends, insisting with loving persistence on better performance and leadership accountability. But when the Lord prompted him to move the Church and stir the nations to open their doors, President Kimball's visionary side took over—always tempered with realistic demands, but the vision was clear. In the *Ensign* article Neal was asked to write in tribute after President Kimball's death, he described President Kimball's attitude toward the sometimes confounding uncertainties of really establishing the Church across the globe:

> Yes, there would be logistical problems as the Church was extended to the people of the world. Yes, there would be challenges funding the growth. . . . Yes, there would be immense leadership training problems. . . . Yes, there would be unevenness and disappointments in connection with the expansion of the work.
>
> He knew all those things, yet . . . he did not wait until everything was perfectly in order before acting. His trust included trust. If one tried to solve in advance all the problems which might occur later, he might never start! The capacity to trust the Lord for *continuous revelation* as to what would later need to be done was clearly a part of the makeup of this very special man.

Neal took this attitude as his guide, then, when he sometimes found himself asking how the Church would manage its growth in places where, for example, the people lacked the income necessary to pay enough tithing to fund their chapels and other costs of operating the Church. He felt the same spiritual urging that President Kimball had felt to just "do it" when an opportunity came to take the Church into a new country. "Partly it's the Spirit," he'd say, "the apostolic thrust, partly my feeling of increasing global awareness." Nevertheless, this didn't mean a helter-skelter process. Neal, joined by his Brethren of the Twelve, would constantly seek to "build the Church so that it's really established, and that we have [enough] active Melchizedek Priesthood holders, and people pay their tithing, and then the Lord will provide."

Elder Maxwell's experiences with the Area Presidencies, missionaries, and Church members in Africa and then in Asia illustrate his approach to globalization. The real beginning of missionary work in West Africa came with the revelation on priesthood in 1978. For twenty years before that time, however, a number of West Africans, mostly in Nigeria, had learned of the Restoration and the Book of Mormon and were asking for missionaries. In 1985, Neal dedicated West Africa's first Church-built meetinghouse at Cape Coast in the Ghana Accra Mission. There were 800 Church members in the Cape Coast District; 1,300 attended the dedication. Considering that Ghana is about the size of Oregon with a population of 13 million, of whom about 3,000 were by then Latter-day Saints, Neal could see immediately both the promise and the hurdles ahead for the Church there, but he was overcome by the promise.

Many Latter-day Saints in West Africa were educated and they spoke English well. Neal discovered for himself what he had heard from others—that the members were "already very religious, wonderful people" who "know their Bibles very well," reflecting their strong Christian heritage from earlier missionary efforts by other churches. As Elder Robert E. Sackley of the Seventy said while on a trip with Neal, "The intellectual African is searching for God. . . . If Africa has any message for us, it is that education ought to bring us closer to God." Yet the people also lived amid great poverty. To Neal, that "deprivation has prepared them for the gospel," giving them a sense of gratitude and "extra

The Aba Nigeria Stake was the first stake in west Africa; Elder Maxwell with the presidency of Aba Nigeria Stake and their wives and Elder and Sister Robert E. Sackley (far right)

gusto to do the work" of the Church. He was moved by the formal statement of welcome presented to him and Elder Russell C. Taylor of the Seventy by the Aba district presidency in Nigeria. They expressed gratitude to the Church for sending them missionaries, who

> marvel us with their high sense of devotion. . . . Kindly bear with us where there are some lapses. We are quite new in the doctrines of the Church. . . . We are optimistic that as we now read books and attend meetings regularly, we shall grow like other countries where the Church has found its foothold.

Then they asked Neal to convey their gratitude to "Spencer W. Kimball, Prophet of God."

On one visit to Africa, Neal called Thomas Appiah to be the new Accra district president in Ghana. The mission president, Miles Cunningham, trusted Brother Appiah so much that he'd always give him cash to purchase from local businesses whatever the Church needed, because if a white person went into a store, the price would be ten times higher. When Neal found that Thomas didn't have suitable clothing for his new Sunday duties, Neal gave him one of his own suits. Three years later, President Cunningham wrote Neal that Brother Appiah still "wears your suit with pride and honor."

More than a decade later, Neal was assigned to meet with a large group of missionaries in New York City. Preparing for the meeting, mission president Ronald Rasband "felt to ponder and prayerfully select [a missionary] whom the Lord would have me ask" to open the meeting with prayer. As he looked over the roster of names, the name of Joseph Appiah from Ghana "boldly stood out" to him. When President Rasband asked Elder Appiah to pray, the missionary wept, telling his mission president that Elder Maxwell had called his father to be district president and had sealed his parents in the Salt Lake Temple. After he was called to the Seventy, Elder Rasband told this story in general conference, illustrating how the Lord "inspired a mission president on behalf of one missionary." Only later did Elder Rasband learn about the suit Elder Maxwell had given to the missionary's father.

In May 1988 Neal joined Elder Robert E. Sackley of the Seventy to create the first stake in West Africa in Aba, Nigeria. David Eka, whom Neal called to be stake president, was surprised at the call, even though he'd been the district president. He worried that he "wasn't from the right tribe." Neal didn't know much about the tribes, he said, but assured the new president that he was acceptable. In 2001 Elder Maxwell set Brother Eka apart as a mission president.

The date of the Aba stake conference was almost exactly ten years after President Kimball's revelation on the priesthood in 1978. Neal had "felt particularly close to President Kimball," who had died in 1985, when the First Presidency and the Twelve approved the creation of this stake. They all knew it was the first stake in any dispensation composed entirely of black Church members. Neal told the Aba members about the handkerchief he had saved from the 1978 temple meeting and then showed them another handkerchief he'd brought for this historic day. He knew he would shed tears, and he did. The handkerchief is tucked safely near the other one in the Maxwell home.

Two years later, in 1990, Elder Maxwell was assigned to dedicate

In Swaziland, Africa, to dedicate that land for the preaching of the gospel; Elder Alexander B. Morrison is second from right on front row. The cloud provided privacy during the dedication

Swaziland and Lesotho, two small mountain kingdoms primarily within South Africa, for the preaching of the gospel. Generally, only Apostles dedicate a country, a special priesthood act and blessing arising from their divine commission, "being sent out, holding the keys, to open the door" of a nation (D&C 107:35). The Church had been established among Europeans in South Africa for many years, but since the 1978 revelation, "the Church of the future there had to take account" of the complete racial spectrum. While he was in the Durban stake conference, Neal kept thinking about the Savior's words that the gospel net gathereth of every kind. A racially mixed Church after a history of apartheid in South Africa created a poignant opportunity and need. It was a good time for the special blessing the dedication of a country allows.

So, joined by Elder Alexander B. Morrison of the Seventy and mission president R. J. Snow, Elder Maxwell and about fifty other people gathered reverently on a beautiful hill overlooking Mbabane, the capital city of Swaziland. Neal was mildly concerned that the hill was part of a local scenic attraction, and he felt a need for privacy. Rain had fallen all morning, but as the appointed time arrived, "the rain stopped and the clouds parted." After brief talks by Swazi members about the Church's history in their land, Neal spoke. Then he offered the dedicatory prayer. As he did so, President Snow said, "the clouds closed in around the small group and enclosed all of us as if we were in a room by ourselves. There was no rain, but we were alone together in the cloud on top of the hill." Neal felt the cloud had seemed to separate them from the outside world.

When Neal dedicated Lesotho, a twelve-year-old boy spoke just before the prayer. As he recounted the story of his people and the blessing of their finding the gospel, the boy began to cry. When he "mopped up his tears with his tie," probably wearing the only white shirt and tie he owned, it was "a very tender, emotional time" for Elder Maxwell and Elder Morrison.

Neal also learned from experiences in Africa about dealing with the opposition that threatens to close the gospel door once it has been opened. Because they'd received misinformation, Ghana's government in 1989 briefly banned the Church from holding meetings or sending missionaries into the country, but local leaders and members adapted and endured impressively. Beverly Campbell, director of the Church's international affairs office in Washington, D.C., learned from Ghana's ambassador to the United States that his people didn't understand what the Church was about, with its "many young men" who "dashed about the villages" but never "told the Village Elders why" they were there.

Beverly and others worked with Neal to develop a response that Area President Jeffrey Holland considered a brilliant handling of a very delicate situation, especially with the follow-through by local leaders. On very short notice, they sent to Ghana two African-American Latter-day Saints—Catherine Stokes from Chicago and Robert Stevenson from Alabama—with no instructions other than to explain what the Church was and how they felt about it. Sister Stokes said Elder Maxwell's only counsel on the phone was that her trip was "very important to the Church." In a press conference sponsored by Ghana's minister for culture and religion, Cathy was asked about the role of women in the Church. She responded that women "are and should be involved" in education and public life but their "most important responsibility" from God is to "preserve what is of value in the society for the children." When asked if Church members wear "magic underwear that makes [them] successful," she "laughed and responded 'we wish,'" adding that "we wear an undergarment that keeps us mindful of our promises [and] covenants to our Heavenly Father." With additional "tours and talk shows," the trip was successful not only for the Church, but for its individual participants. Cathy "marveled" as she realized

> how far the Lord has brought me to trust. That I, a black child of the south, weathered by segregation and the ravages of racial tensions that yet prevail in America, would experience complete trust through the Lord's messenger [Elder Maxwell], who happens to be a white man. Barriers had fallen—for the saints in Ghana—and for me.

In his apostolic role in Africa, Neal learned not only about opening the gospel door and keeping it open but also about keeping the door from blowing off its hinges. Elder Morrison and Elder Holland, who both served in the Area Presidency for the United Kingdom and Africa during Neal's years as first contact, said they all knew that the Church in West Africa "was being born in a day, and it had the potential to become too much too fast." It was a good time to apply Neal's instincts about real growth rather than to seek growth for its own sake. As one response, the Brethren divided the United Kingdom–Africa Area and gave Africa its own Area Presidency in 1990, with instructions to proceed with utmost caution, because, as Neal put it, "this is a continent that could swallow a church." The risk was and still is that the local culture could absorb the Church before its members are fully assimilated into the gospel culture. So the work has proceeded cautiously and steadily, following the guideline from the Twelve to build from "centers of strength."

After years of frustration and often failure among international social programs throughout Africa, Neal saw the Church there as "countercultural." "Our whole assumption is that we change the world by changing individuals. Ours is the original gospel of hope." This has required creative flexibility. In Nigeria, for example, unsafe conditions made it unwise for missionaries to be out of their apartments after dark. Yet activity among the local members was higher than many places in the United States. Neal saw it as a "wheat and tares" environment: it "will be very difficult, but they'll be okay" because the West African Saints are so faithful.

Asia was another part of the world where Elder Maxwell was called upon to exercise the apostolic keys to open new doors to the gospel. During his years as first contact there in the early 1990s, the Asia Area was divided, placing Korea and Japan in the Asia North Area and leaving the Asia Area Presidency with a little time on their hands— along with huge populations in countries long inaccessible to the Church. So Neal told them, "Look, we've got half the world in your area; let's start opening doors." Soon the Area Presidency was knocking on the doors of Asian nations, reaching out to places the Church had never officially entered: Mongolia, Cambodia, Nepal, India, Pakistan, and Laos.

The Asia Area also included that mysterious giant, China, a vast sea of humanity that had taken hold of Neal's heart when he first visited there in 1982 with the Lamanite Generation, a performing group from Brigham Young University. As various BYU groups became widely known and appreciated in China through their tours and their wholesome performances on national television, Neal saw those groups as an "Educational Elias," preparing for the day when the Church itself may be granted entry. Over the next two decades, he returned to China three more times, and each visit showed him another step in the country's economic progress, tantalizing him as it has many other LDS leaders who long for the day when that door of doors will swing open.

So he hasn't been in a hurry, and he repeatedly says that the Church goes in only through the front door. He also says it's been good for him to learn patience in dealing with China, where so much is at stake. In his geographic assignments as well as his role with the Church's Public Affairs Committee, he has cultivated relationships with Chinese officials, "knowing that it might take a long time and that the Lord would just

During Elder and Sister Maxwell's tour of the People's Republic of China in 1982

have to work it out in His way." Elder Monte Brough, who served in the Asia Area Presidency from 1990 to 1993, found that although no General Authority could claim much expertise on China, he's "never seen anybody who could grasp it faster or more completely" than Neal did.

Drawing on his background in CES, Elder Maxwell quietly nurtured for years the visits of retired BYU faculty and other LDS teachers who have gone to China to teach English under strict, and carefully observed, no-proselyting rules. For Neal, just having those Latter-day Saints there, making friends as teachers, was reason enough for their presence. He has also built relationships with Chinese officials, both in the United States and China, hosting the visit of Chinese ambassador Zhu Qizhen to Salt Lake City in 1991 and assisting with the Church's response to the interest of Chinese leaders in the Polynesian Cultural Center (PCC) near BYU–Hawaii. He helped arrange for the PCC's leaders to consult with Chinese officials who were planning their own large theme park.

After Vice Premier Li Lanqing visited the PCC in 1994, he invited Neal to visit China in 1995, along with Elder Russell M. Nelson, who had a long friendship with Chinese doctors after years of helping them to learn about heart surgery. Under normal Chinese protocol, Elders Maxwell and Nelson would not be allowed to enter the country as official representatives of the Church. Both had built such friendly relationships, however, that the government finally accepted the condition that the two could come to Beijing with the acknowledged understanding that "the purpose of the trip was apostolic." The Chinese ambassador to the United States later told Beverly Campbell that the good will of that trip had "positive and unparalleled results."

On a 1992 trip through Asia with Elder Nelson, Neal visited Bangkok, Thailand. The Church had struggled for respect and recognition by Thai authorities ever since two missionaries had been convicted years earlier of showing disrespect toward a statute of Buddha. In 1990, the Church was still unable to own property there in its own name, and missionaries needed to leave the country every ninety days to renew their visas. Assisted by Church Public Affairs personnel, Neal had developed a relationship with the Thai ambassador to the United States in Washington, D.C. That ambassador helped to persuade the Thai authorities to allow local visa renewals and more missionaries. The 1992 trip gave Neal a chance to visit the American ambassador to Thailand to thank him for the U.S. government's help in facilitating the Church's contacts in Washington.

On this same trip, Elder Maxwell had what turned out to be a remarkable, though unanticipated, experience with the Thai government. Thailand had just undergone a dangerous and contentious political upheaval that had displaced the existing government. Conditions were so unstable that for a time missionaries weren't allowed out of their apartments at night, and Bangkok had experienced three days of rioting in the streets. Mission president Larry White said the man widely expected to be named the new prime minister within a few days lacked the popular support needed to restore order. People feared that

Meeting with officials of the Chinese government; left to right: Elder Maxwell; Elder Russell M. Nelson; two interpreters; Li Lanqing, vice premier of China; and Qi Huaiyuan, president of CPAFFC, a Chinese association for friendship with foreign countries

if he were appointed, rioting and civil unrest would resume with further bloodshed.

During the general session of the Bangkok district conference, where Elders Maxwell and Nelson presided, President White whispered to Neal his hope that Neal might somehow leave a special blessing on the country. Although he was generally aware of the unstable climate, Neal really didn't know enough to understand the complete context. Thailand still had a king, but he was a constitutional monarch with little authority to govern. Neal did know that an LDS woman in the congregation was a sister to a lady-in-waiting to the queen.

As the meeting drew to a close, Neal pronounced an apostolic blessing. According to President White's notes, he blessed

> Thailand, the people, the king and leaders at this special hinge point in the history of this nation. I bless all, so there can be a spirit of reconciliation. I plead with Heavenly Father to ratify this blessing upon the king, the leaders, and the people . . . in the spirit of love, friendship, and most importantly as a special witness of Jesus Christ, [speaking for] myself and Elder Nelson.

President White was touched deeply, telling his missionaries at a conference with the two visitors the next day that many would benefit from this blessing.

Elders Maxwell and Nelson left Bangkok the next morning. Three days later, on June 10, the king in a surprise move exerted his moral influence to appoint a former prime minister, Anand Panyarachun, as interim prime minister and to call for general elections. This appointment came as a complete surprise, both to the general population and to the man who had expected to be appointed. Taxi cab drivers in Bangkok honked their horns in celebration. The tense situation was defused, and civil harmony returned as requested in the blessing.

David Phelps, an LDS lawyer who knew the local language and culture well enough to act as Neal's interpreter at the Bangkok meeting, wrote him three years later, describing "the peace I felt in combination with the overwhelming power of the Spirit as you exercised the keys of the holy apostleship on behalf of this land." What the king did was "expected by none yet embraced by all," starting a "healing process which continues to this day." Elder Monte J. Brough, who was present during the conference, said afterward, "I'll go to my grave believing the whole political system in Thailand changed because of the apostolic blessing of a Mormon elder." Any other explanation for what "happened was so unlikely."

During these same years, Elder Maxwell became directly involved in opening the doors of Mongolia to the gospel. This large, landlocked, isolated country of 2.3 million people is located between Siberia on the north and China on the south. It was a Russian satellite nation until the collapse of the Soviet Union in 1989. Once Mongolia adopted a democratic constitution in 1990, its leaders wanted to learn how to create a free-market economy. Elder Monte Brough of the Asia Area Presidency had visited Mongolia many years before his call as a General Authority, and in view of Elder Maxwell's charge to open up new countries, Monte decided to visit Mongolia again.

After sizing up the country's needs and learning that their ambassador to the United States had visited BYU, Elder Brough proposed

Elder and Sister Maxwell with Elder and Sister Kwok Yuen Tai in Mongolia to dedicate that country for the preaching of the gospel; the two men in front are early converts in Mongolia

inviting into Mongolia missionary couples who could help the government modernize its system of higher education and who would be allowed to teach the gospel to people who expressed an interest. As first contact for Asia, Elder Maxwell instinctively liked the link between education and missionary work. He quickly gained approval of the concept by the Twelve and the First Presidency and then went to work to find what he came to call "Green Beret" missionary couples who were experienced in education and also had the fortitude to live in a distant and difficult environment.

Elder John K. Carmack, another member of the Asia Area Presidency, called Elder Maxwell "the father of the Church in Mongolia," because from their location in Hong Kong, the Asia Area Presidency could not arrange for the people and equipment to mount such an innovative start-up operation. "We were sitting out there in a forgotten land [Mongolia], and we had to have somebody [in Salt Lake City] who *cared*." Neal "jumped right in and got his hands dirty."

With this need on his mind, Neal heard that Kenneth Beesley, his former colleague from CES, had retired and was considering serving a mission with his wife. So Neal invited Ken to lunch. The Brethren at first considered Mongolia too primitive and uncertain to warrant a formal missionary call, but if Ken and Donna were willing to volunteer, they seemed perfectly suited. They became the "lead couple" for what became a group of six humanitarian missionary couples, all of them having various education-based specialties, who "just laid aside their lives and went over to start the work in Mongolia."

The first couples began their service in 1992, subsisting under bleak, cold conditions. The only thing they really kept hot was their fax machine—their primary link to the outside world, because mail service was unreliable and telephone calls prohibitively expensive. After concentrating seriously on their educational advisory task for the first several months, the Beesleys felt it was time to dedicate Mongolia for the preaching of the gospel. Elder Maxwell and Elder Kwok Yuen Tai of the Asia Area Presidency arrived in Ulaanbaatar on April 15, 1993. The visitors met first with about seventy-five government, media, and educational leaders, receiving the earnest thanks of this group for the Church's assistance. Then they repaired to a hilltop plaza overlooking the city, joined by the missionary couples, the country's first two converts, and thirty young investigators of the Church. There Neal turned the apostolic key, officially opening Mongolia to the gospel and the Church.

He prayed, "Some of us are far from home and far from our families, but we are comforted to know that no place is distant from Thee." He invoked a blessing on the new converts and asked the Lord to "raise up friends" in this "wind-swept land. May . . . the winds of freedom . . . never cease to blow in Mongolia." Then he dedicated the country, blessing "its leaders and people, its soil, and its sky—all to the end that the nation may . . . respond to the Gospel message so that Thy work may be firmly established here. May Mongolia even be as a beacon light to other nations."

Since that day in 1993, the Church had grown to 3,000 members by 2001, with two districts, seventeen branches, and 130 returned missionaries. Many other Mongolian missionaries have now served in the United States and other missions. The Church is thus the largest organized religion in the country. To Neal, Mongolia was a miraculous "garden spot for the Church," illustrating the value of going to a country when it "still had economic humility" and showing the value of offering genuinely needed educational service. Neal had counseled the Asia Area Presidency all along that when the Church takes such a step of faith, "we go in right, in our full character as missionaries of the Church," with "the right to do missionary work. And if they don't like that, we won't come."

By the time he returned from Mongolia, Neal's experience in dedicating countries for the preaching of the gospel had so stirred him that he realized he had yet to dedicate the Maxwell's most recent home. So on June 23, 1993, exercising the right of any father who holds the Melchizedek Priesthood, Neal gathered Colleen and their family and blessed their home to be

> a place of security, a temple of love, and a haven . . . from the difficulties of the world for all who come here. . . .
>
> Help us to love in a world that is often full of hate. . . . [Bless the family members] who will preach the gospel in other nations [with] a contagion and a feeling of enthusiasm for the great gospel.

In his quest for discipleship, Neal had found once more that missionaries who are drawn to preach the gospel, opening doors in distant lands, return ready to open the doors of their own homes to more fully teaching and living the gospel.

FORTY-SIX

OUT OF OBSCURITY

Iɴ ᴛʜᴇ ʟᴀsᴛ ᴛʜɪʀᴅ ᴏꜰ ᴛʜᴇ ᴛᴡᴇɴᴛɪᴇᴛʜ ᴄᴇɴᴛᴜʀʏ, the Church witnessed significant changes in the way the message of the Restoration was both communicated and perceived in two different audiences—the American media and the general membership of the Church. Many large-scale factors contributed to this transformation, but one influence, if only a modest one, was Elder Maxwell's presence in the Church leadership. His involvement was at once a cause and an effect. In some ways he helped shape the pattern, but on a scale much larger than any one person's role, his own ministry and public expressions also reflected and illustrated it. Thus, Neal's personal contribution and growth are best seen as part of the larger whole of the Church's history. This development partially fulfilled the Lord's promise that He would give His servants "power to lay the foundation of this church, *and to bring it forth out of obscurity*" (D&C 1:30; italics added).

As the Church began to emerge more fully from obscurity, the needs of the times matched Neal's background and skills. From his boyhood onward, he had been a voracious consumer of newspapers, news magazines, political biographies, history books, and many informal sources of historical trends. His interest in journalism and the media had expressed itself when he helped edit his high school newspaper, wrote news stories for hometown papers during World War II, had his own radio interview show as a university student, saw the national political scene from the inside during his years on the Senate staff, interviewed public figures for ten years on educational television, and then engaged the world of public opinion for the University of Utah and as a citizen leader on Utah educational and governmental issues.

Then Neal learned from direct participation how the Church's external and internal communications fit into this world of public affairs. Senior Church leaders increasingly involved him in formulating and implementing such delicate matters as the Church's policy on civil rights, Utah liquor laws, the MX missile, the Equal Rights Amendment, and the Church's relationships with government leaders at all levels. From 1995 to 2000, he was chairman of the Church Public Affairs Committee, working under direction from President Gordon B. Hinckley and President James E. Faust of the First Presidency, both of whom had formerly chaired the Public Affairs Committee. And regarding communications within the Church, Neal's closeness to developments in the correlation movement under Harold B. Lee and later in the Correlation Department involved him over many years in the process of clarifying and communicating the Church's central priorities to its own leaders and members.

Against this background, President Gordon B. Hinckley, himself an astute master of public communications, said in 2000, "I don't know of anybody we have who keeps track of public issues, public figures, which way the wind's blowing, the way Neal Maxwell does." Neal's fundamental viewpoint is that the Church ought to take charge of telling its own story rather than letting others tell it first. President Hinckley agrees: "That's the purpose, of course, of a good public affairs program. . . . You chart the course, instead of letting outsiders chart it for you." President Boyd K. Packer of the Twelve concurs, noting Neal's "ability to view the Church as others see it. He's our number one public affairs man. . . . He's kind of masterminded this." And because of Neal's strategic commitment to having the Church speak for itself, rather than just waiting until events require the Church to respond, "We're really staying ahead of things, as compared to reacting all the time."

A recent change in media attitudes toward the Church, and Neal's view about that process, was illustrated in a cover story "The Mormon Moment" in *U.S. News & World Report* that appeared in November 2000. In his Public Affairs role, Neal was designated by the First Presidency to represent the Church in the interviews for this article. Some excerpts from it:

> By almost any measure, the Church of Jesus Christ of Latter-day Saints is one of the world's richest and fastest-growing religious movements. In the 170 years since its founding in upstate New York, the LDS Church has sustained the most rapid growth rate of any new faith group in American history. Since World War II, its ranks have expanded more than 10-fold, with a worldwide membership today of 11 million—more than half outside the United States. In North America, Mormons already outnumber Presbyterians and Episcopalians combined. If current trends hold, experts say Latter-day Saints could number 265 million worldwide by 2080, second only to Roman Catholics among Christian bodies. Mormonism, says Rodney Stark, professor of sociology and religion at the University of Washington, "stands on the threshold of becoming the first major faith to appear on Earth since the prophet Mohammed rode out of the desert." . . .
>
> [Since its beginning,] the church has continued to face almost unrelenting controversy over its origins. . . .
>
> But today, religion experts note, the LDS church is widely respected for its devotion to faith and family, and its pioneer past is celebrated as an integral part of the American saga. Such a dramatic shift in public perception has not come easily or by accident. In 1995, leaders hired an international public-relations firm to combat what they saw as unfair characterizations of Mormons in the media. One of its first efforts was to encourage the redesign of the church's logo to emphasize the centrality of Jesus Christ in LDS theology. "We don't see it so much

as PR," says [Elder Neal A.] Maxwell, "as trying to define ourselves, rather than . . . letting others define us."

This is not to say that every recent media story about the Church has been so positive. But especially in the 1990s, the willingness of major media sources to speak positively and visibly about the Church's strengths became more obvious than ever before. Some of the most widespread attention came in 1997, when the Church celebrated the anniversary of the pioneers' entry into the Salt Lake Valley in 1847. A picture of the Salt Lake Temple appeared, for instance, on the cover of *Time* magazine in August of that year, with the caption, "Mormons, Inc.: The secrets of America's most prosperous religion." As a summary of the cover story in that issue's table of contents, *Time* said,

> A century and a half ago, Joseph Smith and his followers were reviled and forced into a march across the plains to found a new Zion in Utah. Now the Church of Jesus Christ of Latter-day Saints is making dramatic strides into the mainstream— both as a faith and as a dynamic financial enterprise, a combination of virtues that may make it the religion of America's future.

Other favorable media events during these years included a three-page spread of stories in a 1997 issue of *USA Today* about the Church and its missionaries and a story in the *Washington Post* about the Church welfare program. Then there were President Gordon B. Hinckley's engaging interviews with CNN's Larry King and with Mike Wallace in the CBS television program *60 Minutes,* along with his nationally recognized book, *Standing for Something.* In 2001, *Newsweek* magazine also featured the Church in a cover story. As Neal said, "those were things that were simply not thought of, really, in the 1980s at all." Under President Gordon B. Hinckley's direction, the Church's recent "accessibility, openness, and reaching out to the media . . . to define ourselves" is "unique in this dispensation."

The Wallace interview arose from President Hinckley's disarming remarks at a Harvard Club luncheon in New York City in late 1995. Elder Maxwell accompanied President Hinckley and introduced him at this event. Jan Shipps wrote that, in the *60 Minutes* interview, Mike Wallace had become so friendly that he essentially "made the case for the Mormons' cultural acceptability," even though she thought Wallace should have emphasized more the significance of the Church's international dispersion in the past fifty years.

After the visit to the Harvard Club, Elder Maxwell reported to the First Presidency and the Twelve how well President Hinckley had handled the interchange that led to the Mike Wallace interview. He told them what he has long felt, that President Hinckley's administration will be defined in some significant measure by the able, fearless way he has dealt with the media, thereby informing the public better about the Church. "He is unafraid of the media, and they know it."

Jan Shipps has shown that the media also presented positive images of the Church in earlier years, especially in the 1950s and then again between the mid-1960s and 1970s, when "the dramatic discrepancy between clean-cut Mormons and scruffy hippies" seen in the electronic media "completed the [positive] transformation of the Mormon image" from the generally negative flavor of the nineteenth century. The mid-1980s cast some darker, temporary shadows, but that darkness only provided a sharper contrast for the warm light of the 1990s. Shipps believes the recent media glow may become less friendly, or at least more sophisticated, as the Church's continued growth alters its underdog status as a "model minority" religion.

Several long-term factors contributed to the media's increasingly positive portrayal of the Church in recent years. In a different but important way, similar factors also helped prompt the Church to clarify its core religious themes to its own membership. Elder Maxwell played a role in both dimensions of this change, if only because he emphasized so clearly his conviction that along all communications fronts, from the media to the scholarly community to the Church community, the Church should take the initiative to define itself in an anticipatory way.

First, the Church's own globalization has led it out of obscurity, clarifying and simplifying its central message and the essential themes of the Restoration. Neal welcomed this development, because he has long believed that such basic doctrinal concepts as the mission of Jesus Christ, the Book of Mormon, the family, and personal Christian discipleship are more significant than the more programmatic dimensions of Church membership. And some of the programmatic elements were, in fact, an historical reflection of U.S. culture. In 1998 the Church reached the point of having more members outside than inside the United States. As the Church has become more established in multiple cultures, it necessarily has given priority to its most essential doctrines, which are applied universally, clearly transcending cultural boundaries.

Neal sometimes has compared this process with the early Christian era, when the Lord revealed to Peter that the Apostles must take the gospel to the Gentiles. Just as Peter and Paul had to teach the early Church to avoid imposing the practices of traditional Jewish culture on new Gentile converts, Neal would say, today's Church leaders must avoid imposing the assumed but unnecessary traditions of U.S. culture on Church members in other lands.

Once after returning from a trip to Latin America, for instance, he noted that there is no hymn called "Guatemala the Beautiful" in the Church hymnbook, though at that time "America the Beautiful" was in the hymnbook as a reflection of the unique role of religious freedom in the U.S. Constitution, which made the Restoration possible. He has also expressed concerns about imposing the techniques of American management style on local Church leaders in every culture. And more than once he has said, "They didn't have a Church athletic program in Abraham's day." He was sobered in a stake priesthood leadership meeting in a faraway country when he learned that one leader who had no car was assigned the virtually impossible task of home teaching seventeen families. So he has advocated local flexibility as well as simplicity, encouraging greater programmatic discretion for Area Presidencies and other local leaders. At the same time, because the Church's maturity varies so much from one country to another, he has also been concerned about the risks inherent in imposing an oversimplified set of leadership expectations on fully developed stakes and wards.

The influence of the Church's international expansion on its public affairs efforts is reflected in the work of the Washington, D.C., international affairs office, a group of Church members who have in recent years, often under Neal's guidance, built lasting relationships with ambassadors to the U.S. from other countries. When these leaders have come to know the Church firsthand, they have often played an essential role in helping their home countries to understand the Church. Working with this committee for years, Neal has had a goal to identify individuals like "Colonel Kane" (a friend of the Church during Brigham Young's era who was not a Latter-day Saint) who could say, "Look, I know these people. You can trust them." Building these ties has been a conscious part of Neal's commitment that "we go in the front door or we don't go in at all" to other countries.

A second factor leading the Church to take the initiative in defining itself more clearly has been the influence of critics from outside as well as from within the Church. As the Church became more visible in recent years, for example, the long-standing critical, or sometimes innocent, outsider's question "Are Mormons Christians?" simply acquired more importance. Other areas of questioning that have long interested Neal included the Book of Mormon and Church history. Rather than waiting for more critical attacks, Neal has encouraged the Church, including Latter-day Saint scholars at Brigham Young University and elsewhere, to frame and address the issues on these topics before the questions arise. These efforts have helped bring the historical and doctrinal foundations of ancient and modern scripture ever more out of obscurity.

A third development, which initially had more visible effects within the Church than outside it, has been a gradual but clear increase in the use of the scriptures—especially the Book of Mormon—in LDS homes and classrooms. As this trend increased, it also influenced external perceptions by underscoring Church members' interest in, and appreciation for, the central role of Jesus Christ, both in the Book of Mormon and in general.

The greater use of scriptures in all Church classes, from Sunday School and Relief Society to seminary and institute, reflected the later stages of the correlation movement. When correlation began in the

Elder Maxwell and President Hinckley at the White House in 1995, when they met with U.S. president Bill Clinton

1960s, it was concerned primarily with organizational issues, even though those issues had doctrinal roots. By the early 1970s, under President Harold B. Lee's continued guidance, the leaders of correlation took the natural next step of recommending the four standard works as the primary texts for adult Gospel Doctrine classes. This replaced a tradition of lesson manuals organized around selected gospel principles and illustrated by scriptural verses. This step made it clear that focusing "greater attention on the scriptural texts" was part of "the fundamental mission of correlation." As one Sunday School General Board member said, it was time to "rewrite manuals so they enhanced rather than replaced the scriptures." In addition, the scriptures were a more natural text for an international Church, as distinguished from manuals that had naturally tended to draw on topics and illustrations from U.S. culture.

A fourth factor nudging the Church to be less obscure has been the technological revolution of the past generation. Neal and the other

Church leaders had plenty of reasons to avoid riding the Internet wave with its potential for delivering harmful influences into people's homes. But in the late 1990s, when Neal was chairman of the Temple and Family History Executive Council, he became persuaded—from proposals designed and sponsored by others—that the Church should take the initiative to place its family history records on the Internet. Rather than letting external events overtake the Church and diminish its established world leadership in family history, he believed "we can't lose our place in the world as the ones who really *own* genealogy."

As he had felt about other public communications issues, Neal thought the Church should set the standard and the example for Internet genealogy work, rather than letting others define the terrain and require the Church to react. For him, this attitude was strategic, connected to "what the Church ought to be doing as a leader in family history." So when Elder Monte Brough and others in the Family History Department proposed an Internet search service for family history in 1998, Elder Maxwell and Elder Russell M. Nelson encouraged the Brethren's approval of FamilySearch™ Internet Genealogy Service, which has since recorded millions of hits each day. This paved the way for other Church-sponsored Internet sites for Church members and for other people who have an interest in the Church. Because of the influence of the Internet in the global electronic community, these steps heightened the Church's international visibility. They also increased accessibility to basic Church resources and literature among members in far-off lands.

A fifth factor bringing the Church from obscurity is the secularization of Western society, which especially since the 1960s has altered many public attitudes that previously supported religious and family values. In this climate, although the Church's teachings did not change, its values became more conspicuous when the Church grew stronger just as the surrounding society was growing more secular. Neal believed this development gave the Church the opportunity and the responsibility to carry the message of Christianity to the world. Thus, like President Ezra Taft Benson, he has worked to increase awareness of the Book of Mormon not only to show that the Restoration is true but that a Christian world reeling from rising secularism and higher criticism of the Bible needs the clear second witness of Christ's divinity which the Book of Mormon provides.

Also in a more secular society, Church support for family values in carefully selected causes has influenced the broader community. For example, the First Presidency adopted a statement in 1994 opposing same-gender marriage. The Public Affairs Committee, which Neal chaired, then helped the Church work with citizen groups to encourage public campaigns against same-sex marriage in Hawaii, Alaska, and California. The voters in each state adopted ballot initiatives prohibiting their state's recognition of such marriages. Neal said the Church's association with the "Coalition for the Protection of Marriage" on California's "Proposition 22" was the Church's "biggest ever" involvement in an issue of public morality.

Other specific factors came together around 1995 that added impetus to the Church's public visibility, just as Elder Maxwell became chairman of the Public Affairs Committee. For one thing, President Hinckley became President of the Church, and his unique background and talents immediately enhanced the Church's reputation with public groups of all kinds. As Neal said of him, "The Church can't move forward . . . if we are hidden under a bushel," and President Hinckley is both willing and able to remove the bushel. "He is a man of history and modernity at the same time, and he has marvelous gifts of expression that enable him to present our message in a way that appeals to people everywhere." President Hinckley's informed and gentle candor has signaled to journalists and others "a new openness" about the Church. Salt Lake City's role as host city for the 2002 Winter Olympics also attracted unusual media interest in the Church.

In addition, the First Presidency and the Twelve, assisted by such able staff people as Bruce Olsen and Beverly Campbell, developed several specific steps to enhance the Church's public communications messages. They engaged a consulting firm named Edelman Public Relations Worldwide, stepped up the effort of Church Public Affairs to build bridges with civic leaders at all levels, and launched the pioneer sesquicentennial plans for 1997.

Mike Deaver, who was deputy chief of staff to President Ronald Reagan, works for Edelman. When the Church was considering whether to engage that firm, Neal recalls that Deaver said, "Ronald Reagan knew who he was, and he didn't need anybody to remake him. The Church knows who it is, and they don't need anybody to remake them. They just need to be able to project their message." To this end, Deaver and his associates have been able to work with such media organizations as *Time* magazine in ways the Church "just can't do directly."

As a public affairs leader, Neal has involved himself personally in numerous "bridge-building" visits throughout the United States and elsewhere with governmental leaders, congressmen, ambassadors, and other public figures. Such individuals have found that Neal is "a very cosmopolitan person" who isn't "threatened by any issue or person." At the same time, "he treats everyone from religion writers to U.S. senators the same. He is well read and converses in what interests [other people] with ease. He is a master at telling the Church's story as vibrant and living rather than stuffy and constraining." He has felt especially at home with political leaders, where he has encouraged better recognition of the Church in many countries. His political neutrality has helped, "because he's got so many friends on both sides of the aisle," and "he just stays out of" extraneous political issues.

Neal's long-standing commitment to the two-party system of the United States has also led him to sponsor some initiatives to bring the Church and its members more into the public light. For instance, he encouraged Elder Marlin K. Jensen, a Seventy serving on the Public Affairs Committee, to be interviewed by the Utah media in 1998 about the value of a bipartisan system. To Neal, this proactive step was better than "to sit back passively and have people define us as an ultra-conservative church that's made up solely of Republicans." He also suggested a portion of a First Presidency letter of January 15, 1998, which encouraged Church members to "be willing to serve" in elective or appointive political offices in the party of their choice. Neal is concerned about "the quality of men and women in public office," and he believes Latter-day Saints should "be doing more and having more of

*Meeting President
Ronald Reagan in
the Oval Office in
1985*

an influence," not simply to help the Church but to draw on their religious values to serve better their communities.

Elder Maxwell has reflected his attitudes in occasional breakfasts or lunches with LDS members of the U.S. Congress, who come from both major political parties. He has long worked to ensure that the Church doesn't ask "favors of our own people" in their elective roles, but he has still wanted them to feel closer to and better informed about developments within the Church. On one or two of these occasions, he left an apostolic blessing with the LDS Congressmen. Beverly Campbell in Washington said the Congressmen "valued these visits enormously," though Neal would "never tell them how to vote," whether they asked or not.

In his apostolic years, even when public affairs was the topic, Neal's interests were fundamentally spiritual ones. For example, he told a group of new mission presidents, "The image of the Church will improve in direct proportion to the degree to which we mirror the Master in our lives. No media effort can do as much good, over the sweep of time, as can believing, behaving and serving members of the Church."

In addition, his interaction with political leaders reflects how his personality has matured through the spiritual seasoning of his service.

After watching him deal with legislators and ambassadors in Washington, D.C., Beverly Campbell knew that Neal was not

> born with a natural tolerance for tedious or concealing rhetoric. [And although he could] dazzle everyone, he doesn't. [In our meetings, I found] I was watching someone who, by force of will, had subjugated himself that he might better serve [the Lord]. This humility and generosity of spirit carried with it such power . . . and total submission to his prophetic mission. His gentleness and dignity [enhanced one's] awareness that here was a true moral and intellectual force.

The Church's relationship with the Islamic community offers a final example of Neal's bridge-building, demonstrating the overlap between public affairs and his patient, long-range approach to opening the doors of nations. Chances are, Neal has said, thirty years ago nobody at Church headquarters was wondering how to reach out to the huge Muslim world.

During the late 1980s, Neal talked occasionally with Elders Dallin Oaks and Alexander Morrison about Islam. Aided by Elder Morrison's perspective from his prior experience with the World Health Organization when he was an official in the Canadian government, they all felt the time had come for the Church to open some kind of dialogue with the Islamic people. The Church has much in common with Islam—both religions value family life, and both have an historical relationship with Judaism and the ancient Middle East. Neal had sensed Elder Howard W. Hunter's deep feelings for Muslims when they traveled together to Egypt a few years earlier. And since BYU students had first begun semester abroad programs in Israel in the 1970s, Neal, Dallin, and their successors in the Church Educational System have always nurtured an attitude of compassionate fairness among BYU students toward both Jews and Muslims.

Neal led the members of his Quorum, then, through some position papers on the Church's interface with Islam. He realized that the Church was "so unknown" to them "that we had to find some way of communicating to these wonderful people who we are" rather than "letting other people define us" to them. So Neal invited Daniel Peterson

With Ambassador Marwan Muasher of Jordan; U.S. Senator Harry Reid and his wife, Landra; and Elder Merrill J. Bateman, president of BYU, at a dinner in 1998 celebrating the publication of the first book in a series of Islamic translations by BYU scholars led by Daniel Peterson (far right)

of the BYU Arabic language faculty to join with Elders Oaks, Morrison, and himself in some brainstorming sessions.

Traditional proselyting in Islamic countries was prohibited by law, and Church leaders respected that stance. Still, they wanted to "show Muslims our deep respect for Islam," especially because Muslims often "feel underrated by the West." Thus arose the idea of the Islamic translation project—BYU and the Church, aided by private donations, would sponsor translations into English by the finest Arabic scholars of leading Arabic texts from the Middle Ages. Westerners are generally "unaware of the glorious civilization that Islam had a thousand years ago," in large measure because so many published fruits of Islam's intellectual flowering in that era have never been translated into English. Elder Morrison saw that Neal's desire to "showcase this wonderful civilization" came from his "world view . . . that all people [are] God's children and his deep respect for other cultures"—an attitude that originated in Neal's "feeling heavily his responsibility as an Apostle" to love and reach out to all people.

So Dan Peterson organized a prestigious editorial board, raised funds, and arranged for able translators. Eventually, the first books came off the press—English on one page and Arabic on the facing page. Encouraged by warm support from President Merrill J. Bateman, BYU hosted dinners in 1998 through 2000 in eastern U.S. cities, inviting Muslim leaders and scholars to receive copies distributed by the University of Chicago Press. Neal liked the comment of Parviz Morewedge, editor-in-chief of the series, who told his Muslim friends in Washington that the Mormons are different Christians, the ones with no history of colonialism. Neal hadn't thought of the Church's expansion in that way, but he knew it was true—the LDS global outreach is not designed to create colonies of the U.S. or Europe.

Neal told the gathering in New York about the "many touching points" between "Mormons and Muslims," points he hoped would become bridges of understanding. Those topics include shared general beliefs that God is the source of light, the family is of great importance, we must resist the excesses of the secular world, and faith and knowledge "are not hostile but sequential." Hearing him at this gathering, historian Richard Bushman said Neal spoke "the words of a large soul with a cosmopolitan outlook." Part of that largeness of soul is that Neal, once so impatient to know the end from the beginning, is now content to reach out and then just watch, patiently, for whatever circumstance will allow the opening of another door, or perhaps only a window, to the Islamic world—and China, India, and every other kindred, tongue, and people.

FORTY-SEVEN

FROM THE WORD
TO THE WORD
TO THE *WORD*

THE CHURCH HAS COME EVER MORE "out of obscurity" in the last generation not only externally, in the perceptions shaped by the national media, but also internally, among the Latter-day Saints. The factors mentioned earlier have influenced the Church's internal clarification of its priorities, both among Church leaders and among LDS scholars. This pattern finds a parallel in the development of Neal's own ministry. The growth in his personal sense of direction both influenced and reflected what was going on in the Church at large.

Elder Jeffrey R. Holland has said of Elder Maxwell's interests that he has moved "from the word to the word to the Word." By this he means that Neal "has always loved language"—what Neal calls his love affair with the world of words. His interest in journalism, his habit of constant reading, and the carefully crafted language in his writing and speaking all reflect a lifelong fascination with the English language.

In his years as a General Authority, with this innate affection for words and their pervasive power, Neal's interests gradually shifted from the words of general literature toward the "word of God"—the standard works, especially the Book of Mormon. He developed "a love of *scriptural* language, a love of the scriptures." He continued to read widely, but during the 1970s and especially into the 1980s, his talks and books became increasingly "loaded with scriptures." Now, says Elder Holland, "line for line and paragraph for paragraph," his work includes "more scriptural references than any other" Church leader or speaker. He loves scriptural language. He "treasures favorite scriptural phrases, things that will ring in his ear."

Then, especially since his call to the Twelve, Neal's interest in the scriptural word of God has focused increasingly on the Word, showing "the love of the Word, with a capital W," meaning Jesus Christ. "That's his ultimate maturity." He has "always feasted on the Savior's words," but in his apostolic years, that feast became ever more centered on the Savior Himself—His life, His example, His Atonement, His attributes, and what it means to be His true disciple. In 1991, Neal prepared a list of his principal activities during his first decade in the Twelve. There he wrote, "Focused my Apostolic ministry on Jesus and His Atonement with heavy emphasis on the Prophet Joseph Smith and the Restoration in speeches and writings."

During this same period, the Church generally has become more focused on the centrality of Jesus Christ, the importance of the Book of Mormon and the Restoration, and the preeminence of the family. The growing emphasis on these themes in Neal Maxwell's ministry has both contributed to and been affected by developments within the Church. These were always among the fundamental doctrines and themes of the Restoration, but they have recently emerged like peaks at the highest point of a range of mountains. By 2001, Neal would write that

> the foothills of lesser things . . . merge into the vaulting doctrinal peaks. The colors and hues actually seem to sharpen. The composite silhouette stands out in bold relief, [providing] a striking but subduing sense of the breathtaking range of the glorious Restoration. Even more spectacular in my sunset days, that range has evoked the testimony of Christ.

The Lord has always guided his prophets to emphasize those

principles that apply most directly to the times and seasons of His people. During the days of Joseph Smith, the Church was bathed in an outpouring of revelation, yielding the doctrinal foundations of the Restoration, the authority of the priesthood, and the coming forth of modern scripture. During the Brigham Young era, the Saints were consumed by the process of pioneering, immigrating, and building Zion in the communities of the Intermountain West, a work that laid the organizational and practical foundations of today's Church.

From the pioneer era until about the time of Neal's birth in 1926, the Church reduced its geographical and cultural isolation as it worked out a more integrated relationship with the surrounding American society and consolidated its financial strength with a reemphasis on the law of tithing. The early decades of the twentieth century were also a time for systematizing Church teachings and the record of Church history, as reflected in the publications of Elders James E. Talmage, John A. Widtsoe, and B. H. Roberts.

In Neal's growing-up years, the doctrines of the Word of Wisdom and temporal self-reliance (welfare) were frequently highlighted at general conference, reflecting major concerns in American public life with the regulation of alcohol and the economic chaos of the Depression. Then came the dark war years, followed by the sunnier mid-century season of David O. McKay's presidency in the 1950s and 60s. President McKay's most characteristic themes emphasized the practical living of Christlike attributes, including self-mastery and character development. He gave renewed emphasis to missionary work and family life, preparing the Church for the coming international expansion and the social threats to family stability. This was a season of emphasis on youth programs and education, reflected in Neal's experience on the YMMIA General Board. By the late 1960s, however, the programmatic character of the Church auxiliaries began to decrease, at least as a centralized agenda of activity directed in detail from Salt Lake City. The Church still had a strong American flavor, but the world was beckoning.

The organizational, priesthood, and family-centered themes of the correlation movement in the 1960s were followed by President Spencer W. Kimball's potent expansion of international missionary work in 1974. During this same period, when Neal was working with senior Church leaders on the Leadership Committee and as commissioner of education, the momentum of the principles of correlation led the Church to give greater emphasis to the scriptures generally and the Book of Mormon in particular. The standard missionary discussions, for example, were revised in 1972, giving the Book of Mormon a greater prominence that has continued ever since. A course in the Book of Mormon, rather than a general introduction to theology, became the standard course for freshmen at Brigham Young University in 1961. The scriptures, with the Book of Mormon in growing preeminence, also became the basic texts for seminary and institute classes, which took those same courses throughout the expanding Church when the Church Educational System followed that expansion during Neal's years as commissioner of education.

Similarly, in 1972 the scriptures became the texts for Gospel Doctrine classes in Sunday School, with an eight-year cycle (two years on each of the four standard works). This became a four-year cycle in 1982, largely to give Church members a more frequent return to studying the Book of Mormon. During the late 1980s, President Ezra Taft Benson urged the Church to take the Book of Mormon more seriously—"flooding the earth" with copies of the book, reading it in families, and studying it more in every possible setting.

In 1981 the First Presidency and the Twelve formally adopted a three-fold mission for the Church—proclaim the gospel, perfect the Saints, and redeem the dead—under the unifying vision of assisting the Lord in His "grand and glorious mission 'to bring to pass the immortality and eternal life of man' (Moses 1:39)." Over the next few years, the three-fold mission became increasingly centered on the doctrines and mission of Jesus Christ, although no formal change in the Church mission statement was adopted. This centering process was enhanced by the large-scale forces noted earlier and by several Church-based initiatives that both reflected and accelerated these trends, bringing the core doctrines of the Church out of obscurity both internally and externally. These initiatives included President Benson's emphasis on the Book of Mormon; adding "Another Testament of Jesus Christ" as an official subtitle to the Book of Mormon in 1982; the increasing reference by individual Church leaders to "Come unto Christ" (Moroni 10:32) as a unifying theme for the three-fold Church mission; the growing use of the Christus statue, both in Church visitors' centers and elsewhere (the Danish sculptor Bertel Thorvaldsen had titled his Christus "Come unto Me"); giving greater prominence to *Jesus Christ* in the official name and logo of the Church in 1995; and two public expressions of apostolic testimonies of Christ by the First Presidency and the Twelve in 2000, *The Living Christ* document and the *Witnesses of Christ* video.

The Christ-centered doctrines of the Restoration and the Book of Mormon had always been there, but the simplification and clarification brought on by international growth, by Church responses to questions about its Christianity, and by these initiatives brought its doctrinal Christian core into a bolder relief.

In addition, the prophetic 1995 statement of the First Presidency and the Twelve, *The Family: A Proclamation to the World,* struck a responsive chord among Latter-day Saints, stimulating an unprecedented degree of attention to the doctrinal foundations of the Church's commitment to family life, in and out of the Church.

As with the increasing focus on the Savior, the subject of the family had long since captured Neal Maxwell's imagination with increasing intensity during his service in the Twelve—not only in his talks and writing but also in discussions among his Brethren. He took an active role, for example, during April conference 2001 in teaching General and Area Authorities about building multigenerational families. This was but one visible expression of Elder Holland's comment that in private discussions among the Twelve in recent years, Neal "has become an incomparable defender of the family." He continually wants to know what the Church is doing to strengthen and protect LDS homes and to increase the proportion of homes where LDS children are growing up with parents who are married in the temple. He often points out that no department at headquarters is assigned to watch over the family as such. "He and Brother Packer have become very close, philosophically and theologically," in their emphasis on this theme.

Consider two statistical examples of the general Church trends toward a greater focus on the Book of Mormon and the mission of Christ. A study of scripture usage at general conference conducted by Richard C. Galbraith and verified by Noel B. Reynolds showed that references to the Book of Mormon averaged around 12 percent of the scriptures cited in all general conference talks from 1942 until about 1970. This proportion increased somewhat during the 1970s and then "jumped to 40 percent" when President Benson challenged the Church in the mid-1980s to take the book more seriously. By the early 1990s, the frequency of Book of Mormon references "leveled off at about the 25 percent mark," reflecting, since about 1970, a doubling of "the extent to which Book of Mormon passages have entered the common discourse of Latter-day Saints, as well as indicating the current emphasis placed on the Book of Mormon by Church authorities."

A computer search of the word *atonement* in general conference talks and articles in the *Ensign* also shows a remarkable increase during the 1980s and 1990s, compared to previous years. From 1971 to 1981, *atonement* was used approximately fifteen times per year in conference talks and averaged just under forty times per year in *Ensign* articles. By the 1990s, the number of references to *atonement* had roughly tripled, being used about fifty times a year in conference talks and about 120 times a year in *Ensign* articles. This information is only a sketchy indication, of course, because a single article or talk may use a word such as *atonement* numerous times. Word usage also doesn't tell us how the word was used or why. Still, this comparison confirms the general impression that writers and speakers at the general Church level have begun to talk much more about the Atonement and mission of Christ than was true even as recently as the early 1980s.

Elder Maxwell's speaking and writing—and his own personal quest—have clearly contributed to this development, because of the way he has applied the doctrines of the Atonement and following Christ to the daily process of discipleship. He has spoken frequently about Christ's empathy, about the reach of the Atonement, and about yielding one's will and pride enough to become "a saint through the atonement of Christ the Lord, . . . submissive, meek, humble, patient, full of love, willing to submit to all things which the Lord seeth fit to inflict upon him" (Mosiah 3:19)—one of the verses he has most often quoted since 1981.

As Neal told PBS interviewer Hugh Hewitt, "Not only did [Christ] bear our sins to atone for them—what I call the 'awful arithmetic of the Atonement'—but we're advised by Restoration scriptures that He also took upon Him our sicknesses that He might understand what we go through when we have pain and grief" through His "resplendent empathy." This was a reference to Alma 7:11–12, another passage Neal has quoted with increasing frequency, especially as he has seen and developed the connections between the Atonement, discipleship, and adversity. His point is that Christ went through all he did not only to take upon himself our sins but to prepare himself to empathize, tutor, and teach us without our ever being able to feel that he couldn't possibly understand our personal trauma. That was a major point in Neal's first conference talk as an Apostle in 1981.

Truman Madsen regards Elder Maxwell's greatest doctrinal contribution as his teaching "the nuances of the Atonement and our relationship with Christ," which "in the end leads" to everything else. His frequent references to Alma 7 help "us understand that Christ Himself could not have had the same depth of understanding of our terrible situation unless He had learned according to the flesh." So "the process of Gethsemane was educational to Christ," making him "more available and approachable to us." He didn't come to earth "as a Divine Being who came down in a protective suit and pretended to be a man and went back. He actually experienced mortal grief, whether vicariously or otherwise, and that enabled Him to have His bowels filled with compassion." This puts the Atonement into the here-and-now, because, in Neal's words, "There is no personal problem, but what Jesus understands profoundly. How consoling!"

It was Neal's growing sense about the centrality of this doctrine that led him to realize, after he became so ill with leukemia, that he was finally having the awful but transcending personal experience of learning firsthand what he had been sensing and teaching. Just as the Savior had to learn about empathy from his own suffering, so must we.

The theme of coming to Christ applied to the work of local Church leaders as well, both in Neal's teaching and that of other senior Church leaders. On June 28, 1987, the Church provided a live video training conference for all ward and stake council members in the United States and Canada. In his role as chairman of the Church's Boundary and Leadership Committee, Neal was assigned to conduct and act as moderator for the conference, which was reportedly "the largest and most dispersed gathering for a leadership training meeting" the Church had ever held to that time.

In his introductory message, President Thomas S. Monson of the First Presidency said that "invit[ing] all to come unto Christ" was the "overriding objective of the Church." Eleven other General Authorities gave training instructions, including President Gordon B. Hinckley of the First Presidency, who spoke on the retention of new converts, and President Boyd K. Packer of the Twelve, who taught the importance of concentrating on a single mission of the Church with three parts rather than managing organizations or programs. Elder Maxwell concluded the meeting with a summary of eleven key concepts to help leaders focus on what matters most. He said the chief measure of success is how many people local leaders really help to come unto Christ.

Neal's 1991 list of the "key activities" in which he'd been engaged during his first ten years in the Twelve includes this item: "Worked with Elder Dallin H. Oaks to mobilize the resources of BYU's faculty and others to aid the Church as it is attacked." The list also notes that he helped respond to "attacks on the Prophet Joseph Smith, the Book of Mormon, etc., including a special major talk in Washington, D.C." As hinted by these brief summaries, the 1980s included some years of intense criticism of the Church, but that criticism led to increased clarity, both in Neal's own work and among the LDS scholars whose work he encouraged and facilitated. As he told the October 1985 general conference, "challenges to basic beliefs . . . will aid in the development of even greater convictions. . . . Though it will be the key doctrines which are assailed, after the dust . . . has settled it will be the key doctrines which will have prevailed."

President Thomas S. Monson greeting Elders Boyd K. Packer, James E. Faust, and Neal A. Maxwell at the October 1988 general conference

In retrospect, the mid-1980s seem uncharacteristically negative, especially compared to the favorable reception the media have given the Church in more recent years. But the 1980s indeed had some dark days. The most visible source of trouble was Mark Hofmann, a Utah rare-documents dealer who between 1980 and 1985 brought to the attention of the Church several "historical" documents, many of which he later admitted were forgeries. These included, along with other items, the supposed original copy of a transcript made by Joseph Smith from the Book of Mormon plates and given to Charles Anthon; a purported father's blessing from Joseph Smith to his son Joseph Smith III, implying that the son would be Joseph's successor; and, most notorious of all, a letter allegedly written by Martin Harris to W. W. Phelps. This so-called "salamander letter" referred to an "old spirit" that "transfigured himself from a white salamander," implying that Joseph's dealings with the angel Moroni involved occult treasure-hunting.

Each of these documents ignited spiraling waves of controversy. By August 1984, a religion writer for the *Los Angeles Times* quoted critics who called the salamander letter "one of the greatest evidences against the divine origin of the Book of Mormon." In April 1985, Utah businessman Steven Christensen, who had purchased the salamander letter the previous year, donated it to the Church. Six months later, Christensen and Kathy Sheets, the wife of his former business partner, Gary Sheets, were killed in separate package-bomb incidents in Salt Lake City. The next day, a similar bomb exploded in Hofmann's car, injuring him and leading eventually to his arrest in early 1986 and his conviction for murder in early 1987. Hofmann's detailed confession of his forgeries affirmed that the documents were phony, but some people still criticized the Church for dealing with Hofmann and for not discerning his motives. President Hinckley acknowledged that Hofmann had tricked the Church, as he had tricked document experts everywhere, but he concluded that there was no shame in being victimized.

During the months, even years, of uncertainty about the documents and the tragedy of the bizarre bombings, the Church was also attracting other critics for other reasons, like a wounded deer attracting every predator in the forest. As the debates raged about Joseph Smith and folk magic, a film called *The God Makers* attacked the Church, ridiculing its sacred temple ordinances. The film's proponents showed it everywhere they could, including some locations outside the United States. The Arizona Chapter of the National Conference of Christians and Jews in 1984 found the film "essentially unfair" and inaccurate. Meanwhile, throughout these years, some orthodox Jews were protesting construction of the BYU Jerusalem Center, and old controversies reignited about Church history topics, the role of women in the Church, the attitude of Elder B. H. Roberts toward the Book of Mormon, and other issues.

Although Neal wasn't directly involved in the Hofmann affair, he, like others of his Brethren, had engaged its issues. He wrote the Twelve soon after they'd seen the salamander letter, "We do not yet know *if* [it] is authentic." In October 1985, Elder Maxwell was the Church's spokesman in an Associated Press interview about this entire rash of opposition. He said the Church was experiencing "the most intense" anti-Mormon activities in decades. "Our job," he said, "is to move forward with our work and not to be distracted by criticisms. Jesus, as always, is the controlling example. . . . Rarely did he dignify any criticism with prolonged engagement as he went about his ministry, and that's essentially what we're trying to do."

These unsettling circumstances combined to stir Neal's imagination to reassert basic conviction that the Church must constantly take the initiative to tell its own story, rather than seeming perpetually on the defensive. As had long been the case, he felt an urgency for the Church not only to answer its critics but also to be informed and lead with its own strategic priorities. As Elder Holland described Neal's attitude, "It is a way to answer the critic. But it is also an attitude of, 'Let's know more than anybody else knows. Let's not have anyone else tell our story. . . . What critic should ever be able to tell us anything we haven't already examined in depth?' That's a forthright call to arms." So, as Neal's 1991 list of "key activities" suggested, he became proactive, looking for ways to help restore the Church's control over its own external agenda.

One of Neal's steps was a directly personal one. On February 7, 1986, within days after Mark Hofmann's arrest, Neal found the forum he'd been looking for to give a major address about the Restoration. Months earlier, he had agreed to speak to the BYU Management Society in Washington, D.C. That group of LDS business, political, and other leaders had been meeting for years, but by the mid-80s its annual meeting had become an important setting. This was partly because the Church Public Affairs Committee and the Quorum of the Twelve had seen value in inviting the ambassadors to the United States from many countries, all located in Washington, to see a thousand influential Latter-day Saints meet together with one of the Twelve Apostles. So Neal decided to speak at length about Joseph Smith. He spoke with resounding conviction and directness, informed by months of research. This was among his most thoughtful and stirring messages, as these excerpts suggest:

> If we in the Church were merely non-smoking humanists,
> we would attract little attention. Instead, since we make unusual
> declarations, there are unusual allegations. . . . Moroni [did say]

that Joseph's name would be "good and evil spoken of among all people." . . .

For a number of years, the Church has actually enjoyed relative freedom from attack. Recently there has been a building barrage, partly because, as the Church grows and becomes ever more multinational, it evokes a growing curiosity. . . .

What Church members face now is merely a new generation of fiery salvos, including a few duds and re-used, old darts. . . . A small sampling of the adversary's unrandom target selections discloses his central concerns.

For those for whom any explanation for the Book of Mormon will do but the real one, the trendy thing is to cite Ethan Smith's *View of the Hebrews*. . . .

[But Ethan Smith's work is] not even in the same universe of doctrinal declarativeness or spiritual significance as [the Book of Mormon]. The very opening notes in 'Chopsticks' and Beethoven's Fifth Symphony are substantially the same—but what an enormous difference [in what] follows! . . .

There is a legal doctrine meaning "the thing speaks for itself." The Everest-like peak of ecclesiastical truth . . . from the . . . revelations . . . through the Prophet Joseph Smith speaks for itself, as it towers above the mere foothills of philosophy. . . .

The Restoration responds . . . to the key human questions. Do we actually live in an unexplained and unexplainable universe? Is there really purpose and meaning to human existence? Why such unevenness in the human condition and so much human suffering?

[He then summarizes the] unique dispensational view of mankind's religious history from initiation to completion. . . .

[He also mentions] foreordination, the purpose of this planet, and the wintry doctrine about our mortal tutorials. . . .

More pages of scripture have been received (by translation and by revelation) through the Prophet Joseph Smith—by many, many times—than through any other individual in human history. . . .

Yet in the midst of [his] deprivation, affliction, and obscurity, Joseph received the Lord's stunning assurance, that "the ends of the earth shall inquire after thy name" (D&C 122:1).

How inspired and audacious a prophecy for any nineteenth-century religious leader, let alone one on the American Frontier. . . .

Joseph was promised that during his ministry, "Thy heart shall be enlarged." An enlarged Joseph wrote from Liberty Jail, "It seems to me my heart will always be more tender after this than ever it was before . . . for my part, I think I never could have felt as I now do if I had not suffered for the wrongs which I have suffered." . . .

On April 4, 1839, Joseph wrote his last letter to Emma from Liberty Jail, "Just as the sun is going down" while peeking through "the grates of this lonesome prison" "with emotions known only to God."

[Without so much affliction,] how else could Joseph take his rightful place, "crowned in the midst of the prophets of old?" . . .

Little wonder, as prophesied, the defamation of Joseph is so widespread. Little wonder, as foretold, the inquiries after his name come from the "ends of the earth."

In addition to his personal discourses on critical themes, Elder Maxwell moved to galvanize the skilled and faithful scholars he knew at BYU. In that sense, this season of criticism contributed to a fruitful season of encouragement for LDS scholarship. Elders Maxwell and Oaks, both on the BYU Board of Trustees, began holding quarterly meetings with BYU president Jeffrey Holland and faculty members from Religious Education, the Joseph Fielding Smith Institute for Church History, FARMS (the Foundation for Ancient Research and Mormon Studies), and other groups. Neal told his brethren, "We're going to gather together several people, so that we have that wonderful resource of BYU available to us [for] research that would help with the Church's needs." He was satisfied from past experience that we "can't just wave our arms" in the face of criticism. "We've got to protect our flanks." So he told the BYU scholars about their religious research, "Let's have some peer review, so nobody in your shop publishes a faulty manuscript." He wanted "no more slam dunks" against the Church's history or the Book of Mormon, no more "shoddy, pseudo-scholarship" claims by critics, like the Ethan Smith comparison or the Spaulding manuscript theory.

Neal had a long history of knowing and encouraging LDS scholars. His native curiosity and his appreciation for high-quality, spiritually faithful scholarship had led him to friendships with teachers in many disciplines who were both bright and meek. He had long encouraged them, understood them, and listened to them—and many of them have taken heart from his friendship and encouragement. "Almost every BYU academic department, at one time or another, has had him come and speak to their group and has felt like he encouraged them." Neal genuinely conveys his feeling that they can be "spiritually valuable."

To address the questions of the mid-1980s about the origins of the Book of Mormon, Neal especially encouraged the scholars at FARMS. Their approach to Book of Mormon research was different from that of most earlier LDS scholars, who had "focused heavily on external evidence for the veracity of the book," such as archeology. Rather, the FARMS people looked to Hugh Nibley as their model. He has long been engaged, as Noel Reynolds summarized, in studying parallels between the ancient world and the Book of Mormon:

> The large majority of the parallels were drawn from texts and historical facts that have been uncovered since the Book of Mormon was first published. Nibley asks time after time, how is it that Joseph Smith in 1829 could throw some passing detail into the Book of Mormon . . . that squared with scholarly knowledge that would not be available for years or even decades?

This approach simply made sense to Neal, who had long known, as Truman Madsen said of him, that "there really are so many things about the Book of Mormon that make the notion that it was concocted in the nineteenth century just plain unscientific as a conclusion."

John W. (Jack) Welch had created FARMS as a private nonprofit research foundation in 1979, the year before he joined the law faculty at BYU. In 2000, FARMS officially became part of BYU. Jack had made a Nibley-like discovery about the Book of Mormon when he was on a mission in Germany in 1967. He heard in a university lecture there about a Hebrew literary form called chiasmus, which he intuitively believed would be in the Book of Mormon, because those who wrote the original text came out of a Hebrew culture. Neal loved hearing how Jack had gotten up in the early morning hours one day to find two unmistakable examples of chiasmus in King Benjamin's speech in the Book of Mormon. Citing this as an example of faithful scholarship, Neal would say, "It's because people believe that I think they're led to these things, not because they are skeptical."

Neal could see his own instincts at work here. Applying this model, said Jack, one begins his or her research "with gospel premises . . . with the mind [and scholarly research tools] still involved but not necessarily accepting premises from the non-LDS scholarly context." This was a very different approach from that of some Latter-day Saints who had studied at Protestant divinity schools and would sometimes begin religious research with the "secular vocabulary and viewpoint of non-LDS biblical scholars and import that into a Church setting." This believing approach was basically the same attitude to which Neal had come as a university student himself when he began to integrate secular and religious knowledge by looking to the gospel for the major premises in his reasoning.

As he met with faculty leaders in Religious Education, Church History, and FARMS, Neal conveyed his confidence in the Church's historical roots and urged the scholars to work at "historical contextualizing," such as grounding "the Book of Mormon in ancient history." Jack Welch later said that Elder Maxwell and Hugh Nibley were the two people who most influenced the direction and development of FARMS, although the FARMS scholars always knew that Neal's interest didn't equal Church endorsement.

Neal has occasionally reminded all of these scholars of the reason for his encouragement to them. He has no interest in trying to prove in some scientific way that the Book of Mormon is true. Neal looks to faithful scholarship as a source of defense, not offense, often quoting Austin Farrer's comment on C. S. Lewis: "Rational argument does not create belief, but it maintains a climate in which belief may flourish." Or as Neal put it in 1983: "Science will not be able to prove or disprove holy writ. However, enough plausible evidence will come forth to prevent scoffers from having a field day, but not enough to remove the requirement of faith."

Good research can thus verify the plausibility of religious propositions, offsetting attacks that claim to be based on physical or logical evidence. Neutralizing those attacks—what Lewis called using good philosophy to answer bad philosophy—doesn't seek to prove the gospel's truth; it has the more modest but crucial purpose of nourishing a climate in which voluntary belief is free to take root and grow. Only when belief is not compelled, by external evidence or otherwise, can it produce the growth that is the promised fruit of faith.

What came "out of obscurity" from these efforts, which Neal encouraged rather than directed, is a growing body of sound LDS scholarship that has built enough of a track record that it gradually shifted the momentum of critical debate about many LDS issues. In 1996, for example, two rising Protestant scholars, Carl Mosser and Paul Owen, presented a paper to their colleagues assessing "the state of the debate between believing Latter-day Saint scholars and anti-Mormons regarding the Book of Mormon and related matters." They concluded that it is a "myth" for scholars of other faiths to believe that few LDS scholars have adequate training in "historiography, biblical languages, theology, and philosophy." They found, through visiting BYU and reviewing the relevant literature, that there are indeed "legitimate Mormon scholars . . . 'skilled in intellectual investigation; trained in ancient languages'" who "are not an anti-intellectual group." Further, "Mormon scholars and apologists have . . . answered most of the usual evangelical criticisms." Of greater concern to Mosser and Owen was their finding that

> currently there are (as far as we are aware) no books from an
> evangelical perspective that responsibly interact with contemporary LDS scholarly and apologetic writings. A survey of
> twenty recent evangelical books criticizing Mormonism reveals
> that none interacts with this growing body of literature. Only a
> handful demonstrate any awareness of pertinent works. Many
> of the authors promote criticisms that have long been refuted.

A number of these books claim to be "the definitive" book on the matter. That they make no attempt to interact with contemporary LDS scholarship is a stain upon the authors' integrity and causes one to wonder about their credibility. . . .

At the academic level evangelicals are . . . losing the debate with the Mormons. In recent years the sophistication and erudition of LDS apologetics has risen considerably while evangelical responses have not.

Reading these conclusions and seeing similarly encouraging results in other academic arenas must have reinforced Neal's conviction about the value of "mobilizing the resources" of BYU's trained scholars, especially as these respectful interfaith discussions now continue.

Much of what the two Protestant scholars found was the wide-ranging work of Hugh Nibley's students. Neal has always admired Hugh, whose example set the standard for raising the bar in LDS religious scholarship. He appreciated Hugh for his meekness and unqualified devotion as much as for his intellectual genius. "Isn't it wonderful," Neal said, that "the Lord didn't put him in the Middle Ages in some monastery working with ancient texts, and we'd have lost his genius?" Just after Neal attended Hugh's seventy-fifth birthday party in 1985, Hugh wrote to him:

The whole [birthday] show did have the happy effect of making everybody present feel younger. . . .

[He was interrupted here by a phone call from someone with] the old story of the disaffected who still cannot deny the gospel. . . .

. . . [Such people] can hardly approach the Law of Consecration by refusing obedience because of imperfect men, or making the most significant sacrifice, that of their own self-importance. . . .

As to all this ancient stuff, all my accumulated notes are falling into place . . . and the place where they all meet is, of course, the Temple . . .

[He apologizes for getting off the subject—he had just meant to express thanks.] This sort of thing has got to stop. I hate these overeager IBM typewriters, but my own handwriting is a calamity.

Yours singlemindedly,
Hugh

When Elder Maxwell was in the hospital in 1997, Brother Nibley was one of the few people he had the strength to call on the telephone. Neal honestly thought he might not see him again, and he wanted to thank Hugh one more time for all that he had done to build the Lord's kingdom.

The relationship that emerged among the BYU religious scholars and Elders Maxwell and Oaks during the mid-1980s laid the foundation for a significant but unexpected next project. In 1988, the Macmillan Company, a major publisher, approached Kent Brown of the BYU faculty with the idea of publishing an encyclopedia in which Latter-day Saints would write "what Mormons think is important in their religious experience." The First Presidency and the Twelve approved the idea, and Elders Maxwell and Oaks were appointed as advisors. Their working group included virtually all of the BYU religion scholars with whom they'd been meeting regularly. Daniel H. Ludlow, Neal's former colleague from the Correlation Department, became editor-in-chief, assisted by a fourteen-person editorial board.

The *Encyclopedia of Mormonism* made a quantum leap in bringing the Church out of obscurity. This became the largest and most complete summary of Church doctrine and history ever assembled and was soon available in an electronic format, which eased its placement in libraries everywhere. It was a Neal Maxwell dream come true: the Church telling its own story fully with peer-reviewed LDS scholarship in a respected reference work. As published in 1992, the encyclopedia included 1,848 pages in four large volumes, plus a volume of modern scripture. It contained 1,500 articles by more than 730 different authors, almost all of them Church members. It was a "joint product of Brigham Young University and Macmillan Publishing Company, and its contents do not necessarily represent the official position of The Church of Jesus Christ of Latter-day Saints."

Neal said the encyclopedia "is not, nor was it intended to be, a fully official Church publication, but it will do." Although it wasn't a Church publication, Elders Maxwell and Oaks set up a review process that ensured its overall accuracy and quality. That process included, in addition to the editors, four Seventies—Elders Dean L. Larsen, Carlos E. Asay, Marlin K. Jensen, and Jeffrey R. Holland—as reviewers. Elders Maxwell and Oaks worked hard to balance their intent to keep the publication "unofficial" with the need to ensure that it avoided statements that were demonstrably inaccurate from the standpoint of the Church.

In 1990 the First Presidency appointed Elder Maxwell as one of two advisors from the Twelve to the Church Historical Department, an assignment that has continued into 2002. Until recently, this department has been more involved with the collection and preservation of historical materials than with their dissemination. Meanwhile, the Joseph Fielding Smith Institute at BYU has continued in its role of publishing Church history, with some additional historical publications by *BYU Studies*. Neal has seemed nicely suited to an apostolic advisory role that considers Church historical issues in a mediating and informing way, always anticipating and considering the respective roles and interests of the First Presidency, the Twelve, the Historical Department, BYU, Latter-day Saints, and the general public.

As is by now his pattern, Neal has always been on the lookout for ways to share Church history that let the Church take the initiative rather than waiting for someone less fully informed to publish confusing material that would put the Church on the defensive. He was joined in that attitude by his fellow advisors, first Elder Oaks and then Elder Holland. During the 1990s, they helped behind the scenes to coordinate the best approach to publication by various Church-sponsored entities of William E. McLellin's journals, B. H. Roberts's *The Truth, the Way, and the Life,* and George Q. Cannon's journals.

Elders Maxwell and Oaks also provided sensitive guidance as the Church Historical Department with Richard E. Turley Jr. as managing director, in whom they had much confidence, prepared balanced new criteria for determining which valuable archival materials should be shared publicly. Like most large archival institutions, the department needed to balance a variety of legal and ethical principles in making decisions about access. The new standard they adopted avoided the unreasonable extremes of opening up everything and forbidding all public access. Rather, it balanced the relevant principles to protect "sacred, private, or confidential" information while otherwise encouraging broad access.

Elder Maxwell is among those whom the Lord has empowered "to lay the foundation of this church, and to bring it forth out of obscurity" (D&C 1:30), both within and beyond the Church in the day of its global expansion. His involvement has drawn on his experience in public communication, political affairs, higher education, and his own spiritual journey to clarify and amplify the central messages of the Restoration in his life.

Part XIV

His Thought
and Character

FORTY-EIGHT

THE WORLD
OF WORDS

THE STORY OF NEAL MAXWELL'S LIFE is not complete without some reflections on what he calls his "love affair with the world of words." He is perhaps the most prolific of contemporary General Authority writers, and his style of discourse, written and spoken, is so utterly distinctive that it can only be described as . . . Maxwellian. Both the amount and the nature of his writing have become essential ingredients of his personality and character. In Elder Holland's words, "It's in there, and it's got to come out. . . . I don't know that Neal would be Neal if he couldn't write. It is like people who can't speak if you hold their hands down."

His books and talks speak for themselves, a veritable library of Elder Maxwell's "letters to the Saints." Yet it is worthwhile to explore how and why he has written, partly to gain perspective on his messages and partly because his writing reveals so much about him. As much as any other biographical evidence, the evolving "wordprint" of Neal's writing faithfully tracks and illustrates both his personality and his spiritual growth. Looking at the evolution of his writing with an attitude of grateful realism will show that he was not, in effect, born wearing a white shirt and tie. He learned from experience, and both the form and the content of his work reflect a growth process.

Perhaps most significantly, he writes autobiographically, even if he has never said so—or thought so—about his life's journey. The eventual but central theme of his writing has become discipleship, becoming a true follower of Jesus. Over time, he described discipleship not merely as what one thinks or even does but what one *becomes*, against the hazards of experience. No wonder—discipleship has also been the central preoccupation of his own life, how he has tried to live, and what has made him tick. So most of Neal's writing consists of little notes he has left tacked on the trees for those who come afterward on his path of discipleship—sharing what he found, how it felt, what might be coming next, and what it meant to him. "Having found the only passage," he once wrote, "we should . . . willingly serve as guides for other wanderers."

His writing is like a conversation, then, between hikers stopping along a trail to catch their breath, looking back from where they've come, and looking up at the high country on ahead of them. In this regard, he is like other disciples who wrote their stories and shared their discoveries, people like Nephi, Paul, Moroni, and their fellow travelers. The scriptures are full of stories, life stories, written by disciples of Jesus, speaking honestly about both the hard parts and the wonder of what they found. The Lord has taught us the gospel not with rule books or treatises on theology but by giving us scriptures full of life stories of real people—disciples' lives that show us by example how to live.

Consider first the Maxwell style of prose. President Hinckley has said that Neal "speaks differently from any of the other General Authorities. He just has a unique style all his own. We all admire it." Not that it's always an easy style to absorb. President Hinckley sometimes finds himself reading Neal's talks three times: The first time "just to get a sense of it. The second time to learn what he said. The third time to really appreciate it as gold." President Monson has said, "No one could ever read his material and fail to guess who wrote it. I mean, it's Neal's. We all smile at some of the phrases, because I don't know how far he has to stretch to reach a few of them, but he seems to find just the right word for the right time." Elder Joseph B. Wirthlin of the Twelve finds that the "vintage" Maxwell style is "instructive, thought-provoking, and even brings a smile." Or, as Neal's old friend Tom Korologos put it about the talks he'd heard, "Those talks he gave, boy, it was hard to follow because you had to think every moment of it. . . . Oh, my, yes he was a sensational orator."

Tales about Elder Maxwell's use of language are legendary. A returned missionary who was interpreting live from English into Mandarin Chinese for general conference in about 1993 said the translation staff had categorized each talk in one of "four . . . , well, five levels of difficulty for translators. Levels one through four are for everybody else, and level five is for Elder Maxwell." Elder Cecil Samuelson once attended a fireside meeting with Elder Maxwell in Seoul, Korea. Neal was speaking "a hundred miles an hour, as he always does." A young interpreter was trying very hard to keep up. Neal told a funny story that required several sentences. The translator paused, said about a half dozen words, and the audience roared with laughter. When Elder Samuelson afterward asked the interpreter how he'd handled that, he replied, "I was so far behind and so tired I just said, 'Brothers and sisters, Elder Maxwell just said something very funny. Please laugh.'"

Some Church members are able to follow him better than others. One returned missionary says that when Neal is about to speak in general conference, he and his friends glance at each other and say with awe, "It's the abyss," because Elder Maxwell is "so deep." A few admit they can't quite keep up with him.

It's not that Neal's style is full of long sentences and complicated academic words. On the contrary, what requires the listener's attention is that the language is so compressed, full of carefully chosen imagery, metaphors, and allusions. "One of his talks is like a bouillon cube," said Karen B. Maxwell, using a pretty good metaphor of her own. Metaphors "are a great way to say a lot in a few words," but the listener must bring something to it before "it can expand for you." Consider, for example, his conference comment about religious risk-takers who engage in "intellectual bungee jumping"—not an easy phrase to translate into Chinese.

Jack Welch finds that Neal's talks and books often presuppose a certain level of belief and attention. The language may contain "inside allusions" that actually compliment scripturally literate listeners who can tell that he just assumes they know what he is talking about, needing no explanation. This allows shorthand communication, like that among close friends, for whom "just a word or two evokes an entire memory, and in that sense Neal's speeches are often coded." He might refer, for instance, to "the Pahoran complex," a reference to Moroni's letter to Pahoran, sitting on his throne "in a state of thoughtless stupor," in Alma 60:7. Or he might mention "Martha-like anxiety," a Maxwell favorite he first read in Anne Morrow Lindbergh, referring to Martha in Luke 10:40.

In 1990 Sean Covey, then a student at Brigham Young University, wrote an honors thesis called "An Analysis of the Rhetoric of Neal A. Maxwell." Using Aristotle's classic framework for understanding rhetorical language, Sean analyzed Elder Maxwell's general conference talks from 1981 to 1989. Not that Elder Maxwell was conscious of such an ancient framework or that his style would, or should, fit any preexisting categories, but on balance, Sean concluded that Neal's prose is as close to poetry as it can get and still be prose. One thinks of Jacob in the Book of Mormon, whom Neal has sometimes called the poet-prophet.

After noting the persuasive potential of rhetorical devices, Sean considered the risks of such a style as Elder Maxwell's. Critics could argue that this style can be too archaic, that it can be or seem too calculating, or that its occasional playfulness can detract from a speaker's serious purpose. Neal has had an occasional tendency to mix colloquial and archaic speech, as when, for example, he referred to Satan as an "incurable insomniac"; said the Ten Commandments weren't developed by a focus group; asked whether we can say, "He maketh me to lie down in green pastures" when "put out to pasture" upon release from a Church calling; and wondered if the great and spacious building in Lehi's dream had a bowling alley to provide diversion for its occupants.

Whether rhetorical tools succeed, like the difference between a good pun and a bad one, depends on the user's skill and judgment.

At an old manual typewriter at work in his "world of words"

Puns, alliteration, metaphors, and other devices can, if they're overdone, be distracting. Both Sean and others have felt that Elder Maxwell's skill and thus his effectiveness have steadily increased over time as he has learned from experience. For example, his October 1981 talk about the Savior soon after his call to the Twelve is full of rhetorical devices, but that message is among his most spiritually compelling. Sean found that this talk had thirty-two rhetorical questions in ninety-five sentences, some of them in a rapid onslaught, itself a rhetorical tool: Can we tell Him anything at all about suffering? Can we instruct Him what it is like to be homeless? Can we presume to teach Him about feeling forsaken? The poetic and spiritual force of this pattern spoke for itself— in part because the listener could sense that the phrases came straight from the speaker's heart, with the language serving the core doctrinal message, not the other way round.

Neal's writing offers abundant evidence of several other rhetorical devices, such as figures of speech ("we cannot . . . dress our words and attitudes in tuxedos when our shabby life is in rags"; "the vertical pronoun *I* has no knees to bend, while the first letter in the pronoun *we* does"), maxims presented as universally true statements ("time melts as it touches eternity"; "meekness . . . provides a soft landing for hard doctrines"; "selfishness is really self-destruction in slow motion"), alliteration ("caught up in collecting creature comforts [and] craving carnally convenient codes"), and puns ("The worst form of inflation [is] inflated egos"; "ego trips are almost always made on someone else's expense account").

The quality that has most blessed the Maxwell style has had more to do with his character than with his language. Aristotle said the most persuasive element in any speaking, including the heavily rhetorical, is the believability of the speaker. Conversely, it was the coldly manipulative rhetoric of "hired guns" like the Greek Sophists that first led to criticism of rhetoricians. Most Church members who have listened to Elder Maxwell agree with Elder Oaks: Neal doesn't write or speak just for effect or "to be flowery." "He's very authentic. When I hear him speak, I know that he cares about these things." He speaks as he does "because he is convinced under the power of inspiration that [his message is] important to a lot of people. I have never seen a thread of hypocrisy in this man. He is genuine through and through."

Carried by this quality, as Neal's phrases and images have become sharper, more people have felt the poetic and spiritual power of his words. The comments of rank-and-file Latter-day Saints (Neal calls these faithful ones the "low maintenance, high yield" members) show how and why he has connected with them. One Australian woman was drawn to him when he spoke about the Atonement. As he described the Lord's red robes at the Second Coming, red from the blood of Gethsemane, she saw one tear fall down his cheek, and her feeling for the Atonement was instantly deeper. Asked about his sometimes "fancy words," she replied, "I'm such a simple person. I don't mind the words. It's the depth behind the fancy words that touches my heart. For me, Elder Maxwell is poetry in motion."

Another Australian woman who knows him only from his *Ensign* articles said, "He speaks to my soul. There is so much meaning in the phrases. He draws me to my Heavenly Father." Another said one sentence from him stayed in her mind and changed her life: "The only truly unique gift we can give our Heavenly Father is the complete submission of our will; all else we give him is only returning the things he has given us." She added, "His talks . . . carry messages of hope; and

Elder Maxwell and Elder Russell M. Nelson, in the priesthood session of the April 1998 general conference, display the blanket of ribbons Elder Maxwell won when he raised pigs as a youth

always, he confirms his messages by . . . the scriptures. I love to look up the references." And, as a mother, she concluded, "How sweet is his thought that 'when conscience calls to us from the next ridge, it is not solely to scold but also to beckon'"; moreover, "'we can allow for the agency of others, including our children, before assessing our adequacy.' . . . Through secret prayer, I remain his friend, having experienced in part that medical treatment which he has had to endure."

A priesthood leader from the Midwestern United States said Elder Maxwell's "vessel is often a single phrase of scripture—'all these things,' 'but if not,' 'a perfect brightness of hope'—which he shows to be overflowing with gospel principles. He does so with complete and evident personal commitment. One cannot detect the slightest whiff of pretense."

One reason these people find what they do is that, as Bud Scruggs describes it, Neal's "style is intentional." The content often has "hidden gems" in it. People who mostly like "sophisticated, poetic language" will find it. Beyond that, however, those who want serious doctrinal insights will find thoughtful doctrine—but "he hides it in those talks, so that you really have to want it" to discover it. "If all you want is flowery writing, he'll provide that; but if you want the hard doctrine, he wants you to get it for yourself" because your discovering the meaning with him enhances its value to you.

Introducing Elder Maxwell to a group of English majors at BYU, President Jeffrey Holland recalled

> Kierkegaard's distinction between a genius and an apostle: while we may admire St. Paul for his eloquence . . . we do not believe him because his ideas are clever . . . (any more than we would fail to heed the words of a prophet if his expression were inelegant.) Elder Maxwell's sermons are, as . . . George Herbert urged, not merely witty, learned, or eloquent, but holy—each sentence having been "dipped and seasoned" in the heart until it is "heart-deep."

Neal's touch for "heart-deep" sentences is not just for public or serious discourse. Within the councils of his brethren, says President Faust, "It's his gift to say the appropriate thing at the right time in a clever way, which he can do better than almost anybody I know. . . . In a sentence or two, [he'll] summarize the essence of the whole thing . . . and couple it with his wonderful sense of humor." Elder M. Russell Ballard agrees:

> Few men or women ever attain to the level of spirituality that Neal has while at the same time always maintaining a wonderful sense of humor and an unequaled quick wit. I love to be where Neal is because without fail I always learn something important, enjoy a good laugh, and leave looking forward to the next opportunity to be with him.

It helps to know that Neal has spent a lifetime learning to use poetic language, because he knows and appreciates its power—and its limits. Not everybody, including Neal, who tries to do this always succeeds, and their attempts may at times feel a little clumsy. But he sensed early on, mostly from the "nuggets" he found in his own reading, the lasting energy of the well-turned phrase, and he worked by trial and error to develop the skill. Perhaps he first "felt" such language in the celebrated discourses of political history from Lincoln or Churchill.

The Gettysburg Address is "among the greatest utterances of states-manship" because it, like the Twenty-Third Psalm, is a poem. Its music and rhythms echo, rise, and return "as a passage in music takes flight from the keynote only to conclude, like a bird, by coming to rest on it again." Lincoln's private letters and other speeches have a similar quality, the result of a polished literary gift.

"The greatest political leadership has always expressed itself in poetry—under whatever guise. That is why the Gettysburg Address . . . still says so much." If such language were "mere ornamentation," people would not have valued it so highly for so long. "At its best, prose has always verged on poetry." Lincoln's eloquence was a conscious, developed skill. As a young lawyer in Springfield, he often spent his evenings reading poetry, "some Burns, Byron, and Shakespeare." He was "by nature a literary artist," but young Lincoln also "studied how poets and orators expressed themselves, noting the way they turned a phrase and used a figure of speech, admiring great truths greatly told."

Neal also developed an ear for speeches poetically crafted to move audiences in the best tradition of political leadership—the flash of insight, the quotable line, the exact metaphor. As he once told a Ricks College audience, "Education, for me, . . . underscored the intrinsic beauty and the surprising power of words, especially if words are combined with a good cause and are used effectively and authentically by one with character." Then he quoted William Manchester, who said Winston Churchill's political strength wasn't in his courage or bravery but in "his remarkable mastery of the language. As he used it, the English tongue was a weapon and a benediction. It fascinated him; he adored it, and could spend hours musing over its charms and the ways to employ it with maximum effect." One of Neal's favorite Churchill phrases was from the last volume of his World War II memoirs: "How the great democracies won the war and thus were able to resume the follies which had so nearly cost them their lives."

Such writing and speaking is different from unadorned declarative sentences, or the scholarly development of a complex argument, or the storyteller's gift for dialogue, detail, and plot. It is a precise approach with an honored niche among literary styles. "I have been indulging in

Emerson" lately, wrote young Louis Brandeis. "I have read a few sentences of his, which are alone enough to make the man immortal." Or, as William James said of such prose to Benjamin Blood, "Your thought is obscure,—lightning flashes, darting gleams—but that's the way truth is." James admired Blood's style, despite its occasional lack of coherence. "For single far-flung and far-flashing words and sentences, you're the biggest genius I know; but when it comes to constructing a whole argument . . . it seems to be another kettle of fish."

Truly disciplined metaphors and vivid images "concentrate power in a small space." The English poet John Donne "strained all of his life to concentrate emotional forces [to] summarize . . . meaning." So he gave us "No man is an island" and "Ask not for whom the bell tolls, it tolls for thee." A phrase like the one President David O. McKay often quoted, "No other success can compensate for failure in the home," is a prepoetic form; like a proverb, "irreducible . . . and memorable," it "hook[s] onto the memory" with a "powerful emotional effect." Consider President George W. Bush to Congress on terrorism: "The terrorists are traitors to their own faith, trying in effect to hijack Islam itself." Using such language requires a certain sensitivity that allows one, as W. H. Auden said, to "hang around words in order to overhear them talking to one another."

Some of Neal's word sensitivity is in his sense of play, which, in both his reading and his writing, lets him hear words playing with each other in memorable ways: "Let us have integrity and not write checks with our tongues which our conduct cannot cash." Or "[mothers] rock a sobbing child without wondering if today's world is passing you by, because you know you hold tomorrow tightly in your arms." Or, regarding new Church members, "It will be our job to lift them up—not to size them up." Or, "the laughter of the world . . . is merely a lonely crowd trying to reassure itself."

Poetic language has much to offer religious speech, because it can breathe life into the texture and meaning of everyday religious experience. As Gilbert Meilaender said in describing the work of C. S. Lewis, ordinary language would say, "It was very cold." Scientific language, which is more "theological" than "religious," would say, "It was

-5 degrees Fahrenheit." Poetic language would say, quoting Keats, "bitter chill it was! The owl, for all his feathers, was a-cold." Lewis, whose writing Neal has long admired, wrote poetically about religion, illuminating "the tether and pang of the particular" in everyday Christian living, "so that we may find in it shafts of divine glory that point to God."

When asked if he were a theologian, Lewis once replied, "One is sometimes . . . glad not to be a great theologian. One might so easily confuse it with being a good Christian." The religious writing of both Lewis and Elder Maxwell is clearly more concerned with applied Christian living than with developing the abstract details of theological arguments. Neal's writing, then, generally seeks to illuminate specific insights about the *practice* of living the restored gospel in the light of its unique, Christ-centered doctrines.

This purpose is reflected both in the way he writes and in the way he reads. With his irrepressible creative streak always at work, he'll get an idea or see a scriptural phrase and begin toying with how to put it in a speech. He might work on an idea for months before trying it out on an audience. During some periods, he's "just throwing off sparks like an iron wheel" and has "no idea what he's going to do with it all." Then he'll give something a try in an informal fireside, and it will ripen as he develops it for a more formal setting. His friends "see him integrating what he's learning, what his interests are, in his everyday teachings and in the writing he's doing." Some who have traveled with him have seen "multiple iterations" of a talk, knowing that "he works on his next book over the course of the year . . . developing his thoughts."

He will often chase an idea or a word through the scriptures, using such old tools as his dog-eared copy of George Reynolds's concordance on the Book of Mormon. He has always preferred to read the scriptures topically, rather than reading each chapter as it comes. And he often relies on his sturdy base of Bible knowledge from the "Canadian Bible Belt" days of his mission. As his love for the Book of Mormon grew, in the days before the Topical Guide, he found Reynolds far more useful than any other index—so he kept one copy at home and another at his office. Reynolds has become a primary source for his use of obscure Book of Mormon verses that develop a particular word or point. He has never wanted to master a word processor, much less a computerized word search. Elder Russell Nelson once tried to reveal to him the mysteries of computer usage, but "it made him feel like he was in the cockpit of a B-29."

He uses his trusty old manual typewriter at times, but that wouldn't work for a large writing job. He uses a "hunt-and-peck" system where, if he retypes a page, he "just redistributes his errors." And his handwriting is nearly illegible. President Hinckley said, "Surely a man who has so many virtues must have a vice or two. Have you ever seen Neal's handwriting? . . . I don't know how in the world Colleen ever derived any comfort from the letters Neal sent."

So when he approaches a general conference talk or a CES satellite fireside, he will spread out his notes and dictate to his secretary a rough draft that gets his ideas on paper. Then he'll share a later draft with Colleen or another friend, asking for feedback. Truman Madsen once received an early draft with Neal's note, "This is like a woman being discovered in the morning with her hair curlers and no cosmetics." Said Truman, he doesn't just "spontaneously create one of these masterpiece sermons. People don't understand the creative process of this man. He starts with all kinds of a jumble and then somehow develops it into something."

A typical general conference talk may go through a dozen drafts over the course of several months, and only in the later drafts does the word flow really come together for him. Then, Neal enjoys working to find just the right phrase, because that's "the intellectual process of coming at an idea." A specific use of words will intrigue him, or he'll "find all these little offshoots that . . . make the idea so much richer than he thought at the beginning." The creative writing is often "pressure-filled" and "drudgery" for him, until "the manuscript is quite well shaped, and I'm polishing, going for phrases or refinements. I enjoy that part."

In the refinement phase, he will sometimes sense real inspiration, which has taught him that "teaching by the Spirit does not remove responsibility from the teacher for prayerful . . . preparation." Neal told CES teachers in 1991 that the Spirit can be involved "as much in our preparations as in our presentations." The night before one BYU commencement speech, he wondered how to express the idea that "the world's problems cannot be solved by people who are basically pleasure seekers." Into his mind came the phrase, "pleasure takes the form of 'me' and 'now,' while real joy is 'us' and 'always.'" He felt that idea was "given" to him, expressing "in a condensed way what I was trying to say."

The next question is how that phrase ended up in the book he published the next year. Beginning in about 1970, Neal began a process that soon became almost an annual summer ritual. As he reviewed all of the talks he'd given in the previous year, he wondered if "maybe in them were things that could become a book." So he would look through the talks, identify some possible themes, and then mark ideas or passages he could develop into a few chapters during the month of July—which is why the acknowledgments in his books so often thank Colleen and his family for some "July time" (the "break month" for General Authorities).

Knowing about this process helps explain some otherwise puzzling things about his books. The entire body of his work is huge—some thirty books, of which Elder Maxwell has said, "Having already written and said so much in my ministry—perhaps too much, really . . ." The book titles typically take a phrase from scripture and offer a general theme, but the chapters sometimes need to stretch to fit the theme. His densely packed format, which rarely includes a story or an extended developmental passage, at times lends itself best to shorter bursts, like a fifteen-minute talk, rather than full, chapter-length exposition. And certain ideas, scriptures, and quotations that are staples in Neal's established doctrinal framework are often repeated in several books, offering variations on his basic themes. Several of his friends wish the books could have been edited more, tightening them up to avoid repetitions, developing concepts as well as phrases.

This literary ore contains some rich nuggets, and some of his favorite ideas have undergone valuable metamorphoses over time. Besides, Neal Maxwell is a nugget hunter. He writes the same way he reads, and for him a book is a "good read" if it has even a few memorable images and specific insights. What was said of C. S. Lewis could aptly be said of Neal: "Behind a compulsive writer usually sits a compulsive reader." And Neal's writing taste clearly reflects his reading taste. He's had little interest in fiction, preferring "things concerned with the issues of the day." For years he has devoured biographies of political leaders, works of military and political history, and religious essays, especially those of such British "believers" as George MacDonald, G. K. Chesterton, and C. S. Lewis. One senses a connection here in his curiosity about able leaders, their lives—and their language. He has instinctively wanted to learn from and about people of influence who drew with good motives on the power of the word (see Alma 31:5). A leader's biography should teach us how to be leaders, just as a disciple's biography should teach us how to be followers—of Christ.

He has especially liked reading C. S. Lewis's religious essays, because of the way he finds that Lewis "cuts through," with "phrasing and brevity and . . . 'whiplash sentences' that pop the neck a little, so [the reader] knows what's being said." In his own writing, Neal is "willing to do the work an oyster does to try to produce an epigram, in the hope [it] may survive, whereas three or four paragraphs could be lost pretty fast." And he reads Lewis with the same attitude. He hasn't been as interested in the Lewis children's stories or longer works because he doesn't want to wait for "one of those great lines" if he "can get Lewis in a book where he has to produce them every other paragraph." Neal's speed reading and nugget hunting also explain how he can borrow a long, new biography on John Adams, George Washington, Harry Truman, or Winston Churchill and return it to a friend in two or three days, honestly saying he enjoyed the book.

Both Lewis and Elder Maxwell wanted to write good poetry, but despite the poetic quality of their prose, poetry itself largely eluded them. Moreover, both of them have written many of their religious essays for oral delivery—their style may be best appreciated when listened to aloud but probably not for long stretches, as one does when listening to the chapters of a good novel.

Lewis's grief after the early death of his wife, Joy, taught him in some of the same ways Neal has learned from his leukemia. In his biography of Lewis, A. N. Wilson found that Lewis had been "over-eager" to "defend religious positions which he had really only fallen in love with from the outside, before learning what it was like to *live* them." But with Joy's death, Lewis confronted a "smashing of all his illusions; that religion, if true, must be the ultimate truth, and therefore something which could never be contained in the pat phrases and slick analogies of his earlier self." Indeed, Lewis found that "this shattering is one of the marks of His [God's] presence." Thus his writing after losing Joy was "far more searching, far more deeply religious," than such earlier works as *Mere Christianity*. "This was the real thing," and in the very "suffering which smashed him up," Lewis found "something like sanctification which occurred in him towards the end of his days." In his traumatic years since 1996, Neal Maxwell has found something similar—spiritual discoveries from a realm where mere words cannot go but where suffering provokes a depth from which come new words of fresh authenticity.

Also like Lewis, Neal has not written primarily as a theologian, though the sheer volume of his writing has led some people to think otherwise. He is not a "systematic philosopher" who thinks "in terms of large theological structures," as did Elder Bruce R. McConkie. His writing is more devotional in nature, "a matter of flashes and brilliant insights." Elder McConkie "wrote *theoretically*," said Elder Dallin Oaks, "and Neal writes *practically*" about "applications of Christian doctrine. . . . He is a very practical man." He has also clarified the application of core doctrinal themes in crisp language that often fits this age of the sound bite, as we see in the development of his ideas about discipleship in a secular society. As Jack Welch put it, "People may look back fifty years from now and see Bruce R. McConkie as a Mormon St. Thomas Aquinas, perhaps, and they may see Elder Maxwell as a Mormon St. Francis of Assisi."

Elder B. H. Roberts, an early LDS theologian, once distinguished between "disciples . . . of two sorts." And, says Truman Madsen, the second kind fits Neal "to a T." First is "the disciples pure and simple—people who fall under the spell of a person or a doctrine" and then live "faithful to . . . one formula." Second are the disciples who accept the existing doctrine but also bring to it

> their own personal contribution . . . thoughtful disciples who will not be content with merely repeating some of its truths, but will develop its truths; and enlarge it by that development. [Such followers] will yet take profounder and broader views of the great doctrines [of the Church and] cast them in new formulas; co-operating in the works of the Spirit, until "they help to give to the truth received a more forceful expression" [in] impulses of . . . spiritual affection which the Christian sums up under the term "life."

This observation brings us naturally to consider how the content of Elder Maxwell's writing has changed over the years, as he has developed his understanding of gospel truths.

FORTY-NINE

DEVELOPING
DISCIPLESHIP

Elder Maxwell's writing reflects considerable development since his first book in 1967. "One can see an evolution in style," wrote Jerry Johnston in a book review thirty years later, "from the enchantment of language and poetry in the late 70s . . . to a startling directness—an urgency—in more recent times." Elder Maxwell's 1997 book is "obviously conceived in love. But I'm here to tell you, it's not for the faint of heart." Others have also noticed how his approach, both in form and in content, has led to more disciplined and reflective language, as his skill has increased and as experience has deepened his religious understanding.

Stylistically, he has gradually tamed the ornamentation that some of his friends once thought was simply too much. Tony Kimball, who has shared books with Neal since the 1960s, nearly regrets having introduced him to G. K. Chesterton, who "used alliteration almost to an excess." Acknowledging that Neal "loves to play with words," Alexander Morrison thought he sometimes "plays with words too much and loses people in the process." Elizabeth Haglund, who may have read more of his prepublication manuscripts than anyone else, says some of his books in the 1970s "weren't the books he was capable of" writing. He was "in love with words" and used language "that even erudite readers wouldn't get. . . . I faulted him sometimes for trivializing his subject." Too many of his books were "written too quickly," as if the publishers "needed a piece to take to market." Eventually, however, Liz thinks his "terrific bear-down" discipline "made him a fine writer. He was a *fancy* writer. He's now an *elegant* writer." To Oscar McConkie, Neal has become "much more what I call doctrinal than he used to be."

A similar ripening has occurred in the subject matter of his writing. For example, he said in the 1970s, "I mine the scriptures for those things in which I have a particular and current interest," looking for "insights that can be applied . . . to daily life whether the subject is time management, or delegation, or whatever." Reflecting such interests, his first book was largely a how-to work about leadership skills. That emphasis was natural, given his involvement in the late 1960s with the Church's leadership committee.

The second book, *For the Power Is in Them* (1970), was a sixty-three-page volume of "Mormon Musings," a brief and breezy collection of thought nuggets, though sometimes nuggets without ore. It consisted of short, rapid-fire paragraphs on a wide array of topics, without chapters, without context, and without thematic development. The next two books were also short ones, but they did have chapters, and they typically addressed issues related to youth, education, leadership, and secularism—topics with which Neal dealt frequently as commissioner of education and as a regional representative.

Neal was just learning to glean whatever harvest he found in his previous year's speeches for his books. He was also experimenting with rhetorical devices that occasionally lacked the sharpness that would come later. For instance, consider this metaphor from around 1970: "Our growing asphalt wilderness [in modern Utah] may become, in many ways, more wild and more difficult to tame and to govern than was their [the Utah pioneers'] sagebrush circumstance." Compare it with this more polished one from 1990: "The cares and anxieties of the world occupy us as if we were children making dikes and castles on the beach, unaware that each day's incoming surf will erase sincere but temporal labors." The later metaphor is more disciplined, fusing the principle he's teaching with a sharper image to make his point more clearly.

Neal's early books also contain many doctrinal buds that blossom in his later work. Consider this sample of ideas barely mentioned in his second book in 1970 that would develop in his future writing: discipleship; Mosiah 3:19 ("For the natural man is an enemy to God . ."); the "man of Christ" in Helaman 3:29; things will be in commotion; the fellowship of His suffering; and feasting on the word of God.

Neal brought to his writing in the early 1970s the perspective and concerns of a religious political scientist, whose speeches and writing often tried to encourage Latter-day Saint university students and teachers to use religious insights in their academic and professional fields to help rescue a morally degenerating society. As late as 1980, he told a *Church News* interviewer that he thought secularism in society was the second largest challenge the Church faced, after the issue of international growth. He was concerned about "a despiritualized society with irreligion at its core," and he worried that eventually "misled majorities may sadly reach the conditions noted in Mosiah 29:27," when the majority are so unrighteous that they do not choose what is good. He worried about the threats of secularism to individual Latter-day Saints, but he also worried about the society itself and instinctively wanted to encourage social change.

That My Family Should Partake (1974), his first book as a General Authority, was his most substantial religious book to that point. It reflected his social concerns but also recognized that society must first "look homeward, angel," building on a line from John Milton, because society's best long-term solutions lie in individual families. As he said in one of his better metaphors from this period, "If we poison the headwaters of humanity—the home—it is exceedingly difficult to depollute downstream."

As time went on, and especially after his call to the Twelve in 1981, Neal's thinking and priorities took a gradual turn. After years of experimenting with writing styles laced with extensive quotations from other writers, he began more consistently to find his own voice. And the voice of scriptural passages wove itself increasingly into his voice. He was moving from the word to the word and, ultimately, to the Word.

He still worried about collisions between the sacred and the secular, but he became more pessimistic about, or perhaps just less interested in, social problems as such. Secularism has always interested him, but he moved—in his writing and in his personal priorities—increasingly toward the goal of coming to know the Savior, becoming like Him, and developing His attributes. With this perspective, the earlier social concerns were less compelling—even though he has still urged Church members to care about society enough to be real participants in it.

In 1975, Neal published *Of One Heart,* the first of five books (two in 1975 and then one each in 1976, 1984, and 1992) that used dialogue from imaginary letters or conversations, a creative format quite different from his devotional essays. One challenge with using a dialogue format to present religious topics is that, according to literary theorists, a religious author "cannot produce a truly subversive question [even for a character in an imaginary dialogue] that would undermine his own faith." *Of One Heart* is clearly the best book of the five. Its words flow with a natural freshness through a series of letters written by Mahijah, who is converted by the preaching of Enoch and then joins his community and lives in the city called Zion. "Omner," he writes his friend, "you would not criticize a group of people who sought the same high ground in the midst of a flood; you would not see their presence in one place as an unintelligent act, for they came together in order to be saved. So it is here."

Among his other books, the best ones coincide with key experiences in Neal's own life. His readers, judging by the number of copies sold, and most of his friends agree that *All These Things Shall Give Thee Experience* (1979) is probably his best work. For one thing, says Jim Jardine, this book "starts with an issue and develops it" more fully than do the other books. This was his first attempt to write about adversity in a substantial way, an interest that arose from the poignant empathy he felt for the two cancer victims to whom he dedicated the book, Richard Sharp and David Silvester. What Neal felt and learned through staying very close to these two men during their final months expanded his heart, intensifying his private ministry to people stricken with illness.

Signing copies of his books; Elder Marvin J. Ashton (left) encouraged him to write

The next work that carried a significant freshness and depth was *Even As I Am* (1982), a collection of essays that expressed Elder Maxwell's feelings about Jesus Christ in the months after his call to the Twelve, including his moving talk from the October 1981 general conference. Whatever his tasks now, he wrote, "there stands the Savior. . . . What *He* is presses in upon me in relentless reminder of what *I* should be." Now he could hardly sing of Him without tears coming to his eyes. Now he must "earnestly . . . strive to accept His generous but genuine invitation and direction to become, as He has said, 'Even as I am.'"

Another book that conveyed unusual spiritual vitality was *But for a Small Moment* (1986), which grew from the historical research Neal undertook during the Mark Hofmann era, when he rose so passionately to the defense of Joseph Smith. In so doing, Neal was especially drawn to Joseph's haunting experience in Liberty Jail, the place B. H. Roberts called the "prison temple" because of the profound religious inspiration the Prophet received there in the midst of his oppressive captivity. By immersing himself in Joseph's thought and feelings, Neal found himself looking at the Church, his life, and the lives of others during the stresses of the mid-1980s through the narrow grates of

Joseph's windows in the thick walls of the ironically named "Liberty" Jail. *But for a Small Moment* includes, in a different form, most of the content from Neal's stirring 1986 talk in Washington, D.C., on Joseph Smith.

If Thou Endure It Well (1996) was significant especially for the almost eerie way it anticipated the leukemia that would strike him within months after the book was published. Here he wrote that "adversity must be part of the pattern rather than always an aberration." And, "how could our personal empathy be genuinely and lastingly established and enlarged without refining experiences in the furnace of affliction?" Its most striking anticipatory signal was the book's epilogue, which consisted of Neal's poem "Submission." He had actually expressed this poem's same line of thought in various prose versions in his earlier books—indeed, it is one of his oldest nuggets, a theme he has mentioned in numerous places dating back more than twenty years. But these lines, his best effort at poetry, captured his thinking about Jonah and applied it to the reader—and himself—in a way his prose never quite could and with shuddering accuracy about what was waiting for him just around the corner:

> When from Thy stern tutoring
> I would quickly flee,
> Turn me from my Tarshish
> To where is best for me.

> Help me in my Nineveh
> To serve with love and truth–
> Not on a hillside posted
> Mid shade of gourd or booth.

> When my modest suffering seems
> So vexing, wrong, and sore,
> May I recall what freely flowed
> From each and every pore.

> Dear Lord of the Abba Cry,
> Help me in my duress
> To endure it well enough
> And to say, . . . "Nevertheless."

One More Strain of Praise (1999) should be mentioned because it is such sober evidence of what Elder Maxwell honestly believed in 1999—that he might not live more than a few months, barring divine intervention. The book is based on the hymn "Sing We Now at Parting," which is quoted fully in the introduction, its lines providing all of the chapter headings. There is a real sadness about the valedictory tone of this volume, but that heaviness would later be alleviated by the miraculous extension of Neal's life, which medical science really could not have predicted. In that sense, this book stands as evidence for the spiritual power that intervened in his life.

Consider a few other samples of the way doctrinal phrases that appeared early in his writing expanded in his later works.

Alma's phrase, for example, "I ought to be content with the things which the Lord hath allotted unto me," first came to Neal's attention decades before this idea became one of his most insightful conference talks in April 2000. In at least two different books (1978 and 1986), Neal noted the phrase briefly, without much comment. In 1978, he quoted a 1952 conference talk by Elder Henry D. Moyle, "We . . . might as well take to heart the admonition of Alma and be content with that which God hath allotted us." By 2000, Neal would put Alma's phrase into its nine-verse context, comparing his desire to speak, like an angel, "with the trump of God" (Alma 29:1) with his humble acceptance of being but "an instrument in the hands of God" (Alma 29:9)—thereby content with his allotment. For Neal, his illness barely in remission, the once-brash young man full of limitless hopes had meekly come to accept the "allotted 'acreage'" of a probably shortened life—with hope of a different kind.

Another seed Neal planted for future germination was a quotation from G. K. Chesterton, which he used in 1973: "We have to love our neighbor because he is there. . . . He is the sample of humanity which is actually given us. Precisely because he may be anybody he is everybody." Later Neal would draw on this idea for his larger concept that we should live the gospel most fully among family and friends because they are the "clinical material" God gave us for practicing our Christianity.

One more sample of many is that Neal was intrigued from a very early stage by the doctrine of the premortal existence. He mentioned this doctrine repeatedly, but usually only briefly, in his early books. As he explored the meaning of adversity, his treatment of premortality took on increased meaning as a perspective on adversity and God's omniscience (1979). This meaning expanded when he considered the doctrinal light that came to Joseph in Liberty Jail (1986) and even more when he explained premortality as one of the Restoration's most distinctive and powerful doctrines (1986, 1988, and 1990).

Neal's understanding of the Atonement of Jesus Christ and his feelings for it developed considerably over the course of his writing. He used the phrase "the Atonement with its awful arithmetic" in his second book, in 1970, the same sixty-three-page book in which he also mentioned "the awful arithmetic of alcoholism." The book's mention of the Atonement referred to Christ's loneliness as an example of not being appreciated. Neal used the "arithmetic of the Atonement" phrase again in his first talk at October conference in 1974, a statement of gratitude that this arithmetic included his own sins.

Along with other occasional brief references in the 70s, at the end of a 1977 book he wrote, "It is the Garden Tomb, not life, that is empty!" But in 1981, after his call to the Twelve, the doctrine and meaning of the Atonement really embraced him and expanded his understanding. In 1981 he described how the Atonement flowed from Christ's attributes. By 1982 he was especially drawn to Alma 7:11–12, which explains how Christ could succor us in all our "infirmities" because of what he learned "according to the flesh." After Allen Bergin first drew his attention to this verse, Neal returned to it again and again. In his 1982 book, he also observed that Joseph Smith couldn't have written with the loving forgiveness he expressed in an oft-quoted letter to W. W. Phelps had the occasion been ten years earlier—because Joseph needed experience in order to understand, a point Neal applied to himself as well.

By 1988, Neal was increasingly consumed with his appreciation of the Atonement's meaning and reach, writing of "the infinite Atonement," with its triumph of mercy over justice, the healing reach for all mankind, the intensity of Christ's suffering, and the sheer breadth of the blessing: "In addition to bearing our sins—the required essence of the Atonement," he said, "the full intensiveness of the Atonement involved bearing our pains, infirmities, and sicknesses as well as our sins." In 1994 and 1999 he wrote at length about the meaning of faith in the Atonement of Jesus and understanding Christ as our advocate with the Father.

Finally, the concept of "discipleship" moved from bud to blossom as its roots sank deeper into Neal Maxwell's heart. Neal talked about "disciples" at his first stake conference visit as a YMMIA board member in the mid-1960s, and he used the word often in his first books and talks as a general Church officer. But in those days, he used the term essentially as a synonym for "Church member." During the 1970s, he would say such things as "discipleship . . . involves citizenship," "the disciple of Christ is urged . . . to seek out the best books," "one who desires discipleship [should] 'give place' in his busy life for . . . gospel morality," and "the disciple does not disdain facts, for they are useful and helpful."

After reading all of Elder Maxwell's books and published talks, Eric d'Evegnee, a BYU graduate student, found that his "writing over the last thirty years is marked by a narrowing from a generalized idea of discipleship to a culminating emphasis on being fully consecrated to the Father's will." Eric saw that early in his life Neal talked in youth and leadership settings about being faithful disciples, sometimes to distinguish "how the disciple is different from 'the world.'" In the late 1970s, he began talking about the implications of the plan of salvation for a disciple. As the 1980s began, he focused on the Lord's plan for each person, which was designed to teach "certain virtues" that would create "true disciples," virtues demonstrated in Christlike attributes and in the life of Joseph Smith. Within a few years, these virtues emphasized meekness and submissiveness, until the 1990s, when his teaching focused more sharply on becoming "a *celestial* disciple, or one that is fully swallowed up in the will of the Father."

The major steps in Neal's increased understanding of discipleship were clearly marked by new insights that emerged in his key books. By about 1976, discipleship was becoming Neal's dominant theme, emphasizing the relationship between "disciple" and the "discipline" of forsaking the world and following Christ. But with *All These Things* in 1979, he began to see discipleship more as a process than a single choice, and the process got moving only after one began the journey of becoming Christ's true follower. Through watching his believing, cancer-stricken friends deal with their adversity, Neal saw the connection between faithfulness and suffering—the theme of that book.

In that context, he explained that we may suffer because of our sins or because of life's adversities, but, in addition, God may "inflict" suffering on disciples "because [He] deliberately chooses to school us." That's why Neal wrote, in terms that would take on such autobiographical meaning by the mid-1990s, "the very act of choosing to be a disciple . . . can bring to us a certain special suffering." So the general relationship between adversity and discipleship was now becoming more clear, but the deeper connection to Christ—His Atonement and developing His attributes—was still to come.

With Elder Maxwell's call to the Twelve in 1981, he began to focus intently on discipleship as a personal relationship with Jesus Christ—a master-apprentice tutorial in which the disciple has the duty to become more like the master. *Even As I Am* (1982) thus emphasized what Neal was feeling so deeply for his own ministry as he quoted, "The disciple is not above his master: but every one that is perfect shall be as his master" (Luke 6:40), noting that "to strive to be like Him means that we must be genuinely serious about developing" the qualities "in the Master's personality." And the Master would teach the apprentice: "The most advanced disciples—far from being immune from further instruction—experience even deeper and more constant tutorials." Discipleship was now definitely becoming an exercise in personal development.

Another insight came in *But for a Small Moment* in 1986, as Neal began to empathize with the experience of Joseph Smith in Liberty Jail. His reflections on the "prison temple" brought a fresh appreciation of how the Lord had used that frightful adversity to tutor Joseph—and not

With Hugh Hewitt, who interviewed him for a television program that aired on PBS

just to test him in general but to teach him the Christlike attributes a disciple must have. Joseph's experience with "these things" (D&C 122:7, written in Liberty Jail) was "part of the essence of significant spiritual development, the end for which all serious disciples are to strive."

Now Neal could see, and teach, that the disciple, like his Master, must *learn* obedience "by the things which he *suffered*" (Hebrews 5:8; italics added). Suffering, when it is part of the divine tutorial, can be sanctifying—in the sense of developing the very virtues the disciple needs to learn. By 1988 it was clear, then, that the only way to learn Christlike attributes—the whole point of following after Christ—was to accept and internalize whatever trial the Father "seeth fit to inflict" (Mosiah 3:19). By this means, as costly as it may be, the virtues reflected in Christ's nature "reflect the outcome of serious discipleship." As we "become His children," then, "a change begins in us. As we . . . strive to become one with Him, . . . we come to resemble Him."

During the late 1980s and into the 90s, Neal built upon this foundation to focus on the particular Christlike virtues His disciples need to develop by the tutorial process—especially meekness. And, as with all else he'd written, the emphasis in Neal's talks and books reflected his own process: He wrote about being meek and lowly precisely because he now wanted to develop those qualities more fully within his own nature. He had come to see that meekness was the quality that would allow his total submission to the Lord's will—not only to accept the commandments in general but to accept whatever "He seeth fit to inflict" for the disciple's uniquely personal growth toward being "as his Master": "Some suffering actually comes in striving to become like Christ as well as in obeying him." And "meekness makes sublime submissiveness possible, without which no real spiritual development would be possible."

One issue in this understanding of spiritual growth is how much the individual can, and should, develop spiritual attributes through sheer self-discipline. In Neal's younger days he made very conscious, focused efforts at self-improvement, a trait that continued into the spiritual realm of his maturity. But is meekness something we "do" because we think we should, or are we truly meek only when that's the way we are? Neal used to express admiration for President Kimball's meekness, saying that part of what made him special was that he wasn't conscious of how special he was. Similarly, Leo Tolstoy once wrote about a man who was trying to discipline himself to "sainthood." Tolstoy thought that one who "trains himself to attain sainthood by grand gestures and noticeable acts of self-sacrifice" will "fail, because no matter what he does to humble his pride, he is still proud of his very humility." So when Tolstoy's character "meets a true saint, he discovers that she is unaware of her exceptionality."

In 1998 PBS interviewer Hugh Hewitt asked Neal about this same theme of consciously acquired Christian virtues. Hewitt wondered, "Can you really put in what wasn't there to begin with?" Neal responded that personal effort develops character if one is meek enough, because "meekness [is] seeing ourselves in relationship to . . . what we have the power to become." He has tried consciously to develop more Christlike attributes, "even though the journey is long and mine is far from through." And "in that sense my story can be everybody's story who is serious about values."

Then he added that "all who are serious about being disciples" will begin to live better as *the unconscious result of a consciously chosen way of life.* We're "conscious that we need to be better, and we choose to do this, but we're probably, and mercifully, not conscious of all that's happening." Also, conscious effort with the right intent carries "the tacit acknowledgment of imperfections." The result, through personal striving and the Lord's bestowal of spiritual gifts in "the gospel of hope," is that "incremental improvement can occur."

The true disciple develops, then, from accepting to appreciating, to adoring, and then to emulating Christ. Now Neal was seeing that emulating One who suffered as Jesus did also means the follower must somehow yield his own kind of full sacrifice. "If we are serious about our discipleship, Jesus will eventually request each of us to do those very things which are most difficult for us to do." Within that process, the Savior blesses us with the gifts of the Spirit—including charity—after all we can do (see 2 Nephi 25:23).

As the process of discipleship blossomed in his writing and in his experience, Elder Maxwell gave this subject his most complete pre-illness explanation in "Becoming a Disciple" in the June 1996 *Ensign* and then treated it in "The Pathway of Discipleship" in the September 1998 *Ensign*. The second version reflects but makes no attempt to describe his own recent encounter with becoming utterly submissive. He could only say that when the disciple is fully and ultimately tested, "not shrinking is more important than surviving, and Jesus is our exemplar." These themes continued in *The Promise of Discipleship*, published in 2001.

Neal's experience then, reflected in the totality of his writing, is that disengaging from the unclean things of the secular world is only the introductory course in the curriculum of discipleship. Then comes an incremental process—not just a decision to accept Christ but also a willingness to follow Him, learning to become like Him against the grain of opposition. As one submits to the tests and growing pains that come next, the process finally becomes something one experiences more than something one can explain. Through dealing with his illness, Neal found that words and reasoning can take us only so far, as valuable as words and reasons often are. True disciples of Jesus, if they want the real fruits of their deepest desires, eventually move beyond reason into the realm of sanctification by sacrifice.

FIFTY

AN
UNDERSTANDING
HEART

THE STORY OF NEAL MAXWELL'S LIFE has now found its way back to the time of his memorable appearance at April conference 1997. His leukemia was in remission, his energy and his hair were both in short supply, but the conference experience had rejuvenated his spirits after the debilitating weeks of chemotherapy in LDS Hospital. It was a time of great hope.

After conference, Neal and Colleen slipped quietly home for the long, slow months it would take to build up his blood supply. They received a few visitors, but most friends silently understood that these two, and their family, needed privacy and peace. The remission had officially begun in February 1997, but no one knew how long it would last.

The daily mail brought an outpouring of support, words of love from friends across the globe and from each era of their lives. Yet one of the more poignant letters came from a Latter-day Saint they had never met. The letter prompted Neal to call her. In that and subsequent phone visits, he found "an authenticity" in this mother, and no self-pity. Her attitude, the absence of drama, and her matter-of-fact good cheer were an inspiration to him. She wrote:

> Thank you for your words of encouragement this conference. I am the single mother of five children. (One is serving in the Cebu Philippines Mission.)
>
> I have experienced two brain tumors and have a son who is fourteen who now has leukemia. I have a place in my heart for you and all that you and your family have been through.
>
> I have personal knowledge that it is our relationship with Christ that comforts us when needed. I know that the Holy Ghost fits in there somewhere but have much more to learn. My [missionary] son would love you to know of his concern.
>
> Best wishes and may you be comforted continually.

Another letter came from former President George Bush, who had lost a child to leukemia. He wrote, "Leukemia is a tough disease. We learned that the hard way years ago. But . . . medicine is making dramatic strides in treating [it]. . . . Barbara and I just wanted to wish you the speediest possible recovery." In his reply, Neal told the Bushes that the leukemia survival rate for children had moved from 17 to 70 percent since the death of their child.

Within several weeks, Neal felt well enough that Colleen invited Dr. Clyde Ford and Dr. Larry Staker and their wives to the Maxwell home for a "thanksgiving" dinner. Then, reflecting Neal's growing strength, the Maxwells took the entire family to San Diego for a vacation in July. By August he was back in the office and soon resumed much of his normal schedule of meetings, trips, and appointments. Not long afterward, he even began playing tennis again, so vigorously that the following spring he fractured his elbow while diving to return a shot. These events troubled physician Cecil Samuelson, who knew that Neal's chemotherapy had thinned his bones enough to make tennis a little risky. But Cecil couldn't argue with the symbolism of seeing his friend "in the game." His determination to play was "a continuing affirmation that he's not giving up. . . . He's the old Neal Maxwell."

Weeks before returning to the office, Neal found himself drawn like a magnet to other cancer patients as well as to those with other afflictions. He and Colleen expanded what they called their "cancer network," which increased the number of phone calls they made almost nightly. Colleen and Neal had much earlier developed the practice of looking after people in their neighborhood and beyond. Their ward Relief Society president once told her husband that every time she went to see someone who was sick or in need, the Maxwells had already been there. Now that circle kept growing, as Neal began to drop other after-hours activities in favor of staying close to more people whose sorrows he now understood better than he ever could before.

Since the mid-1970s, when he had been so moved by the example of President Spencer W. Kimball, Neal's very personal ministry to "the sick and afflicted" had matured into a significant feature of his priorities and even his character. At the risk of diminishing that private realm of service by disclosing details, many people have expressed the hope that something could be said here, even in general terms, about what he has done to comfort so many who have been stricken with adversity and what he's learned from doing it.

Neal's personal ministry was learned behavior—he didn't spend much time at it in his younger years. Later on, "the more he did it, the better he got at it." Perhaps he took counsel from a phrase in his patriarchal blessing, which blessed him with a gift of healing, giving him power "to rebuke the destroying agencies . . . that the sick may be healed." He was also influenced by the cancer patients he met in the late 1970s and by the thoughts that came to him during and after those years about the connections between adversity, divine tutorials, and learning to be true followers of Christ. That's one reason he began writing about those themes as much as he did.

Neal's "incredible pastoral outreach to people who have suffered" is "a major development in his discipleship in the last decade," says Elder Dallin H. Oaks. This is, indeed "an important part of Neal's personality, analogous to that of Spencer Kimball, who did so much work with individuals." "The Lord has twelve Apostles; they're not all stamped out of the same mold, and that has been a deliberate choice on His part." Neither Neal nor his Brethren, each of whom has his own private ministry of some kind, can do all that they wish were possible,

At "thanksgiving dinner" with Dr. Clyde Ford and his wife, Cheryl (left), and Dr. Larry Staker and his wife, Michelle (right)

but Latter-day Saints generally understand that the gifts of healing and blessing are not confined to Church leaders; they are gifts and priesthood privileges spread among all true disciples.

Neal has learned from experience about constructive ways to help people. Especially with the terminally ill, he is careful to avoid raising unrealistic expectations, even while acknowledging that at times a miracle does come. Each blessing and moment of counsel varies, but he sometimes invites the sick person and his or her family to read several scriptures aloud and then talk about each one. One verse he likes to read with them is this: "I know that he loveth his children; nevertheless, I do not know the meaning of all things" (1 Nephi 11:17). Neal discusses with the family the meaning of both principles from that passage. Especially since his own recent illness, he may also share with them what they will probably learn about the Atonement.

Elder Maxwell converses with a tone of sensitive realism, listening attentively and sharing experiences, keeping a steady rein on emotion. With the terminally ill, he will also talk matter-of-factly about ways the patient and the family can make the most of whatever time they have—such as giving father's blessings, tape-recording a personal testimony or history, writing letters of particular advice and counsel, and planning special experiences together.

Neal doesn't wait to be invited to make a visit. The stories are legion about his calling or just showing up in some unexpected place to express support. And he shows great interest in people who are not Latter-day Saints, along with people who are less active or otherwise estranged from the Church. Some of the most touching stories involve people among his old friends from the University of Utah who were once chilly toward the Church but who have now returned, some to be baptized, some for temple ordinances, all with Neal's presence and support.

He will also often make multiple calls and visits, staying close, remembering details, and giving encouragement—sometimes for months, sometimes for years. Neal has also paid particular attention to the "secondary sufferers," the spouses and family members of the stricken ones. Colleen, who knows something of this perspective, often joins him in these visits.

Among the children in these families, nine-year-old Melissa Howes sent Neal a large paper doll that still hangs on his office wall. When her young father was dying of cancer in 1998, Melissa said in her family prayer, "Heavenly Father, bless my daddy, and if you need . . . him more than us, you can have him. We want him, but Thy will be done. And please help us not to be mad at you."

Elder Maxwell's experience with the family of Shirley Scruggs (the wife of his friend Bud) illustrates his pattern. Shirley's sister Lisa developed cancer not long after Neal returned home from his own chemotherapy. When Neal gave Lisa a blessing, he surprised her by blessing her not only with comfort but with increased empathy. She had long felt an intuitive empathy for others, but the blessing answered her unspoken specific need—she'd been troubled by not knowing how to act toward people who knew she had cancer. Neal's own empathy let him see that she needed to let people minister to her, and she needed to know how imperfect some of that ministering would be. Then she could give more in her receiving.

When Lisa passed away, Neal groaned at the news. Now he was

asking the "why not me" question. He was puzzled, even troubled, each time he learned that much younger patients whom he had met during his own therapy had not survived. He would gladly have traded places with any of them, for their families' sakes.

He had developed enough of a relationship with Lisa that he wondered aloud how he could help. Shirley told him she was to speak at the funeral in California and didn't know what to say. How could an energetic young mother be taken when her children had such needs? Neal thought about her question and called her back the next day. Don't try to explain, he said. We don't understand why God takes people. The key points are from Nephi—I don't understand everything, but I do know that God loves each one of us. Then he shared the content of letters Lisa had written him. Her story corresponded almost perfectly with the course of his own illness—except for the conclusion.

After the funeral, when Lisa's husband and children visited Salt Lake, Neal invited them to his office. He gave the father a blessing but was otherwise "remarkably unsentimental." He told the children they had great parents and then said, "Let me tell you what your mother is doing right now in the spirit world." He seemed to understand what they were feeling and how to offer specific encouragement.

By May 1998, Neal's remission had lasted fifteen months. Admittedly not eager to line up for another turn at the chemo ward, he was thankful for his unexpected return to near-normal activity. Dr. Ford continued to monitor his monthly blood samples with close scrutiny and Sphinx-like reactions. He didn't want to let on that he fully expected the leukemia to return.

On Friday, May 29, a new painting of Joseph Smith in Liberty Jail was delivered to Elder Maxwell's office. While he was away that afternoon, his secretary Susan had the painting hung in the place prepared for it. As she stood back to see how it looked, she was drawn to Joseph's blue eyes, which seemed to carry a mellow kind of sadness. Something about the pleading eyes remained with her, creating a kind of quiet, heavy feeling.

Neal had the splint removed from his fractured tennis elbow the next Monday. Later that morning he met with Dr. Ford, who reported the results of the latest tests, which had included a bone marrow biopsy. The news was not good. The leukemia had returned. The remission was over. That which they most feared had come to pass.

Neal and Colleen decided to tell only their children that night. He would find a way to tell his Brethren, but he wasn't ready to talk to others. It felt like a time for silence. When his secretary first saw Neal on Tuesday, he didn't tell her the bad news, but he didn't need to. He couldn't have hidden the diagnosis. She thought his eyes were like Joseph's eyes in the painting, reflecting that same feeling of pleading sadness.

The new round of chemotherapy would begin on Wednesday, June 10. When Neal told President Faust on June 8 what was happening, his long-time friend said, "Neal, you're needed here." He suggested a blessing the next day before Neal checked into the hospital. At the appointed hour, President Faust brought five members of the Quorum of the Twelve to Neal's office, where they gave him a priesthood blessing, with President Faust as voice. As each one embraced him, once more a sure spirit of peace remained behind—the same spirit Neal had felt in the temple with them nearly two years before.

After several days of new chemotherapy, Neal returned home. He had beat the odds again: The cancer was once more in remission. On June 29, President Packer visited his home to give him another blessing. Neal returned to the hospital with a high fever during early July. By mid-August, he was back in his office, his hair gone once more. Of this period, President Packer said, "He doesn't take himself very seriously. He hasn't hidden the illness . . . but you can't get him to complain about it. When he's about to take [another] treatment, he tells his brethren he's 'going down under now.'"

Meanwhile, Dr. Clyde Ford was deeply unsettled about how to proceed. He knew that the odds of Neal's staying long in the second remission were slim. So he plunged into the medical literature, determined, especially for this patient, to find something in the reports of new medical experiments. He found a brief description of new work by some Swedish doctors; however, the treatment regime hadn't yet been

Greeting people on National Cancer Survivors Day at Hogle Zoo in Salt Lake City

tested in sufficient numbers of patients to justify predictable effects. So Dr. Ford told Neal and Colleen that it was completely experimental, but it looked like their best option. This wasn't the first time Neal had found himself on the cutting edge of experience, and he wasn't afraid to be there again. "Let's go," he said.

The "Swedish protocol" is, according to Neal, "not as exotic as it sounds." The medications alternate between suppressing the cells and building up the white count, Dr. Ford explains. Neal takes two injections of Interleukin-2 daily for three weeks and then goes without medication for two weeks. Next he takes oral and injectable chemotherapy for three weeks, takes another week off, and goes back to the Interleukin-2. He has followed this regimen for nearly four years, and despite usually being somewhat "washed out" by the injection periods, he has resumed most of his normal activities. To Dr. Ford, a believing Church member, "Elder Maxwell's very long second remission is miraculous. It seems more than chance to me."

Neal has developed two names for this otherwise undefined season of experience. Sometimes he calls it his "delay en route," reflecting his early use of military jargon. At other times it is his "pincushion period." For example, flying back from meetings in Spain in November

1999, he had to give himself injections en route. This prompted him to share with Colleen the remark from columnist Erma Bombeck that airplane lavatories are so small you have to stand on the toilet seat to shut the door.

Asked if the experimental process actually kills leukemic cells the way conventional chemotherapy does, Dr. Ford answers that he doesn't know. He only knows that, for Neal, it has worked—so far. "If I could explain in detail why it works, I'd be world famous." So how long will Neal follow this pattern? Indefinitely? We'll have to see. Medically, this is "way out on a statistical fringe of what you expect to happen. Spiritually, it's a miracle."

President Gordon B. Hinckley observed that Elder Maxwell, after two remissions, is "constantly expressing appreciation and gratitude. He's grateful for the gift of life, but I think he has lost all fear of death. I think he's adjusted his feelings so that death holds no terror for him. He has come to recognize that his life under these circumstances is a bonus from the Lord, and he wants to make the most of it."

At the same time, Neal has been cautious about drawing "hasty conclusions to his own advantage." Rather than feeling this extension of life was his to claim, he prefers to quote C. S. Lewis: "If we were stronger, we might be less tenderly treated. If we were braver, we might be sent, with far less help, to defend far more desperate posts in the great battle."

Neal's attitude is grounded in the doctrine of his October 1998 conference talk, titled "Hope through the Atonement of Jesus Christ." This was his first conference talk after his second complete immersion in chemotherapy. He again began with an understatement—"I am very grateful to be with you today"—and then added that his medical treatments "are encouraging in spite of my alternating conference hairstyles."

The central point of his talk distinguished between "proximate hope," which can easily be dashed by life's disappointments, and "ultimate hope," which, through the power of the Atonement, can consecrate our afflictions to our spiritual gain. In direct reflection of his daily experience, he said that ultimate hope keeps us engaged in "good causes, even if these appear to be losing causes on the mortal score-board." It is "with us at funerals," and it "inspires quiet Christian service, not flashy public fanaticism." Disciples blessed with this special hope reach out to those who have "moved away from the hope of the gospel," entreating them "by the patience of hope and the labor of love," until at last they hear the words, "well and faithfully done, enter into my joy, sit down on my throne."

During the time since the second remission began, Neal and Colleen have tried to do what they have long counseled other cancer survivors to do. Often patients with a terminal illness delay "bringing things to closure," thinking, almost subconsciously, that if they "don't have that final discussion with the kids, don't call that person they're estranged from," they can somehow delay the inevitable. But there was none of that for the Maxwells, whose priorities clearly included resolving the most important issues. These ranged from rethinking the most spiritual dimensions of his public ministry to very personal matters, such as deciding to give each grandchild an apostolic blessing.

Elder Maxwell's family members and closest friends have noticed that, as fully mature as he was in 1996, his experience has somehow altered him. They say such things as, he's not quite the same person since coming out of the hospital. He reflects a new depth of *feeling*, as well as new levels of understanding, about the Atonement. He was always tender, but there is a new tenderness, more emotion. He is simply different from the younger Neal Maxwell, good as he was.

As Elder Russell M. Nelson has watched at close range, he has seen Neal's empathy "augmented because of his own illness," reminding Elder Nelson of the way multiple illnesses increased President Spencer W. Kimball's awareness of other people's feelings and needs. Neal has also developed "an objectivity . . . that most patients don't have" in looking at his own circumstances. Most people focus more subjectively on "I'm miserable, I'm hurting. . . . But Brother Maxwell sees himself going through this period of testing and trying," never losing "sight of his place in the work of the Lord." Not imprisoned by his own misery, Neal is free to reflect on what his new understanding can teach him and how it helps him teach others.

Elder John K. Carmack, who worked closely with Neal for years, joined him for area training meetings in Spain in 1999. He saw "a new dimension in him" there, and "it was obvious to everybody. It was like he transported everybody there into a more eternal, spiritual realm. His manner contained all of the talented rhetorical abilities he always had, but we all felt something different . . .—a greater empathy for people, a greater sense of what life is about." In private he talked with great interest about all of his favorite subjects—politics, history, and current events. But one could sense that his ultimate interests "were definitely turned toward eternity."

Nolan Archibald, a stake president in Washington, D.C., found the same thing at Area training there, among a chapel full of stake presidents and other leaders in the fall of 2000. He had heard Elder Maxwell many times before, but found this meeting one of the spiritual feasts of his life, taught by a timeless Apostle who somehow left the group feeling what it would be like for Paul or Alma to teach them. Brother Archibald had always found Neal to be a gifted teacher, but this time he felt a new spiritual dimension as the group talked together of scriptural doctrines, with tangible two-way feelings of affection, gentleness, humility, and tears frequently in the eyes of his brethren.

Elder Maxwell views whatever has happened as a gift, not an achievement. He knows that something about the experience has brought him more compassion. The Lord, he said,

> gives us a "new heart" (Ezek. 18:31). Our heart has to be broken, in a way, so that it can be re-made. By that I mean more spiritual sensitivity, more empathy, and more capacity to be responsive to people. The natural man['s] . . . heart . . . is pretty self-centered and hard. If we can put off the natural man [see Mosiah 3:19], we can be given a new heart, and it will be enlarged . . . without hypocrisy (see D&C 121:42). Adversity can squeeze out of us the hypocrisy that's there.
>
> [So, for me,] it's been a great spiritual adventure, one I would not want to have missed. I feel a little about it the way I do about Okinawa. If I'd waited my turn to be drafted, I would never have seen any action. It wasn't that I was anything special as a soldier. Even though it cost me some hearing, I'm glad I saw

The Quorum of the Twelve Apostles, 1995

that action. And even though this has cost, it's been a great blessing. I know people may think I'm just being patriotic to say that, but it's true.

Understanding the nature of Elder Maxwell's experience is enhanced by comparing it with that of another person whose lifelong quest for discipleship was strikingly similar to Neal's.

In 1963, B. West Belnap was dean of the College of Religious Instruction at BYU and was, like Neal, a close associate of Elder Harold B. Lee in the correlation committees. One semester he taught a small class called "Your Religious Problems." In the first class, Brother Belnap demonstrated his intended class format by sharing the religious question that had the greatest personal meaning to him: How can I obtain the gift of charity? With endearing candor, he told the students how his religious faith had developed over his lifetime.

As a child with very bad eyesight, he once prayed anxiously to find a lost pair of glasses. He was awestruck when the Lord answered his prayer by guiding his footsteps. Over time, his soul came to delight increasingly in the scriptures. His yearning to understand and live the deep things of God influenced his daily life, his family, his career. At the time he taught this class, West was just past forty years old and the father of seven children. He was a thoughtful, well-balanced man of sound judgment who had enjoyed an unusually high degree of Church experience for one his age.

After telling his students about his more recent spiritual experiences, he told them how puzzled he was that he didn't feel he had been able to obtain charity—the pure love that Christ has for all people. He read from the scriptures what charity was, that it reflected the Lord's very nature, and that God has promised it to "all who are true followers of his Son, Jesus Christ" (Moroni 7:48). A poignancy accompanied his earnest reflection that, despite years of trying to live as pure a daily life as he knew how, the gift had eluded him.

A few years later, by then only in his mid-forties, West Belnap died from a terribly painful brain tumor. At his funeral, Elder Harold B. Lee spoke of his close friendship with West. He said that when the cancer persisted after two surgeries, West asked for counsel about additional treatments. The pain was so unbearable and the prognosis so dim that he wondered if he shouldn't forgo further efforts and let himself go quickly. Elder Lee had told him,

> West, you and I . . . know that life is a very precious thing and . . . has a very important meaning. Every minute of it, even the suffering of it. . . . How do you and I know but what the suffering you're going through is a refining process by which obedience necessary to exaltation is made up? . . .
>
> Live it out to the last day, West. . . . Who knows but what the experience you are having now will pay dividends greater than all the rest of your life. Live it true to the end, and we'll bless you and pray to God that pains beyond your endurance will not be permitted by a merciful God.

West followed that counsel, accepting an unknowable degree of suffering before finally being released in death.

West had developed in his early life an earnest desire to follow the Savior as far as it is possible to follow Him. He couldn't have known where this desire might take him or what it might cost, but he, like Neal

Elder and Sister Maxwell with President and Sister Gordon B. Hinckley at the dinner establishing the Neal A. Maxwell Presidential Endowed Chair at the University of Utah

Maxwell in his own way, pursued his desire a step at a time, disciplining himself, learning, accepting correction, and making clear to the Lord his commitment to full discipleship, regardless of the cost.

Perhaps his excruciating illness somehow gave him access to his heart's desire—charity. He had wanted to possess what the Savior felt in His love for every human being. To attain that charity, West was willing to give the Lord anything that was his to give, although he knew that, finally, charity is a spiritual gift "*bestowed*" by the grace of the Atonement "upon all who are true followers of his Son, Jesus Christ . . . that when he shall appear we shall be *like him*" (Moroni 7:48; italics added). Could West have sensed how dear the price might be—that, perhaps, to assimilate attributes of divinity from the core of the Savior's love might require some hauntingly tangible contact with the core of his afflictions? "All those who will not endure chastening . . . *cannot* be sanctified" (D&C 101:5; italics added).

Truman and Ann Madsen have known the Maxwells since their college days together. Truman said that the people with whom he has counseled about the hardest of life's problems tend to have two concerns about those who try to help them. One is, "You don't know what I'm talking about, how hard this is; you've never been there, never faced real adversity." The other concern is, "You don't really care about me. You're listening, but you want to go home and have dinner." Elder Maxwell has taught that we'll never be able to level either of those charges at Christ. And now, says Truman after watching Elder Maxwell's experience with his illness, "You'll never be able to say any of those things to Neal Maxwell, either."

Perhaps the experiences of such people as Neal Maxwell and West Belnap teach us that those who seek apprenticeship with the Master of mankind must emulate his sacrificial experience to the fullest extent of their personal capacity. Then they might taste His empathy and His charity. For only then are they like him enough to feel his love for others *the way he feels it*—to love others "as I have loved you" (John 13:34). That is a deeper, different love from "love thy neighbour as thyself" (Matthew 19:19). Perhaps it isn't possible to have Christ's charity without submitting to some form of His affliction—not only through physical pain but in many other ways—because they are two sides of the same, single reality.

The Savior's love for all mankind is fully bound up in his exquisite pain. "How sore you know not . . . how hard to bear you know not" (D&C 19:15). Perhaps we cannot know his love without knowing his pain. If so, the personal suffering we confront in the sanctification process—"the fellowship of His suffering"—could move the pure love of Christ from a concept in one's head to a substance in one's heart. And once in the heart, charity will circulate all through the body, because it is being moved by "a new heart."

In March 2000, when he was in a pondering mood about his illness, with its implications both dreadful and miraculous, Neal had a sacred experience that he could only compare with what happened that night in 1945 on Okinawa. The soul voice of the Spirit came into his mind to whisper, "I have given you leukemia that you might teach my people with authenticity." The words sank in deeply, confirming his belief that the Lord had authored his tutorial—and his recovery. What did this mean about the length of his ministry? That part remained

Carrying the Olympic torch in Salt Lake City, 7 February 2002

unclear. He wondered if the statement meant future teaching only. Yet whatever the future holds, his recent experience also bears a personal witness that reaffirms and enriches his previous attempts to teach people about meekness, adversity, discipleship, not shrinking, and finding charity in the midst of affliction.

In that personal witness, the way Neal Maxwell has lived is more vital than what he has taught. For him to receive more empathy, which in its fulness is charity, fulfills a desire he has long nourished. And even though he may be best known among Church members for his distinctive use of language, a closer search of his life reveals dimensions of that desire that have much deeper substance.

His talks to less active members and converts carry between their lines an empathy for the less included that is both kind and disarming. He understands them. His talks to the women of the Church reflect an honest sensitivity to their questions and priorities. He understands them. His messages to college students and teachers have let them feel his openness, his awareness, and his serenity about their hardest questions. He understands them. His relationships with political communities, whether close at hand or far away, have built bridges of trust that make it natural for opinion leaders in and out of the Church to sense that in him they have a friendly ear. He understands.

The Saints in Africa, Asia, and other remote places of new beginning for the Church have felt he somehow understands intuitively where the gospel fits into their personal cultural context. Those afflicted with illness or the death of family members sense that he has unusual, personal reasons for understanding what they are feeling. All of this is why those who know Elder Maxwell best say, "There are many people in the Church who feel he understands them," and they have therefore felt "understood by the general leadership of the Church." "His greatest qualities are not those of his head but of his heart."

The educated may think he is approachable because he was an educator. Converts to the Church, those interested in social issues, or those wounded with adversity may sense in him a special interest in their concerns. Political and media leaders may feel he understands their world because of his background in it. His family knows him as an unusually devoted father. And in a way, they are all correct. But cutting through all the dimensions of Neal Maxwell's broad interests is a core quality of empathy that has increasingly manifested itself in every context. In recent years, especially since his illness, that empathy has expanded more and more toward charity.

This may well be the charity Neal sensed at the time of his call as an Apostle that he must somehow come to claim, the charity of which his mentor Harold B. Lee spoke when he said he realized that he must learn to "love and forgive every soul that walked the earth." Because charity is a gift of the Spirit, the knowing tenderness Elder Maxwell now feels is larger than anything he could possess of himself alone.

The source of that tenderness looks this way to Elder Henry B. Eyring:

> Some of the people who love his wonderful insights and his gorgeous language underestimate how close he is to the Savior. [I would tell them,] you don't know him. You don't know that as brilliant as he is, as gifted as he is in language . . . there's no one as brave and as determined to do only what the Savior wants . . . For some reason [his writing style] results in many people seeing him as the intellectual. . . . But he's way closer to Peter than he is to C. S. Lewis. . . . And when it comes time to say, "The world be hanged, we'll go the Lord's way," no one is braver.

At the time an endowed chair was created in Neal's name at the

© John Snyder

In December 2001

University of Utah, President Hinckley said that whoever occupies the chair "will find a hand resting on his shoulder" from "one who loved mercy, one who practiced charity, one who had a great love for learning, one who had a mind to think objectively, one who made a contribution in whatever he did."

Neal Maxwell, said Elder Alexander Morrison, is "a man of the last half of the twentieth century, when secularism" is rampant, and "Christianity is dying around the world." His "defense of Christianity, and his reconciliation of faith and the intellect" are a great legacy. But more important than all of that is what he has learned, and lived, about "the struggle to be pure . . . to put away the natural man." He has shown that, with the Savior's help, "it is possible to purify yourself, to change." So "the transformation . . . in his own life . . . is the great miracle of his apostleship, because it holds out hope for ordinary people [showing them that they] can be better . . . less competitive and more loving.

That's the great theme of Neal's life . . . that if you take your discipleship seriously, you really can change."

This kind of change is a process that is available to all. Ultimately it is a gift—given, paradoxically, only to those who pay its full price. Its source is the grace given to faithful followers of Jesus. As they expend all of their own strength and all of their own will, the gift comes: "Lo, I have given thee . . . an understanding heart" (1 Kings 3:11). It comes through the Savior's mercy—"mercy cometh because of the Atonement" (Alma 42:23)—to those who put off the natural man enough to be forgiven and then press beyond forgiveness toward becoming "a saint through the Atonement of Christ the Lord, . . . full of love [charity], willing to submit to all things which the Lord seeth fit to inflict" (Mosiah 3:19).

The same gift also comes to disciple-leaders not just to enrich them, but to validate their teaching and to bless God's people: "And the priests were not to depend upon the people for their support; but for their labor they were to receive the grace of God, that they might wax strong in the Spirit, having the knowledge of God, that they might teach with power and authority" (Mosiah 18:26).

And that they might teach His people with authenticity.

It is the way of a Disciple's life—and a disciple's life.

SOURCE NOTES

PREFACE

Page

xiv "are too large": Wilson, *C. S. Lewis*, 126.
xv "history's gold": Gilbert, *In Search of Churchill*, 20.
xv "idealizing or idolizing biography": *Merriam-Webster's Collegiate Dictionary*, s.v. "hagiography."
xv "It isn't that we're searching": NAM-Irving oral history, 388.
xv "We must be careful": NAM, *More Excellent Way*, 130.
xvi "interweave what [Johnson] privately wrote": Boswell, *Life of Samuel Johnson*, 2–3.

1. I Should Have Seen It Coming

Page

3 "needed to make": NAM, "Discussion of Values."
4 "his courage": Stack, "Pain Is Part of Progress," C3.
4 "That is how": Unnamed BYU staff member, quoted to Hafen in conversation with Eric d'Evegnee, 30 March 2000.
4 "My thanks": NAM, "From Whom All Blessings Flow," 11; paragraphing altered.
8 "remind me": Jackson to Hafen, 15 August 2001.
8 "So how are you": Scruggs oral history, 21.
9 "pre-leukemic condition": Ford oral history, 4.
11 "I will never forget": Holland oral history, 50.
12 postgraduate course: NAM, *Not My Will*, 4.
12 "come to us": NAM, *All These Things*, 30, 32, 34, 36, 39; some italics added; paragraphing altered.
12 "wintry verse": NAM, *Men and Women of Christ*, 61.
12 "The enlarging": NAM, "Endure It Well," 34–35; italics added.
12 the very act of choosing: NAM, *All These Things*, 32.

2. WINTRY DOCTRINE

Page

13 "something awful": Olsen to Hafen, 5 January 2000.

14 "pre-leukemic condition": "Elder Maxwell Fulfilling Duties," B1.

14 "comforted by the afflicted": Olsen to Hafen, 5 January 2000.

14 "to promote": Scruggs oral history, 22.

16 "I have no concept": Ford oral history, 32.

16 As the wintry: Orson F. Whitney, "The Wintry Day, Descending to Its Close," *Hymns*, no. 37.

16 "I just don't want to *shrink*": See D&C 19:18.

16 "Certain forms of suffering": NAM, "Enduring Well," 8.

17 "Please know that I": NAM to Katie Anderson and Timothy Maxwell, 27 February 1997, in 1997 scrapbook.

18 "Truman and Ann": Madsen oral history, 43.

18 "the weakest": Staker oral history, 8 December 2000, 15.

19 "It is required": Holmes, *Memorial Day Address*, 643.

20 "constant conversation": Douglas Parker, remarks at Joseph S. Clark funeral, 23 February 1996, in Parker oral history, 52.

20 "Joe had a special": NAM, remarks at Joseph S. Clark funeral, 23 February 1996, in Parker oral history, 55–57.

21 "I do not believe": Lindbergh, quoted in "Lindbergh Nightmare," 35.

22 "probably terminal": Staker oral history, 13 December 2000, 12.

22 "the awful C-word": Hafen notes, Jackie Moody funeral, 15 July 1996.

22 "to learn": NAM, *One More Strain*, 4.

22 "That's what Jesus did": Staker oral history, 13 December 2000, 12.

22 Jesus, in his hours: Hafen notes, General Authority temple meeting, 7 June 2001.

22 "instructed his disciples": Colleen H. Maxwell, "Hope Everlasting," 383.

22 "many people felt": Colleen H. Maxwell, untitled address, 14 February 1998, 1–2.

23 "realistic about": Colleen H. Maxwell, "Hope Everlasting," 383.

23 "The pain then": quoted in Meilaender, "Everyday C. S. Lewis," 31.

23 "character": NAM, "From Whom All Blessings Flow," 11.

3. CONVERT ORIGINS

Page

28 "a Christian from": Minerva Maxwell obituary, NAM ancestry file, 119.

28 "man of strong character": John Maxwell obituary, NAM ancestry file, 118.

28 "was brought up poor": Martin Lundwall journal, NAM ancestry file, 127.

28 "gave out": Anders Lundwall to Martin Lundwall, 21 July 1862, NAM ancestry file, 128, 134.

29 "now thanks to the Lord": Anders Lundwall to Martin Lundwall, 2 November 1862, NAM ancestry file, 135.

30 "It was mostly": Martin Lundwall journal, April 1863, NAM ancestry file, 135.

30 "they persuaded them": Anders Lundwall to Martin Lundwall, 8 August 1863, NAM ancestry file, 136.

30 "They had left": Martin Lundwall journal, 19 November 1864, NAM ancestry file, 136.

32 "Nothing seemed to be the same": Clarence Maxwell personal history, NAM ancestry file, 11, 13.

4. PIONEER ORIGINS

Page

35 "literary turn": Alma Ash autobiography, NAM ancestry file, 197–99, 201–3, 206.

36 "Well, Sir Thomas": Thomas Ash biographical sketch, NAM ancestry file, 194.

36 "received [him] rather coldly": Alma Ash autobiography, NAM ancestry file, 209–10, 215–16, 219–20.

37 "genteel, kindly manners": Thomas Ash biographical sketch, NAM ancestry file, 192, 195.

38 "'I don't want'": George Albert Ash biographical sketch, NAM ancestry file, 175–77.

40 "wind-rocked": Charles Augustus Cobbley personal history, NAM ancestry file, 224.

42 "I will merely state": Cobbley to Woodruff, 7 January 1893, NAM ancestry file, 233.

42 "without a five-cent piece": Charles Augustus Cobbley personal history, NAM ancestry file, 228.

42 "had little time": Emma Louise Davis biographical sketch, NAM ancestry file, 237.

5. CLARENCE AND EMMA

Page

44 "an event": Clarence H. Maxwell autobiography, NAM ancestry file, 21.

45 other more "impish": Emma A. Maxwell personal history, NAM ancestry file, 152–53.

46 "When Judd": NAM, remarks at George Truman "Judd" Flinders funeral, 1 December 1998, 2.

46 "Angrily I went": Clarence H. Maxwell loose-leaf journal, NAM ancestry file, 157.

48 "critical mass": NAM, *Look Back at Sodom*, 33; *Time to Choose*, 46.

48 "He comes": Packer oral history, 2.

6. BORN IN SALT LAKE CITY'S ROARING TWENTIES

Page

51 "Emerging from": Morris and Morris, *Encyclopedia of American History*, 352.

52 "benign presence": Brokaw, *Greatest Generation*, 4.

52 Church membership stood: Allen and Leonard, *Story of the Latter-day Saints*, 498.

53 "covered from one side": Lois Maxwell autobiography, in 1988 scrapbook, 4.

53 Utah was among: Sillitoe, *History of Salt Lake County*, 129, 153.

54 "loaded with converts": NAM-Irving oral history, 10–11.

55 "talked too much": NAM, "Unto the Rising Generation," 11.

55 New buildings rose: Sillitoe, *History of Salt Lake County*, 148.

56 "healthful enjoyment": From Bishop Nibley's remarks at the dedication of Nibley Park, quoted in Alexander and Allen, *Mormons and Gentiles*, 176.

56 "was good for": NAM personal history, 3.
56 enticed the office-bound: Talmage, *Talmage Story*, 227–28.
56 "maze of urban": Sillitoe, *History of Salt Lake County*, 128, 150.
56 "from thoroughfares": Alexander and Allen, *Mormons and Gentiles*, 179.
57 "didn't lose any time": Clarence H. Maxwell to NAM, 6 July 1987, in 1987 scrapbook.

7. Clarence Maxwell and Son: Master and Apprentice

Page

59 shy and unassuming: McConkie oral history, 6.
59 about five: NAM-Hafen oral history, 25, 27.
59 a favorite: Wright to Cory H. Maxwell, 4 September 2000.
59 "Dad didn't need": Skankey to Cory H. Maxwell, 4 September 2000.
60 "which gave me": NAM-Hafen oral history, 1, 5.
61 "your part": Clarence H. Maxwell to NAM, 6 July 1987, in 1987 scrapbook.
61 "his gentleness": Karen B. Maxwell oral history, 51–52.
62 "life seemed to have": Peterson, "Friend to Friend," 7.
62 "Neal was not as methodical": Colleen H. Maxwell–Hafen oral history, 7–8.
62 "just throwing things together": Lois Maxwell to NAM, 4 July 1987, in 1987 scrapbook.
62 "loving but exacting": NAM, "Put Your Shoulder to the Wheel," 37.
62 "you were never through": Peterson, "Friend to Friend," 7.
63 "heart full of song": NAM, "Put Your Shoulder to the Wheel," 37.
63 "the importance of pride": NAM, *More Excellent Way*, 134.
63 "constantly faced": NAM, "My 4-H Club Experiences," in 1926–59 scrapbook.
64 "though joyful": NAM, "Put Your Shoulder to the Wheel," 38.
64 "better disciples": NAM, "Friend to Friend," 7; paragraphing altered.
64 "Your 4-H achievements": Clarence H. Maxwell to NAM, 6 July 1987, in 1987 scrapbook.
65 "why this question": Smith to Clarence H. Maxwell, 20 January 1947.
66 "if you got him talking": NAM-Hafen oral history, 26.
67 "kept [up] a steady": NAM, remarks at Clarence H. Maxwell funeral, in 1993 scrapbook, 14.
67 "tells me I'm not": NAM-Irving oral history, 88.
67 He vividly remembers: Heslop, "He Built on Parents' Example," 5.
68 "I watched my father": Hewitt, *Searching for God*, 122.
69 "sandbagged him": NAM-Hafen oral history, 88.
69 "one of His faithful servants": Clarence H. Maxwell, father's blessing of NAM, in 1976 scrapbook, 1.

8. Emma, Lois, and Life at Home

Page

71 "equal partnership": Clarence H. Maxwell, "Eternal Investments," in 1988 scrapbook.
71 "give her an A": NAM, remarks at Emma A. Maxwell funeral, 4 May 1983, in 1983 scrapbook.
72 "If plants know": Lois Maxwell to Hafen, 13 September 2001.

72 "We know": NAM, remarks at Emma A. Maxwell funeral, in 4 May 1983, 1983 scrapbook.

72 "she lined up": NAM-Hafen oral history, 76.

72 "He's the bishop": NAM sisters oral history, 4, 17.

73 "for talks with Mom": Wright to Hafen, 13 September 2001.

73 "the local medical association": NAM-Irving oral history, 5.

73 "really cared": Skankey to Hafen, 24 August 2001.

74 "crying and coming home": NAM personal history, 2.

74 "I remember looking": Emma Ash Maxwell to NAM, 6 July 1982, in 1982 scrapbook.

75 "play like mad": Emma Ash Maxwell personal history, in NAM ancestry file, 167.

75 "the cloud": NAM personal history, 2.

75 "a stringer": NAM-Irving oral history, 48.

75 "duet brother and sister": NAM personal history, 1.

75 most all: Lois Maxwell to NAM, 4 July 1987, in 1987 scrapbook.

76 "she has never": NAM sisters oral history, 16.

76 "unhurried, unlimited": Skankey to Hafen, 24 August 2001.

76 "when you get there": NAM sisters oral history, 20–23.

77 "picked her successor": NAM-Hafen oral history, 135.

9. A True Story? Or Were You Just Preaching?

Page

78 "Church, church": Emma A. Maxwell to NAM, 6 July 1982, in 1982 scrapbook.

79 "Tithing. The law": NAM personal history, 5.

79 "I look so": NAM-Irving oral history, 9–10, 12, 16–17, 19.

79 "much less": NAM-Allen oral history, 111.

80 "wooden benches": NAM-Irving oral history, 10, 21, 392.

80 "a set of givens": NAM-Irving oral history, 392; NAM, "Discussion of Values"; NAM, "Insights from My Life" (2000), 13.

81 "felt a sense": NAM-Reeves oral history, 2.

81 "a warm": NAM personal history, 2.

81 "That makes me": NAM sisters oral history, 19.

81 "If I could": NAM-Irving oral history, 23.

81 "I still remember": NAM, *"But a Few Days,"* 3.

82 "steadying the ark": NAM-Irving oral history, 78. During the time of King David, God had commanded that no one should touch the sacred ark of the covenant. When an Israelite named Uzzah touched the ark to steady it on the back of shaking oxen, "God smote him" dead (2 Samuel 6:6).

10. Hoops and Hogs

Page

83 "Tom Sawyer solitude": NAM personal history, 4.

85 "It was a bitter": Knight, "Language Is a Key to His Life," 5.

85 "a very difficult": NAM-Judd dictation, 4.

86 "one of the": NAM, "My 4-H Club Experiences," in 1926–59 scrapbook, 1.

86 "outstanding in education": Lois Maxwell to NAM, 4 July 1987, in 1987 scrapbook.

86 "there is pigs": NAM, "Story of My Project," in 1926–59 scrapbook, 1–2.

87 "with an experienced": NAM, "My 4-H Club Experiences," in 1926–59 scrapbook, 1.

87 "prestige enough": NAM, "Story of My Project," in 1926–59 scrapbook, 1–2.

87 "one of the competent": Broadbent to County Scholarship Committee, 22 November 1942, in 1926–59 scrapbook.

87 "the best year": NAM, "Story of My Project," in 1926–59 scrapbook, 3–4.

11. Adolescent Disappointments and Directions

Page

89 "being at home": NAM, "Insights from My Life" (1976), 189.

89 "Adolescence is a": Armour, *Educated Guesses,* 65.

90 He enouraged them: Rex Allen, notes from Madrid Area training conference, in 1999 scrapbook.

90 "he wasn't gifted": Hewitt, telephone conversation with Hafen, 31 July 2001.

91 "I seem to hear": Holland, introduction of NAM, in 1982 scrapbook.

91 "Carolyn Fagg did most": NAM personal history, 8.

92 "quite a speech": NAM-Irving oral history, 20, 90.

92 "The Lord was nudging": Hewitt, *Searching for God,* 122.

12. Volunteering for Immediate Induction

Page

95 "Mr. President": Brokaw, *Greatest Generation,* 9.

96 "4-H Victory Achievement": NAM, "4-H Victory Achievements," in 1926–59 scrapbook.

96 "Two German Strongholds": *Deseret News,* 18 May 1944.

96 "anxious to be involved": NAM personal history, 9.

96 "I felt it was": NAM-Irving oral history, 25.

96 "had a fairly well developed sense": NAM, Granite High School 55th Reunion, in 1999 scrapbook.

96 "I didn't want to wait": NAM-Irving oral history, 27.

97 "hearts were full": Emma A. Maxwell to NAM, 6 July 1982, in 1982 scrapbook.

97 "didn't even need to shave": NAM personal history, 9.

97 "be a real man": NAM to family, 18 September 1944.

97 "I've been shooting the M-1": NAM to family, 2 November 1944.

97 "Our home was heaven": NAM to family, 18 September 1944.

97 "I owe $5.50": NAM to family, 2 November 1944.

98 "go overseas": NAM personal history, 10.

98 "needed to go": NAM, "Discussion of Values."

98 "we were in a righteous": NAM-Allen oral history, 116.

99 "falling exhausted": Longford, *Wellington,* 1:490.

99 "came of age": Brokaw, *Greatest Generation,* jacket flap.

99 "seemed familiar": Morrison oral history, 28.

99 "They answered the call": Brokaw, *Greatest Generation,* xix-xxi, 271–72, 276–78, 329; paragraphing altered.

101 "A people may prefer": John Stuart Mill, quoted in NAM, "Constitution . . . Wisest," 2.

101 "have a hard time": Scruggs oral history, 14.

101 "He had a severe": Haglund oral history, 11.

13. OKINAWA

102 "Have [now] seen": NAM to family, 25 April 1945.

103 "the artillery blazing": NAM personal history, 10; NAM-Allen oral history, 116.

104 "Tennozan": Feifer, *Tennozan*, flyleaf; Leckie, *Okinawa;* Gailey, *War in the Pacific.*

104 "the key to": Ivan Morris, quoted in Feifer, *Tennozan*, vi.

104 "monster ambush": Leckie, *Okinawa*, 20–21.

104 Ironically, as it turned out: NAM personal history, 10, 13–14. Another member of L Company Neal saw on that same morning was Seldon K. Nowers from Beaver, Utah.

105 To begin with: Feifer, *Tennozan*, xiv. Many of those serving were members of the Church. During World War II, more than 100,000 Latter-day Saints served in the armed forces of various nations on both sides of the conflict, and approximately 5,000 of them died. Mark E. Peterson, "In Defense of Liberty," 288.

105 "mortal contact with": Feifer, *Tennozan*, xiv.

105 "I've been assigned": NAM to family, 13 May 1945.

106 "vicious sprawling struggle": Hanson W. Baldwin, quoted in Feifer, *Tennozan*, vii.

106 "measured by sheer": Feifer, *Tennozan*, xi, xiii.

106 "bristled with mortars": Leckie, *Okinawa*, 177.

106 "could barely put": NAM-Allen oral history, 117.

106 He heard soon: Feifer, *Tennozan*, 295.

106 The first American: NAM personal history, 11.

107 "rendered the entire": NAM to Cory H. Maxwell, 10 October 1973.

107 "turned the battlefield": Gailey, *War in the Pacific,* 439; paragraphing altered.

107 "sometimes you slept": Feifer, *Tennozan*, 299–307.

108 "Had a dream": NAM to family, 13 May 1945.

108 "Mormon boy who": Seil to NAM, quoted in NAM, *One More Strain,* 106.

109 "Still haven't drunk": NAM to family, 8 June 1945.

109 "You never know": C. S. Lewis, quoted in NAM, *More Excellent Way,* 129.

110 "one of those": NAM-Judd dictation, 3.

110 "After that triangulation": NAM personal history, 12.

111 "I foolishly thought": NAM-Judd dictation, 3.

112 "May [no date]": NAM to family, May, June, August, and September 1945; May 1946.

115 "Decades after the war": Summary of events of May 1996, in 1995–96 scrapbook.

115 "which, for me": NAM, "Insights from My Life" (1976), 190; paragraphing altered.

116 "still trying to keep": NAM-Reeves oral history, 4.

116 "sensed that the Lord": Avant, "Elder Maxwell Personifies," 4.

116 "With this blessing": NAM, "Becoming a Disciple," 19.

116 "We became acquainted": McKay, "Pioneer Women," 8.

116 "a great spiritual adventure": NAM-Irving oral history, 27, 560.

14. Learning and Leadership in Wartime

Page

117 Learning in wartime: Lewis, *Weight of Glory*, 21.
117 "primitive though they": NAM-Irving oral history, 53.
117 "the memory of black days": NAM to family, 30 June 1945.
118 "drafting those letters": Eyring, "Neal A. Maxwell," 7.
118 "Hear much about": NAM to family, July 1945.
118 Then he began: NAM-Irving oral history, 91.
119 Years later: Brough-Irving oral history, 8.
119 "How about Maxwell?": NAM, conversation with Hafen, 24 January 2001.
119 "I sure have some": NAM to family, 6 January 1946.
120 "I get a little thrill": NAM to family, 25 January 1946.
120 "I suppose you know": NAM to family, 2 February 1946.
120 "one of the significant": NAM personal history, 14.
120 "I'm in an awkward": NAM to family, 17 August 1945.
120 "armies of occupation": NAM personal history, 14.
121 "I still wander": NAM to family, 27 March 1946.
121 "Time is heavy": NAM to family, 2 May 1946.
121 "friendly fire": NAM personal history, 12.
122 "it was a privilege": NAM to family, 31 October 1945.
122 "a rugged sergeant": NAM, *More Excellent Way*, 135.
122 "You were a good": Buesing to NAM, 14 April 2000.
123 as "old Mac": Gardea and Felshaw, "Reunion with Army Buddy," A4.
123 "the boasting words": NAM, "Insights from My Life" (1976), 199.
123 "The Dilemma of Madame Butterfly and Mary Jones": In 1926–59 scrapbook.
123 "had quite an effect": NAM to family, 26 August 1945.
124 "visual aid": NAM-Irving oral history, 41.
124 "[his] people": NAM to family, 26 August 1945.
125 "strove to put on": NAM, "Jesus, the Perfect Mentor," 7.
125 Neal and Boyd didn't: Packer oral history, 19.

15. Teaching the Gospel

Page

129 "had promises to keep": NAM-Judd dictation, 3.
129 "ark-steadying tendencies": NAM-Irving oral history, 341; NAM, *One More Strain of Praise*, 110.
130 "Thirty years ago": NAM, "Notwithstanding My Weakness," 12.
131 "avoid political discussions": NAM-Irving oral history, 94.
131 "I say Dewey": NAM to family, n.d.
131 The mission had: Annual Report of Canadian Mission, 1948, in Church Archives.
131 "We were there": NAM-Allen oral history, 118; NAM-Irving oral history, 35.
132 "the greatest generation": Brokaw, *Greatest Generation*, xxx.
132 "veterans with a maturity": Newton, "My Family, My Friends, My Faith," 9.
132 "things were in": NAM personal history, 15.
133 "It gets about": NAM to family, 7 February 1947.
133 "My first three": NAM to Cory H. Maxwell, 3 November 1972.
133 "No'th o' th' Boda'": NAM to family, 19 February 1947.
134 "reading ability": Call to Hafen, 27 July 2000.

134 "Am through with all": NAM to family, 7 February 1947.
134 "Finished B. H. Roberts": NAM to family, 19 February 1947.
134 "Sorry if I disturbed you": NAM to family, 24 February 1947.
134 "I could use": NAM to family, 29 November 1947.
135 "binge reading": NAM-Irving oral history, 36, 38–39, 361.
135 was "a student": Adams oral history, 6, 14.
135 "Local minister slammed": NAM to family, 7 February 1947.
136 "there on the": NAM, "Discussion of Values."
136 The indifference: NAM-Irving oral history, 37.
136 "were all fumbling": NAM-Allen oral history, 118–19.
137 "the least efficient": NAM-Irving oral history, 38.
137 "I never thot": NAM to family, 19 July 1947.
138 "Do not feel": NAM, "Sword of Truth," 1.
139 President Eyre liked: Joseph R. Smith to Hafen, 15 September 2001. Elder Smith was a missionary in the Canadian Mission when Elder Maxwell's plan was adopted.
139 "better by far": NAM-Hafen oral history, 25.

16. Establishing the Church

Page

141 "As they sustained": NAM missionary file, 14 September 1947.
141 "My testimony is": NAM to family, 16 September 1947.
141 "Elder, because we": NAM to LaPriel R. Eyre, 30 April 1973, in 1973 scrapbook.
142 "My mission president": NAM, "I Will Arise," 67.
142 "I know I": NAM, "Jesus of Nazareth," 27.
142 "Your son is a scholar": Merrill to Clarence and Emma Maxwell, Christmas 1947.
142 "I am old enough": Merrill to Clarence and Emma Maxwell, 25 January 1948.
142 "because you really": NAM-Irving oral history, 40.
143 "a really good": Adams oral history, 9, 14, 19, 23.
143 "how to answer": NAM to family, 30 October 1947.
144 "better than average": NAM to family, 20 September 1948.
144 "imprudently" and "foolishly but": NAM personal history, 16.
144 "Can one holder": NAM to family, 24 April 1948.
144 "What do you know": NAM to family, 26 January 1948.
145 "God's strengthening help": NAM to family, 8 May 1948.
145 "isolated Saint": NAM to family, 24 February 1947.
146 "More than 30 years ago": Arbuckle, "Conversion Story," in 1984 scrapbook; paragraphing altered.
146 "May I take": NAM to Wandamere Ward, 25 March 1947.
146 "It gave me a great thrill": NAM to family, 19 November 1947.
147 "Samaras": "Samaras" is a seed from a Canadian tree. "At maturity it is blown with the winds, only to reestablish itself elsewhere and be self-perpetuating." Joseph R. Smith to Hafen, 15 September 2001.
147 "big production": Colleen H. Maxwell–Hafen oral history, 20.
147 "I was not late": NAM, remarks at inauguration of John A. Widtsoe Chair in Chemistry, in 1995–96 scrapbook, 4.
148 "He has with": Eyre to Eldred C. Bergeson, 22 January 1949, in 1926–59 scrapbook.

17. A POSTWAR STUDENT'S LIFE

Page

152 the "greatest generation": Brokaw, *Greatest Generation,* xxx.

152 the number of enrollments: Bennett, *When Dreams Came True,* 7–11, 201, 236.

153 "sat in old": NAM, remarks at inauguration of NAM Presidential Endowed Chair, in 1999 scrapbook.

153 In that field: G. Homer Durham later became academic vice president at the University of Utah, president of Arizona State University, commissioner of education for the Utah System of Higher Education, and then a member of the First Quorum of Seventy of The Church of Jesus Christ of Latter-day Saints.

153 "thousands of undergraduate students": Durham to Citizenship Clearing House, 15 August 1959, in 1966–69 scrapbook.

154 "in too big a hurry": NAM-Irving oral history, 54.

154 "A sooty, sweaty hand": "Shortest Distance," in 1926–59 scrapbook, 23.

154 "ominous voice": NAM-Irving oral history, 82.

155 "fun loving": Adams oral history, 8, 20, 27.

155 "most outrageous and memorable": Parker oral history, 9.

155 "unnecessarily insecure": McConkie oral history, 4.

155 "East High crowd": NAM-Irving oral history, 57–58.

155 "an incredible conversationalist": Madsen oral history, 2–3.

155 "how it takes": Parker oral history, 38.

18. INTELLECTUAL AWAKENING AND MENTORING

Page

157 "There are only": Madsen oral history, 4.

158 "thoroughgoing isolationist": Mecham to Hafen, 1 March 2000, 3.

158 "as an individual": Allen and Leonard, *Story of the Latter-day Saints,* 513.

159 "may have been": Manchester, *Glory and the Dream,* 683.

159 "his voice dropping": McCullough, *Truman,* 851.

160 "If he'd spoken": NAM, remarks at inauguration of NAM Presidential Endowed Chair, in 1999 scrapbook.

160 "place in history": NAM, "Meekness," 73.

160 "I couldn't figure out": Alder to Hafen, 20 May 2000.

160 He was also: Lythgoe, "G. Homer," C1.

160 "go to the wall": L. Ralph Mecham, quoted in Lythgoe, "G. Homer," C2.

161 "one of Homer's boys": NAM, "Tribute to a Special Man," in 1987 scrapbook, 1, 3–4, 7.

19. CONNECTING THE SECULAR AND THE SACRED

Page

163 "didn't see how": NAM-Irving oral history, 40, 42, 61, 68.

164 "the learning of": Goates, *Harold B. Lee,* 615.

165 "the most distinguished": NAM, "In Memoriam," 3–4.

165 "Many years ago": Nelson, "Living by Scriptural Guidance," 17.

165 "the lessons from": NAM-Irving oral history, 391.

165 "the gospel is relevant": Nelson, "Living by Scriptural Guidance," 38.

166 "In my own education": NAM, "But Behold . . . These Are My Days," in 1984 scrapbook, 5.

166 "The Lord sees": NAM, "Disciple-Scholar," 3.
166 "there is a danger": Oman, review of *Zion in the Courts,* 132.
167 "early on [Neal]": Samuelson oral history, 13, 85.
167 "a confused mankind": NAM, "These Last Records," 8.
167 "a miracle": Bowen, *Miracle at Philadelphia,* xi.
167 "so many bright minds": NAM-Irving oral history, 63.
167 "the most remarkable": Schlesinger, *Birth of a Nation,* 245–46.
167 "It would be invaluable": Tuchman, *March of Folly,* 18, quoted in NAM, "Constitution . . . the Wisest," 2.
168 "some misguided monk": NAM-Irving oral history, 69; NAM, "'From the Beginning,'" 18.
168 "May I express": NAM to Lewis, 23 November 1960, in 1960–62 scrapbook.
168 "institutional chafing": NAM-Irving oral history, 71.
168 "I thought, All right": Hewitt, *Searching for God,* 123.
169 "whether you like": NAM-Allen oral history, 120.
169 "When you get": NAM-Reeves oral history, 8.
170 "We do not": In NAM, "Spencer, the Beloved," 13.
170 "was very nice": NAM-Allen oral history, 120.
171 "a perfectly abysmal place": NAM-Irving oral history, 71–72.
171 When the general committee: NAM-Hafen oral history, 18.
171 "He's so bright": Holland oral history, 24.

20. Early Life

Page
175 "the same considerate": Parker oral history, 5.
176 "a very able": Hinckley oral history, 4.
176 "a certain resilience": Faust oral history, 7.
176 "influence on him": Oaks oral history, 40.
176 "a strong woman": Holland oral history, 79–80.
176 "I cannot help": Holland, introduction of NAM, in 1982 scrapbook.
176 "I don't think you could": Jensen oral history, 36.
177 "he frequently heard": Dew, *Go Forward with Faith,* 10.
177 "I think I have never seen": Quoted in Dew, *Go Forward with Faith,* 16.
178 "We have had": Ira N. Hinckley to Ira N. Hinckley Jr., 2 March 1883.
178 "Although you have": Ira N. Hinckley to Ira N. Hinckley Jr., 24 May 1883.
178 "in those pioneering": George Hinckley personal history notes.
178 "Do you have time": Ada Robison Hinckley to George Edwin Hinckley, 2 November 1931.
179 "When it seemed": NAM, remarks at George E. Hinckley funeral, 5 January 1989, in 1989 scrapbook, 2.
180 "Hinckley eyebrows": Colleen H. Maxwell–Hafen oral history, 32, 50.
180 "didn't know what": Fern J. Hinckley personal history notes.
181 "Well, he's a nice-looking": NAM-Irving oral history, 327.
181 "one of the most appreciative": NAM, remarks at Fern J. Hinckley funeral, 2 April 1983, in 1983 scrapbook, 2.
181 "advertisement for the Church": NAM, remarks at George E. Hinckley funeral, 5 January 1989, in 1989 scrapbook, 2.
182 "many of the young men": Colleen H. Maxwell, "My Life Story," 7–8, 13–15.
182 "It was kind of": Colleen H. Maxwell–Cory H. Maxwell oral history, 10.
182 "a more stimulating vocation": Colleen H. Maxwell, "My Life Story," 16.

184 "passed out our awards": NAM-Irving oral history, 335, 338.
184 "seemed a bit": Colleen H. Maxwell, "My Life Story," 16–17.
185 "Who is this guy?": Colleen H. Maxwell–Hafen oral history, 10.
185 writing "nice things": Colleen H. Maxwell–Cory H. Maxwell oral history, 8.
186 that "he talked so fast": NAM-Irving oral history, 326.
186 "just for spunk": Colleen H. Maxwell–Cory H. Maxwell oral history, 9.
186 "was impressed": NAM-Reeves oral history, 6.
186 "was this kid": NAM-Hafen oral history, 51.
186 "really cute and interesting": Notes from Colleen H. Maxwell–Hafen interview, 1981.
186 "was so knowledgeable": Colleen H. Maxwell–Cory H. Maxwell oral history, 15.
186 "spiritual impetus": NAM-Irving oral history, 326.
186 "used so many": Ward, "Sister Colleen Hinckley Maxwell," 16.
187 "I don't know him": Colleen H. Maxwell–Hafen oral history, 21–22.
187 "Our first introduction": Emma A. Maxwell to NAM, 6 July 1982.

21. Speaking the Truth in Love

Page
189 "married up": NAM, quoted in Hafen, "Elder Neal A. Maxwell," 12.
189 "There is romantic": NAM-Irving oral history, 330.
190 "didn't think of herself": NAM, quoted in Ward, "Sister Colleen Hinckley Maxwell," 16.
190 "recommit themselves to": Colleen H. Maxwell–Cory H. Maxwell oral history, 16.
191 "I knew I was": NAM-Irving oral history, 334.
191 "We hadn't been": NAM, quoted in Ward, "Sister Colleen Hinckley Maxwell," 16.
191 "smarter than you think": NAM-Irving oral history, 335, 343.
191 "My life cannot implement": Lindbergh, *Gift from the Sea,* 124, quoted in NAM-Irving oral history, 343.
192 "love personified": Kathy Jones to NAM, 28 December 1987, in 1987 scrapbook.
192 "You've always had": Eyring to Colleen H. Maxwell, 20 August 1984, in 1984 scrapbook.
192 "she just has to say": NAM-Irving oral history, 341–42.
192 "Colleen is superb": Haglund oral history, 95.
192 "Colleen way": NAM-Irving oral history, 338.
193 "Dearest Husband": Colleen H. Maxwell to NAM, 8 February 1990, in 1990 scrapbook.
194 "calming influence": Adams oral history, 29.
194 "stress-free environment": Porter oral history, 4.
194 "is in high speed": Maxwell children oral history, 17.
194 "very prayerful": NAM-Irving oral history, 357.
194 his "auxiliary conscience": NAM to Colleen H. Maxwell, 24 January 1975, in 1981 scrapbook.
195 "an additional prompter": NAM-Irving oral history, 335, 339, 342, 349.
196 "What she says": NAM, quoted in Ward, "Sister Colleen Hinckley Maxwell," 15.
196 "source of strength": NAM to Nancy Maxwell, 5 October 1977, in 1981 scrapbook.

196 "leftovers wisely": Karen B. Maxwell oral history, 46.
197 "overly bowled over": NAM-Irving oral history, 333–36, 341, 349.

22. WASHINGTON, D.C.

Page
203 "loved that political thing": Colleen H. Maxwell–Cory H. Maxwell oral history, 22.
203 "Lead, Kindly Light": John Henry Newman, "Lead, Kindly Light," *Hymns*, no. 97.
204 "was almost in": Ellis, "Bennett Says He'll Leave," A3.
205 "opened with a silent prayer": Manchester, *Glory and the Dream*, 794.
205 "she was unthreatened": NAM, *More Excellent Way*, 136.
206 "in one federal": NAM, "Insights from My Life" (1976), 197.
206 Logistical support for: Mecham to Hafen, 13 January 2000, 2.
207 reflected the "brashness": NAM-Irving oral history, 118.
207 called "Uranium Millionaire": LeRoy Howard to Mecham and NAM, 4 October 1954, in 1926–59 scrapbook.
207 "I got to": NAM-Reeves oral history, 8.
207 "Which way am": NAM-Irving oral history, 108.

23. THE SPIRIT OF PUBLIC SERVICE

Page
209 "McCarthyism": "A mid-20th century political attitude characterized chiefly by oppostion to elements held to be subversive and by the use of tactics involving personal attacks on individuals by means of widely publicized . . . allegations esp. on the basis of unsubstantiated charges." *Merriam-Webster's Collegiate Dictionary.*
209 "the most famous": Manchester, *Glory and the Dream*, 636–37, 682, 879.
209 "handmaidens of the": NAM-Allen oral history, 123.
209 "taken this thankless": Mecham to Hafen, 1 March 2000, 5.
209 "now they were standing": NAM-Allen oral history, 123.
210 "knew [McCarthy] was through": NAM-Irving oral history, 110.
210 "In their final": NAM, "Insights from My Life" (1976), 194.
210 "inept and phony": NAM-Allen oral history, 123.
210 "craving power and": NAM, "Tugs and Pulls," 35.
210 "a legitimate veteran": NAM-Irving oral history, 112.
211 "by and large": NAM-Reeves oral history, 9.
211 "incessant strivings": NAM, "Disciple-Scholar," 17.
211 "addicting nectar of": NAM, "Jesus, the Perfect Mentor," 6.
211 "towering genius": Fehrenbacher, *Abraham Lincoln*, 41, quoted in NAM, "Disciple-Scholar," 17.
212 "the situation": NAM-Irving oral history, 112, 205–6.
213 The passage: Ellis, "Bennett Says He'll Leave," A4.
214 "the American Congress": NAM-Reeves oral history, 8.
214 "self-confidence enclosed in meekness": NAM-Irving oral history, 86–87, 98, 102, 182, 216.
215 "world of public service": NAM, "Insights from My Life" (1976), 195.
216 "probably the most": Flexner, *Washington*, 174.
216 "'Gentlemen, you must'": MacDowell, *Revolutionary War*, 190–91, quoted in NAM, "Integrity," 14.
216 "This homely act": Flexner, *Washington*, xvi, 38, 174–75.

24. Family Beginnings

Page

218 "Happy families are": Tolstoy, *Anna Karenina*, 3.
219 "protracted self-education": Flexner, *Washington*, 38, quoted in NAM, "Integrity," 14.
219 "Winning points": Eyring, "Neal A. Maxwell," 10.
219 "We will be": NAM, in *Growing Edge*, October 1975, in 1975 scrapbook.
219 "life's most demanding": NAM, "Thanks Be to God," 53.
219 "He's a great": Faust oral history, 2.
220 Yet the Maxwells: Hales, "Strengthening Families," 35.
220 "slept with his head": NAM-Hafen oral history, 127.
221 "Before you turn": Colleen H. Maxwell–Hafen oral history, 29, 31, 49.

25. The Maxwell Family

Page

224 "impressed that someone": Maxwell children oral history, 10–11, 99, 126.
224 "Friends of the Forest": NAM-Irving oral history, 348.
224 Cory Cucumber: Maxwell children oral history, 9, 42, 93.
226 "Let the record show": NAM, "Proclamation," 9 July 1986, in 1986 scrapbook.
227 "suggestion-box climate": NAM, *That My Family Should Partake*, 65.
227 they "butted heads": Maxwell children oral history, 3, 5, 30, 43, 122.
227 "Okay, I'm going": NAM-Hafen oral history, 66.
228 "back to the": Maxwell children oral history, 4–5, 16, 33, 45.
229 "in every case": Ward, "Sister Colleen Hinckley Maxwell," 15.
229 "down on their luck": Colleen H. Maxwell–Hafen oral history, 36.
230 "gospel conversations": Maxwell children oral history, 8, 34.
230 relaxed "exit interview": NAM-Irving oral history, 350.
230 "Let me tell you": Maxwell children oral history, 154, 166.
231 "If I were to make": NAM to family members, 3 December 1970, in 1993 scrapbook.
232 "stood at the kitchen": Maxwell children oral history, 1.
232 He told Cory: Lee, *Teachings of Harold B. Lee*, 279.
232 "real impact": Maxwell children oral history, 96.
233 "Do all you": NAM to family, 13 January 1988, in 1988 scrapbook; paragraphing altered.
233 "Remember to allow": NAM to family, 5 February 1988, in 1988 scrapbook; paragraphing altered.
234 "missed a fair amount": Maxwell children oral history, 37, 124.
234 "probably the world's worst": Brough-Irving oral history, 11.
235 "politely declined": Nelson oral history, 18.
235 "you never just": Maxwell children oral history, 100, 128.
236 "We're probably within": Maxwell family videotape, 1994.
236 "He does it even": Karen B. Maxwell oral history, 14.
237 "peacemaker": Maxwell children oral history, 102.
237 "Should I bring": Stack, "LDS Apostle Finds Lessons," A9; paragraphing altered.
238 "In honor of our": Maxwell grandchildren's pledge, 22 November 1990, in 1990 scrapbook.
238 "just trusted that": Karen B. Maxwell oral history, 21–23, 55.

238 "I never would have": Maxwell children oral history, 136–37.

239 "Neal doesn't like": Ahlander, remarks at Anderson wedding breakfast, in 1977–78 scrapbook.

240 "warming and mellowing": Karen B. Maxwell oral history, 49.

240 "Peter tells us": NAM to Mike and Becky Ahlander, 12 September 1975, in 1981 scrapbook.

240 "We really have": Karen B. Maxwell oral history, 20.

240 "angels are coming": William W. Phelps, "The Spirit of God," *Hymns,* no. 2.

240 "I knew that our": Karen B. Maxwell to NAM and Colleen H. Maxwell, January 1995, in 1995–96 scrapbook.

241 "'Anna Jo, when'": NAM, "Content with the Things Allotted," 74.

241 "is already lighting": Hewitt, *Searching for God,* 137.

242 "Good! You did": Colleen H. Maxwell, "Hope Everlasting," 382.

242 "conviction of God's": Hewitt, telephone conversation with Hafen, 31 July 2001.

242 "you'd have a": NAM-Irving oral history, 352–53, 356.

26. Singularity in Diversity

Page

247 "the governmental approach": Eyring, "Neal A. Maxwell," 8.

247 "mission field": Parker oral history, 37.

247 preprogrammed to return: Mecham to Hafen, 13 January 2000, 2.

247 "totally consuming": NAM-Irving oral history, 215–16.

247 "hadn't dealt with": Nelson oral history, 2, 4, 6.

248 was "understandable" but: Ezra Taft Benson to NAM, 23 November 1956, in 1926–59 scrapbook.

248 "You will be": Ezra Taft Benson to NAM, 9 April 1956, in 1926–59 scrapbook.

248 "splintered oak desk": Haglund oral history, 60.

248 "disengagement from the": "Business Portrait," C2.

249 "protégé newly returned": Lowell M. Durham to NAM, 25 August 1970, in 1970 scrapbook.

249 "very frank and": A. Ray Olpin journal, 29 June 1957.

250 "Regionalism in the": NAM-Irving oral history, 132.

250 "sort of *Larry King Live*": L. Ralph Mecham, remarks at inauguration of NAM Presidential Endowed Chair, in 1999 scrapbook.

251 "fairly amateurish": NAM-Irving oral history, 128–30.

252 "evidence of Neal's": Haglund oral history, 3, 43.

252 "witty 1950s television": Death notice of Arlene Francis, age ninety-three, in *Time,* 11 June 2001, 22.

252 "is network material": Haglund oral history, 43, 83.

252 "grasp of public": NAM personal history, 20.

252 "the small talk": NAM, "Insights from My Life" (1976), 193.

252 "Your father [Joseph F.": NAM-Irving oral history, 128.

253 "one of the": Pearson, "Legislature, Salute to Ike Slated on TV," B8.

253 "Channel Seven's big": Martin, "Checking the Channels," 26.

254 "intellect was so": Haglund oral history, 13–14, 21, 43.

27. PRESIDENT OLPIN AND POLITICAL SCIENCE

Page

255 "more than any": Durham, remarks at Olpin funeral, 10 March 1983, 1.

255 With a historic: Hodson, *Crisis on Campus,* 1.

256 "the boys that": Durham, remarks at Olpin funeral, 10 March 1983, 5–6.

256 The university soon: Hodson, *Crisis on Campus,* 8.

256 "it was preferable": G. Homer Durham, in Haglund, *Remembering,* 26.

257 "did remarkable things": Haglund oral history, 25, 27.

257 He was nonetheless: NAM-Irving oral history, 125.

257 "deep caring for": NAM, remarks at Olpin funeral, 10 March 1983, 3–4.

257 "stern, but strong": NAM-Irving oral history, 125.

257 "took criticism": NAM, *More Excellent Way,* 137.

257 "Hard work and quick": *Utonian,* 1961, 20.

257 "my executive assistant": Olpin journal, 2 July 1962.

258 "a hundredfold and": "Maxwell Speech Reflects Historical Past," 2.

258 "While I have": Hanks to Olpin, 29 August 1960, in 1926–59 scrapbook.

258 that a mind expanded: Jardine, remarks at inauguration of NAM Presidential Endowed Chair, in 1999 scrapbook.

259 "all over the": Haglund, quoted in Eyring, "Neal A. Maxwell," 8.

259 "saw his commitment": Haglund oral history, 38.

259 "a bit officious": Unnamed former student, quoted in Madsen oral history, 4.

259 "seen the metamorphosis": Madsen oral history, 4.

259 "humble and spiritual-minded": Unnamed former student, quoted in Madsen oral history, 4.

260 "political patriarchs": NAM, "West on Capitol Hill," 469–70.

260 "all members": A. J. Wann to Milton Voigt and William F. Prokasy, 23 January 1970, in 1966–69 scrapbook.

260 "Neal is worth": J. D. Williams to A. J. Wann, 2 February 1970, in 1966–69 scrapbook.

261 "could teach students": NAM-Hafen oral history, 81.

28. DEAN OF STUDENTS

Page

262 "participative" leadership: NAM, *More Excellent Way,* 28.

262 "wouldn't be kept": Olpin journal, 6 June 1962.

263 "if someone untrained": Olpin journal, 18 June 1962.

263 "a matter of": Olpin journal, 19 June 1962.

263 "we didn't know": Olpin journal, 2 July 1962.

263 "came to work": NAM-Irving oral history, 143.

264 "Dean Maxwell": "Human Side," 14.

264 "as only Lowell": NAM-Irving oral history, 145.

264 "gap locally between": NAM to Olpin, 28 June 1963, in 1966–69 scrapbook.

264 "hilltop hideaway": Haglund oral history, 7.

265 "rendezvous with destiny": Briscoe, "Maxwell: LDS Should Participate," in 1963–65 scrapbook.

265 "nine copies": Bronson oral history, 40.

265 "The man of religion": NAM, "But Speaking the Truth," 6.

265 "inability to be": Brown to NAM, 15 June 1964, in 1963–65 scrapbook.

266 "flap over an": NAM to Douglas H. Parker, 20 January 1964.

267 "didn't know exactly": Bronson oral history, 21.

267 "The issue is not": Ravitch, *Troubled Crusade*, 199–200, 223.
268 "Anybody who watched": NAM-Reeve oral history, 9.
269 "power sharing": NAM-Irving oral history, 145–46.
269 "the capacity to": NAM, "Dean Maxwell Tells of 'Two Worlds,'" in 1963–65 scrapbook.
269 "a major personnel": NAM, "Our Crises in Self-Esteem," 38, 40.
270 "self-esteem through achievement": *Dimensions,* National 4-H publication, in 1966–69 scrapbook.
271 "always fitting those ideas": Christensen oral history, 28.
271 "was not a University of Utah": YMMIA General Board minutes, Church archives.

29. Utah Statesman and University Vice President

Page
272 "a Harold Stassen": NAM-Hafen oral history, 118.
272 "credentials and capacity": Parker to University of Utah board of regents, 22 January 1964.
273 "absolutely incapable": Haglund oral history, 51.
274 "intellectually arrogant": Hodson, *Crisis on Campus,* 267.
274 "interacting with them": Haglund oral history, 52.
274 "I struck gold": Fay Fletcher, remarks at inauguration of NAM Presidential Endowed Chair, in 1999 scrapbook.
274 "interpreting the university": *Utonian,* 1967.
274 "Though still": "Good Men at the 'U,'" A12.
275 "I have long admired": Lee to NAM, 8 December 1964, in 1963–65 scrapbook.
275 "one of the most": Fletcher, telephone interview with Hafen, July 1981.
276 "is not Utah's": NAM, "Unseen University," 5.
276 "nervous and impatient": Haglund oral history, 9, 22.
277 "million dollar angel": Lela Ence, remarks at inauguration of NAM Presidential Endowed Chair, in 1999 scrapbook.
277 He confided: NAM to Douglas Parker, 9 December 1963, Parker oral history, 44.
277 "tied to the state": "Business Portrait," C2.
277 "He'll cross the": Faust oral history, 9.
278 "drunken molecule": NAM-Irving oral history, 70, 156, 163.
279 "the biggest bonding": Haglund oral history, 70.
279 "'tidal wave' of": "Higher Education's Cart Before Horse," A18.
280 "philosophically more comfortable": Tarbox, "Origins of the Utah System," 240–41, 243, 245.
281 "At no time": National Municipal League statement, quoted in Hafen, "Legislative Branch," 416 n. 4.
281 "the most serious": Jefferson Fordham, quoted in Hafen, "Legislative Branch," 417 n. 7.
281 "the ideal guy": McConkie oral history, 29.
281 The public was: Third Interim Report, 2.
282 "rarely . . . seen anyone": Porter to Hafen, 25 July 2000, 3–5.
282 *Salt Lake Tribune:* NAM, "Amendments Offer Way," B6.
283 "All the amendments": NAM to Cory H. Maxwell, 17 November 1972.
283 "knack of identifying": "Neal Maxwell Service Achievements," A18.

283 "irenic" quality: Bushman to Hafen, 7 July 2000.
284 The university years: Morrison oral history, 22.

30. THE MAXWELL STYLE

285 "nice certificate": Bronson oral history, 23.
286 "drive to win": Haglund oral history, 22.
286 Edith signaled to him: Jardine oral history, 40.
287 "as if it were": Mecham to Hafen, 1 March 2000, 5.
287 was "novel": Jardine oral history, 40.
287 "swipe the ball": Phillip C. Smith to Hafen, 31 January 2000.
287 "solicitous concern for": certificate, 31 July 1970, in 1970 scrapbook.
287 "he'll dive for": Jardine oral history, 25.
287 "A one-minute": Haglund oral history, 96.
287 "somewhere between": Maxwell children oral history, 138.
287 "a clean desk man": J. D. Williams, remarks at inauguration of NAM
     Presidential Endowed Chair, in 1999 scrapbook.
288 When he visited: McConkie oral history, 49.
288 Then he'd rise: Campbell to Hafen, 27 December 1999.
289 "bridled his passions": Haglund oral history, 14, 16, 21.
289 For example, Neal: Phillip C. Smith to Hafen, 31 January 2000.
289 "has tried very": Morrison oral history, 19–20.
289 "No one I know": Haglund oral history, 94.
289 "with a capital": Samuelson oral history, 20.
290 "Avoid trifling conversation": Franklin, *Benjamin Franklin,* 72–74.
290 "We talk glibly": NAM talk to Honors 315 students, 9.
290 when Neal ran across: Bronson oral history, 6.
290 "Deliberately cultivate what": NAM to Cory H. Maxwell and Karen B.
     Maxwell, 2 November 1979, in 1979 scrapbook.
290 "naturally patient" person: Maxwell children oral history, 62, 65.
290 "I don't know": Heslop, "He Built on Parents' Example," 5.
291 "more likely to *listen*": McConkie oral history, 2, 43.
291 "the capacity for": Jardine oral history, 25.
291 "less than worthy": NAM, "Insights from My Life" (1976), 191.
291 "just buried it": Jardine oral history, 25.
291 "talents in ministering": McConkie oral history, 47.
291 "Look, somebody is": NAM-Irving oral history, 207, 247.
292 As Neal spoke: Jardine oral history, 23.
292 "even when he's": Faust oral history, 5.
292 He might ask: NAM to Cory H. Maxwell, 13 December 1972.
293 He might also: NAM to Cory H. Maxwell, n.d. [October or November],
     1973.
293 "a tool for": Samuelson oral history, 25.
293 "there is generally": NAM to Cory H. Maxwell, 28 February 1974.
293 "very significant question": Oaks oral history, 24.
293 "How do you": Carmack oral history, 2.
293 "wonderful, warm, meaningful": McConkie oral history, 41.
293 "I have found": NAM, "Insights from My Life" (1976), 199.
294 "If you didn't": Haglund oral history, 18, 30–31, 37.
294 "understand in part": NAM letter, January 1976; paragraphing altered.

294 Rather than whispering: Nelson oral history, 11–12.
295 "anything left over": Bronson oral history, 13, 26.
295 "In their young": Garrett transcript, 2.
295 "had a talk": NAM to Cory H. Maxwell, 2 November 1979, in 1981 scrapbook.
296 "because he's too": Monson oral history, 5.
296 He still often: Jackson to Hafen, 15 August 2001.
296 "so anxious to": Bronson oral history, 7.
296 "humanized": McConkie oral history, 42.
296 "likes to get": Packer oral history, 3.
296 "When it's time": Monson oral history, 17.
297 "his talks are so hard": Bronson oral history, 7.
297 "You take that": Carmack oral history, 11.
297 "the younger kids": Bronson oral history, 13.
297 "A distinctive, differential": NAM, "Address to Graduates," BYU Commencement, in 1973 scrapbook.
298 "I'm now down": NAM-Irving oral history, 415.
298 "laugh himself almost": Oaks oral history, 51–52.
298 "complete spiritual commitment": Snow to Hafen, 9 March 2000, 3.
299 "instead of allowing": Haglund oral history, 31–32.
299 "[Neal's] warmth did": Loos to Hafen, 26 August 2001.
299 "the local culture": NAM-Irving oral history, 157.
299 "was so unarguably": Nelson oral history, 8–9.
300 "hugely important that": McConkie, remarks at inauguration of NAM Presidential Endowed Chair, in 1999 scrapbook.
300 "learn to defend": NAM-Irving oral history, 206.
300 "a great source": Snow to Hafen, 9 March 2000, 3.
300 "non-Mormons and less-active": Jardine oral history, 9.

31. Student Ward Bishopric

Page

305 "going to the": Bronson oral history, 25.
306 "A few of": NAM-Irving oral history, 219, 221.
306 "fit candidates for": McConkie oral history, 6.
306 "could have been": NAM-Irving oral history, 226, 231.
307 "Well, I'm glad": McConkie oral history, 3, 14–15, 23, 47.
308 "I don't know": NAM-Irving oral history, 241.
308 "touch people's lives": NAM-Reeves oral history, 20.
309 One of the: See page 9.
309 "I don't know why": NAM-Irving oral history, 238.
310 "The Lord has": McConkie oral history, 24.

32. YMMIA General Board and *A More Excellent Way*

Page

311 "Neal Maxwell's reputation": Monson oral history, 2.
312 "forth as if": NAM-Irving oral history, 264.
312 "a *disciple* should": Minutes for Ben Lomond South Stake conference, 28 November 1964, in 1963–65 scrapbook.
312 "not being our": NAM-Irving oral history, 261, 279.

313 "impression of the man": Packer oral history, 1–2.
315 "developing a climate": NAM, *More Excellent Way*, 3, 28, 30, 56, 60–62, 65, 90, 99.
316 "acquired and cultivated": "Business Portrait," C2.
316 "I am supposed to": NAM-Irving oral history, 253–55, 261.

33. Correlation and the Church Leadership Committee

Page
318 "one of the": Allen and Leonard, *Story of the Latter-day Saints*, 593.
318 "some historians may": Goates, *Harold B. Lee*, 363–64, 374.
321 "You may have": Monson oral history, 3.
321 "like Larry Csonka": NAM-Allen oral history, 138.
321 "young, vigorous, and": Monson oral history, 8–9.
322 "Now Neal Maxwell": NAM-Irving oral history, 310.
322 "felt about as": NAM personal history, 23.
323 "act as an advisor": Allen and Leonard, *Story of the Latter-day Saints*, 599.
323 "line authority": NAM-Allen oral history, 56–57.
324 "You've told us": NAM-Irving oral history, 297.
324 "Revelation works in": NAM-Allen oral history, 59–61.
325 "the Priesthood as": Lee, regional representatives' seminar, 2–3.
325 "devolving into 'little'": Sheler, "Mormon Moment," 63; quotation within the quotation is from Shipps.
325 "disintegration . . . into a": Shipps, quoted in Sheler, "Mormon Moment," 63.
325 "more centralized system": Sheler, "Mormon Moment," 63.
325 "'standardized and simplified'": Shipps, quoted in Sheler, "Mormon Moment," 63.
325 "that emphasizes families": Sheler, "Mormon Moment," 63.
325 "correlation is the key": "Jan Shipps—Sojourner," 7.
326 "emerged as being": Goates, *Harold B. Lee*, 376.
326 "put him on": NAM-Irving oral history, 254, 314.
327 "immense personal skills": Holland oral history, 38.
327 to field-test certain: NAM-Allen oral history, 63.
327 "saw the Lord reveal": NAM personal history, 24.
328 The First Presidency: Goates, *Harold B. Lee*, 380.
328 "shows some faith": Lee, regional representatives' seminar, 5, 9.
328 "We are losing ground": NAM, in Lee, regional representatives' seminar, 9.
328 "We are losing more": Lee, regional representatives' seminar, 9–10.
328 "widows and the": NAM in Lee, regional representatives' seminar, 10.
328 "And so on": Lee, regional representatives' seminar, 11.
328 Neal gave him: NAM-Irving oral history, 306–7.
329 "We were all": NAM, remarks to former YMMIA and YWMIA board members, 12 April 1995, in 1995–96 scrapbook.

34. Commissioner of Education

Page
331 "open, candid": Sale, "Men of Low Profile," 36, quoted in Wilkinson, *Brigham Young University*, 4:323.

331 "a compassionate spirit": President's Commission on Campus Unrest (1970), 209, quoted in Wilkinson, *Brigham Young University,* 4:323–24.
333 "sources of strain": O'Dea, *Mormons,* 222, 225–27, 235–36, 240.
334 "break camp and": NAM-Hafen oral history, 105.
335 "had never thought": NAM-Irving oral history, 199.
335 "I believe we are": Knight, "Language Is a Key to His Life," 5.
336 "the only master's": Oaks oral history, 46–47.
336 "Native distinction needs": Madsen oral history, 14.
336 "has a reputation": Johnston, "Favorites of an 'Intensive' Reader," C2.
337 "who does not have": Lee, "Iron Rod," 7.
337 "by the lamp": Joseph F. Smith, *Gospel Doctrine,* 373, quoted in Lee, "Iron Rod," 7.
337 "schoolmen of spiritual": Madsen to Hafen, 21 July 2000.
338 "felt free to make": McConkie oral history, 25.
338 "upon the delightful": Lee to NAM, 1 July 1970, in 1970 scrapbook.
339 "from going off": NAM-Irving oral history, 208.
339 "feeling back in the early 50s": Mecham to Hafen, 13 January 2000, 3.

35. Creating the Church Educational System

Page

343 "reviving the old": Durham diary, 21 July 1970.
343 "I don't really": "Neal Maxwell Honored," A5.
344 "exceptionally beset by": "Neal Maxwell's Big Job," A18.
344 "This is Neal": Bronson oral history, 9, 35.
344 Caught off guard: McConkie oral history, 25.
344 a mild cuss word: Maxwell children oral history, 59.
344 "above all, Neal": Bronson oral history, 9, 25.
345 "the inexhaustible gospel": NAM-Irving oral history, 71.
345 "much more free": Christensen oral history, 30.
345 "a flight to freedom": Martin B. Hickman, quoted in Wilkinson, *Brigham Young University,* 4:63–64.
345 "I think he": Bronson oral history, 39.
345 "blessed if I": NAM-Baldridge oral history, 6.
345 as noted earlier: See page 161.
347 "This independence of": Berrett, *Miracle in Weekday Religious Education,* 75.
347 as "chancellor" of: NAM-Irving oral history, 62 n. 21.
348 "had an idea of": Monson oral history, 9.
348 "era of intense creativity": Christensen oral history, 16–17, 21.
349 "I don't suppose": Palmer to NAM, 29 June 1976, in 1976 scrapbook.
349 "More than anyone": Oaks oral history, 16.
349 "as significant as": Christensen oral history, 56.
349 "genius [is the": Bushman to Hafen, 7 July 2000.
350 during Neal's years: Madsen oral history, 16.
350 "much more subtle": Oaks oral history, 16.
351 "together in a": Packer oral history, 3.
351 "Neal created this": Holland oral history, 31.
351 "our scope": Beesley oral history, 11.
353 "They respected him": Oaks oral history, 7.

36. New Leaders

Page

354 "Neal likes a": Holland oral history, 16.

354 "80 percent of": NAM-Allen oral history, 11.

355 "He's about as": Christensen oral history, 11.

355 all young outsiders: Holland oral history, 5–6.

356 "Hal, are you": Eyring oral history, 2, 4.

356 "went back to my": NAM, *"But a Few Days,"* 1.

356 "Hal, I'd like": Eyring oral history, 6, 8.

358 "whom the Lord": NAM, remarks following Lee, *Decades of Distinction,* 5–6.

359 "'We all know": Goates, *Harold B. Lee,* 446.

359 "impress upon BYU's": Wilkinson, *Brigham Young University,* 4:202–3.

359 "the Brethren probably": Oaks oral history, 2, 4, 7.

359 One day Elder: NAM, conversation with Hafen, 29 October 2001.

359 "more harmony in": Oaks oral history, 5, 42.

360 "I wouldn't even": Holland to NAM, 7 April 1999, in 1999 scrapbook.

360 "my mentor and tutor": Holland oral history, 52.

37. Religious Education and Church Schools

Page

362 called "reaction papers": Christensen oral history, 21, 34–35.

362 "an excellent history": "Reaction Paper," in 1970 scrapbook.

363 "Seek Learning Even": Church Educational System, "Seek Learning Even by Study and by Faith."

363 "the best illustration": Holland oral history, 19–20.

364 an "eloquent appeal": Berrett, *Miracle in Weekday Religious Education,* 147–53.

365 wherever the Church: Christensen oral history, 8, 42.

365 "I know of": Christensen, "Globalization of the Church Educational System," 9.

365 CES leaders hired: Peterson-LeBaron oral history, 1–12.

366 "virtually the same": Christensen oral history, 31.

366 CES had expanded: Board of Education minutes for 1 September 1976, cited in Gentry, "History of Latter-day Saint Religious Education," 37.

366 "This whole dream": Holland oral history, 26–27, 30.

366 By 2001, the: Christensen, "Globalization of the Church Educational System," 15.

366 President Kimball challenged: Eyring oral history, 37.

367 "history of the": NAM, *"But a Few Days,"* 2.

367 The closer they looked: NAM-Allen oral history, 34.

368 Many of these: Beesley oral history, 3–4.

368 The international loan: Hinckley, "Perpetual Education Fund," 51–53.

369 "The first country": NAM, "Meaning of a Centennial," in 1975 scrapbook, 1.

369 primarily with "returnability": NAM-Baldridge oral history, 12.

371 Competent expatriate Americans: Peterson oral history, 17.

371 "We are in": NAM to Cory H. Maxwell, 10 February 1974.

371 "Well, [the man]": Christensen oral history, 51.

38. Higher Education and Brigham Young University

Page

372 By 1970, Latter-day: Allen and Leonard, *Story of the Latter-day Saints,* 615.
373 "didn't want to": NAM–Allen oral history, 36.
374 "unique and deeply": Wilkinson, *Brigham Young University,* 4:149.
374 his "most complicated": NAM–Baldridge oral history, 12.
374 "make fresh exploration": Church Educational System, *Report of the Select Committee,* 2.
374 Interestingly, many concepts: Eyring oral history, 14.
375 "Mormonism's . . . encounter with": O'Dea, *Mormons,* 222.
375 "knew what [Dallin]": Oaks oral history, 5, 9, 11, 32, 36, 51.
377 "jump a nearby": Oaks to Hafen, 13 August 2001.
377 "major contribution": Oaks oral history, 22, 31, 50–51.
377 And Neal would: NAM, conversation with Hafen, 11 September 2001.
378 "who weren't totally": Oaks oral history, 18.
379 "a Church institution": Romney, quoted in Wilkinson, *Brigham Young University,* 4:200.
379 He would tell them: NAM, *Deposition of a Disciple,* 15–16.
379 "For a disciple of": NAM, "Disciple-Scholar," 7–22.
380 "into the fray": NAM, *Mormon Milieu,* 5.
380 "turned inward": NAM, address at BYU Administrative Workshop, 6–7, 10.
383 "religious education [should]": Packer, quoted in Wilkinson, *Brigham Young University,* 4:194.
384 "Now let's talk": Romney interview with Hafen, 1973.
384 "could not have been": NAM, quoted in Wilkinson, *Brigham Young University,* 4:207–8.

39. Becoming a Spiritual and Educational Leader

Page

385 "the nerve center": Rea, "Nerve Center Role for Y.," B1.
385 Leaders, he said, should: NAM, Conference Report, October 1970, 94–98.
386 "an ecclesiastical Everest": "Interview with Neal A. Maxwell," 48.
386 "With so much": NAM, "Democracy and Dissent," 4.
386 "impatient with marshmallow": NAM, "Now and Future Student," 3, 6.
387 "You are my only": NAM to Cory H. Maxwell, 10 February 1974.
387 "We savored your": NAM to Cory H. Maxwell, 17 November 1972.
387 "We fasted for": NAM to Cory H. Maxwell, 13 February 1973.
388 "There's mundaneness in": NAM to Cory H. Maxwell, 23 October 1972.
388 "Often, when I": NAM to Cory H. Maxwell, 29 March 1973.
388 "I had a busy": NAM to Cory H. Maxwell, 19 February 1974.
388 "You work for": NAM to Cory H. Maxwell, 24 October 1973.
388 He had first been: Lloyd to John T. Bernhard, 12 April 1962, in 1960–62 scrapbook.
388 His name was: Teuscher, "Predicting Politics."
389 "It's an open secret": "About Our Authors," in NAM, "Unseen University."
389 "All of Lincoln's": Oates, *With Malice toward None,* 175.
389 "somewhat tempted": NAM, *One More Strain of Praise,* 103.
390 "would have been": Scruggs oral history, 33–34.
390 "I am not presently": NAM to Cory H. Maxwell, 17 November 1972.

390   "fire in his belly": NAM-Irving oral history, 119.
390   "was gentle and": NAM, *One More Strain of Praise,* 103.
390   "wasn't that excited": NAM personal history, 30.
390   "wasn't too keen": NAM to Cory H. Maxwell, 11 December 1972.
390   He soon felt: NAM personal history, 30.
390   "to make one": NAM to Cory H. Maxwell, 29 March 1973.
391   "If the Lord": Haglund oral history, 34.
391   "Discipleship may keep": NAM, "Tugs and Pulls of the World," 35.
391   "made up his": NAM personal history, 31.
391   "A giant redwood": Kimball and Kimball, *Spencer W. Kimball,* 1.
391   "It is my sad duty": NAM to Cory H. Maxwell, 27 December 1973.
392   "No man can come": NAM to Harold B. Lee, 5 July 1972, in 1974
       scrapbook.
392   "I had a comfort": Goates, *Harold B. Lee,* 460.
392   "trusted me so": NAM-Allen oral history, 137.
392   "the sweetest spirit": NAM personal history, 31.
393   "There is no": Tanner to NAM, 15 April 1974, in 1974 scrapbook.
394   "The sociological implications": Manchester, *Glory and the Dream,* 1226.
394   Some 2.3 million: Tanner to Hafen, 17 November 2000 and 4 December
       2000.
395   "by encouraging [higher]": O'Dea, *Mormons,* 224–26.
395   "had once belonged": Manchester, *Glory and the Dream,* 1226.
395   "rural and quite": O'Dea, *Mormons,* 226.
395   Indeed, reliable research: Albrecht and Heaton, "Secularization, Higher
       Education, and Religiosity," in Duke, *Latter-day Saint Social Life,* 293–314.
396   "asked them what": O'Dea, *Mormons,* 262–63.
397   "striving for excellence": Hickman, introduction of NAM, G. Homer
       Durham Lecture Series, in 1987 scrapbook.
397   "ability to have": Morrison oral history, 2, 15, 22, 25.
398   "ranged widely over": Jensen oral history, 40.
398   "I began to realise": Raeside to NAM, 29 April 1997.
399   "Probably it is his": Oaks oral history, 25.

40. Called to His Ministry

Page
403   "No greater address": Quoted in NAM, "Spencer, the Beloved," 10.
403   "the greatest speech": NAM to Cory H. Maxwell, 8 April 1974.
404   It would permanently: Ashton oral history, 156–57.
405   "you may use your": NAM personal history, 33.
405   "you could see": Christensen oral history, 55.
406   "felt the weight": NAM–Allen oral history, 75.
406   "Included in the": NAM, "Response to a Call," 112.
406   "The living of one": NAM, "Why Not Now?" 12–13.
407   "a great deal": Morrison oral history, 1–2.
407   "What would you": Jensen oral history, 8, 12.
408   "to increase the": NAM-Irving oral history, 438.
408   "If we are to": NAM, address at Utah Technical College Commencement, 3.
409   "Secularists so often": NAM, address at Utah Social Security Conference, in
       1977–78 scrapbook, 61.
409   "A religion of ten": NAM, "Public Service in a Time of Paradoxes," 494–95.

409 "filled with Martha-like": NAM, "Some Thoughts about Our Constitution," 105, 109.
410 the "safety": "LDS Official Says," B1.
410 "Have you ever": NAM, "Response to a Call," 112.
411 "There is such an": Holland oral history, 37.
411 "I know personally": NAM to Cory H. Maxwell, 12 January 1973.
412 "then comes the": Hewitt, *Searching for God,* 128.
412 "went to the mailbox": Letter, 22 May 1980, in 1980 scrapbook.
412 "the voice in": Hewitt, *Searching for God,* 128.
413 After hearing him: Colleen H. Maxwell–Hafen oral history, 55.
413 "Unlike the roar and crash": NAM, "Becoming a Disciple," 19.

41. Lengthening the Church's Stride

Page
414 "the volume of": NAM-Allen oral history, 59.
414 "had never happened": NAM-Reeves oral history, 11.
415 They were the organization: McConkie, *Sermons and Writings,* 236.
416 "everything that shall": Quoted in Tate, *Boyd K. Packer,* 235.
416 The First Presidency had: Madsen, *Defender of the Faith,* 203.
416 "The First Quorum": Widtsoe, *In a Sunlit Land,* 163.
416 the entire First Council: Young to First Presidency and Council of the Twelve, 15 March 1968, in Young, *History of the Seventies.*
416 the Quorum's creation: NAM personal history, 36.
416 "the call of a Seventy": Tate, *Boyd K. Packer,* 236.
416 "clearly involved with": Holland oral history, 51.
417 "revelation, not accommodation": NAM personal history, 41.
417 He later recalled: See page 470.
418 "that was the telegram": Jardine oral history, 4.
418 "Major quantitative growth": "Church Can Now Be Universal," 20.
419 "we're in a global": NAM-Irving oral history, 466.
419 "When any credit or": NAM to Hafen, 29 October 2001.
420 "you just keep going": NAM-Allen oral history, 138–39.
420 "as long as he": NAM to Cory H. Maxwell, 4 February 1974.
420 "just show up": Bronson oral history, 55.
420 "I am mighty glad": Kimball to NAM, 19 February 1975, in 1975 scrapbook.
421 "I am wondering if": Kimball to NAM, 23 May 1977, in 1977 scrapbook.
421 "Surely you can": Hafen, "Elder Neal A. Maxwell," 13.
422 "Yes, I know": Eyring, "Neal A. Maxwell," 9.
422 "Do you know that": NAM personal history, 42, 55.
422 "how uniquely beloved": NAM, "Spencer, the Beloved," 8, 12–13.
423 "the authority of [her]": NAM, remarks at Camilla E. Kimball funeral, 26 September 1987, in 1987 scrapbook, 1–3.

42. The Correlation Department

Page
425 the "correlation review": Goates, *Harold B. Lee,* 540.
425 and "final filter": NAM-Irving oral history, 318.
426 "A federal army": NAM, "Insights from My Life" (1976), 187–88.
427 "evaluate the effectiveness": NAM-Allen oral history, 93.

427 "victimized by our": NAM-Reeves oral history, 13.
428 "analytical vision": Oaks oral history, 50.
428 "data about the": NAM-Reeves oral history, 13.
429 "realizes that data": Welch oral history, 33.
430 That study, a summary: "Key to Strong Young Men," 66–68.
431 "the research efforts": Stark, "Rise of a New World Faith," 26–27.
432 the Church can: Oaks oral history, 43.
432 "All Neal Maxwell": Holland oral history, 57–59.
432 "junction box": NAM-Irving oral history, 455.
433 "take correlation to": NAM-Allen oral history, 91.
433 "It was an awkward": NAM personal history, 37.
433 Within a few months: NAM-Irving oral history, 457, 471.

43. The Holy Apostleship

Page

437 "The mission of the": Kimball, "Report of My Stewardship," 5.
438 the unusual step: The most recent examples of similar calls were those
     made during the presidency of David O. McKay, who called as additional
     counselors Hugh B. Brown (1961), Thorpe B. Isaacson (1965), and Alvin R.
     Dyer (1968).
438 "For some time prior": D. Arthur Haycock, quoted in Dew, *Go Forward with
     Faith*, 385.
439 "It's not his heart": NAM-Irving oral history, 421–22.
440 "I stood there just": Cory H. Maxwell to NAM, 23 July 1981, in 1981
     scrapbook.
441 "I'm glad you're": Emily Maxwell to NAM, 23 July 1981, in 1981 scrapbook.
441 "get himself together": NAM personal history, 48.
441 "Even though I'd": NAM-Irving oral history, 423–25.
441 "array of scriptures": NAM, conversation with Hafen, 1981.
442 "a pupil or learner": LDS Bible Dictionary, 657.
442 "I came to a night": Quoted in NAM, *More Excellent Way*, 139.
442 "My fumbling response": NAM to Kimball, 29 July 1981, in 1981 scrapbook.
443 "My solemn obligation": NAM notes from testimony to Twelve, March 1982,
     in 1982 scrapbook.
444 "his ability to love": Faust oral history, 10.
444 Neal and Dan: Mitchell, conversation with Hafen, January 2000.
444 "be the least": NAM, "'O, Divine Redeemer,'" 8.
445 "life had been": NAM-Hafen oral history, 22.
445 "Can we, even": NAM, "'O, Divine Redeemer,'" 8–10.
446 "This is the Lord's": NAM, "Insights from My Life" (2000), 13.
447 "Neal is an Apostle": Packer oral history, 12.
447 "the bank of": Nichols, "Light That Shone in a Dark Place," in 1983
     scrapbook.
448 "The highlight [of": Garff to NAM, 18 May 1987, in 1987 scrapbook.
448 "the Spirit of our": NAM personal history, 53.
448 "an incredibly touching": Howell to NAM, 8 June 1987, in 1987 scrapbook.
448 "Your inspired and informative": Hawkins to NAM, 8 June 1987, in 1987
     scrapbook.

44. The Twelve as a Council

Page

450 "Brethren, we've come": NAM-Hafen oral history, 7.
451 "a big deal": NAM-Irving oral history, 427–28, 432.
454 "one gets a chance": Hewitt, *Searching for God,* 142.
454 "sail" and the "anchor": NAM-Irving oral history, 434.
455 "how delightful it": NAM personal history, 53.
455 "grown into the office": Holland oral history, 39–40.
456 "bring forward aggressive": Eyring oral history, 39.
456 "When I awakened": NAM, "Meek and Lowly," 61.
456 "akin to that": Faust oral history, 1, 8.
457 "Conferences come and": Faust to NAM, 4 May 1976, in 1976 scrapbook.
457 "the privilege of sitting": Nelson to NAM, 18 April 1984, in 1984 scrapbook.
457 "how much you": Nelson to NAM, 17 September 1985, in 1985 scrapbook.
457 "fertile mind": Haight to Hafen, 10 September 2001.
457 "remarkable ability": NAM-Allen oral history, 137.
457 "President Tanner had": NAM, *Wonderful Flood of Light,* 124.
457 "in this dispensation": NAM-Allen oral history, 137.
458 "Needless to say": Tanner to NAM, 6 July 1975, in 1975 scrapbook.
458 no one at: Samuelson oral history, 5.
458 "enormous credibility": Brough-Irving oral history, 30.
458 "circumspect about not": Scruggs oral history, 37.
460 "Let the Twelve Apostles": Smith, *History of the Church,* 5:366.

45. Opening the Doors of the Nations

Page

462 "Since President Kimball": NAM-Irving oral history, 525, 527–28.
462 "characteristic . . . of the": Hinckley oral history, 5.
463 "shrink in the face": NAM-Irving oral history, 430.
463 "to look at the": Morrison oral history, 5, 13, 24.
463 the retention issue: NAM-Irving oral history, 480, 502, 506.
464 "he was the entire": Holland oral history, 55.
464 "it will be easier": NAM-Hafen oral history, 10.
464 "a major contribution": Oaks oral history, 33.
464 a "lost sheep" project: Holland oral history, 55.
465 "Ammon" pilot project: Figuerres to Hafen, 20 November 2001.
466 "very clearly": Morrison oral history, 6.
467 "Yes, there would": NAM, "Spencer, the Beloved," 17.
468 "Partly it's the": NAM-Hafen oral history, 10, 12.
468 The real beginning: Morrison, *Dawning of a Brighter Day.*
468 "already very religious": NAM-Irving oral history, 514.
468 "The intellectual African": "Nigeria Marks Twin Milestones," 7.
468 "deprivation has prepared": NAM-Reeves oral history, 15–16.
469 "marvel us with": Statement from Aba District Presidency, in 1985 scrapbook.
470 "wears your suit": Cunningham to NAM, 13 June 1988, in 1988 scrapbook.
470 "felt to ponder": Rasband, "One by One," 30.
470 "wasn't from the": NAM-Irving oral history, 507–8, 510, 512.
472 "the rain stopped": Snow to Hafen, 9 March 2000, 4.

472   "mopped up his tears": Morrison oral history, 4.
472   "many young men": Campbell to Hafen, 27 December 1999.
472   Beverly and others: Holland oral history, 55.
472   "very important to": Stokes to Hafen, 30 November 2001.
473   "was being born": Holland oral history, 54.
473   "this is a continent": NAM-Irving oral history, 507.
473   "centers of strength": Holland oral history, 55.
473   "Our whole assumption": NAM, quoted in Morrison, *Dawning of a Brighter Day*, 46.
474   "will be very": NAM-Irving oral history, 512, 517.
475   "never seen anybody": Brough-Irving oral history, 4.
476   "the purpose of": Campbell to Hafen, 27 December 1999, 4.
477   "Thailand, the people": White to Hafen, 17 August 2001.
478   "the peace I": Phelps to NAM, 18 June 1995.
478   "I'll go to my": Brough-Barney oral history, 4.
479   call "Green Beret" missionary: NAM-Hafen oral history, 13.
479   "the father of the": Carmack oral history, 30–31.
480   "just laid aside": NAM-Irving oral history, 516.
480   "Some of us": Dedicatory prayer for Mongolia, 15 April 1993, in 1993–94 scrapbook.
480   The Church is thus: Brough-Irving oral history, 28.
481   "garden spot for": NAM-Hafen oral history, 12–13.
481   "we go in right": Brough-Irving oral history, 25.
481   "a place of security": NAM, "Dedication of Neal A. Maxwell and Colleen Hinckley Maxwell Home, June 20, 1993," in 1993–94 scrapbook.

46. Out of Obscurity

483   "I don't know of": Hinckley oral history, 5, 7.
483   "ability to view": Packer oral history, 3, 7.
484   "By almost any": Sheler, "Mormon Moment," 62.
485   "Mormons, Inc.: The": Van Biema, "Mormons, Inc.," 3, 50–59.
485   three-page spread: Kelly, "Mormons on Mission to Grow," D3–D5.
485   about the Church welfare: Chesnutt, "Y2K or Not," A22.
485   CNN's Larry King: On 8 September 1998, 24 December 1999, and 14 September 2001.
485   with Mike Wallace: On 18 December 1995 and 10 March 1996.
485   *Standing for Something:* Hinckley, *Standing for Something.*
485   In 2001, *Newsweek:* Woodward, "Mormon Moment," 44–51.
485   "those were things": NAM-Irving oral history, 535, 537, 539.
486   "made the case": Shipps, "Mormon Metamorphosis," 786.
486   "He is unafraid": NAM to Hafen, 30 July 2001.
486   "the dramatic discrepancy": Shipps, *Sojourner,* 100, 111–16.
488   "Colonel Kane": NAM-Irving oral history, 551.
488   "we go in the": Sheler, "Mormon Moment," 63.
489   "greater attention on": Reynolds, "Coming Forth," 31.
490   "we can't lose": Brough-Irving oral history, 19.
490   Thus, like President: Elder Maxwell underscored this point during informal remarks to scholars from the Joseph Fielding Smith Institute of Church History at BYU, 28 June 2001.

491   "biggest ever" involvement: NAM-Irving oral history, 546.

492   "The Church can't move": Dew, *Go Forward with Faith*, 536.

492   "Ronald Reagan knew": NAM-Irving oral history, 535, 539.

492   "bridge-building" visits: Jensen oral history, 27, 37–38.

492   "he treats everyone": Olsen to Hafen, 5 January 2000.

493   "because he's got": Scruggs oral history, 36.

493   For instance, he encouraged: NAM-Irving oral history, 546–47; Harrie, "GOP Dominance," A1.

493   "be willing to": Scruggs oral history, 38.

493   "favors of our": NAM-Irving oral history, 555.

494   "valued these visits": Campbell to Hafen, 27 December 1999, 7.

494   "The image of the Church": NAM, in "Notable Quotes by Leaders," 4.

494   "born with a": Campbell to Hafen, 27 December 1999, 7.

494   Chances are, Neal: NAM-Irving oral history, 521, 533.

495   "show Muslims our": Morrison oral history, 21–22.

496   "many touching points": Carter, "Diplomats Hail Y.'s Islamic Translations," B5.

496   "the words of a": Bushman to Hafen, 7 July 2000, 1.

47. From the Word to the Word to the *Word*

Page

497   "from the word": Holland oral history, 41.

498   "Focused my Apostolic": NAM, ten-year review list, in 1991 scrapbook.

498   "the foothills of": NAM, *Promise of Discipleship*, 129.

500   This became a: Reynolds, "Coming Forth," 19.

500   "grand and glorious": Kimball, "Report of My Stewardship," 5.

501   "has become an": Holland oral history, 42–43.

502   "jumped to 40": Reynolds, "Coming Forth," 10.

503   "Not only did": Hewitt, *Searching for God*, 128–29.

503   "the nuances of": Madsen oral history, 13.

503   "There is no personal": NAM, "These Last Records," 13.

504   In his role as chairman: "June Videoconference," 73.

504   the "key activities": NAM, ten-year review list, in 1991 scrapbook.

504   "challenges to basic": NAM, "Premortality," 15.

505   "old spirit": "1830 Harris Letter Authenticated," 6.

505   "one of the greatest": Dart, "Mormons Ponder 1830 Letter," 6; for a complete treatment of the Church's role in the Hofmann case, see Turley, *Victims*.

506   President Hinckley acknowledged: Dew, *Go Forward with Faith*, 432.

506   "essentially unfair": Quoted in Dew, *Go Forward with Faith*, 404.

506   "We do not yet": Turley, *Victims*, 94.

506   "the most intense": White, "LDS Church Says," 32.

507   "It is a way to": Holland oral history, 64.

507   "If we in the Church": NAM, "'Good and Evil Spoken of,'" 1–3, 5, 8, 11–12, 15–16.

509   "We're going to": NAM-Hafen oral history, 61, 98.

509   "Let's have some": NAM-Irving oral history, 369–70, 373.

510   "Almost every BYU": Karen B. Maxwell oral history, 44–45.

510   "focused heavily on": Reynolds, "Coming Forth," 34–36.

510   "there really are so": Madsen oral history, 37–38.

511   "It's because people": NAM-Irving oral history, 373.
511   "with gospel premises": Welch oral history, 10–11, 18, 34, 62.
511   "Rational argument does": quoted in NAM, "Discipleship and Scholarship," 5.
511   "Science will not be": NAM, *Plain and Precious Things*, 4.
512   "the state of the": Reynolds, "Coming Forth," 39.
512   a "myth": Mosser and Owen, "Mormon Scholarship," 180–81.
513   "Isn't it wonderful": NAM-Irving oral history, 372.
513   "The whole [birthday] show": Nibley to NAM, 15 April 1985, in 1985 scrapbook.
514   "what Mormons think": Welch oral history, 43.
514   "joint product of Brigham": Ludlow, *Encyclopedia of Mormonism*, lxii.
515   "is not, nor was": NAM-Irving oral history, 373.
516   "sacred, private, or": Richard E. Turley Jr., "Confidential Records," in Ludlow, *Encyclopedia of Mormonism*, 309–10; Richard E. Turley Jr., general introduction to Cannon, *To California in '49*, xvi.

48. The World of Words

Page
519   "It's in there": Holland oral history, 75, 73.
520   little notes he has: I thank Eric d'Evegnee for the image of "notes left tacked on the trees."
520   "Having found the": NAM, *Time to Choose*, 19.
520   "speaks differently from": Hinckley oral history, 1.
520   "just to get": Hinckley, remarks at inauguration of NAM Presidential Endowed Chair, video recording.
520   "No one could": Monson oral history, 7.
521   the "vintage" Maxwell: Wirthlin to Hafen, 8 August 2001.
521   "Those talks he": Tom C. Korologos, remarks at inauguration of NAM Presidential Endowed Chair, in 1999 scrapbook.
521   "four . . . , well, five": David K. Hafen, conversation with Hafen, about 1993.
521   "a hundred miles": Samuelson oral history, 31.
521   "One of his talks": Karen B. Maxwell oral history, 30–31.
522   "inside allusions": Welch oral history, 64.
522   "incurable insomniac": NAM, *Even As I Am*, 75.
522   Ten Commandments weren't: NAM, "Lessons from Laman and Lemuel," 8.
522   "put out to pasture": NAM, "Christ-Centered Life," 15.
522   great and spacious building: NAM, "Becometh As a Child," 68.
523   "we cannot": NAM, *All These Things*, 96.
523   "the vertical pronoun": NAM, "Put Off the Natural Man," 14.
523   "time melts as": NAM, *All These Things*, 100.
523   "meekness . . . provides a": NAM, *Meek and Lowly*, 60.
523   "selfishness is really": NAM, "Put Off the Natural Man," 16.
524   "caught up in": NAM, *Wherefore, Ye Must Press Forward*, 22.
524   "The worst form": NAM, *If Thou Endure It Well*, 15, 42.
524   "to be flowery": Oaks oral history, 31.
524   "fancy words": Helen Conlon, conversation with Hafen, February 2000.
524   "He speaks to": Judith Grimes, conversation with Hafen, March 2000.
524   "The only truly": Maureen Young to Hafen, July 2000.
525   "vessel is often": Eric Andersen to Hafen, 26 September 2000.

525 "style is intentional": Scruggs oral history, 42.

526 "Kierkegaard's distinction between": Holland, introduction of NAM, in 1982 scrapbook.

526 "It's his gift to": Faust oral history, 4.

526 "Few men or women": Ballard to Hafen, 20 September 2001.

527 "among the greatest": Halle, "Language of Statesmen," 30–31.

527 "some Burns, Byron": Oates, *With Malice toward None*, 49–50.

527 "Education, for me": NAM, talk at Ricks College graduation, in 1984 scrapbook.

527 "his remarkable mastery": Manchester, *Last Lion*, 647, quoted in NAM, talk at Ricks College graduation, in 1984 scrapbook.

527 "How the great democracies": Churchill, quoted in NAM, *Wherefore, Ye Must Press Forward*, 6.

527 "I have been": Mason, *Brandeis*, 38.

528 "Your thought is": Perry, *Thought and Character of William James*, 212.

528 "concentrate power in": Ciardi, *How Does a Poem Mean?* 870–71.

528 "No man is": Donne, *Devotions upon Emergent Occasions*, Meditation 17.

528 "No other success": McKay, Conference Report, April 1935, 116.

528 "irreducible . . . and memorable": Ciardi, *How Does a Poem Mean?* 774–75; italics omitted.

528 "The terrorists are": "President Bush's Address on Terrorism Before a Joint Meeting of Congress," nytimes.com, 21 September 2001.

528 "hang around words": Ciardi, *How Does a Poem Mean?* 667, 775.

528 "Let us have": NAM, "Meeting the Challenges of Today," 151.

528 "[mothers] rock a": NAM, "Women of God," 10.

528 "the laughter of": NAM, "These Are Your Days," 6.

528 "It was very cold": Meilaender, "Everyday C. S. Lewis," 27–28, 31.

529 "just throwing off": Scruggs oral history, 41.

529 "see him integrating": Jensen oral history, 31.

529 "multiple iterations": Samuelson oral history, 9.

530 "it made him": Madsen oral history, 19.

530 "just redistributes": NAM-Irving oral history, 407.

530 "Surely a man": Hinckley, remarks at inauguration of NAM Presidential Endowed Chair, video recording.

530 "This is like a": Madsen oral history, 19.

530 "the intellectual process": Karen B. Maxwell oral history, 33.

530 "pressure-filled": NAM-Irving oral history, 391.

530 "teaching by the Spirit": "Teaching by Spirit," 12.

531 "the world's problems": NAM to Cory H. Maxwell, 23 April 1973.

531 The next question: NAM, *That My Family Should Partake*, 38.

531 "maybe in them": NAM-Irving oral history, 394.

531 "Having already written": NAM, *One More Strain of Praise*, 112.

532 "Behind a compulsive": Adey, *C. S. Lewis*, 1.

532 "things concerned with": NAM-Irving oral history, 359, 379–81.

533 been "over-eager": Wilson, *C. S. Lewis*, 282, 284.

533 "this shattering is": Lewis, *Grief Observed*, 76.

533 "far more searching": Wilson, *C. S. Lewis*, 285, 292.

533 Also like Lewis: Elder Maxwell is "arguably the best theologian among" the Twelve. "He is certainly the most published." Stack, "Apostle Speaks of Faith," C1.

533 "systematic philosopher": Bushman to Hafen, 7 July 2000.

533 "wrote *theoretically*": Oaks oral history, 30.
533 "People may look": Welch oral history, 71.
533 "disciples . . . of two": Roberts, *Defense of the Faith and the Saints*, 1:309.
533 fits Neal "to a T": Madsen to Hafen, 21 July 2000.
533 "the disciples pure": Roberts, *Defense of the Faith and the Saints*, 1:309–11.

49. DEVELOPING DISCIPLESHIP

Page

535 "One can see": Johnston, "Tidbits of Truth," E1.
535 "used alliteration almost": Kimball to Hafen, 10 July 2001.
535 "loves to play": Morrison oral history, 7.
536 "weren't the books": Haglund oral history, 6, 11, 25.
536 "much more what": McConkie oral history, 35.
536 "I mine the scriptures": NAM-Judd dictation, 2.
536 "Our growing asphalt": d'Evegnee to Hafen, 1 February 2001, 7.
536 "The cares and anxieties": NAM, *Wonderful Flood of Light*, 83.
537 "a despiritualized society": "Church Can Now Be Universal," 20.
537 "look homeward, angel": Milton, quoted in NAM, *That My Family Should Partake*, 8.
537 "If we poison": NAM, Conference Report, October 1970, 97.
538 "cannot produce a": d'Evegnee to Hafen, 1 February 2001, 27.
538 "you would not": NAM, *Of One Heart*, 51.
538 "starts with an": Jardine oral history, 30.
539 "there stands the Savior": NAM, *Even As I Am*, 10–11.
539 the "prison temple": Roberts, *Comprehensive History of the Church*, 1:526.
540 This book includes: See pages 507–9.
540 "adversity must be": NAM, *If Thou Endure It Well*, 2–3, 133.
541 "We . . . might as": NAM, "More Determined Discipleship," 73.
541 the "allotted 'acreage'": NAM, "Content with the Things Allotted," 72.
541 "We have to": Quoted in NAM, *Smallest Part*, 34.
541 "clinical material": NAM, "Jesus, the Perfect Mentor," 13.
542 "the Atonement with": NAM, *For the Power Is in Them*, 3, 27.
542 "It is the Garden": NAM, *Wherefore, Ye Must Press Forward*, 133.
542 In 1981 he described: NAM, *Even As I Am*, chapter 2.
542 "according to the": NAM, *We Will Prove Them Herewith*, 48–49, 96.
543 "In addition to": NAM, *Not My Will*, 51.
543 In 1994 and 1999: NAM, *Lord, Increase Our Faith*, chapter 1; *One More Strain*, chapter 3.
543 "discipleship . . . involves citizenship": NAM, "Meeting the Challenges of Today," 149.
543 "the disciple of Christ": NAM, *Smallest Part*, 6, 27.
543 "the disciple does": NAM, *Things As They Really Are*, 4.
543 "writing over the": d'Evegnee to Hafen, 1 February 2001, 1.
544 "because [He] deliberately": NAM, *All These Things*, 30, 32.
544 "to strive to": NAM, *Even As I Am*, 14, 43.
545 "part of the": NAM, *But for a Small Moment*, 105.
545 "reflect the outcome": NAM, *Men and Women of Christ*, 47, 49.
546 "Some suffering actually": NAM, *Not My Will*, 5.
546 "trains himself to": Morson, "Prosaics," 523.

546 "Can you really": NAM, "Discussion of Values."
546 "all who are": NAM-Hafen oral history, 77.
547 "the gospel of": NAM, "Discussion of Values."
547 "If we are serious": NAM, *Time to Choose*, 46.
547 "not shrinking is": NAM, "Pathway of Discipleship," 13.

50. An Understanding Heart

Page

548 "an authenticity": NAM, "Discussion of Values."
549 "Thank you for": Letter to NAM, 9 April 1997, in 1997–98 scrapbook.
549 "Leukemia is a": Bush to NAM, 11 June 1997, in 1997–98 scrapbook; paragraphing altered.
549 "a continuing affirmation": Samuelson oral history, 44.
550 "cancer network": NAM-Irving oral history, 557–58.
550 "the more he did": McConkie oral history, 47.
550 "incredible pastoral outreach": Oaks oral history, 27–28.
552 "secondary sufferers": NAM-Hafen oral history, 56.
552 "Heavenly Father, bless": Howes to NAM, quoted in NAM, "Testifying of the Great," 14.
553 "why not me": NAM-Irving oral history, 558.
553 "remarkably unsentimental": Scruggs oral history, 27–28.
554 She thought his: Jackson to Hafen, 15 August 2001.
554 "He doesn't take": Packer oral history, 4.
555 "not as exotic": NAM-Irving oral history, 551.
555 "washed out": Samuelson oral history, 43.
555 "Elder Maxwell's": Ford oral history, 34; Ford to Hafen, 2 August 2001.
556 This prompted him: NAM-Irving oral history, 81.
556 "If I could explain": Ford oral history, 24–25.
556 "constantly expressing": Hinckley oral history, 5.
556 "If we were stronger": Lewis, *World's Last Night*, 11.
556 "I am very grateful": NAM, "Hope through the Atonement," 61–63.
557 "bringing things to": Samuelson oral history, 49.
557 "augmented because of": Nelson oral history, 19–22.
558 "a new dimension": Carmack oral history, 7–8.
558 found the same thing: Archibald, telephone conversation with Hafen, 5 September 2001.
558 "gives us a 'new heart'": NAM, "Discussion of Values."
558 [So, for me,]: NAM-Irving oral history, 558.
560 "West, you and I": Lee, remarks at B. West Belnap funeral, transcript from tape.
562 "You don't know": Madsen oral history, 42.
562 Elder Maxwell has taught: NAM, "O, Divine Redeemer," 8–10.
562 "You'll never be able": Madsen oral history, 42.
562 "I have given": NAM-Hafen oral history, 17.
564 "There are many": Karen B. Maxwell oral history, 43, 52.
564 "His greatest qualities": Jardine, quoted in Stack, "LDS Apostle Finds Lessons," A9.
564 "Some of the people": Eyring oral history, 41–42.
565 "will find a hand": Hinckley, remarks at inauguration of NAM Presidential Endowed Chair, video recording.
565 "a man of the last": Morrison oral history, 25–27.

BIBLIOGRAPHY

The research for this biography drew upon many unpublished documents, along with published books, newspaper and magazine articles, and other materials. To simplify documentation while also accurately identifying where source materials can be found, source notes briefly describe the relevant source but should be read in conjunction with this statement. Unpublished sources are listed with their present locations; published works are listed in full, allowing identification in the notes with brief author-title references.

The archives of the Family and Church History Department, The Church of Jesus Christ of Latter-day Saints, Salt Lake City, Utah, contain most of the unpublished material. Gordon Irving of that department recorded eighteen interviews between November 1999 and May 2000, referenced in the notes as NAM-Irving oral history. Eight additional interviews recorded between June 1976 and March 1977 by James B. Allen are cited as NAM-Allen oral history, Kenneth W. Baldridge's August 1981 interview is referenced as NAM-Baldridge oral history, and an interview recorded on videotape in August 1991 by Brian D. Reeves is cited as NAM-Reeves oral history. The transcript of a September 1979 audiotape recorded for Mary Lu E. Judd's Sunday School class in a Salt Lake City ward is cited as NAM-Judd dictation.

In 1999 and 2000 Gordon Irving also conducted oral history interviews with Orval W. "Web" Adams Jr., Edith H. Bronson, Monte J. Brough, John K. Carmack, Joe J. Christensen, Henry B. and Kathleen J. Eyring, James E. Faust, Elizabeth M. Haglund, Gordon B. Hinckley, Jeffrey R. Holland, James S. Jardine, Marlin K. Jensen, Cory H. Maxwell, Karen B. Maxwell, Oscar W. McConkie Jr., Thomas S. Monson, Alexander B. Morrison, Dallin H. Oaks, Boyd K. Packer, Douglas H. and Corene C. Parker, Roger B. Porter, Cecil O. Samuelson Jr., H. E. "Bud" Scruggs Jr., and John W. Welch. Transcripts of all these interviews are on file in the Church Archives. The Haglund, Jardine, McConkie, Oaks, Parker, Porter, and Samuelson transcripts are accompanied by copies of letters and other written reminiscences that they supplied. The Maxwell children oral history includes transcripts of interviews Cory H. Maxwell recorded early in 2000 with his sisters and their respective husbands—Rebecca M. and Michael B. Ahlander, Nancy M. and Mark L. Anderson, and Jane M. and Marc N. Sanders.

Also in the Church Archives are records of the Canadian Mission during the time Elder Maxwell served there in the late 1940s, video recordings and partial transcripts of remarks from the January 1999 dinner announcing the Neal A. Maxwell Presidential Endowed Chair at the University of Utah, an oral history recorded with Wendell J. Ashton by Gordon Irving between January 1984 and May 1985, an oral history recorded with Monte J. Brough by Ronald O. Barney in February 1997, an oral history recorded with Kenneth H. Beesley by David J. Whittaker in July 1977, an oral history recorded with Stanley A. Peterson by Jeffery L. Anderson in February 2000, a microfilm copy of G. Homer Durham's diary, the text of President Harold B. Lee's October 1971 address to the regional representatives' seminar, and a history of the Seventies written by S. Dilworth Young in the late 1970s.

I consulted President A. Ray Olpin's journal in the archives of the University of Utah, Salt Lake City, Utah, for key events in Elder Maxwell's career as a University of Utah administrator. These archives also contain Elder Maxwell's personnel file, including papers related to his faculty rank.

Although Elder Maxwell has not kept a formal journal, he and his secretaries have compiled an extensive set of scrapbooks containing the texts of some talks he has given, letters and other correspondence, photographs, and newspaper clippings. The scrapbooks also contain a very brief personal history he wrote as a few annual pages in the 1970s and early 1980s, cited as NAM personal history. Other unpublished items in the scrapbooks are identified by the volume in which they are housed. Individual letters are cited by author, addressee, and date. Newspaper clippings and other printed items in the scrapbooks for which publication information is available are cited without reference to the scrapbooks.

Elder Maxwell also has in his possession the texts of other unpublished talks he has delivered, as well as letters he wrote to his family during World War II and while he served as a missionary. The letters were preserved by his father and later returned to Elder Maxwell. Cory Maxwell has the letters his father wrote him during Cory's mission.

My files contain copies of material supplied by Maxwell family historians, including biographical information created by or about Alma Ash, Charles Augustus Cobbley, Martin Lundwall (printed in the Lundwall family newsletter), Clarence H. Maxwell, Emma A. Maxwell, John Maxwell, and Lois Maxwell. Colleen H. Maxwell has supplied copies from her own file of personal history materials, including written statements by her parents, George and Fern Hinckley.

My files include transcripts of recordings or handwritten notes from my interviews for the biography with Elder Maxwell (cited as NAM-Hafen oral history), Nolan D. Archibald, Clyde Ford, DeLora Garrett, Hugh Hewitt, Truman G. Madsen, Colleen H. Maxwell, Russell M. Nelson, H. E. "Bud" Scruggs Jr., and Larry Staker, as well as an interview that Cory Maxwell recorded with his mother. I also have older files from interviews I conducted in 1981 with Elder Maxwell, Colleen H. Maxwell, James C. Fletcher, and others for the biographical article about Neal Maxwell I wrote for the February 1982 *Ensign*. I also consulted files from my work on a portion of the history of Brigham Young University from 1973 through 1976.

Additionally, my files include notes taken in meetings and communications to me from Rex Allen, Richard L. Bushman, Stephen W. Call, Beverly J. Campbell, Eric F. d'Evegnee, Cyril I. A. Figuerres, Susan Jackson, Tony Kimball, William Loos, L. Ralph Mecham, Bruce L. Olsen, Joseph R. Smith, Philip C. Smith, R. J. Snow, Catherine Stokes, Jeff Tanner, and Larry White. These files also hold the transcribed text of remarks at the funerals for B. West Belnap, George Truman "Judd" Flinders, and A. Ray Olpin; notes from Lyman Moody's talk at the funeral for his wife, Jackie; a transcription of the funeral service for George E. Hinckley; transcriptions of talks given by Colleen H. Maxwell; Marjorie Newton's unpublished essay entitled "My Family, My Friends, My Faith"; and an oral history Dale LeBaron recorded with Stanley A. Peterson.

I have relied on my memory for some facts and impressions, some of which have not previously been written or filed. These memories deal primarily with 1976 to 1978, when I worked daily with Elder Maxwell in the Correlation Department, and with 1978 to 1996, when I had contact with him because I was an administrator and faculty member at BYU and at Ricks College while he was a member of the BYU and Ricks College boards of trustees. I also had several unrecorded conversations with Neal and Colleen Maxwell between October 1999 and December 2001 while working on the book. Because the Maxwells have reviewed the entire text, I consider that review an acceptable check on the accuracy of my memory. If no other citation is given to phrases attributed to them, that language or paraphrase comes from these memories and conversations.

Those interviewed for the biography were given an opportunity before publication to review any page that quoted or paraphrased their comments or mentioned their name. The language as published thus reflects editing from this process and may be slightly different from the original interview transcripts. Quotations from a few unrecorded conversations have been similarly reviewed and thus are not individually documented in the notes.

Other unpublished works by Elder Maxwell and by others, as listed below, are also in my files. When the publication process is completed, documents now in my possession that were gathered for the biography will be placed in the Church Archives.

Works by Neal A. Maxwell

Books

All These Things Shall Give Thee Experience. Salt Lake City: Deseret Book, 1979.
But for a Small Moment. Salt Lake City: Bookcraft, 1986.
The Collected Works of Neal A. Maxwell. 6 vols. Salt Lake City: Deseret Book, 2001.
Deposition of a Disciple. Salt Lake City: Deseret Book, 1976.
Even As I Am. Salt Lake City: Deseret Book, 1982.
For the Power Is in Them. Salt Lake City: Deseret Book, 1970.
If Thou Endure It Well. Salt Lake City: Bookcraft, 1996.
Look Back at Sodom. Salt Lake City: Deseret Book, 1975.
Lord, Increase Our Faith. Salt Lake City: Bookcraft, 1994.
Men and Women of Christ. Salt Lake City: Bookcraft, 1991.
A More Excellent Way. Salt Lake City: Deseret Book, 1973.
Neal A. Maxwell Quote Book. Salt Lake City: Bookcraft, 1997.
Not My Will, but Thine. Salt Lake City: Bookcraft, 1988.
Of One Heart. Salt Lake City: Deseret Book, 1990.
One More Strain of Praise. Salt Lake City: Bookcraft, 1999.
Plain and Precious Things. Salt Lake City: Deseret Book, 1983.

The Promise of Discipleship. Salt Lake City: Deseret Book, 2001.
The Smallest Part. Salt Lake City: Deseret Book, 1973.
That My Family Should Partake. Salt Lake City: Deseret Book, 1974.
That Ye May Believe. Salt Lake City: Bookcraft, 1992.
Things As They Really Are. Salt Lake City: Deseret Book, 1978.
A Time to Choose. Salt Lake City: Deseret Book, 1972.
We Will Prove Them Herewith. Salt Lake City: Deseret Book, 1982.
Wherefore, Ye Must Press Forward. Salt Lake City: Deseret Book, 1977.
A Wonderful Flood of Light. Salt Lake City: Bookcraft, 1990.

Talks and Articles

"Amendments Offer Way to Better Government." *Salt Lake Tribune,* 5 November
     1972, B6.
"Becometh As a Child." *Ensign,* May 1996, 68–70.
"Becoming a Disciple." *Ensign,* June 1996, 12–19.
"But a Few Days." Address to Church Educational System religious educators, 10 Septem-
     ber 1982. Salt Lake City: The Church of Jesus Christ of Latter-day Saints, 1982.
"The Christ-Centered Life." *Ensign,* August 1981, 13–17.
"The Conference of Western Senators." *Western Political Quarterly,* December 1957,
     902–10.
"Congress Abdicates on Foreign Policy." *Nation,* 8 November 1958, 339–41.
" 'The Constitution . . . the Wisest Ever Yet Presented to Men.' " Talk in Grant Stake,
     Salt Lake City, 7 May 1987.
"Content with the Things Allotted unto Us." *Ensign,* May 2000, 72–74.
"Dean Maxwell Tells of 'Two Worlds.' " *Daily Utah Chronicle,* 21 May 1964, 1.
"Democracy and Dissent." *Perspectives on Utah Education,* December 1970, 4–5.
"The Disciple-Scholar." In *On Becoming a Disciple-Scholar.* Edited by Henry B.
     Eyring. Salt Lake City: Bookcraft, 1995.
"Discipleship and Scholarship." *BYU Studies,* Summer 1992, 5–9.
"A Discussion of Values, Family, and Personal Conviction: A Conversation with
     Neal A. Maxwell." Interview by Hugh Hewitt. Videocassette. KUED, 1998.
"Endure It Well." *Ensign,* May 1990, 33–35.
"Enduring Well." *Ensign,* April 1997, 7–10.
"Friend to Friend: Gospel of Work." *Friend,* June 1975, 6–7.
"From the Beginning." *Ensign,* November 1993, 18–20.
"From Whom All Blessings Flow." *Ensign,* May 1997, 11–12.
The Growing Edge 8, no. 2 (October 1975): 1.
"Hope through the Atonement of Jesus Christ." *Ensign,* November 1998, 61–63.
"In Memoriam: Henry Eyring 1901–1981." *BYU Studies,* Winter 1982, 3–4.
"Insights from My Life." *1976 Devotional Speeches of the Year.* Provo, Utah: Brigham
     Young University Press, 1977, 187–201.
"Insights from My Life." *Ensign,* August 2000, 6–13.
"Integrity: The Evidence Within." *Clark Memorandum,* Fall 1993, 10–17.
"I Will Arise and Go to My Father." *Ensign,* September 1993, 65–68.
"Jesus of Nazareth, Savior and King." *Ensign,* May 1976, 26–27.

"Jesus, the Perfect Mentor." Address to Church Educational System personnel, 6 February 2000. Salt Lake City: The Church of Jesus Christ of Latter-day Saints, 2000.

"Lessons from Laman and Lemuel." *Ensign,* November 1999, 6–8.

"Meek and Lowly." In *1986–87 Devotional and Fireside Speeches.* Provo, Utah: Brigham Young University, 1987, 52–63.

"Meekness—A Dimension of True Discipleship." *Ensign,* March 1983, 70–74.

"Meeting the Challenges of Today." In *1978 Devotional Speeches of the Year.* Provo, Utah: Brigham Young University Press, 1979, 149–56.

"A More Determined Discipleship." *Ensign,* February 1979, 69–73.

The Mormon Milieu. Brigham Young University Speeches of the Year, Provo, Utah, 23 February 1971.

"The Net Gathers of Every Kind." *Ensign,* November 1980, 14–15.

"Notwithstanding My Weakness." *Ensign,* November 1976, 12–14.

"'O, Divine Redeemer.'" *Ensign,* November 1981, 8–10.

"Our Crises in Self-Esteem—A Major Personnel Problem." *Journal of College and University Personnel Association,* May 1966, 38–41.

"The Pathway of Discipleship." *Ensign,* September 1998, 7–14.

"Premortality, a Glorious Reality." *Ensign,* November 1985, 15–18.

"Public Service in a Time of Paradoxes." *Vital Speeches of the Day,* 1 June 1979, 494–96.

"Put Off the Natural Man, and Come Off Conqueror." *Ensign,* November 1990, 14–16.

"Put Your Shoulder to the Wheel." *Ensign,* May 1998, 37–39.

Remarks following *Decades of Distinction: 1951–1971,* by Harold B. Lee. Brigham Young University Speeches of the Year. Provo, Utah, 1971.

"Response to a Call." *Ensign,* May 1974, 112.

"Ricks College Graduation—A Good Time to Take Inventory." *Church News,* 29 April 1984, 6.

"Some Thoughts about Our Constitution and Government." In *Five Essays on the U. S. Constitution.* Edited by Ray C. Hillam. Provo, Utah: Brigham Young University, 1977.

"Spencer, the Beloved: Leader–Servant." *Ensign,* December 1985, 8–19.

"Spiritual Ecology." *New Era,* February 1975, 35–38.

"Testifying of the Great and Glorious Atonement." *Ensign,* October 2001, 10–15.

"Thanks Be to God." *Ensign,* July 1982, 51–55.

"These Are Your Days." *New Era,* January–February 1985, 4–6.

"3,638 Receive Degrees at BYU Graduation." *Church News,* 21 April 1973, 3.

"The Tugs and Pulls of the World." *Ensign,* November 2000, 35–37.

"The Unseen University." *Utah Alumnus,* Fall 1964, 5–7.

"Unto the Rising Generation." *Ensign,* April 1985, 11.

"The West on Capitol Hill." In *Politics in the American West.* Edited by Frank H. Jonas. Salt Lake City: University of Utah Press, 1969.

"Why Not Now?" *Ensign,* November 1974, 12–13.

"The Women of God." *Ensign,* May 1978, 10–11.

Unpublished Works

Address at BYU administrative workshop, Timp Lodge, 9 July 1974.

Address at Utah Technical College commencement, 3 June 1976.

Baccalaureate address at Utah State University, 5 June 1981.

"'But Behold . . . These Are My Days.'" Address at Ricks College graduation, 19 April 1984.

"'But Speaking the Truth in Love.'" Baccalaureate address at University of Utah, 7 June 1964.

"'Good and Evil Spoken of among All People.'" Address to BYU Management Society in Washington, D.C., 7 February 1986.

Lecture on C. S. Lewis to Honors 315 students, Brigham Young University, 30 May 1973.

"The Now and Future Student." Address to 49th Annual Conference of Association of College Unions International, St. Louis, Missouri, 28 March 1972.

Remarks at inauguration of John A. Widtsoe Chair in Chemistry, 20 January 1995.

"Sword of Truth." Lessons for missionaries, 1949.

"'These Last Records . . . Shall Establish the Truth of the First'" [ca. 1987].

"A Tribute to a Special Man from 'One of His Boys.'" G. Homer Durham Lecture Series, 4 November 1987.

WORKS BY OTHER AUTHORS

Books

Adey, Lionel. *C. S. Lewis: Writer, Dreamer, and Mentor.* Grand Rapids, Mich.: William B. Eerdmans, 1998.

Alexander, Thomas G., and James B. Allen. *Mormons and Gentiles: A History of Salt Lake City.* Vol. 5 in the Western Urban History Series. Boulder, Colo.: Pruett Publishing, 1984.

Armour, Richard. *Educated Guesses.* Santa Barbara, Calif.: Woodbridge Press Publishing, 1983.

Allen, James B., and Glen M. Leonard. *The Story of the Latter-day Saints.* 2d ed. Salt Lake City: Deseret Book, 1992.

Bennett, Michael J. *When Dreams Came True: The GI Bill and the Making of Modern America.* Washington, D.C.: Brassey's, 1996.

Berrett, William E. *A Miracle in Weekday Education: A History of the Church Educational System.* Salt Lake City: Salt Lake Printing Center, 1988.

Boswell, James. *Life of Samuel Johnson, LL.D.* Edited by Mortimer J. Adler. Vol. 44 of *Great Books of the Western World,* edited by Robert Maynard Hutchins. Chicago: Encyclopedia Britannica, 1952.

Bowen, Catherine Drinker. *Miracle at Philadelphia: The Story of the Constitutional Convention, May to September 1787.* Boston: Little, Brown, 1986.

Brokaw, Tom. *The Greatest Generation.* New York: Random House, 1998.

Ciardi, John. *How Does a Poem Mean?* Boston: Houghton Mifflin, 1959.

Dew, Sheri L. *Go Forward with Faith: The Biography of Gordon B. Hinckley.* Salt Lake City: Deseret Book, 1996.

Donne, John. *Devotions upon Emergent Occasions,* 1624.

Duke, James T., ed. *Latter-day Saint Social Life: Social Research on the LDS Church and Its Members.* Provo, Utah: Religious Studies Center, Brigham Young University, 1998.

Fehrenbacher, Don E., ed. *Abraham Lincoln: A Documentary Portrait through His Speeches and Writings.* New York: The New American Library, 1964.

Feifer, George. *Tennozan: The Battle of Okinawa and the Atomic Bomb.* New York: Ticknor and Fields, 1992.

Flexner, James Thomas. *Washington, the Indispensable Man*. Boston: Little, Brown, 1974.

Franklin, Benjamin. *Benjamin Franklin: A Biography in His Own Words*. Edited by Thomas Fleming. New York: Newsweek Book Division, 1972.

Gailey, Harry A. *The War in the Pacific: From Pearl Harbor to Tokyo Bay*. Novato, Calif.: Presido Press, 1995.

Gilbert, Martin. *In Search of Churchill: A Historian's Journey*. New York: John Wiley & Sons, 1994.

Goates, L. Brent. *Harold B. Lee: Prophet and Seer*. Salt Lake City: Bookcraft, 1985.

Haglund, Elizabeth M., ed. *Remembering the University of Utah*. Salt Lake City: University of Utah Press, 1981.

Hewitt, Hugh. *Searching for God in America*. Dallas, Texas: Word Publishing, 1996.

Hinckley, Gordon B. *Standing for Something: Ten Neglected Virtues That Will Heal Our Hearts and Homes*. New York: Times Books, 2000.

Hodson, Paul W. *Crisis on Campus: The Exciting Years of Campus Development at the University of Utah*. Salt Lake City: Keeban Corporation, 1987.

Holmes, Oliver Wendell, Jr. *Memorial Day Address*. 1884. In John Bartlett, *Bartlett's Familiar Quotations*. Boston: Little, Brown and Company, 1980.

Hymns of The Church of Jesus Christ of Latter-day Saints. Salt Lake City: The Church of Jesus Christ of Latter-day Saints, 1985.

Jonas, Frank. *Politics in the American West*. Salt Lake City: University of Utah Press, 1969.

———. *Western Politics*. Salt Lake City: University of Utah Press, 1961.

Kimball, Edward L., and Andrew E. Kimball. *Spencer W. Kimball*. Salt Lake City: Bookcraft, 1977.

Leckie, Robert. *Okinawa: The Last Battle of World War II*. New York: Viking, Penguin, 1995.

Lee, Harold B. *The Teachings of Harold B. Lee*. Edited by Clyde J. Williams. Salt Lake City: Bookcraft, 1996.

Lewis, C. S. *A Grief Observed*. New York: Bantam Books, 1961.

———. *The Weight of Glory*. New York: Macmillan, Collier Books, 1949.

———. *The World's Last Night and Other Essays*. New York: Harcourt Brace Jovanovich, 1960.

Lindbergh, Anne Morrow. *Gift from the Sea*. New York: Random House, 1955.

Little Hoover Commission. Utah State Archives, Salt Lake City, 433, 434.

Longford, Elizabeth. *The Years of the Sword*. Vol. 1 of *Wellington*. New York: Harper & Row, 1969.

Ludlow, Daniel H., et al., eds. *Encyclopedia of Mormonism: The History, Scripture, Doctrine, and Procedure of The Church of Jesus Christ of Latter-day Saints*. 4 vols. New York: Macmillan, 1992.

MacDowell, Bart. *The Revolutionary War: America's Fight for Freedom*. Washington, D.C.: National Geographic Society, 1967.

Madsen, Truman G. *Defender of the Faith: The B. H. Roberts Story*. Salt Lake City: Bookcraft, 1994.

Manchester, William Raymond. *The Glory and the Dream: A Narrative History of America, 1932–1972*. Boston: Little, Brown and Company, 1973, 1974.

———. *The Last Lion, Winston Spencer Churchill: Visions of Glory, 1874–1932*. Boston: Little Brown, 1983.

Mason, Alpheus Thomas. *Brandeis: A Free Man's Life*. New York: The Viking Press, 1946.

McConkie, Bruce R. *Sermons and Writings of Bruce R. McConkie.* Edited by Mark L. McConkie. Salt Lake City: Bookcraft, 1989.

McCullough, David. *Truman.* New York: Simon and Schuster, 1992.

Merriam-Webster's Collegiate Dictionary. 10th ed. Springfield, Mass.: Merriam-Webster, 1999.

Morris, Richard B., and Jeffrey B. Morris, eds. *Encyclopedia of American History.* 7th ed. New York: Harper Collins, 1996.

Morrison, Alexander B. *The Dawning of a Brighter Day: The Church in Black Africa.* Salt Lake City: Deseret Book, 1990.

Oates, Stephen B. *With Malice toward None: The Life of Abraham Lincoln.* Ontario: Penguin Books, 1977.

O'Dea, Thomas. *The Mormons.* Chicago: University of Chicago Press, 1957.

Perry, Ralph Barton. *The Thought and Character of William James.* New York: Harper & Row, 1948.

Ravitch, Diane. *The Troubled Crusade: American Education, 1945–1980.* New York: Basic Books, 1983.

Roberts, B. H. *A Comprehensive History of The Church of Jesus Christ of Latter-day Saints, Century One.* 6 vols. Salt Lake City: The Church of Jesus Christ of Latter-day Saints, 1930.

———. *Defense of the Faith and the Saints.* 2 vols. Salt Lake City: Deseret News, 1907–12.

Schlesinger, Arthur M. *The Birth of the Nation: A Portrait of the American People on the Eve of Independence.* New York: Knopf, 1968.

Shipps, Jan. *Sojourner in the Promised Land: Forty Years among the Mormons.* Chicago: University of Illinois Press, 2000.

Sillitoe, Linda. *A History of Salt Lake County.* Salt Lake City: Utah State Historical Society, 1996.

Smith, Joseph. *History of The Church of Jesus Christ of Latter-day Saints.* Edited by B. H. Roberts. 7 vols. 2d ed. rev. Salt Lake City: The Church of Jesus Christ of Latter-day Saints, 1932–51.

Smith, Joseph F. *Gospel Doctrine.* 5th ed. Salt Lake City: Deseret Book Company, 1939.

Storr, Richard J. *Harper's University: The Beginnings.* Chicago: University of Chicago Press, 1966.

Talmage, John Russell. *The Talmage Story: The Life of James E. Talmage—Educator, Scientist, Apostle.* Salt Lake City: Bookcraft, 1972.

Tate, Lucile. *Boyd K. Packer: A Watchman on the Tower.* Salt Lake City: Bookcraft, 1995.

Tolstoy, Leo. *Anna Karenina.* New York: Random House, 1965.

Tuchman, Barbara Wertheim. *The March of Folly: From Troy to Vietnam.* New York: Knopf, 1984.

Turley, Richard E., Jr. *Victims: The LDS Church and the Mark Hofmann Case.* Urbana: University of Illinois Press, 1992.

———. Introduction to *To California in '49,* by George Q. Cannon. Edited by Michael N. Landon. Vol. 1 of *The Journals of George Q. Cannon,* edited by Adrian W. Cannon and Richard E. Turley Jr. Salt Lake City: Deseret Book, 1999.

Utonian (yearbook). Salt Lake City: University of Utah, 1961, 1967.

Widtsoe, John A. *In a Sunlit Land: The Autobiography of John A. Widtsoe.* Salt Lake City: Deseret Book, 1952.

Wilkinson, Ernest L., ed. *Brigham Young University, the First One Hundred Years.* 4 vols. Provo: Brigham Young University Press, 1976.

Wilson, A. N. *C. S. Lewis: A Biography.* New York: W. W. Norton & Company, 1990.

Talks and Articles

Avant, Gerry. "Elder Maxwell Personifies Poetry at Pulpit." *Church News,* 19 January 1986, 4–5.

Briscoe, David. "Maxwell: LDS Should Participate in Party Politics." *Daily Utah Chronicle,* 26 October 1964, 1.

"Business Portrait: U. Aide's Product Is 'Awareness.'" *Salt Lake Tribune,* 4 August 1968, C2.

Carter, Edward L. "Diplomats Hail Y.'s Islamic Translations." *Deseret News,* 11 February 2000, B5.

Chesnutt, Jim. "Y2K or Not, Mormons in Utah Are Ready." *Washington Post,* 26 December 1999, A22.

"The Church Can Now Be Universal with Priesthood Revelation of 1978." *Church News,* 5 January 1980, 20.

Church Educational System. *Report of the Select Committee on Post-Secondary Education in the Church Educational System.* Salt Lake City: The Church of Jesus Christ of Latter-day Saints, 1972.

———. "Seek Learning Even by Study and by Faith: Report for 1971." Salt Lake City: The Church of Jesus Christ of Latter-day Saints, 1971.

Conference Report. October 1970. Salt Lake City: The Church of Jesus Christ of Latter-day Saints, 1970.

Dart, John. "Mormons Ponder 1830 Letter Altering Idealized Image of Joseph Smith." *Los Angeles Times,* 25 August 1984, 6.

"1830 Harris Letter Authenticated." *Church News,* 28 April 1985, 6.

"Elder Maxwell Fulfilling Duties Despite Illness." *Deseret News,* 26 October 1996, B1.

Ellis, Dexter. "Bennett Says He'll Leave Senate Seat in 1974." *Deseret News,* 23 June 1973, A3–A4.

Eyring, Henry B. "Neal A. Maxwell: Pursuing 'A More Excellent Way.'" *Ensign,* January 1987, 6–11.

Gardea, Richard, and Jacque Felshaw. "Reunion with Army Buddy to Have Special Meaning for Duncan Man." *Eastern Arizona Courier,* 15 February 1978, A4.

"Good Men at the 'U.'" *Deseret News,* 9 September 1964, A12.

Hafen, Bruce C. "Elder Neal A. Maxwell: An Understanding Heart." *Ensign,* February 1982, 6–13.

———. "The Legislative Branch in Utah." *Utah Law Review,* 1996, 416–61.

Hales, Robert D. "Strengthening Families: Our Sacred Duty." *Ensign,* May 1999, 32–35.

Halle, Louis J. "The Language of Statesmen." *Saturday Review,* 16 October 1971, 30–31.

Harrie, Dan. "GOP Dominance Troubles Church." *Salt Lake Tribune,* 3 May 1998, A1.

Heslop, J. M. "He Built on Parents' Example." *Church News,* 11 May 1974, 5

"Higher Education's Cart before Horse." *Salt Lake Tribune,* 26 July 1966, A18.

Hinckley, Gordon B. "The Perpetual Education Fund." *Ensign,* May 2001, 51–53.

"The Human Side." *Salt Lake Tribune,* 28 July 1962, 14.

"Interview with Neal A. Maxwell." *Improvement Era,* September 1970, 48.

"Jan Shipps—Sojourner." *Exponent II,* Winter 2001, 4–7, 28–30.

Johnston, Jerry. "Favorites of an 'Intensive' Reader." *Deseret News,* 2 May 1980, C2.

———. "Tidbits of Truth Are Not for Faint of Heart." *Deseret News,* 11 October 1997, E1.

"June Videoconference: 'Accomplishing the Mission of the Church.'" *Ensign,* September 1987, 73.

Kelly, Katy. "Mormons on Mission to Grow." *USA Today,* 21 October 1997, D3–D5.

"Key to Strong Young Men: Gospel Commitment in the Home." *Ensign,* December 1984, 66–68.

Kimball, Spencer W. "A Report of My Stewardship." *Ensign,* May 1981, 5–7.

Knight, Hal. "Language Is a Key to His Life." *Church News,* 15 August 1981, 5.

"LDS Official Says ERA 'Threat to Family.'" *Salt Lake Tribune,* 24 March 1977, B1.

Lee, Harold B. "The Iron Rod." *Ensign,* June 1971, 5–10.

"Lindbergh Nightmare." *Time,* 5 February 1973, 35.

Lythgoe, Dennis. "G. Homer." *Deseret News,* 10 January 2000, C1–C2.

Martin, Richard O. "Checking the Channels." *Salt Lake Tribune,* 10 October 1962, 26.

Maxwell, Colleen. "Hope Everlasting." In *The Arms of His Love.* Salt Lake City: Deseret Book, 2000.

"Maxwell Speech Reflects Historical Past." *Daily Utah Chronicle,* 29 February 1960, 1–2.

"Maxwell Views Foreign Relations Committee." *Daily Utah Chronicle,* 6 November 1958.

McKay, David O. "Pioneer Women." *Relief Society Magazine,* January 1948, 4–9.

Meilaender, Gilbert. "The Everyday C. S. Lewis." *First Things,* August/September 1998, 31.

Morson, Gary. "Prosaics." *American Scholar,* Autumn 1988, 523.

Mosser, Carl, and Paul Owen. "Mormon Scholarship, Apologetics and Evangelical Neglect: Losing the Battle and Not Knowing It?" *Trinity Journal of Theology,* 1998, 179–205.

"Neal Maxwell Honored at Farewell Fete." *Deseret News,* 8 August 1970, A5.

"Neal Maxwell Service Achievements Are in Best Tradition of Public Help." *Salt Lake Tribune,* 11 May 1974, A18.

"Neal Maxwell's Big Job: World Is His Campus." *Deseret News,* 22 June 1970, A18.

Nelson, Russell M. "Living by Scriptural Guidance." *Ensign,* November 2000, 17.

"Nigeria Marks Twin Milestones." *Church News,* 21 May 1988, 6–7.

"Notable Quotes by Leaders on Missionary Work." *Church News,* 3 July 1983, 4.

Oman, Nathan. "Review of *Zion in the Courts.*" *FARMS Review of Books* 12, no. 1, 113–35.

Pearson, Howard. "Legislature, Salute to Ike Slated on TV." *Deseret News,* 9 January 1961, B8.

Petersen, Mark E. "In Defense of Liberty." *Improvement Era,* May 1946, 288.

Peterson, Janet. "Friend to Friend." *Friend,* February 1984, 6–7.

The President's Commission on Campus Unrest. *Campus Unrest.* Washington, D.C.: U. S. Government Printing Office, 1970, 209.

Rasband, Ronald A. "One by One." *Ensign,* November 2000, 29–30.

Rea, Dorothy. "Nerve Center Role for Y., Says Maxwell." *Deseret News,* 14 September 1970, B1.

Reynolds, Noel B. "The Coming Forth of the Book of Mormon in the Twentieth Century." *BYU Studies*, vol. 38 no. 2, 6–49.

Sale, J. Kirk. "Men of Low Profile." *Change*, July–August 1970, 36.

Sheler, Jeffery L. "The Mormon Moment." *U. S. News & World Report*, 13 November 2000, 58–67.

Shipps, Jan. "Mormon Metamorphosis: The Neglected Story." *Christian Century*, 14–21 August 1996, 784–87.

Stack, Peggy Fletcher. "Apostle Speaks of Faith." *Salt Lake Tribune*, 20 July 1996, C1.

———. "LDS Apostle Finds Lessons in Life, Literature." *Salt Lake Tribune*, 4 April 1997, A9.

———. "Pain Is Part of Progress, Maxwell Says." *Salt Lake Tribune*, 26 September 1998, C1.

Stark, Rodney. "The Rise of a New World Faith." *Review of Religious Research*, September 1984, 18–27.

"Teaching by Spirit Encourages Students' Intellectual Honesty." *Church News*, 14 September 1991, 12.

Teuscher, DeMar. "Predicting Politics Always Risky." *Deseret News*, 3 June 1965, A9.

Third Interim Report of the Constitutional Revision Commission. Salt Lake City, January 1975.

Van Biema, David. "Mormons, Inc.: The Secrets of America's Most Prosperous Religion." *Time*, 4 August 1997, 50–59.

Ward, Maurine Jensen. "Sister Colleen Hinckley Maxwell." *New Era*, July 1977, 14–16.

White, Michael. "LDS Church Says Anti-Mormons Have Little Effect on Membership." *Daily Herald*, 6 October 1985, 32.

Woodward, Kenneth. "A Mormon Moment." *Newsweek*, 10 September 2001, 44–51.

Unpublished Works

Christensen, Joe J. "The Globalization of the Church Educational System." Address to the International Society, 19 August 2001.

Gentry, Leland. "A History of LDS Religious Education," n.d.

Maxwell, Colleen H. Talk to single adult ward, 14 February 1998.

Tarbox, Norman C. "Origins of the Utah System of Higher Education." Doctoral dissertation, University of Utah, 2000.

INDEX

activities, 506–7; delivers major
address about Joseph Smith to BYU
Management Society, 507–9; enjoys
relationship with Hugh Nibley,
513–14; oversees preparation of
Encyclopedia of Mormonism, 514–15;
serves as advisor to Church
Historical Department, 515–16

Teachings
Adversity, 4–5, 12; Atonement, 5,
23–24, 502–3, 542–43; suffering,
12, 16–17; wintry doctrines, 20;
work, 64; connecting secular and
sacred, 165, 166; U.S. Constitution,
167; American political process
and public service, 215; home and
family, 219, 242; gospel's ability to
solve problems, 247; eternal
progression, 290; leadership, 314–16;
revelation, 324; correlation between
growth of seminary and institute
program and of full-time missions,
367; academic scholarship and
discipleship, 379–80; helping
society versus escaping from it,
380–81; commitment, 406–7;
government, 408–9; community
service, 409; personal revelation,
413; effect of revelation extending
priesthood, 418; Joseph Smith,
507–9; discipleship, 543–47;
meekness, 545–46; hope,
556–57

University of Utah administrator
University experience as preparation
for future Church assignments,
245–46; holds variety of jobs, 246;
turns down Washington, D.C., job
offers and returns to Utah, 246–48;
Deseret News publishes opinion
piece by, 248; as assistant director of
public relations, 248; assists
university president, 249;
coordinates scholarships, 249;
publishes article in political science
journal, 249; completes master's
degree, 250; publishes article in
Nation, 250; moderates weekly

interview series *Tell Me,* 250–53;
becomes professional colleague of
Elizabeth Haglund, 251–52, 254;
works as editor for educational
television network and comments on
1968 election results, 253–54; assists
university president and board of
regents secretary, 257; speaks at
university functions, 257–58; teaches
political science, 258–60; weathers
controversy over academic rank,
259–61; becomes dean of students,
262–64; released as assistant to
university president, 264; released as
campus bishop, 264; strengthens
university's relationship with
business community, 264; speaks at
baccalaureate service, 265; speaks on
Utah voter attitudes at institute
devotional, 265; learns lessons in
conflict resolution, 266–67; becomes
defender of well-established values,
269; learns lessons in participative
leadership, 269; becomes interested
in concept of self-esteem, 269–70;
called as member of Young Men's
MIA General Board, 270; coauthors
1966 MIA leadership manual, 270;
university experience influences
approach to Church leadership,
270–71; as candidate for university
president, 272–73; appointed
executive vice president, 274;
develops relationship with James C.
Fletcher, 274, 275–76; becomes vice
president for planning and public
affairs, 274–75; becomes interpreter
between university and community,
276, 277–78; assists in organizing
university's National Advisory
Council, 276–77; chairs United
Fund drive, 277; serves in other
leadership positions in community,
277; represents university and
Utah higher education to
legislators, 277–80; chairs
Legislative Study Committee
and Constitutional Revision
Commission, 280–83; receives